Economic Complexity and Evolution

For further volumes:
http://www.springer.com/series/11583

Andreas Pyka • Esben Sloth Andersen
Editors

Long Term Economic Development

Demand, Finance, Organization, Policy and Innovation in a Schumpeterian Perspective

Springer

Editors
Andreas Pyka
Lehrstuhl für Innovationsökonomik
University of Hohenheim
Stuttgart, Germany

Esben Sloth Andersen
Department of Business and Management
Aalborg University
Aalborg, Denmark

ISBN 978-3-642-35124-2 ISBN 978-3-642-35125-9 (eBook)
DOI 10.1007/978-3-642-35125-9
Springer Heidelberg New York Dordrecht London

Library of Congress Control Number: 2013937717

Printed on acid-free paper

Springer is part of Springer Science+Business Media (www.springer.com)

Contents

Introduction

Andreas Pyka and Esben Sloth Andersen

The general theme of the thirteenth International Joseph A. Schumpeter Society Conference, held during June 21th–24th, 2010 at Aalborg University in Denmark, was the exploration of the interrelated phenomena of innovation, organization, sustainability and crises. By addressing these phenomena an attempt was made to confront some of the underexplored parts the Schumpeterian legacy, but there was also room for new results concerning more well-developed parts of evolutionary economics.

The five plenary sessions concerned: advances in the understanding of industrial evolution; new research on entrepreneurship, spill-overs and regional development; the analysis of innovation-based growth, fluctuations and crises; the current crises in a long-term historical perspective; and the processes of development in relation to the problems of catching-up, falling behind and forging ahead.

The scope of the conference can be recognized by the broad range of topics that was covered by the 62 parallel sessions. The session titles included: finance and innovation; evolutionary economic development; perspectives on patenting and licensing; creative destruction and labor mobility; consumption and evolution; evolution and development; incentives, learning and complexity; agent-based modeling; financial innovation and financial crisis; innovation in pharmaceuticals; knowledge networks; capitalism, labor markets and reorganization; innovation in the medical industry; the environment and sustainability; clusters and industry

---

Modified and extended version from Journal of Evolutionary Economics 22(4), 621–625, Springer (2012).

A. Pyka (✉)
University of Hohenheim, Stuttgart, Germany
e-mail: a.pyka@unihohenheim.de

E.S. Andersen
Aalborg University, Aalborg, Denmark

A. Pyka and E.S. Andersen (eds.), *Long Term Economic Development*,
Economic Complexity and Evolution, DOI 10.1007/978-3-642-35125-9_1,

evolution; innovation in consumption goods; modeling technical change and growth; modeling industry dynamics; discontinuities and continuities; technological and regional relatedness; perspectives on innovation studies; R&D and patents; survival of firms; public policy and innovative growth; growth and resilience; eco-innovations; Schumpeterian analyses of growth and fluctuations; structural change and growth; firm practices and innovation; outsourcing and offshoring; public action and innovation; financial constraints on innovation; regulation and innovation; environmental policy and innovation; Schumpeter and innovation; entrepreneurship and evolution; high-tech clusters; sustainable emergence; firm growth and innovation; technological regimes and change; biotechnology; persistent performance; diversity and knowledge creation; innovation in Africa; innovation policy and policy innovation; universities and business innovation; entrepreneurship in regions; learning and locating; perspectives on catching up; innovation and market concentration; organizational forms; small and new firms; perspectives on networks; entrepreneurship and self-organization; Schumpeterian creative destruction; innovation and interaction; perspectives on Chinese transitions; environmental sustainability and innovation; the role of patents; technology and cycles; R&D, spillovers, and innovation; and preferences and evolution.

The proceedings following the 2010 conference of the International Schumpeter Society starts with the presidential address given by Esben Sloth Andersen with the title "Schumpeter's Core Works Revisited: Resolved Paradoxes and Remaining Challenges". The chapter begins with an analysis of Schumpeter's core works in German and English that serves to characterize the Schumpeterian legacy and its challenges for modern evolutionary economics. The analysis is partly made through the distinction between microevolution and macroevolution, and major tasks for future research concern the latter phenomenon. Other research issues emerge from the distinction between Schumpeter's three major evolutionary models: the entrepreneur-driven model (Mark I), the oligopoly-driven model (Mark II), and the model of socio-economic coevolution (Mark SC).

Evolutionary economics sometimes is still characterized as dominantly supply-side oriented. In this view the relationship between innovation and demand are not at the forefront of evolutionary research. This is without doubt rather surprising given that no innovation could have successfully diffused without consumers adopting the new technology. In 2001 the *Journal of Evolutionary Economics* pioneered with the publication of a special issue "Economic growth—What happened on the demand side" edited by Witt (2001) and triggered a continuously increasing number of publications dealing with the dynamic interplay between innovation, demand, income generation, consumer capabilities and changing distributions of consumption expenditures. Therefore the criticism of an exclusive supply-side orientation of evolutionary economics is no longer justified. The third chapter in the proceedings takes up this rich research agenda. Andreas Chai and Alessio Moneta ask the question "Back to Engel?" and give empirical evidence for Ernst Engel's hierarchy of needs which he published already in (Engel 1857). The challenging question addressed in this paper deals with the dynamics of consumption patterns. Is the order of consumption which Engel has introduced more than

150 years ago still observable and how do rising incomes and increasing choices of consumption influence the behavior of consumers?

In the fourth chapter by Christian Garavaglia, Franco Malerba, Luigi Orsenigo and Michele Pezzoni demand aspects also matter even if the focus of the paper is on the developing industrial structure of biopharmaceutical industries. In their chapter "Technological regimes and demand structure in the evolution of the pharmaceutical industry" the authors apply a history-friendly simulation model to analyze the mutual interaction between the nature of the demand and the development of industry concentration. They show that the fragmented feature of the demand in pharmaceuticals expressed in the competition for new market niches leads to a seemingly high degree of competition in the pharmaceutical market despite the high R&D and marketing intensities.

Francesco Bogliaciono and Mario Pianta connect R&D investments, techno-economic opportunities and the potential for entrepreneurship with demand factors. In Chap. 5 the authors test these relationships at the industry level for 38 manufacturing and service sectors in six European countries over two time periods from 1994 to 2006. They show that an increase in overall demand increases profits, but is not necessarily responsible for improved innovative performances. Instead, growing innovation activities are positively associated to export growth alone. Accordingly, industries with a marked international openness are inclined to improve technological competitiveness through new products. Contrary, increased demand due to household consumption slows down the introduction of new products. Domestic demand seems to lead to an expansion of output of existing goods and services without a significant effect on innovation.

Supply relationships, intermediate demand and real as well as financial interactions in supply chains are the topic of the contribution by Giulio Cainelli, Sandro Montresor and Giuseppe Vittucci Marzetti in Chap. 6. To bring together the complex interactions between firms comprising different forms of exchange the authors apply the network metaphor and develop an analytical model to analyze "Production risk sharing and financial linkages in inter-firm networks" concerning the "structural variety, risk sharing and resilience" in these networks. The authors use the network terminology also to highlight the important geographical dimension of innovation. Different occurrences of network indicators like connectivity measures are applied to assemble various forms of industrial clusters which show to be characterized by specific possibilities to process shocks among the network members.

Kenneth Carlaw and Richard Lipsey challenge core neoclassical theories like Real Business Cycles (RBC) in their contribution "Does history matter? Empirical analysis of evolutionary versus stationary equilibrium views of the economy" and dispose their discussion in a tradition which started with Nelson and Winter (1982). With their evolutionary growth model they produce artificial macro data which they analyze for stylized facts of RBC theory. When applying the same econometric tests which are applied to real time series the artificial macro data exhibit stationarity features although they were created by an evolutionary model with strong path dependencies. Therefore, the question of the role of history cannot meaningful answered with standard econometric methodology. Carlaw and Lipsey go one step further and take real data from six OECD countries and show that the stationarity conditions do not hold among others with respect to the short-run, negatively sloped Philips curve, nor the short and long-run general equilibrium conditions or a vertical long-run Phillips curve. Thus, the answer to the question asked in their title is an unconditional "Yes".

In Chap. 8 Harry Bloch and David Sapsford also take up business cycles considerations but reflect the long term relations between "Innovation, real primary commodity prices and business cycles". They focus on the impact of innovation on the long-run changes in real prices of primary commodities like agriculture and mining products. Their time dimension covers multiple business cycles, including long waves which run for over half a century per cycle. They found that the influence of innovation has been sufficient to result in negative trends in real prices for numerous individual commodities and for aggregate indexes of commodities and conclude that the world economy is currently entering a downswing phase of a long cycle.

In Chap. 9 of the proceedings Bo Carlsson takes up a core topic in Neo-Schumpeterian Economics and analyses "knowledge flows in high-tech industries—dissemination mechanisms and innovation regimes". He is comparing discovery-driven and design-driven innovation processes in various different industry clusters in the North America and Europe. For his analysis he is referring to several strands of the theoretical and empirical literature in industry dynamics to work out regularities of knowledge flows. Central are the different sources of new knowledge and the mechanisms for its dissemination. From this also follows the question whether it is appropriate to refer to spillovers in order to tackle knowledge diffusion.

The contribution by Jorge Niosi, Petr Hanel and Susan Reid "The international diffusion of biotechnology—the arrival of developing countries" addresses a similar question on the sectorial level. The hypothesis challenged is the one which deals with economic and technological convergence processes among countries prevalent in conventional economic approaches. In an empirical study including eight developing countries, namely China, India, Korea, Singapore, Argentina, Brazil, Chile and Mexico the countries' endeavors to establish biopharmaceutical industries are analyzed. Their results show that a trickling down of technologies can be observed; however, the particular trajectories are different, path dependent and strongly shaped by national institutions.

Gunnar Eliasson is digging deeper into the issues of the global organization of production and focuses on the impact of modern ICT on engineering industries. In his contribution entitled "The internet as a global production reorganizer—the old industry in the new economy" he investigates the reasons of why some developing economies are successfully adopting new technologies and jump on faster growth paths compared to mature industrial economies which experience severe difficulties of reorganizing. The difficulties, however, are not equally distributed among the former industrialized countries and in those economies that manage this transition, the engineering industries are likely to play the backbone role also in future.

Piergiuseppe Morone, Carmelo Petraglia and Giuseppina Testa are interested in finding out the determinants of Italian SMEs to innovate. In Chap. 12 entitled "Looking around: the smart way of Italian SME's to innovate" it becomes clear that geography matters for Italian SMEs. Being located in the South, however, does not affect the firm's choice of starting R&D projects, but affects negatively the amount of R&D investments. Furthermore, knowledge diffusion via geographical proximity increases the probability to innovate depending on the human capital of the companies. Finally, for small companies the probability to innovate is also positively related to sectoral spillovers.

So far in many contributions of the proceedings the idea of technological and geographical clustering, the exploitation of regional and sectoral spillovers and the organization of innovation processes in networks are thematized. Nobuya Fukugawa in Chap. 13 in his contribution "Strategic fit between regional innovation policy and regional innovation systems: the case of local public technology centers in Japan" focuses on the policy implications from this. In particular he addresses local public technology centers in Japan and finds that the characteristic features of regional innovation systems in Japan are not reflected adequate in the design of policy instruments and offer scope for substantial improvement.

Schumpeter's contradictory statements concerning the size of firms and their potential to innovate has triggered a very long scientific discussion. The question is whether path breaking innovation activities are to be found dominantly among small entrepreneurial start-ups (Schumpeter Mark I, Schumpeter 1911) or whether large, diversified companies in high concentrated markets are responsible for radical innovation (Schumpeter Mark II, Schumpeter 1942). Exactly this question is addressed by Roberto Fontana, Alessandro Nuvolari, Hiroshi Shimitzu and Andrea Vezulli in their contribution "Schumpeterian patterns of innovation and the sources of breakthrough inventions: evidence from a data-set of R&D awards" by exploiting the "R&D 100 awards" data set of the magazine Research & Development, which yearly awards since 1963 technologically significant new products. Today, the picture is even more complex because many industries are characterized by a co-existence of large established and new entrepreneurial companies. E.g. after the deregulation of telecommunication industries the former national monopolists co-exist with smaller technology-oriented companies and also in the pharmaceutical industries the biotechnology companies did not replace the large diversified pharmaceutical companies but co-exist and cooperate in innovation. In their paper, however, the authors show, that breakthrough innovations are more likely in the turbulent world with small entrepreneurial companies engaged in innovation competition which corresponds to Schumpeter Mark I.

Of course, innovation and entrepreneurial activities are not restricted to the industrial pillars and the demand side of economies but encompass also their financial and public pillars (Hanusch and Pyka 2007). Public sector innovation, public entrepreneurship, social innovation and innovation and venture financing are some keywords which express the comprehensive nature of the required approach to design the future-orientation of economic systems. What characterizes the symbiotic and twin-track relationship between innovation and finance? Mariana

Mazzucato and Massimiliano Tancioni test in their contribution "R&D, Patents and Stock Return Volatility" the direct relationship between innovation and stock return volatility. Their results reveal positive relationships between R&D activities with volatility and the level of returns. Their major conclusion, however is that Knightian uncertainty is a major ingredient of a Schumpeterian theory of finance.

Related Giovanni Cerulli and Bianca Potì focus on the immediate relationship between firms' profitability and their innovation activities. They find in their empirical investigation which builds on a merger of three waves of Capitalia/ Unicredit data set on Italian manufacturing firms that indeed persistent innovative activities are positively reflected in the profitability of the companies and confirm with this result the meaning of dynamic capabilities which are accumulated in persistent innovation endeavours.

Chapter 17 by Gustav Martinsson and Hans Lööf also explores the relationship between innovation and finance. The authors investigate the relationship between patenting and equity capital—for innovative firms it is important to have access to equity in order to maintain a smooth patenting strategy over time. The empirical test confirming their hypotheses were done for Swedish companies in the period 1997–2005.

In the contribution "Building Systems", Brian Loasby also takes the comprehensive view: He characterizes economic systems as a set of elements which are connected in characteristic ways. The viability of the system stems from its decomposability which allows for sane development. Intentional innovation processes are a strong, even not the only force which spurs the development of economic systems. Referring to the system of selective connections in the Human brain, Brian Loasby disentangles the immanent conflict between structure and dynamics. Both co-ordination (structure) and development (dynamics) are ordered processes and can only meaningful interpreted within this radical process-oriented view.

Michael Joffe asks the question "What causes creative destruction?" in Chap. 19 of these proceedings. Although Schumpeter's notion is very powerful and has been invoked most often it is not exactly clear to the author how this mechanism works in different periods and forms of capitalistic organization. In his chapter Michael Joffe shows this ambiguity of the notion in Schumpeter's own work.

The dichotomous model of markets and organization is challenged in Maria Brouwers contribution "Markets and Organizations—Individualism and Economic Theory". She stresses the point that markets and organizations are complementary from a theoretical point of view. Therefore, both principal-agent theory and perfect competition run short in the explanation of real phenomena, in particular dynamic processes. To illustrate her argument Maria Brouwer gives the examples ranging from the rising individualism in Medieval England to collective opinion formation on financial markets.

The last contribution to the proceedings is written by Muhammad Nadeem Javaid and Pier-Paolo Saviotti and applies the strong process-orientation emphasized by Brian Loasby in Chap. 18 by focusing in a fine grained-way on the particular patterns which characterize economic structures, namely on related and unrelated variety with respect to the exports of 97 countries and their changes in a period of more than 10 years. The authors empirically analyze "Financial System and Technological Catching-up: An Empirical Analysis; Is there a recipe for increasing the export variety of nations?" the interactions between the financial system of an economy and its exports. Like Mazzucato and Tancioni in Chap. 15 they found a crucial determinant for the explorative activities in an economy to be manifested in the role of stock markets.

The contributions to this proceedings volume are all selected from the contributions of the 2010 conference of the International Schumpeter Society and illustrate the scope of Schumpeterian economics today. Confronted with a higher degree of complexity than other scientific disciplines, evolutionary economics strongly contributes to a better understanding of the rich and varied patterns of economic systems and their development.

References

Engel E (1857) Die Produktions- und Consumtionsverhältnisse des Königreichs Sachsen. Bulletin de Institut International de Statistique 9:1–54

Hanusch H, Pyka A (2007) The principles of Neo-Schumpeterian economics. Camb J Econ 31 (2):275–289

Nelson RR, Winter SG (1982) An evolutionary theory of economic change. Cambridge University Press, Cambridge, MA

Schumpeter JA (1911) Theorie der wirtschaftlichen Entwicklung. Duncker & Humblot, Berlin

Schumpeter JA (1942) Capitalism, socialism and democracy. Harper & Brothers, New York

Witt U (2001) Economic growth – what happened on the demand side. J Evol Econ 11(1):1–5

Schumpeter's Core Works Revisited

Resolved Problems and Remaining Challenges

Esben Sloth Andersen

Abstract This paper organizes Schumpeter's core books in three groups: the programmatic duology, the evolutionary economic duology, and the socioeconomic synthesis. By analysing these groups and their interconnections from the viewpoint of modern evolutionary economics, the paper summarises resolved problems and points at remaining challenges. Its analyses are based on distinctions between microevolution and macroevolution, between economic evolution and socioeconomic coevolution, and between Schumpeter's three major evolutionary models (called Mark I, Mark II and Mark SC).

1 Introduction

Modern evolutionary economics can learn much from revisiting the older type of evolutionary economics that is found in Joseph Schumpeter's core works. He provided many of our core concepts and basic questions, and revisiting his works helps us to clarify these concepts and questions. We can also learn from what, in retrospect, might be considered wrong steps he took during his lifelong attempt to develop his version of evolutionary economics. These are major reasons why we celebrate the centenary of *Theorie der wirtschaftlichen Entwicklung*, which is the first edition of *The Theory of Economic Development*. However, he would probably have disliked this type of celebration of his book. In its preface, Schumpeter (1912c, vii) expressed two wishes. His first wish was that the 'facts and arguments' of his book

Reprinted version from Journal of Evolutionary Economics 22(4), 621-625, Springer (2012)

E.S. Andersen (✉)
Department of Business and Management, Aalborg University, Fibigerstraede 4, 9220 Aalborg, Denmark
e-mail: esa@business.aau.dk

A. Pyka and E.S. Andersen (eds.), *Long Term Economic Development*, Economic Complexity and Evolution, DOI 10.1007/978-3-642-35125-9_2,

would become acknowledged by economic theorists. His second wish was that these theorists would 'as soon as possible' make his book 'surpassed and forgotten'. Nevertheless, there was no quick 'surpassing', since practically none of his contemporaries cared to think about the 'facts' of what we now call Schumpeterian dynamics and his 'arguments' for grasping the essence of economic evolution by means of his system of concepts. This situation changed with the emergence of a modern evolutionary economics that ranges from explicit Schumpeterian dynamics (relating to Nelson and Winter 1982) to more abstract evolutionary game theory (relating to Maynard Smith 1982). Through the increased efforts to analyze economic evolution, we seem to be approaching the point at which we have surpassed and can largely forget about Schumpeter's works. However, we probably still need at least a couple of decades before we can say that the fulfilling of Schumpeter's two wishes has been accomplished.

When revisiting Schumpeter's works, we have to recognize two important facts. First, he was not the only great economist who confronted the difficulties of handling economic evolution analytically. We should also appreciate efforts that range from Adam Smith and Marx via Marshall and Menger to Veblen and Hayek. However, Schumpeter is exceptional since he, until very recently, was the only major economist who made evolutionary analysis the turning point of practically all his research efforts. These efforts reflect a second important fact: Since he felt nobody took his arguments seriously and surpassed his evolutionary theory, Schumpeter decided to perform the further development and application of this theory on his own. The consequence is that practically all his major research efforts can depicted as the preparation for and the following up on his first formulation of his theory of economic evolution in *Entwicklung*. Thus, we have to move from celebrating the centennial of a single great book to the revisiting of an evolutionary research program that is presented and implemented in Schumpeter's core works.

The appreciation of Schumpeter's works is eased if we distinguish between his three different models of evolutionary processes. The Mark I model describes economic evolution as the outcome of the interaction between individual innovative entrepreneurs and routine-based incumbent firms. The Mark II model describes economic evolution as the outcome of the innovative oligopolistic competition between incumbent firms. The Mark SC model describes socioeconomic evolution as a coevolutionary process between the major sectors of society. Although all these models are important, Schumpeter's efforts concentrated on developing Mark I. In contrast, he left Mark II and Mark SC as mere sketches. Furthermore, he developed the Mark I model in a one-sided way. This can be recognized by making the distinction between microevolution and macroevolution. Microevolution is the process of evolution that takes place within a population of entities that face more or less uniform selection pressures, such as the firms of an industry. Macroevolution is the long-term transformation of a complex system of evolving and branching populations. It is more difficult to analyze macroevolution than microevolution, but a formal analysis of Schumpeter's different accounts of Mark I demonstrates that he focused on macroevolution—although this phenomenon is not described in any detail. The reason seems to be that he wanted to relate to Walras's general equilibrium model and that he prematurely rejected Marshall's industry-level analysis. Although the Mark I model could also have been developed for analyzing microevolution, his analysis of this process was largely postponed to the sketchy Mark II model of oligopolistic competition. This peculiar use of his core models created many difficulties for Schumpeter—and still provide challenges for modern evolutionary economists.

2 Grouping Schumpeter's Core Books

Modern evolutionary economists find Schumpeter's core works among his books and not among his 200 papers (listed in Augello 1990). He followed the old-fashioned rule that the size of a publication should reflect its scientific importance; his smaller papers are normally made for the occasion, while the longer papers present more ambitious research, and his major books present the core scientific contributions. By revisiting two of these books, we can find three more or less precisely described models of evolution. *The Theory of Economic Development* is dedicated to the presentation of a model that describes economic evolution as the interaction between new innovative firms and the system of economic routines. This model has been called Schumpeter's Mark I model. The second part of *Capitalism, Socialism and Democracy* from Schumpeter (1942) presents, much more sketchily, two additional models. The most obvious is the Mark II model that depicts economic evolution as a process that is driven by the innovative oligopolistic competition between larger firms. It is also possible to detect elements of a Mark SC model of the socioeconomic coevolution between the economic sector, the science sector, the family sector, and the political sector. These three evolutionary models are mentioned throughout this paper, but Mark II and Mark SC are primarily discussed in Section 5.

To understand Schumpeter's evolutionary research program, we should revisit three more of his voluminous books (see Table 1). Between *Development* and *Capitalism*, Schumpeter in (1939) published *Business Cycles: A Theoretical, Historical, and Statistical Analysis of the Capitalist Process*. On the more than thousand pages of this book, he made very complex analyses of the process of economic evolution in capitalist economies. These analyses are normally considered failures, but *Cycles* includes many scattered but important discussions of the phenomenon of innovation, a restatement of the Mark I model, and the extension and application of this model for the analysis of waveform economic evolution. Furthermore, Schumpeter started his academic career by publishing his book on the essence and main contents of theoretical economics, which is still only available in

Table 1 Schumpeter's core works

1908	*Das Wesen und der Hauptinhalt der theoretischen Nationalökonomie*	*Wesen* analyzes 'The Essence and Main Contents of Theoretical Economics'. It focuses on the essence and limits of Walrasian equilibrium economics and it uses these limits to emphasize the necessity of developing the complementary evolutionary economics as a fundamental field of economics. Its 626 pages have not been translated
1912	*Theorie der wirtschaftlichen Entwicklung*	*Entwicklung* presents on 548 pages the essence of Schumpeter's Mark I evolutionary economics with heavy emphasis on the personality of the innovative entrepreneur. Chapter 7 includes a sketch of a general theory of socioeconomic evolution (Mark SC). Translations of core parts are now available (Schumpeter 1910, 1912a, b)
1934	*The theory of economic development: an inquiry into profits, capital, credit, interest and the business cycle*	*Development* is the translation on the 255 pages of the radically revised and shortened 2nd edition of *Entwicklung* (Schumpeter 1926). Its focus on the basic Mark I modelling of economic evolution is obtained by concentrating on the entrepreneurial function and by removing the last chapter of *Entwicklung*
1939	*Business cycles: a theoretical, historical, and statistical analysis of the capitalist process*	*Cycles* presents a Mark I theory waveform economic evolution that is used for a sketchy analysis of 200 years of capitalist economic evolution. For most purposes many of the 1077 pages can be skipped by reading the Rendigs Fels's excellent abridged edition (Schumpeter 1964)
1942	*Capitalism, socialism and democracy*	*Capitalism* has, in the 1950 edition, 425 pages. Part 2 can be read as relating to the last chapter of *Entwicklung* as well as to some of the arguments in *Business Cycles*. Thereby it becomes clear that we are facing a Mark II extension of the theory of economic evolution as well as the applications of a general theory of socioeconomic coevolution (Mark SC)

German (*Das Wesen und der Hauptinhalt der theoretischen Nationalökonomie*, Schumpeter 1908). This book 'contains the statement of his fundamental views which constitute the basis of Schumpeter's whole scientific *weltanschaung* [world view]' (Leontief 1950, 105). It is in *Wesen* that he analyzes the limits of Walrasian equilibrium economics and the need for complementing it with evolutionary economics. To understand how he developed the latter fundamental field of economics, we have to consider the first German edition of *Development* separately. Actually, the many pages of *Theorie der wirtschaftlichen Entwicklung* demonstrate that it can fruitfully be considered a distinct book rather than a first edition that was replaced by *Development*.

The way in which Schumpeter's five core books contribute to his evolutionary research program becomes clear if we group them in two duologies and an additional book. First, *Wesen* and *Entwicklung* form the duology of early programmatic books. This programmatic duology starts by analysing economic theory in the narrow sense, then adds the analysis of economic evolution, and finally ends up with a proposal of an encompassing analysis of all aspects of socioeconomic evolution. Second, *Development* and *Cycles* can be called his evolutionary economic duology. *Development* streamlines the evolutionary economic theory of *Entwicklung* and ends with the announcement of a major application of this theory: the analysis of the waves of economic evolution. *Cycles* extends this theoretical analysis and complements it with historical and statistical analyses of long-term capitalist economic evolution. Finally, *Capitalism* can be interpreted as the socioeconomic synthesis that has roots back in the historical analyses of *Cycles* as well as in *Entwicklung*'s programmatic statement of a general theory of economic and social evolution.

3 Equilibrium Economics and Evolutionary Economics

The name of the game. The idea of considering *Wesen* and *Entwicklung* as Schumpeter's programmatic duology forces us to confront several terminological and theoretical problems that do not stand out clearly when applying the standard focus on *Development* and *Capitalism*. Let me start by arguing that the title *The Theory of Economic Development* is not an adequate translation of *Theorie der wirtschaftlichen Entwicklung*. The most obvious problem is that the English title uses the definite article, whereas Schumpeter is actually proposing an alternative to, for example, the Smithian and Marshallian theory of growth and evolution through the gradually increasing division of labor. However, the main problem is that the translated title ought to have been 'A Theory of Economic *Evolution*'.

The argument for this title is not that 'economic development' later became connected to the transformation of underdeveloped countries. The argument is instead that the concept 'development' was, even when *Development* was published in (1934), denoting pre-programmed processes, and this is not the type of process that he analyzed. What Schumpeter analyzed can better be described as 'evolution', that is, an open-ended process that combines innovation, behavioral inertia, and selection. He emphasized that such a process is characterized by a degree of indeterminateness that makes it impossible to predict its long-term outcomes, but it is possible to analyze scientifically the mechanisms of evolution. It was on these mechanisms that Schumpeter focused, while he was uninterested in the predictable

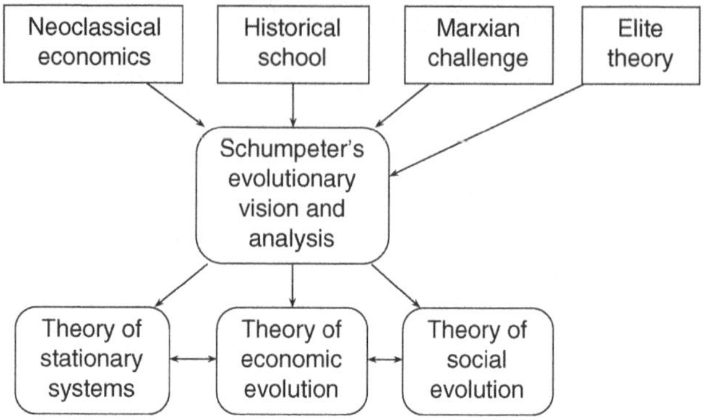

Fig. 1 Main sources and components of Schumpeter's evolutionary theories (from Andersen 2011, 91; modified from Andersen 2009, 36)

outcomes of processes of growth and development. Since the German word 'Entwicklung' cannot only be translated by 'development' but also by 'evolution', it seems clear that Schumpeter made the wrong choice of title for his (1934) book. This conclusion is supported by the fact that his large (1939) book, *Cycles*, only speaks of 'economic evolution'.

Synthesis and research program. Schumpeter developed his theory of economic evolution through a kind of synthesis between several sources (see Fig. 1). The first source of his evolutionary synthesis is neoclassical economics. He was an Austrian who, by the members of Menger's Austrian School, was taught theoretical economics in a way that seems to have included considerations on economic evolution. But he, somewhat paradoxically, preferred an independent study of Walras's non-evolutionary formalization of equilibrium economics. The second source is the economic sociology and the historical analyses of the German Historical School, where he related to considerations on socioeconomic evolution by scholars such as Schmoller and Max Weber. The third source is the challenge provided by the ideas about long-term capitalist evolution by Marx and the so-called Austro-Marxist School. The fourth and final source is more difficult to grasp, but Schumpeter wanted to rescue what he considered the important messages of innovative leadership and resistance to change that he found in the elite theories of Pareto and Nietzsche.

Schumpeter combined these sources into an evolutionary vision and analysis. His evolutionary economics started from his theory of stationary and routine-based systems in which evolution has come to a halt. To this he added the theory of a type of economic evolution that is driven by innovative entrepreneurs, and, furthermore, he generalized the theory to cover the evolutionary processes in each sector of society and the coevolution between these sectors. However, Schumpeter's most important tools and more direct inspirations seems to have come from equilibrium economics; and he initially considered evolutionary statics and evolutionary dynamics to be at the very core of his research program.

The programmatic formulations in *Wesen* and *Entwicklung* relate to a peculiar intellectual situation within economics at the beginning of the twentieth century. On the one hand, Schumpeter emphasized that neoclassical equilibrium economics had provided much-needed clarity and many important results. On the other hand, he argued that neoclassical leaders such as Alfred Marshall (1898) had an unrealistic ambition when they wanted to move gradually from equilibrium economics toward the much more important and difficult topic of economic evolution (or transformative dynamics). A core formulation in *Wesen* (pp. 182–183) is: 'Statics [equilibrium economics] and Dynamics [evolutionary economics] are completely different fields, they concern not only different problems but also different methods and different materials. They are not two chapters of one and the same theoretical building but two completely independent buildings. Only Statics has hitherto been somewhat satisfactorily worked up and we essentially only deal with it in this book. Dynamics [evolutionary economics] is still in its beginnings, is a "land of the future".' *Entwicklung* (p. 465) added that equilibrium economics is essentially the theory of a stationary economy. Its motto is: everyone adapts as good as possible under given conditions. In contrast, evolutionary economics is essentially the theory of the endogenous change of the routines of the economic system. Its main theme is that some economic agents create new routines, while other agents adapt to these routines.

The Walras connection. This way of defining the essence of equilibrium economics and evolutionary economics can most easily be understood respectively when we recognize that the early Schumpeter was a rebellious disciple of the economist he considered the greatest master of equilibrium economics, Léon Walras. Actually, Schumpeter (2000, 43–44) not only sent him a copy of *Wesen* but also a couple of letters in which he told Walras that it 'is a book of a disciple' and that he wanted to work under the Walrasian 'leadership'. Schumpeter had carefully studied the logic of the Walrasian equilibrium system as well as of the tâtonnement process that, after an exogenous perturbation, brings this system back to equilibrium (Walras 1954). It is the competition between Walrasian entrepreneurs (the W-entrepreneurs) that adjust the economic system to changed production functions and changed consumption functions. We might add that the changes of production functions and consumption functions are produced by changes in psychology, scientific knowledge and institutions, but this would just imply a fuller account of the meaning of the exogenous factors (see Fig. 2). It was not purely for analytical convenience that Walras made the assumption that any change in the Walrasian equilibrium system is the result of the change of exogenous factors. Schumpeter (1937, 166) later remembered that 'Walras would have . . . said (and, as a matter of fact, he did say it to me the only time that I had the opportunity to converse with him) that of course economic life is essentially passive'. In other words, if the economic system 'changes at all, it does so under influences that are external to itself'.

Schumpeter (1937, 166) strongly opposed the Walrasian idea that economic life is only an adaptive process: 'I felt very strongly that this was wrong, and that there

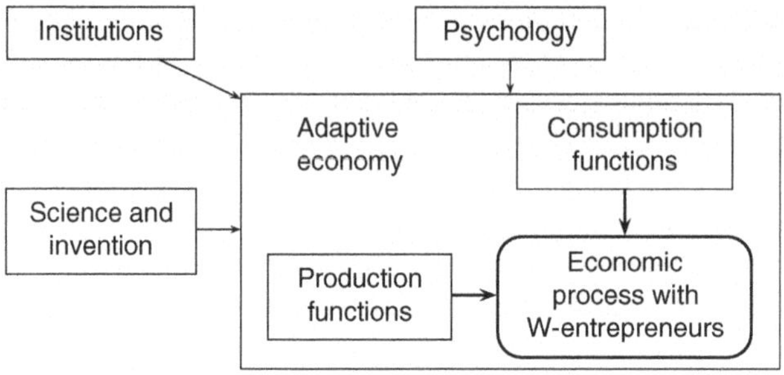

Fig. 2 The exogenous determination of economic change in the Walrasian paradigm

was a source of energy within the economic system which would of itself disrupt any equilibrium that might be attained.' He implemented this idea in the Mark I model in which Schumpeterian entrepreneurs (the S-entrepreneurs) create innovation-based firms (see Fig. 3). The creation of each innovative firm requires the will and energy of an S-entrepreneur as well as a loan from a banker who expects repayment from the profits of the entrepreneurial project. As soon as the routinized production of the new firm has become established, an S-manager is hired and the S-entrepreneur retires and spends the part of temporary profits left after repaying the loan. This behavior explains the conservatism of incumbent firms in the Mark I model. If all profits are shared between the retired entrepreneur and the banker, then the firm has no resources for expansion and for significant improvements of its knowledge. Even in the rare case where the firm has some degree of sustainable monopoly power, its surplus is extracted and it will sooner or later find its conservative place in the circular flow of economic life. This conservatism also implies that the firm will be driven to extinction by some future wave of innovation.

The evolutionary process of the Mark I model requires interplay between S-entrepreneurs who introduce new routines of production and consumption and the S-managers whose responses serve to adapt the economic system to the new routines. The analysis of the functioning of this model starts in an economic situation that comes close to the Walrasian general economic equilibrium. It is important to notice that we are facing a situation in which the stoppage of S-entrepreneurship and the competition between S-managers has brought evolution to a halt. Evolution is restarted by a new wave of S-entrepreneurs who, by means of borrowed money, establish new innovation-based firms and overcome the resistance against economic change. Thus, the entrepreneurs and the bankers are the drivers of Schumpeter's evolutionary process, but the system-level implementation of innovative change cannot take place without the adaptation of the routine behavior of the rest of the economic agents, that is, the S-managers, the workers and the consumers. These agents do not give up their routines willingly; their resistance is normally overcome in the capitalistic economic system. It is interaction between S-entrepreneurs and the routine-oriented agents that produces an evolutionary process. It is the analysis of this process that gives the new

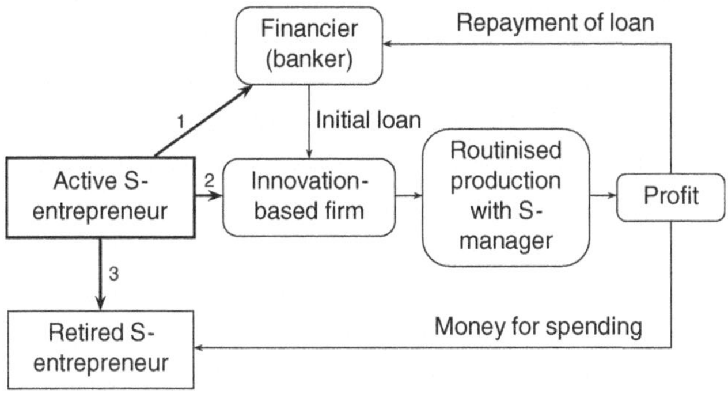

Fig. 3 The creation of an innovation-based firm in Schumpeter's Mark I model (modified from Andersen 2011, 59)

Schumpeterian meaning to core economic concepts such as profits, capital, interest, and credit and that might help explaining the business cycle phenomenon.

Toward socioeconomic coevolution. The macroevolutionary version of Schumpeter's Mark I model of capitalist economic evolution deals with a long-term historical process that does not take place within a given framework (see Fig. 4). The process of economic evolution can change from a situation in which innovations are introduced by individual entrepreneurs to another situation in which innovations are primarily made by established firms. To reflect such a change he produced the Mark II model, which is only found in *Capitalism*. Furthermore, the process of economic evolution can be influenced by changes within the political sector, the family sector and the science sector. Some of these changes are clearly exogenous to the economic process. But many such changes seem to be propelled by changes in the economic sector, and the opposite direction of causation is also possible.

Although Schumpeter's evolutionary analyses (except those in *Capitalism*) were based on the Mark I model, he occasionally pointed out feedbacks from the economic sector to the other sectors. These remarks point at his ambition of developing what might be called the Mark SC model of socioeconomic coevolution. This model is sketched in the last pages of chapter 7 of *Entwicklung* (see Schumpeter 1912a, 208–218). The starting point is the proposition that every sector of social life has an evolutionary process in which innovators interact with agents who merely adapt. Given such sectoral processes, we can study the coevolutionary processes between the sectors. However, the overall process of socioeconomic evolution is characterized by the different speeds of the individual sectoral processes. The consequence of these asynchronous sectoral processes is that the outcomes of overall societal evolution are highly indeterminate.

After having published *Entwicklung*, Schumpeter did not move directly to the analysis of the transformation of the mechanisms of economic evolution and to socioeconomic coevolution. On the contrary, he largely postponed these important topics to the socioeconomic synthesis of *Capitalism*. Instead, he chose to dedicate

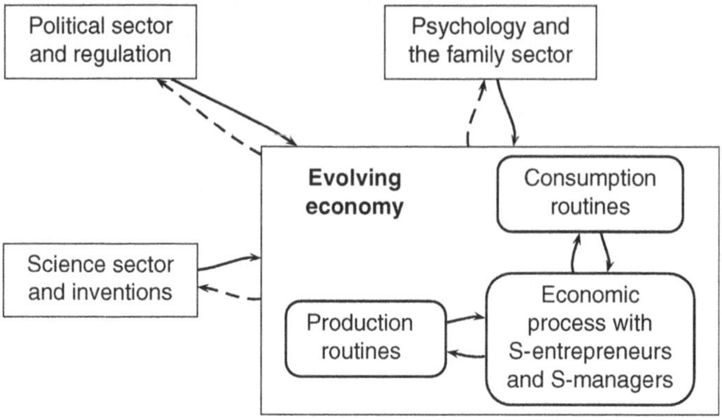

Fig. 4 The evolving Schumpeterian economy, where the S-entrepreneurs innovate the routines while S-managers are forced to adapt (modified from Andersen 2011, 44)

Development and *Cycles* to the further development and application of his Mark I model.

4 Combining Macroevolution with Microevolution

The evolutionary economic duology consists of *Development* and *Cycles*. The former book excludes *Entwicklung*'s broad discussions of heroic entrepreneurship and socio-economic coevolution. It also streamlines the exposition of the Mark I model and contains a total rewrite of what now is the last chapter of the book: the interpretation of business cycles as reflecting waves of economic evolution. Thereby the book explicitly points at *Cycles*, but it is the fact that both books rely on the cyclical functioning of the Mark I model that is most important for the coherence of the duology. Actually, Schumpeter tried to use extensions of this model to explain why 200 years of capitalist economic evolution had been characterized as business cycles. This explanation has been considered shaky ever since Kuznets (1940) presented his devastating criticism of *Cycles*. In retrospect, the shortcomings of this book can be traced back to its depiction of macroevolution as a sequence of circular flows. This is probably the reason why Freeman (1990, 28) suggested that 'it was Schumpeter's misfortune that he attempted to marry it [Walrasian equilibrium theory] with his own theory of dynamic destabilizing entrepreneurship'. However, we should not ignore the important materials that are presented in *Cycles*. We should especially notice the important but scattered contributions to the understanding of microevolution. For instance, the term 'innovation' occurs on 185 pages of *Cycles*, while it is only is found on 11 of the pages of *Development*.

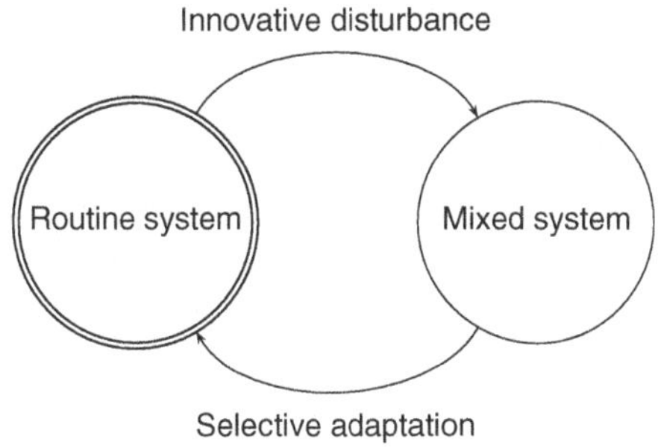

Fig. 5 Schumpeter's cyclical Mark I scheme of economic macroevolution (modified from Andersen 2009, 149)

Waves of evolution and business cycles. According to the macroevolutionary version of the Mark I model (see Fig. 5), evolutionary analysis starts from a situation in which evolution has reached an initial halt and where routine behavior reigns in the circular flow of economic life. Then, evolution is restarted because of the innovative disturbance by a smaller or larger swarm of Schumpeterian entrepreneurs. The evolutionary process is continued by a phase in which selection (or adaptation) dominates and where we see the creative destruction of old routines. This selective process not only serves to adapt the routine system but also to bring the evolutionary process to a new halt. Then the process is restarted by another swarm of entrepreneurs. Thus, the routine system evolves through repeated rounds of innovative disturbances, mixed and evolutionarily unstable situations, and processes of selective adaptation that bring the system to the 'neighborhood' of an economic equilibrium (according to *Cycles*).

Schumpeter thought he could easily introduce an explicit time dimension into the cyclical scheme of the Mark I model. The result is depicted by Fig. 6. Here, waves of evolution and related business cycles still start from non-evolving routine systems, the circular flows. Then prosperities are interpreted as innovation-based upswings, whereas recessions are periods of enforced adaptation. It is assumed that the next business cycle cannot start before the economic system has reached another equilibrated routine system. The main problem of this cyclical scheme is that it is very difficult to define an operational wave indicator. Actually, we need two different indicators: one for macroeconomic conditions and one for economics evolution. Some measure of the price level might reflect the 'pressure' of the system of economic activity. However, among the many wave indicators considered in *Cycles* (e.g. pp. 14–17), not any single one directly measures the underlying evolutionary process.

Cycles is based on a stepwise refinement of the Mark I scheme of Fig. 6. This scheme represents Schumpeter's first approximation with its simple application of the circular flow, the innovative disturbance, and a process selective adaptation. His second approximation adds oligopolistic competition and macroeconomic mechanisms. The result is, from an evolutionary viewpoint, that the upswing is not only characterized by innovative investment but also by derived investments that will in the long run show up as 'erroneous'. Therefore, the system's return to a new circular flow not only requires the adaptive recession of the first approximation

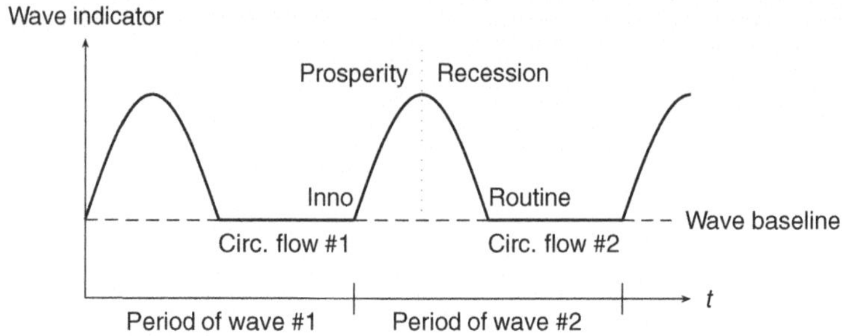

Fig. 6 Two-phase waves with innovation-based prosperity and adaptation-based recession (from Andersen 2011, 161; modified from Andersen 2009, 219)

but also a depression and recovery that serve to get rid of 'erroneous' investments. Even here Schumpeter ought to have paused to handle a lot of very difficult questions on the relationship between evolutionary waves and the macroeconomic business cycles. Nevertheless, he moved directly to his third approximation that is based on the realistic assumption that different types of innovation require different time spans for being embedded in the economic system. This is the background for the famous three-cycle version of the Mark I model. He used this version to decompose the history of capitalism into long Kondratieff waves that consist of several Juglar cycles which in turn consist of Kitchin cycles of even shorter length. We can simplify by recognizing that it is only Kondratieff waves and Juglar cycles that are connected with the process of economic evolution.

The waveform evolutionary process of Mark I and the related business cycles can be interpreted in two ways. On the one hand, it can be seen as a stylized version of a real macroscopic process of economic evolution that by necessity progresses in waves and produces a type of business cycle that starts from evolutionary resting points. This unproven assumption caused Schumpeter much trouble in *Cycles*. On the other hand, we can consider Mark I as a tool that provides an analytically convenient starting point for the study of evolutionary process. Even if we do not make the assumption that real evolution starts and ends at resting points, we still can learn much by thinking in such terms. In this context, we can hardly consider Schumpeter's focus on the short-term stops of evolution and the related combination of equilibrium and evolution an error. On the contrary, any analysis of evolution requires a notion of a state where the evolutionary process has come to a halt. Furthermore, the use of the Schumpeterian scheme for analytical convenience does not necessarily imply any endorsement of strong coupling of evolutionary waves with business cycles. In addition, we can emphasize the radical difference between Walrasian equilibrium and Schumpeter's evolutionary halts. Finally, we can try to develop an indicator of the waves of evolutionary change that he failed to deliver. Such an indicator will probably have to be based on explicit microevolutionary analysis.

The statistical approach to microevolution. Schumpeter failed to distinguish clearly between the analysis of the macroevolutionary process (depicted by Fig. 5) and the more elementary study of microevolution. Microevolutionary processes take place within a population with similar selection pressures, such as the firms of an industry. In retrospect, it can be argued that Schumpeter's main problem was that he lacked a statistical operationalization of such microscopic processes. When Schumpeter worked on his evolutionary economic duology, this operationalization was actually being delivered by the great statistician and evolutionary biologist Fisher (1930), but most biologists and all economists ignored this fact. Today, the situation has changed (see e.g. Andersen 2004). We can simply define the total microevolutionary change as the change of the statistical average of an evolutionarily relevant characteristic of a population of, e.g., firms. If we only study incumbent firms, we can easily decompose total evolutionary change into the selection effect and what I call the 'innovation' effect. Then it becomes clear that we arrive at the stop of evolution through a process that reduces both the innovation effect and the selection effect to zero. It should be mentioned that it is also possible to include the evolutionary effects of the entry of new firms and the exiting of old firms to provide a fuller description of the Schumpeterian process. (See the mathematical treatment in pp. 436–445 Andersen (2009).)

Schumpeter hardly paused to analyze such microevolutionary processes. Instead, he used his Mark I model directly to confront macroevolution, that is, the long-term transformation of a complex system of evolving populations. There are no statistically operational ways of measuring long-term macroevolutionary processes. We might more modestly think of the statistical variances of some of the evolutionarily relevant characteristics of the firms of the whole economy. We might also define the Schumpeterian circular flow as a situation in which these variances are zero (or very low), while at least some of them are increased by the innovative disturbance—and again reduced during the process of selective adaptation. But the highly complex and multidimensional nature of the macroscopic process of economic evolution suggests that we can never produce statistical indicators that are relevant for long periods of evolution. Furthermore, we have no chance of tracing the movement from one circular flow to the next because of the complex and changing 'ecological' interactions between the many individual populations of firms. Nevertheless, *Cycles* treated some of these interactions in the voluminous chapters on economic history.

The ecological approach to evolution. Given the difficulties of macroevolutionary analysis, it seems obvious that the Mark I model can be used most convincingly for cases where macroeconomic evolution is relatively closely connected to the microevolutionary process of a single industry. Furthermore, the analysis is eased if the industry-level evolution is dominated by a single major innovation. This explains why Schumpeter's favorite example of macroevolution is based on the replacement of horse-driven mail-coaches by railroads in the nineteenth century (Andersen 2002). He saw this replacement as the core of the process of 'railroadization of the world', which produced a wave of change of the routines of whole economic system. Schumpeter provocatively used this example to reject the evolutionary gradualism that was preferred by most economists. However, his account for innovative jump that was related to the railroad innovation demonstrates that he did not embrace the idea of the sudden emergence of 'Hopeful Monsters', which is rightly rejected by evolutionary biology. The railroad was already prepared, and it mainly needed a new combination of existing elements to emerge as a major innovation that served to define the agenda and the selection pressures for a long evolutionary trajectory.

The core microevolutionary process of railroadization can be described as the diffusion of the railroads. This diffusion roughly takes the form of an S-shaped logistic curve. By using the standard notation of evolutionary ecology, this curve of the replication of an innovation describes the movement of the number of its applications, N. The increase of N—for instance, the number of standard-length railroads—can be described by the logistic differential equation that includes two parameters, r and K. Thus, the equation is

$$\frac{\mathrm{dN}}{\mathrm{dt}} = rN\left(\frac{K-N}{K}\right).$$

The starting point is the basic railroad innovation, which I call an S-innovation (see Fig. 7). Initially the speed of diffusion is solely determined by its 'potency of spread', r. But the diffusion slows down because of the increasing closeness to the temporary 'carrying capacity' of the economic system, K.

Although it is primarily the diffusion of an S-innovation that is used to explain the long Kondratieff wave of the nineteenth century, the historical part of *Cycles* add many complications. Of special importance is that the diffusion of the railroad innovation induced a lot of minor innovations, which are obvious when we compare the early railroads with the later ones. Two types of additional innovations can be understood in relation to the logistic diffusion process. On the one hand, during the early stages of railroadization, we recognize r-innovations that speed up the diffusion process. On the other hand, we see K-innovations that increase the demand for railroad services. These K-innovations are made when the industry has come close to the (temporary) maturation of demand. They seem to formalize parts of Schumpeter's (1939, 497) remark that 'no industry can go on expanding output at the rate of its [S- and r-] innovation stage. Each reaches maturity in the sense that it finds its place in the economic organism and the amount of output beyond which it cannot profitably go, unless that amount be increased by some further [K-] innovation within it or in some 'complementary' industry and by the general effects of ... Growth.'

Toward macroevolutionary modelling. The idea of S-innovations, r-innovations, and K-innovations helps us to understand microevolutionary processes in terms of the density of the populations in which they take place. They also point at the important of the ecological interactions between different industries (the 'mesoevolution' of Dopfer and Potts 2008). They even point at the way

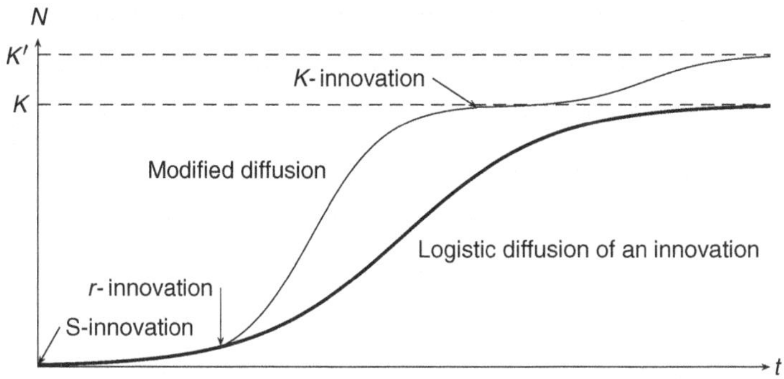

Fig. 7 Logistic industrial dynamics with added types of minor innovation (from Andersen 2011, 200; modified from Andersen 2009, 432)

macroeconomic change influences microevolution through fluctuations of the carrying capacity for individual industries. It is, however, obvious that the ecological approach serves to complicate the task of combining microevolution and macroevolution in the analysis of the relation between waves of evolution and business cycles. Here we probably need an aggregative analysis that focuses on the role of the financial sector. The ecological approach suggests that this role cannot solely be analyzed in terms of the externally financed innovations of the Mark I model. Since *K*-innovations are largely implemented by means of the internal finance of incumbent firms, we have include some aspects of the Mark II model (of *Capitalism*). The discussion of the feasibility and characteristics of more complex models is beyond the scope of the present paper. However, it should be noted that even those who consider the model of *Cycles* insufficient and misleading can learn much from searching Schumpeter's evolutionary economic duology for its scattered but important microevolutionary insights. Furthermore, we should recognize that the ultimate goal is to be able to analyze macroevolution convincingly and that a strong microevolutionary bias might lead us to forget this goal.

5 The Socioeconomic Synthesis

In *Capitalism*, Schumpeter largely ignored the Mark I model. This was done without explicit argument, but we get the impression that he thought that Mark I hindered the further development of his evolutionary economics. Having freed himself of this straitjacket and having chosen an informal writing style, he could quickly solve two tasks that he had previously defined (e.g. in Schumpeter 1912a, 1928, 1939). On the one hand, he could present the Mark II model of a microevolutionary process that is driven by the innovative oligopolistic competition between larger firms. On the other hand, he could present some of the elements the Mark SC model of societal macroevolution as determined by the coevolution between the economic sector, the science sector, the family sector, and the political sector.

Innovative oligopolistic competition. Microevolutionary interpretations of the Mark I model describe an evolutionary process in which established firms of an industry are conservative upholders of unchanging routines and are, in the long run, replaced by new innovation-based firms—such as when mail-coach firms were replaced by railroad companies. In contrast, the Mark II model describes established firms as combining two activities: they replicate given routines; and they engage in innovative moves and counter-moves. Schumpeter used Mark I to analyze macroevolution, while Mark II is a microevolutionary model. It is unclear whether Schumpeter really wanted to delimit his model of innovative oligopolistic competition in this way. But *Cycles* demonstrates that he knew that it was possible to produce a large number of different models of non-evolutionary oligopolistic competition and that the emergence of collusive monopoly is often plausible. Adding innovation and imitation would simply increase the number of models and add the possibility that monopoly emerges from the oligopolistic process. Thus, for Schumpeter it probably seemed impossible to produce a realistic oligopoly model of macroevolutionary dynamics, but he did succeed in describing the microevolutionary process of Schumpeterian competition that tended to increase productivity and the quality of goods.

The core of the Mark II process can be understood from the viewpoint of individual firms. Whereas innovation-based firms of the Mark I model quickly become conservative (see Fig. 3), the growth of Mark II firms is influenced by feedback loops (see Fig. 8). If we apply a pure-labor model, then the Mark II firm largely uses any positive profits to expand its workforce. This means a firm with a sustainable productivity lead will ultimately take over the whole industry. The evolutionary process becomes more complex when we add the possibility that the firm uses part of its workforce to produce innovations and imitations. But unless imitation is unrealistically easy, we have strong feedback loop between innovative performance and the growth of the firm. The informal writing style of *Capitalism* meant that he did not feel obliged to explain why monopoly in the strict sense is not the rule but rather the exception. However, an easy answer could have been made by combining the Mark II model with the Mark I model: the individual entrepreneurs might be those who undermine established monopolies. If this is not sufficient, he could have added the activities of the firms of other industries and the international dimension of economic evolution.

Major transitions in evolution. It is hardly necessary to discuss most aspects of the microevolutionary Mark II model since it is has been widely applied and extended by evolutionary economists since Nelson and Winter (1982). These pioneers even produced a Mark II model of economic growth, but, according to the present interpretation, this growth model is a microevolutionary model for a whole economy. However, there is one aspect of Schumpeter's use of the Mark II model that relates to macroevolution in the sense of the long-term transformation of the complex system of evolving populations. This is Schumpeter's (1928, 384–385)

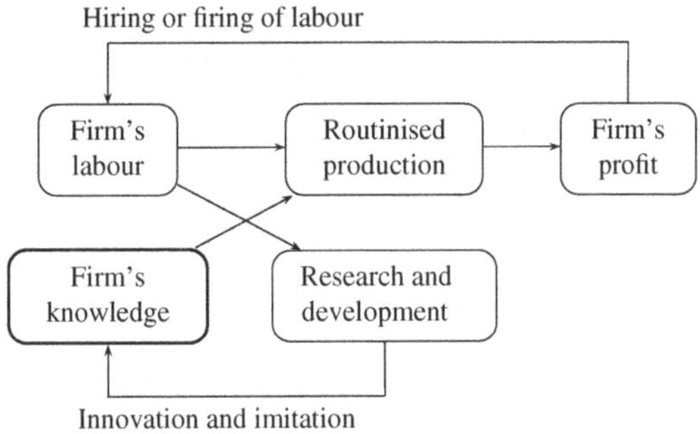

Fig. 8 Feedback loops of an incumbent firm in the pure-labor version of the Mark II model (modified from Andersen 2011, 208)

idea that there has been a real historical transition from the firms and mechanisms of the Mark I model to the firms and mechanisms of Mark II. This transition became obvious in the late nineteenth century when, in a few industries, it became a competitive necessity for firms to have departments of research and development. Since then, this type of innovative investment has spread to more and more industries. Another major transition had taken place a few centuries earlier when credit-based Mark I firms largely replaced artisan workshops (*Cycles*, pp. 223–230). What was gradually replaced can also be described as the Mark Zero model of guild-based artisan production, which had been shaped under feudalism. Thus Mark I marked a transition that started from a model in which the replication of routines was emphasized and major innovative change were actively discouraged.

Although such transitions in the units and mechanisms of evolution are the results of microevolutionary processes, they clearly influence macroevolution. Three characteristics can be recognized by comparing with the major transitions in the units and mechanisms of biological evolution (Maynard Smith and Szathmáry 1997). First, the transition from single-cell organisms to multi-cell organisms did not mean that single-cell organisms became extinct. Similarly, we see the continued coexistence of Mark II firms, Mark I firms, and even some artisan workshops of the Mark Zero type. Second, major transitions in both natural and economic evolution influence the possible types of mutations and innovations. In economic life, the artisan workshops of Mark Zero had only room for incremental innovations, while radical innovations became possible through the independence and external finance of Mark I innovators. The innovative oligopolistic competition of the Mark II model does not exclude such innovations, but it seems clear that the bulk of the activities of R&D departments concerns minor innovations. Third, the emergence of multi-cell organisms led to a radical increase in the speed of macro-evolutionary change. Similarly, the transition from Mark Zero workshops to Mark I firms was accompanied by an immediate increase in the average speed of evolution within industries and a long-term increase in the number of industrial specializations. Further increases in the speed of macroevolutionary change followed the emergence of Mark II firms; and the step-wise increases in the level of R&D that is needed for operating in most industries means that we have reached the present astonishing speed of macroevolution.

Socioeconomic coevolution. Although the microevolutionary analyses of *Capitalism* are based on the Mark II model, Schumpeter still mainly thought of the macroscopic evolution of the routine system in terms of the Mark I model. He assumed the alternation of routinized equilibria and innovative disturbances that challenges pre-existing routines. He dramatized the socioeconomic meaning of this process by means of two related concepts. 'Creative destruction' is the selecting out of firms (or their routines) by the pressure from radical innovations; and 'the process of creative destruction' is the combination of this kind of selection and the innovative activities that drives the process. Many of the old firms cannot make a smooth upgrade of their competencies and switch their areas of specialization. They instead tend to perish in the evolutionary process; and their employees face great stress and significant welfare losses, which to them seem more obvious than the long-term advantages of economic evolution. The reactions of the old firms and their employees can, directly or indirectly, slow down the process of economic evolution. This effect can be depicted by adding two brakes on the Mark I model (see Fig. 9). The primary brake functions by making conditions for innovation more difficult. The secondary brake concerns the avoidance of creative destruction for those involved; its use implies that the selective adaptation of the routine system is slowed down.

The idea of adding brakes on the Mark I model of economic evolution seems to have brought Schumpeter back to his early idea of developing a Mark SC model of socioeconomic coevolution. We have already (in Section 3) seen that *Entwicklung* suggested that every sector of social life has an evolutionary process analogous to that of economic evolution. *Capitalism* (chapter 22) implemented this idea in relation to its analysis of the functioning of democratic political systems. Here, politicians are competing for votes. Most of them do so in a routinized manner, but there are also innovators who create new parties or modify the policies of established parties. The resulting process can be depicted by models of political evolution. Here we can start from a situation in which the evolution of the routines of political life has stopped. Then innovative politicians produce an evolutionary disequilibrium, while the process of selective adaptation brings the political system to a new Schumpeterian equilibrium.

An obvious area for political innovation is the use of the two brakes during long periods that are dominated by the destructive part of the economic process of creative destruction. The major reason is that, during the same depressive periods, the evolution of the family sector emphasizes the norm of stable and secure standards of life. Thus, we have a major example of the coevolution between the family sector, the political sector, and the economic sector. However, it is not easy to develop the analysis of coevolution, since it depends on the way the evolutionary process is organized in each of the sectors. This can be understood by considering *Capitalism*'s (pp. 273–283) two models of political evolution (see Andersen 2009, 174–180). The Mark I model is based on innovations by individual political

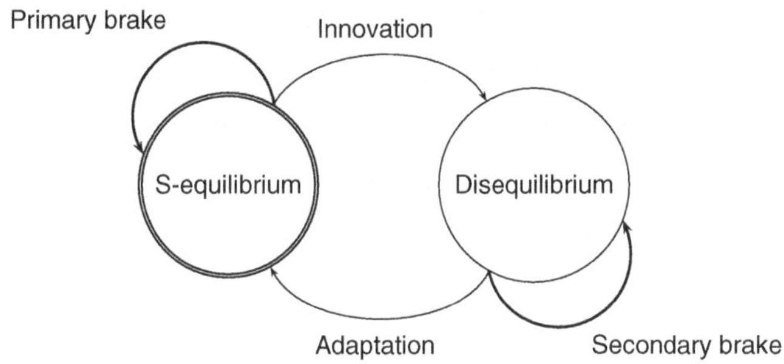

Fig. 9 Adding two brakes on the Mark I model of economic macroevolution (from Andersen 2011, 222)

'entrepreneurs', such as in the classical British parliamentary system. The Mark II model is based on the minor innovations and marketing by oligopolistic political parties, such as in the USA. The latter model might be more likely to evolve policies that make use of the brakes on economic evolution.

Although Schumpeter probably returned to the Mark SC model of his youth because he was interested in the problem of the brakes on economic evolution, we are actually facing a model that can be used for many analytical purposes. For the sake of generality, it is helpful to add the science sector to the already mentioned economic sector, political sector, and family sector. The general process of coevolution between these sectors (see Fig. 10) is hardly analytically manageable unless we, for a specific historical period, are able to reduce the number of significant interactions and to consider the selected sectoral interactions asymmetric. The previous discussion of the use of the brakes is based on a sequential logic. We started with the influence of economic evolution on family sector evolution. Then the family sector defined an agenda for political evolution. Finally, the political sector tried to brake economic evolution. However, Schumpeter's standard case is capitalist economic evolution with little braking. This implies an alternative sequence of sectoral interactions. During the upswing of the long wave of railroadization, it was economic evolution that largely provided the circumstances to which the other three sectors adapted. Furthermore, the politicians promoted the spread of the railroads and did not bother to save the mail coaches. A similar sequence of causations seems to characterize recent processes of globalization. More generally, it seems to be the most internationally exposed sectors (the economy and science) that tend to dominate the sectoral coevolution with the political sector and the family sector, which are largely nationally organized. However, the uneven internationalization of the sectors seems to be a major source of global instabilities.

The above discussion of the sequences of asymmetric causation has reduced analytical complexity at a high cost: the result can hardly be called an analysis of socioeconomic coevolution. Since the processes of coevolution are immensely complex and still beyond the reach of solid analysis, we have to consider an alternative stepwise procedure. This procedure becomes clear when we realize

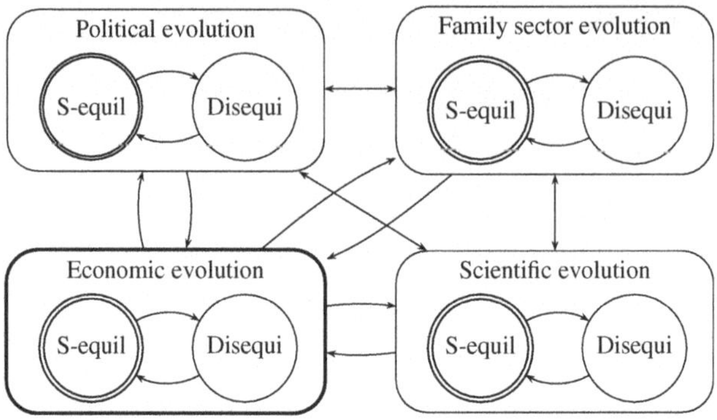

Fig. 10 The Mark SC model of sectoral coevolution (modified from Andersen 2011, 226)

that most of our analyses of economic evolution are made under the assumption that the other sectors do not evolve. We can approach the coevolution between two sectors by gradually changing this assumption. We first study the evolutionary process of one sector under different assumptions of the state of the other sector. Then we do the same for the other sector. Finally, we try to study the simultaneous evolutions within the two sectors. By gradually adding more and more sectoral processes of evolution, we might in the end obtain some analytical clarity about the overall process of socio-cultural evolution. This seems to be the way Schumpeter wanted to approach the Mark SC modelling of socioeconomic coevolution.

Economic evolution and the natural environment. There is no reason to constrain modern evolutionary models to those developed or suggested by Schumpeter. On the contrary, it seems important to start developing a family of 'Mark NE models' that he rather discouraged than promoted. This label might be used to denote models that include the impact of the natural environmental on economic evolution, and vice versa. Environmentally oriented models have tended to ignore economic evolution. This was at least the case when Christopher Freeman in (1973) contributed to a book called *Models of Doom* (Cole et al. 1973). Here he characterized much of the contents of the famous report called *The Limits to Growth* as 'Malthus with a Computer' (Freeman 1973). The problem was that the report ignored the evolutionary responses to the challenges from the environment and population growth. Freeman later promoted the analysis of the evolutionary responses of the capitalist engine to environmental challenges. However, the challenge to evolutionary researchers is to develop a family of more formal models of these issues. For convenience, this family of models might be called 'Schumpeter Mark NE'. Mark NE modelling can start from either Mark I or Mark II. But ultimately these Mark NE models have in some way to deal with the complexities of socio-economic coevolution, and thus they become developments of the Mark SC model.

6 Conclusions

This paper has argued that evolutionary economists can still learn much from revisiting the type of evolutionary economics that Joseph Schumpeter started to develop one hundred years ago. Actually, we can fruitfully explore and exploit his evolutionary economics in largely the same way as biologists have used Charles Darwin's evolutionary biology for 150 years. However, while Darwin in all respects has been surpassed by modern evolutionary biologists, Schumpeter's core books still contain important challenges for modern evolutionary economists. Furthermore, we cannot appreciate his efforts by reading a single great book such as the *Origin of Species*. I suggested that we instead can organize Schumpeter's books in three groups. The first of them is the programmatic duology that consists of his two early German books (*Wesen* and *Entwicklung*). The second is the evolutionary economic duology that consists of *Development* and *Cycles*. The third is the socioeconomic synthesis that is found in parts of *Capitalism*. Then I analyzed the internal logic of and the interconnections between these groups of works.

My analyses of these groups of books were supported by the distinction between Schumpeter's three different models of evolutionary processes and by the distinction between microevolution and macroevolution. The Mark I model of the interaction between individual innovative entrepreneurs and routine-based firms dominates in *Entwicklung*, *Development* and *Cycles*. Inspired by Walrasian economics, he used this model to analyze the macroscopic evolution of the system of economic routines—and neglected the analysis of the microevolution that takes place within individual industries. Today an important task is to operationalize the concept of macroevolution by adding microevolutionary processes that includes both innovation and selection. When this is done, we might be able to combine the microscopic and macroscopic aspects of something like a Mark I process of economic evolution. However, we should in this connection not ignore *Capitalism*'s well known Mark II model of oligopolistic competition. This model describes a microevolutionary process, and the remaining question is how Mark II in detail influences macroevolution. Furthermore, Schumpeter presented the major historical transition from Mark I to Mark II. The analysis of such transitions in evolution is still an important challenge for evolutionary economics. *Capitalism* also contains elements of the Mark SC model that describes socioeconomic evolution as a coevolutionary process between the major sectors of society. It is a major challenge to develop Mark SC into something that can rightfully be called a model. Since such a model would include political evolution, family-sector evolution, and scientific evolution, its development presupposes transdisciplinary research. This is even more important for the development of Mark IV models of the interaction between economic evolution and the natural environment.

Acknowledgements This paper is based on my presidential address presented at the 13th International Schumpeter Society Conference, Aalborg University, 21–24 June 2010. A revised version was presented at the European Association for Evolutionary Political Economy Conference on Schumpeter's Heritage, Vienna, 27–30 October 2011. I wish to thank for useful comments given by participants of these conferences. I also thank Palgrave Macmillan for permission to reproduce and modify figures from Andersen (2011) and Anthem Press for permission to modify figures from Andersen (2009).

References

Andersen ES (2002) Railroadization as Schumpeter's standard example of capitalist evolution: an evolutionary-ecological account. Ind Innov 9:41–78

Andersen ES (2004) Population thinking, Price's equation and the analysis of economic evolution. Evol Inst Econ Rev 1:127–148

Andersen ES (2009) Schumpeter's evolutionary economics: a theoretical, historical and statistical analysis of the engine of capitalism. Anthem, London

Andersen ES (2011) Joseph A. Schumpeter: a theory of social and economic evolution. Palgrave Macmillan, Basingstoke and New York

Augello MM (1990) Joseph Alois Schumpeter: a reference guide. Springer, Berlin

Cole HSD, Freeman C, Jahoda M, Pavitt KLR (eds) (1973) Models of doom: a critique of the limits to growth. Universe Books, New York

Dopfer K, Potts J (2008) The general theory of economic evolution. Routledge, London and New York

Fisher RA (1930) The genetical theory of natural selection. Clarendon, Oxford

Freeman C (1973) Malthus with a computer. In: Cole HSD, Freeman C, Jahoda M, Pavitt KLR (eds) Models of doom: a critique of the limits to growth. Universe Books, New York, pp 5–13

Freeman C (1990) Schumpeter's *Business Cycles* revisited. In: Heertje A, Perlman M (eds) Evolving technology and market structure: studies in Schumpeterian economics. University of Michigan Press, Ann Arbor, pp 17–38

Kuznets S (1940) Schumpeter's *Business Cycles*. Am Econ Rev 30:257–271

Leontief W (1950) Joseph A. Schumpeter (1883–1950). Econometrica 18:103–110

Marshall A (1898) Distribution and exchange. Econ J 8:37–59

Maynard Smith J (1982) Evolution and the theory of games. Cambridge University Press, Cambridge

Maynard Smith J, Szathmáry E (1997) The Major Transitions in Evolution. Oxford University Press, Oxford

Nelson RR, Winter SG (1982) An evolutionary theory of economic change. Harvard University Press, Cambridge

Schumpeter JA (1908) Das Wesen und der Hauptinhalt der theoretischen Nationalökonomie. Duncker & Humblot, Leipzig

Schumpeter JA (1910) On the nature of economic crises [in practice a translation of Chapter 6 of *Entwicklung*]. In: Boianovsky M (ed) Business cycle theory: selected texts 1860–1939, vol 5, 2005. Pickering & Chatto, London, pp 5–50

Schumpeter JA (1912a) The economy as a whole (translation of Chapter 2 of *Entwicklung*). In: Becker MC, Knudsen T, Swedberg R (eds) (2011) The entrepreneur: classical texts by Joseph A. Schumpeter. Stanford University Press, Stanford, pp 155–226

Schumpeter JA (1912b) The fundamental phenomenon of economic development (translation of Chapter 2 of *Entwicklung*). In: Becker MC, Knudsen T, Swedberg R (eds) (2011) The entrepreneur: classical texts by Joseph A. Schumpeter. Stanford University Press, Stanford, pp 79–154

Schumpeter JA (1912c) Theorie der wirtschaftlichen Entwicklung. Duncker & Humblot, Leipzig

Schumpeter JA (1926) Theorie der wirtschaftlichen Entwicklung: Eine Untersuchung über Unternehmergewinn, Kapital, Kredit, Zins und den Konjunkturzyklus. Duncker & Humblot, Munich and Leipzig

Schumpeter JA (1928) The instability of capitalism. Econ J 38:361–86
Schumpeter JA (1934) The theory of economic development: an inquiry into profits, capital, credit, interest and the business cycle. Harvard University Press, Cambridge
Schumpeter JA (1937) Preface to Japanese edition of 'Theorie der wirtschaftlichen Entwicklung'. In: Essays: on entrepreneurs, innovations, business cycles, and the evolution of capitalism. Transactions Books, New Brunswick, 1989, pp 165–168
Schumpeter JA (1939) Business cycles: a theoretical, historical, and statistical analysis of the capitalist process. McGraw-Hill, New York
Schumpeter JA (1942) Capitalism, socialism and democracy, 1st edn. Harper, New York
Schumpeter JA (1964) Business cycles: a theoretical, historical, and statistical analysis of the capitalist process, Rendigs Fels's abridged edn. McGraw-Hill, New York
Schumpeter JA (2000) Briefe/letters. Mohr, Tübingen
Walras L (1954) Elements of pure economics or the theory of social wealth. G. Allen, London

Back to Engel? Some Evidence for the Hierarchy of Needs

Andreas Chai and Alessio Moneta

Abstract Using UK household expenditure data spanning over four decades (1960–2000), this paper employs Engel's needs-based approach to analyzing household expenditure patterns and finds evidence for the existence of a stable hierarchy of expenditure patterns at low levels of household income. Second, we investigate how rising household income influences the manner in which total expenditure is distributed across Engel's expenditure categories. Our results suggest that i) total household expenditure is distributed across Engel's expenditure categories in an increasingly even manner as household income increases and ii) over time, there has been an acceleration in the rate at which household expenditure patterns become diversified as household income rises. Finally, we consider how the shape of Engel Curves may help shed light on the relationship between goods and the underlying needs they serve.

1 Introduction

The set of needs that motivate consumption activity is an important theoretical concept which has a long tradition in economic thought (see inter alia Menger 1871; Marshall 1890; Georgescu-Roegen 1954). Many scholars posit that some of these needs are related to the biologically-evolved nature of *homo sapiens* (e.g. Witt

Reprinted from Journal of Evolutionary Economics 22(4), 649-676 , Springer (2012)

A. Chai (✉)
Griffith Business School, Gold Coast Campus, Griffith University, Gold Coast, Qld 4222, Australia
e-mail: a.chai@griffith.edu.au

A. Moneta
Laboratory of Economics and Management, Scuola Superiore Sant'Anna, Piazza Martiri della Libertà, 33, 56127 Pisa, Italy
e-mail: moneta@econ.mpg.de

A. Pyka and E.S. Andersen (eds.), *Long Term Economic Development*, Economic Complexity and Evolution, DOI 10.1007/978-3-642-35125-9_3,

2001). Moreover, the fact that some of these needs are subject to satiation can provide important behavioral micro foundations for models in which changes in the industrial composition of growing economies are linked to compositional changes in household expenditure patterns (see inter alia Aoki and Yoshikawa 2002; Metcalfe et al. 2006; Saviotti and Pyka 2008). Beyond models of structural change, the existence of a universally-shared set of needs has fundamental implications for the analysis of household expenditure patterns.

In this regard, it is a little known fact that Ernst Engel devised a classification method to measure how different needs affect household spending patterns. In particular, he found empirical regularities in the expenditure patterns of low income households. Engel claims that these regularities support the existence of a hierarchy amongst needs (Engel 1857). Using UK household expenditure data spanning four decades (1960–2000), we examine whether the distribution of consumption expenditure across Engel's expenditure categories at the lowest income levels is stable and reflects the same order found by Engel. This is done by employing Engel's classification system by which goods are classified according to the needs they serve. It would seem unlikely this conjecture would be confirmed in light of the major changes in the number and variety of goods available to households, as well as the growth of real household income levels that has taken place since Engel's era. Nevertheless, we find evidence that the order Engel inferred to exist in the spending patterns of low income households in 1857 is still present in the expenditure patterns of low income households of today.

Second, we examine how rising household income leads to changes in the manner in which total expenditure is distributed across expenditure categories. This is done by measuring how evenly total expenditure is distributed across Engel's expenditure categories at high and low household income levels using the Gini measure of inequality. Here, our results suggest that total household expenditure is distributed across Engel's expenditure categories in an increasingly even manner as household income increases. In other words, as households become rich, they diversify their spending patterns. There appears to exist a tendency for this diversification to take place in a way that the differences between the budget shares dedicated to different needs fall as income increases. This new 'addendum' to Engel's Law has implications for understanding demand-driven structural change. Moreover, when examining the way in which household diversification patterns change over time, we find evidence that there has been an acceleration in the rate at which household expenditure patterns become diversified as household income rises. Whilst a stable hierarchy of expenditure patterns is present among low income households across all of the observed years, the rate at which this order breaks down with additional increases in household incomes appears to have accelerated in more recent years.

Finally, we discuss the shortcomings of Engel's classification method in which the link between goods and the needs they serve are made with little theoretical justification. An important question in this regard is whether it is possible to develop a way of empirically identifying the number of needs that goods are connected to particular expenditure categories. We explore such a possibility by building on a theoretical insight from the literature on lexicographic preferences about how the shape of the Engel Curve (EC) for a good may be affected by the range of needs to which the good is linked. Comparing the shapes of ECs, we find certain 'lower order' goods that directly serve needs possess relatively similar EC shapes relative to 'higher order' goods.

This paper is structured as follows. Section 2 briefly reviews Engel's results, while Section 3 discusses both the opportunities and pitfalls of pursuing Engel's evolutionary approach to analyzing household expenditure patterns. Section 4 examines whether modern household expenditure data supports Engel's claim of a hierarchy amongst needs. Section 5 examines the manner and pace at which the uncovered order breaks down as household income levels rise. Finally, Section 6 considers what the shape of Engel Curves may reveal about the relationship between the goods and the range of underlying needs they serve.

2 Engel's Hierarchy

More than 150 years ago, Ernst Engel undertook one of the earliest attempts to study empirically the expenditure patterns of low incomes household in order to shed light on their living standards. Despite its well-known reputation, it is a little known fact that, in this study, Engel claims to have found evidence that the evolved biological nature of humans generate empirical regularities in the distribution of households expenditure at low income levels. This section briefly reviews Engel's results and discusses both the opportunities and pitfalls of pursuing his evolutionary approach to analyzing household consumption expenditure patterns in the context of the prevailing economic literature.

Writing some seventy years before income was systematically analyzed in economic theory (Stigler 1954:102), the theoretical starting point for Engel's inquiry was to analyze the *Bedürfnisse* (needs) which motivate consumption and how their influence changes as household income rises. A key facet of his work is to understand why a change in the income levels of households affects the composition of consumption expenditure and why preferences are not constant with rising income (in modern parlance, why preferences are non-homothetic). While the use of the concept of needs in economic theorizing was certainly not unique to Engel (e.g. Menger 1871), what was unique was his empirical approach in analyzing the effects of needs and his argument that needs have their origins in human evolution.[1] As Engel put it:

[1] In the literature, Engel was thus perceived as a pioneer of an evolutionary approach to economics: "By his study on consumption alone Engel came to appreciate the modifiable nature of human beings. This is a central thought in modern economics which many students have only recently been coerced into accepting by the triumph of evolutionary philosophy" (A. G. Warner, *Publications of the American Statistical Association*, 1896).

> All living things are born with a number of needs, whose non-satisfaction leads to death. The human being is not an exception. Also in him works the urge to satisfy (these needs) with a natural power that can overcome strong constraints that either carry humans away from or lead them to victory (Engel 1895: 8).[2]

Engel proceeds by studying how household expenditure is distributed across *needs* rather than goods and services. Therefore, a real innovation in his work is that he developed a method for empirically measuring the impact that particular needs have on consumption patterns over a range of observed income. He does this by aggregating preexisting expenditure data on individual goods and services, found in Ducpétiaux (1855), into larger expenditure groups that are related to the satisfaction of particular needs. In doing so, Engel assumes that all individuals share the same set of needs at low income levels and possess the same potential for developing higher-order needs, such as education. Engel justifies this assumption on the basis of the aforementioned conjecture that needs have their origins in the evolved biological nature of humans. The list of needs includes the need for nourishment, clothing, accommodation, heating and light, household goods, intellectual education (which included some forms of entertainment), public safety, health and recreation and personal services (Engel 1857:6). Shown in Table 1, the resulting taxonomy of consumption expenditure was far more detailed relative to standard expenditure taxonomies of the time.

In terms of the way in which needs are linked to the consumption of goods, Engel makes a priori assumptions about the connection between goods and the underlying needs they serve. He assumes all households consume goods and services for the same purpose. For example, all households consume food specifically for the sake of nourishment. Thus, households possess a common understanding about the function that goods and services serve. Most goods and services are also assumed to have a single purposes in that they are linked to the satisfaction of a single need. Thus, expenditure on travel is grouped with recreational expenditure as Engel reasons that both types of expenditure served the same need for health and recreation. No real theoretical justification is provided for why he thought these expenditure categories served the same underlying need.

In other cases, Engel assumes *a priori* that goods and services *do* have multiple purposes. He constructs two special categories for these, which he labels 'tools and means for work' as well as 'personal services'. Engel acknowledges that it is difficult to identify the needs that these particular goods and services satisfied (Engel 1857:7) and that this issue requires more attention, as such expenditures do not serve their specific needs but are incurred by consumers in the process of satisfying other needs. In this regard, Engel recognizes that there exists not only an order amongst needs, but also another type of order amongst goods: some goods

---

[2] "Niemand weiss, warum es so ist, aber es ist so, dass alles Lebende mit einer Reihe von bedürfnissen geboren wird, deren Nichtbefriedigung den Tod herbeiführt. Der Mensch macht hiervon am wenigsten eine Ausnahme. Auch in ihm wirkt der Drang der Befriedigung mit der Gewalt einer Narturkraft, dies selbst über starke Fesseln den Sieg davon trägt oder aber darin zu Grunde geht."

Table 1 Engel's expenditure categories

Needs (*Bedürfnisse*)	Relevant expenditures
1. Nourishment (*Nahrung*)	Daily nourishment from meals and beverages, spices, stimulants (e.g. alcohol, coffee), tobacco, occasional dining out, etc.
2. Clothing (*Kleidung*)	Clothing and shoes of all kinds; underwear, jewelry and toiletries; clothing accessories
3. Housing (*Wohnung*)	Shelter, furniture, household appliances; beds and bedding; insurance for housing and furniture.
4. Heating and Lighting (*Heizung*)	Wood, coal and gas heating; lighting via candles, oil and gas
5. Tools for work (*Geräthe*)	Tools, machines, mechanical instruments; crockery and vessels etc.; all kinds of metal, earths, stones, glass, porcelain, leather, pulp, rubber etc.; wagons, boats, saddles and equipment etc.; means of communications etc.
6. Intellectual education (*Erziehung*)	Education, tuition; church; tools for education, tuition and worship; scientific equipment, literary and artistic production; intellectual rejuvenation and educations, music, theater etc.; musical instruments
7. Public safety (*öffentliche Sicherheit*)	Legal protection; administration; police; state defence; care for the poor etc.
8. Health and recreation (*Gesundheitspflege*)	Medical treatment and pharmaceutical expenses, bathing; outdoor recreation, play, recreational travel.- Life insurance
9. Personal service (*Dienstleistungen*)	Personal services attained from use of domestic servants of all kinds

Source: Engel (1857: 5–6).

directly satisfy the consumer's needs, while others are used by consumers to satisfy needs in a more indirect fashion. This will be discussed further in Section 5.

In contrast to existing expenditure aggregation methods, we argue that the approach pursued by Engel has some methodological advantages. Current approaches that are widely used in the modern literature on household expenditure make their own assumptions about the separability of preferences and the household budgeting process (Strotz 1957; Gorman 1959). These approaches assume that agents allocate total expenditure first to broad groups of goods, based on a price index for each group, and then further allocate expenditure within each of these groups, based on group individual prices and group expenditures. A benefit of these modern approaches is that they only rely on the assumption that households respond to price and income effects. However, Engel's approach suggests that it may be fruitful to let aggregation methods be also informed by scientific knowledge of the nature of consumer's needs and how these are satisfied. This strategy will not necessarily lead to the creation of more testable assumptions. It will, however, lead to the creation of more realistic assumptions that are at least consistent with what is known about the underlying motivations that drive household expenditure patterns.

The main conclusion of Engel's work was an observation about how the expenditure patterns of low income household reflect a ranking amongst needs (see Table 2). He explicitly claims that his results show that needs are not of equal

Table 2 Budget shares of Belgian workmen's families

	Family type		
Needs	On relief	Poor but independent	Comfortable
Nourishment	70.89	67.37	62.42
Clothing	11.74	13.16	14.03
Housing	8.72	8.33	9.04
Heating and lighting	5.63	5.51	5.41
Tools for work	0.64	1.16	2.31
Intellectual education	0.36	1.06	1.21
Public safety	0.15	0.47	0.88
Health and recreation	1.68	2.78	4.30
Personal services	0.19	0.16	0.40

Source: lines 1–10: Table 6 in Engel (1857: 27)

importance to households, but rather that a hierarchy existed amongst needs (Engel 1857:27). As stated in the later book:

> Needs are not of the same rank. At the top stand those needs whose satisfaction is key to physical sustenance: nourishment, clothing, housing, heating and lighting and health. Of a second order follow: intellectual and spiritual care, legal protection and public safety, public provisions and assistance. (Engel 1895:8)[3]

Engel argues that the observed hierarchy is in line with what typically happens in families experiencing a decline in income: When a family can not properly satisfy all their existing needs, they tend to sacrifice the satisfaction of higher order needs in order to satisfy more basic needs. Hence the lowering of income essentially acts as a litmus test on the consumer's priorities, in that it forces out expenditures related to needs that are less basic, and leaves those expenditures related to more fundamental needs. Therefore, it is possible to identify the most important needs by examining which types of expenditure dominate household spending at the lowest observed level of household income. The well-known 'Engel law' is based on his observation that expenditure on the need for nourishment increases as household income falls (Chai and Moneta 2010). Because of its importance, Engel reasons that a rough proxy for household living standards is the size of the budget share dedicated to nourishment: the lower it falls, the better off households are, as they are able to dedicate more expenditure to other, higher-order needs (Engel 1857:50).

All in all, Engel uses the concept of needs as an explanatory vehicle to account for 'Engel's Law' and, more broadly, how household consumption patterns change as income rises. The idea that the need for nourishment is the most important need explains why low income households spend a large share of their budget on goods

[3] "Allein die Bedürfnisse sind nicht alle von gleichem Range. Obenan stehen die von deren Befriedigung die physiche Erhaltung abhängt: Nahrung Kleidung, Wohnung, Heizung und Beleuchtung derselben und Gesundheitspflege. In Zwieter Linie folgen: Geistespflege, Seelsorge, Rechtsschutz und öffentliche Sicherhiet, Vor- und Fürsorge, Erholung und Erquickung."

related to the satisfaction of this need. As households become more affluent, the budget share dedicated to other needs becomes more prominent as the household begins to dedicate more expenditure to the satisfaction of lower order needs.

3 An Evolutionary Approach to Needs

The existence of a hierarchy amongst needs has the potential to provide an important account of how the composition of household expenditure systematically alters as households become more affluent. Since Engel's time, there has been considerable progress in both developing a theory of how consumer respond to marginal changes in price and their incomes, as well as the empirical analysis of household expenditure patterns (Deaton and Muellbauer 1980a; Aitken and Irongmonger 1995). However, a discussion of the underlying motivations of consumption is absent from much of this literature. It is widely recognized that marginalist consumer theory is unable to explain how budget expenditure shares will change in the face of rising income - as embodied in the basic shape of the Engel curve. As Prais puts it, "traditional theory of consumption deals only with infinitesimal changes, does not give any insight into the general shape of Engel Curves" (Prais 1953). More recently, Lewbel observes that contemporary models of demand systems "still fail to explain most of the observed variation in individual consumption behavior" (Lewbel 2007). The inescapable conclusion is that "influences other than current prices and current total expenditure must be systematically modeled if even the broad pattern of demand is to be explained in a theoretically coherent and empirically coherent way" (Deaton and Muellbauer 1980b:323).

A start to tackling this open question can be found in lexicographic demand systems (Day and Robinson 1973; Earl 1983; Drakopoulos 1994). Lexicographic choice theory explicitly models ordered preferences that constrain substitution possibilities between goods. In the recent literature, this idea has been used to model the concept of bounded rationality in the consumption context (Aversi et al. 1999; Nelson and Consoli 2010). Originating from Simon (1956), bounded rationality states that because agents have a limited amount of reasoning power and that decisions incur 'energy costs' (Loasby 1998:22), then any conception of the consumer 'perfectly optimizing' decisions would be logically impossible as it would require an infinite amount of time and thought.

Beyond modeling decision-making, lexicographic preference systems are also useful when considering how the broad composition of demand changes with rising income. In their strongest form, lexicographic preferences imply that the indifference curve is strictly vertical in certain regions, since consumers have no interest in substituting away from a certain good that serves first order needs until they have attained a critical quantity of this good. Only when this threshold is reached is it possible for consumers to substitute between this good and goods serving needs of a lower order. More weaker versions if lexicographic preferences model the same phenomenon via a change in the slope of the indifference curve, thus allowing some substitution between goods (Drakopoulos 1994). However, what is lacking in this approach is any hard predictions about precisely what type of expenditures consumers are less willing to substitute at low levels of expenditure.

Elsewhere, such a lexicographic structure of demand can be found implicitly hidden in many contemporary macroeconomic models of demand-driven structural change. These models examine what economic effects may result from changes in the composition of household expenditure patterns that take place as household rises. A key message of demand-driven structural change theory is that the industrial composition of growing economies can be altered by the manner in which household expenditure patterns change as household income rises (Metcalfe et al. 2006; Saviotti and Pyka 2008). This growing body of literature assumes that household expenditure on *any* particular good has an upper limit which causes the specific growth rate of demand faced by each sector to follow an S-shaped path, whereby demand growth will slow down and eventually cease as more households reach the saturation level of income (see inter alia Aoki and Yoshikawa 2002; Metcalfe et al. 2006; Foellmi and Zweimüller 2008; Saviotti 2001).[4]

The theoretical basis for the presence of saturation in demand patterns is the notion that some of the underlying needs that motivate consumption are 'satiable' as they can be effectively satisfied at some consumption level (see inter alia Menger 1871; Marshall 1890; Georgescu-Roegen 1954). Pasinetti argues that, because of the *physiological* nature of needs, they may be satisfied at certain income levels and the marginal utility of successive increments of the same good tend to fall dramatically and can even become negative (Pasinetti 1981:72). The basic example is food. Once the consumer has eaten enough, they possess no willingness to pay for additional amounts of food. Once a need is satiated, the corresponding consumption expenditure dedicated to its satisfaction ceases to rise and additional increases in income are dedicated to the satisfaction of other needs which are not yet satiated. More recently, Witt (2010, 2001) makes some useful remarks on this issue from a naturalistic perspective. Similar to Engel, his starting point is the biologically evolved nature of humans, which has imprinted a certain number of 'basic needs' on the human genetic endowment. The degree to which a need influences consumption depends on the consumer's state of deprivation.

A general pitfall of the needs-based approach to consumption is that there is no clear consensus on precisely how many universally-shared needs exist. Needs schemas developed elsewhere have attempted to shed light on the functional nature of consumption, such as those developed by Maslow (1954), Galtung (1980) and Max-Neef (1991). Here it should be noted that there are important differences to the 'psychological' approach to defining the needs of consumers, compared to earlier 'physiological' approaches. For a detailed discussion of these see Deci and Ryan

[4] For a discussion of the extent to which saturation can be found across the wide variety of goods and services present in modern economies see Moneta and Chai (2010).

(1975). Psychological schemas are difficult to apply as they tend to include relatively difficult to observe higher order needs, such as the need for self determination.[5] Moreover, because such needs have no basis in the biologically evolved nature of humans, it becomes hard to justify why they are universally shared by consumers and why they are fixed over time. In this respect, Witt argues that only needs with obvious reproductive value in times of fierce selection pressure should be considered as basic needs in the sense that they are innate and, indeed, they are commonly shared by humans (Witt 2010). In particular, he argues that these can be roughly identified as motivations associated with such activities as drinking, sleeping, eating, keeping body temperature, physical activity, sex, and seeking pain relief, shelter, affection, social recognition, sensory arousal, cognitive consistency, and achievement (Millenson 1967:386).

Another complication is the idea that the number of needs that agents possess may grow or decline over time. Beyond 'basic' needs, Witt conjectures that there exists another class of needs that are not universally shared, and may be acquired or lost through experience. Via the laws of associative learning (Hergenhahn and Olson 1997), formerly neutral stimuli that have repeatedly become associated with primary reinforcers may become reinforcing in their own right: for example, aesthetic tableware that has been regularly perceived while an agent has consumed food and enjoyed the company of others (Witt 2001:35). With enough experience, the consumer may find such tableware pleasing, even if it is not experienced in the company of food or friends. If developed further, this approach could enable scholars to relax the assumption that consumers share the same set of needs and that these are constant over time, as different consumers with different learning histories will possess different sets of needs. Hence, an important phenomenon accompanying the growth of consumption could be the growth and diversification of acquired needs that have emerged and expanded as households become more affluent. This idea suggests that investigating the type of reinforcement to which consumers are exposed, as well the type of goods and services that are likely to become associated with this reinforcement, could yield insights into how the large diversity present in household consumption expenditure patterns may have arisen.[6]

If indeed it is feasible that certain consumer motivations are a product of the consumer's particular past experiences, this opens the door to understanding how the scale and quality of goods supplied in an economy can endogenously influence not only the knowledge that consumers possess, but also the motivations that stimulate consumers to purchase goods in the first place. In this respect, there is a growing awareness among contemporary scholars about how the structure of demand and supply may have important mutual influence on each other. For

[5] For one attempt, see Jackson and Marks (1999).

[6] A number of case studies have begun to study the evolving link between particular goods & services and the underlying needs they serve. The general aim is to uncover general regularities in how product innovations may be linked to satiation of the needs original served by goods and services, such as food (Ruprecht 2005; Manig and Moneta 2009), shoes (Frenzel Baudisch 2006), tourism services (Chai 2011) and washing machines (Witt and Woersdorfer 2010).

example, the economic historian de Vries (2008) points out that important historical changes in household economic activity led to increases in *both* the supply of market-orientated money earning activities *and* the demand for goods offered in the market place. Key here was that a change in consumer aspiration levels altered household's willingness to supply labor between 1650 and 1850 in such a way that households were prepared to work longer and harder than in previous generations. This 'industrious revolution' is an important macro-historical process necessary to understand patterns of long run economic development. Several other studies have highlighted the way in which the structure of technology and the nature of market institutions may foster creativity amongst consumers (Bianchi 2002) that, via the close interaction with producers, lead to the emergence of new product innovations (von Hippel 2005). In this sense, the search for consistent patterns of household expenditure patterns across large periods economic growth (see below) can be thought of as a way of examining the extent to which household consumption patterns are malleable and tend to be influenced by changing economic conditions. If indeed economic conditions play a strong role in shaping the nature of consumer needs, then it is highly unlikely that the composition of spending would stay constant over many decades of economic growth.

4 Evidence for a Hierarchy of Needs

This section examines what evidence exists for Engel's claims of a hierarchy amongst needs using modern household expenditure data. If Engel's conjecture is correct that certain needs of consumers are fixed and universally-shared across all consumers, then some possibility exists that a stable pattern of household expenditure could be found at the lowest observable levels of household income. We investigate this by using Engel's original classification schema in order to examine to what extent his results about the hierarchy of needs are robust. This does not imply that we fully agree with his proposed set of needs and how they relate to goods and services. Clearly, it is difficult to justify some of the assumptions Engel made in his classification methodology. However, given their historical precedence and the lack of a better alternative, we adopt Engel's classification methodology to see whether his findings about the existence of a hierarchy still hold. This exercise will shed light on the existence of a stable pattern in household consumption patterns. Yet the extent to which this stable patterns can be used as evidence for a hierarchy needs is an open question. In this regard, we leave it for future work to develop a more refined list of needs and an associated classification scheme for aggregating goods and services.

There are several foreseeable reasons why it is unlikely that the ordering of budget shares in modern consumption data is similar to that found by Engel in 1856. Clearly, consumer needs are not the only factor that influence relative levels of consumption expenditure. Changes in supply side conditions could lead to significant changes in expenditure patterns over time via the growth of production capacity and the realization of economies of scale, that would affect the cost of consumption. It is foreseeable that technological progress and increased competition may enable households to satisfy their most basic needs in a relatively inexpensive fashion compared to households of the 19th century. Furthermore, the difference in income between households observed in the 1850s and those observed in the present day are large. Since 1820, there has been an eightfold increase in world per capita income (Maddison 2001). As a result, it is possible that even at the lowest observed income level, household income may have increased sufficiently over time to lead to alterations in the order of budget shares due to expenditure on certain needs being subject to satiation at some real level of expenditure. In other words, if preferences are truly non-homothetic, then sufficiently large increases in household income over time can be predicted to cause major changes in the spending patterns at even the lowest observed household income level.

Using the classification scheme devised by Engel, we proceeded to re-categorize and aggregate household expenditure data from the UK Family expenditure survey. We choose to use observations from 5 years that span over four decades 1961, 1970, 1980, 1990 and 2000. These years were chosen for two reasons: First, we sought to cover a long time span in order to ensure that any results are not a consequence of conditions specific to any one particular sample year. Second, due to the time consuming nature of re-categorizing expenditure using Engel's schema, the number of survey years used was limited to five. To avoid the complications arising from differences in household size, we focus on three person households, since these have the largest number of observations relative to other household sizes.[7]

Table 3 below reports the summary of income statistics. To control for changes in price levels, the Retail price (RPI - all items percentage change over 12 months) was used to derive real values. Average income (as proxied by total expenditure) has clearly risen considerably between 1960 and 2000, and the changes in the standard deviation of income indicate that there were also substantial changes in the income distribution of households. The budget shares for these expenditure grouping were then calculated for ten income deciles for each year included in the sample.

Table 4 reports results for the lowest income decile observed for each sample year. The most salient feature of these results is the surprising consistency of the budget shares across the four decades. Between 1960 and 1980 none of the budget shares changed by more than 2%: the budget share of expenditure dedicated to nourishment dropped marginally from 62 to 60%, while the budget share of

[7] We avoided aggregating across households of different sizes as this would involve using equivalence scales that feature a priori assumptions about how the proportion of family spending dedicated to needs changes with family size. To check the robustness of our results, we aggregated spending data across different household sizes. We found similar results to those reported below, These results are available upon request. In the reclassification exercise, some unavoidable inaccuracies emerged, as there was insufficient information to properly allocate the expenditure category within Engel's schema.

Table 3 Summary income statistics of three person household in FES data, 1960–2000

	1960	1970	1980	1990	2000
Number observations	642	1218	1208	1106	990
Mean real weekly total expenditure	£13.81	£42.23	£125.71	£314.05	£468.18
Standard deviation	£8.86	£48.05	£112.71	£206.93	£294.28
Lowest observed total expenditure	£3.83	£8.32	£15.30	£20.45	£44.58
Highest observed total expenditure	£271.84	£1373.77	£2006.60	£2535.86	£3789.67

Note: measured in pounds, where 2000 is the base year. The Retail Price Index (RPI - all items percentage change over 12 months) was used to derive real values.

Table 4 Budget shares for the lowest income decile, 1960–2000

Needs	1960	1970	1980	1990	2000
1. Nourishment	62	60	60	40	38
2. Clothing	8	9	10	9	9
3. Housing	1	1	1	13	17
4. Heating and lighting	6	5	4	6	9
5. Tools	7	7	7	7	6
6. Intellectual education	3	3	5	3	6
7. Public safety	1	0	1	0	0
8. Health and recreation	3	4	3	6	3
9. Personal services	2	2	1	1	0
10. All other	7	9	8	15	11

Note: entries denote per cent of total expenditure.

expenditure dedicated to clothing rose slightly from 8 to 10%. Other small changes occurred in the budget shares relating to intellectual goods and heating and lighting expenditure. This stability in the household budget shares of expenditure occurred in spite of a large increase in the average real income of three-person households in the lowest income decile: the weekly average real total expenditure rose from 6.81 pounds in 1960 to 123.46 pounds in 2000. It is only after 1980 that and significant changes can be observed: expenditure on nourishment declined significantly, while housing expenditure increased significantly. We note that the upward trend in housing expenditure budget shares reflects the substantial increase in house prices since the 1980s, reductions in the government provision of housing subsidies to low income households, as well as other well known measurement changes related to the manner in which housing expenditure was recorded in the UK Family Expenditure Survey (Tanner 1999).

Contrasting these results to Table 2, they appear to be surprisingly consistent with Engel's observed patterns. Expenditure on nourishment for the poorest observed category of workers was roughly 71% of total expenditure in 1856, while in 1960 it was 62% of total expenditure. In other words, the budget share of nourishment dropped by merely nine per cent in 104 years- a century which witnessed unprecedented economic growth in Europe and an eightfold increase in world per capita income (Maddison 2001).

More generally, the spending on needs that Engel identified as being key to physical sustenance consistently dominate low-income household consumption patterns across all sample years. Summed together, expenditure dedicated to the first order needs represents around 70% of total expenditure across the observed years 1960–2000. The budget share for heating and lighting in the contemporary data also appears to be roughly the same of what it was in the 19th century, although more recently this has increased which reflects the rising price of energy services. As such, these results provide evidence for the conjecture that a stable pattern of expenditure does exist at the lowest levels of observable household income, and has remained considerably stable in spite of the growth in real household income, as well as the goods and services available to households.

We use a comparison of means test to examine formally Engel's specific claim that needs related to physical sustenance, including nourishment, clothing, housing, heating and lighting and health, are of a higher order to needs related to intellectual spiritual care, legal protection and public safety, public provisions and assistance (see previous section). We do this by aggregating the relevant expenditure categories and performing two-sample mean-comparison test, where the hypothesis is that the mean expenditure dedicated to physical sustenance is greater than the mean expenditure dedicate to second order needs. Table 5 below shows that this can not be rejected at an $\alpha = 1\%$ level of significance. As such, it provides some evidence to support Engel's argument that expenditure dedicated to physical sustenance tends to dominate expenditures related to second order needs in the consumption patterns of low income households, and does so consistently over the four decades analyzed in this study.

5 An Addendum to Engel's Law

We now turn to investigate the manner and pace at which the composition of household expenditure patterns evolve as household income levels rise. Previous studies using highly aggregated, national spending data have found preliminary evidence for a positive correlation between expenditure diversification and income (Theil and Finke 1983; Falkinger and Zweimüller 1996). However, these studies have used highly aggregated country level data in which inferences about the relationship between income and expenditure diversification have been drawn from comparing the aggregate expenditure patterns of a rich country to those of a poor country. To date, we are not aware of any study that has used actual household spending data to examine diversification patterns across a wide range of expenditure categories. So far, it appears that only diversification patterns *within* certain categories, e.g. food, have been studied (Thiele and Weiss 2003). Therefore, to gain a deeper understanding of how evenly total expenditure is distributed across expenditure categories at different household income levels, we use household level data and employ the Gini measure of inequality in order to show how it fluctuates across household income and time. If one accepts the notion that Engel's

Table 5 Mean comparison test for lowest income decile, 1960–200

	1960	1970	1980	1990	2000
Lowest income decile					
Mean expenditure dedicated to physical sustenance	7222.69***	1999.17***	26576***	67.42***	90.41***
Mean expenditure dedicated second order needs	348.61	885.562	1721.41	2.96	7.78

Note: Large differences in values arise across years due to changes in the reporting methods of the FES. Three stars indicate that hypothesis that the means of expenditure dedicated to sustenance is larger than the mean of expenditure dedicated to second order needs can not be rejected at the $\alpha = 1\%$ level of significance.

classification schema does, to some extent, measure the relative influence of certain needs on household expenditure patterns, then investigating changes in this distribution may provide some insight into how the hierarchy of needs changes household income rises.

We begin by examining the distribution of expenditure at high income levels. Table 6 reveals that, while nourishment is still the most dominant expenditure category, there is much more variability in the budget share of household expenditure on tools, housing, and clothing. Compared with the highest income level observed by Engel, the budget expenditure on nourishment has more than halved, from 62.42% in 1856 to 27.86% in 1960. Between 1960 and 2000, considerable fluctuations can be found in the budget share related to shelter, tools and 'all other' cateogries.

Comparing these results with the expenditure patterns of contemporary low income households (see Table 5), an interesting pattern emerges. Clearly, as predicted by Engel's Law, food expenditure dedicated to food is much lower relative to low-income households. Also, in the lowest income decile there is a very uneven distribution of expenditure as most of the expenditure is concentrated in expenditure related to nourishment. At high income levels, household expenditure appears to be distributed much more evenly across the different expenditure categories. To get a more precise picture of how unevenly household expenditure is distributed across these expenditure categories, we calculate the Gini coefficient, which is a measure of the inequality of a distribution, a value of 0 expressing total equality and a value of 1 maximal inequality. Using Deaton's (1997) formula:

$$G = \frac{N+1}{N-1} - \frac{2}{N(N-1)\mu}\left(\sum_{i=1}^{n} P_i X_i\right) \tag{1}$$

where

N is the set of consumption expenditures (See Table 1)
μ is the mean budget share of the set
P_i is the budget share rank of expenditure i with budget share X_i.

Table 6 Budget shares for the highest income decile, 1960–2000

Needs	1960	1970	1980	1990	2000
1. Nourishment	28	21	23	15	16
2. Clothing	15	9	10	8	8
3. Housing	17	16	18	15	25
4. Heating and lighting	2	2	1	0	9
5. Tools	17	7	10	14	10
6. Intellectual	3	3	4	5	3
7. Public safety	2	1	0	2	0
8. Health and recreation	7	11	9	7	9
9. Personal services	2	2	2	1	2
10 All other	8	29	24	33	18

Note: Entries denote per cent of total expenditure.

The results, as found in Table 7, reveal what appears to be evidence for a general regularity describing the way in which consumption expenditure becomes more diversified as households become more affluent.[8] As household income grows, not only is there a decline in the budget share dedicated to nourishment, but household expenditure is distributed across consumption expenditure categories in a more even fashion. This is reflected in the fact that, across all of the observed years, the Gini coefficient for the highest decile is lower than the Gini coefficient for the lowest income decile. This indicates that total expenditure is distributed more evenly across expenditure categories at high income levels than it is at low income levels. In other words, the budget share of the various expenditure categories exhibit a tendency to converge to a common level, as household income increases. This implies that diversification of household expenditure does not take place in such a way that any one particular non-food expenditure category tends to dominate other non-food expenditure categories. Rather, it appears that diversification takes place in such a way that additional income is distributed in increasingly equal proportions across non-food expenditure categories.

It should be noted that this finding is not encapsulated in Engel's law, which describes how the budget share of household expenditure on food declines in response to an increase in household income. While Engel's law does imply that the budget share of non-food expenditure will rise, it has no implications for how consumption expenditure will be distributed across non-food categories. The above finding suggests that, as the food budget share declines, the budget shares of all other non-food expenditure categories will tend to converge.[9] To attain an

[8] This finding should be interpreted as a "generic invariance" in the statistical properties of consumption behavior in the spirit advocated by Aversi et al. (1999:384).

[9] This result is also different from Prais' (1953) statement that, as income rises, a greater number of goods will enter the household consumption basket (see Jackson 1984). The fact that a greater number of goods enter the consumption basket does not imply that there will be a more even distribution across expenditure categories. It is a possible that the number of items found in the household consumption basket increases, without affecting the distribution of total expenditure across expenditure categories.

Table 7 Gini coefficient for expenditure shares, 1960–2000

	1960	1970	1980	1990	2000
Lowest income decile	0.74	0.75	0.76	0.61	0.61
Middle income decile	0.69	0.66	0.68	0.60	0.56
Highest income decile	0.53	0.52	0.54	0.48	0.54

increasingly even distribution across these expenditure categories, there must be an additional regularity at work that relates to how expenditure is distributed *in increasingly equal proportions* across different expenditure categories. In this respect, we claim this result to be an additional insight into understanding the manner in which the composition of household expenditure changes as household income grows. Of course, it is likely that this result will not hold if expenditure is highly aggregated into two or three categories, such as 'food' and 'non-food', or food, goods and services. We speculate that the finding holds if at least four different expenditure categories are specified.[10]

In terms of understanding how the order of needs changes as household income rises, this finding also suggests that, if Engel's expenditure categories are an accurate reflection of the influence of needs, the actual hierarchy of needs appears to have a very different character to those proposed by social scientists such as Maslow (1954). Rather than there being a clear order among several needs, it appears that there exists only an order to the extent that the need for nourishment predominates over other needs at low income levels, but no other needs clearly predominate at higher income levels.

An examination of how these Gini coefficient changes across time (see Fig. 1) reveals a downward trend among households located in the lowest income decile, from around 0.73 in 1960 to approximately 0.60 in 2000. Among households in the middle income decile, the Gini coefficient also exhibited a downward trend, from around 0.70 in 1960 to around 0.57 in 2000. This finding suggests that the expenditure patterns of households located in these income deciles are becoming increasingly diversified over time. Thus, while we found evidence for the existence of a stable pattern of household expenditure at low income households in the previous section, these results suggest that it would be misleading to conclude that no significant changes have occurred in the expenditure patterns of low income households. This negative trend Gini coefficients appears to indicate an acceleration in the rate at which household expenditure patterns become diversified. Historically, it was only in the expenditure patterns of high income households that one

[10] Regarding how sensitive these results are to demographic factors, we found that these results were robust when comparing ECs for households of different sizes (two and three person households). For reasons of space we do not report these results here. They are available on request.

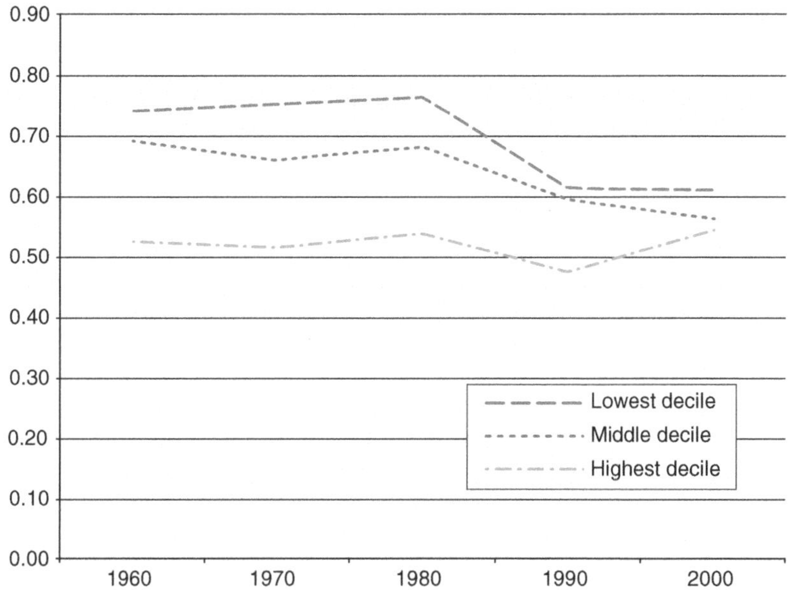

Fig. 1 Evolution of Gini coefficients, 1960–2000. Gini coefficients are calculated to measure how evenly total expenditure is distributed across expenditure categories. This is done separately for low, middle and high income households. The results show that, as household income increases, total expenditure tend to become more evenly distributed across expenditure categories. Note that differences between high income and low income households appear to be declining over time

can find a large amount of expenditure diversity. However, this results suggest that this is increasingly not the case in the modern era, as the household expenditure patterns of middle and low income households have become increasingly diversified across expenditure categories.

Finally, it is also interesting to note that the relative differences in how unevenly spread household expenditure patterns are between low income and high income households appear to be falling over time. In 1960 the difference in the Gini coefficient between low income and high income households was 0.21. This dropped to 0.07 in 2000. To some extent, a factor contributing to this drop is the rise of housing expenditure, which has a large influence on the expenditure patterns of high income households and is mainly a result of rapidly increasing house prices in the UK (as discussed above). Nevertheless, the fact that low income households are increasingly able to distribute their expenditure patterns more evenly across Engel's expenditure in a manner that is increasingly similar to the expenditure patterns of high income households, may provide new information about household living standards and how they differ across income groups.

6 Needs and Engel Curves

Finally, we turn to consider what the shape of ECs may reveal about the relationship between the goods and services and the range of underlying needs they served. In doing so, we begin to tackle one of the major shortcomings of Engel's original approach, namely the a priori assumptions made about the relationship between goods and services and the needs they served.[11] In terms of how household expenditure patterns may evolve over time, these assumptions are particularly vulnerable in light of the rapid pace at which product innovations take place in modern market economies which may take place in precisely such a way so as to ensure goods serve multiple needs (Witt 2001). Even holding time constant and only thinking about how expenditure patterns change across different household income levels, these assumptions are vulnerable. Given the range of goods and services that are present in low income versus high income expenditure patterns, it is clear that many luxury versions of goods, such as luxury pens, luxury wristwatches, luxury cars and so on, do not serve the same needs as their relatively cheaper counterparts. To uncover comprehensively the link between goods and the needs they serve, one would require detailed micro level data on consumer expenditure, product characteristics and information on individual's consumption experiences, which are not available on the aggregate level.

Nevertheless, an interesting question is whether it is possible to uncover empirically any insights about this relationship from the shape of ECs. The EC describes the relationship between an expenditure category and income. It is typically expressed as a share of total expenditure. The EC relative to a particular expenditure g is estimated by regressing the budget share of expenditure b_i allocated to g on total expenditure x_i:

$$b_i = m(x_i) + \epsilon_i \tag{2}$$

The subscript i refers to households 1, ..., n. The broad shape of the EC is commonly used to infer the income elasticity of a good. It is notable that, for much of the twentieth century, the parametric approach to estimating ECs was dominant, which required researchers to make a priori assumptions about the shape of the EC. Via the gradual shift away from linear towards log-linear and eventually nonlinear functional forms (Prais 1953; Banks et al. 1997), some consideration was given to functional forms that imposed a saturation level of expenditure (Aitchison and Brown 1954).

In the following, we adopt a nonparametric approach in which there is more scope to discovering and verifying general regularities because the shape of the regression curve is derived from the data without assuming any functional form a priori (see Engel and Kneip 1996 for a discussion). It should be noted that the nonparametric approach cannot avoid dealing with two major problems that must

[11] Similar assumption are made in Jackson and Marks (1999).

be faced when working with household expenditure data. First, the functional form is influenced by the distribution of observations. As most household expenditure surveys have fewer observations at high levels of household income, some doubt may be cast on the properties of nonparametric ECs at these levels. However, in the case of the UK Family Expenditure Survey, Tanner (1999) studied the reliability of FES expenditure data by comparing it to spending figures found in the UK National Accounts. She found that the ratio of non-housing total FES expenditure to non-housing total expenditure in the National Accounts was around 90% between 1974 and 1992.[12]

A hypothesis about how the shape of the EC shape may reveal information about the set of needs that a good serves can be found in the literature on lexicographic preferences. This literature suggests that the more needs a particular expenditure category serves, the greater are the number of changes one would expect to observe in the slope of the EC (for details see Day and Robinson 1973; Drakopoulos 1994). Consequently, when examining the shape of ECs estimated with nonparametric techniques, one would to expect find some common properties in the shape of the EC for expenditure categories that serve multiple needs, relative to goods that serve a smaller range of needs. To this end, we use household expenditure data to investigate whether any similarities can be found among the shape of Engel curves for goods that we hypothesize tend to serve a relatively limited range of needs.

In particular, we hypothesize that certain perishable goods, such as food, tobacco and alcohol, tend to serve a relatively limited range of needs, while other durable goods and services tend to serve a relatively wider range of needs. Perishable goods can be thought of as 'first order' goods, in that they possess a specific purpose and are directly used by consumers to satisfy their needs. According to Menger (1871), these can be distinguished from *higher order* goods that do not directly satisfy consumers' needs, but are instead used by consumers to transform other goods in a consumption process (e.g. an oven is used to make cake which is then consumed).[13] Menger notes that the use of such higher order goods is heavily dependent on the consumer's knowledge and their ability to combine its use with other higher order goods and services (e.g. a consumer must use electricity to power the oven).[14] In addition, another higher order good used by modern households is services. In using services, consumers are buying a set of processing operations to be undertaken by a service provider (Gallouj and Weinstein 1997). For example, instead of cooking their own meals, cleaning their own houses, or fixing their own cars, consumers

[12] This compares favorably to the US Consumer Expenditure Survey (CES) in which Slesnick (1992) found that 1989 per capita total expenditure only captures 65% of per capita total expenditure recorded in the National Income and Product Accounts.

[13] To be distinguished from Becker's (1996) approach; see Steedman (2001) and Elster (1997).

[14] Similarly, Witt (2001) distinguishes between goods used to directly satisfy needs, such as food and drink, which he calls 'basic inputs' (2001). They are non-renewable in that once they have been used, they cannot be used again. On the other hand, 'tools' are different in that they include relatively more durable goods such as ovens and clothing which are used by consumer to produce lower order goods(see Witt and Woersdorfer 2010).

may purchase services to undertake these activities. In other cases, services are used because consumers seek 'expert' advice, e.g. medical and legal services, which are required in order to take advantage of knowledge accumulated in society (Earl and Potts 2004). A major part of the growth in the consumption of services can be viewed as an outcome of an outsourcing exercise on the part of consumers who have little time or high opportunity costs to manipulate lower order goods and services themselves (Lindner 1970).

Because of the relatively specific and direct fashion in which they are used to satisfy needs, we argue that lower order goods are less likely to serve a wide range of needs in comparison to higher order goods. For example, food only describes perishable and edible materials that are all closely linked to the need for nourishment. On the other hand, higher order goods such as services can include everything from hairdressing, lawyer's fees, catering, mechanical services, music lessons that relate to a wider range of needs as social recognition, transport, legal protection and intellectual fulfilment. The intangible nature of service and the tendency for these to be modified in accordance with the consumer's specifications implies they possess a greater flexibility in serving a wide range of needs. Perhaps some forms of food can be used as a status signalling device (caviar) or as an aphrodisiac (oysters), but it is highly unlikely that food can serve such needs as legal protection or transport. Similar arguments can be made about other lower order goods such as alcohol and tobacco in that they are perishable goods with unique material properties that are used directly in the satisfaction of needs. Thus we build a preliminary hypothesis that basic inputs that serve a relatively limited set of needs will possess relatively similar EC shapes.

Hypothesis A: Engel curves for lower order goods possess shapes that are more similar to each other than to the shapes of Engel Curves for higher order goods.

Hypothesis B: Engel curves for higher order goods possess shapes that are more similar to each other than to the shapes of Engel Curves for lower order goods.

It should be noted that there are other possible explanations that account for the shape of ECs. For example it is common in the literature to assume that all consumer's face the same price (the law of one price). However, regional differences in prices across geographic locations with different socioeconomic conditions may influence the shape of the Engel curve. Also, the EC shape may be the product of the distribution of observations. Especially at high income levels, the density of observations decreases rapidly, which tends to influence the shape of ECs at high income levels. In this regards, the rank correlation method (described below) used in this paper takes this into account, as it allocates a higher weighting to observation at lower income levels.

In contrast to Engel's concept of hierarchy, which is couched in terms of an order of needs, the concept of lower and higher order goods is linked more to the manner in which goods are used by consumers to satisfy any given need. Both higher and lower order goods can thus be found *within* the expenditure dedicated to any given need. For this reason, we can not use the same classification method used in the previous section. Instead, to test these hypotheses, we classify goods according into thirteen aggregate expenditure categories found in the UK Family Expenditure Survey. The data is taken from the UK Family Expenditure Survey 1986–2001 jointly with the expenditure and food survey (EFS) 2002–2006. The data are about household expenditures on various categories of goods and services. Each year, approximately 7,000 households were randomly selected, and each of them recorded expenditures for two weeks. We are able to recover information about total expenditures and expenditures on thirteen aggregated categories: (1) housing (net); (2) fuel, light, and power; (3) food; (4) alcoholic drinks; (5) tobacco; (6) clothing and footwear; (7) household goods; (8) household services; (9) personal goods and services; (10) motoring, fares and other travel; (11) leisure goods; and (12) leisure services.[15] In order to have samples of households which are demographically homogeneous, we only consider families which have a number of members between two and three. Families of this type are approximately 3,000 each year.

We estimate the ECs in a nonparametric fashion for the 13 categories using the kernel smoothing method proposed by Gasser and Müller (1984) and Gasser et al. (1991). This estimator, besides having an asymptotic bias that is nevertheless preferable to the Nadaraya-Watson estimator, has the advantage of being easily applicable to the problem of estimating the derivatives of regression functions. The kernel function used is a fourth-order kernel, and the bandwidth parameter is chosen via the *plug-in* approach proposed by Herrmann (1997), which has the advantage of being able to deal with heteroscedasticity.

To measure the similarity in shape between estimated regression curves, we use the rank correlation method proposed by Heckman and Zamar (2000). In contrast with the L_2 distance between two functions m_1 and m_2 ($\int\{m_1(x) - m_2(x)\}^2$), the rank correlation is able to capture *qualitative* features of the curves such as kinks and spikes (cf. Marron and Tsybakov 1995). But what does it mean that two ECs (derivatives or variances) $m_1(x)$ and $m_2(x)$ have the same shape? They have the same shape if there exists a strictly increasing function g such that $m_1(x) = g\{m_2(x)\}$, that is the plot of $y = m_1(x)$ is the same of $y = m_2(x)$ after a deformation of the y axis. The measure of similarity proposed by Heckman and Zamar presupposes the definition of a probability measure μ on the the interval in which

[15] The 12 categories, together with "miscellaneous and other goods", add up to total expenditures. From 1987 to 2006 the survey contains a macro-code for each of the 13 categories. For 1986, the FES contains macro-codes only from the first six categories (from housing to clothing and footwear), plus other macro-categories which are not consistent with the other seven categories listed above (household goods, household services, personal goods and services, motoring, fares and other travel, leisure goods, and leisure services). We thus constructed, for 1986, these seven macro-categories aggregating micro-categories (disaggregate expenditures) in order that they be consistent with the way they are formed in the years 1987–2006.Due to the quality of the data, it was not possible to control for other factors, such as geographic location. For a discussion of the empirical significance of these socio-demographic factors, we refer the reader to Calvet and Common (2003) and references therein.

$m_1(x)$ and $m_2(x)$ are defined (which is the unit interval after standardizing the data). We use as measure $\mu(A) = (\# \ x \in A)/(\# \ x \in [0, 1])$ (that is, the proportion of x points that are in A), for any subinterval A of the unit interval. The rationale for using this measure is to give more weight to the portion of the curve for which there are more observations. The rank correlation measure between $m_1(x)$ and $m_2(x)$ is defined as:

$$\rho_\mu(m_1, m_2) = \frac{\int \{r^{m_1}(w) - R^{m_1}\}\{r^{m_2}(w) - R^{m_2}\}d\mu(w)}{\sqrt{\int \{r^{m_1}(w) - R^{m_1}\}^2 d\mu(w) \int \{r^{m_2}(w) - R^{m_2}\}^2 d\mu(w)}}, \qquad (3)$$

where $r^{m_1}(x) = \mu\{t : m_1(t) < m_1(x)\} + \frac{1}{2}\mu\{t : m_1(t) = m_1(x)\}$ and $R^{m_1} = \int r^{m_1}(w) \, d\mu(w)$ ($r^{m_2}(x) = \mu\{t : m_2(t) < m_2(x)\} + \frac{1}{2}\mu\{t : m_2(t) = m_2(x)\}$ and $R^{m_2} = \int r^{m_2}(w) \, d\mu(w)$). A consistent estimator of ρ_μ is given by Heckman and Zamar (2000:137). Having calculated these distances for each year under observation, a good overview of the magnitude of differences in EC shapes among the expenditure categories is attained via cluster analysis. We perform a hierarchical cluster analysis using as distance measure $d = (1 - \rho_\mu)$.[16]

In terms of Hypothesis A, the cluster analysis reveals that the EC shapes for two of the three hypothesized lower order goods possess a relatively similar shape across the observed years (1986–2006). In 14 out of the 20 years observed, the ECs for food and tobacco were located within the same cluster at a very low height; see for example the cluster dendrogram for 1991 and 1996 in Fig. 2. In the remaining six years, food and tobacco still display relatively similar shapes, and tend to be situated in the same cluster at a relatively low height of 0.2; see, for example, the cluster dendrogram for 2001 and 2006 in Fig. 2. It was also found that the shape of the EC for alcohol was found to be relatively dissimilar to food and tobacco throughout the observed time period. Interestingly, a surprising result was that there is also a tendency for Energy Services to be consistently clustered with food, alcohol or tobacco. This category includes household expenditure on fuel, light and power which are used for cooking, heating and lighting. It is interesting to note the essentially perishable nature of this type of expenditure. All in all, it appears there is some preliminary evidence for the Hypothesis A that the Engel curves for lower order goods possess shapes that do appear to be more similar to each other, relative to the shapes of ECs for lower order goods.

In terms of Hypothesis B, the results are less promising. No discernable clusters of higher order goods and services emerge consistently across the observe time period. There is a weak tendency for the ECs of personal services and leisure services to possess similar shapes, as they appear in the same cluster at a very low height in four out of the 20 years observed; see for example the cluster dendrogram for 2001 and 2006 in Fig. 2. In an additional seven years, these two categories appear in the same cluster at the height of 0.5. None of the other higher order goods

[16] Note that since $-1 \leq \rho_\mu \geq 1$ we have $0 \leq d \geq 2$.

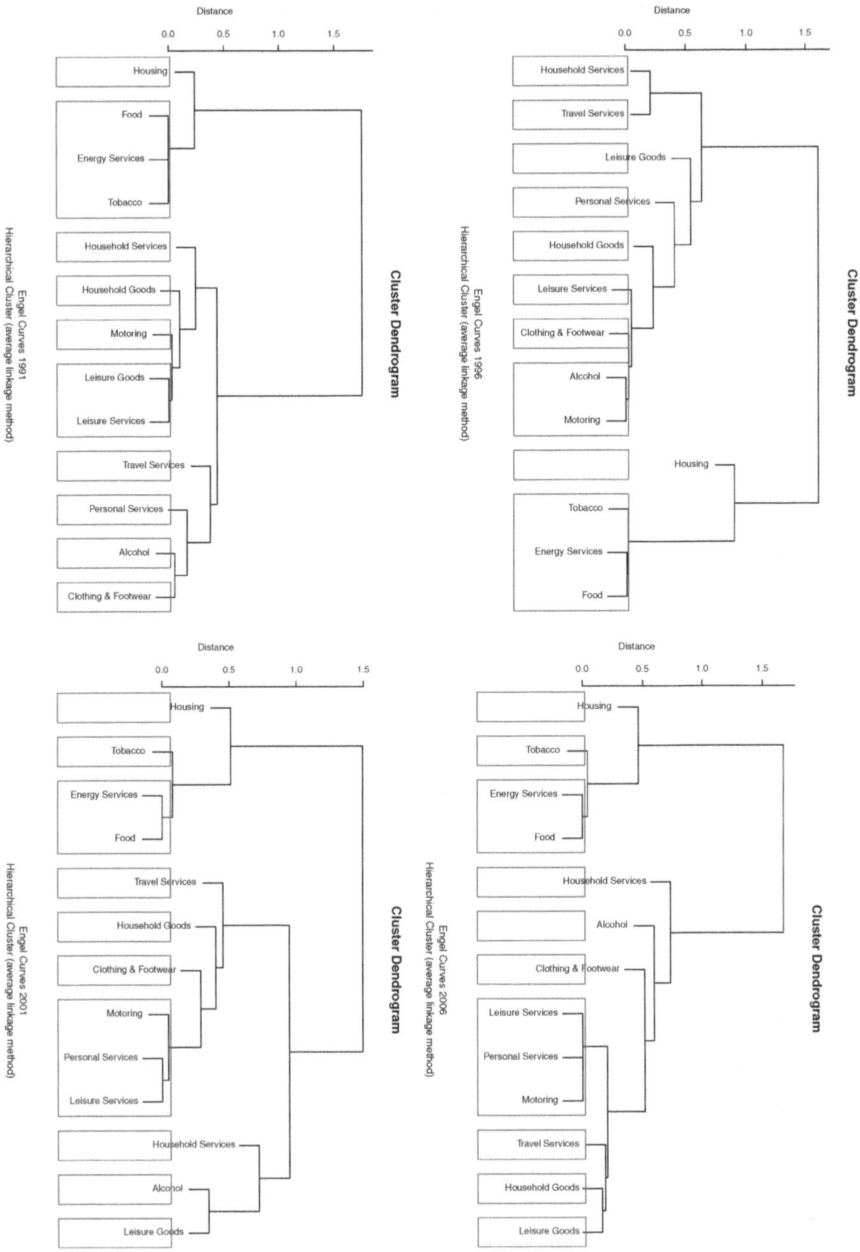

Fig. 2 Cluster Analysis of EC Shapes, 1991–2006. *Note:* A separate cluster analysis was undertaken for each year between 1986 and 2006. This figure above displays results for 1991, 1996, 2001 and 2006. Results for other years available upon request

and services, such as leisure goods, household goods and travel services display any tendency to exhibit a similar EC shape. All in all, these results suggest that hypothesis B can be rejected in that the Engel curves for higher order goods possess shapes do not appear to be more similar to each other, relative to the shapes of ECs for lower order goods.

7 Conclusion

This paper has taken a small step towards finding evidence for, and understanding the implications of, the existence of a hierarchy among the needs of consumers. Our results reveal that income patterns of low income households are remarkably stable over several decades: a stability that could be attributed to the basic needs of consumers which are the product of the biological evolution. In particular, expenditure classified by Engel as being related to a group of needs that together constitute physical sustenance is significantly larger than expenditure on other, lower order needs.

Moreover, we examined the manner in which rising household income affects the distribution of total expenditure across expenditure categories. Our results reveal that, as household income rises, household expenditure is distributed across these expenditure categories in an increasingly even fashion. In other words, the budget share of the various expenditure categories exhibits a tendency to converge to a common level as household income increases. If indeed Engel's classification schema is broadly accurate in classifying goods and services according to the underlying needs they serve, this finding suggests that a hierarchy of needs appears to consist of two levels, in that it is only the most important needs, the need for nourishment, that appears to dominate other needs. There appears to exist no order between other, lower order needs. We also observed that, across time, an increase in the ability for households located at the low and medium income deciles to diversify their consumption patterns. An important research question for future work should uncover what supply and demand factors are responsible for this convergence. This would involve accounting for the effects of the lexicographic nature of household preferences on the demand side, as well as important qualitative differences in the nature of goods that are purchased by high and low income households (Witt 2001).

In sum, there is a great potential in adopting Engel's approach to studying changes in consumption through understanding the nature of the consumer's needs, their basis in human biology, and how their influence on consumption changes as household income increases. In particular, this may shed more light on how economic growth can lead to significant endogenous changes in the composition of household demand which, in turn, may have important implications for how the industrial composition of economies undergo transformation as they grow. At the same time, several important obstacles facing this approach still remain. Precisely how many needs are there? Do the set of needs possessed by consumers change significantly over time as a result of their past experiences? If we are to avoid making the same a priori assumptions that Engel made 150 years ago, it is also important to conduct work on developing a plausible way of uncovering empirically the relationship between particular goods and the needs they serve. This paper has yielded some preliminary evidence for the hypothesis that goods that serve a relatively limited range of needs, such as food and tobacco, tend to possess Engel curves with similar shapes, in comparison to the shapes of Engel curves of other goods and services that serve a wider range of needs.

All in all, while the challenges facing this approach are considerable, it should be remembered that the potential reward is large: To date, there exists no proper explanation for the shape of Engel curves and the income elasticity of goods and services that is properly couched in terms of how the behavior of individual households changes with rising income. An important task for progressing any science is to develop theories within which discovered laws have their place. As Engel himself recognized, an appropriate account for these shapes begins with a consideration of the motivations of consumption, and how these tend to change as households become more affluent. For evolutionary economists, this represents an opportunity to highlight the benefits of adopting a new approach to economics, since the observed stability of low income household expenditure observed across four decades suggests that the needs driving these regularities are inherent and linked to the evolved, biological nature of humans. Thus, what Engel's approach ultimately offers us is the beginning of a comprehensive theoretical framework that can account for the manner in which household expenditure patterns evolve as household income rises.

Acknowledgements We would like to thank Ulrich Witt, Paolo Saviotti, Giorgio Fagiolo, Nicholas Rohde, Liana Wortley, the anonymous referee who provided comments on the paper during the submission process, the participants at the 13th conference of the International Joseph A. Schumpeter Society International Schumpeter Society held in Aalborg (2010), as well members of the Evolutionary Economics Group at the Max Plank Institute of Economics, for very useful comments. We thank the UK Data Archive for providing access to the UK Family Expenditure Survey. The usual disclaimer applies.

References

Aitchison J, Brown JAC (1954) A synthesis of Engel curve theory. Rev Econ Stud 22(1):35–46

Aitken CK and Irongmonger DS (1995) Household time use surveys. Aust Econ Rev 28:89–92

Aoki M, Yoshikawa H (2002) Demand saturation-creation and economic growth. J Econ Behav Organ 48:127–154

Aversi R, Dosi G, Fagiolo G, Meacci M, Olivetti C (1999) Demand dynamics with socially evolving preferences. Ind Corp Change 8:2

Banks J, Blundell R, Lewbel A (1997) Quadratic Engel curves and consumer demand. Rev Econ Stat 79(4):527–539

Becker GS (1996) Accounting for tastes. Harvard University Press, Cambridge, MA

Bianchi M (2002) Novelty, preferences and fashion: when new goods are unsettling. J Econ Behav Organ 47:1–18

Calvet L, Common E (2003) Behavioral heterogeneity and the income effect. Rev Econ Stat 85 (3):653–669

Chai A (2011) Consumer specialization and the romantic transformation of the British grand tour of Europe. J Bioecon 13:181–203

Chai A, Moneta A (2010) Retrospectives: Engel curves. J Econ Perspect 24(1):225–240

Day R, Robinson S (1973) Economic decision and the L^{**} utility. In: Cochrane J and Zeleny M (eds) Multiple criteria decision making. University of South Carolina Press, Colombia

Deci E, Ryan R (1975) Intrinsic motivation and self-determination in human behavior. Plenum Press, New York

Deaton A (1997) Analysis of household surveys. Johns Hopkins University Press, Baltimore

Deaton A, Muellbauer J (1980a) Economics and consumer behavior. Cambridge University Press, Cambridge

Deaton A, Muellbauer J (1980b) An almost ideal demand system. Am Econ Rev 70:312–326

de Vries J (2008) The industrious revolution. Cambridge University Press, Cambridge

Drakopoulos SA (1994) Hierarchical choice in economics. J Econ Surv 8(2):133–153

Ducpétiaux E (1855) Budgets économiques des classes ouvriéres en Belgique. Bruxelles

Earl P (1983) The Economic Imagination. Wheatsheaf Books, Brighton

Earl P, Potts J (2004) The market for preferences. Camb J Econ 28:619–633

Elster J (1997) More than enough. Univ Chic Law Rev 64:749–764

Engel E (1857) Die produktions- und consumtionsverhältnisse des Königreichs Sachsen. Reprinted in Bull Inst Int Stat (1895) 9:1–54

Engel E (1895) Das Lebenskosten Belgischer Arbeiterfamilien früeher und Jetzt. Bull Inst Int Stat 9:1–124

Engel J, Kneip A (1996) Recent approaches to estimating Engel curves. Journal of Economics 63 (2):187–212

Falkinger J, Zweimüller J (1996) The cross-country Engel curve for product diversification. Struct Chang Econ Dyn 7:79–97

Frenzel Baudisch A (2006) Continuous market growth beyond functional satiation. Papers on Economics and Evolution 0603

Foellmi R, Zweimüller J (2008) Structural change, Engel's consumption cycles and Kaldor's facts of economic growth. J Monet Econ 55(2):1317–1328

Gallouj F, Weinstein O (1997) Innovation in services. Res Policy 26:537–556

Galtung J (1980) The basic needs approach. In: Lederer K (ed) Human needs. Oelgeschlager, Gunn and Hain, Cambridge

Gasser T, Kneip A, Köhler W (1991) A flexible and fast method for automatic smoothing. J Am Stat Assoc 86(14):643–652

Gasser T, Müller HG (1984) Estimating regression functions and their derivatives by the Kernel method. Scand J Statist 11:171–185

Georgescu-Roegen N (1954) Choice, expectation and measurability. Quart J Econ 68:503–534

Gorman M (1959) Separable utility and aggregation. Econometrica 27:469–481

Heckman NE, Zamar RH (2000) Comparing the shapes of regression functions. Biometrika 87 (1):135–144

Herrmann E (1997) Local bandwidth choice in Kernel regression estimation. J Comput Graph Stat 6(1):35–54

Hergenhahn B, Olson M (1997) An introduction to theories of learning. Prentice Hall, New Jersey

Jackson L (1984) Hierarchic demand and the Engel curve for variety. Rev Econ Stat 66:8–15

Jackson T, Marks N (1999) Consumption, sustainable welfare and human needs - with reference to UK expenditure patterns between 1954 and 1994. Ecol Econ 28:421–441

Lewbel A (2007) Engel Curves. The New Palgrave Dictionary of Economics

Loasby BJ (1998) Cognition and innovation. In: Bianchi M (ed) The active consumer: novelty and surprise in consumer choice. Routledge, London

Lindner S (1970) The harried leisure class. Columbia University Press, New York
Maddison A (2001) The world economy: a millennial perspective. OECD, Paris
Marron JS, Tsybakov AB (1995) Visual error criteria for qualitative smoothing. J Am Stat Assoc 90(430):499–507
Marshall A (1890) The principles of economics. Prometheus Books, London
Maslow A (1954) Motivation and personality. Harper and Row, New York
Max-Neef M (1991) Human-scale development- conception, application and further reflection. Apex Press, London
Menger C (1871) Grundsätze der Volkswirthschaftslehre. Wilhelm Braumüller, Wien
Metcalfe S, Foster J, Ramlogan R (2006) Adaptive economic growth. Camb J Econ 30:7–32
Millenson JR (1967) Principles of behavioral analysis. New York: Macmillan
Manig C, Moneta A (2009) More or better? Quality versus quantity in food consumption. Papers on Economics and Evolution 0918
Moneta A, Chai A (2010) The evolution of Engel curves and its implications for structural change. Discussion Paper, Griffith University
Nelson R, Consoli D (2010) An evolutionary theory of household consumption behavior. J Evol Econ 20:665–687
Pasinetti L (1981) Structural change and economic growth. Cambridge University Press, Cambridge
Prais SJ (1953) Non-linear estimates of the Engel curves. Rev Econ Stud 20(2):87–104
Ruprecht W (2005) The historical development of the consumption of sweeteners a learning approach. J Evol Econ 15:247–272
Saviotti P (2001) Variety, growth and demand. In: Witt U (ed) Escaping satiation. Springer, Berlin, pp 115–138
Saviotti P, Pyka A (2008) Product variety, competition and economic growth. J Evol Econ 18 (3):323–347
Simon H (1956) Rational choice and the structure of the environment. Psychol Rev 63:129–138
Slesnick D (1992) Aggregate consumption and saving in the postwar United States. Review Econ Stat 18(3):323–347
Steedman I (2001) Consumption takes time. Routledge, London
Stigler GJ (1954) The early history of empirical studies of consumer behavior. J Polit Econ 62 (2):95–113
Strotz RH (1957) The empirical implications of a utility tree. Econometrica 25:269–280
Theil H, Finke R (1983) The consumer's demand for diversity. Eur Econ Rev 23:395–400
Thiele S, Weiss C (2003) Consumer demand for food diversity: evidence for Germany. Food Policy 28:99–115
von Hippel E (2005) Democratizing innovation. MIT Press, London
Tanner S (1999) How much do consumers spend? Comparing the FES and national accounts. In: Banks J, Johnson P (eds) How reliable is the family expenditure survey? Institute for Fiscal Studies, London
Witt U (2010) Product characteristics, innovations and the evolution of consumption. A behavioral approach, paper prepared for the conference on "Technical change: history, economics and policy" in honor of GN Tunzelmann, SPRU, March 2010
Witt U, Woersdorfer JS (2010) Parting with 'blue monday' – preferences and consumer responses to innovations. Papers on Economics and Evolution, Max Planck Institute of Economics, Jena, Nr 1110
Witt U (2001) Learning to consume - a theory of wants and the growth of demand. J Evol Econ 11:23–36

Technological Regimes and Demand Structure in the Evolution of the Pharmaceutical Industry

Christian Garavaglia, Franco Malerba, Luigi Orsenigo, and Michele Pezzoni

Abstract This paper examines how the nature of the technological regime governing innovative activities and the structure of demand interact in determining market structure, with specific reference to the pharmaceutical industry. The key question concerns the observation that—despite high degrees of R&D and marketing-intensity—concentration has been consistently low during the whole evolution of the industry. Standard explanations of this phenomenon refer to the random nature of the innovative process, the patterns of imitation, and the fragmented nature of the market into multiple, independent submarkets. We delve deeper into this issue by using an improved version of our previous "history-friendly" model of the evolution of pharmaceuticals. Thus, we explore the way in which changes in the technological regime and/or in the structure of demand may generate or not substantially higher degrees of concentration. The main results are that, while

Reprinted from Journal of Evolutionary Economics 22(4), 677-709, Springer (2012)

C. Garavaglia
DEMS, University of Milano-Bicocca, via Bicocca degli Arcimboldi 8, 20126 Milano, Italy

CRIOS, Bocconi University, via Roentgen 1, 20136 Milano, Italy

F. Malerba (✉)
CRIOS, Bocconi University, via Roentgen 1, 20136 Milano, Italy

Department of Management and Technology, Bocconi University, Milano, Italy
e-mail: franco.malerba@unibocconi.it

L. Orsenigo
CRIOS, Bocconi University, via Roentgen 1, 20136 Milano, Italy

IUSS (University Institute for Advanced Studies), Piazza della Vittoria 15, 27100 Pavia, Italy

M. Pezzoni
DEMS, University of Milano-Bicocca, via Bicocca degli Arcimboldi 8, 20126 Milano, Italy

CRIOS, Bocconi University, via Roentgen 1, 20136 Milano, Italy

Observatoire des Sciences et des Techniques, boulevard Pasteur 21, 75015 Paris, France

A. Pyka and E.S. Andersen (eds.), *Long Term Economic Development*,
Economic Complexity and Evolution, DOI 10.1007/978-3-642-35125-9_4,

technological regimes remain fundamental determinants of the patterns of innovation, the demand structure plays a crucial role in preventing the emergence of concentration through a partially endogenous process of discovery of new submarkets. However, it is not simply market fragmentation as such that produces this result, but rather the entity of the "prize" that innovators can gain relative to the overall size of the market. Further, the model shows that emerging industry leaders are innovative early entrants in large submarkets.

1 Introduction

Pharmaceuticals are traditionally a high R&D and marketing intensive sector. Both factors would suggest that—as a first approximation—the industry should be characterized by high degrees of concentration. However, concentration has been consistently low over the whole history of the industry. Yet, adding to the puzzle, competition does not occur among many small (relative to the market) firms of approximately similar size. Rather, the industry is largely dominated by a core of innovative firms which has remained quite small and stable for a very long period of time.

Standard explanations of these patterns refer essentially to the following main factors (e.g. Schwartzman 1976; Comanor 1986; Sutton 1998; Scherer 2000; Malerba and Orsenigo 2002):

a) the patterns of imitation;
b) the random nature of the processes of drug discovery;
c) the fragmented nature of the market.

The first two factors are key features defining a "technological regime" (Nelson and Winter 1982; Winter 1984; Pavitt 1984; Breschi et al. 2000). A research tradition, nested in the tradition of innovation studies and evolutionary economics, suggests that the patterns of innovation and market structure are essentially determined by the nature of the relevant technological regime, described in terms of opportunity and appropriability conditions and cumulativeness of technological advances. In this context, the role played by the structure of demand has been less well explored, at least in formal terms. Here, using an updated version of a "history-friendly" model of the evolution of pharmaceuticals (Malerba and Orsenigo 2002), we address this issue directly and ask how the properties of the technological regime interact with market fragmentation (and size) in influencing the patterns of innovation and the evolution of market structure. In a nutshell: how do the relevant variables interact in producing the observed outcomes?

Our analysis links closely with other recent contributions, mainly Sutton (1998), Klepper (1996, 1997) and Klepper and Thompson (2006) which explicitly identify in market fragmentation a main limit to concentration. In this paper, we relate our results to this literature, but we depart from it in many respects. First, coherently with an evolutionary approach, we do not assume full rationality on the part of the agents and pre-impose equilibrium conditions. Second, we do not assume that the number of submarkets is fixed or exogenously generated, nor that any potentially profitable submarket is actually occupied (the "arbitrage principle", see Sutton 1998). Rather, although there is a fixed number of "potential" submarkets, only some of them are actually discovered through R&D efforts. Third, our analysis is cast in an explicit dynamic setting. Fourth, we suggest that the variables that define a technological regime are indeed fundamental determinants of the mechanism governing the relationship between market structure and innovation.

In previous papers (Malerba and Orsenigo 2002; Garavaglia et al. 2010), we began to explore these issues through a history-friendly model of the evolution of the pharmaceutical industry and biotechnology. The model did a good job in replicating the main patterns of evolution of the industry. In this paper, we develop an updated version of the model, which introduces significant improvements compared to Malerba and Orsenigo (2002), and we expand significantly the analysis by examining systematically the manner in which the properties of the technological and demand regimes interact in determining concentration. It must be stressed that, although this paper is based on a history-friendly model, the analysis developed here is not strictly a history-friendly exercise. Rather, we use the history-friendly model to investigate a set of more general questions which might be relevant also for other industries and contexts. (For a discussion of this procedure, see Malerba et al. 2007 and Garavaglia 2010).

The paper is organized as follows: Section 2 discusses the interpretations of the features of market structure in pharmaceuticals provided by the literature. Section 3 presents the model, and Section 4 discusses the standard simulation results. Section 5 investigates the effects of technological regimes and demand structure on concentration. Section 6 concludes.

2 Innovation and Market Structure

2.1 Suggested Interpretations for the Case of Pharmaceuticals

The essential features of the pharmaceutical industry and of its history are rather well known and we shall not recount them here.[1] The central question raised in this paper is the following: why such a high R&D (and marketing) intensive industry such as pharmaceuticals has never been and it is still not highly concentrated? And why, at the same time, is this sector largely dominated by a handful of large firms, which entered early in the history of the sector and which have maintained their

[1] See, among others, Pisano (1996), Henderson et al. (1999), Sutton (1998), Pammolli (1996), Grabowski and Vernon (1994), Chandler (2005), Galambos and Sturchio (1996), Gambardella (1995) and Bottazzi et al. (2001).

leadership for decades? The literature is almost unanimous in suggesting three factors which may explain the patterns observed in pharmaceuticals.

a) Imitation

First, it is noted that imitation plays a crucial role. Innovation and the introduction of really new drugs is only part of the competitive story in pharmaceuticals. "Inventing-around" existing molecules, or introducing new combinations among them, or new ways of delivering them, etc., constitute a major component of firms' innovative activities broadly defined. Thus, while market competition centers around new product introductions, firms also compete through incremental refinements of existing drugs over time, as well as through imitation after (and not infrequently even before) patent protection has expired. This latter in particular allows a large "fringe" of firms to thrive through commodity production and development of licensed products. Thus, many firms do not specialize in R&D and innovation, but rather in imitation/inventing around, as well as in the production and marketing of products often invented elsewhere. Additionally, generic competition after patent expiration is becoming increasingly strong.

b) The properties of the innovation process

Second, it is emphasized that, in this industry, the innovative process is characterized by extreme uncertainty and, above all, by the difficulty of leveraging the results of past innovative efforts into new products. In other words, economies of scope and cumulativeness of technological advances are limited. In fact, the process of discovery and development of new drugs has been based for a long time on an approach customarily labelled "random screening". Lacking a precise knowledge of the causes of the diseases and of the mechanisms of action of drugs, researchers screened randomly thousands of natural and chemically derived compounds in test tube experiments and in testing on laboratory animals for therapeutic activity. Unsurprisingly, only a very small fraction of them showed promising potential. Hence, innovative firms have only limited room for establishing dominant positions. Market leadership can be easily contested by new innovators. Concentration can arise through success-breeds-success processes: an innovative firm enjoying high profits may have more resources to invest in R&D and therefore higher probabilities to innovate again as compared to non-innovators. However, to the extent that the probability of the success of any one project is independent from past history, the tendency toward rising concentration is weakened. Thus, the process of discovery and development of a drug closely resembles a lottery (Sutton 1998).[2]

[2] From the mid 1970s, basic scientific progress led to a deeper understanding of the causes of the diseases as well as of the mechanisms of the action of drugs. This advance opened up the way for new techniques of searching, that have been named "guided search" and "rational drug design". It is not the aim of this paper to study the advent and the consequences of biotechnology: a preliminary attempt in this direction can be found in Malerba and Orsenigo (2002). For the purposes of the present, suffice it to mention here that the "biotechnological revolution" and

c) Market fragmentation

A third crucial factor limiting concentration is the fragmented nature of the pharmaceutical market. The pharmaceutical market results from the aggregation of many independent submarkets—corresponding to different therapeutic categories (*TCs*)—with little or no substitution between products. Thus, even monopolistic positions in one submarket do not translate into overall concentration, if the number of submarkets is large and their size (relative to the overall market) is not too skewed. As the number of submarkets increases, it becomes more difficult for one firm to dominate a larger, fragmented market. Pharmaceuticals fits this picture rather well. The industry is actually composed by a series of fragmented, independent markets, such as, e.g. cardiovascular, diuretics, tranquilizers, etc. The largest firms hold dominant positions in individual *TCs*.

2.2 The Theoretical Background

Recent theoretical literature has emphasized the role of market fragmentation, coupled with high entry costs and the absence of economies of scope or cumulativeness in preventing the onset of concentration in innovative industries.

Sutton (1998) provides a simple and compact framework in a game theoretic setting for analyzing this question. In his approach, the key determinant is the "escalation parameter" *alpha*: how large is the profit that a firm outspending its current or potential competitors might gain? If such profit is large, then an escalation mechanism is set in motion which leads to high concentration. In Sutton's approach, the degree of market fragmentation plays a crucial role: if the overall market is composed by many independent sub-markets, then the value of *alpha* is necessarily lower. When the overall market is composed of several independent product groups, firms may pursue alternative research trajectories which have different relevance for the various submarkets. At one extreme, the same trajectory might be applicable to a wide range of products. At the other extreme, each trajectory is applicable only to one specific submarket. Thus, the effectiveness of an escalation strategy depends on two factors. First, it depends on the effectiveness of R&D investment on any single trajectory in raising consumers' willingness to pay for the firm product within the associated submarket. Second, it depends also on the strength of the linkages between different R&D trajectories and their associated submarkets, i.e. on the economies of scope characterizing any one trajectory and on the degree of substitutability among products in the eyes of the consumers (Matraves 1999). A further prediction of the model is that an increase of the size of the market should lead to higher concentration: as market size grows, so does the

genomics have not yet substantially modified the intrinsically uncertain nature of the process of drug discovery and development.

value of the profits achievable through higher R&D spending, and the stronger becomes the escalation mechanisms.

Klepper's approach takes a different route. In the analysis of the life cycle patterns (Klepper 1996), the main engine is given by a process of dynamic increasing returns to R&D: larger firms benefit most from process R&D—and hence choose to invest more in R&D—because they apply the resulting unit cost reductions to the largest amounts of output. As entry and growth occur over time, industry output expands, causing price to fall. Over time, the requisite R&D capabilities to enter arise. Eventually, even the most capable potential entrants cannot profitably enter, and entry ceases. The convex costs of growth limit the ability of later entrants to catch up with earlier entrants in terms of size, and as price continues to fall, the smallest firms and least able innovators are forced to exit the industry. This leads to a shakeout of producers that continues until the entire output of the industry is taken over by the most capable early entrants.

This model assumes homogeneous demand. Klepper (1997) suggests that product differentiation and demand fragmentation into many niches may prevent shakeouts and the emergence of concentration. Generalizing this intuition, Klepper and Thompson (2006) develop a model in which the process of (exogenous) creation and destruction of submarkets drives industry evolution. Firms expand by exploiting new opportunities that arrive in the form of new submarkets, while they shrink when the submarkets in which they operate are destroyed. The model predicts that a shakeout occurs and concentration increases if the rate of creation of new submarkets slows down and/or a new very large submarket appears. The exploitation of economies of scale and especially economies of scope across different product varieties reinforces this tendency. The tire, laser, automobile and disk drive industries are examples (Buenstorf and Klepper 2010). The link between innovation, demand and market structure thus explains the patterns of industry evolution.

A third approach focuses attention on the nature of the relevant technological regime (Nelson and Winter 1982; Winter 1984; Pavitt 1984; Breschi et al. 2000) in determining the patterns of innovation and the evolution of market structure. In extreme summary, a technological regime is defined in terms of opportunity and appropriability conditions and the cumulativeness of technological advances. In particular, tight (weak) appropriability conditions and strong (weak) cumulativeness in innovation give big (small) and self-reinforcing advantages to (early) innovators. Thus, one would expect technologies characterized by these properties to be associated with high (low) levels of concentration and large (small) firm size, as in the so-called Schumpeter Mark II (Schumpeter Mark I) model. The role of opportunity conditions is less direct. In Schumpeter Mark II contexts, high opportunities may reinforce the tendency towards concentration or allow the survival and/or entry of new innovators. Moreover, under these conditions, "lucky" new innovators introducing major innovations can also end up displacing incumbents. Conversely, in Schumpeter Mark I technologies, ample innovative opportunities are likely to sustain competition, as innovation can come from every quarter and its advantages are transient.

In this paper, we suggest that the variables that define a technological regime are indeed fundamental determinants of the mechanism governing the relationship between market structure and innovation in Sutton's approach (Sutton 1998). However, in the technological regimes approach, the role played by the structure of demand has been less well explored, at least in formal terms. A number of models have focused attention on differences in consumers' preferences as an important factor influencing the industry life cycle (Saviotti 1996; Dalle 1997; Windrum and Birchenhall 1998), particularly by allowing for the emergence of multiple, distinct market niches. Other studies focus attention on the way in which heterogeneity in consumers preferences influences the conditions by which a new technology can survive and eventually displace the old one (Dalle 1997; Adner and Levinthal 2001; Adner 2002; Windrum and Birchenhall 2005; Malerba et al. 2007). Similarly, Malerba et al. (1999, 2008) show the manner in which the appearance of new market niches can (or fail to) lead to stronger competition. These models, however, were based on environments characterized by "Schumpeter Mark II" regimes, i.e. by strong appropriability conditions and cumulative technological advances. Here, we delve deeper into the analysis of the way the demand regime—defined in terms of market size and market fragmentation—interacts with the technological regime in shaping market structure and its evolution.

Specifically, we ask:

a) how do changing opportunity, appropriability and cumulativeness conditions affect market concentration in a setting of fragmented market?
b) are the same results obtained with more homogeneous markets?
c) in other words: do the predictions of the technological regimes approach still hold under different demand regimes?

3 The Model

3.1 The Appreciative Model

The industry is composed of many submarkets, called therapeutic categories *(TC)*. Firms compete to discover, develop and market new drugs for a large variety of diseases, which are then sold in one of the *TCs*. Consistent with an evolutionary approach, neither firms nor customers are assumed to be fully rational, in the sense that they do not completely understand the world in which they are living, and no equilibrium conditions are pre-imposed to the model. Firms are characterized by different propensities towards innovation, imitation and marketing. Thus, firms explore randomly the "space of molecules" until they find one or more promising compounds, i.e. one which might become a useful drug, and patent them. Reflecting the "random screening" procedure, the search process is by definition completely random. The patent provides protection from imitation for a certain period of time and over a given range of "similar" molecules. After discovery, firms begin to develop the drug, without knowing what the quality of the new drug will be. If successful, the drug is sold on the market, the size of which is defined by the number of potential patients. Marketing expenditures allow firms to increase the number of patients they can access. At the beginning, the new drug is the only product available on that particular *TC*. But other firms can discover competing drugs or—after patent expiry—imitate. Thus, over time, the innovator's sales and profits will be eroded away.

The discovery of a drug in a *TC* does not entail any advantage in the discovery of another drug in a different *TC*—except for the volume of profits they can reinvest in research and development. As a consequence, diversification into different *TCs* is also purely random. Firms' growth, then, depends on the number of drugs they have discovered, on the size and the growth of the submarkets in which they are present, on the number of competitors, on the relative quality and price of their drug vis-à-vis competitors. Given the large number of *TCs* and the absence of any form of cumulativeness in the search and development process, no firm can hope to be able to win a large market share of the overall market, but – if anything—only in specific *TCs* for a limited period of time. As a result, the degree of concentration in the whole market for pharmaceuticals will be low.

3.2 The Formal Model

In this section, we describe the basic structure of the model.[3]

3.2.1 The Topography

The number of the submarkets (*TCs*) is given and equal to n. Each *TC* has a different number of patients (Pat_{TC}), which determines the potential demand for drugs in each *TC*. This number is set at the beginning of each simulation by drawing from a normal distribution truncated at 0 to avoid negative values, and it is known by firms. Patients of each *TC* are grouped according to their willingness to buy drugs characterized by different qualities. Some of them, for example, may be unwilling to buy low quality drugs at the current price because of the presence of side effects.

Other things being equal, *TCs* having a larger number of patients tend to be more attractive for firms. The economic value of each *TC* is endogenously determined by summing the revenues of each drug j sold at a given time-variable price ($Price_{j,t}$). Therefore, even if the number of patients is exogenously given, the economic value

[3] As compared to the previous version (Malerba and Orsenigo 2002), the model has been modified in many respects. The main change concerns the possibility of running parallel projects. Also, the development process, the demand equation, the pricing rule and the marketing module have been considerably modified. For a more detailed presentation of the model, see Garavaglia et al. (2010).

of the TC changes during the simulation according to the monopolistic power stemming from to patents and the degree of competition among firms.

Each TC is characterized by a given spectrum of opportunities, represented by the number of molecules Mol_{TC} having a therapeutic and (therefore potential) commercial value (quality Q) which firms aim to discover. Q is randomly set, drawn from a normal distribution (Fig. 1). On average, the probability of finding a "zero quality" molecule is equal to φ.

When a molecule is discovered, a patent is granted and is stored in a firm-specific portfolio of molecules available for future development projects. Patents have a specific duration, PD, and width, PW. That is to say, a patent prevents competitors from developing similar molecules located in the neighborhood (spatial location represents the similarity) for PD simulation periods. Once the patent expires, the molecule becomes available to all firms, i.e. it is put it in a public portfolio shared by all the firms.

3.2.2 The Firms

The industry is populated by an exogenously given number[4] of potential entrants, nF, which may possibly enter the market at any given *time*. Each potential entrant is endowed with a budget B_{start}, equal for all firms. All firms engage in three activities: search, development (i.e. research activities) and marketing. In each simulation period, firms search for promising molecules and, if successful, start to develop the drug. If the process of drug development is successful, firms actually enter the market and start marketing and selling the new drug. Firms have a limited understanding of the environment in which they act and behave, and follow simple, firm-specific rules of thumb (routines).

Firms are heterogeneous: each firm is characterized by a different "strategy", or propensity, with regard to research and marketing activities. This propensity is quantitatively represented by a parameter, h, extracted from a uniform distribution. Consequently, firms invest a different amount of resources to each activity, according to their propensity. Thus, the firm's budget, B, is divided each period among search, development and marketing activities as follows:

$$B_{M,t} = (h)B_t \tag{1a}$$

$$B_{S,t} = (1 - h)\omega B_t \tag{1b}$$

$$B_{D,t} = (1 - h)(1 - \omega)B_t \tag{1c}$$

where ω is invariant and firm-specific.

[4] The choice of parameters nF, n and *time* has been taken according to a process of calibration of the model in order to avoid meaningless outcomes.

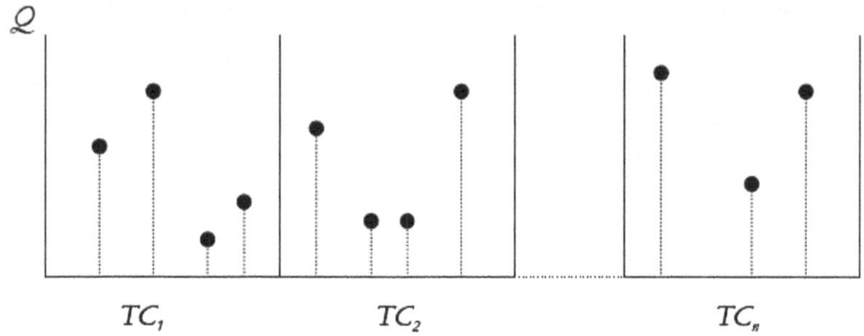

Fig. 1 Therapeutic categories (*TCs*) and molecule quality (*Q*)

Firms are heterogeneous for another reason as well: they can behave as innovators or imitators. Innovators look for new molecules, randomly screening the market environment and incurring a search cost. Imitators select among the molecules the patents on which have expired and thus avoid the cost of search. Imitators also benefit from facing a lower cost of drug development.

3.2.3 Innovative and Imitative Activities

Innovators invest in a search process which involves the payment of a fixed cost, (C_s), in order to draw a molecule. Thus, the number of molecules drawn by a firm in each period (X_t) is determined by the ratio between the fraction of the budget allocated to search, $B_{s,t,}$ and the cost C_s:

$$X_t = \frac{B_{S,t}}{C_S} \tag{2}$$

Firms do not know the "height" (quality) Q of the molecule that they have drawn: they only know whether Q is greater than zero or not. If the molecule has $Q > 0$ and it has not been patented by others, then a patent for that molecule is obtained. The patented molecules become part of an individual 'portfolio' that each firm maintains for potential drug development. When drug development ends, the quality of the molecule (the new drug) is revealed.

Imitative firms differ from innovative firms because they pick up an already discovered molecule the patent on which has expired,[5] without paying the cost of drawing.

[5] The portfolio of molecules includes not only the molecules from which other firms generated a drug, but also molecules not developed because firms fail or the molecules was not economically attractive.

3.2.4 Development Activities

Both innovator and imitator develop products from molecules by engaging in drug development activities. A firm starts a development project using the budget allocated to this kind of activity, $B_{D,t}$, to pay for the cost of development. The time and the cost necessary to complete a development project are assumed—for sake of simplicity—to be fixed and equal for all molecules and firms, the only difference being that both the cost and the time spent for innovation are larger than for imitation. Products must have a minimum quality, indicated with ν_Q, to be allowed to be sold in the marketplace. In other words, products are subject to a "quality check" by an external agency (e.g. the FDA). Below this value, the drug cannot be commercialized and the project fails.

When a product originates from a molecule which has never been used before, it is labelled as an innovative product; otherwise it is considered an imitative product.

In every simulation period, firms choose how many projects to start and which are the most promising molecules to develop: firms run parallel projects. The choice of how many projects to be conducted simultaneously and of the molecules to be developed is governed by routines. Firms consider two features of the molecules for choosing the molecules to be developed: the economic value[6] of the *TC* to which the molecule belongs and the residual length of the molecule's patent protection. Given the number of projects compatible with the budget constraint, the top ranked molecules are chosen and the related development projects are started.

3.2.5 Marketing Activities

If the quality check is successful, in order to get access to a larger number of patients, firms invest in marketing activities, which yield a certain level of "product image" for the consumers.

The marketing expenditure for a given product, M_t, is borne entirely at the launch of the drug at time *t*. This level of "image" is eroded with time at a rate equal to *eA* in each subsequent period, according to:

$$M_{t+1} = M_t(1 - eA). \tag{3}$$

3.2.6 Demand

Drugs are bought on the marketplace by groups of heterogeneous consumers[7] (patients). Their decision to buy a drug depends on several factors, which together

[6] This value depends on the degree of competition among firms in the *TC*.

[7] For reasons of simplicity, we do not distinguish between patients who use the drug and physicians who prescribe it.

yield a specific "merit" to each j-th drug at time t. Formally, the value of this "merit", $U_{j,t}$, is given by:

$$U_{j,t} = Q_j^a \left(\frac{1}{Price_{j,t}} \right)^b M_{j,t}^c \tag{4}$$

where: Q_j is the quality of the drug, M_t the level of marketing "image" at time t, $Price_{j,t}$ is the level of price of drug j at time t defined by the firm according to a mark-up rule,[8] exponents a, b and c are specific to each TC and drawn from uniform distributions (see Appendix 1).

The quality of the drug impacts the diffusion among patients. Each patient is assumed to buy one unit of the drug. Patients of each TC are classified according to their sensitivity to drug's quality. Low quality drugs will be in competition only for patients with the lowest request in terms of quality. Only high quality drugs are able to satisfy all the demand, even if there is only one firm in the TC. This stylized mechanism accounts the heterogeneity of the demand, where some patients face problems of side-effects and tolerability of the drugs.

Other things being equal, the higher the share of patients the higher will be firm's sales and market share and, consequently, the higher will be the mark-up and price. The product's price, the unit cost of manufacturing (assumed to be constant) and the number of patients determine the profits earned by a firm associated to a given product. Because a firm may have more than one product, total profits are given by the sum of profits obtained from all the products of the firm.

3.2.7 Exit Rules

There are three rules governing the firm's exit. First, if the number of draws of potentially valuable molecules per period in the search process is 0 more than x times, the firm fails. This rule aims at reflecting research inefficiencies (obviously this rule does not work for those firms who follow an imitative strategy). The second rule states that, when a firm does not have the minimum budget needed to complete one project and is not selling or making other products, it fails. This rule reflects financial difficulties of the firm. Finally, firms exit when their overall market share is lower than χ. This reflects the unattractive position of the firm in the market. In the model, there is also an exit rule at the product level: firms consider marginal a product that is purchased by a share of consumers lower than 5 %, and consequently withdraw this product from the market.

[8] The mark-up is structured in order to take into account the competitive pressure in the market TC. See Garavaglia et al. (2010).

4 Simulation Runs: "History-Friendly" Results

The "history-friendly" parameterization of the model (the "Standard Set") reflects some fundamental theoretical hypotheses and, in a highly qualitative way, some empirical evidence, some strongly simplifying assumptions and, of course, our ignorance about the "true" values of some key parameters. Thus, for example, there are no economies of scale, no economies of scope and no processes of mergers and acquisitions, no exogenous advances in knowledge that allow firms to focus their search activities. As a consequence, the Standard Set is broadly considered as "history-friendly" and it serves the purpose to produce a benchmark for subsequent analyses.

The calibration of the model is the result of a process of repeated changes in the parameters and methods of the model in order to obtain a satisfactory specification. Some parameters are selected on the basis of the knowledge we have about their meanings and values as shown by the empirical literature and the evidence provided by industry's specialists. The value of other parameters has been selected with the view to preserve coherence.

In our model, the landscape explored by firms is sufficiently rich in terms of opportunities of discovery to allow for the survival of the industry and the introduction of a large number of new drugs. However, search remains a very risky and most of the time unsuccessful activity: the parameter describing the probability of finding a "zero quality" molecule, φ, is set equal to 0.97: this means that only 3 % of the available molecules are potentially valuable. Moreover, the quality value of the molecules is highly skewed.

Search, development and marketing activities are expensive and take time. The development of a drug takes, respectively, eight and four periods (approximately, one period can be thought as corresponding to one year) for innovative and imitative products. The relative costs of search, development and marketing broadly reflect the costs currently observed in the industry (Di Masi et al. 2003). Patent duration is set equal to 20 periods. The number of submarkets (*TCs*) is also very high (200). Marketing expenditures have an important role in accessing a large number of customers and the sensitivity of demand to price is rather low.

The results of the "history friendly" analysis are described in detail in Garavaglia et al. (2010) and, for reasons of space, they will not be recounted here again. Suffice it to say that the so-called "Standard Set" succeeds in reproducing many of the stylized facts of the pharmaceutical industry: low and relatively stable concentration, strong competition between innovators and imitators, firms diversification in many submarkets, skewed size distribution of firms. In particular, it might just be worth remembering that, in each submarket, concentration (measured by the Herfindahl index, H_{TC}) tends to decrease quickly after an initial upsurge (Fig. 2): early entrants gain monopoly power in each *TC* but gradually, after the introduction of new competitive innovative and imitative products in the same *TC*, the degree of competition rises and concentration decreases.

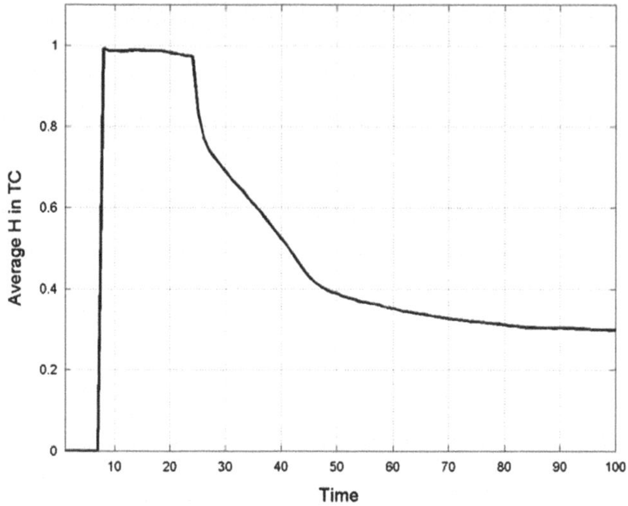

Fig. 2 H_{TC} index

Overall market concentration (measured by Herfindahl index in the overall market, *H*) is, however, always much lower than in individual TCs and it remains low throughout the simulation (Fig. 3). The reasons of this result are described and discussed in the following sections.

5 The Simulation Runs: Technological Regimes and Demand Regimes

The Standard Set is broadly considered as "history-friendly" and it serves the purpose to produce a benchmark for subsequent analyses.

In this section, we investigate the relationships between the variables defining the technological regime (appropriability, cumulativeness, opportunity) and the structure of demand (market fragmentation and market size). Results are averages over 100 runs.

5.1 Technological Regimes and Market Fragmentation

5.1.1 Appropriability

Imitation is the first candidate for explaining the low overall level of concentration. Figures 4 and 5 show how different appropriability regimes—defined in term of the duration of patent protection (*PD*)—affect concentration. In the Standard Set,

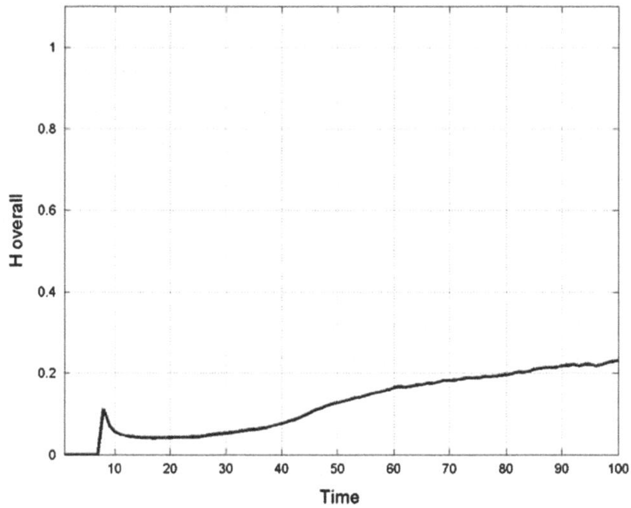

Fig. 3 *H* index in the overall market

unsurprisingly, H_{TC} increases as patent protection becomes longer (Fig. 4). However, changes in *PD* induce somewhat unexpected outcomes in terms of overall concentration *H* (Fig. 5). First of all, changes are not drastic. Second, in a regime with basically no patent protection ($PD = 1$), *H* is actually higher in the earlier periods of the simulation: immediate imitation cuts the profits of both innovators and imitators and therefore the probability of discovering new products. Thus, entry becomes more difficult and the number of active firms is small. When the number of innovative products has grown enough, concentration begins to fall because firms are small and easy imitation starts to bite. At the end simulation, the value of *H* is halved as compared to the Standard Set.

However, *H* decreases also when patent duration is doubled, as compared to the Standard Set ($PD = 40$). The reason is that longer patent protection entails higher profits for innovators and hence higher probability to discover new drugs: while stronger patent protection extends the ability to maintain market power in each individual *TC*, innovative firms discover more *TCs* (about +30 %). Overall concentration declines accordingly because the number of active submarkets increases. Imitating firms also benefit from this scenario because there are now more products to imitate; both the number of innovative and imitative products increase (respectively, about +70 % and +23 %). As a result, H_{TC} declines over time, reaching values only slightly superior to those obtained in Standard Set by the end of the simulation, and a larger number of active *TCs* allows more firms (innovators and imitators) to survive and prosper.[9]

[9] In this paper, we do not discuss the effects of patent protection on prices. In general, though, lower patent protection implies lower prices, as expected.

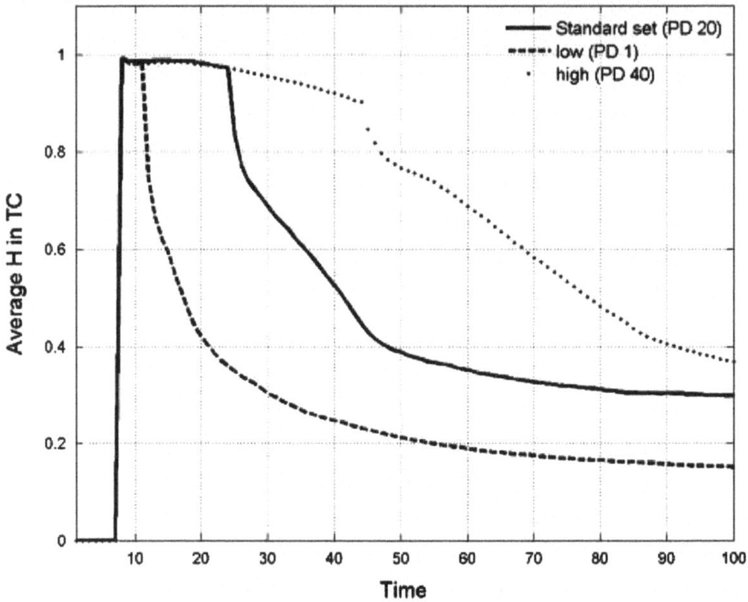

Fig. 4 H_{TC} index

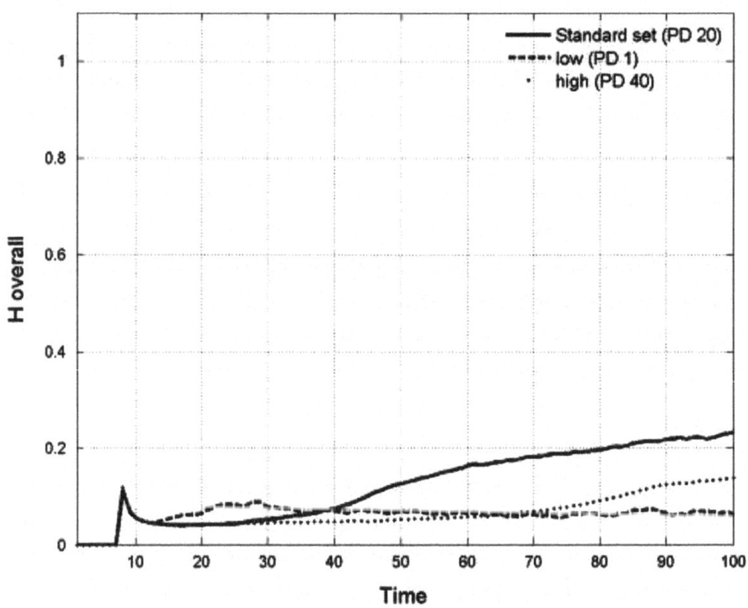

Fig. 5 *H* index in the overall market

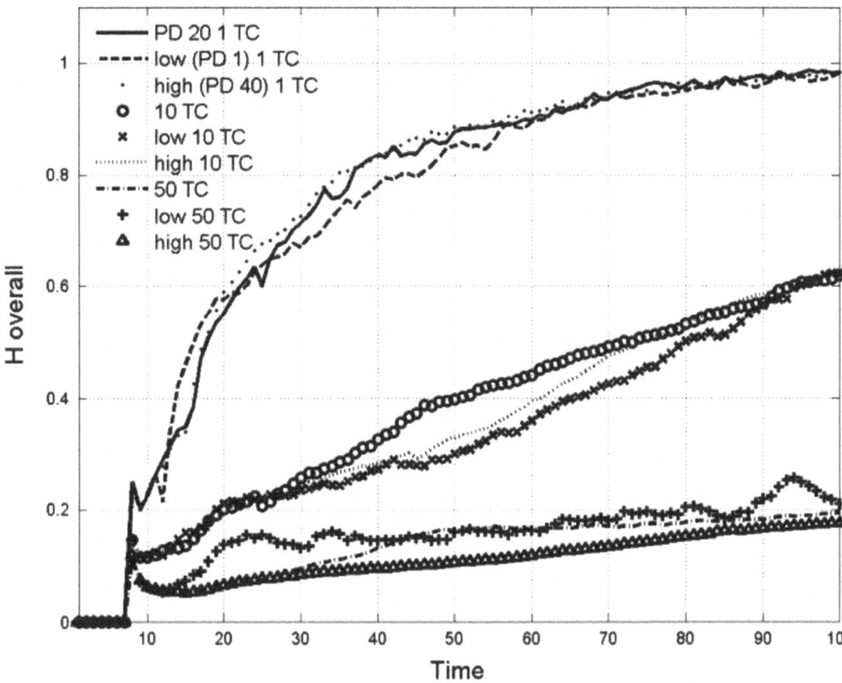

Fig. 6 *H* index in the overall market

Let us now investigate the effects of shorter or longer *PD* in a less fragmented market. Figure 6 reports the value of *H* when the number of submarkets *TCs* is equal to 50, 10 and 1, for the cases of low, standard and high patent protection (respectively: $PD = 1$, 20 and 40). First, as the number of *TCs* decreases, the *H* index increases and, again, *PD* does not modify concentration substantially. More specifically, the effect of longer *PD* tends to decrease *H* with a large number of *TCs*. This effect becomes smaller as the number of *TCs* is reduced, but it never becomes positive. Conversely, low *PD* tends to increase slightly the *H* index (at least until period 40) with fewer *TCs*, i.e. $TC = 50$. When the number of submarkets becomes very low (i.e. $TC = 10$ or less), a shorter *PD* decreases again *H* (but still marginally), such that there is an inverted U effect of lower patent duration on *H* as the market becomes less fragmented. In the extreme case of a homogenous market ($TC = 1$), the industry converges quite rapidly towards monopoly, but even with no patent protection, concentration remains lower but still very high.

These results suggest that concentration depends much more on the degree of fragmentation of the market than on the appropriability regime. Competition in the industry does not appear to be substantially determined by the ease of imitation. Rather, the effects of changes in patent protection are constrained by the structure of demand. In "homogeneous" markets, concentration tends to be high anyway and stronger patent protection has practically no effect, while weaker appropriability can only limit but not reverse the tendencies towards monopoly power. Vice versa, if the industry is competitive (as a result of market fragmentation), a stronger appropriability regime may even reduce (already low) concentration precisely because—through higher profits—it makes the discovery of new submarkets easier.

5.1.2 Cumulativeness

A second factor that induces low concentration in pharmaceuticals is customarily identified in the random nature of search and the low level of cumulativeness in innovation. Thus, firms are unable to exploit past research to improve their chances to innovate again in the future, both in each *TC* and even more so in different *TCs*.

In this simulation, we introduce a technical cumulative effect in the search process of firms by modifying Eq. 2: the number of draws in the search space in each period for a firm is now defined as an increasing function of the number of products owned by the firm (Pr_t):

$$X_t = \frac{B_{S,t}}{C_S} + cum \cdot Pr_t^k \tag{5}$$

where Pr_t is the number of products already developed by the firm and *cum* and k are parameters.

In general, more cumulative search processes have no significant effects on H.[10] When $k = 1$, if anything, stronger cumulativeness tends to lower H. Why? An "equalizing effect" prevails: all firms benefit from the cumulative effect in the process of search,[11] so that they increase their probability to develop more innovative products. This also leads to a higher opportunity for imitative firms to survive and to prosper by imitating and introducing new products. On the other hand, big firms with rich budgets benefit relatively less than small firms from cumulativeness, since they have already access to a large number of draws. In any case, as new *TCs* are discovered, overall concentration is lowered and coherently average concentration in each *TC* increases. With higher values of the parameter k, concentration does indeed increase, but the effect is still small (from 0.22 to 0.26): higher cumulativeness increases concentration only when the parameter k is very high.

This result holds also when the number of submarkets is changed. Changes in the degree of cumulativeness have very small effects in all scenarios. Similar results are obtained if a different form of cumulativeness is introduced in the model, namely economies of scale and scope in product development rather than in drug discovery.

[10] See Figures in Garavaglia et al. (2010) regarding results with different values of the parameters *cum* and k, not included here for reasons of space.

[11] The number of draws by each firm, calculated according to equation 5, are the same as draws given by Eq. 2 plus an additional term. Both large or small firms in terms of product owned benefit from this counterfactual experiment.

5.1.3 Innovative Opportunities

How would market structure and innovation evolve in "richer" and "poorer" environments in terms of innovative opportunities? The effect of these changes are ex-ante uncertain: on the one hand, higher opportunities might reduce concentration, making it easier for firms to find molecules and to introduce new products; imitation would becomes easier, too. On the other hand, higher opportunities might increase concentration to the extent that success-breeds-success processes favor the growth of the larger firms, even in the absence of cumulativeness in the search process (Nelson and Winter 1982).

In order to investigate this question, we focus on the properties of the search space in our model. We run simulations with different probabilities of finding a promising molecule in order to start a new project (probability $1 - \varphi$ in Section 3.2.1), comparing the Standard Set, where the probability of finding a "zero quality" molecule is $\varphi = 0.97$, with a simulation in which opportunities are "richer" ($\varphi = 0.9$) and with one where are "poorer" ($\varphi = 0.99$).

The results are similar to the case of patent protection: the higher the probability of finding promising molecules, the higher (but only slightly) is the H_{TC} (Fig. 7), the lower is H (Fig. 8), the greater are the number of firms, the number of explored *TCs*, the number of innovative and imitative products, and the size of both innovative and imitative firms.

These patterns can be explained by the interaction of different processes. First, when discovery is easier (higher opportunities), more *TCs* are discovered: firms distribute their innovative and imitative activities over a wider spectrum of submarkets. Second, within each *TC*, innovators can maintain higher market shares simply because they face fewer competitors (who are active in different *TCs*). Larger firms can grow more, enjoy higher profits and higher further chances to discover new drugs. But again, successful efforts are distributed over many different submarkets.

Results are partially different under alternative scenarios of the demand structure. In situations of high market fragmentation, higher opportunities reduce concentration, making it easier for firms to introduce new products in new submarkets. As the number of submarkets shrinks, higher opportunities induce higher concentration both in individual submarkets and in the aggregate. Firms have still better chances to discover new products, but the scope for entering new submarkets is now more limited. Larger firms have still better chances to innovate, but in a smaller set of *TCs*. Competitors may well introduce new products, but the submarkets are more crowded, profits are lower and chances to innovate again are comparatively reduced. Thus, success-breeds success processes lead to comparatively higher H. However, the effect of higher opportunities on H is positive at a decreasing rate as the number of *TCs* decreases. As the number of submarkets becomes very small—the extreme case being a completely homogeneous market—a firm becomes quickly a (quasi)-monopolist; in this case, higher opportunities for innovation and

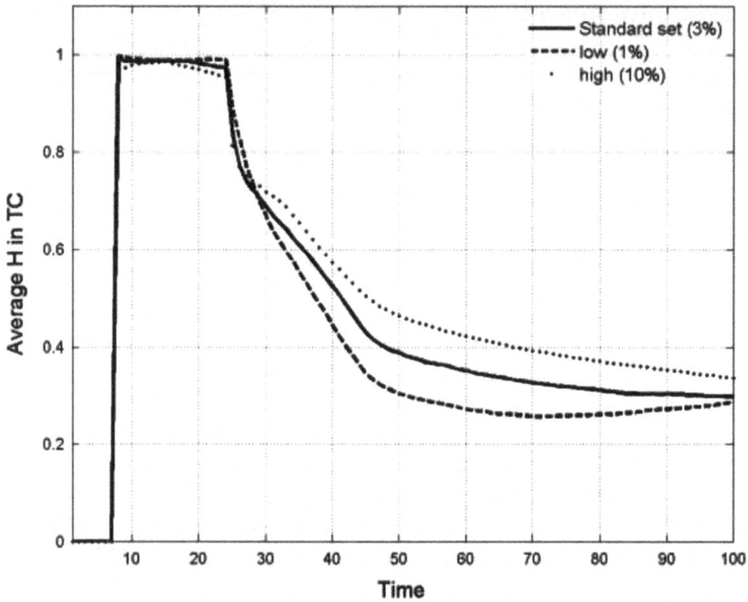

Fig. 7 H_{TC} index

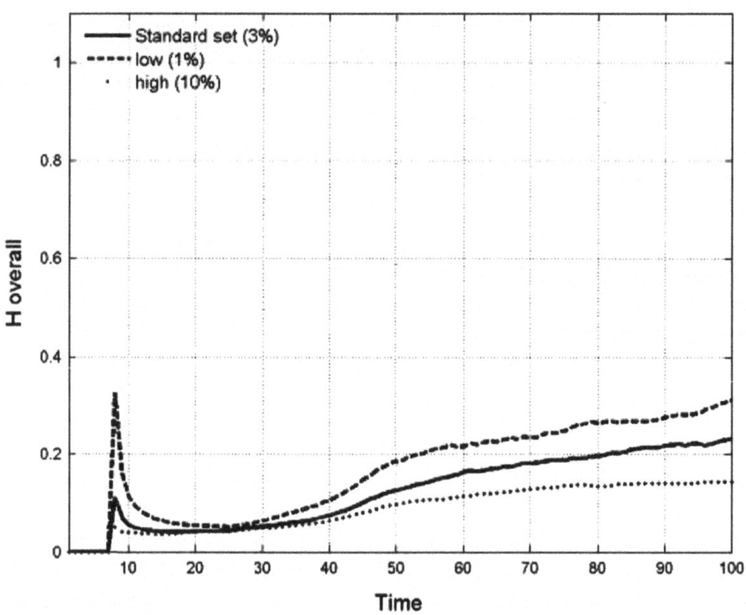

Fig. 8 *H* index in the overall market

additional profits bear only smaller additional advantages, also because new products cannibalize old ones.

5.1.4 Schumpeter Mark I and Mark II

Finally, we summarize the results obtained so far by changing simultaneously the values of the parameters which define a technological regime. First, we create a "Schumpeter Mark I" context (SM1), with plenty of opportunities to innovate ($\varphi = 0.9$), low appropriability ($PD = 1$) and no cumulativeness. Then, we construct a "Schumpeter Mark II" context (SM2), where $\varphi = 0.99$, $PD = 40$ and cumulativeness is high (k in Eq. 5 is equal to 3). We compare these two regimes with the Standard Set for different numbers of potential submarkets. We should expect, in principle, that concentration should decrease in the SM1 regime and increase in the SM2 regime.

In the SM1 regime (Figs. 9 and 10), both $H_{TC}$and H are always lower than in the Standard Set for every given demand structure, although the effects are small and disappear by the end of the simulation. The fall in the indexes is more pronounced with a large number of submarkets. It becomes smaller as the number of *TCs* is reduced.

In the SM2 regime (Figs. 11 and 12), the effect is less obvious. On the one hand, concentration increases within individual submarkets up to a degree of market fragmentation equal to $TC = 10$, where, as we have discussed, the effect of low opportunities associated with the "Schumpeter Mark II" regime leads to lower average concentration levels. Moreover, overall concentration H decreases, contrary to our initial expectation. Our previous findings, however, explain this result. As appropriability and cumulativeness are stronger, firms gain larger profits in any one *TC* and have greater chances to discover new molecules and to open new submarkets. Thus, while concentration increases within each individual *TC* (H_{TC}), overall concentration H falls as the number of active *TCs* grows. As the number of potential submarkets is reduced, this effect becomes weaker. In the extreme case of a homogeneous market ($TC = 1$), the industry converges to monopoly.

5.2 Demand Regimes: Potential Submarkets and the Size of the Market

Previous results indicate that the variables defining the technological regime exert their effects on concentration—coherently with expectations—only within any given demand structure, but have limited effects when the demand structure changes. Indeed, one of the most important channels through which the technological regime influences market structure is through the discovery of new submarkets.

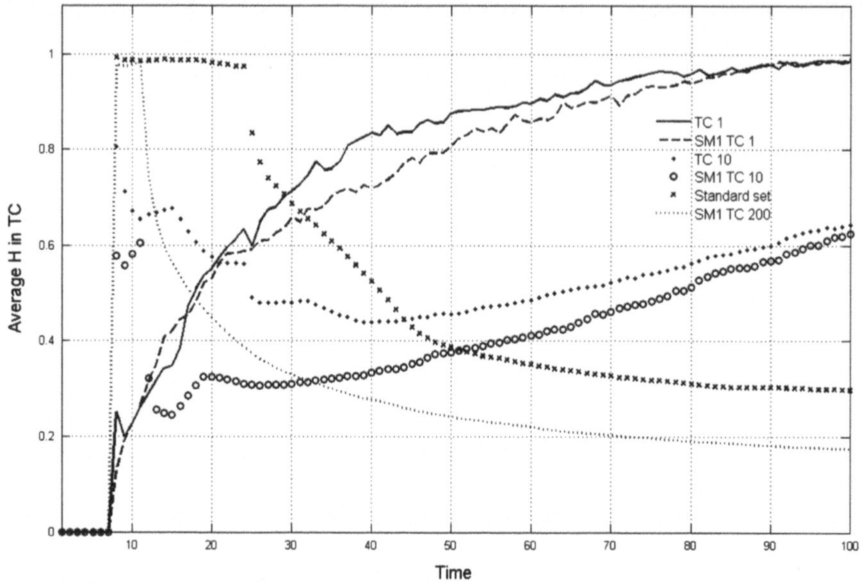

Fig. 9 H_{TC} in Schumpeter Mark I regime in different fragmentation settings

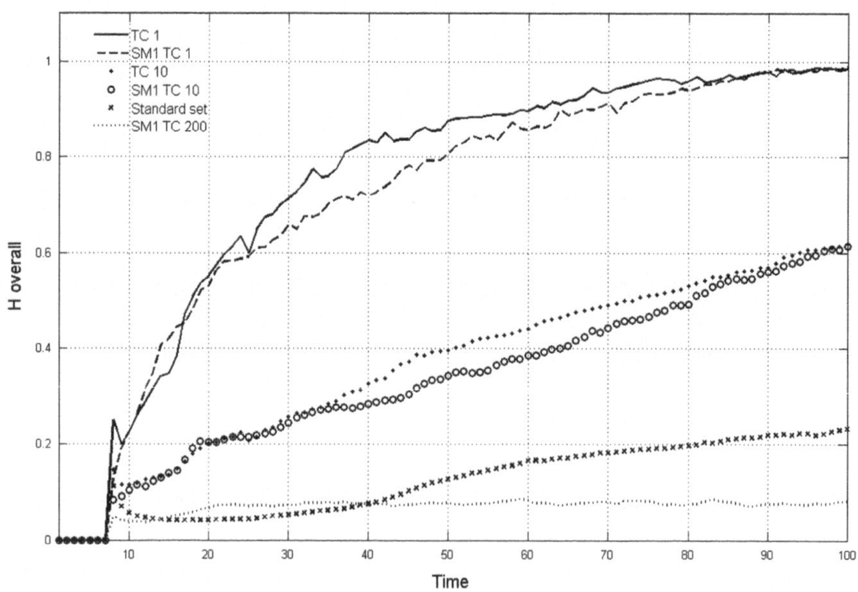

Fig. 10 Overall H in Schumpeter Mark I regime in different fragmentation settings

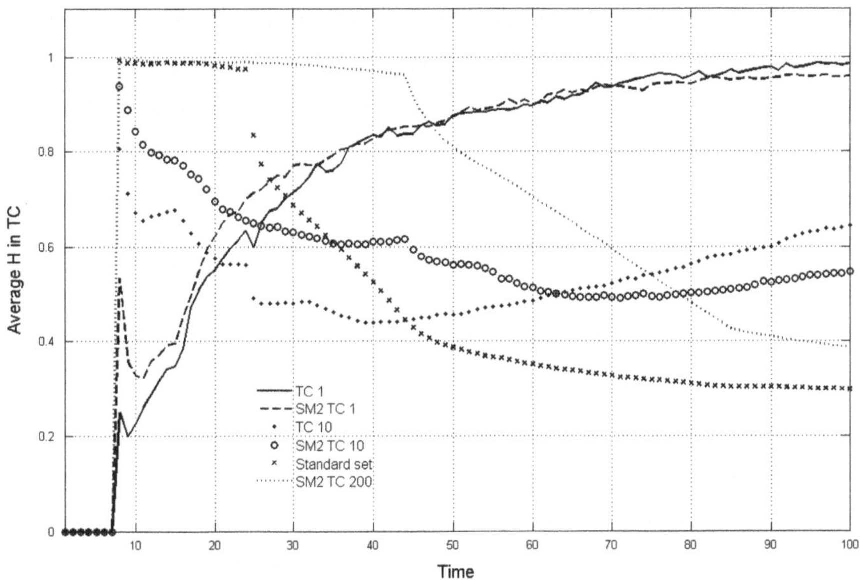

Fig. 11 H_{TC} in Schumpeter Mark II regime in different fragmentation settings

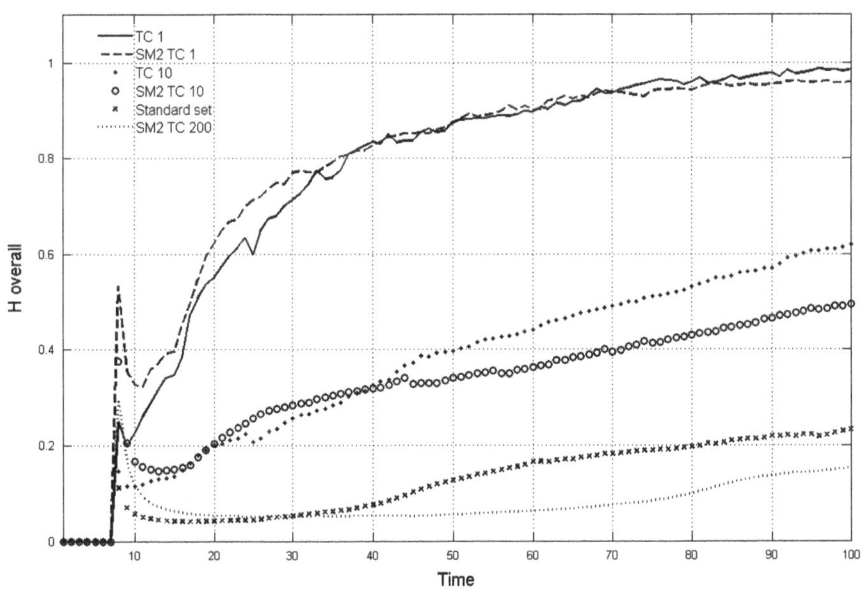

Fig. 12 Overall H in Schumpeter Mark II regime in different fragmentation settings

The crucial questions, then, are: how and why do different degrees of market fragmentation affect concentration?

5.2.1 Number of Potential Submarkets

Keeping unchanged the value of the other relevant parameters, we modify the number of potential submarkets. Holding the value of the overall market constant, the number of *TCs* is gradually reduced from 200 to one. Results are straightforward: concentration increases as market fragmentation decreases. In the extreme case of a homogeneous market ($TC = 1$), the H index converges progressively and rapidly towards monopoly. This result squares neatly with the simple intuition described in the Introduction and in Section 3 and, in particular, with Sutton's model (1998).[12]

With regard to the dynamics of concentration in individual submarkets, at the end of the simulations, average concentration is higher, the lower is fragmentation, as expected. However, at the beginning of the simulations, the reverse holds: in the early stages of the simulation, only a few *TCs* have been discovered. Hence, more firms enter the same *TCs*, fostering competition and lowering concentration (see Garavaglia et al. 2010 for details).

This result is in tune with theoretical expectations. In particular, Sutton's model predicts that market fragmentation leads to lower concentration because the "escalation parameter", *alpha*, is lower. When markets are fragmented, the additional profits obtainable by a firm outspending rivals are limited: concentration remains low. Our model confirms this intuition: the key variable is the size of the "prize" that innovators can gain relative to the value of the overall market (and hence also the distribution of these prizes across submarkets): in pharmaceuticals, firm growth and changes in concentration are strongly dependent on the discovery of few blockbusters. However, the mechanism linking market fragmentation and concentration is somewhat different: it has to do essentially with success-breeds-success processes and first mover advantages.

When the market is fragmented, the prize accruing to an innovator is limited. An early innovator gains only a modest advantage vis-a-vis competitors, who maintain their chances to discover a molecule, mainly by opening new *TCs*. In an extreme case, one can think of many firms holding monopoly power in a single submarket and few early innovators being present in different *TCs*. This process increases concentration within each therapeutic category, but decreases it overall. Conversely, when the "prize" is big—because there are few *TCs*—early innovators gain a disproportionate advantage vis-a-vis competitors. Through their large profits, they gain further chances of discovering new molecules, while competitors are left with little possibilities to invest and find new drugs. Early innovators gradually end

[12] See the robustness of these results in Appendix 2.

up dominating individual submarkets and—through diversification—the overall market.

More generally, it is the distribution of the "prizes" accruing to innovators that matters. Results (not reported here) show clearly that, holding constant the number of *TCs* and the value of the overall market, changes in the variance and in the skewness of the values of individual submarkets have a substantial impact on concentration (Garavaglia et al. 2010). The explanation is that, if the overall market is composed by very few extremely rich *TCs* and many poor ones, concentration increases drastically: the firm discovering the large submarket gains also a large fraction of the overall market; the "size of the prize" matters. In dynamic terms, this observation implies also that the discovery of a rich submarket will raise abruptly concentration, as in Buenstorf and Klepper (2010).

5.2.2 The Size of the Market

We now explore the behavior of the model for varying size of the markets. Holding the number of submarkets fixed, we change the number of patients and (as a consequence) the economic value of the market. Figure 13 shows an inverted U effect.

In the Standard Set, concentration declines (slightly) as the size of the market shrinks: the value of the prize is lower and the first mover advantage is smaller. However, larger markets do not induce substantially higher concentration because additional profits lead primarily to the discovery of new submarkets, keeping thus the level of concentration low. That is to say, irrespective of market size, fragmented markets are clearly related to low concentration and changes in the size of the market do not lead to substantially different results when the number of submarkets is high.

Next, we examine the effects of changes in market size in a different scenario of market fragmentation ($TC = 10$), as reported in Fig. 14. The results confirm the previous intuition. As the number of submarket declines, poorer markets induce lower concentration and larger markets increase it, although at decreasing rates: when the market is sufficiently large (twice as much as compared to the Standard Set), further increases in market size do not bear any significant change. This is consistent with our previous finding: even if larger markets imply richer firms and consequently higher probabilities of discovering new *TCs*, with little market fragmentation, the negative effect of discovering new *TCs* on concentration vanishes: the degree of concentration shows a lower bound and remains relatively high.

In other words, the size of the "prize" matters: but it is its relative size rather than its absolute value that matters more.

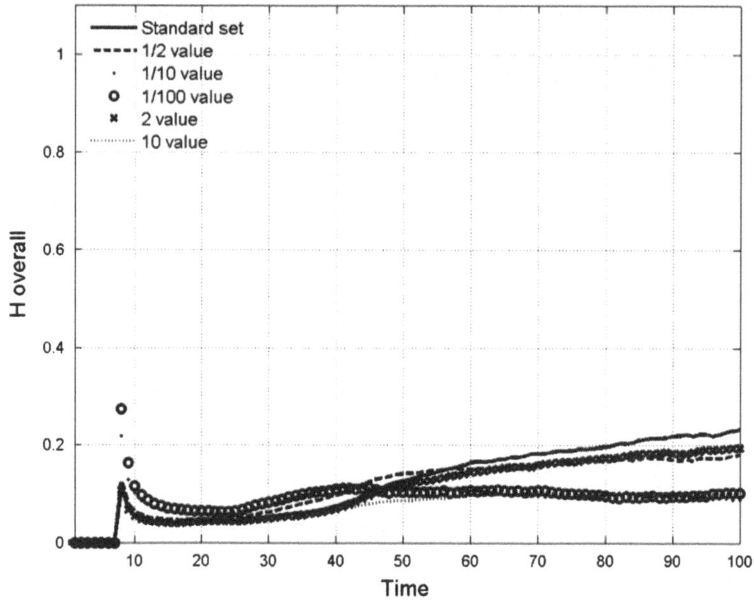

Fig. 13 Overall *H* with different values of market size

5.2.3 Market Leaders

Both empirical evidence for pharmaceuticals and Klepper's models (Klepper 1996; Klepper and Simons 2000a, b) suggest the relevance of innovative strategies and first-mover advantages in the evolution of the industry. Simulation results obtained so far suggest also that the size of the market (of the "prize" for innovators) should provide a strong advantage to innovators. To explore these issues, we implement a simple econometric analysis with simulated data. We define two different specifications of the model in order to test whether firms that dominate the market at the end of simulation are innovators and early entrants in large markets. We run 100 simulations and register data about 50 firms per simulation,[13] at the end of simulation, for the following variables: *share* (firms' market share), *size* (firms' profit), *alive* (status of firms), *nTC* (firms' diversification, i.e. number of submarkets explored by each firm). Moreover:

- we construct three dummies relating to the period of entry of firms; *cohort1* if the firm enters in periods [1–3], *cohort2* if the firm enters in periods [4–8], *cohort3* if the firm enters after period 8;

[13] The number of firms included in the regression should be 5000 (50 firms for 100 simulations). Among the 5000 firms, 20 do not enter the market (i.e. they do not discover and sell any drug). These firms are not included in the regression sample.

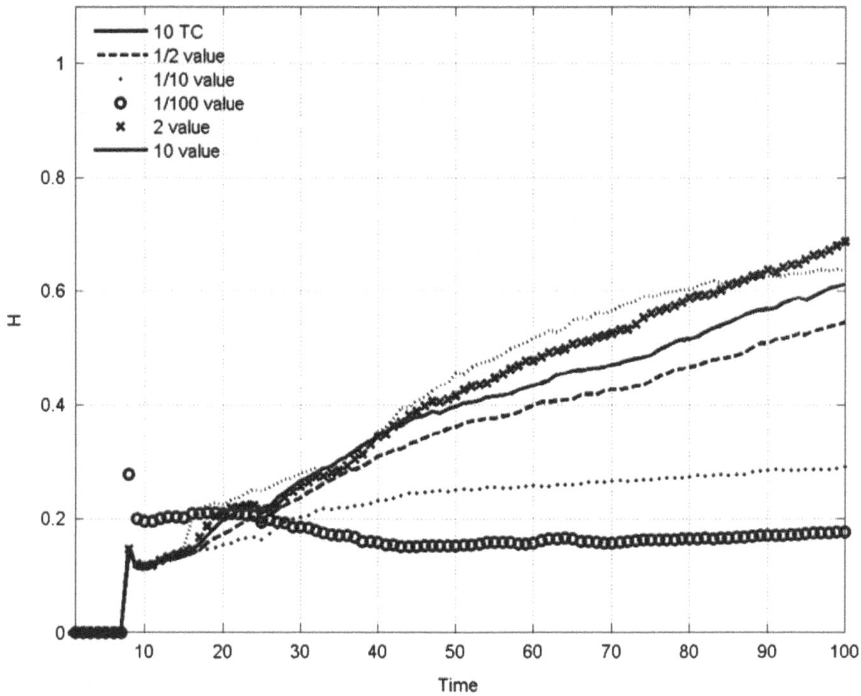

Fig. 14 Overall H with different values of market size, when $TC = 10$

- we register *market_size*: size of the market, in terms of patients, in which firms enter first;
- we define four dummies for the propensity of firms to invest in research in comparison to marketing, equal to (1–h), as defined in Section 3.2.2: *high_propensity, medium_propensity, weak_propensity, low_propensity*, respectively if $h < 0.25$, $0.25 \leq h < 0.5$, $0.5 \leq h < 0.75$, $h \geq 0.75$.

We estimate a Probit model (column 1 of Table 1) with *alive* as the dependent variable. The results show that the earlier the entry period and the larger the first market entered, the higher the probability of being still alive at the end of the simulation period. The variables indicating the propensity to invest in research are not significant.

In another specification (column 2 of Table 1), we estimate an OLS on the subsample of firms conditional on being active in the end of the simulation. The dependent variable is the logarithm of *share*. Results are reported in column 2 of Table 1. Firms entering during the first cohort have a *share* 18 % larger at the end of the simulation. The same does not apply for the firms entering during the second cohort, while the difference is not statistically significant if compared to the firms that entered later. These results confirm that the first mover advantage is crucial and its effect is stronger at the very beginning of the simulation and disappears quickly.

Table 1 Regression table

Variables	(1) Probit alive	(2) OLS log(share)
cohort1	0.87*** (0.064)	0.18** (0.085)
cohort2	0.63*** (0.073)	0.057 (0.093)
high_propensity	0.062 (0.059)	1.47*** (0.058)
medium_propensity	−0.015 (0.059)	0.37*** (0.059)
weak_propensity	−0.031 (0.059)	0.12** (0.060)
log(market_size)	1.06*** (0.037)	0.35*** (0.035)
Constant	−6.42*** (0.20)	−6.35*** (0.22)
Observations	4980	1991
R-squared	(pseudo) 0.29	0.307

The size of the first *TC* explored by the firm affect positively the market share at the end of the simulation: a 1 % larger *TC* grants, on average, a 0.35 % larger share. Further, firms having a high propensity to innovate reach on average a market share 147 % larger then low propensity firms. To conclude, the model predicts that industry leaders are the early innovative entrants in large submarkets.

6 Conclusions

The history-friendly model of the pharmaceutical industry is able to reproduce the main stylized facts of the evolution of that industry. Moreover, our more theoretically oriented exploration provides results which might have a broader interest for the dynamic analysis of the relationships between innovation, demand and market structure.

First, the structure of demand matters in determining market structure. Fragmented markets are always less concentrated than homogeneous markets, irrespective of the relevant technological regime.

Second, technological regimes matter also, but their influence is modulated by the demand regime. Given a degree of market fragmentation, while in Schumpeter Mark I regimes, the nature of the technological regime influences market structure according to expectations (i.e. concentration tends to be lower as compared to the Standard Set), in a Schumpeter Mark II regime, overall concentration tends to be lower.

This seemingly negative result is explained by the third finding of this paper. Competition takes place in the model largely through the discovery of new submarkets. Within each submarket, the variables that define the technological regime produce indeed the expected results: stronger cumulativeness, richer opportunities to innovate and tighter appropriability conditions favor the emergence of market leaders. However, the opening of new submarkets reduces overall concentration.

Fourth, is not the number of submarkets as such that determines market structure, but rather the size of the "prize" that the innovators gain, both in absolute terms and relative to the value of the market. From this perspective, our result is in line with Sutton (1998) emphasis on the role played by the "escalation mechanism" in determining the relationship between market structure and innovation. However, our model reinterprets this finding in a dynamic, evolutionary context, where the value of the escalation parameter is crucially influenced by the nature of technological regime, the number of submarkets is partially endogenous and no assumption that profitable submarkets will be left unoccupied is required.

Moreover, the model embodies, at the same time, further results concerning the factors leading to industry leadership. Similarly with Klepper (1996), Klepper and Simons (2000a) and Klepper and Thompson (2006), but through different processes, and consistently with empirical evidence for pharmaceuticals, the model predicts that industry leaders will be early innovative entrants in large submarkets.

Fifth, the emergence of concentration (or lack of it) is explained in our model by the working of dynamic processes such as success-breeds-success, and increasing returns and strong cumulativeness, bandwagon effects in the demand side, as well as by the (partially endogenous) process of the creation of new submarkets.

We believe that these results increase our understanding of the factors affecting the relationship between market structure and innovation in an evolutionary and Schumpeterian approach. We believe also that they can foster dialogue and cross-fertilization between different approaches, identifying not only differences but also similarities, beyond fundamental diversity in basic methodological commitments.

Acknowledgements The authors acknowledge the financial support of the Italian Ministry for Education, Universities and Research (FIRB, Project RISC - RBNE039XKA: "Research and entrepreneurship in the knowledge-based economy: the effects on the competitiveness of Italy in the European Union"). Christian Garavaglia would like to thank the participants of the 13th Conference of the International Schumpeter Society (Aalborg, 21–24 June 2010). The authors thank two anonymous referees for their useful suggestions. The usual disclaimers apply.

Appendix 1: Parameters and variables reported in the text

f	index for firms
t	index for time
TC	index for therapeutic categories

General model parameters.

$nF = 50$	Initial number of possible entrants (firms)
$n = 200$	Number of *TCs*
$time = 100$	Periods of simulation

Exogenous industry characteristics.

$a = \mathrm{U}(0.5,0.6)$	Exponent of product quality (PQ)
$b = \mathrm{U}(0.15,0.20)$	Exponent of inverse of price $1/\mathrm{Price}_{j,t}$
$c = \mathrm{U}(0.35,0.4)$	Exponent of launch marketing expenditures M
$eA = 0.01$	Erosion coefficient of launch marketing expenditure
$Mol_{TC} = 400$	Number of molecules per *TC*
$PD = 20$	Patent duration
$PW = 5$	Patent width
$\varphi = 0.97$	Probability of drawing a zero-quality molecule
$Pat_{TC} \sim N(\mu_p, \sigma_p)$	Number of patients per *TC*
$\mu_p = 600$	Mean of normal distribution of number of patients per *TC*
$\sigma_p = 200$	Standard deviation of normal distribution of the number of patients per *TC*
$Q \sim N(\mu_Q,\sigma_Q)$	Quality of the molecule
μ_Q	Mean of normal distribution of positive quality molecules
σ_Q	Standard deviation of normal distribution of positive quality molecules
$\nu_Q = 30$	Minimum quality of the product to be sold on the market
$\varepsilon = 1.5$	Price sensitivity of demand

Endogenous industry characteristic.

H_{TC}	Average Herfindahl index in submarkets (*TCs*)
H	Herfindahl index in the overall market

Exogenous firm characteristics.

$B_{start} = 4500$	Starting budget given to each entrant
$h = \mathrm{U}[0.25, 0.75]$	Firm's strategy
$\omega = \mathrm{U}(0.05, 0.15)$	Firm's share of budget dedicated to search
$C_s = 20$	Firm's cost of draw new molecules
$x = 7$	blank periods of search that leads to exit the market
$\chi = 0.4\ \%$	lower bound to exit the market

Endogenous firm characteristics.

$B_{D,t}$	Budget dedicated to development of products at time *t*
$B_{M,t}$	Budget dedicated to marketing of products at time *t*
$B_{S,t}$	Budget dedicated to search of molecules at time *t*
X_t	Number of draws of a firm *f* at time *t*
Pr_t	Number of products belonging to firm *f* at time *t*
M_t	marketing expenditure at time *t*
$Price_{j,t}$	Price of drug *j* at time *t*

Table 2 Parameters' values of the robustness check

	Benchmark	Upper bound	Lower bound
Starting budget given to each entrant	4500	4000	5000
Cost of single step in developing process (innovative products)	60	50	70
Cost of single step in developing process (imitative products)	20	16	24
Firm's cost of draw new molecules	20	16	24
Interest rate of remuneration	0.08	0.07	0.09
Mean of normal distribution of positive quality molecules	30	26	34
Erosion coefficient of launch marketing expenditure	0.01	0.009	0.011
Eta parameter in mark-up equation	0.5	0.4	0.6

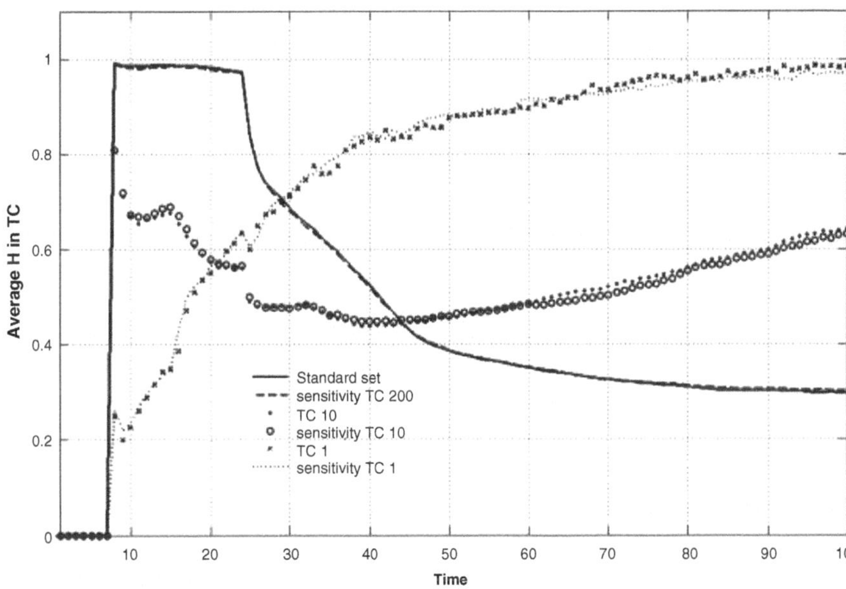

Fig. 15 Robustness check: average H_{TC} index

Appendix 2: Robustness of results

We check the robustness of our results with a Monte Carlo exercise for different degrees of fragmentation of the market: $TC = 1$, 10 and 200. For each of these three cases, we draw 100 different parameterizations of the model from a uniform multinomial distribution. Each marginal distribution of the multinomial is the

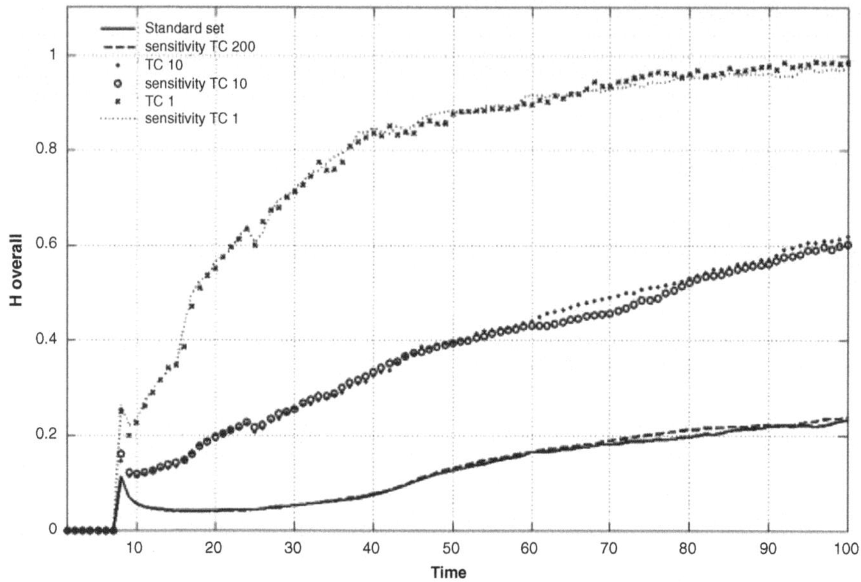

Fig. 16 Robustness check: overall *H*

value of the parameter i for the parameterization n, where i is between 1 and 8, and n between 1 and 100. Table 2 reports the parameters of the robustness check. We exclude the parameters that are the center of our analysis in order to isolate the effects of the i.

Robustness check is successful (Figs. 15 and 16). In the three baseline cases ($TC = 1$, 10 and 200), the effect of market fragmentation on H_{TC} and H is confirmed, according to the analyses in the text, even applying the random parameterization of the model.

References

Adner R (2002)1 When are technologies disruptive: a demand-based view of the emergence of competition. Strat Manag J 23:667–688

Adner R, Levinthal D (2001) Demand heterogeneity and technology evolution: implications for product and process innovation. Manag Sci 47(5):611–628

Bottazzi G, Dosi G, Lippi M, Pammolli F, Riccaboni M (2001) Innovation and corporate growth in the evolution of the drug industry. Int J Ind Organ 19(7):1161–1187

Breschi S, Malerba F, Orsenigo L (2000) Technological regimes and schumpeterian patterns of innovation. Econ J 110:388–410

Buenstorf G, Klepper S (2010) Submarket dynamics and innovation: the case of the U.S. tire industry. Ind Corp Change 19(5):1563–1587

Chandler AD (2005) Shaping the industrial century: the remarkable story of the modern chemical and pharmaceutical industries (Harv Stud Bus Hist), Harvard University Press, Cambridge, MA

Comanor WS (1986) The political economy of the pharmaceutical industry. J Econ Lit 24:1178–1217
Dalle J-M (1997) Heterogeneity vs. externalities in technological competition: a tale of possible technological landscapes. J Evol Econ 7:395–413
Di Masi J, Hansen R, Grabowski H (2003) The price of innovation: new estimates of drug development costs. J Health Econ 22(2):151–185
Galambos L, Sturchio J (1996) The pharmaceutical industry in the twentieth century: a reappraisal of the sources of innovation. Hist Technol 13(2):83–100
Gambardella A (1995) Science and innovation in the US pharmaceutical industry. Cambridge University Press, Cambridge
Garavaglia C (2010) Modelling industrial dynamics with 'history-friendly' simulations. Struct Chang Econ Dyn 21(4):258–275
Garavaglia C, Malerba F, Orsenigo L, Pezzoni M (2010) A history-friendly model of the evolution of the pharmaceutical industry: technological regimes and demand structure, KITeS Working Paper
Grabowski H, Vernon J (1994) Innovation and structural change in pharmaceuticals and biotechnology. Ind Corp Change 3(2):435–449
Henderson R, Orsenigo L, Pisano GP (1999) The pharmaceutical industry and the revolution in molecular biology: exploring the interactions between scientific, institutional and organizational change. In: Mowery DC, Nelson RR (eds) The sources of industrial leadership. Cambridge University Press, Cambridge
Klepper S (1996) Entry, exit, growth and innovation over the product life cycle. Am Econ Rev 86:562–583
Klepper S (1997) Industry life cycles. Ind Corp Change 6(8):145–181
Klepper S, Simons K (2000a) Dominance by birthright: entry of prior radio producers and competitive ramifications in the US television receiver industry. Strateg Manag J 21:997–1016
Klepper S, Simons K (2000b) The making of an oligopoly: firm survival and techniological change in the evolution of the U.S. tire industry. J Polit Econ 108:728–760
Klepper S, Thompson P (2006) Submarkets and the evolution of market structure. RAND J Econ 37(4):861–886
Malerba F, Nelson R, Orsenigo L, Winter S (1999) History-friendly models of industry evolution: the computer industry. Ind Corp Change 8(1):3–40
Malerba F, Nelson R, Orsenigo L, Winter S (2007) Demand, innovation, and the dynamics of market structure: the role of experimental users and diverse preferences. J Evol Econ 17:371–399
Malerba F, Nelson RR, Orsenigo L, Winter SG (2008) Vertical integration and disintegration of computer firms: a history-friendly model of the co-evolution of the computer and semiconductor industries. Ind Corp Change 17:197–231
Malerba F, Orsenigo L (2002) Innovation and market structure in the dynamics of the pharmaceutical industry and biotechnology: towards a history-friendly model. Ind Corp Change 11 (4):667–703
Matraves C (1999) Market structure, R&D and advertising in the pharmaceutical industry. J Ind Econ 47(2):169–194
Nelson R, Winter S (1982) An evolutionary theory of economic change. The Belknapp Press of Harvard University Press, Cambridge
Pammolli F (1996) Innovazione, Concorrenza a Strategie di Sviluppo nell'Industria Farmaceutica, Guerini Scientifica
Pavitt K (1984) Sectoral patterns of technical change: towards a taxonomy and a theory. Res Policy 13(6):343–373
Pisano G (1996) The development factory: unlocking the potential of process innovation. Harvard Business School Press
Saviotti P (1996) Technological evolution. Variety and the economy. Edward Elgar, Cheltenham

Scherer FM (2000) The pharmaceutical industry. In: Culyer AJ, Newhouse JP (eds) Handbook of health economics, I. Elsevier, Amsterdam, pp 1297–1336

Schwartzman D (1976) Innovation in the pharmaceutical industry. John Hopkins University Press, Baltimore

Sutton J (1998) Technology and market structure: theory and history. MIT Press, Cambridge

Windrum P, Birchenhall C (1998) Is product life cycle theory a special case? Dominant designs and the emergence of market niches through coevolutionary-learning. Struct Chang Econ Dyn 9:109–134

Windrum P, Birchenhall C (2005) Structural change in presence of network externalities: a co-evolutionary model of technological successions. J Evol Econ 15:123–148

Winter S (1984) Schumpeterian competition in alternative technological regimes. J Econ Behav Organ 5(3–4):287–320

Innovation and Demand in Industry Dynamics: R&D, New Products and Profits

Francesco Bogliacino and Mario Pianta

Abstract The links between three interconnected elements of the Schumpeterian sources of economic change are explored, conceptually and empirically, and related to the role played by demand factors. First, we examine the commitment of industries to invest profits in cumulative R&D efforts; second, the ability of industries' R&D to introduce to new products in markets; third, the impact of new products on entrepreneurial profits. We consider the nature and variety of innovative efforts—distinguishing in particular between strategies of technological and cost competiveness—and we introduce the role of demand in pulling technological change and supporting profits. We develop a simultaneous three-equation model and we test it at industry level—for 38 manufacturing and service sectors—on six European countries over two time periods from 1994 to 2006. The results show that the model effectively accounts for the dynamics of European industries and highlights the interconnections between the different factors contributing to growth.

F. Bogliacino
Fundación Universitaria Konrad Lorenz, Carrera 9Bis, No 62-43 Bogotá, Colombia
e-mail: francesco.bogliacino@gmail.com

M. Pianta (✉)
University of Urbino, Urbino, Italy

Centro Linceo Interdisciplinare, Accademia Nazionale dei Lincei, Rome, Italy
e-mail: mario.pianta@uniurb.it

A. Pyka and E.S. Andersen (eds.), *Long Term Economic Development*,
Economic Complexity and Evolution, DOI 10.1007/978-3-642-35125-9_5,

1 Introduction[1]

Economic change in advanced countries can be seen—in a Schumpeterian perspective—as the result of three processes that are closely interconnected. First, the cumulative nature of knowledge and R&D, supported by *technology push* and *demand pull* factors, and by the commitment of firms and industries to invest profits in research activities. Second, the ability of industries' R&D to lead to successful innovations, combining developments on the supply and the demand side. Third, the impact of new products, new processes, and demand growth on entrepreneurial profits.

This article explores these complex relationships and investigates the links between innovation and economic performance in an integrated perspective. Much economic research has investigated these issues either considering externalities and spillovers as major channels for the diffusion of knowledge and technologies (Griliches 1979, 1992, 1995; Griffith et al. 2004), or focusing on R&D driven technological change that leads to endogenous growth (see Aghion and Howitt 1998 for a general discussion of the literature). We aim to enlarge the picture, considering the *diversity* of innovative efforts—that include not just R&D, but also innovative investment, adoption of new technologies, learning processes, etc. -, the *uncertainty* of technological change—addressing innovative *outputs* as well as *inputs*, such as R&D—and the *feedback* effects that may exists among the different relationships.

A few contributions have explored the links between innovation and economic performance by breaking down this sequence of relationships and estimating empirically different phases: the decision to invest in R&D, the relationship between inputs ad outputs and the effect of R&D on economic performance (Crepon et al. 1998; Parisi et al. 2006). In a recent work (Bogliacino and Pianta 2012) we develop a model with a three-equation system that explains R&D intensities, the importance of innovative in sales and the growth of profits; an empirical test is carried out at the industry level for major European countries. We find that R&D supports successful innovations and that they lead to higher profits, which in turn finance R&D, with a complex structure of lags and feedbacks.

In this chapter we build on that approach and provide two main novelties. First, we integrate the analysis of the innovation-performance link with the demand side, exploring the role of different demand factors—exports, domestic consumption, intermediate demand, etc.—in the equations. Second, we consider the determinants of product innovations, that reflect a strategy of *technological competitiveness*, and

[1] This article develops the paper presented at the thirteenth International Schumpeter Society conference in Aalborg; for the discussion there we thank Kenneth Carlaw, Giovanni Cerulli, Giovanni Dosi, Marco Grazzi, Marco Valente and Sydney Winter; a special thank to our discussant Thorbjorn Knudsen. We thank two anonymous referees and the editor Andreas Pyka for their comments. We are indebted to Matteo Lucchese for help with data. The usual disclaimer applies.

we investigate in parallel the impact of process innovations and acquisition of new machinery, associated to a search for *cost competitiveness*.

The role of demand has often been neglected in neo-Schumpeterian approaches (see the discussion in Crespi and Pianta 2007, 2008a, b); while the importance of new markets and demand pull effects in stimulating innovation is usually acknowledged, few studies have empirically examined the specific sources of demand that affect innovation. A major contribution of this chapter is the integration in our model of different demand variables, using information drawn from Input–output tables—based on the work on structural change in European industries by Lucchese (2011). By considering the evidence on demand dynamics we can reliably test the importance of different demand sources in the emergence of new products and in the dynamics of profits.

The chapter proceeds as follows. Section 2 presents the model; Sect. 3 data and methodology, Sect. 4 the results and Sect. 5 the concluding remarks.

2 The Model: Linking R&D, New Products and Profits

We estimate a system of equations that account for R&D efforts, product innovation and profits growth. In the following subsections we put forth the theoretical basis of each part of analysis and we discuss the points of contact with the existing literature.

2.1 The Decision to Carry Out R&D Efforts

We follow evolutionary approaches to R&D efforts in firms and industries. R&D is a path dependent process because the paradigm (and trajectory) related development of technology makes the process of search eminently localized (Atkinson and Stiglitz 1969; Nelson and Winter 1982; Dosi 1982, 1988). R&D is affected by demand pull (Schmookler 1966; Scherer 1982) and technology push effects (Mowery and Rosenberg 1979). According to the former perspective, innovation is brought to the market when firms anticipate strong demand; in the latter view innovation is supported by science-related developments and is triggered by relative prices in a feasible production set. Moreover, innovation is persistently characterized by the presence of specific technological and production capabilities (Pavitt 1984; Dosi 1988; Malerba 2004; Metcalfe 2010).

R&D may be cash constrained (Hall 2002), due to the intangible nature of R&D which is difficult to collateralize and due to informational problems, namely the "radically uncertain" nature of research and the asymmetric distribution of information in the classical lender–borrower case (Stiglitz and Weiss 1981). Under these conditions, profits from past innovation play a major role in financing R&D. Our first equation is the following:

$$R\&D_{ijt} = \alpha_0 + \alpha_1 R\&D_{ijt-1} + \alpha_2 DP_{ijt} + \alpha_3 FR_{ijt} + \alpha_4 \pi_{ijt-1} + \varepsilon_{ijt} \tag{1}$$

where, from now on, i indicates industry, j country, t time. R&D is research and development (thousands of euros per employee in our data), and is affected by its lag; DP stands for *demand pull* and reflects the potential for the introduction of new products, captured by the objective of opening up new markets reported by innovation surveys, FR is the distance from the capability frontier, calculated as the difference in labour productivity from the industry leader, π represents operating profits (with a one period lag) and the last term is the standard error. In Sect. 3.2 we discuss the proxies used from our database.

The *demand pull* versus *technology push* debate has led to several contributions that have investigated the respective influences on R&D and innovation, and controlled for capabilities. Kleinkecht and Verspagen (1990) find a significant effect of demand after controlling for path dependency. Piva and Vivarelli (2007) estimate demand pull effects for different groups of firms; the effect of demand is higher for firms which export, do not receive public subsidies, are liquidity constrained, diversified, large and in medium and low tech sectors. Bogliacino and Gómez (2010) found a negative and significant effect of the distance from the production frontier, which is a proxy for technological capabilities. A more recent strand of research has used data from innovation surveys (for a review see Mairesse and Mohnen 2010), finding that R&D efforts are positively influenced by size and public support to innovation.

A further strand of literature has tried to detect the effect of firm size on R&D (Cohen and Levine 1989; Cohen 2010). This line of research has been criticized for being unclear on whether it is innovation input or output that is affected by size and for the risk of endogeneity, given that both market structure and innovation are codetermined by the fundamental features of the sector (appropriability, cumulativeness and the knowledge base, see Breschi et al. 2000).

The importance of profits in supporting innovation was pointed out by Schumpeter[2] but has led to a limited literature; studies on financial constraints in R&D investment are reviewed by Cincera and Ravet (2010). In their empirical exercise—using data from the R&D Scoreboard which covers the largest R&D investors—they found that cash constraints are important for EU but not US firms. Their argument is indirectly supported by Brown et al. (2009) who found that the "dot.com bubble" played a major role in allowing R&D expenditure growth in the US in the 1990s. Finally, in the previous version of our model (Bogliacino and Pianta 2012) we find a negative effect of the distance from the frontier—i.e. more R&D is carried out when industries are closer to the capability frontier—and a positive effect of profits from past innovation.

[2] "Whence come the sums needed to purchase the means of production necessary for the new combinations if the individual concerned does not happen to have them? (...) By far the greater part (...) consists of funds which are themselves the result of successful innovation and in which we shall later recognise entrepreneurial profit" (Schumpeter 1955, 71–72). See also O'Sullivan (2006).

By carrying out our investigation at the industry level—for both manufacturing and services—we are able to consider broad feedbacks between economic performance, innovative efforts and demand dynamics.

Studies at the firm level have focused on the role of profits as sources of finance for cash constrained R&D, have provided controversial evidence on the ability of higher profits to support greater R&D[3] and—according to the performance feedback theory (Greeve 2003)—have argued that firms with profits below expected targets could increase R&D and adjust their organizational routines in order to meet their objectives. On the other hand, when we move to the industry level of analysis, the positive association between past profits and R&D is more straightforward as the overall R&D efforts of a sector can be driven by past profits of incumbent firms that attract entry by new innovative firms. The performance feedback is also taken into account by the relationships at the industry level; firms can define their target profits in relation to industry averages; when they operate in high profit sectors their increase in R&D efforts can contribute to the overall high levels of R&D; when they operate in low profit industries, expectations will be lowered, driving down R&D efforts.

Studies at the firm level consider a perfectly elastic demand for individual firms and therefore do not consider the presence of demand constraints. At the industry level, on the other hand, the dynamics of demand is constrained—it is defined by the distribution across industries of the growth of aggregate demand—and a consideration of the different sources of demand becomes important (for a discussion, see Bogliacino and Pianta 2012).

2.2 *Explaining Product Innovation*

Economic change is shaped by successful innovations, rather than by R&D inputs. For this reason several models—such as Crepon et al. (1998), Parisi et al. (2006) and Bogliacino and Pianta (2012)—add a second equation on the relationship between innovation inputs and outputs. The conceptualisation of innovation is important in this context; a large evolutionary literature has pointed out the role of different modes of innovation depending on the technological trajectory associated with each sector (Pavitt 1984; Dosi 1988; Malerba 2002, 2004 among the others). Pianta (2001) suggested to return to the original Schumpeterian distinction between product and process innovation; although they often are complementary, they are usually associated with different objectives and generate different effects in terms of growth, employment and distribution (see Crespi and Pianta 2007, 2008a, b; Pianta and Tancioni 2008; Bogliacino and Pianta 2010, 2012) and should be kept analytically distinct. As a result Pianta (2001) proposed the concepts

[3] Among several studies, Bogliacino and Gómez (2010) found a positive link between profits and R&D, while Coad and Rao (2010) found a weak association.

of *technological* and *cost competitiveness* to summarise on the one hand innovation strategies focusing on new markets, new products and R&D, as opposed to efforts directed at labour saving new machinery, efficiency gains and cost reductions.

Technological competitiveness is explained in our second equation by R&D efforts, demand dynamics and market structure.[4] Conversely, efforts for cost competitiveness and process innovation—measured by the adoption of new machinery and equipment—have an effect on economic performance; and are included in the profit equation [(3) below].

Our second equation is the following:

$$TC_{ijt} = \beta_0 + \beta_1 R\&D_{ijt-1} + \beta_2 D_{ijt} + \beta_3 MS_{ijt} + \varepsilon_{it} \tag{2}$$

where TC stands for technological competitiveness—proxied by the share of firms that are product innovators in each industry -, R&D is the variable estimated by (1) with one lag, D stands for one or more variables on the rates of growth of demand directed to the industry, and MS is a measure of market structure, namely average firm size in the industry.

Successful innovation leading to new products and new markets requires R&D inputs and—as in the Schumpeterian "mark II" models—is often characterised by the presence of large firms with strong capabilities for exploiting knowledge, and oligopolistic market structures, where high incentives to generate product innovations exists. Finally, demand may play a role in several ways. The *demand pull* perspective and the literature on structural change (Pasinetti 1981) emphasises the positive effect that a strong demand dynamics has on the development and diffusion of new products. This is a complementary approach to the Schumpeterian analysis of the way major innovations change the economy. However, when an economy—or an industry—operates in the Schumpeterian "circular flow", without major innovations, current demand for standard products may reduce the incentive to develop new products and delay their introduction. Therefore, demand that matches relevant technological change—the most dynamics components of demand, such as exports—is likely to support the introduction of new products in a virtuous circle between capabilities, innovations and markets (as in the "learning by exporting" hypothesis, see Crespi et al. 2008). Conversely, demand that is related to the activity of industries where a "circular flow" prevails—such as demand for consumption and for intermediate goods—may lead to less incentives for the introduction of new products.

[4] Some studies have tried to explore the relationships of (2) using patents as a measure of product innovation; a review can be found in Denicolò (2007). However, a large literature has shown that patents are a biased indicator and capture very poorly the innovation output outside Science Based industries (for a discussion on measuring innovation, see Archibugi and Pianta 1996; Smith 2005).

2.3 Explaining the Dynamics of Profits

Following Bogliacino and Pianta (2012), we add a third equation for the dynamics of profits. We depart from previous work such as Crepon et al. (1998) and Parisi et al. (2006), where the performance equation explains productivity growth. These contributions use productivity because, at the firm level and with a short time dimension, any measure of profits is likely to be highly volatile. Our use of industry level data and our time structure (broader, and based on long differences as discussed below) allows using stable indicators of profit growth as the most appropriate measure of industry performance.

In our formulation, profits are affected by technological and market factors. On the one hand profits are supported by successful efforts to achieve both technological and cost competitiveness; the former is the variable—importance of product innovation—resulting from (2); the latter is the relevance of technology adoption and investment in new machinery. On the other hand, strong market demand for industries' output is reflected in growth of production and sales. Our third equation of the system is the following:

$$\pi_{ijt} = \gamma_0 + \gamma_1 TC_{ijt} + \gamma_2 CC_{ijt} + \gamma_3 PR_{ijt} + \varepsilon_{ijt} \qquad (3)$$

where π is the growth of profits—proxied by data on industries' operating surplus—TC and CC are technological and cost competitiveness as defined above; the former is the predicted value from (2), the latter is proxied by expenditure in new machinery (thousand of euros per employee); finally PR stands for growth of total production—proxied by growth of industry sales—that reflects overall industry demand.

The literature on the determinants of profits and on the impact of innovation is not very large (Teece 1986; Geroski et al. 1993; Cefis and Ciccarelli 2005; Pianta and Tancioni 2008; Bogliacino and Pianta 2012) and has generally found a significant effect of all types of innovation on profits.

3 Data and Methodology

3.1 Data

In the empirical analysis we use industry level data from the Urbino Sectoral Database (USD) developed at the University of Urbino (Pianta et al. 2012) that includes data from three European Community Innovation Surveys—CIS 2 (1994–1996), CIS 3 (1998–2000) and CIS 4 (2002–2004)—matched with data from OECD-STAN for production (that we use as a proxy for sales), value added, employment and operating surplus and data from OECD Input–output tables to calculate demand components. Data are available for the two-digit NACE

Table 1 List of variables from the USD database

Variables	Unit	Source
In-house R&D expenditure per employee	Thousands euros/ empl	CIS
New Machinery expenditure per employee	Thousands euros/ empl	CIS
Share of product innovators	%	CIS
Share of firms innovating with the aim to open new markets	%	CIS
Average firm size	Number empl per firm	CIS
Compound rate of growth of export	Annual rate of growth	OECD I-O Tab.
Compound rate of growth of intermediate demand	Annual rate of growth	OECD I-O Tab.
Compound rate of growth of household final demand	Annual rate of growth	OECD I-O Tab.
Distance in labour productivity from the frontier	%	Elab. on STAN
Compound rate of growth of production	Annual rate of growth	STAN
Compound rate of growth of operating surplus	Annual rate of growth	STAN

classification for 21 manufacturing and 17 service sectors; all data refer to the total activities of industries.[5]

The country coverage of the database includes six major European countries—Germany, France, Italy, Netherlands, Spain, and United Kingdom—that represent a large part of the European economy. The selection of countries and sectors has been made in order to avoid limitations in access to data (due to the low number of firms in a given sector of a given country, or to the policies on data released by national statistical institutes).

Time periods are the following. Economic and demand variables are calculated for the periods 1995–2000 and 2000–2005. Innovation variables refer to 1994–1996 [used for the lagged R&D variable in (1) and (2)]; 1998–2000 (linked to the first period of economic variables); 2002–2004 (linked to the second period of economic variables). The variables used are listed in Table 1.

In order to use these data in panel form, we need to test that the sample design or other statistical problems in the gathering of data are not affecting the reliability of data. Besides considering the time-effects capturing macroeconomic dynamics, we have examined the stability of the database. A very detailed empirical investigation on the characteristics of the database has been carried out (see Bogliacino and Pianta 2012) and we report in the following table the main descriptive statistics (Table 2):

[5] CIS data are representative of the total population of firms and are calculated by national statistical institutes and Eurostat through an appropriate weighting procedure. Economic variables are deflated using the GDP deflator from Eurostat (base year 2002) corrected for PPP (using the index provided in Stapel et al. 2004).

Table 2 Descriptive statistics

Variables	Mean	SD overall	SD between	SD within
In-house R&D expenditure per employee	2.66	4.89	4.10	2.06
New machinery expenditure per employee	1.78	2.68	2.31	1.74
Share of product innovators	36.66	20.36	18.98	9.18
Share of firms innovating with the aim to open new markets	32.14	20.04	16.80	11.57
Average firm size	223.72	455.35	357.10	278.42
Compound rate of growth of export	6.39	16.81	11.09	12.64
Compound rate of growth of intermediate demand	3.01	7.20	5.10	5.09
Compound rate of growth of household final demand	2.64	10.67	6.64	8.49
Distance in labour productivity from the frontier	29.84	22.14	20.57	8.27
Compound rate of growth of production	2.92	5.51	4.15	3.71
Compound rate of growth of operating surplus	2.57	15.43	15.57	8.62

3.2 Methodological Issues

We address the problem of endogeneity in three ways. First of all, we estimate the model by Three Stages Least Squares (3SLS) in order to explicitly model the endogenous variables and to control for simultaneity. Secondly, we use the time structure; we introduce lags whenever we have a suspect of endogeneity. Since our time lags are of 3–4 years, the autoregressive character (and the implied endogeneity) is considerably softened. Third, our use of average growth rates is equivalent to the use of long (log) differences which is a standard way in the literature to address the problem of endogeneity (see Caroli and Van Reenen 2001; Piva et al. 2005), besides removing individual time invariant effects. Finally the variables that are not expressed as rates of growth are scaled by the number of employees or firms (the ones expressed as shares), so we are correcting for the potential bias deriving from using groups of unequal size.

Our specification of the model is based on the choice of the following variables.

The R&D equation. The lag of R&D per employee accounts for path dependence and cumulativeness of knowledge. Technology push effects are likely to be internal to the sector, or controlled for by the autoregressive nature of R&D. As a proxy for *demand pull* effects we use the share of firms which innovate to expand the range of products, reflecting expectations on the presence of strong demand for new and improved goods and services.[6] As a proxy for capabilities we use the distance in

[6] We use a variable of objective and not a direct measure of demand for two reasons: first, given the time lag necessary to obtain results from R&D, putting a contemporaneous term would be meaningless; second, the inclusion of a future term would be seriously affected by endogeneity problems and would have implied some form of rational expectations which are unrealistic in a radical uncertainty domain.

percentage points from the labour productivity of the industry in the country where the productivity is the highest.[7] Closeness to the frontier indicates accumulated capabilities and a greater need to carry out R&D as the opportunities for imitating leaders are modest; in this case a negative relationship is therefore expected. Finally, the rate of change of lagged profits is proxied by the operating surplus and is expected to support higher R&D.

The product innovation equation. In order to explain the relevance of technological competitiveness, as dependent variable we use the share of firms that have introduced a product innovation (with or without the parallel introduction of new processes). Lagged R&D per employee has been defined above. The structure and dynamics of demand is measured as the change in demand for goods produced by the industry (calculated from input–output tables), and is accounted for by different variables: the most dynamic component of demand is the rate of change of export, that is expected to have a positive impact on the new products introduced by industries; the rate of change of household final demand and the rate of change of change of intermediate demand for the industry's output may be associated to standard products and may delay the introduction of new ones. Finally, as a measure of market structure we use the average size of firms in the industry.

The profit equation. The share of product innovators in the industry, defined above, is again the proxy we use for accounting for technological competitiveness. The innovation-related expenditure for new machinery per employee is the proxy we use for cost competitiveness. In order to account for the market dynamics of industries we use the rate of growth of production, reflected in industry sales.

4 Results

In the OLS estimation we do not find any particular diagnostic problem, in particular multicollinearity is not an issue: computing the variance inflation factors we found 1.06 for the first equation, 1.14 for the second and 1.21 for the third one. We therefore estimate the system with 3SLS as explained above.

The results of our three equation model are reported in Table 3.

[7] See Bogliacino and Pianta (2012) for a discussion of this variable. For every observation (sector-country) we calculate the labour productivity (value added per employee) in the initial year of the sub-period. Then for each industry we individuate the leader (e.g. for sector x1 the highest labour productivity is in country y2) and we compute the distance in percentage points. At the industry level this variable may be affected by the pattern of countries' competitive advantages; unfortunately with our dataset it is the only available measure.

Table 3 The results of the system: the relationships between R&D, new products and profits three stage least squares

	(1) R&D per employee	(2) Share of product innovators	(3) Rate of growth of profits
R&D per employee (first lag)	0.53 [0.06]***	2.71 [0.28]***	
Rate of growth of profits	0.19 [0.04]**		
New market objective	0.06 [0.02]***		
Distance from the frontier	−0.00 [0.01]		
Size		8.95 [5.38]*	
Rate of growth of export		0.40 [0.16]**	
Rate of growth of final consumption		−0.23 [0.09]***	
Rate of growth of intermediate demand		−0.59 [0.17]***	
Share of product innovators			0.35 [0.09]***
New machinery per employee			0.72 [0.38]*
Rate of growth of production			0.51 [0.19]**
Constant	−0.92 [1.49]	24.80 [1.42]***	−12.71 [3.19]***
Obs	204z	204	201
RMSE	5.30	15.36	17.71
Chi-2	198.91	127.90	35.36
(*p*-value)	(0.00)	(0.00)	(0.00)

S.e. in brackets
Source: USD
*significant at 10 %, **significant at 5 %, ***significant at 1 %

In the R&D equation past R&D and past profits support R&D efforts that are pulled by the presence of a potential market for new products; the distance from the frontier of labour productivity is not significant.

In the product innovation equation, past R&D and firm size have a positive and significant impact, confirming the assumptions of the "Schumpeter mark II" perspective. Demand variables have, as expected, different effects on new products. Export growth is associated to a higher presence of product innovators, in line with the "learning by exporting" hypothesis (Crespi et al. 2008); a high growth of household consumption and intermediate demand, conversely, is associated to lower product innovation; an increase in such components of demand may lower the need to introduce new products, a relationship that is typical of "traditional" industries and services with little R&D, more standard goods and less international openness.[8]

In the third equation profits are pushed in parallel by innovation-driven gains in technological and cost competitiveness, and are pulled by demand-led growth in sales.

The estimated coefficients come out as expected, and the results are consistent with those found in the previous version of our model (Bogliacino and Pianta 2012). In Appendix we provide an additional version of the model without the demand variables, further showing the stability of our results.

In order to check the robustness of our estimations, we address three potential problems: (a) size may be important also in explaining the decision to do R&D, (b) our specification may not control adequately for technology push, (c) there may exist omitted institutional factors at country level.

The relation between size and R&D has been addressed by a large literature that, however, did not lead to clear cut results; we ran estimations adding size among the explanatory variables in the R&D equation, but it did not come out significant. This may be a further indication that size is capturing other effects, such as cash constraints, capabilities effects or, simply, endogeneity. As stressed by Dosi et al. (2007) the heterogeneity is such that no robust evidence is found on support of this hypothesis once the proper control variables have been added. This should be kept into account when assessing previous results with CIS data which usually suggest a size-innovation relationship (see the review in Mairesse and Mohnen 2010).

In order to address point (b) we also included time dummies in the R&D equation, but the results are unchanged, and the dummies are not significant. Indeed, the use of long differences, industry level data, average rate of change and autoregressive specification is a satisfactory strategy to account for time varying production possibilities frontier.

Finally, institutional differences are mainly accounted for through national level fixed effect. It is possible to use specific data on institutional factors at the country level, but given the higher level of aggregation it would be impossible to identify the effect, and the t-test will be unreliable (see Moulton 1986). In our estimation, since we are considering rate of changes, we are eliminating the time invariant dimension. In order to test whether institutional frameworks affect rates of change—that is, whether they have a time-trend impact—we ran the estimations with country dummies in all three equations, and the results do not show appreciable changes in the coefficients.[9]

[8] A systematic analysis of the links between innovative dynamics, demand factors and structural change is in Lucchese (2011).

[9] We remind also that, technically, the effects captured through country dummies cannot be identified; since our unit of analysis is the industry, which are in fixed numbers, the only way to increase the number of observations is by increasing the number of countries. Asymptotically, the number of country effects diverges at the same rate as the sample size, thus we would face an incidental parameter problem. As a result, we do not report these estimations. All three robustness check regressions are available from the authors upon request.

5 Conclusions

Our model and the empirical results we obtain—focusing on the industry level—appear capable to account for important dimensions of the interconnected engines of economic change in a Schumpeterian perspective. Our three equation system links several insights of the evolutionary literature on innovation and supports them with its empirical results.

In explaining R&D intensities, the cumulative nature of research and knowledge, the *demand pull* effect of the potential for new products, and access to finance through the reinvestment of lagged profits play a significant role.

In explaining the importance of product innovation, the same cumulative nature of R&D and firm size are important on the supply side, while demand factors either stimulate the introduction of new products, in the case of strong export growth, or may delay it when consumption and intermediate demand characterise industries' markets.

In explaining the dynamics of profits we find a direct effect of the previous variable—the importance of product innovation, reflecting a strategy of technological competitiveness—in addition to significant effects of gains in cost competitiveness—through process innovations introducing new machinery. Moreover, fast growing sales reflecting demand growth also contribute to higher increases of profits.

Three improvements on the existing literature emerge from our model and findings.

First, we provide a simultaneous explanation of three interconnected sources of change in advanced economies—R&D, new products and profits. We move from one-way relationships to a system that accounts for simultaneous links and feedback effects, developing Schumpeterian insights and providing support for several evolutionary assumptions. In this chapter we expand the model and test developed in Bogliacino and Pianta (2012), extending the approach by introducing demand variables; the results confirm the strength of the model and the relevance of the empirical findings.

Second, our findings confirm the importance of the diversity of innovative efforts—pointed out by evolutionary approaches—and the strength of our previous work on the distinction between technological competitiveness (based on new products) and cost competitiveness (based on new processes) (Pianta 2001).

Third, while much of the evolutionary literature has neglected the role of demand, we integrate—in our industry-level analysis—both technological and demand factors, showing that innovation in products and profits are deeply affected—in a complex way—by demand factors. This extension of the empirical evidence has been possible thanks to the combination in our database—the USD of the University of Urbino—of innovation survey and economic data with information on demand dynamics drawn from input–output tables for both manufacturing and service industries.

In our model we show that the role of demand emerges in different ways. An increase in overall demand, leading to higher production, drives up profits, but may not be relevant for improved innovative performances. In fact, the increase in product innovations is positively associated to export growth alone; industries with a greater international openness and operating in more competitive markets are pushed to improve their technological competitiveness through new products. Conversely, increased demand due to household consumption or to intermediate demand from other industries may, in effect, slow down the introduction of new products; when domestic demand for existing products in less competitive internal markets increases, firms may be under less pressure to innovate their product range and strengthen their technological capabilities; they may just expand output of existing goods and services, easily obtaining increased profits (as shown by the results of the profit equation).

This diversity of outcomes from different components of demand may have relevant policy implications, emphasising the importance of the "virtuous circle" between R&D efforts, innovation in products, technological competitiveness, export growth—that in last decades has been the most dynamics demand component for EU economies—and higher profits obtained from an expansion of output—rather than from a restructuring driven by labour saving new processes; such profits, in turn, can support larger R&D efforts. Our approach is able to model these complex relationships in an integrated way, with appropriate lags and feedback effects, and to test them empirically. This appears as an improvement on current approaches and opens up novel directions for conceptual and empirical work aiming to explain the complex dynamics of economic change in advanced economies.

Appendix

In order to appreciate the relevance of the inclusion of demand variables in our results in Table 3, we report in Table 4 the results of a different estimate that excludes the proxies for demand and considers other variables only. The structure of results is the same as in Table 3.

Table 4 The system: baseline formulation three stage least squares

	(1) R&D per employee	(2) Share of product innovators	(3) Rate of growth of profits
R&D per employee (lagged)	0.46 [0.06]***	2.69 [0.28]***	
Rate of growth of profits (lagged)	0.18 [0.07]**		
New market objective	0.07 [0.03]**		
Distance from the frontier	0.01 [0.02]		
Share of product innovators			0.38 [0.10]***
New machinery per employee			0.82 [0.36]**
Rate of growth of sales			0.50 [0.20]**
Constant	−0.92 [1.49]	24.80 [1.42]***	−14.13 [3.30]***
Obs	204	204	204
RMSE	5.27	16.07	17.71
Chi-2 (p-value)	130.80 (0.00)	86.48 (0.00)	38.45 (0.00)

S.e. in brackets
Source: USD S.e. in parenthesis. *significant at 10 %, **significant at 5 %, ***significant at 1 %

In the first equation, as expected, R&D is path dependent, is pulled by demand, and is finance constrained, with profits playing a supporting role. The only coefficient that does not meet our expectation is the distance from the frontier which is not significant. In order to explore this variable a graphical examination is provided below

In the second equation product innovation is driven by lagged R&D alone. In the third equation product innovation and the adoption of new technology, together with sales growth, explain the variance of the growth rate of profits

These results are consistent with those found in the previous version of our model (Bogliacino and Pianta 2012), and with those of Table 3 above. The inclusion of demand variables strengthens the explanation of new products in (2)

In (1) the distance from the frontier of labour productivity does not emerge as significant (the same is in Table 3 above). In order to explore in greater detail this variable, we can examine it graphically. If we regress R&D per employee on its lag and we take the residuals, we can plot their distribution for different intervals of the distance. In order to choose the threshold for the distance from the frontier variable, we first look at the distribution of the distance and we see that it is bimodal, with a first mass of probability between 0 and 20 %. Then we plot the empirical density of

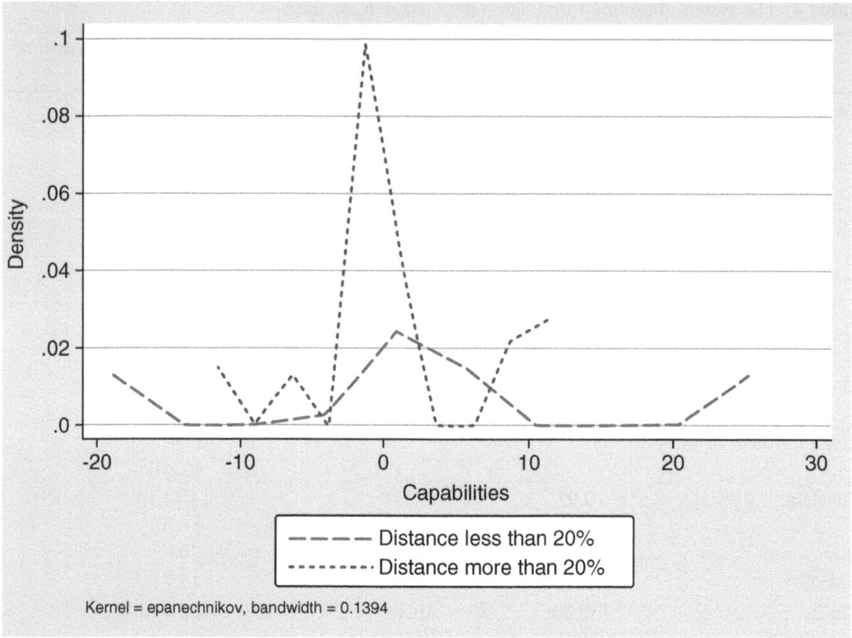

Fig. 1 The density of R&D for different value of the capability proxy

the residuals for the distance from the frontier below and above 20 %. The results are shown in Fig. 1 below. As we can see from the graph, for distances lower than 20 % (closer to the frontier) there is higher R&D expenditure and—one would say—higher right tail skewness. However, for distances less than 20 % there is also much more variability in the distribution of R&D expenditure. This evidence contributes to explain the lack of significance for this variable in the model

References

Aghion P, Howitt P (1998) Endogenous growth theory. MIT Press, Cambridge

Archibugi D, Pianta M (1996) Innovation surveys and patents as technology indicators: the state of the art, in OECD, innovation, patents and technological strategies. OECD, Paris, pp 17–56

Atkinson AB, Stiglitz JE (1969) A new view of technological change. Econ J, LXXIX, pp 573–578

Bogliacino F, Gómez S (2010) Cash flows and capabilities are the main determinants of R&D expenditures. IPTS Working Paper on Corporate R&D and Innovation 2010–10

Bogliacino F, Pianta M (2010) Innovation and employment. A reinvestigation using revised Pavitt classes. Res Pol 39(6):799–809

Bogliacino F, Pianta M (2012) Profits, R&D and innovation: a model and a test. Indus Corp Change. http://icc.oxfordjournals.org/content/early/2012/09/09/icc.dts028.full.pdf+html

Breschi S, Malerba F, Orsenigo L (2000) Technological regimes and Schumpeterian patterns of innovation. Econ J 110:388–410

Brown JR, Fazzari SM, Petersen BC (2009) Financing innovation and growth: cash flow, external equity, and the 1990s R&D boom. J Finance 64:151–185
Caroli E, Van Reenen J (2001) Skill biased organizational change? Evidence from a panel of British and French establishments. Q J Econ 116:1449–1492
Cefis E, Ciccarelli M (2005) Profit differentials and innovation. Econ Innovat New Tech 14 (1–2):43–61
Cincera M and Ravet J (2010) Financing constraints and R&D investments of large corporations in Europe and the USA. Ipts Working Paper on Corporate R&D and Innovation, 3/2010
Coad A, Rao R (2010) Firm growth and R&D expenditure. Econ Innovat New Tech 19 (2):127–145
Cohen W (2010) Chapter 4: fifty years of empirical studies of innovative activity and performance. In: Hall B, Rosenberg N (eds) Handbook of the economics of innovation. Elsevier, Amsterdam
Cohen WM, Levine RC (1989) Empirical studies of innovation and market structure. In: Schmalensee R, Willig RD (eds) Handbook of industrial organization, 2nd edn. Elsevier, North-Holland, pp 1059–1107
Crepon B, Duguet E, Mairesse J (1998) Research and development, innovation and productivity: an econometric analysis at the firm level. Econ Innovat New Tech 7(2):115–158
Crespi F, Pianta M (2007) Innovation and demand in European industries. Econ Politic J Inst Anal Econ 24(1):79–112
Crespi F, Pianta M (2008a) Demand and innovation in productivity growth. Int Rev Appl Econ 22:5, forth., September 2008
Crespi F, Pianta M (2008b) Diversity in innovation and productivity in Europe. J Evolut Econ 18:529545
Crespi G, Criscuolo C, Haskell J (2008) Productivity, exporting, and the learning-by-doing hypothesis: direct evidence from UK firms. Can J Econ 41(2):619–638
Denicolò V (2007) Do patents over-compensate innovators? Econ Pol 22:679–729
Dosi G (1982) Technological paradigms and technological trajectories: a suggested interpretations of the determinants and directions of technical change. Res Pol 11:147–162
Dosi G (1988) Sources procedures and microeconomic effects of innovation. J Econ Lit 26:1120–71
Dosi G, Gambardella A, Grazzi M, Orsenigo G (2007) Technological revolutions and the evolution of industrial structures. LEM Working Paper Series, 2007–2012
Geroski P, Machin S, Van Reenen J (1993) The profitability of innovating firm. Rand J Econ 24 (2):198–211
Greeve HR (2003) Organizational learning from performance feedback. Cambridge University Press, Cambridge
Griffith R, Redding S, Van Reenen J (2004) Mapping the two faces of R&D: productivity growth in a panel of OECD industries. Rev Econ Stat 86(4):883–895
Griliches Z (1979) Issues in assessing the contribution of research and development to productivity growth. Bell J Econ 10:92116
Griliches Z (1992) The search for R&D spillovers. Scand J Econ 94:29–47
Griliches Z (1995) R&D and productivity: econometric results and measurement issues. In: Stoneman P (ed) Handbook of the economics of innovation and technological change. Blackwell Publishers, Oxford, p 5289
Hall BH (2002) The financing of research and development. Oxford Rev Econ Pol 18(1):35–51
Kleinkecht A, Verspagen B (1990) Demand and innovation: Schmookler re-examined. Res Pol 19:387–394
Lucchese M (2011) Demand, innovation and openness as determinants of structural change. University of Urbino DEMQ working paper
Mairesse J, Mohnen P (2010) Using innovations surveys for econometric analysis. NBER working paper, w15857
Malerba F (2002) Sectoral systems of innovation and production. Res Pol 31:247–264
Malerba F (ed) (2004) Sectoral systems of innovation. Cambridge University Press, Cambridge

Metcalfe JS (2010) Technology and economic theory. Camb J Econ 34(1):153–171
Moulton BR (1986) Random group effects and the precision of regression estimates. J Econometr 32:385–397
Mowery DC, Rosenberg N (1979) The influence of market demand upon innovation: a critical review of some recent empirical studies. Res Policy 8:102–153
Nelson RR, Winter S (1982) An evolutionary theory of economic change. Belknap Press of Harvard University Press, Cambridge, MA
O'Sullivan M (2005) Finance and innovation. In: Fagerberg J, Mowery D, Nelson R (eds) The Oxford handbook of innovation. Oxford University Press, Oxford
Parisi ML, Schiantarelli F, Sembenelli A (2006) Productivity, innovation and R&D: micro evidence for Italy. Eur Econ Rev 50:2037–2061
Pasinetti L (1981) Structural change and economic growth. Cambridge University Press, Cambridge
Pavitt K (1984) Patterns of technical change: towards a taxonomy and a theory. Res Policy 13:343–374
Pianta M (2001) Innovation, demand and employment. In: Petit P, Soete L (eds) Technology and the future of European employment. Elgar, Cheltenham, pp 142–165
Pianta M, Tancioni M (2008) Innovations, profits and wages. J Post Keynesian Econ 31 (1):103–125
Pianta M, Lucchese M, Supino S (2012) The Urbino Sectoral Database 1994–2009 (USD). Sources and methodologies, University of Urbino, Faculty of Economics, Discussion Paper
Piva M, Vivarelli M (2007) Is demand-pulled innovation equally important in different groups of firms? Camb J Econ 31:691–710
Piva M, Santarelli E, Vivarelli E (2005) The skill bias effect of technological and organisational change: evidence and policy implications. Res Pol 34(2):141–157
Scherer FM (1982) Demand-pull and technological invention: Schmookler revisited. J Indus Econ 30:225–237
Schmookler J (1966) Invention and economic growth. Cambridge University Press, Cambridge, MA
Schumpeter JA (1955) Theory of economic development. Harvard University Press, Cambridge, MA (1st edn 1911)
Smith K (2005), Measuring innovation. In: Fagerberg J, Mowery D, Nelson R (eds) pp 148–179
Stapel S, Pasanen J, Reinecke S (2004) Purchasing power parities and related economic indicators for EU, candidate countries and EFTA. Eurostat—statistics in focus
Stiglitz JE, Weiss A (1981) Credit rationing in markets with imperfect information. Am Econ Rev 71(3):393–410
Teece D (1986) Profiting from technological innovation. Res Pol 15(6):285–305

Production and financial linkages in inter-firm networks: structural variety, risk-sharing and resilience

Giulio Cainelli, Sandro Montresor, and Giuseppe Vittucci Marzetti

Abstract The paper analyzes how (production and financial) inter-firm networks can affect firms' default probabilities and observed default rates. A simple theoretical model of shock transfer is built to investigate some stylized facts on how firm-idiosyncratic shocks are allocated in the network, and how this allocation changes firm default probabilities. The model shows that the network works as a perfect "risk-pooling" mechanism, when it is both strongly connected and symmetric. But the "risk-sharing" does not necessarily reduce default rates, unless the shock firms face is lower on average than their financial capacity. Conceived as cases of symmetric inter-firm networks, industrial districts might have a comparative disadvantage in front of heavy crises.

Reprinted from Journal of Evolutionary Economics 22(4), 711-734, Springer (2012).

G. Cainelli
CERIS-CNR, Milan, Italy

Department of Economics and Management "Marco Fanno", University of Padua, via del Santo 33, 35122 Padua, Italy
e-mail: giulio.cainelli@unipd.it

S. Montresor (✉)
JRC-IPTS European Commission, Seville, Spain

Department of Economics, University of Bologna, Bologna, Italy
e-mail: sandro.montresor@unibo.it

G. Vittucci Marzetti
Department of Sociology and Social Research, University of Milano-Bicocca, via Bicocca degli Arcimboldi 8, 20126 Milan, Italy
e-mail: giuseppe.vittucci@unimib.it

A. Pyka and E.S. Andersen (eds.), *Long Term Economic Development*, Economic Complexity and Evolution, DOI 10.1007/978-3-642-35125-9_6,

1 Introduction

The world is now experiencing the economic tail of the sub-prime financial crisis. The idiosyncrasy of this crisis (e.g. Shiller 2008; Reinhart and Rogoff 2008, 2009) and the different resilience exhibited by countries (e.g. Frenkel and Rapetti 2009) have already been investigated. Quite interestingly, this investigation has led to a certain "revitalization" of some past interpretations of financial crises, which seem to fit the current one as well as more recent theories, although with important amendments: the Minsky approach to asset bubbles and crises is just an example (e.g. Dymski 2010; Arestis and Singh 2010; Eggertsson and Krugman 2011).

On the contrary, at the best of our knowledge, the resilience of the different models of production organization to the crisis has not yet received attention. Nonetheless, this is a further test for the alleged superiority of the "flexible specialization" model of production (e.g. Storper and Christopherson 1987; Hirst and Zeitlin 1989; Storper 1995; Herrigel 1996; Le Heron 2009), and of industrial districts in particular (e.g. Harrison 1992; Guerrieri et al. 2003). From an evolutionary perspective to urban and regional studies (Ter Wal and Boschma 2011), the current crisis brings to the front the selection mechanisms that macroeconomic fluctuations entail at the meso-level, depending on the features of local production systems.

In trying to fill this gap, the paper analyzes how inter-firm (production and financial) networks affect the firm's resilience to financial shocks. In particular, it focuses on the risk of default entailed by firm-specific credit constraints and investigates: (i) how the allocation of risk depends on the structure of such networks; and (ii) how this allocation changes firms' default probabilities.

The remainder of the paper is organized as follows. In Section 2, we review and combine the theoretical literature on network models of risk-sharing, contagion and financial stability, with the empirical literature on the different typologies of inter-firm networks. In Section 3, we build up a simple stylized model to analyze the transfer mechanisms of firm's idiosyncratic financial shocks in inter-firm networks. Section 4 presents the main results of the model. Section 5 discusses their empirical implications and concludes.

2 Background literature and stylized facts

The scope and speed of diffusion of the recent financial crisis have stimulated the analysis of the conditions under which *financial contagion* can actually arise. This literature dates back at least to Diamond and Dybvig (1983), who refer to phenomena of "bank run" and self-fulfilling panic in the banking system. Drawing on them, Allen and Gale (2000) analyze how interbank lending brings about domino-like effects, which could increase the risk of collapse of the whole financial system, that is "systemic risk". Iori et al. (2006), Nier et al. (2007), Gallegati et al. (2008) and Battiston et al. (2009) have recently re-examined this issue and found a possible trade-off between the mutual insurance of financial institutions and the systemic risk.

Out of the financial literature, the conditions for domino effects (here called "cascading failures") to occur and produce "global cascades" have been studied by Watts (2002), Motter and Lai (2002) and Whitney (2009). Along the same research stream, diffusion and contagion in networks have been investigated by, among the others, Pastor-Satorras and Vespignani (2001; Pastor-Satorras and Vespignani (2002), Dodds and Watts (2005) and López-Pintado (2008). Finally, recent economic studies have analyzed the efficient and stable configurations of "risk-sharing networks", i.e. networks the links of which guarantee the nodes bilateral mutual insurance (Bramoullé and Kranton 2007a, b; Fafchamps and Gubert 2007; Bloch et al. 2008).

In spite of its consistency, this literature has not yet been applied to investigate the way in which inter-firm networks affect the resilience of firms to external shocks. This is unfortunate, as a number of empirical and theoretical studies have addressed inter-firm relationships in clusters and their actual structures. Taxonomies of them (e.g. constellations, hub-and-spokes, satellite platforms and different kinds of industrial districts) have been put forward by Markusen (1996), Paniccia (1998) and Carbonara (2002). Their evolutionary patterns have been studied in an *industry life-cycle* perspective by Carbonara et al. (2002) and Albino et al. (2006, 2007)—for supply chains in industrial districts—and by Ter Wal and Boschma (2011)—in terms of co-evolutionary processes of industries, firms and networks in clusters. Finally, the structure of ownership and non-ownership ties in industrial districts, their evolution over time and the presence of business groups in industrial districts have been investigated by Brioschi et al. (2002, 2004).

These inter-firm networks are mainly made up of production linkages between different typologies of firms (e.g. final producers vs. subcontractors) with heterogeneous capabilities.[1] These production linkages become extremely important in the aftermath of crises that expose firms to demand declines and credit restrictions from formal banking institutions.[2]

Indeed, inter-firm *production* relationships usually entail inter-firm *credit* relationships. On the one side, firms can obtain credit from subcontractors through payments delays, i.e. *trade credit*, which requires different contractual power between the parties (Peterson and Rajan 1997). On the other side, the supplier may obtain credit from the buyer on the basis of an underlying commercial transaction, possibly by discounting the refunding from the relative payment.

[1] Firms look for networking also in other spheres, such as innovation. For an analysis of the networks of R&D collaborations see, for instance, Orsenigo et al. (2001), Goyal and Moraga-Gonzalez (2001) and Goyal and Joshi (2003).

[2] Alessandrini et al. (2008, 2009) and Alessandrini and Zazzaro (2009) suggest that local banking systems, affecting information asymmetries between lenders and borrowers at the local level, can reduce firms' financing constraints. As a matter of fact, physical proximity, involving long-lasting relationships and in-depth cultural affinity, allows local banks to collect a greater amount of "soft" information on local borrowers, thus increasing the quality of screening and monitoring. Nonetheless, since bank decision centers have been concentrated over the last decade in a few places, the "functional" distance between banks and local production systems has increased, thus counterbalancing the positive effects of local closeness. Their findings show that these negative effects

While the nature of trade-credit has been largely investigated, that of the latter deserves more attention. As Dei Ottati (1994) argues, this is a kind of credit which a final firm might want to "interlink" with the underlying subcontracting relationship with the supplier, in order to allow it to deliver what is required, according to certain technical specifications. Unlike trade-credit, which is somehow indirect, the "interlinking of credit and subcontracting" is actually a direct credit, as the client firm actually provides the supplier with financial resources, usually before the underlying production transaction occurs, and in order to make it occur should the provider face some financial difficulties. In a sense, the outcome of the subcontracting contract, to which the parties mutually commit, is the collateral of such a particular kind of credit.

On the one hand, because of its peculiar nature, this interlinking requires a minimum level of cooperation and mutual trust between firms. On the other, it helps reducing the emergence of opportunistic behaviors and thus raises the level of social capital in the socio-economic cluster. It is not by chance that this kind of relationship has been detected for the first time in the investigation of the industrial district of Prato (Florence, Italy) (Dei Ottati 1994). In general, it may be seen in those contexts where spatial proximity, face-to-face contacts, long-lasting relationships and in-depth social and cultural closeness play an important role (Cainelli 2008).

As is well-known, the Italian manufacturing system is an emblematic example of the coexistence of all these features. Accordingly, although to a certain extent idiosyncratic, it could be taken as a good empirical test to support the relevance of our theoretical arguments. On the one hand, most of the Italian manufacturing activities are concentrated within local systems of small and medium sized firms and industrial districts. In 2001, the 199 Italian industrial districts, identified according to the National Statistical Office's (Istat) definition, accounted for about 38 % of the total value added, 44 % of the total employment and 46 % of the total manufacturing exports of the country (ISTAT 2005). The relevance of these local production systems increases if their production specialization is considered. For example, the textile districts accounted for about 58 % of the Italian manufacturing employment, while those operating in the footwear industry for 61 % (Cainelli and Zoboli 2004). On the other hand, in Italian local production systems, subcontracting and trade credit are very pervasive, too. As for subcontracting, in presenting the results of a survey conducted by the Bank of Italy on the Italian industrial districts, Omiccioli (2000) shows that 32.3 % of the surveyed firms were actually sub-contractors, 43.5 % of which were with respect to final producers as such, and the rest with respect to final firms which were in turn subcontractors. According to the same study, the incidence of sub-contracting firms is higher among small firms (about 35 % of the total) and in those sectors in which Italian industrial districts are typically specialized, such as textiles (40.2 %) and

prevail over the positive ones due to "operational" distance, making firms' financial constraints actually more binding.

mechanics (40.2 %). As far as trade credit is concerned, with reference to the same Bank of Italy study, Cocozza (2000) shows that about 27 % of Italian manufacturing firms in the survey (both subcontractors and final producers) used trade credit as one of the main sources of external financing. Omiccioli (2000) supports these findings and qualifies them by noticing that final firms are generally larger than subcontractors and that, for the latter, the incidence of trade credit out of total sales is as much as 7.3 %. Moreover, trade credit relationships are found to be particularly widespread among firms operating in such district-like sectors as textiles (9.2 % of the total sales) and mechanics (8.1 %).

Quite interestingly, the intertwining of these production and credit relationships, both empirically documented, turns out to be crucial in periods of financial crisis such as the current one. As is shown in a recent report by the Bank of Italy about the effects of the international crisis on the Italian economy (Bugamelli et al. 2009), first of all, final producers have been transferring to their subcontractors part of their non-diversifiable risk due to their credit constraints. In so doing, subcontracting relationships have allowed final firms to benefit from a greater production and financial flexibility, thus mitigating the effects of the crisis itself. On the other hand, a number of final producers have financed some of their suppliers through "factoring" operations, in order to allow them to continue in their production activities. As shown by the interviews of the report, the need to protect these long-lasting supplier relationships was the main reason for these strategic choices.

In general, the empirical evidence about firm reaction to the crisis is quite rich and complex.[3] The underlying mechanisms are as usual difficult to disentangle, unless by simplifying the picture, an exercise to which the following model is dedicated.

3 Model

Let us consider a network of n firms. Assume these firms are linked through production relationships only, in which one firm acts as supplier (S) of intermediate commodities or labor services for another final producer (F).[4] On the basis of the arguments developed in Section 2, these production relationships could entail two possible credit relationships between S and F: (i) trade credit, that is, the credit granted by S to F via payments delays, the extent of which depends on the relative contractual power of the parties; and (ii) the credit to the subcontractor, which is granted by F to S in an interlinking of subcontracting and credit, as a means to reduce opportunistic behaviors and sustain long-term relationships (Fig. 1a).

[3] The 2009 Innobarometer survey (Kanerva and Hollanders 2009), although limited to innovation, is a significant example of this richness.

[4] Although at the price of a certain lack of realism, the model is kept in its simplest benchmark version, in order better to show its functioning and potentiality.

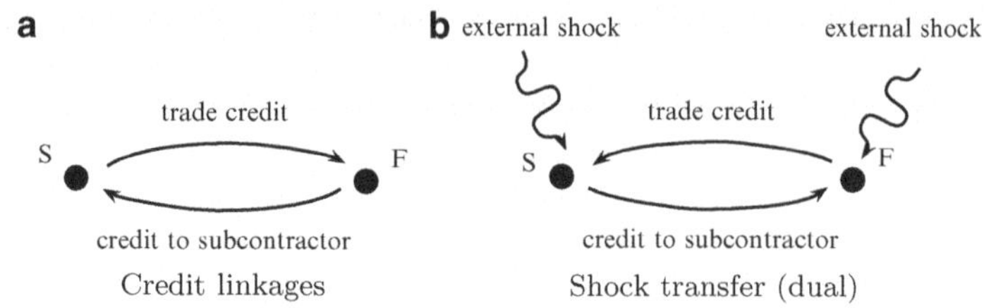

Fig. 1 Inter-firm credit relationships and shock transfer

These credit channels are very important. They can act as possible transfer mechanisms, between S and F, of the shocks which could hit them. In particular, trade credit can allow F to transfer part of its own shock to S. The credit granted to the subcontractor, as well as the pre-existence of a credit relationship, can instead enable S to transfer part of its shock to F (Fig. 1b).

The shock which could hit the firms—in a way we will clarify below—is assumed to be exogenous. With respect to the issue at stake in this paper, it can be thought of as a credit shortage, originating from bank downturns and collapses—external to the model—which make F and S suffer from financial constraints in operating their businesses. However, providing it has repercussions on the financial conditions of S and F, the shock could be of any kind, such as a macroeconomic or an industrial one.

The working of the transfer mechanisms crucially depends on the network structure. In order to study this effect, assume that each firm i of the n in the network is hit by an external shock x_{i0}. We then represent the transfer mechanisms of these idiosyncratic shocks by a *weighted directed network* Γ, where the *valued directed edge* from firm/node i to firm/node j (δ_{ij}) measures the share of the total idiosyncratic shock of i that i can transfer to j ($\sum_{j=1}^{n} \delta_{ij} = 1$) (Fig. 2).

With this assumption, the shock experienced by firm i after one *round* (x_{i1}) is simply equal to:

$$x_{i1} = \sum_j \delta_{ji} x_{j0}$$

and:

$$\left(x_{11} \ldots x_{n1}\right) = \left(x_{10} \ldots x_{n0}\right) \begin{pmatrix} \delta_{11} & \ldots & \delta_{1n} \\ \vdots & \ddots & \vdots \\ \delta_{n1} & \ldots & \delta_{nn} \end{pmatrix}$$

or, in matrix form:

$$\mathbf{x}_1' = \mathbf{x}_0' \mathbf{T} \tag{1}$$

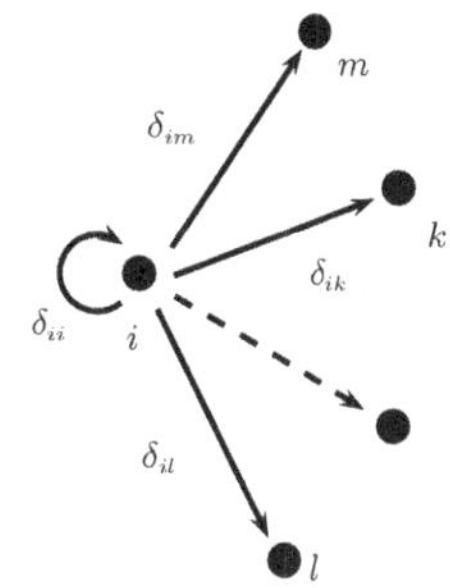

Fig. 2 Shock transfer

where $\mathbf{T}$ is the *adjacency matrix* of the network Γ, and $\mathbf{x}'_1$ the row vector of firm-specific shocks after one round of interaction.

It follows that:

$$\mathbf{x}'_t = \mathbf{x}'_{t-1}\mathbf{T} = \mathbf{x}'_0\mathbf{T}^t \tag{2}$$

where $\mathbf{x}_t$ is the allocation vector after t rounds of interactions, assuming that the network Γ stays constant throughout the process.

If the process converges in the limit, so that, by further increasing the rounds of interactions, the allocation vector does not change:

$$\hat{\mathbf{x}}' = \mathbf{x}'_0\left(\lim_{t\to\infty}\mathbf{T}^t\right) = \mathbf{x}'_0\left(\lim_{t\to\infty}\mathbf{T}^t\right)\mathbf{T} \tag{3}$$

we can retain such vector $\hat{\mathbf{x}}$ as the vector of the equilibrium allocation of the idiosyncratic shocks. It is a function of the initial allocation $\mathbf{x}_0$, given the adjacency matrix $\mathbf{T}$: $\hat{\mathbf{x}}(\mathbf{x}_0;\mathbf{T})$.

Just to give an example, in a simple transfer network made up of three firms—1, 2, 3—with the following structure (Fig. 3a):

$$\mathbf{T} = \begin{pmatrix} \frac{1}{3} & \frac{1}{3} & \frac{1}{3} \\ 1 & 0 & 0 \\ 0 & 1 & 0 \end{pmatrix}$$

we have:

$$\mathbf{T}^{25} \approx \mathbf{T}^{26} = \ldots = \begin{pmatrix} \frac{1}{2} & \frac{1}{3} & \frac{1}{6} \\ \frac{1}{2} & \frac{1}{3} & \frac{1}{6} \\ \frac{1}{2} & \frac{1}{3} & \frac{1}{6} \end{pmatrix}.$$

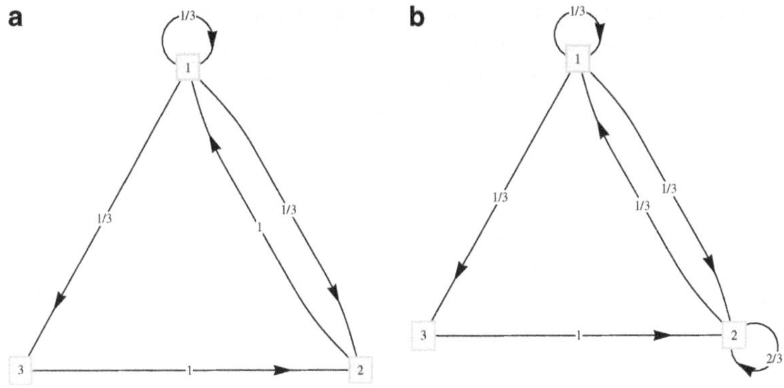

Fig. 3 Asymmetric strongly connected networks

So the system soon converges to the equilibrium and thus:

$$\hat{\mathbf{x}}' = \mathbf{x}_0'\left(\lim_{t\to\infty}\mathbf{T}^t\right) = (x_{10}, x_{20}, x_{30})\begin{pmatrix} \frac{1}{2} & \frac{1}{3} & \frac{1}{6} \\ \frac{1}{2} & \frac{1}{3} & \frac{1}{6} \\ \frac{1}{2} & \frac{1}{3} & \frac{1}{6} \end{pmatrix} = \left(\frac{1}{2}, \frac{1}{3}, \frac{1}{6}\right)\sum_{i=1}^{3} x_{i0}.$$

As for the initial exogenous shock $\mathbf{x}_0$, we model it as a random vector, which generic element x_{i0} is made up of a common trend (μ) and an idiosyncratic random component (ϵ_i):[5]

$$x_{i0} = \mu + \epsilon_i \tag{4}$$

Moreover, each node/firm i is characterized by a given *threshold* θ_i, which represents its resistance to external shocks.[6]

Assuming that $\hat{\mathbf{x}}$ exists and is in fact unique, the default condition for firm i can be stated as follows:

$$\hat{x}_i(\mathbf{x}_0; \mathbf{T}) > \theta_i. \tag{5}$$

---

[5] This idiosyncratic component can capture the individual differences in the experienced shock or in the buffer level of the internal absorption of the shock.

[6] Such parameter can be conceived as a resistance threshold to unexpected losses. As such, it is not simply a threshold to the loss distribution. If the shock was somehow expected or if the firm was usually operating in a high volatile environment, the firm would tend to accumulate resources to better resist to the possible losses.

The reference to the equilibrium allocation of the shocks in the default condition greatly simplifies the analysis. However, the higher (lower) the speed of convergence of the system to the equilibrium, the more (less) reasonable is such assumption. We address this issue in Section 4.2.3.

4 Results

Of the simple model above, we first search for the limit distribution of the idiosyncratic shocks in the network. Provided that it exists and is indeed unique, we then investigate its impact on firms' *default probabilities*—that is, the probability that the shock overcomes the firm's financial capacity (i.e. threshold)—and on expected *default rates*—i.e. the number of defaulted firms over the total number of firms in the network—induced by the network of shock transmissions formalized by **T**.

4.1 Shock transfer and risk distribution

As far as the analysis of the limit distribution of the idiosyncratic shocks in the network is concerned, it is important to note that, in spite of the fact that, for what concerns the shock transfer, our model is not probabilistic, **T** is formally a *right stochastic matrix*. Hence, in order to study the allocation of shocks in equilibrium, we can use a number of useful results from the theory of finite Markov chains.[7]

First of all, following the standard definitions, we define the network Γ (and the related matrix **T**) as *strongly connected* if each node can reach every other by a *directed path*, i.e. a sequence of distinct nodes $i_1, i_2, \ldots, i_K$ such that $T_{i_k, i_{k+1}} > 0$, for each $k \in \{1, 2, \ldots, K\}$.

Let us say that the network Γ (and the related matrix **T**) is *aperiodic* if the greatest common divisor of the lengths of its directed cycles is 1, where a *directed cycle* is a directed path joining a node to itself, and the *length* of the cycle is the number of distinct nodes in the path.[8]

We can therefore state our first proposition.

[7] For a textbook treatment of Markov chains, see Karlin and Taylor (1975, 1981) and the references therein. Iterated matrices have been used also in studies on the convergence of beliefs in networks (DeGroot 1974; DeMarzo et al. 2003; Golub and Jackson 2010), prestige and status (Bonacich 1987), and in strategic games for networks with neighbors' influence (Ballester et al. 2006).

[8] Strictly speaking, a cycle is not a path because the starting (and ending) node appears twice. However, apart from this minor inconsistency, the definition is correct and is made here for convenience.

Proposition 1 *If the inter-firm network Γ is strongly connected and aperiodic, the system always reaches an equilibrium in which each firm bears a definite proportion (s_i) of the sum of all the idiosyncratic shocks ($\sum_i x_{i0}$):*

$$\hat{\mathbf{x}}' = \mathbf{s}'\left(\sum\nolimits_i x_{i0}\right)$$

where $\mathbf{s}'$ *is the left eigenvector of* $\mathbf{T}$ *corresponding to eigenvalue* 1 *the entries of which sum to 1:* $\mathbf{s}'(\mathbf{I} - \mathbf{T}) = \mathbf{0}$, $\sum_i s_i = 1$.

Let us note that the condition of aperiodicity for the network is rather weak, and can be assumed as almost always satisfied in the present framework. Indeed, a sufficient condition for the network to be aperiodic is that there is at least one loop ($\delta_{ii} > 0$ for some i), that is, at least one firm which is not able to transfer all the experienced shock in each round.

A formal proof of the proposition is provided in the Appendix. Here we instead discuss the simple three-firm example in Section 3 (Fig. 3a). In that example, although firms 2 and 3 are able to transfer all the one-round shock to the others, the system soon converges to the equilibrium and such equilibrium entails the following redistribution of the sum of all the shocks: $\left(\frac{1}{2}, \frac{1}{3}, \frac{1}{6}\right)$. Thus, when firms are hit by the same initial shock, the system of relations is detrimental (beneficial) for firm 1 (3).[9]

As we will say in the discussion, this is what could be expected when a generic cluster of firms—that is, a cluster in which all the firms are either directly or indirectly connected among them, but with no need of reciprocity—is hit by a shock. Its distribution in the network has, for the firms that constitute it, ambiguous effects. In other words, in absence of qualified forms of network relationships—such as, for example, those occurring in an industrial district—being part of a network will not necessarily reduce the severity of the shock the firms face, although that might be possible. In the light of this result, the expectations about the destiny of small and medium enterprises based in non-firmly embedded networks in front of the crisis are at most misty.

Therefore, in general, the proportion of the sum of all the shocks that, in equilibrium, accrues to each firm is not the same. On the contrary, given a *symmetric* network, i.e. a network whose adjacency matrix is symmetric ($\delta_{ij} = \delta_{ji}$ for each i, j), the following holds:

Proposition 2 *If the network is strongly connected, aperiodic and symmetric, the risk distribution is egalitarian, i.e. each firm gets in equilibrium a common shock amounting to an average of all the shocks:*

[9] So, for instance, if $\mathbf{x}'_0 = (100{,}100{,}100)$, we have $\hat{\mathbf{x}}'_0 = (150, 100, 50)$.

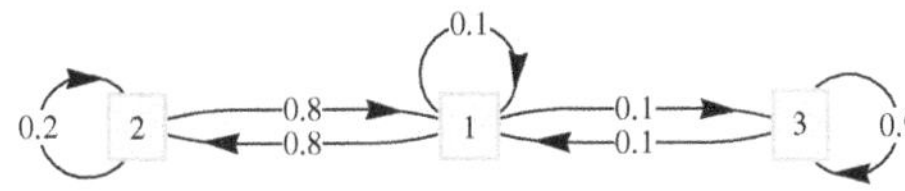

Fig. 4 A symmetric strongly connected network

$$\hat{x}_i = \frac{\sum_{i=1}^{n} x_i}{n} = \bar{x}, \qquad \forall i \in N.$$

A formal proof of the statement is given in the Appendix. Here we just note that, apart from the strong connectivity and aperiodicity, the condition for this "egalitarian" distribution to occur is not that all the linkages are equal, but only that they are perfectly reciprocated, as the example of Fig. 4 illustrates. In this simple three-firm network, the equilibrium values are: $s_1 = s_2 = s_3 = \frac{1}{3}$, in spite of the fact that the structure of relations of the three firms is strongly different.[10]

As we better argue in Section 5, the symmetry condition could be retained proper of a network configuration toward which industrial districts would tend "asymptotically". It can be understood by thinking that the higher the level of social capital in a local production system, that is, the more the system resembles an industrial district—in the characterization given of it by the famous Becattini's tradition (Pyke et al. 1990)—the more the interlinking of credit and subcontracting is used to re-balance the contractual power of the parties in the supplier-user relationships (Dei Ottati 1994), the more the correspondent network turns out to be symmetric.

In general, when the symmetry condition does not hold, the risk distribution is not egalitarian and a different portion of the total shock accrues to firms ($s_i \neq s_j$). Still, industrial districts are such that, being part of them tends to align firms as far as the supported shock is concerned. In other words, in industrial districts, the shock distribution is more "democratic'" than in other networks, even when it is not perfectly egalitarian (such as in a symmetric network). As we will see, this is not necessarily a good thing for district firms.

What is important is that the portion of the supported shock depends on the overall structure of relations. An example is provided in Fig. 3b, where, despite the symmetry in the reciprocal relationship, 1 and 2 get different parts of the total shock because of the differences in their relation with 3: $(s_1, s_2, s_3) = (.3, .6, .1)$.

The final network structure that we consider is that of a network which is not strongly connected, where one or more nodes/firms may have zero *outdegree* or *indegree*: in economic terms, firms with no forward or backward linkages, respectively.

It is self-evident that nodes with zero indegree and a positive outdegree turn out to be *shock releasers*: firms which, in the limit, are always able to transfer their

[10] Indeed, at a first glance, firm 1 might look in a better position than 3, because it is able to transfer a much greater portion of its initial shock to the others (0.9 against 0.1 of firm 3).

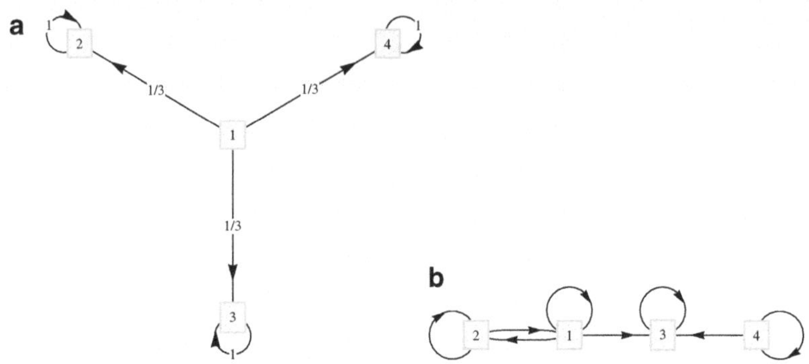

Fig. 5 Shock releasers/absorbers in non strongly connected networks

shock to the others completely. This is the case shown in Fig. 5a, where firm 1 transfers all of its shock to the others. As we will say in the discussion, this might be thought as the case of strongly hierarchical networks, where the suppliers do not have any contractual power (in the limit position) over the client firm, which dominates them.

On the other hand, nodes with zero outdegree and a positive indegree turn out to be *shock absorbers*. In other words, these are firms that sustain the shock of the others without being able to transfer theirs. This is the case of firms 2, 3 and 4 in the previous example,[11] as well as of firm 3 in Fig. 5b.

4.2 Risk distribution and default probabilities

By affecting the actual allocation of idiosyncratic shocks, inter-firm networks can change firms' *default probabilities* and, via this, observed *default rates*.

In this section, we investigate only the two most paradigmatic cases, namely, (i) the default probability of a supplier in a subcontracting relation without interlinking credit (Fig. 6); and (ii) the default rate of firms in a symmetric and strongly connected network. These cases are quite extreme, and this necessarily lead to a loss of generality. They can, nonetheless, deliver clear-cut results and, therefore, be a useful starting point in the analysis of more complex situations. To this end, we also provide some insights for the case of strongly and asymmetric networks.

The section ends with a discussion on the speed of convergence, which is of utmost importance. In fact, given our analysis of default probabilities at the equilibrium, the lower the speed at which the system reaches the equilibrium, the

[11] In the example, each supplier (firms 2–4) faces its idiosyncratic shock plus a fraction (1/3) of the buyer's shock.

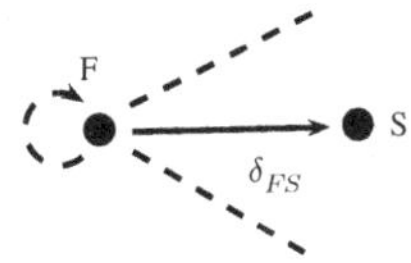

Fig. 6 A supplier-buyer relation

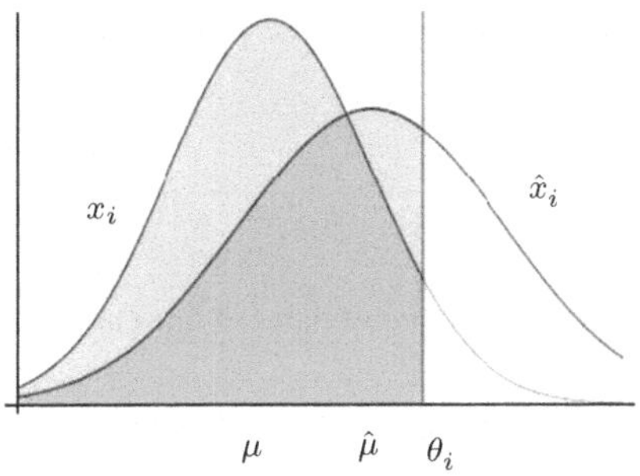

Fig. 7 Default probabilities of supplier

more unrealistic is our operational suggestion to analyze default probabilities at the equilibrium allocation.

4.2.1 Default probabilities of suppliers in supplier-buyer relations

Given the idiosyncratic shock:

$$x_i = \mu + \epsilon_i$$

and assuming that $\epsilon_i \sim (0, \sigma^2)$, the shock faced by the supplier is:

$$\hat{x}_S = x_{S0} + \delta_{FS} x_{F0} \sim \left((1 + \delta_{FS})\, \mu,\ (1 + \delta_{FS}^2)\, \sigma^2 \right).$$

Thus, the shock experienced by the supplier ($\hat{x}_S$) is higher on average and it is also more volatile than its initial shock (x_{S0}). Clearly, this increases its default probability with respect to the one of an isolated firm facing the shock x_i (Fig. 7).

The economic correspondent of this result is pretty intuitive. The suppliers of a hierarchical network, with a pivotal client firms—in the following, we will refer as an example to the case of the Fiat automobile value chain—suffer twice as much the consequence of the shock than if they were isolated, not only because of the higher scale of the shock, but also because of its lower predictability.

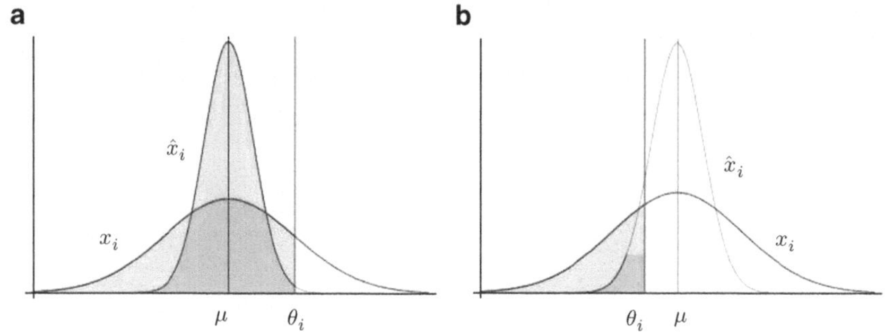

Fig. 8 Default probabilities of firms in symmetric networks

4.2.2 Default rates in strongly connected networks

In case of firms in a symmetric and strongly connected network, from Proposition 2 it follows that $\hat{x}_i = \hat{x}_j = \bar{x}_0$, for each i, j. Still assuming that $\epsilon_i \sim (0, \sigma^2)$, this implies:[12]

$$\hat{x}_i = \bar{x}_0 \overset{a}{\sim} N\left(\mu, \frac{\sigma^2}{n}\right)$$

Thus, given that each firm faces in equilibrium an average of all the shocks, its volatility is reduced. This leads us to state two further propositions.

Proposition 3 *Assume that the idiosyncratic components of the shocks are independently distributed and the number of firms in the network sufficiently large. Then, the default probability of a firm in a symmetric and connected network is higher (lower) than that of the same firm in isolation when the expected value of the random shock is higher (lower) than its threshold.*

A formal proof of this proposition is in the Appendix. In intuitive terms, Fig. 8 shows the case of a normally distributed shock for a firm i with a certain threshold θ_i. The shadow area under the curves measure the probability that the shock is lower than the firms' threshold, that is, the probability of survival for the firm. As clearly emerges from the Figure, this area for x_i—the random shock faced by the firm in isolation—is higher (lower) than the corresponding area for $\hat{x}_i$—the random shock

[12] Let us note that the assumption of an equal distribution of ϵ is not strictly needed for any of the results and even the assumption of equality in variance can be relaxed. Indeed, by using the Lindeberg-Lévy central limit theorem, one can show that, if $\epsilon_i \sim (0, \sigma_i^2)$, then:

$$\hat{x}_i = \bar{x}_0 a{\sim} N\left(\mu, \frac{\bar{\sigma}^2}{n}\right)$$

with $\bar{\sigma}^2 = \sum_{i=1}^{n} \sigma_i^2 / n$ as long as the Lindeberg condition holds, that is, $\bar{\sigma}^2$ is not dominated by any single term.

faced by the firm in the network—when the average of the shock (μ) is lower (higher) than the firm's threshold (θ_i).

As we will emphasize in the discussion, this is one of the most interesting results of the paper. A district firm, or a firm in a district-like environment, is not necessarily safer than an isolated one. It depends on the severity of the (financial) crisis firms face. Should we able to conclude that the current crisis is indeed a very large one, with respect to others, firms in industrial districts are expected to have a comparative disadvantage.

Moving from the individual firm to the network of firms, if the threshold is heterogeneous across firms, but drawn from a common distribution, the following holds:

Proposition 4 *Assume the idiosyncratic components of the shocks are independently distributed, and so are the threshold values (θ_i), and in addition the number of firms sufficiently large. Then, the average default rate in a symmetric and connected network is higher (lower) than the one for isolated firms if* $\Pr(\theta_i < \mu) > \Pr(\theta_i - x_{i0} < 0)$ ($\Pr(\theta_i < \mu) < \Pr(\theta_i - x_{i0} < 0)$).

For the simpler case of a homogeneous threshold, the previous proposition reduces to the following one:[13]

Proposition 5 *Assume the idiosyncratic components of the shocks are independently distributed, the threshold value is homogeneous across firms, and the number of firms sufficiently large. Then, the average default rate in a symmetric and connected network is higher (lower) than the one for isolated firms if the expected value of the random shock is higher (lower) than the common threshold.*

Finally, let us consider the case of strongly connected asymmetric networks, in which the allocation of the total shock is not equal across firms. As it depends on the overall structure of bilateral relations, no easy generalization can be made. In general, if s_i is the fraction of the total shock accruing to firm i, i will face in equilibrium a shock which is asymptotically normally distributed (by the central limit theorem) with expected value:

$$\mathrm{E}[\hat{x}_i] = \mathrm{E}\left[s_i \sum_i x_{i0}\right] = s_i n \mu$$

and variance:

$$\mathrm{Var}[\hat{x}_i] = \mathrm{Var}\left[s_i \sum_i x_{i0}\right] = s_i^2 n \sigma^2$$

[13] In reality, there could be a relation between the firm size, the value of θ and the network structure. So, for instance, in strongly hierarchical networks, more central firms are usually bigger and therefore likely associated with higher thresholds. However, the assumption of a homogeneous threshold across firms seems to be less unrealistic in the case of strongly connected-(nearly) symmetric networks, because such inter-firms networks are usually Marshallian districts where differences in size tend to be small.

Hence, if $s_i < 1/n$, the firm in the network have to face a shock which is less volatile and lower on average than the one it faced in isolation. If instead $1/n < s_i < 1/\sqrt{n}$, the firm's shock in the network is higher on average but still less volatile. Finally, when $1/\sqrt{n} < s_i \leq 1$, the firm's shock is both higher on average and more volatile.

In any case, asymptotically, the following proposition holds (proved in the Appendix):

Proposition 6 *Assume the idiosyncratic components of the shocks are independently distributed and the number of firms in the network sufficiently large. Then, the default probability of a firm in a strongly connected asymmetric network is higher (lower) than that of the same firm in isolation if the expected value of the random shock is higher (lower) than* $\frac{\theta_i}{s_i n}$.

In the case of a heterarchical network, therefore, but without the symmetric ties of an industrial districts, the results in terms of default crucially depend on the size of the shock. In particular, we need to take into account the share of the overall shock the firm gets in equilibrium and whether this share actually makes the expected value of the shock exceed the firm's threshold.

At the level of the overall network, what matters is the correlation between the equilibrium shares, as determined by the network, and the firms' thresholds. So, for instance, if the firms that in equilibrium get the higher shares of the overall shocks are those with the lowest thresholds, the default rate exhibited by these networks can be relatively high in the case of low shocks, but comparatively lower in case of strong common shocks. Indeed, the system of relations makes the weakest firms, which would have died anyway, take a larger share of the total shock.

4.2.3 Default analysis and speed of convergence

Our default analysis strongly relies on the operational device to work out default probabilities at the limiting distribution of shocks. In fact, the slower the rate at which the system converges to the equilibrium, the less realistic is our assumption.

Hence, understanding the relationship between the structure of the firms' network and the speed of convergence is crucial. In formal terms, the question amounts to calculate how long it does take the Markov matrix **T** to approach its limit.

This is a well known issue, on which there is in fact a large literature. As reported by Golub and Jackson (2010), the convergence time is proportional to 1/log(|λ2 (**T**)|), where λ2(**T**) stands for the second largest eigenvalue of **T**. Therefore, a second eigenvalue close to 1 implies a very low speed of convergence.

As for the relationship between this mathematical condition and its insights for our model, a useful perspective is the one provided by the approach based on measuring *bottlenecks* (Diaconis and Stroock 1991). The basic idea is that if there are pieces of the network connected only by narrow linkages, the convergence is slow.

5 Discussion and final remarks

The results of the model suggest a number of interesting interpretations, related to the background literature and stylized facts we reviewed.

First of all, the network capacity of working as a "system" in financial terms—in which individual firms exchange their idiosyncratic shock for a certain portion of the total shock of the network—crucially depends on the structure of the network itself. In particular, the strong connectivity of the network is crucial. Should some or even only one of the firms be "isolated" from the twofold transfer mechanism we have described, the network would lose its system properties.

This can be considered in the case of clusters, in which firms are linked through subcontracting relationships but with little socio-economic embeddedness. In these chains of "atomistic" producer-user relationships, the client firms exploit their larger market power to transfer, via trade credit, their risk to the subcontractors themselves, which thus get subject to financial default exclusively and/or earlier than the former.

This result can be used to interpret what is happening, for example, in the supply-chain network of Fiat automobile in Italy (Abatecola 2009). Here, the small subcontractors of components are actually providing the producer with a remarkable margin of flexibility both in production and financial terms. The FIAT contractual power and the absence of a district-like environment for the supply-chain are crucial for this to occur.

While strongly connected networks are able to work as financial systems, on the other hand, their capacity to translate the idiosyncratic risk of each firm into an average of the risk of all the firms in the cluster is not guaranteed. In order to have such "egalitarian" risk-pooling, the inter-firm bilateral relationships need to be perfectly reciprocated. With benefit of hindsight, we could say that the district atmosphere the network in which it is embedded must be such as, to compensate exactly, or tend to compensate, the asymmetries in contractual powers which emerge from user-supplier differences in size. Quite interestingly, this result is consistent with the trade-off local studies find between contractual opportunistic behaviors, on the one side, and social capital, on the other. For example, this has been shown to be the case of the footwear district of San Mauro Pascoli in the Italian region of Emilia-Romagna (Brioschi et al. 2004).

Interesting implications can be drawn also in terms of default probability, that is, of the actual capacity of the network firms to bear a financial risk such as the current one. In the case of non strongly connected networks, when "isolated firms" are present, those firms which act as pure absorbers have been shown to be two times in trouble: not only because they end up receiving a shock larger on average than the one would have accrued in isolation, but also because such a shock encapsulates the variability of that faced by the other firms.

Definitely more interesting is the result for the district network, where trade credit and interlinking of credit and subcontracting coexist. District firms have been shown to be more resilient than isolated ones *only* under two important conditions: in the case of symmetric relationships, and providing the average shock is lower than the threshold of the firm itself. Conversely, belonging to the district could even increase the default probability of the firm.

This is possibly the most important result of the model. Indeed, it seems to show that the industrial district model, while enabling firms to share the risk of a moderate shock, and to be actually more resilient in "normal" conditions, does not help and is actually disadvantageous in front of "heavy" financial crisis (such as possibly the current one).[14] Quite interestingly, this result is invariant with respect to the actual structure of the relationships in the district: "canonically" or not Paniccia (1998) does not make any difference for its financial behavior. Indeed, recent data seem to show that the crisis have had a major impact on more traditional districts, such as those in textiles and footwear, no matter their actual structure of the network. See, for instance, the recent report on the textiles district of Carpi (R&I 2011).

If, in strongly connected networks, the twofold credit relationships we have envisaged are asymmetric, the implications of the model becomes more blurred, as they depend on the ratio between the share of the overall shock firms get (in equilibrium) and the firms' threshold. Still, the insight is that, in this case, the networked firms actually split into two groups: the "winners", so to say, which are able to transfer to the others part of both the average and the variance of their shock, and the "losers", whose default rate increases both because of a higher and a more variable shock. This is another interesting result, which recovers the relevance of the structure of local production systems in evaluating their resilience to the crisis: indeed, such a structure turns out to be more important than the bilateral relationships on which local studies usually focus.

The results of this paper contribute to the evolutionary analysis of the dynamics of local production systems and of industrial districts at least in two respects. First of all, we extend to financial linkages the array of factors which intervene in the adjustment processes that clusters of firms experience in front of external shocks (Boschma and Lambooy 2002). As we said, rather than on the peculiarities of local banks and local credit, which have already received attention in urban and regional studies (e.g. Ughetto 2009; Alessandrini and Zazzaro 2009), these financial linkages depend on the network structure and on the mutual coordination mechanisms (in particular, on the "interlinking of subcontracting and credit") that social capital and institutions allow local firms to undertake. The second contribution concerns the extension of the manifold co-evolutionary processes through which regional dynamics go. Indeed, in addition to a life-cycle perspective—which has also received a certain attention (c.g. Neffke et al. 2011; Albino et al. 2007)—the local interlinking of industrial dynamics, evolution of firm capabilities

[14] Under a different perspective, the same result points to the production specialization of the districts, making more (less) fragile those which are specialized in sectors more (less) exposed to international competition: the different destiny of the ceramic tales district of Sassuolo and of the mechanical one of Bologna in Italy, for example, can also be read in this terms.

and industry-wide knowledge (Ter Wal and Boschma 2011) should also consider a business-cycle perspective, in which the "shocks" we have addressed in this paper are of crucial importance.

We think the main value added of the paper is that the stylized model we propose is analytically tractable and can deliver very striking predictions. However, as usual, such tractability comes at a price. In particular, we make the implicit assumption that the dynamics of propagation of the shocks do not significantly differ. In fact, the shock transfer mechanisms implied by the different credit channels linking together suppliers and final producers can exhibit very different dynamics. Moreover, we assume that the structure of the network stays constant all along the process. In fact, the network structure will probably change along the process of propagation as the result of the firm's strategies aimed at minimizing the default probabilities.[15] In order to analyze these issues, one probably needs to give up the analytical tractability and build an agent-based model relying on simulations. This is the next step, and we think that the results of this paper can prove useful in such a step.

Acknowledgements The authors would like to thank Stefano D'Addona and the participants to the II Workshop of the PRIN2007 (Padua, January 22–23, 2010), the "DRUID Summer Conference 2010" (London, June 16–18, 2010), the "13th Conference of the International Schumpeter Society" (Aalborg, June 21–24, 2010), the internal seminar of Orkestra, Basque Institute of Competitiveness (San Sebastian, January 31, 2012) and two anonymous referees for their useful suggestions. The authors gratefully acknowledge support for this research from the PAT (Provincia Autonoma di Trento), post-doc scholarship 2006, Giuseppe Vittucci Marzetti, and OPENLOC-Project, Giulio Cainelli and Sandro Montresor. The usual disclaimers apply.

Appendix

Proof of Proposition 1. When $\mathbf{T}$ is strongly connected, it is a standard result of the theory of Markov chains that aperiodicity is a necessary and sufficient condition for $\mathbf{T}$ to be convergent (e.g. Kemeny and Snell 1960). Moreover, when this happens, $\mathbf{T}$ is also *primitive*, i.e. $\mathbf{T}^t$ has only strictly positive entries for some $t \geq 1$ (e.g. Perkins 1961), and there is a unique (up to scale) left eigenvector $\mathbf{s}$ of $\mathbf{T}$, corresponding to the unit eigenvalue, such that for any $\mathbf{v}$:

$$\lim_{t\to\infty} \mathbf{T}^t \mathbf{v} = \mathbf{s}'\mathbf{v}.$$

Since $\mathbf{T}$ is convergent, $\mathbf{S} \equiv \lim_{t\to\infty} \mathbf{T}^t$ exists and hence:

$$\mathbf{ST} = \lim_{t\to\infty} \mathbf{T}^t\,\mathbf{T} = \lim_{t\to\infty} \mathbf{T}^t = \mathbf{S}$$

[15] In this respect, it seems plausible that the slower the propagation, the higher the probability that such changes occur.

where each row of $\mathbf{S}$ is equal to $\mathbf{s}'$.

It follows that:

$$\hat{\mathbf{x}}' = \mathbf{x}_0'\left(\lim_{t\to\infty}\mathbf{T}^t\right) = \mathbf{x}_0'\mathbf{S} = \mathbf{x}_0'\begin{pmatrix}\mathbf{s}'\\ \vdots \\ \mathbf{s}'\end{pmatrix} = \mathbf{s}'\left(\sum_i x_{i0}\right). \qquad \square$$

Proof of Proposition 2. A symmetric network implies $\mathbf{T} = \mathbf{T}'$ and therefore:

$$\mathbf{S}' = \left(\lim_{t\to\infty}\mathbf{T}^t\right)' = \lim_{t\to\infty}\mathbf{T}'^t = \mathbf{S}$$

i.e. $\mathbf{S}$ must be symmetric too ($s_{ij} = s_{ji}$). As in $\mathbf{S}$ by definition $s_{ji} = s_{ii}$, the symmetry implies $s_{ii} = s_{ij}$.

Moreover, since the sum by column of each row is one, it follows that:

$$\sum_{j=1}^{n} s_{ij} = n\ s_{ii} = 1$$

for each i and all the elements of $\mathbf{S}$ are equal to $1/n$. Hence:

$$\hat{x}_i = \mathbf{x}_0'\begin{pmatrix}\frac{1}{n}\\ \vdots \\ \frac{1}{n}\end{pmatrix} = \frac{\sum_i x_{i0}}{n} = \bar{x}$$

for each $i \in N$. $\square$

Proof of Proposition 3. Given that, in a connected-symmetric network $\hat{x}_i = \bar{x}_0$ and this variable is asymptotically normally distributed with variance σ^2/n and mean μ, when n gets larger it converges in probability toward μ. Therefore, we have:

$$\lim_{n\to\infty}\Pr(\hat{x}_i > \theta_i) = \begin{cases} 1 \text{ if } \theta_i > \mu \\ 0 \text{ if } \theta_i < \mu. \end{cases}$$

By contrast, since $\sigma^2 > 0$, there is always a $\epsilon > 0$ such that $\epsilon < \Pr(x_{i0} > \theta_i) < 1 - \epsilon$ and this probability is so strictly bound between 0 and 1. $\square$

Proof of Proposition 4. Assuming that θ_i are identically and independently distributed, and so are x_{i0}, the number of firm defaults follows a binomial distribution with expected value $n\Pr(\theta_i - x_{i0} < 0)$. The expected value of the default rate is, therefore, simply $\Pr(\theta_i - x_{i0} < 0)$.

For firms in a symmetric-connected network, the expected value of the binomial is instead: $n\Pr(\theta_i - \bar{x} < 0)$, with an expected default rate equals to $\Pr(\theta_i - \bar{x} < 0)$.

Given that $\bar{x} \xrightarrow{p} \mu$ we have that:

$$\lim_{n\to\infty} \Pr(\theta_i - \bar{x} < 0) = \Pr(\theta_i < \mu)$$

Hence, the expected default rate of firms when the number of firms gets large is higher (lower) in isolation than in a symmetric-connected network if $\Pr(\theta_i - x_{i0} < 0) > \Pr(\theta_i < \mu)$ ($\Pr(\theta_i - x_{i0} < 0) < \Pr(\theta_i < \mu)$). □

Proof of Proposition 5. For a common threshold ($\theta_i = \theta$), we have :

$$\lim_{n\to\infty} \Pr(\bar{x} < \theta) = \begin{cases} 1 \text{ if } \theta > \mu \\ 0 \text{ if } \theta < \mu \end{cases}$$

while $\Pr(x_{i0} < \theta)$ remains strictly bound between 0 and 1. □

Proof of Proposition 6. The probability of default in a strongly connected asymmetric network for firm i is:

$$\Pr(\hat{x}_i > \theta_i) = \Pr\left(s_i \sum_i x_{i0} > \theta_i\right) = \Pr\left(s_i n \frac{\sum_i x_{i0}}{n} > \theta_i\right) = \Pr\left(\bar{x} > \frac{\theta_i}{s_i n}\right)$$

$\bar{x}$ converges in probability toward μ, therefore we have that $\Pr(\hat{x}_i > \theta_i)$ tends to 1 if $\bar{x} > \frac{\theta_i}{s_i n}$ and 0 if instead $\bar{x} < \frac{\theta_i}{s_i n}$.

By contrast, since $\sigma^2 > 0$, there is always a $\epsilon > 0$ such that $\epsilon < \Pr(x_{i0} > \theta_i) < 1 - \epsilon$ and the probability in this case is strictly bound between 0 and 1. □

References

Abatecola G (2009) Crisis in the European automobile industry: an organizational adaptation perspective. DSI Essays Series 5, University of Rome "Tor Vergata", Department of Business Studies

Albino V, Carbonara N, Giannoccaro I (2006) Innovation in industrial districts: an agent-based simulation model. Int J Prod Econ 104(1):30–45

Albino V, Carbonara N, Giannoccaro I (2007) Supply chain cooperation in industrial districts: a simulation analysis. Eur J Oper Res 177(1):261–280

Alessandrini P, Zazzaro A (2009) Bank localism and industrial districts. In: Becattini G, Bellandi M, De Propris L (eds) A handbook of industrial districts. Edward Elgar, Cheltenham

Alessandrini P, Presbitero A, Zazzaro A (2008) Banche e imprese nei distretti industriali. Quaderni di ricerca 309, University of Ancona, Department of Economics
Alessandrini P, Presbitero A, Zazzaro A (2009) Global banking and local markets: a national perspective. Camb J Reg Econ Soc 2(2):173–192
Allen F, Gale D (2000) Financial contagion. J Polit Econ 108(1):1–33
Arestis P, Singh A (2010) Financial globalisation and crisis, institutional transformation and equity. Camb J Econ 34(2):225–238
Ballester C, Calvo-Armengol A, Zenou Y (2006) Who's who in networks. Wanted: the key player. Econometrica 74(5):1403–1417
Battiston S, Delli Gatti D, Gallegati M, Greenwald B, Stiglitz J (2009) Liaisons dangereuses: Increasing connectivity, risk sharing, and systemic risk. NBER Working Paper 15611
Bloch F, Genicot G, Ray D (2008) Informal insurance in social networks. J Econ Theory 143 (1):36–58
Bonacich P (1987) Power and centrality: a family of measures. Am J Sociol 92:1170–1182
Boschma R, Lambooy J (2002) Knowledge, market structure, and economic coordination: dynamics of industrial districts. Growth Change 33(3):291–311
Bramoullé Y, Kranton R (2007a) Risk sharing across communities. Am Econ Rev 97(2):70–74
Bramoullé Y, Kranton R (2007b) Risk-sharing networks. J Econ Behav Organ 64(3–4):275–294
Brioschi F, Brioschi M, Cainelli G (2002) From the industrial district to the district group: an insight into the evolution of local capitalism in Italy. Reg Stud 36(9):1037–1052
Brioschi F, Brioschi M, Cainelli G (2004) Ownership linkages and business groups in industrial districts. The case of Emilia Romagna. In: Cainelli G, Zoboli R (eds) The evolution of industrial districts. Physica, Heidelberg
Bugamelli M, Cristadoro R, Zevi G (2009) La crisi internazionale e il sistema produttivo italiano: un'analisi su dati a livello di impresa. Occasional Paper 58, Bank of Italy
Cainelli G (2008) Industrial districts: theoretical and empirical insights. In: Karlsson C (ed) Handbook of research on cluster theory. Edward Elgar, London, pp 189–202
Cainelli G, Zoboli R (eds) (2004) Evolution of industrial districts. Changing governance, innovation and internationalisation of local capitalism in Italy. Physica, Heidelberg
Carbonara N (2002) New models of inter-firm networks within industrial districts. Entrep Reg Dev 14(3):229–246
Carbonara N, Giannoccaro I, Pontrandolfo P (2002) Supply chains within industrial districts: a theoretical framework. Int J Prod Econ 76:159–176
Cocozza E (2000) Le relazioni finanziare nei distretti industriali. In: Signorini L (ed) Lo Sviluppo Locale. Un'Indagine della Banca d'Italia sui Distretti Industriali. Meridiana Libri, Corigliano Calabro
DeGroot M (1974) Reaching a consensus. J Am Stat Assoc 69(345):118–121
Dei Ottati G (1994) Trust, interlinking transactions and credit in the industrial district. Camb J Econ 18:529–546
DeMarzo P, Vayanos D, Zwiebel J (2003) Persuasion bias, social influence, and unidimensional opinions. Q J Econ 118(3):909–968
Diaconis P, Stroock D (1991) Geometric bounds for eigenvalues of Markov chains. Ann Appl Probab 1(1):36–61
Diamond D, Dybvig P (1983) Bank runs, deposit insurance, and liquidity. J Polit Econ 91 (3):401–419
Dodds P, Watts D (2005) A generalized model of social and biological contagion. J Theor Biol 232 (4):587–604
Dymski G (2010) A spatialized approach to asset bubbles and Minsky crises. In: Papadimitriou D, Wray L (eds) The Elgar companion to Hyman Minsky, chapter 12. Edward Elgar, London
Eggertsson G, Krugman P (2011) Debt, deleveraging, and the liquidity trap: a Fisher–Minsky–Koo approach. Mimeo
Fafchamps M, Gubert F (2007) The formation of risk sharing networks. J Dev Econ 83(2):326–350

Frenkel R, Rapetti M (2009) A developing country view of the current global crisis: what should not be forgotten and what should be done. Camb J Econ 33(4):685–702
Gallegati M, Greenwald B, Richiardi M, Stiglitz J (2008) The asymmetric effect of diffusion processes: Risk sharing and contagion. Global Econ J 8(3):1–20
Golub B, Jackson M (2010) Naïve learning in social networks: convergence, influence, and the wisdom of crowds. AEJ: Microeconomics 2(1):112–149
Goyal S, Joshi S (2003) Networks of collaboration in oligopoly. Games Econom Behav 43:57–85
Goyal S, Moraga-Gonzalez J (2001) R&D networks. Rand J Econ 32(4):686–707
Guerrieri P, Iammarino S, Pietrobelli C (eds) (2003) The global challenge to industrial districts: small and medium-sized enterprises in Italy and Taiwan. Edward Elgar, Cheltenham
Harrison B (1992) Industrial districts: old wine in new bottles? Reg Stud 26(5):469–483
Herrigel G (1996) Crisis in German decentralized production: unexpected rigidity and the challenge of an alternative form of flexible organization in Baden Wurttemberg. Eur Urban Reg Stud 3(1):33–52
Hirst P, Zeitlin J (1989) Flexible specialisation and the competitive failure of UK manufacturing. Pol Q 60(2):164–178
Iori G, Jafarey S, Padilla F (2006) Systemic risk on the interbank market. J Econ Behav Organ 61 (4):525–542
ISTAT (2005) Distretti industriali e sistemi locali del lavoro 2001. VIII Censimento Generale dell'Industria e dei Servizi, Rome
Kanerva M, Hollanders H (2009) The impact of the economic crisis on innovation. Analysis based on the Innobarometer 2009 survey. Report, ProInno Europe—Innometrics
Karlin S, Taylor H (1975) A first course in stochastic processes. Academic Press, New York
Karlin S, Taylor H (1981) A second course in stochastic processes. Academic Press, New York
Kemeny J, Snell J (1960) Finite Markov chains. van Nostrand, Princeton
Le Heron R (2009) Globalisation and local economic development in a globalising world: critical reflections on the theory-practice relation. In: Rowe J (ed) Theory of local economic development. linking theory to practise. Ashgate, Farnham
López-Pintado D (2008) Diffusion in complex social networks. Games Econom Behav 62 (2):573–590
Markusen A (1996) Sticky places in slippery space: a typology of industrial districts. J Econ Geogr 72(3):293–313
Motter A, Lai Y-C (2002) Cascade-based attacks on complex networks. Phys Rev E 66:065102
Neffke F, Henning M, Boschma R, Lundquist K, Olander L (2011) The dynamics of agglomeration externalities along the life cycle of industries. Reg Stud 45(1):49–65
Nier E, Yang J, Yorulmazer T, Alentorn A (2007) Network models and financial stability. J Econ Dyn Control 31(6):2033–2060
Omiccioli M (2000) L'organizzazione dell'attività produttiva nei distretti industriali. In: Signorini L (ed) Lo Sviluppo Locale. Un'Indagine della Banca d'Italia sui Distretti Industriali. Donzelli-Meridiana, Roma
Orsenigo L, Pammolli F, Riccaboni M (2001) Technological change and network dynamics lessons from the pharmaceutical industry. Res Policy 30(3):485–508
Paniccia I (1998) One, a hundred, thousands of industrial districts. Organizational variety in local networks of small and medium-sized enterprises. Organ Stud 19(4):667–699
Pastor-Satorras R, Vespignani A (2001) Epidemic spreading in scale-free networks. Phys Rev Lett 86(14):3200–3203
Pastor-Satorras R, Vespignani A (2002) Epidemic dynamics in finite size scale-free networks. Phys Rev E 65(3):035108
Perkins P (1961) A theorem on regular matrices. Pac J Math 11(4):1529–1533
Peterson M, Rajan R (1997) Trade credit: theories and evidence. Rev Financ Stud 10(3):661–691
Pyke F, Becattini G, Sengenberger W (eds) (1990) Industrial districts and inter-firm co-operation in Italy. International Institute for Labour Studies, Geneva

Reinhart C, Rogoff K (2008) Is the 2007 US sub-prime financial crisis so different? An international historical comparison. Am Econ Rev 98(2):339–344

Reinhart C, Rogoff K (2009) The aftermath of financial crises. Am Econ Rev 99(2):466–472

R&I (2011) Osservatorio del settore tessile abbigliamento nel distretto di Carpi. Rapporto X, Comune di Carpi. Assessorato Economia, Commercio, Agricoltura, Turismo

Shiller R (2008) The subprime solution: how today's global financial crisis happened, and what to do about it. Princeton University Press, Princeton

Storper M (1995) The resurgence of regional economies, ten years later: the region as a nexus of untraded interdependencies. Eur Urban Reg Stud 2(3):191–221

Storper M, Christopherson S (1987) Flexible specialization and regional industrial agglomerations: the case of the US motion picture industry. Ann Assoc Am Geogr 77 (1):104–117

Ter Wal A, Boschma R (2011) Co-evolution of firms, industries and networks in space. Reg Stud 45(7):919–933

Ughetto E (2009) Industrial districts and financial constraints to innovation. Int Rev Appl Econ 23 (5):597–624

Watts D (2002) A simple model of global cascades on random networks. Proc Natl Acad Sci 99:5766–5771

Whitney D (2009) Cascades of rumors and information in highly connected networks with thresholds. In: Second international symposium on engineering systems. MIT, Cambridge

Does History Matter? Empirical Analysis of Evolutionary Versus Stationary Equilibrium Views of the Economy

Kenneth I. Carlaw and Richard G. Lipsey

Abstract The evolutionary vision in which history matters is of an evolving economy driven by bursts of technological change initiated by agents facing uncertainty and producing long term, path-dependent growth and shorter-term, non-random investment cycles. The alternative vision in which history does not matter is of a stationary, ergodic process driven by rational agents facing risk and producing stable trend growth and shorter term cycles caused by random disturbances. We use Carlaw and Lipsey's simulation model of non-stationary, sustained growth driven by endogenous, path-dependent technological change under uncertainty to generate artificial macro data. We match these data to the New Classical stylized growth facts. The raw simulation data pass standard tests for trend and difference stationarity, exhibiting unit roots and cointegrating processes of order one. Thus, contrary to current belief, these tests do not establish that the real data are generated by a stationary process. Real data are then used to estimate time-varying NAIRU's for six OECD countries. The estimates are shown to be highly sensitive to the time period over which they are made. They also fail to show any relation between the unemployment gap, actual unemployment *minus* estimated NAIRU and the acceleration of inflation. Thus there is no tendency for inflation to behave as required by the New Keynesian and earlier New Classical theory.

This is a revised version of a paper presented at the 44th Annual Conference of the CEA May 28–30, 2010, Quebec City and the 13th ISS Conference 2010 in Aalborg, Denmark June 21–24, 2010

Modified and extended version from Journal of Evolutionary Economics 22(4), 735–766, Springer (2012).

K.I. Carlaw (✉)
Department of Economics, University of British Columbia, 3333 University Way, Kelowna, BC, Canada V1V 1V7
e-mail: kenneth.carlaw@ubc.ca

R.G. Lipsey
Simon Fraser University, 1125 west 26th Street North Vancouver, BCV7R 1A4, Canada
e-mail: rlipsey@sfu.ca

A. Pyka and E.S. Andersen (eds.), *Long Term Economic Development*, Economic Complexity and Evolution, DOI 10.1007/978-3-642-35125-9_7,

We conclude by rejecting the existence of a well-defined a short-run, negatively sloped Philips curve, a NAIRU, a unique general equilibrium with its implication, a vertical long-run Phillips curve, and the long-run neutrality of money.

Economists face two conflicting visions of the market economy, visions that reflect two distinct paradigms, the Newtonian and the Darwinian. In the former, the behaviour of the economy is seen as the result of an equilibrium reached by the operation of opposing forces—such as market demanders and suppliers or competing oligopolists—that operate in markets characterised by negative feedback that returns the economy to its static equilibrium or its stationary equilibrium growth path. In the latter, the behaviour of the economy is seen as the result of many different forces—especially technological changes—that evolve endogenously over time, that are subject to many exogenous shocks, and that often operate in markets subject to positive feedback and in which agents operate under conditions of genuine uncertainty.[1]

One major characteristic that distinguishes the two visions is *stationarity* for Newtonian economics and *non-stationarity* for the Darwinian. In the stationary equilibrium of a static general equilibrium model and the equilibrium growth path of a Solow-type growth model, the path by which the equilibrium is reached has no effect on the equilibrium values themselves. *In short, history does not matter*. In contrast, an important characteristic of the Darwinian vision is path dependency: what happens now has important implications for what will happen in the future. *In short, history does matter*.

In this paper, we consider, and cast doubts on, the stationarity properties of models in the Newtonian tradition. These doubts, if sustained, have important implications for understanding virtually all aspects of macroeconomics, including of long term economic growth, shorter term business cycles, and stabilisation policy.

1 Two Worlds Views[2]

1.1 Views in Which History Does Not Matter

Virtually all mainline macro theories share a stationary equilibrium approach to understanding the economy. The old fashioned Keynesian model, expressed in its simplest form as IS-LM, had a short run equilibrium that did not necessarily

[1] The use of the terms Darwinian and Newtonian here is meant to highlight the significant difference in equilibrium concept employed in the two groups of theories that we contrast, the evolutionary and what we call equilibrium with deviations (EWD) theories. Not all evolutionary theories, including the one employed here, are strictly speaking Darwinian in the sense that they embody replication and selection. We use the term, Darwinian to highlight the critical equilibrium concept of a path dependent, non-ergodic, historical process employed in Darwinian and evolutionary theories and to draw the contrast between that and the negative feedback, usually unique, ergodic equilibrium concept employed in Newtonian and EWD theories.

[2] We have compared and contrasted many aspects of these two views in Lipsey et al. (2005: Chapter 2, hereafter LCB) and here we give only a brief outline to set the stage for what follows.

produce full employment. When it was subsequently closed by a simple Phillips curve, it had the property that, for any given money supply, a long run equilibrium emerged. Price level changes restored equilibrium income, Y^*, whenever actual income, Y, deviated from Y^* because of either expenditure or monetary shocks. In their critiques of the simple Phillips curve, Phelps and Freidman assumed a general equilibrium determination of Y^* and its corresponding equilibrium level of unemployment, U^*, the natural rates of national income and unemployment, deviations from which were caused by misperceptions of price signals. This treatment led to the expectations-augmented Phillips curve and the accelerationist hypothesis. According to the latter, any deviations from Y^* and U^* would set up price level changes that restored equilibrium or, if the monetary authorities insisted on validating the inflation with corresponding increase in the money supply (or 'validating' a deflation with corresponding reductions in the money supply), the inflation rate would accelerate in the face of a persistent positive output gap ($Y > Y^*$) or decelerate in the face of a persistent negative gap ($Y < Y^*$). The early New Classical models associated with Robert Lucas also used this concept of a general equilibrium in which markets were always cleared and were now inhabited by agents who had rational expectations and who maximized inter-temporally. These individuals did confuse relative and absolute price changes and were thus led to depart from equilibrium temporarily until the real market conditions were understood. Later, the new Keynesian models, and the so-called New Keynesian synthesis, followed New Classical economists in assuming rational inter-temporal maximisation and, since money wages were not sticky, a labour market that cleared continually. But output gaps still occurred because of assumed costs of changing goods prices. This implied that real marginal cost deviated temporarily from its full equilibrium value, and so output gaps continued to be part of this class of models. This branch of modern macroeconomic analysis uses the new Keynesian Phillips curve (as in Calvo) and despite its many NeoClassical features, including no involuntary unemployment, fully rational expectations and long run maximization, is referred to as 'New Keynesian.'

In all of these theories history does not matter (unless the system becomes unstable). There is a unique equilibrium which, if disturbed, is restored by an automatic adjustment mechanism and the path of the economy following on any disturbance and subsequent adjustment (if modelled at all) has no effect on the final outcome, which is to a restoration of the situation *ante bellum*. These a-historical theories all share the following characteristics: (1) there is an equilibrium or natural rate of national income, Y^*; (2) output gaps that are positive ($Y - Y^* > 0$) or negative ($Y - Y^* < 0$) can occur (for various reasons depending on the theory in question); (3) the rate of inflation is positively related to the output gap; (4) if the money supply is held constant (or changing at a slower rate than the price level is changing), output gaps of either sign will be removed by price level adjustments (possibly faster in the face of negative gaps than positive gaps); (5) if the money supply is changing at a rate that equals or exceeds the rate of change of the price level, the inflation rate will accelerate in the face of a positive gap and decelerate in the face of a negative gap; (6) in all but the New Keynesian theory, there is also a natural rate of unemployment, the NAIRU or U^*, deviations from which are a function of deviations of Y from its natural rate, Y^*. In New Keynesian theory, although employment changes as Y changes, the labour market clears continuously so that full employment is always maintained. (Very recently, a few new Keynesians have been extending this framework to admit unemployment.) It follows from these characteristics that there is only one level of income and of unemployment that are consistent with a constant, non-accelerating rate of inflation, the natural rates.[3] It is this implication of all of these equilibrium theories that we investigate in Sect. 3. In contrast, with evolutionary theories, which are all subject to constant not fully foreseeable changes and the latest New Classical Theories in which the economy is always in optimal equilibrium, these theories all have an equilibrium (either of the static or balanced growth variety), from which the economy can diverge, but to which it is returned by equilibrating forces. Since there is no collective name for the theories in this group, we name them *equilibrium with deviations*, or "EWD," theories.

The latest versions of New Classical macroeconomics do not contain income gaps nor Phillips curves of any form. Instead the behaviour of fully informed representative agents creates an equilibrium growth path by acting in response to an exogenous, stationary, stochastic, process that generates a constant long run trend of technological change. The level of output (the identical actual and natural levels) follows a cyclical pattern since there are persistence-generating mechanisms in the model. For example, the capital-stock accumulation identity makes technology shocks in one period matter for a number of future periods but not in the long run. Since all markets always clear, and all agents are farsighted and rational, all realised levels of income are equilibrium levels, representing optimal adjustments to the long term growth path and the disturbances around it. It follows that there are no output gaps and no role for policy to improve the behaviour of the whole economy. The proponents of this view regard the theory's ability to track the observed (and in some cases stylised) macroeconomic facts as a test of the theory, and it is this "test" that we investigate in Sect. 2 of our paper.

1.2 The Evolutionary Theory in Which History Matters

The assumptions concerning technology in evolutionary economics stand in sharp contrast to the stationarity assumptions of New Classical and EWD theories. Evolutionary economics accepts and builds on the understanding that continual but uneven endogenously induced technological changes are a fact of ordinary observation. These continually alter the structure of the economy, causing waves of

[3] U^* must be a NAIRU for reasons given in the text. However, in a model in which markets are allowed to be temporarily out of equilibrium, there may be another level of U that is a temporary NAIRU because of asymmetries in the speed of upward and downward adjustment to excess demands and excess supplies. See Tobin (1998).

serially correlated investment expenditure that are a major cause of cycles. These also drive long term growth in the sense that, without it, growth would eventually stop. In doing so, they continually transform our economic, social and political structures.

This is not the place to give an historical discussion of the origins of evolutionary economics. Suffice it to mention that the nineteenth century economist Rae (1905) saw that the existence of endogenous technological change upset many of the apparent policy implications of classical and neoclassical economics. Marx (1957) understood the transforming effects of technological changes on the social, economic and political structures of society. Veblen (1953) emphasised the importance of institutions and a deeper understanding of consumers' tastes beyond mere self-centred utility maximisation. Schumpeter (1934) made the entrepreneur-innovator the centrepiece of his dynamic view of the economy. Nelson and Winter (1982) wrote a seminal piece that pointed the way to the modern analysis of evolutionary change. Arthur (1994) and Lipsey et al. (2005) studied the scale effects that typically accompany technological developments, while Nathan Rosenberg (e.g., 1982) pioneered empirical research into the anatomy, causes and consequence of endogenous technological change.

Although evolutionary economics has no agreed canonical model, it's theorising has many common characteristics. The economy is seen as evolving continuously along path-dependent trajectories that are largely driven by technological changes generated endogenously by private-sector, profit-seeking agents competing in terms of new products, new processes and new forms of organisation and by public sector activities in such places as universities and government research laboratories. Because agents in both of these sectors make R&D decisions under conditions of genuine uncertainty (not just risk), there is no unique line of behaviour that maximises their expected profits. Thus agents are better understood as groping into an uncertain future in a purposeful, profit- or utility-seeking manner, rather than as maximizing their profits or utility.

When an economy is evolving under conditions of uncertainty, it cannot have a unique equilibrium balanced growth path (trend or difference stationary) along which agents wish to do the same thing period by period and to which it will return if disturbed. Such an equilibrium requires that the past be repeatable and that disturbances leave no trace once their effects have been worked out—history does not matter. In contrast, in evolutionary economics the trajectory of economic growth is non-unique because if agents could return to the same initial conditions, there is no guarantee that they would retrace their steps exactly since the outcome of successive actions subject to uncertainty may be different at each point in time. Technological changes are also path dependant. Scientific and technological advances build on themselves and those technological advances that firms decide to search for today depend on their current capabilities, and these in turn depend on what they have decided to search for in the past, and on how successful they were in these endeavours.[4] Thus, the concept of a unique stable equilibrium growth path is not applicable to an economy whose growth is being driven by endogenous technical change—history does matter.[5]

The discussion in this section goes a long way towards explaining why, in spite of much work both theoretical and empirical on the characteristics and behaviour of evolving economies, no generally agreed canonical model has been expounded. Canonical models, of theories such as the New Classical, the neoclassical and the New Keynesian, tend to be universal. Even when they contain random elements, they are deterministic at a quite abstract level in the sense that, given certain conditions, growth will always occur, while booms and slumps are always generated by the same disturbance mechanism and market disturbances are eliminated by a negative feedback mechanism. In short, the details of economic history do not matter for what we observe over all time periods. In contrast, the evolutionary view makes specific historical events matter. With growth, the Industrial Revolution happened when and where it did for very specific historical reasons. Although there is debate about the actual causes, most historians agree that these causes were specific to Europe at the time.[6] With cycles, although a major cause of cycles are successive waves of investment expenditure following on the innovation of new technologies, many other historical events can exert major influences. For example, major causes of the great recession that began in 2008 were the new financial innovation of derivates (enabled largely by the information handling capabilities of electronic computers) and a change in the regulatory structure followed, for example, by a change Wall Street partnerships becoming public corporations and in the process altering the incentive structure from concern with long term profitability to concern with short term volume. Agents often learn from transitory disturbances in ways that significantly affect their subsequent behaviour. For example, the exceptionally high interest rates in the early 1980s (short term rates of over 20 %) provided the incentive to learn how to manage previously idle transactions balances and because the fixed costs of such learning was then a bygone, the behaviour persisted when interest rates returned to more normal levels. No one-size-fits-all canonical model can handle such diverse, context-specific, current and historical events.

[4] See LCB (2005: 77–82) for a discussion of the relevance of path dependence and a reply to those who doubt its importance.

[5] Most evolutionary economists accept that for many issues in micro economics, comparative static equilibrium models are useful. Also, there is nothing incompatible between the evolutionary world view and the use of Keynesian models—of which IS-LM closed by an expectations-augmented Phillips curve is the prototype—to study such short run phenomenon as stagflation and the impact effects of monetary and fiscal policy shocks. Problems arise, however, when such analyses are applied to situations in which technology is changing endogenously over time periods that are relevant to the issues being studied. Depending on the issue at hand, this might be as short as a few months.

[6] Pomeranz (2000) gives a dissenting view and we give our objections to it in LCB: 267.

2 Does History Matter for Growth and Cycles?

Nelson and Plosser's (1982) paper, and the subsequent voluminous time series empirical work on unit roots and cointegration, are generally taken to indicate that most macro time series are stationary, at least in differences (if not levels). These results are assumed to justify the assumptions of New Classical growth models and RBC theory in which growth takes place along a stationary trend or balanced (first difference stationary) path. The conclusion that the business cycle is stationary is then taken to support the classical dichotomy in which monetary and other shocks have no permanent effect on the equilibrium values of the real variables.

In this section we investigate these accepted propositions by conducting empirical analysis on data generated from a model whose structure we know. In this model, endogenous behaviour that determines the pattern of technological development and economic growth is explicitly non-stationary (trend and difference) and also contains significant elements of genuine uncertainty. Thus the model exhibits non-stationary behaviour and path-dependence because historical events and context have persistent effects—history matters. Following the practice of RBC theorists we analyse the business cycle properties of the simulated data generated by this model by matching its growth rates to actual Canadian data from the period 1961–2007 and find that their growth properties match the Canadian data. We then filter the simulated data and match it to the standard RBC properties. Then, following the practice of time series econometricians, we perform a time series econometric analysis of the unfiltered data.

2.1 The Simulation Model

The simulations performed in this paper utilize the model of Carlaw and Lipsey (2011), which is an elaboration of the model presented in Carlaw and Lipsey (2006). The following paragraphs outline the model whose details can be seen in Appendix. Italicised statements indicate alterations made to the model for purposes of the present paper. The model we now use has three sectors, each with several production activities and each containing many agents. Each has a production function that displays diminishing marginal returns to a fixed aggregate stock of a composite resource, R. Research labs in the pure knowledge sector produce a set of flows of pure knowledge concerning the various classes of technology such as power, organization, materials, transportation and information and communication: g_t^x, $x \in [1, X]$, where X is the number of such labs. The labs occasionally discover a new technology that has the potential to evolve into a GPT in one of these classes. The timing of these discoveries is determined by a random process that is not known by the labs *but that is influenced by the allocation of resources to both pure and applied R&D.*[7] *Increasing the resources to such R&D increases the likelihood of GPTs arriving in any period, making the distribution of the random arrival process for GPTs non-stationary.*

The existing stock of potentially useful pure knowledge is embodied in the new technology and then its efficiency slowly evolves according to a logistic function to become increasingly useful in applied research and in most cases to eventually become a fully fledged GPT. The Y research facilities in the applied R&D sector produce flows of knowledge, a_t^y, $y \in [1, Y]$, that are useful both in the consumption sector's I industries and the pure research sector's X labs, the latter being a feedback that is well established in the technology literature.[8] The consumption sector produces consumption goods that use the results of the various forms of applied research in their production functions. Technological structure is modelled in two ways. First, each sector has a number of production units, each with its own distinct production function that allows for variation in intra-sector technology.[9] Second, there is variation across the distinct characteristics embedded in the set of production functions for each of the three sectors—consumption, applied R&D and pure knowledge. *To simulate the technology shocks of the real business cycle model, we allow stationary random processes to influence the period by period realizations of investment and output by pre-multiplying the production functions within each sector by a normally distributed random variable with a mean of unity and a variance calibrated to match the stylized RBC facts.*The model contains many sources of uncertainty in invention and innovation with respect to any new technology including those that eventually become GPTs. In particular, the following things are uncertain: (1) how much potentially useful pure knowledge will be discovered by any given amount of research activity; (2) the timing of the discovery of new technologies; (3) just how productive a new technology will be over its lifetime *although the prior accumulation of GPTs within a given class positively influences the maximum productive potential of each subsequent potential GPT within that class, making the distribution of the potential impact of each non-stationary*; (4) how well the new technology will interact with technologies of other classes that are already in use; (5) how long a new technology that becomes a GPT will continue to evolve in usefulness; (6) when it will begin to be replaced by a new superior version of a GPT of the same class (7) how long that displacement will take and (8) if the displacement will be more or less complete (as were mechanical calculators) or if the older technology will remain entrenched in particular niches (as does steam that remains an important source of power for generating electricity).

As a result of these uncertainties the model displays considerable path dependency with both favourable and unfavourable occurrences affecting the future course of national income. Thus the model never settles down into a growth path that is stationary in its first differences.

[7] We allow the critical value of the arrival parameter λ^* in Carlaw and Lipsey (2011) to be a decreasing function of the accumulated amount of resources devoted to pure and applied R&D.

[8] See, for example, Rosenberg (1982: Chapter 7).

[9] For simplicity in the simulations reported below we let $X = Y = I = 3$.

2.2 Business Cycle Properties of the Simulated Data

We ran two classes of simulations of the model, calibrating it to produce annualized data. In Class 2 simulations we used all of the italicised additions to our 2011 JEE model listed above. In Class 1 simulations, we did not use the random disturbances on the production functions in the consumption and investment sectors designed to simulate the disturbances postulated in real business cycle theory. From each class of simulation we generated artificial time series data for (1) output, measured as consumption plus investment, (2) consumption, measured as the aggregate of all types of consumption goods, (3) labour, measured as the marginal product of labour times the total of all resources R,[10] (4) investment, measured as the flow output from all lines of applied R&D plus the input value of resources devoted to pure knowledge creation and (5) capital, measured as the stocks of useful accumulated knowledge from the pure and applied sectors. We ran hundreds of simulations in each of the two classes of simulation to ensure that the real growth properties that we use here were consistent with the average results produced by the model. Here we present a representative run from each class of the simulations, both containing 450 observations.

In Table 1 we compare the growth properties of the simulated data with those of the Canadian aggregate data for the period 1961–2007. For Canada, output is GDP, consumption is consumption of non-durables, semi-durables and services, investment is gross investment in non-residential capital, and labour is total hours worked. We find that the growth properties of the simulated data closely match the Canadian data, except for the very large Canadian figure of a 5.29 % annual investment growth over the last 25 years. In our simulation, the investment growth rate is only about 3.4 %.[11]

We then filtered each of the simulated time series using a Hodric–Prescott filter set for annual data and compared their properties to the filtered Canadian data. According to RBC theory the filtered Canadian data should exhibit the following properties when compared with output: investment should be about 2.5 times more volatile, consumption should be slightly less volatile, and labour should exhibit about the same volatility. All variables except capital should be highly correlated with output.

Table 2 shows the simulated data properties for Classes 1 and 2. Investment is about as volatile as output in Class 1 but slightly more than twice as volatile in Class 2. Consumption and labour are about as volatile as output in both cases. Investment,

[10] When we came to calculate an equivalent to labour in our model, we were forced to make some simplifying assumptions. First, we assumed that R is a composite of land and raw labour and that each unit of land is uniformly endowed to each unit of labour. Second, we assumed that labour will take out some of the value of its marginal product in consumption and some in reproduction that will expand the labour supply. For simplicity, we assumed a 50:50 split.

[11] The data used for these calculations are from the Canadian Socio-economic Information and Management System Database (CANSIM).

Table 1 Actual and simulated growth properties

Average growth rate %	Class 1 simulated data (450 annual periods)	Class 2 simulated data (450 annual periods)	Canada (1961–2007)
Output	3.44	3.32	3.85
Consumption	3.44	3.33	3.03
Investment	3.46	3.27	5.29
Labour	1.91	1.85	1.58

Table 2 Basic business cycle properties

	Class 1		Class 2	
Simulated data	Standard deviation (%)	Correlation with output	Standard deviation (%)	Correlation with output
Output	8.3724	1	9.2874	1
Consumption	6.9800	0.8329	7.7145	0.8730
Investment	8.1372	0.8851	18.6727	0.7033
Labour	7.3469	0.9893	7.2318	0.9598
Capital	7.1994	0.4955	6.8392	0.4594

consumption and labour are all highly correlated with output.[12] All of these comparisons indicate that our simulated data match well with the stylized RBC facts derived from the filtered Canadian data.

2.3 *Time Series Properties of the Simulated Data*

To analyze the time series properties, we first took logs of the simulated time series data, we then ran augmented Dickey–Fuller (ADF) tests on each individual time series for levels and first differences. In all cases we also ran the KPSS and Phillips-Peron unit root tests to confirm the ADF findings. These test all indicate that the testing results presented are consistent. The data are confirmed to be either levels or difference stationary by the tests.

For the first ADF test on the log of the levels we included an intercept but no trend because we believed that this is the case least likely to reject the null hypothesis of a unit root and therefore indicate that the data are non-stationary in the log of the levels. We found, as is shown in columns 2 and 3 of Table 3, that each series from both Class 1 and Class 2 rejected the null hypothesis of a unit root at the 5 % confidence level and all but investment in Class 2 rejected the null of a unit root at the 1 % confidence level. So according to this test, all of the series were stationary in the level!

[12] The simulated data are more volatile than the Canadian data and the usual RBC simulation models. Much of the additional volatility in our simulation comes from the arrivals of the major new technologies.

Table 3 Augmented Dickey–Fuller unit root test, levels, ADF, t-statistics

	Intercept, no trend		Intercept and trend	
Log of the time series	Class 1	Class 2	Class 1	Class 2
Output	−6.134979	−5.212397	−2.237547	−7.685560
Consumption	−6.377878	−5.853145	−2.117475	−8.022857
Investment	−6.689336	−3.221415	−2.452014	−0.204417
Labour	−6.716565	−3.729299	−1.972472	−0.165856
Capital	−7.923275	−5.055750	−0.493023	−5.331387

The critical t-statistic values for the ADF test are −2.570323 at the 10 % confidence level, −2.868089 at the 5 % confidence level and −3.445445 at the 1 % confidence level for this form of the ADF test

Next we ran the ADF test on the log of the levels but included a trend in the procedure. Columns 4 and 5 of Table 3 report these results for the two classes of data. In this case for Class 1 the null hypothesis that all of the series have a unit root cannot be rejected. However, for Class 2 the null is rejected for output, consumption and capital, indicating that these are stationary in the levels while investment and labour each exhibit a unit root, indicating non-stationarity in these variables. This is closer to what we expect given the non-stationary data generating process. However, there is still a puzzle with the Class 2 data in that output, consumption and capital from the simulation that most closely matches the RBC facts exhibit trend stationarity. This is what the RBC model predicts from its stationary data generating process but not what we would expect from our non-stationary data generating process.

Having discovered that all of the data in Class 1 and some of the data in Class 2 pass the tests for unit roots in the levels, we turned our testing to first differences of the data to see if the growth rates exhibit stationarity. In first differences we initially ran the ADF test including an intercept but no linear trend. These results are reported in the second and third columns of Table 4.

We next ran the ADF test on the first differences and included both an intercept and a trend. We report these results in the fourth and fifth columns of Table 4. According to the test Class 1 seems most likely to have a trend and no unit root. (This is because the null is most strongly rejected in the case where we run the unit root tests with the intercept and trend included). Class 2 appears to have no trend and no unit root. (This is because there is very little difference between the tests run with intercept and no trend those run with both trend and intercept.) Once again this is curious because the only difference between Class 1 and Class 2 is the addition of random noise on the production functions for consumption and applied R&D activities in the model.[13] In any case, the data appear either to be stationary in first differences or, in some cases, in levels. In Class 1 the data appear to exhibit stationarity in the first difference with a trend. This comes closest to what we would expect given the non-stationary data generating process, however, as we report in the last paragraph of this section even this result is somewhat misleading.

[13] The critical value for this ADF test is −3.445445 at the 1 % confidence level.

Table 4 Augmented Dickey–Fuller unit root test, first differences, ADF, t-statistics

	Intercept, no trend		Intercept and trend	
Log of the time series	Class 1	Class2	Class 1	Class 2
Output	−5.540376	−31.63073	−8.115891	−31.83105
Consumption	−4.806436	−15.75234	−8.752848	−15.81485
Investment	−12.78157	−15.04974	−14.37239	−15.55301
Labour	−6.390322	−14.97234	−8.733609	−15.49406
Capital	−17.46262	−19.20608	−19.86257	−15.75635

The critical value for this ADF test is −3.445445 at the 1 % confidence level

We wished to verify our interpretation of our analysis thus far: that the simulated data from a non-stationary data generating process appear to exhibit stationarity, in some cases in levels and in all cases in first differences. To do this, we ran a Johansen maximum likelihood-based cointegration test on both classes of simulated data. These tests are run on the simulated data in log form with a number of lags for the vector autoregression (VAR).[14] Tables 5 and 6 support the interpretation that the data are difference stationary and possibly stationary in levels for Class1 and Class 2.

These cointegration tests can be reported in a number of ways but in all of these it appears that Class 1 exhibits four cointegrating equations according to the trace test and two cointegrating equations according to the maximum eigenvalue test while Class 2 exhibits five cointegrating equations according to both the trace and the eigenvalue tests.[15] The cointegration tests appear to confirm that the Class 1 data are difference stationary. However, the Class 2 data appear to be levels stationary as indicated by the unit root tests presented in Table 4.

When we included a trend in the unit root estimations, they seemed to better detect the underlying data generating process. So for a final exercise we ran the cointegration tests with both an intercept and a trend. These results are reported in Tables 7 and 8. It appears from these results that the Class 1 data has three cointegrating equations and Class 2 has four cointegrating equations. Thus, each set of data appears to follow a difference stationary (I1) process but with a constant trend.

We make one final empirical observation. When we look at sub-periods of the Class 1 output growth rate series and fit trends using univariate regressions, we find significant negative trends in the growth rate for some subperiods while for others we find significant positive trends in the growth rate. This leads us to conclude that while the Unit Root and cointegration tests suggest that the data are at least difference stationary (if not levels stationary) with a constant trend, they are in

[14] We use the Eviews defaults of 1 through 4.

[15] This should not be surprising since the Class 2 data showed stationarity in the unit root test of the levels for each individual time series when run with no intercept and trend. So the cointegration test should show all series as being stationary. This is strictly speaking a slight abuse of the cointegration test because it is only valid for I(1) or higher orders of integration processes.

Table 5 Unrestricted cointegration rank test, class 1, variables in logs, intercept no trend

		Johansen trace				Maximum eigenvalue		
Hypothesised no. of CE(s)	Eigenvalue	Trace statistic	0.05 critical value	Prob.[a]	Hypothesised no. of CE(s)	Max-eigen statistic	0.05 critical value	Prob.[a]
None[b]	0.175839	160.7016	69.81889	0.0000	None[b]	82.19043	33.87687	0.0000
At most 1[b]	0.089460	78.51115	47.85613	0.0000	At most 1[b]	39.82990	27.58434	0.0008
At most 2[b]	0.044385	38.68125	29.79707	0.0037	At most 2	19.29485	21.13162	0.0886
At most 3[b]	0.038305	19.38639	15.49471	0.0123	At most 3[b]	16.59963	14.26460	0.0210
At most 4	0.006536	2.786762	3.841466	0.0950	At most 4	2.786762	3.841466	0.0950

[a]MacKinnon–Haug–Michelis (1999) p-values
[b]Denotes rejection of the hypothesis at the 0.05 level

Table 6 Unrestricted cointegration rank test, class 2, variables in logs, intercept no trend

		Johansen trace				Maximum eigenvalue		
Hypothesised no. of CE(s)	Eigenvalue	Trace statistic	0.05 critical value	Prob.[a]	Hypothesised no. of CE(s)	Max-eigen statistic	0.05 critical value	Prob.[a]
None[b]	0.303026	333.2193	69.81889	0.0001	None [b]	160.6483	33.87687	0.0001
At most 1[b]	0.177553	172.5711	47.85613	0.0000	At most 1[b]	86.98447	27.58434	0.0000
At most 2[b]	0.124996	85.58662	29.79707	0.0000	At most 2[b]	59.41944	21.13162	0.0000
At most 3[b]	0.046397	26.16718	15.49471	0.0009	At most 3[b]	21.14113	14.26460	0.0035
At most 4[b]	0.011231	5.026052	3.841466	0.0250	At most 4[b]	5.026052	3.841466	0.0250

[a]MacKinnon–Haug–Michelis (1999) p-values
[b]Denotes rejection of the hypothesis at the 0.05 level

Table 7 Unrestricted cointegration rank test, class 1, variables in logs, intercept and trend

		Johansen trace				Maximum eigenvalue		
Hypothesised no. of CE(s)	Eigenvalue	Trace statistic	0.05 critical value	Prob.[a]		Max-eigen statistic	0.05 critical value	Prob.[a]
None[b]	0.177238	175.0674	88.80380	0.0000	None[b]	82.91243	38.33101	0.0000
At most 1[b]	0.089540	92.15496	63.87610	0.0000	At most 1[b]	39.86719	32.11832	0.0046
At most 2[b]	0.071274	52.28777	42.91525	0.0045	At most 2[b]	31.42529	25.82321	0.0082
At most 3	0.041637	20.86248	25.87211	0.1853	At most 3	18.07476	19.38704	0.0767
At most 4	0.006538	2.787718	12.51798	0.9007	At most 4	2.787718	12.51798	0.9007

[a]MacKinnon–Haug–Michelis (1999) p-values
[b]Denotes rejection of the hypothesis at the 0.05 level

Table 8 Unrestricted cointegration rank test, class 2, variables in logs, intercept and trend

		Johansen trace				Maximum eigenvalue		
Hypothesised no. of CE(s)	Eigenvalue	Trace statistic	0.05 critical value	Prob.[a]		Max-eigen statistic	0.05 critical value	Prob.[a]
None[b]	0.303087	339.9031	88.80380	0.0000	None[b]	160.6874	38.33101	0.0000
At most 1[b]	0.184238	179.2157	63.87610	0.0000	At most 1[b]	90.61677	32.11832	0.0000
At most 2[b]	0.127701	88.59897	42.91525	0.0000	At most 2[b]	60.79735	25.82321	0.0000
At most 3[b]	0.048845	27.80153	25.87211	0.0284	At most 3[b]	22.82459	19.38704	0.0184
At most 4	0.012321	5.517037	12.51798	0.5240	At most 4	5.517037	12.51798	0.5240

[a]MacKinnon–Haug–Michelis (1999) p-values
[b]Denotes rejection of the hypothesis at the 0.05 level

fact not stationary. The trend in the growth rate is neither constant nor of the same sign throughout the data. Yet the time series econometrics would suggest that the growth rate is stationary with a constant (very small)[16] negative trend at least in our Class 1.[17]

2.4 Implications

Our findings are that the business cycle properties of the Canadian data for the period 1961–2007 when HP filtered can be closely replicated by data generated by the inherently non-stationary model in Carlaw and Lipsey (2011) when it has been HP filtered. This finding casts doubt on the implicit conclusion of New Classical theory that the macro-economy is stationary because the RBC model with its assumed stationary equilibrium fits the filtered data. In our analysis a clearly non-stationary data generating process, once filtered, also exhibits the RBC properties of the filtered real data for Canada.

Another important finding is that standard empirical time series analysis implies that the simulated data generated from our model is difference stationary, even though we know that the data generating process bears no resemblance to the theoretically stationary equilibrium of the New Classical RBC model and New Classical growth models. The unit root and cointegration tests indicate that the simulated data is at least difference stationary with a trend and in the Class 2 example appears to be levels stationary with a trend.

Our analysis casts serious doubt on the conclusion typically drawn by New Classical theorists that the passing of tests for stationarity by real time series data shows that they were generated by stationary processes in which history does not matter. Our data also pass these tests even though (1) they were generated by a model whose processes are non-stationary and in which history does matter and (2) the differing but significant trends in the sub-periods of generated Class 1 data show that its overall growth rate is not stationary.[18]

[16] The coefficient on the trend for the ADF test (with intercept and trend) on the log difference of output in Class 1 is $-2.02e^{-05}$ with a t statistic of -5.742228.

[17] Both Class 1 and Class 2 output series exhibit a very small negative trend. This is likely due to the large initial growth rates that occur because of how the simulation is initially seeded with values.

[18] Further analysis to choose between these two interpretations will entail generating a number of simulated data sets from a model that is explicitly non-stationary to see under what conditions time series analysis will detect its non-stationary properties. For example, one stylised fact that emerges out of the historical analysis of general purpose technologies and economic growth is that sometimes the early stages of technologies that become transforming GPTs cause structural disruptions to the economy that lead to economic slowdowns for a period while they gestate and mature. This can be modelled explicitly within the Carlaw and Lipsey (2011) framework and can provide another source of non-stationarity (in terms of first differences) in the simulated data. Further analysis will reveal if the time series econometric techniques will detect these sources of

3 Does History Matter for the Economy's Output Gap/Inflation Behaviour?

We now come to the group of theories that we have termed EWD—equilibrium from which the economy can diverge temporarily. All of these theories are closed by one version or another of a Phillips curve that relates the rate of inflation to the output gap. Their key characteristics, as well as being found in the theories mentioned in the introduction, are incorporated in many econometric models of the economy. Belief in their relevance is also implicit in the behaviour of most central banks and treasury departments who measure output gaps, assume they can influence them by changes in fiscal and monetary policy, and worry about expanding the economy into the range of accelerating inflation.

In all of these theories, history does matter in the trivial sense that the economy's movement along a path towards equilibrium depends on where it was on the path yesterday. But history does not matter is the sense that the equilibrium to which the economy returns (either a static or a stationary balanced growth path) is the same as existed before it was disturbed by some shock. Because of this characteristic, most of these models display a long-run neutrality of money. A monetary disturbance can cause a gap-creating shock, but the equilibrium to which the economy returns after the effects of the shock have been worked out is not affected by the economy's behaviour during the adjustment process.

To investigate these theories empirically, we chose a key characteristic: the necessary existence of equilibrium values for output, Y^*, and unemployment, U^*. These are often called the natural rates of output and unemployment. They are the only values that are consistent with a constant level of prices and wages, or any fully anticipated, constant, non-zero rate of change of these variables. All other sustained values of Y and U must be associated either with an accelerating rate of inflation (a positive output gap) or a decelerating rate (a negative output gap). It is this basic accelerationist prediction of this group of models that we investigate in this section.

Empirical attempts to locate this required stable NAIRU over the last several decades have not been successful.[19] In response, more recent efforts have been directed at locating a time varying NAIRU, often by using a Kalman filter. In this section, we attempt the same and argue that our results cast serious doubt on the existence of a NAIRU that has any operative significance. We study data for five OECD countries, France, Italy, Spain, the UK and the US.[20] Space limitations allow

---

non-stationarity in the data. Until that time, we conclude that existing tests do not support the conclusion that the real data have been generated by stationary processes in which the details of history do not matter.

[19] The voluminous empirical work concerning the Phillips curve and the NAIRU is briefly discussed in the last section of this paper.

[20] The data are for the standardised unemployment rates and consumer prices provided by the OECD at http://oecd-stats.ingenta.com and accessed 1 August 2010. They begin at different years: France 1977, Italy 1978, Spain 1977, the UK 1970, and the US 1960. We use all the data available from that source since inter-country comparisons are not of major importance to our study.

us to present most of our graphs for only one country and we chose the UK. Most of the results for the other countries are given verbally or in tables.

3.1 The Kalman Filter Estimates of a Time-Varying NAIRU

We estimate a time-varying NAIRU using the Kalman filter which calculates the time series of the NAIRU through a recursive error adjustment mechanism:

$$U^*{}_t = U^*_{t-1} + \varepsilon_t \tag{1}$$

subject to the existence of some form of the accelerationist hypothesis, which is almost invariably imposed in linear form:

$$\dot{\pi}_t \equiv \pi_t - \pi_{t-1} = \beta(U_t - U^*{}_t) + \xi_t \tag{2}$$

The fitting procedure seeds the recursive process in (1) with some initial U, usually the U of the first period under consideration, and then uses a maximum likelihood procedure subject to (2). This procedure makes the estimated NAIRU vary from period to period so as to make it the best possible fit for the accelerationist hypothesis. It is meant, therefore, to account for shifts in the NAIRU caused by auto regressive processes in factors that influence it.

If we let $\pi^e_t = \pi_{t-1}$ and $\xi_t \sim N(0, \sigma)$ in (2), we get its implied Phillips curve:

$$\pi_t = \beta(U_t - U^*_t) + \pi^e_t, \quad \text{where}\, \beta < 0. \tag{3}$$

Although (2) is commonly used in Kalman filter estimates, the implied linear Phillips curve is not altogether satisfactory (1) because with $U \in [0, 100]$ the inflation rate approaches a maximum as U approaches zero, a maximum that is lower the lower is the value of U^* and (2), the Phillips curve is symmetric around U^* rather than being steeper when $U < U^*$ than when $U > U^*$.

A Phillips curve that has more desirable characteristics is:

$$\pi_t = b\left[\left(\frac{U^*}{U}\right) - 1\right] + \pi^e_t, \quad \text{where b} > 0. \tag{4}$$

This curve shows inflation increasing without limit as U approaches zero and deflation increasing at a diminishing rate as U approaches 100 %. However, it has a positive slope in contrast to the usual negative slope of the Phillips curve. This reversal is made solely because the Kalman filter that we use in EViews cannot handle non-linear values of the state variable U^*.

If we again let $\pi^e_t = \pi_{t-1}$, the acceleration equation for this curve becomes:

$$\dot{\pi}_t = \pi_t - \pi_{t-1} = b\left[\left(\frac{U^*}{U}\right) - 1\right] \tag{5}$$

In what follows, we estimate the time varying U^* using both the non-linear constraint of (5) and the more commonly used but less satisfactory linear constraint

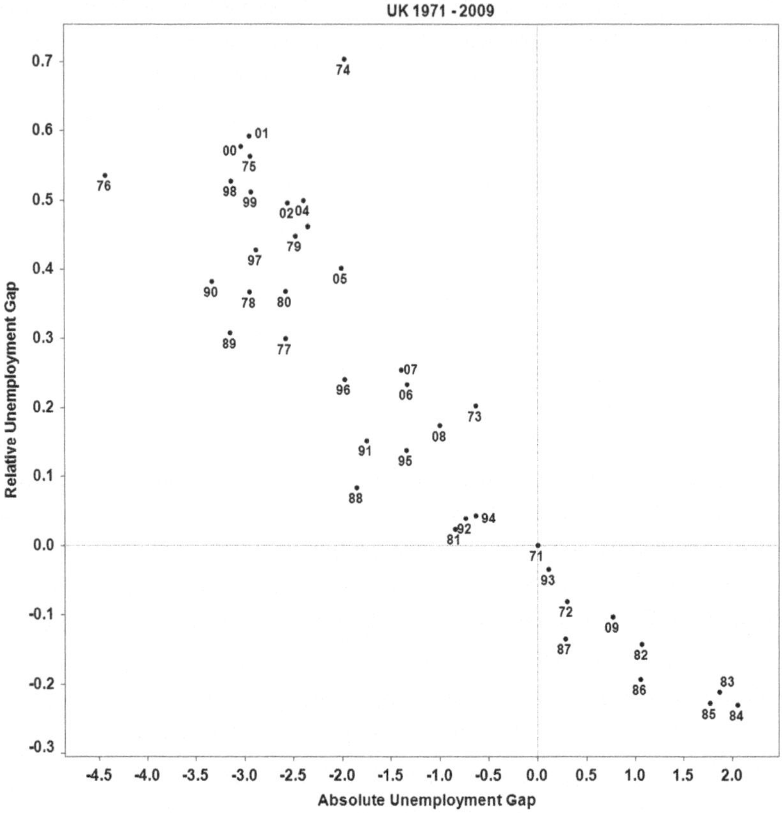

Fig. 1 The relative and absolute measure of the unemployment

of (2).[21] We refer to the NAIRU estimated using the linear constraint as U^{*1} and estimated by the nonlinear constraint as U^{*2}. We call $U - U^{*1}$ 'the absolute form of the unemployment gap', and $(U^{*2}/U) - 1$ the 'the relative form'. Figure 1 compares these two measures for the UK. As expected, the two are negatively related in all five countries with the dispersions being smaller the larger the absolute unemployment gap $(U - U^{*1})$.[22]

3.2 *The Sensitivity of the* U* *Estimates*

A little experimentation showed that the Kalman filter estimates of U^* for any one year are sensitive to the period over which the estimation is made. Figure 2 shows

[21] The data used in the following estimations can be obtained in an excel spreadsheet form from either author email: kenneth.carlaw@ubc.ca or rlipsey@sfu.ca.

[22] If each absolute gap is associated with the same U^*, the two measures will be perfectly correlated along a curved line. If some absolute gap's are associated with different U^{*s}, there will be a scatter of these relative gap values around their associated absolute gap values.

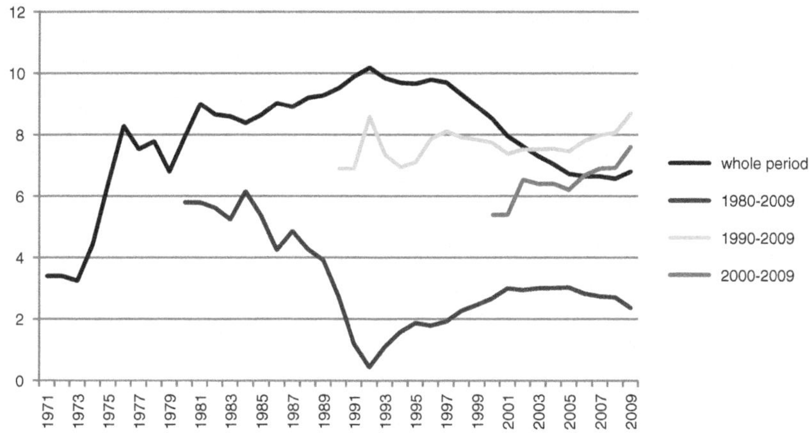

Fig. 2 UK NAIRU estimated over various time periods

Table 9 Estimated 2009 values for the U^{*2} when the estimation period begins in various years

Country	U^{*2f} (estimations begin in bracketed year)	U^{*2s} (all estimations begin in 1990)
France	10.3 (1978)	12.9
Italy	9.2 (1979)	9.6
Spain	5.4 (1978)	15.6
UK	6.8 (1971)	8.7
USA	5.8 (1960)	8.5

four different estimates for United Kingdom's U^{*2} that start in 1971, 1980, 1990 and 2000 respectively and all end in 2009. The value of U^* for the year 2009 estimated from each of these U^{*2} series is respectively 6.8, 2.4, 8.7 and 7.6.[23]

Inspection of the scatters for inflation and unemployment for the whole period suggested to us that there may have been a change in the relation somewhere around 1990. This is about the time that many central banks had got inflation more or less under control after a bout of deflation-inducing unemployment in the 1980s, after which expectations of a low and stable inflation rate became established. To give the NAIRU the best chance of doing what is expected of it in EWD theories, we estimated U^{*1} and U^{*2} over two periods, the full range over which we had data, which we termed U^{*1f} and U^{*2f}, and over the shorter period starting in 1990, which we termed U^{*1s} and U^{*2s}. The values of U^* for the year 2009 estimated from U^{*2f} and U^{*2s} are shown in Table 9. With the exception of Italy, the 2009 values for NAIRU are substantially different when they are estimated from a U^* fitted over the entire period and over the shorter period.

[23] The surprisingly low figure where the filter estimation starts in 1980 illustrates how sensitive U^* estimates are to the historical period over which they are made.

3.3 Does the Estimated Gap Explain Acceleration?

The Kalman filter will always provide estimates of a time varying U^* that is independent of the structure of any EWD model. So obtaining statically significant estimates of β in the linear version of the gap or a b in the non-linear version is not a test of the predicted existence of a NAIRU with the required properties. We consider two ways in which these estimated time-varying values can be used to make such a test.

The first way is to test some key prediction of the GE model that involves U^*. For this we use the accelerationist hypothesis that is basic to all equilibrium models that assume full rationality in the neoclassical sense. We relate the acceleration in the inflation rate to the unemployment gap measured as $U - U^{*2}$. In doing this, we are not just rediscovering the Kalman filter estimates. The filter estimates U^* as a value that varies in each time period so as to give the best fit to the acceleration hypothesis, the variations being assumed to be the result of the influences that cause U^* to shift. In our test, we use the estimated U^{*2} to calculate the relative unemployment gap and then relate this to the acceleration of inflation, forcing the regression line to pass through the origin in conformity with the prediction that zero acceleration should occur if and only if $U = U^*$.[24] This test has the advantage that it goes directly to the theoretical prediction that is of most concern to policymakers: that at any one time there is one and only one value for U (and correspondingly for Y) that is consistent with a stable inflation rate; for other values that rate either accelerates or decelerates continually.

We fitted the relation

$$\dot{\pi}_t = c\left[\left(\frac{U_t^{*2}}{U_t}\right) - 1\right] + \xi_t \qquad (6)$$

to the data for all five countries, first using U^{*2f} and then U^{*2s}, expecting a significant positive value for the slope coefficient c. We made this test over our two time periods. Because the series for U^{*s} seemed less volatile than U^{*f}, we thought U^{*s}, being less volatile than U^{*l} would give the hypothesis a better chance of passing test than U^{*f}. Figure 3 shows the results for the UK for both periods. The two relations have the right sign but are not statically significant.

The results for all the countries are reported in Table 10. The c coefficients estimated over the long and short periods for France and the long period for Italy have the wrong sign. Only the US and Spain over the long period show any a statistically significant relation. Over the shorter period, however, none of the c

[24] There is a possible problem in conducting this test since $U = U^*$ is predicted to be consistent with any stable inflation rate. For this to be a problem in practice we would have to have two or more successive years in which U stayed approximately equal to U^* (say $U = \pm\, 0.5U^*$ while the inflation rate stayed approximately constant over the period. However, such a situation has not arisen in any of our data.

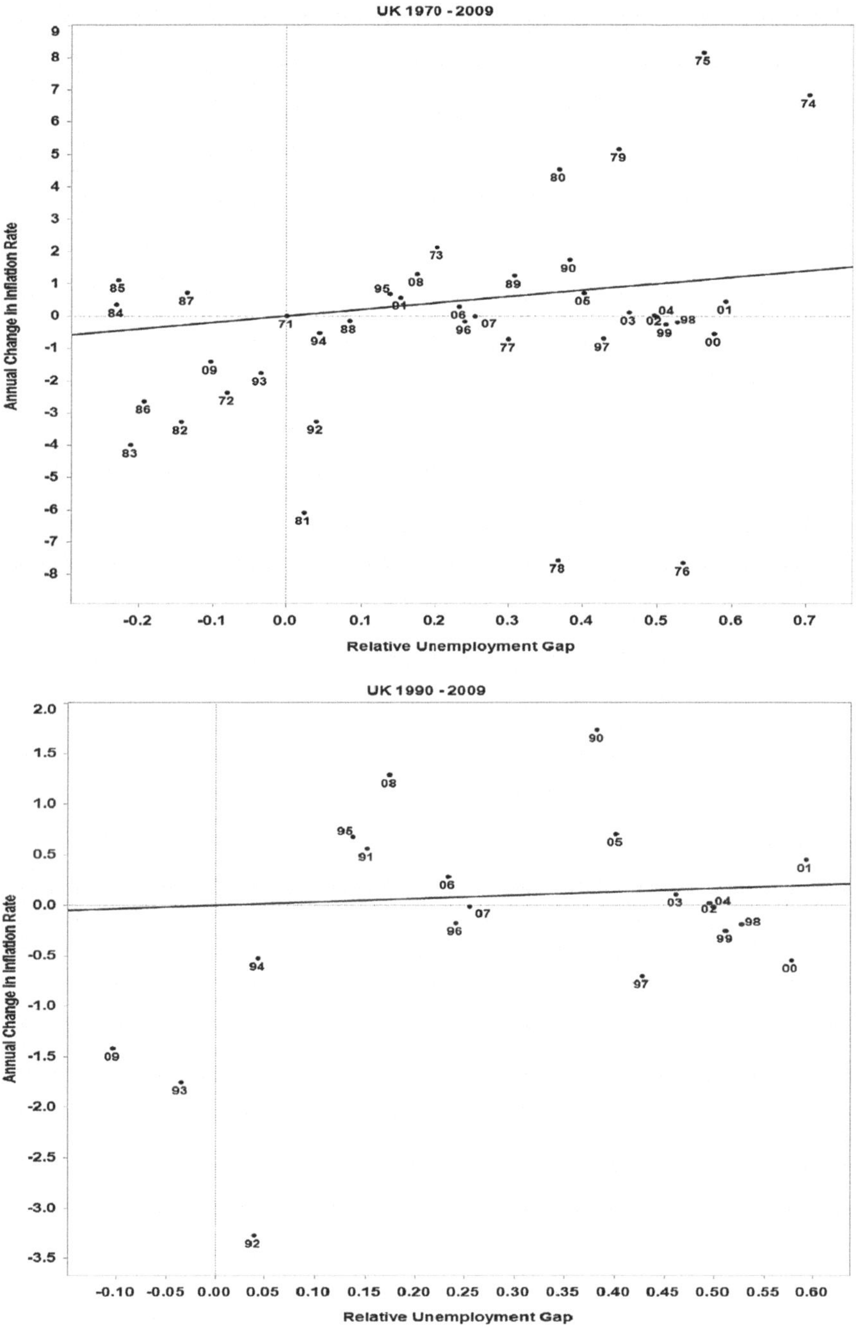

Fig. 3 Acceleration of inflation related to the relative unemployment gap

Table 10 Changes in the inflation rate related to two relative unemployment gap measures (estimates printed in Italic are significant)

Country	Whole period	Whole period	1990–2009	1990–2009
	Estimated *b*	Estimated *c*	Estimated *b*	Estimated *c*
France	*4.25445*	−0.199	1.811685	−0.087
	(1.309119)	(0.917)	(1.305114)	(0.707)
Italy	*4.854445*	−1.812	0.131584	0.233
	(1.186975)	(0.827)	(0.995747)	(1.081)
Spain	−0.084508	*1.205*	0.968721	0.479
	(0.631162)	*(0.464)*	(1.169691)	(0.668)
UK	3.134990	2.001	0.646443	0.539
	(2.104695)	(1.447)	(1.16911)	(0.670)
USA	*3.126144*	*2.519*	1.622797	0.134
	(1.330744)	*(0.941)*	(1.120825)	(0.449)

values are statistically significant, including those for the US and Spain. Indeed the *t* statistics are less than unity in all five cases.

Notice that the slope coefficient, *c*, differs from, and always has a lower significance coefficient than that of the *b* in the Kalman filter equation. The reason is that the Kalman filter provides the estimate of *U** in each year that makes the accelerationist hypothesis look as favourable as possible, while in our regressions we are testing the ability of the *U** so estimated for each year in conjunction with the actual *U* to predict the acceleration of inflation in that year. (Almost identical results were found when we related the absolute measure of the gap, U^{*1f} and U^{*1s}, to the acceleration of inflation, $\pi = d\left(U_t^* - U_t\right) + \in_t$, the only qualitative difference being that the long-period coefficient for Italy had the correct sign.)[25]

A second method of testing this aspect of the EWD model is by relating changes in *U** to changes in the model itself rather than using a mechanistic filter to do the job. Strictly speaking, the EWD models, or any other model with a stationary equilibrium, implies that *U** and *Y** are constant. (When there is growth and an unchanged structure, *U** and *Y*/Y* should be constant.) If they do change, this must be caused by changes in the model's exogenous variables and/or the parameters on one or more of its behavioural equations. For a direct test of the NAIRU theory, one would need to develop a formal theory of the determinants of the NAIRU's value—more formal, for example, than Friedman's statement that it was "the value ground out by the Walrasian equations". Then, when these determinants changed, alterations in the value of the NAIRU would be predicted. These predicted values could then be checked against the U^{*s} estimated from the Kalman equation. To the best of our knowledge no one has attempted to do take this crucial second step.

[25] The estimated *d* coefficient values, this time expected to be negative, were for the short and long periods respectively, France: 0.046 (0.115), 0.024 (0.056); Italy: −0.136 (0.105), −0.064 (0.134); Spain: *−0.090 (0.031)*, 0.078 (0.065); UK: −0.116 (0.239), −0.079 (0.118); USA: −0.*746 (0.176)*, −0.097 (0.120).

In the absence of such a test, we can attempt to calculate what changes in U^* would have to occur from year to year to make the acceleration hypothesis fit the data. To do this fully would require a major study of its own. In the absence of such a study, we can make a rough approximation as follows. First, we use the absolute value of the unemployment gap. As shown in Fig. 1, this is not a bad approximation to the more satisfactory relative gap and it is the definition that has been used by those writers who have used the Kalman filter to estimate U^*. Thus using

$$\pi_t = e\left(U_t - U_t^*\right) \tag{7}$$

yields a new estimate for U^* which we term U^{*3}

$$U_t^{*3} = U_t - \frac{\dot{\pi}_t}{e} \tag{8}$$

The obvious way to obtain a value of e for each country is to use the β value from the Kalman filter in the linear form of the acceleration equation. We show the series for all our countries in Fig. 4 for the period 1990–2009. We use only this later period because all of the data show much less variability than they do over the earlier period so that the NAIRU would also be expected to be less variable than over the longer period. Nonetheless, an inspection of the four parts in Fig. 4 makes it clear that U^{*3} (shown as U^{*3} in the figure) is highly variable even over this more stable period. We summarise these results by calculating the ratio of the variance in U^{*3s} to U over the period. These values are 8.01 for France, 7.53 for Spain, 15.85 for the UK and 1.83 for the US.[26] So to explain the observed acceleration of inflation using a linear acceleration curve, the NAIRU would have to change nearly twice as much as the unemployment figures themselves changed in the US and many, many time more than twice in the other four countries. Thus, as a first approximation, the supporters of a time varying NAIRU that is explained from within any EWD model would have to show how changes in the model's parameters and exogenous variables, plus some random noise, combined to produce the highly variable time series of U^{*3s} as shown in Fig. 4. This seems to us to be a nearly impossible task and, even if it could be accomplished, it would spell the end of predictions based on a U^* that was changing only slowly or occasionally.

---

[26] Italy is omitted because the Kalman filter estimate of its β coefficient over the shorter period is almost zero and completely insignificant statistically. Thus massive variations in U^{*3} are required to create a sufficiently large unemployment gap to explain the observed variations in the acceleration of inflation. To check Italy, we estimated its coefficient e in (8) by the alternative method of fitting that equation to the data for U and $\dot{\pi}$. We then calculated its U^{*3} for each period and found it to be not dissimilar from those for the other countries, but still more variable with a ratio of the variance of U^{*3} to U of 84.57.

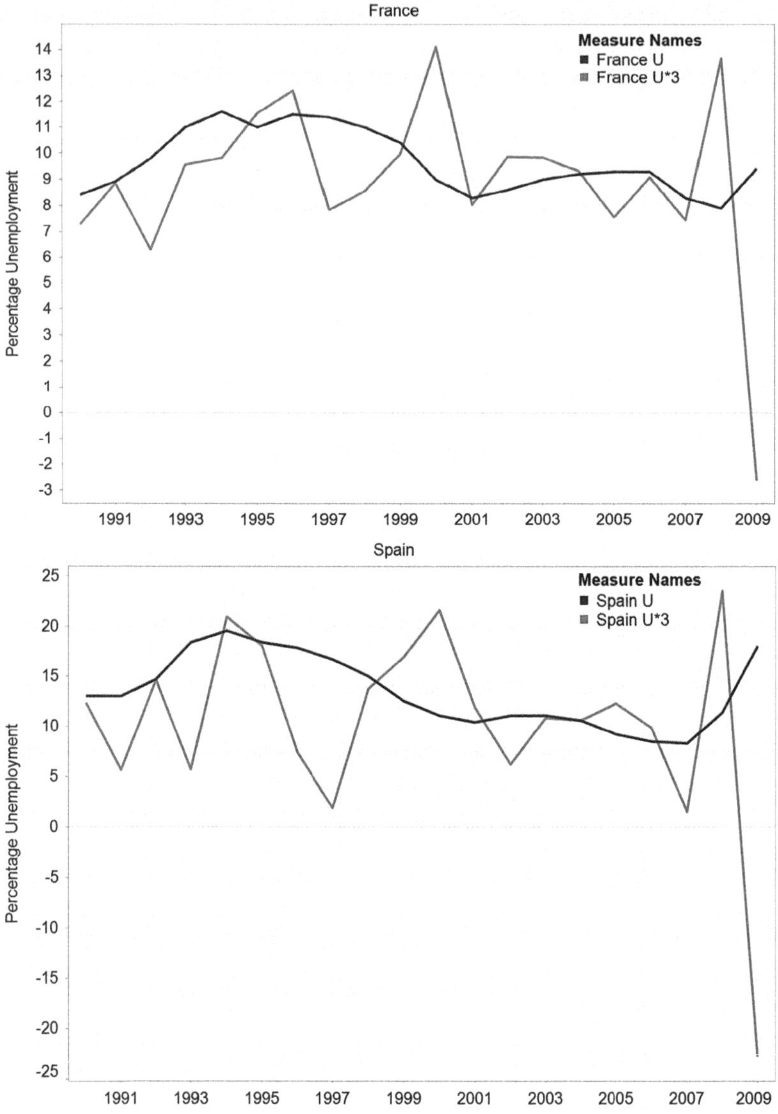

Fig. 4 (continued)

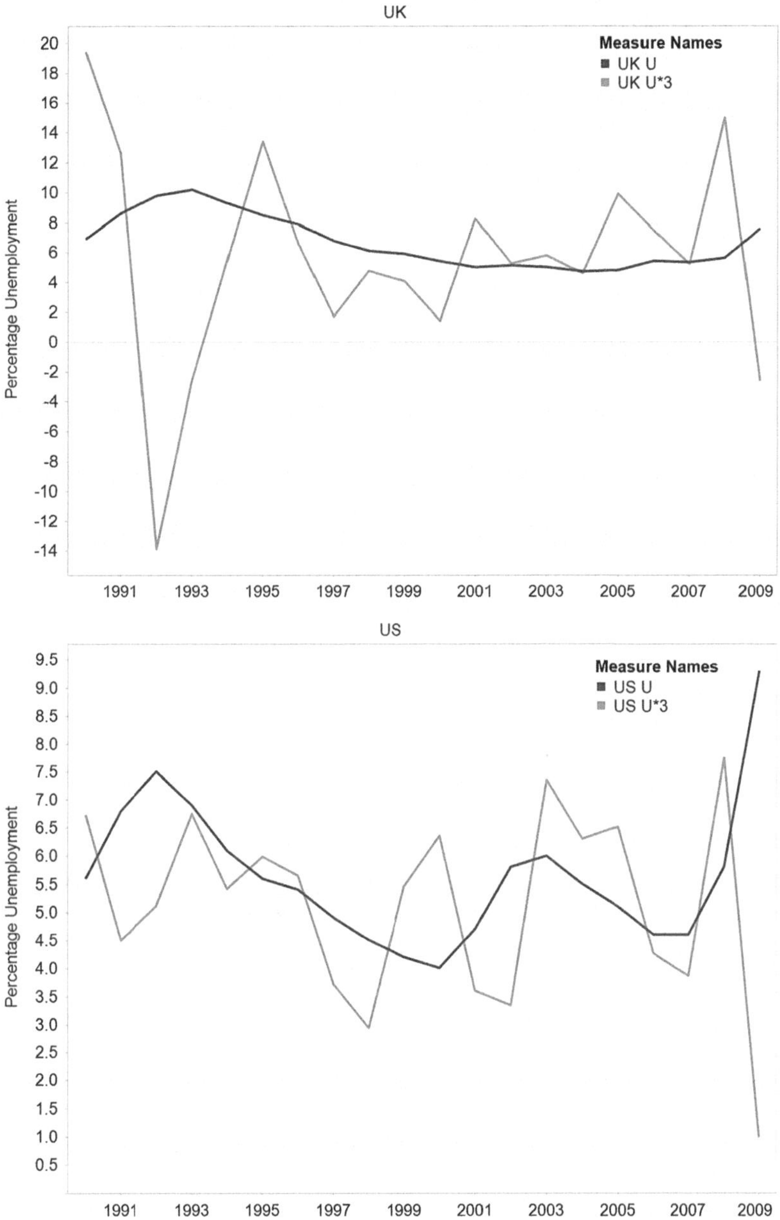

Fig. 4 U^{*3}: estimated value that U^* must take on to make the New Classical theory correctly predict the acceleration of inflation from 1990 to 2009

3.4 Implications

Much earlier econometric work has shown that no static NAIRU can be discerned in the data from most countries over the last 2–3 decades. Our Kalman filter estimates of the NAIRU for each of the six countries confirms this lack of structural stability over either the whole period for which comparable OECD data are available or the shorter one starting in 1990.

This leaves the possibility to save the accelerationist hypothesis and all the EWD models that require it, as a NAIRU that varies over time. When estimates are made of a varying NAIRU that give the best fit on the assumption that the accelerationist hypothesis does hold ((1) and (2) and (1) and (8)), the results do not provide any reliable data for dividing a range of accelerating inflation in which $U < U^*$ from a range of decelerating inflation in which $U > U^*$. Finally, if reasons why the NAIRU varies were to be specified from within EWD model, the reasons would have to vary substantially from year to year in order to explain the time series shown in Fig. 4. We conclude that our evidence conflicts with a key prediction of EWD models in which history does not matter in determining the short run behaviour of key macro variables.[27]

4 Conclusions

It is interesting to note that some of the concerns of those who accept the so called Neoclassical synthesis can be resolved by the evolutionary approach outlined in this paper.[28]

- The low and apparently trendless inflation rates that have prevailed in many countries since the early 1990s when their central banks accepted achieving such rates as their main goal requires EWD theorists to hold that each achieved level of unemployment and output are the natural rates, even though they have fluctuated considerably over the period. Structural changes that could cause these natural rates to fluctuate so widely from year to year are hard to imagine. In contrast, the obvious explanation, one that agrees with evolutionary economic theory, is that that there is no unique NAIRU so that the unemployment rate can vary over quite a wide range with no induced changes in the rate of either price or wage inflation (i.e., all unemployment rates within this range are NAIRUs).

[27] The NAIRU is not a merely part of what Imré Lakatos called a theory's protective belt. Instead it is part of the core of all EWD theories. Without it, the whole concept of a unique equilibrium for the economy, departure from which sets up equilibrating forces which can only be frustrated by agents making repeated errors, fails.

[28] The material in the bullet points that follow in the text are paraphrases of material in Lipsey and Scarth 2011, xxxii–xxiii).These authors give an extensive survey of the Phillip curve and NAIRU literature from the earlier times until the early twenty-first century.

For example Fortin (2001) makes this argument but without its application to evolutionary economics.

- In recent times, one common way of dealing with the empirical problems facing the new Keynesian versions of the Phillips curve and related concepts has been to assume that a subset of agents face such high decision-making costs that inter-temporal optimisation is not sensible for them. Instead, these agents follow a simple rule of thumb—they mimic the optimising agents with a one-period time lag. (See, for example, Gali and Gertler 1999.) In evolutionary theory, agents do look ahead but pervasive uncertainty implies that none can fully optimise over a very long time horizon, let alone the infinite one, as long as they are causing, or are being affected by, technological change (which applies to most producers as well as many workers and consumers). Of course, some turn out after the fact to have made good decisions and prosper while others turn out to have made bad decisions and do poorly. But this is groping behaviour based on knowledge, judgement, intuition and luck, not long-term optimisation and it does not appear to be well modelled by a dichotomy between long term maximizers and short term followers.
- There is strong evidence in the literature to support the proposition that the Phillips curve is better regarded as a band, not as a precise curve. For example, in the Federal Reserve Bank of Richmond's recent surveys on the Phillips curve, Nason and Smith (2008: i) conclude that "estimates of the slope of the NKPC (New Keynesian Phillips Curve) are imprecise and confidence intervals that are robust to weak identification are wide." In his overview essay for the Richmond Fed collection, Hornstein (2007: 305) indicates that this conclusion is "bad news for the NKPC as a model of inflation and for monetary policy." Be that as it may, it is good news for the evolutionary view of the economy.

As Lipsey and Scarth (2011, xxxiii) observe: "Today's prevailing paradigm involves the injunction that explicit dynamic optimisation is required as an under-pinning for a macro analysis to have pedigree." Evolutionary economists reject this injunction arguing that is its directing macroeconomics in the wrong direction because economic behaviour in the uncertain world in which endogenous techno-logical change is a major factor cannot be understood as rational inter-temporal maximisation. Instead, it is a more empirically based, striving and groping into the fog of an uncertain future in which what is good, let alone optimal, can only be known after the event.

Few experienced economists are naïve enough to believe, however, that major paradigmatic theories die just because they have met with serious refutations of some of their predictions. Instead, repeated refutations, revealed contradictions, and inadequacies, plus some more attractive alternative are all needed before this happens. Nonetheless it is interesting to see just what is left of the theories we have criticized and what would be left behind were they to exit.

4.1 Goodbye To All That and Does it Matter?

First to go is the stable long run vertical aggregate supply curve, indicating a unique equilibrium level of national income, Y^*. Accepting that there are good reasons why the economy does not oscillate between hyperinflation and zero employment, is a long way from accepting the existence of a unique Y^* that persists for any length of time or that changes on a stable trend. Although the economy clearly does cycle, there has never been any serious evidence that it cycles around a stable equilibrium national income, Y^*, such that whenever current Y does not equal Y^* pressures will be clearly operating to return the economy to Y^*.

Second to go is the concept of a unique relation between the unemployment gap and wage and price inflation as shown by the Phillips curve. The original Phillips curve implied that *money* wage rates were highly sensitive to the state of demand in the labor market. It is one thing to say that the labor demand and supply will have some influence on wage changes, to which many would agree, and quite another thing to say that the rate of change in wages is uniquely and negatively related to the unemployment gap such that successive reductions in U will be reflected in ever higher rates of wage inflation. This auction-market view of the labor market denies the voluminous evidence that wages respond to many things other than just excess demand, or, as Hall (1980) put it many years ago, wages are more responsive to the economic climate than to the economic weather.

Next to go is the concept of the NAIRU, which puts the labor market on a fine edge equilibrium, any sustained departure from which causes the rate of wage changes to accelerate at an ever increasing rate (or decelerate at an ever falling rate).[29] Gone with it is the expectations-augmented Phillips curve which has the same properties as the NAIRU.

Note that the original Phillips curve and the NAIRU are distinct relations requiring separate refutations. The original Phillips curve implied only a negative relation between the unemployment gap and wage inflation. The NAIRU and the expectations-augmented Phillips curve required the existence of a *unique equilibrium level of unemployment*, departures from which could be sustained only if people were making repeated errors.

The original Phelps Friedman critique of the "naïve" Phillips curve that led to the concept of a NAIRU and of an expectations-augmented Phillips curve was based on an unquestioning acceptance of a unique general equilibrium of the economy. It is interesting that in the debate that followed the publications by these two economists, few questioned this basic assumption. However, once we abandon the concept of a unique general equilibrium for the economy and adopt the concept of an economy that is growing and constantly changing under the driving force of endogenous, path-dependent technological change, the theoretical

[29] At U^*, wages will be constant in a static model, or changing at the same rate as productivity is changing in a growth model. In either case, this results in the absence of any inflationary pressure emanating from the labour market.

justification for the NAIRU and the expectations-augmented Phillips curve disappears. Furthermore, as we have seen above, we find no empirical evidence for the existence of either of these as operational concepts.

Finally, what goes conclusively is the commonly held doctrine of the long run neutrality of money. There is no challenge to the proposition that the number of zeros on the monetary unit is of no economic significance, nor that changing all of them in unison, as in a comprehensive monetary reform will have no significant real economic effects. What is challenged by our results is the proposition that a monetary disturbance has real effects in the transition period but none in the long run. Since according to evolutionary economics there is no static, long-run equilibrium to which the economy returns after a disturbance, and since the response to any disturbance can alter the path taken by future technological change, there is nothing to support the theory that monetary disturbances are without long-term effects on the economy. The competing vision is of an economy whose parts and whole are changing constantly along paths that can be altered more or less permanently by such shocks as a sharp monetary expansion, a temporary oil shortage or an embargo that raises the price of oil to unprecedented heights for a long but not indefinite time.

What is seriously challenged, if not totally dismissed, is New Classical real business cycle theory. This theory which employs the ergodic axiom of an assumed stationary equilibrium never seemed reasonable to evolutionary theorists, and to many others. The critics see cycles as having many causes, some of which originate in the financial sector and others in the real sector, including serially correlated changes in the flows of investment and/or consumption expenditures. *Random* shifts in tastes and technology seem low on the list of potential and observed causes of cycles. We have shown that a model that bears no relation to the core theoretical model of RBC theory, one that is inherently non-stationary and exhibits path dependencies, generates data that when filtered using a Hodric–Prescott filter pass the same tests as are used by RBC theorists to match stylized RBC growth facts. RBC theory asserts that because the observed real data, once filtered, match the data generated by the stationary RBC model, the real data are generated by a stationary process in which history does not matter. While we have not refuted all of real business cycle theory, what we have done certainly puts this conclusion into question and calls for further critical investigation of that model.

Next to be seriously challenged, even if not totally dismissed, is the New Classical concept of growth being a process that is stationary in its first differences. Most growth models employ an explicitly stationary equilibrium concept. Many empirical tests of the real world data seem to verify this assumption. We employ the same empirical tests and find that they indicate that data generated from a model that is explicitly non-stationary appear to be stationary. At the very least this raises serious doubt about the belief that the stationary equilibrium assumption of most of growth theory has in fact been empirically verified. Our observation that the growth rate significantly changes sign in sub-periods even though the whole period passes stationarity tests, suggests that the power of these empirical tests may simply be too low to tell us if history does or does not matter in growth processes.

What seems to us to be overwhelming evidence shows that economic growth is not a stationary process. There are large differences in growth rates for any one country over time and among countries at any one time. More importantly, all growth models that are based on an aggregate production function contain nothing that would distinguish one country from another structurally, such as institutions, culture or past history. Yet economic historians and development economists are clear that country specific contexts have large effects on economic growth. This is attested to by such economic historians as Jacob (1997), Jones (1988), Landes (1969, 1998), Mokyr (1990, 2002), Musson and Robinson (1989), and North (1981) to mention just a few. Although they argue about the importance of various context-specific causes, they are clear that macro growth models based on a single aggregate production function are unable to explain why economic growth occurs at different periods in history in various countries at different rates (including zero). Also some evolutionary economists have provided historical and theoretical studies showing the importance of context specific issues including the evolution of key technologies. For example, Freeman and Louçã (2001) provide strong evidence that growth in the West over the last three centuries came in the kinds of long waves that Schumpeter hypothesized while Carlaw and Lipsey have built models of GPT driven economic growth, including the model used to generate the simulation data used in Part 2 of this paper.

Finally and more broadly, what must go is the GE theory of a perfectly or monopolistically competitive economy inhabited by representative agents who produce an equilibrium that is always the optimal response to whatever shocks are impinging on the economy and that carry no implication for the behaviour of the inflation rate (which is determined separately by a quantity theory equation). The New Classical model that supplanted the Keynesian model in most macro text books during the 1980s, swept into prominence on two main arguments. On the empirical side was the erroneous belief that the stagflation of the 1970s had refuted the Keynesian model. Lucas and Rapping spoke of "the spectacular failure of the Keynesian models in the 1970s" (1972: 54) and asked what could be salvaged from the "wreckage". In fact, the stagflation of the 1970s and early 1980s was initially caused by a supply shock that raised prices but lowered unemployment. It was soon explained within the corpus of Keynesian economics by emphasising aggregate supply as well as aggregate demand (the text-book AD-AS model).[30] Also the Phillips curve was maintained as a short run adjustment equation by adding a price expectations term to produce what came to be called an 'expectations-augmented Phillips curve'. On the theoretical side, was the argument that Keynesian economics lacked micro underpinnings, which the New Classical model supplied. In contrast, Lipsey (2000) has argued that Keynesian economics did have strong microeconomic underpinnings. However, because they captured the reality of small group competition in both product and labour markets, they could not be

[30] Robert Gordon's triangle model is another approach that also does the same job.

formally aggregated into a single set of macro relations. The underpinnings of the New Classical model that replaced the Keynesian ones were typically based on atomistic competition and the aggregation problem was solved by assuming a representative consumer and representative firm each of which could be multiplied by the total number of such agents to represent the aggregation of that type of agent over the whole economy.

4.2 Hello to All This

What is left after all of these deletions? In the short term, the economy can exist with a range of Y and U and at various stable rates of inflation, provided that the central bank has a creditable policy to maintain the rate within a fairly narrow band that includes the present rate.[31] As a result, instead of the Phillips curve, there is a band shown by the broken lines in Fig. 5. The midpoint of the band is at the expected rate of inflation, shown by the solid line. The actual rate will vary around the expected rate depending on a number of variables including productivity and supply shocks, such as large changes in the price of oil and food, but not significantly on variations in U. At either end of this band, there may be something closer to a conventional Phillips curve. At the upper end U^u, a really major depression might cause changes in money wage rates and prices to fall to zero, or even become negative (the downward pointing arrow). At the lower end of U^l, a really major boom financed by money creation could cause wage and price inflation at very low levels of unemployment (the upward pointing arrow). Also anything that changes in the expected rate of inflation will shift the whole band.

In the medium and long term, the economy is evolving and constantly changing in structure, undergoing recessions and booms but not on a highly regular cycle, and growing on a non-stationary path that depends on many context-specific circumstances, some of the most important of which are technological changes generated endogenously at the micro economic level. Agents make decisions under conditions of Knightian uncertainty and some of these decisions may have consequences that persist for a very long time, perhaps to be latter displaced by future decisions made by other agents with consequences that in their turn persist for a very long time, and so on.

[31] This lack of uniqueness is reinforced by two important characteristics. First, many firms (probably most) have short run cost curves that are flat, allowing a wide range of output fluctuations over the short run with little or no changes in product prices. Second, at some times, such as the last two decades, the nature of technological change creates a great deal of uncertainty in the labour market that puts strong pressure on labour to be fairly docile, not pushing aggressively for higher wages at the first sign of an economic expansion or even the onset of an output boom. See Lipsey 2010 for a full discussion of the importance of these two characteristics.

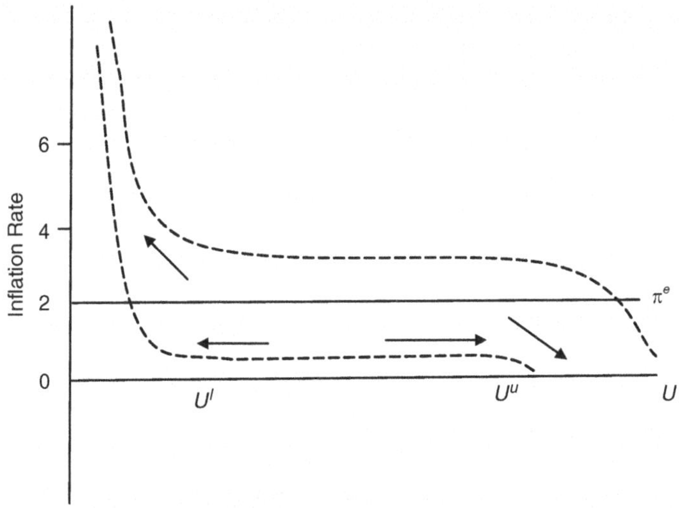

Fig. 5 The band of non-accelerating inflation: all unemployment rates between U^l and U^u are NAIRUs

Acknowledgements We are indebted for funding support to the Economic and Social Sciences and Humanities Research Council of Canada and to the Centre for International Governance and Innovation – Institute for New Economic Thinking grant number 2881. We are also grateful to Steven Kosempel, Bill Scarth and Les Oxley for comments on earlier drafts.

Appendix: Summary of Carlaw and Lipsey (2011) Model

The fixed supply of the composite resource, R, is allocated by private price-taking agents in the consumption and applied R&D sectors and by a government that taxes the applied R&D and consumption sectors to fund pure research at an exogenously determined level.

The constraint imposed by the composite resource is:

$$R_t = \sum_{i=1}^{I} r_t^i + \sum_{y=1}^{Y} r_t^y + \sum_{x=1}^{X} r_t^x \tag{9}$$

The Applied R&D and the Consumption Sectors

The output of applied knowledge from each applied R&D facility, y, depends on the amount of the resource it uses and its productivity coefficient, which is the geometric mean of each $(G_{n_x})_t$ term multiplied by its corresponding v term, as shown in (10).

$$a_t^y = z_t^y \left[\prod_{x=1}^{X} \left(\nu_{y,z}^{n_x} (G_{n_x})_{t-1}\right)^{\beta_x} \right]^{\frac{1}{X}} (r_t^y)^{\beta_{X+1}}, \tag{10}$$

$$\beta_x \in (0,1] \ \forall x \in X, \ \ \beta_{X+1} \in (0,1)$$

where z_t^y is drawn from a Normal distribution with mean 1 and variance 0.2.

The stock of applied knowledge generated from each facility accumulates according to:

$$A_t^y = a_t^y + (1-\varepsilon) A_{t-1}^y, \tag{11}$$

where $\varepsilon \in (0,1)$ is a depreciation parameter.

In the consumption sector, we make the simplifying assumptions (1) that there are the same number of applied R&D facilities and consumption industries, $Y = I$, and (2) that the knowledge produced in each of the facilities, y, is useful only in the one corresponding consumption industry, i. The production function for each of the I industries in the consumption sector is then expressed as follows:

$$c_t^i = z_t^i (\mu A_{t-1}^y)^{\alpha_y} (r_t^i)^{\alpha_{Y+1}}, \ \alpha_y \in (0,1] \ \forall y \in Y, \ \alpha_{Y+1} \in (0,1) \text{ and } i = \text{y} \tag{12}$$

where z_t^i is drawn from Normal distribution with mean 1 and variance 0.06

The Pure Knowledge Sector

There are X labs each producing one class of pure knowledge that leads to the occasional invention of a new version, n_x, of that class of GPT. The productivity coefficient in each lab is the geometric mean of the various amounts of the Y different kinds of applied knowledge that are useful in further pure research (one for each applied R&D facility and each raised to a power σ_y). The output of pure knowledge in lab x, g_t^x, is a function of the geometric mean of the various amounts of applied knowledge produced from the Y facilities doing applied R&D and the amount of the composite resource devoted to that lab.

$$g_t^x = \left[\prod_{y=1}^{Y} \left((1-\mu) A_{t-1}^y\right)^{\sigma_y} \right]^{\frac{1}{Y}} (\theta_t^x r_t^x)^{\sigma_{Y+1}}, \tag{13}$$

$$\sigma_y \in (0,1], \ \ \forall \ y \in Y \text{ and } \sigma_{Y+1} \in (0,1).$$

The stocks of *potentially useful* knowledge produced by each of the X labs accumulate according to:

$$\Omega_t^x = g_t^x + (1-\delta)\Omega_{t-1}^x \tag{14}$$

where $\delta \in (0,1)$ is a depreciation parameter.

New GPTs are invented infrequently in each of the X labs and their invention date is determined when the drawing of the random variable $\lambda_t^x \geq \lambda^{*x}$. For simplicity, we let the critical value of lambda for each of the X labs be the same: $\lambda^{*x} = \lambda^*$ $\forall\, x \in X$. When at any time, t, $\lambda_t^x \geq \lambda^*$, indicating that a new version of class-x GPT is invented, the index t_{n_x} is reset to equal the current t, and n_x is augmented by one.

Here we alter the arrival condition to make it a function of endogenous behaviour as follows. At any point in time, t, $\lambda_t^x \geq \frac{\lambda^*}{\left(\sum_{\tau=\tau last}^{t}\sum_{y=1}^{Y}(r_\tau^y)\right)}$,where $\tau last$ is the date that the last GPT of any class arrived in the economy.

Agents make their adoption decisions with incomplete information. In each applied R&D facility the only ν that agents expect to change is the one associated with the challenging x-class GPT, so, we can compare the productivities for any of the y facilities by simply comparing the $v_{y,z}^{(n-1)_x}\left(G_{(n-1)_x}\right)_{t_{nx}}$ that would result if the incumbent were left in place with the $\bar{v}_{y,z}^{n_x}(G_{n_x})_{t_{nx}}$ that is expected to result if the challenger were adopted. This comparison is made in each of the Y applied R&D facilities at time $t = t_{n_x}$ so the test, stated generally for all applied R&D facilities, is:

$$\left[\bar{v}_{y,z}^{n_x}(G_{n_x})_{t_{nx}}\right] \geq \left[v_{y,z}^{(n-1)_x}\left(G_{(n-1)_x}\right)_{t_{nx}}\right] \text{ for each y} \in [1, Y]. \tag{15}$$

If the test is passed, the new GPT is adopted in facility y.

The evolving efficiency with which the GPT delivers its services is shown in (16) below.

$$(G_{n_x})_t = \left(G_{(n-1)_x}\right)_{(t-1)_{nx}} + \left(\frac{e^{\tau+\gamma(t-t_{nx})}}{1+e^{\tau+\gamma(t-t_{nx})}}\right)\left(\psi_t\Omega_{t_{nx}}^x - \left(G_{(n-1)_x}\right)_{(t-1)_{nx}}\right), \tag{16}$$

where

$$\psi_t = \frac{e^{n_t}/X}{10+e^{n_t}/X}$$

and n_t is the total number of GPT arrivals in the economy up to date t.

The equation shows the efficiency of the GPT, $(G_{n_x})_t$, increasing logistically as the full potential of the GPT is slowly realized. t_{n_x} is the invention date of the version n_x, of the class-x GPT, $\Omega_{t_{nx}}^x$ is the full *potential* productivity of the new version of GPT x, $\left(G_{(n-1)_x}\right)_{t_{(n-1)_x}}$ is the *actual* productivity of the version that it replaced, evaluated at the time at which that earlier version was last used, $t_{(n-1)_x}$ and γ and τ are calibration parameters that control the rate of diffusion. The evolution of efficiency proceeds as follows. Initially, since $t_{n_x} = t$ (and because γ is very small, 0.07 in our simulations), the value of the efficiency coefficient is close to zero so that the initial productivity of the challenging GPT is close to that of the incumbent. As t increases over time the value of the efficiency coefficient approaches unity so that the GPT's productivity approaches its full potential.

In the subsequent periods, the test in (15) is modified to note the productivity changes that occur over time:

$$\left[\bar{v}_{y,z}^{n_x}\left(G_{n_x}\right)_t\right] \geq \left[v_{y,z}^{(n-1)_x}\left(G_{(n-1)_x}\right)_t\right] \tag{15'}$$

for each $y \in [1, Y]$ that has not yet adopted GPT G_{n_x}.

Resource Allocation

As we have already noted, in the pure knowledge sector the government pays for and allocates a fixed amount of the generic resource, R, to each of the pure knowledge producing labs. Producers in the applied R&D and consumption sectors maximize their profits each period taking prices as given.[32] The prices for output from the I consumption industries are derived from the maximization of an aggregate utility function, which we assume is additively separable across the I consumption goods.

$$U = \sum_{i=1}^{I} \left(c^i\right)^{\phi^i} \text{ and } \phi^i = \phi^{i'} = 1, i \neq i' \forall i, i' \in I \tag{17}$$

Maximizing this utility function and rearranging the first order conditions (FOCs) yields:

$$\frac{MU^{i=1}}{MU^{i\neq 1}} = \frac{P^{i=1}}{P^{i\neq 1}} = \frac{\phi^{i=1}\left(c^{i=1}\right)^{\phi^{i=1}-1}}{\phi^{i\neq 1}\left(c^{i\neq 1}\right)^{\phi^{i\neq 1}-1}} \tag{18}$$

Since $\phi^i = 1 \ \forall \ i \in I$ it follows that $P^{i=1} = P^{i\neq 1}$, i.e., the relative prices of all consumptions goods are unity.

---

[32] We suppress time subscripts in (17) through (24) because agents are not foresighted and are consequently performing a static maximization in each period.

We assume a competitive equilibrium in the market for the composite resource. This implies that it earns the same wage, w, regardless of where it is allocated.

Each consumption industry maximizes its profits taking the price of its consumption output, P^i, and the prices of its inputs, composite resource, w, and applied knowledge, P^y, as given. Profits are expressed as:

$$\pi^i = P^i c^i - wr^i - P^y A^y \tag{19}$$

Profit maximization yields the following FOCs in each of the I consumption industries:

$$\begin{aligned} P^i mpr^i - w &= 0 \\ P^i mpA^y - P^y &= 0 \end{aligned} \tag{20}$$

where mp represents marginal product. From the first FOC, the assumption the $P^i = 1$, and the definition of the production function for industry i we get:

$$r^{i*} = \left[\frac{\alpha_{Y+1}}{w}(\mu A^y)^{\alpha_y}\right]^{\frac{1}{1-\alpha_{Y+1}}}, \tag{21}$$

which is the reduced form expression for the demand for the composite resource in each consumption industry, i.

From the combination of both FOCs from the profit function for consumption industry i and the definition of the production function we get:

$$\frac{w}{P^y} = \frac{\alpha_{Y+1}}{\alpha_y}\frac{A^y}{r^i}$$

which implies that:

$$P^{y*} = \frac{\alpha_y w}{\alpha_{Y+1} A^y}\left[\frac{\alpha_{Y+1}}{w}(\mu A^y)^{\alpha_y}\right]^{\frac{1}{1-\alpha_{Y+1}}} \tag{22}$$

Each applied R&D facility maximizes profits taking the price of its applied knowledge output, P^y, and the composite resource, w, as given. The pure knowledge input in the form the currently adopted set of X GPTs is provided freely to the applied R&D facilities by the government financed labs. Profits are expressed as:

$$\pi^y = P^y a^y - wr^y \tag{23}$$

Maximization of the profit function and algebraic manipulation yields the following FOC:

$$P^y mpr^y - w = 0$$

The demand for the composite resource from each of the Y applied R&D facilities is thus:

$$r^{y*} = \left[\beta_{X+1}\left[\prod^{X}\left(v_{y.z}^{n_x}(G_{n_x})_t\right)^{\beta_x}\right]^{\frac{1}{X}}\frac{P^{y^*}}{w}\right]^{\frac{1}{1-\beta_{X+1}}} \tag{24}$$

With these resource demand equations we now have a complete description of the allocation of the composite resource across the three sectors.

References

Arthur B (1994) Increasing returns and path-dependence in the economy. University of Michigan Press, Ann Arbor, MI

Carlaw KI, Lipsey RG (2006) GPT-driven, endogenous growth. Econ J 116:155–174

Carlaw KI, Lipsey RG (2011) Sustained endogenous growth driven by structured and evolving technologies. J Evol Econ 21(4):563–593

Fortin P (2001) Interest rates, unemployment and inflation: the Canadian experience in the 1990s. In: Banting K, Sharpe A, St-Hilaire F (eds) The review of economic performance and social progress: the longest decade – Canada in the 1990s, vol 1. Centre for the Study of Living Standards & The Institute for Research on Public Policy, Ottawa), pp. 113–130

Freeman C, Louçã F (2001) As time goes by: from the industrial revolutions to the information revolution. Oxford University Press, Oxford

Gali J, Gertler M (1999) Inflation dynamics: a structural econometric approach. J Monet Econ 44 (2):195–222

Hall RE (1980) Employment fluctuations and wage rigidity. Brookings Economic Papers, 10th Anniversary Issue, pp 91–123

Hornstein A (2007) Evolving inflation dynamics and the new Keynesian Phillips curve. Econ Q 93 (4):317–339

Jacob MC (1997) Scientific culture and the making of the industrial west. Oxford University Press, Oxford

Jones E (1988) Growth recurring: economic change in world history. Oxford University Press, Oxford

Landes D (1969) The unbound prometheus: technological change and industrial development. Cambridge University Press, London

Landes D (1998) The wealth and poverty of nations. W.W. Norton, New York

Lipsey RG (2000) IS-LM, Keynesianism and the new classicism. In: Blackhouse RE, Salanti A (eds) Macroeconomics and the real world, volume 2: Keynesian economics, unemployment, and policy. Oxford University Press, Oxford, pp 57–82

Lipsey RG (2010) Schumpeter for our century. In: Hanusch H, Kurz HD, Seidl C (eds) Homo oeconomicus. Accedo Verlagsgessellschaft, Muchen, Special Issue, 27(1/2), pp 145–176

Lipsey RG, Scarth W (2011) The history, significance and policy context of the phillips curve. In: Lipsey RG, Scarth W (eds) Inflation and unemployment: the evolution of the Phillips curve. Edward Elgar, Cheltenham

Lipsey RG, Carlaw KI, Bekar C (2005) Economic transformations: general purpose technologies and long-run economic growth. Oxford University Press, Oxford

Lucas RE Jr, Rapping LA (1972) Unemployment in the great depression: Is there a full explanation? J Polit Econ 80(1):186–191

Marx K (1957) Capital: a critique of political economy (3 vols), translated from the 3rd German Edition by Samuel Moore and Edward Aveling, Fredrick Engles (eds). Foreign Language Publishing House, Moscow

Mokyr J (1990) The Lever of riches: technological creativity and economic progress. Oxford University Press, New York

Mokyr J (2002) The gifts of athena: historical origins of the knowledge economy. Princeton University Press), Princeton, NJ

Musson AE, Robinson E (1989) Science and technology in the industrial revolution. Gordon and Breach, Ogdensburg, NY

Nason JM, Smith GW (2008) The new Keynesian Phillips curve: lessons from single-equation econometric estimation. Econ Q 94:361–395

Nelson C, Plosser C (1982) Trends and Random walks in macroeconomic time series: some evidence and implications. J Monet Econ 10:139–169

Nelson R, Winter S (1982) An evolutionary theory of economic change. Harvard University Press, Cambridge

North DC (1981) Structure and change in economic history. Norton, New York

Pomeranz K (2000) The great divergence: China, Europe and the making of the modern world economy. Princeton University Press, Princeton

Rae J (1905) The sociological theory of capital. Macmillan, New York, first published in 1834 as Statement of some new principles on the subject of political economy exposing the fallacies of the system of free trade and of some other doctrines maintained in the wealth of nations

Rosenberg N (1982) Inside the black box: technology and economics. Cambridge University Press, Cambridge

Schumpeter J (1934) The theory of economic development. Harvard University Press, Cambridge, MA

Tobin J (1998) Supply constraints on employment and output: NAIRU versus natural rate. In: Paper presented at the international conference in memory of Fausto Vicarelli, Rome, 2–23 Nov, manuscript

Veblen T (1953) The theory of the leisure class (revised ed.). New American Library, New York

Innovation, Real Primary Commodity Prices and Business Cycles

Harry Bloch and David Sapsford

Abstract Schumpeter emphasizes the role of innovation in explaining long-run economic development. This contrasts to the emphasis on scarcity in classical and neoclassical models. Our research shows the fruitfulness of Schumpeter's approach in explaining movements in real prices of primary commodities since 1650. In models that emphasize resource scarcity, rising real prices of these products are identified as limiting growth. However, in examining the historical data we find a dominance of negative price trends across individual commodities, particularly when allowing for long-run cyclical behavior. We then provide examples to show how innovations for particular commodities have contributed to the negative price trends. Overall, innovation has meant that increased supplies of primary commodities have been available at reduced real prices, thereby providing a positive contribution to growth. Of course, as Schumpeter suggests, the development process associated with innovation is uneven, so price movements are heterogeneous across long-run cycles and commodities.

1 Introduction

Our objective in this paper is to develop and apply a framework for understanding the impact of innovation on the long-run movement in the real prices of primary commodities, namely the products of land and other natural resources, specifically

---

An earlier version of this paper was presented to the International Schumpeter Society conference in Aalborg, Denmark in June 2010.

H. Bloch (✉)
School of Economics and Finance, Curtin University of Technology, GPO Box U1987, Perth, WA 6845, Australia
e-mail: h.bloch@curtin.edu.au

D. Sapsford
Management School, University of Liverpool, Chatham Street, Liverpool L69 7ZH England, UK
e-mail: D.Sapsford@liverpool.ac.uk

A. Pyka and E.S. Andersen (eds.), *Long Term Economic Development*, Economic Complexity and Evolution, DOI 10.1007/978-3-642-35125-9_8,

agriculture and mining products. By real price we mean the price of these products relative to other prices, especially the prices of manufactured products. By long run we mean over the course of multiple business cycles, including the long wave or Kondratieff cycle that runs for over half a century per cycle. We apply the framework to data for real prices of primary commodities that cover a period of up to more than three centuries.

Our framework is developed from Schumpeter's theory of economic development and the business cycle. Here, innovation is the force released by capitalist organization of the economy, driving progress through a process of discontinuous change. The influence of innovation is reflected in prices having a wave-like motion over time, with prices rising and then falling by an even larger amount before partially recovering over the course of the Kondratieff cycle.

We follow Rostow (1980) in extending Schumpeter's analysis of Kondratieff cycles by considering the influence of gestation lags that slow adjustment in the production of primary commodities in addition to the impact of technological breakthroughs. Primary commodities have a special role in the process of development, as they are the basic raw materials for production of finished consumer and producer goods. Any tendency for primary commodity prices to rise in the prosperity phase of a cycle enhances the incentives for exploration, enhanced recovery technology and development of substitute products or more efficient use in further production. As Schumpeter (1939) notes history is replete with examples of commodity price rises followed by opening of new production provinces, use of innovative technology to extend mine life and development of synthetic substitutes, all of which encourage prices to fall back towards long-run norms. Rostow systematizes this response of productive capacity for primary commodities thereby generating a distinctive pattern of movement for commodity prices over the Kondratieff cycle.

In addition to the analyses of Schumpeter and Rostow, we draw on the work of Prebisch (1950) and Singer (1950) regarding trend in the terms of trade between primary producers and manufacturers in the long run. Particularly important is the suggestion that the terms of trade are influenced by different degrees of market power for primary producers and manufacturers, as well as by different labor market conditions in industrialized versus developing countries. Prebisch and Singer argue that these differences in market structure along with different rates of technological change contribute to a declining trend in the price of primary commodities relative to the price of manufactured goods.

Our analysis leads to an expectation of a long-run downward trend for the real (or relative) prices of primary commodities along with a distinctive cyclical pattern, rising in the upswing of the Kondratieff cycle and declining by a larger amount in the downswing. This characterization of price movements applies in general, but is subject to disturbance by history. For the aggregate of all commodities this is reflected in larger historical events, such as wars, population migrations and financial crises, albeit with recognition that these events may have roots in the ongoing process of economic development. For individual commodities the application of the general characterization occurs against the specific technological breakthroughs in the production and consumption of that commodity.

In the next section we discuss the opposing impacts on productivity in primary production arising from natural resource constraints and technological innovation. We then review evidence on long-run trends for real primary commodity prices, both for aggregate real commodity price indexes and for real prices of individual commodities over long periods, extending back in some cases to 1650. In the third section we examine the data on an aggregate index of real primary commodity prices to identify Kondratieff cycles as suggested by Rostow's analysis of lags in the supply response of commodity production. In Sect. 4, we examine similarities and differences in the trend in the real price series across commodities and over different cycles. The final section contains our conclusions and a discussion of the implications for the future course of real commodity prices.

2 The Long-Run Trend in the Real Prices of Primary Commodities

Natural resources have long been recognized in economics as posing a limit to economic growth. In the classical economic analysis of limits to the amount of arable land by Ricardo (1911) this is reflected in declining marginal productivity of labor in the production of agricultural commodities as the economy grows. Further analysis of nonrenewable resources by Hotelling (1931) suggests that there will be declining marginal productivity over time for all variable inputs in the production of mining commodities, even without growth in the level of output. Yet, real wages have risen strongly in both agriculture and mining in advanced countries, implying equivalent rises in the marginal productivity of labor according to the marginal productivity theory of wages.

Schumpeter puts innovation at the center of the analysis of long-run economic development. In *Business Cycles*, Schumpeter (1939, pp. 237–240) notes the contribution of entrepreneurial innovations to the rise in output per acre in English agriculture over the period from 1500 to 1780. This was also a period of rural depopulation associated with enclosures (one of the entrepreneurial innovations identified by Schumpeter). The resulting rise in output per worker contradicted the dire predictions of classical economists and provided plentiful and cheap food for the manufacturing labor force required for the beginnings of the Industrial Revolution.

Schumpeter is clear that innovations in primary production continued beyond the early years of the Industrial Revolution. He notes innovations in English, German and American agriculture that vastly expanded production. While prices followed an erratic path due to the effects of variable harvests, wars and protectionism (op. cit., pp. 266–270), he cites a consistent pattern in the example of the expansion of areas of wheat cultivation in the United States, 'Each process of this kind spells an increase in production and, at the same time, prosperity in the new and depression in the old' (op. cit., p. 270). This is a nice example of the process of creative destruction that is more commonly applied to innovation in manufacturing.

Innovation and the expansion of primary production is in part a reaction to high demand and rising prices. However, the drive to innovate continues even when demand abates, shifting from a focus on capacity expansion to one of cost reduction.[1] Historically, the net result has been a long-run improvement in productive capability that has more than offset the force of the natural limits emphasized by classical and neoclassical approaches to natural resource pricing. The improvements have been so strong that the real prices of primary products have generally fallen.

Real price measures deflate the nominal price of a good measured in a particular currency by a measure of the general price level in the same currency, removing the influence of generic factors that affect prices of all goods. The resulting measure is meant to reflect factors that are specific to the individual good or group of goods. A falling trend in the real price for a primary commodity suggests that the innovations in the production and consumption of the commodity are more than sufficient to offset any effect of the finite limits to the natural resource.

Harvey et al. (2010) examine whether there are long-run trends in the prices of 25 primary commodities. The series for eight of the primary commodities (beef, coal, gold, lamb, lead, sugar, wheat and wool) go back to 1650, while the other series go back at least as far as 1900 (bananas and jute). They find evidence of a long-run downward trend in the real price of eight commodities (aluminum, coffee, jute, silver, sugar, tea, wool and zinc) without allowing for structural breaks. They also find evidence of a long-run downtrend including structural breaks for a further three commodities (hides, tobacco and wheat). No evidence of a statistically significant long-run trend, either up or down, is found for any of the other fourteen commodities.

The findings of Harvey et al. support the hypothesis of a declining long-run trend in real commodity prices as put forward in the seminal work of Raul Prebisch (1950) and Hans Singer (1950). Most of the empirical literature dealing with the Prebisch-Singer hypothesis has focused on aggregated indexes of primary commodity prices.[2] For comparison with this literature, we illustrate the phenomenon of declining real commodities prices in Fig. 1, which shows the time path since 1650 of the natural logarithm of the simple average of the real price index for the 25 commodities examined by Harvey et. al.[3] There is clearly downward movement over the full period, but many episodes of rising prices, including some substantial price spikes. This suggests there are complex dynamics at play rather than a steady

[1] Tilton and Landsberg (1999) provide an illuminating discussion of the response of US copper producers to declining copper prices from the 1970s through the 1990s. Output and productivity first declined and then rose substantially as the real price of copper fell by more than 50 %.

[2] A recent overview of this literature that also contains a discussion of volatility in commodity prices is Nissanke (2010a).

[3] We thank Jakob Madsen for supplying the data used in Harvey et al. (2010). We have extended the data series from 2005 to 2008 by chain linking, with the primary commodity index linked to the IMF all commodities world price index series and the manufacturing price series linked to the OECD total manufacturing price index series. We use the logarithm of the price index so that equal proportionate changes in price show as movements of equal distance along the vertical index, thereby reducing the potential distortion caused by very comparisons over a large range of prices.

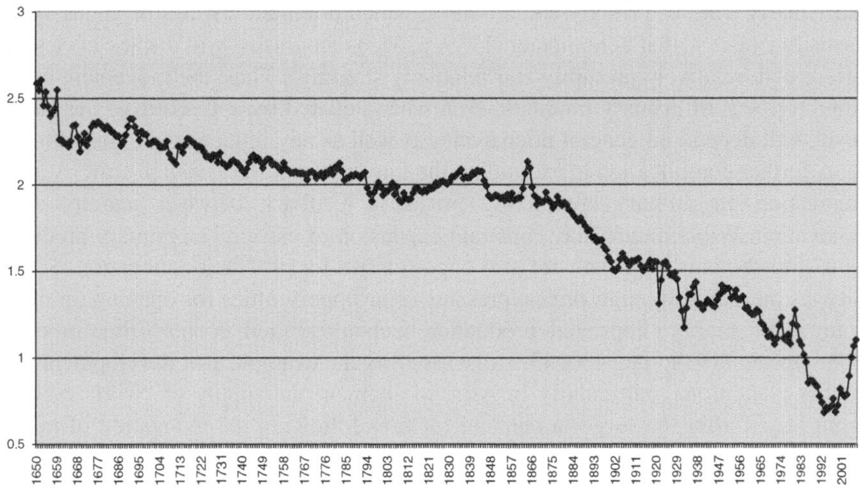

Fig. 1 Logarithm of aggregate index of real commodity prices, 1650–2008 (2005=1)

down (or up) movement over the full period. The dynamics of commodity prices are the subject of the next section of the paper.

3 Kondratieff Cycles in Real Prices of Primary Commodities

In *Business Cycles*, Schumpeter (1939) argues that innovation does not have smooth impact on the pace of economic life. Rather, it causes disturbances that lead to uneven development of the economy. Yet, he suggests a degree of regularity to this process involving cyclical fluctuations of various lengths. His stylized representation of cycles (see Schumpeter 1939, Chap. 5, Chart 1) has three overlapping cycles, a Kitchin cycle lasting slightly more than 3 years, a Juglar cycle of about 9 and a quarter years and a Kondratieff cycle of 55 and a half years. The cycles are shown as overlapping in that each Kondratieff cycle contains six Juglars and each Juglar contains three Kitchins.

Schumpeter's argument that major innovations lead to alternating long periods of expansion and decline in economic activity has been adopted in a number of works dealing with the history of capitalism, for example, Mensch (1979), Tylecote (1992) and Freeman and Louçã (2001). However, Schumpeter's characterization of regular cycles has been discarded in favor of a pattern with irregular amplitude and duration. The terminology of a long wave is used in place of the Kondratieff cycle, with the long wave having the duration of something like a half century.

The key variable in Schumpeter's characterization of the cycle is the price level rather than the level of output that features in most discussions of the business cycle. This reflects Schumpeter's emphasis on innovation as leading to structural change and uneven development. The price level rises during the upswing of a cycle and falls during the downswing. These cyclical swings in prices obscure the working of innovation on the trend in particular goods or groups of goods. This is particularly true for primary commodities, which dominate listings of goods with "sensitive prices" that Schumpeter (1939, p. 525) recognizes 'will display cycles in prices both relatively promptly and relatively strongly'. Thus, the movement over time in prices of primary products, even when deflated by a measure of the price level, will depend on general price cycles as well as any influences of innovation.

A further complication in examining the impact of natural resource scarcity and innovation on primary commodity prices is feedback between scarcity and innovation. While nature may constrain expansion of capacity in primary production, impediments to growth are also opportunities for profitable innovation. Scarcity, as measured by high prices, presents clear opportunities for opening up new sources of supply, improved production technology and economizing in use. Schumpeter (1939, pp. 430–432) discusses as an example the development of rubber plantations, particularly in Asia, to augment the supply of "wild" rubber from Brazil after the surge in demand for tires following the innovation of mass produced motor cars. Under capitalism the dictum "necessity is the mother of invention", can be aptly rephrased as "profitability is the mother of innovation".

Rostow (1980, Chapter 2) formalizes the process of delayed expansion of natural resource production capacity, incorporating long lags in feedback from prices to expanded capacity. Rostow's model includes two sectors, one producing industrial goods and the other producing basic commodities. Natural resources in the form of land only enter into the production of basic commodities. In contrast to neoclassical models, where land is assumed to be fixed in quantity forever, Rostow assumes that amount of land can be augmented. However, the augmentation occurs with a substantial lag behind growth in labor and physical capital, taking up to three decades to match the growth rate of labor and physical capital. Simulations of the model generate a growth cycle of some 50 years, with the relative price of the basic commodity and the rent of land rising in the early decades of the cycle and then falling back towards the original levels.

Augmentation of natural resources in Rostow's model is meant to capture the pattern observed in his historical work (see Rostow 1978). Rostow argues that spurts in industrial production following on major technological innovations drive up the relative price of basic commodities as supplies are inelastic in the short run. He identifies three types of lags that slow the augmentation of the natural resource in response to an increase in relative price. Recognition lags occur because it takes time for commodity producers to become convinced that the higher prices are not temporary. Gestation lags occur because large scale infrastructure, such as rail links or pipelines, is often necessary to open up new production provinces. Finally, exploitation lags occur because it takes time to reach full potential as the number of production units expand to take advantage of the infrastructure.

Rostow's simulations are based on parameter values calibrated to match his characterization of the stylized facts of economic history. In a related two-good model, we (Bloch and Sapsford 2000) estimate the parameters of pricing equations for primary products and manufactured goods in world markets using annual data for the period from 1948 to 1993. Primary commodities in this model take the place of Rostow's basic commodities, while manufactured goods take the place of industrial goods. However, there are important differences in the structure of our model and that of Rostow.

Rostow assumes competitive market clearing in product markets for both industrial goods and basic commodities. We also treat primary commodity prices as determined by competitive market clearing, but manufactured goods are sold under conditions of imperfect competition with price equal to unit cost times one plus a gross profit margin.[4] Rostow assumes that both industrial goods and basic commodities go directly into final consumption, while we have primary commodities as inputs into the production of manufactured goods. A final important difference in structure is that Rostow has a single wage in both sectors, while we allow for different wages in the two sectors following Prebisch's (1950) arguments regarding the impact of unionization and income support programs in the industrialized countries that dominate exports of manufactures versus generally surplus labor in the developing countries that dominate exports of primary commodities.

The estimates obtained in Bloch and Sapsford (2000) imply a trend rate of decline in the price of primary commodities relative to manufactured goods of about one half percent per annum over the sample period, 1948–1993. This estimate of the trend decline in the "real" price of primary commodities is determined based on the observed average rates of change for the exogenous variables in the model, which are an increase in manufacturing output of about 5 % per annum and the average rate of increase in the manufacturing gross profit margin of about one third of a percent per annum.[5] Importantly, the results indicate that real primary commodities prices tend to increase relative to trend during periods of substantially above average growth in manufacturing output and fall relative to trend during periods of average or slower than average growth in manufacturing output. These results are consistent with Rostow's observation that spurts of rapid growth in industrial output lead to rises in the relative price of basic commodities. Unfortunately, the shortness of the time span covered does not allow any statistical test for the type of long gestation lags suggested by Rostow.

Putting the trend aside, we expect the rhythm of "sensitive" prices to be reflected in rising real prices of primary commodities in the upswing of a Kondratieff cycle and falling real prices in the downswing. If these cyclical fluctuations dominate trend in the short run as suggested in Fig. 1, then the peak of the Kondratieff cycle should be reflected in a local maximum for real prices of primary commodities and the trough in a local minimum. The long-run downward trend also needs to be taken into account when choosing minima and maxima.[6] When this procedure is applied to the real commodity price series shown in Fig. 1, we obtain the dating of peaks

[4] This asymmetric treatment follows that in Kalecki (1971).

[5] This estimate is based on a simplified version of the model that excludes rates of growth of capital stock in the manufacturing and industrial sectors as exogenous variables. We prefer the results from the simplified model as the measures for the capital stock growth variables are imprecise and the estimated coefficients of these variables have low statistical significance when they are included in regressions.

[6] Local minima are reasonably clear against a falling trend, but local maxima are not. A later observation can be higher relative to the trend line, even though it has a lower value. For example, we choose 1954 as the peak of the cycle with troughs in 1932 and 1993, even though the real price index is lower in 1954 than in 1937.

Table 1 Peaks and troughs in real primary commodity price index, 1650–2008

Year	Peak or trough?	Index value (logarithmic units)	Change in value from preceding extreme	Annual rate of change (%)
1669	Trough	2.193		
1691	Peak	2.382	0.189	0.859
1711	Trough	2.119	−0.163	−0.815
1716	Peak	2.216	0.097	1.940
1741	Trough	2.070	−0.146	−0.584
1745	Peak	2.170	0.100	2.500
1796	Trough	1.904	−0.266	−0.522
1835	Peak	2.086	0.182	0.467
1848	Trough	1.923	−0.163	−1.254
1864	Peak	2.133	0.210	1.312
1902	Trough	1.500	−0.633	−1.666
1905	Peak	1.602	0.102	3.400
1932	Trough	1.173	−0.429	−1.589
1954	Peak	1.387	0.314	1.427
1993	Trough	0.681	−0.706	−1.810
2008	Peak	1.180	0.499	3.327

and troughs that is shown in Table 1.[7] Table 1 also shows the change in the logarithmic value between adjacent peaks and troughs along with the implied annual rate of change in percentage.

The pattern of peaks and troughs in Table 1 helps to explain why there has been so much controversy about whether there is a negative trend in real primary commodity prices. Each cyclical peak exceeds the previous trough and there is even a period in the nineteenth century when there is an increase from peak to peak and trough to trough (from the trough in 1796 to that in 1848 and from the peak in 1835 to that 1864). Otherwise there is a decrease between all adjacent peaks or troughs, especially in the twentieth century, which leads to the overall downward movement in commodity prices shown in Fig. 1. Increasing volatility over time, especially in the twentieth century, is a further complication in discerning trends in real primary commodity prices, which makes even the pronounced decline in prices from the mid nineteenth century onwards subject to doubt depending on the choice of starting and ending dates.[8]

The peaks and troughs in the aggregate primary commodity price index reflect the factors that affect each component price. Some of these are specific to the particular commodity, such as innovations in the production or use of the commodity, while other factors have more general impact, such as the growth of industrial

[7] Not all local maxima and minima are chosen as peaks and troughs, respectively. In particular, we avoid choosing closely coincident local maxima and minima as these would not fit the concept of a long cycle.

[8] The sharp upward spike shown in 2008 at the end of the series in Fig. 1 has been followed by a precipitous decline in 2009 and then almost complete recovery before another downturn.

output, manufacturing profit margins and wages in both primary production and manufacturing. Having identified turning points in terms of the aggregate index, we next turn to examining movements in prices of individual commodities over the cycles in the aggregate index.

4 Trends in Real Prices for Individual Primary Commodities

Tables 2a and 2b show the rates of price change in percent per annum for each of 25 primary commodities for each of the trough-to-trough cycles shown in Table 1.[9] The top panel shows price changes for agricultural commodities, while the bottom panel shows price changes for metal and energy commodities. Annual rates of change are used to enable comparisons across cycles of different lengths.[10]

The data in Tables 2a and 2b show clear differences in the rate of change of prices of primary commodities across both commodities and cycles. While the comparison across troughs of the cycles in real primary commodity prices is meant to remove the common cyclical component of price movements, there is still substantial variation across commodities remaining in the price change. This reinforces the fragility noted above of conclusions regarding the presence of trend in real primary commodity prices. Different commodities have different measured trend rates of change in different cycles.

Statistical analysis is used to determine whether the variation in rates of price change is consistent with a single trend rate for the whole of the period for which data are available, with or without allowing for structural breaks. As noted in the previous section, Harvey et al. (2010) are able to identify statistically significant negative price trends for eight commodities (aluminum, coffee, jute, silver, sugar, tea, wool and zinc) without allowing for a structural break and a further three commodities (hides, tobacco and wheat) after allowing for structural breaks. Further evidence of statistical significant negative price trends with or without structural breaks for the shorter period from 1900 to 2007 is provided by Sapsford et al. (2010) for six commodities (aluminum, hides, rice, rubber, sugar and wheat).

The bulk of the statistically significant negative price trends in both Harvey et al. (2010) and Sapsford et al. (2010) are for agricultural commodities. In addition, in Tables 2a and 2b the price trends for bananas are negative in both cycles for which data are available. Also, rice shows all negative price changes except for the cycles in the nineteenth century. Indeed, there are only three agricultural commodities that lack statistically significant negative price trends and have an ambiguous mix of positive and negative price trends in Tables 2a and 2b. These are beef, cocoa and lamb.

[9] As discussed in note 6 above, cyclical troughs are more readily identified than are peaks. Also, 2008 is too recent to be sure that it will remain a local maximum relative to years in the near future, particularly given the volatility of commodity prices in recent years.

[10] The annual rate of change is calculated as the change in the natural logarithm of the price index for the cycle divided by the number of years elapsed in the cycle.

Table 2a Rate of price change for agricultural commodities in percent per annum (measured trough to trough)

Period	Banana	Beef	Cocoa	Coffee	Cotton	Hides	Jute	Lamb	Rice	Sugar	Tea	Tobacco	Wheat	Wool
1669–1711		−0.694						−0.824		−0.781			−0.714	−1.756
1711–1741		0.339		−0.416	−0.835			0.307	−0.440	0.017	−0.548		0.293	0.170
1741–1796		−0.112		−0.442	0.980			−0.206	−0.408	−0.196	−1.085	0.364	−0.044	−0.044
1796–1848		1.333		−0.179	−0.139			0.656	0.466	−0.072	0.206	1.202	0.164	1.103
1848–1902		1.155	1.196	−0.562	−0.323	0.030		−0.171	0.202	−1.870	−1.267	0.883	−0.634	0.405
1902–1932	−0.390	0.110	−1.826	0.347	−1.225	−1.710	−1.351	2.242	−2.456	−2.318	−1.887	0.216	−0.188	−0.435
1932–1993	−1.540	−0.600	−0.549	−2.160	−2.687	−1.610	−4.384	0.359	−1.876	−1.574	−2.370	−0.789	−1.013	−3.045

Table 2b Rate of price change for metal and energy commodities in percent per annum (measured trough to trough)

Period	Aluminium	Coal	Copper	Gold	Lead	Nickel	Oil	Pig iron	Silver	Tin	Zinc
1669–1711		−0.486		−0.734	−1.228						
1711–1741		0.238		0.170	0.392				0.197		
1741–1796		−0.188		−0.563	−0.388			−1.388	−0.593		
1796–1848		1.683		1.799	2.397			1.308	1.786		
1848–1902		3.111	1.287	2.500	3.514	−1.033		1.940	1.915	0.694	
1902–1932	−0.297	0.494	0.937	0.109	−2.373	0.327	2.799	−1.866	−0.155	−0.380	−0.545
1932–1993	−0.571	−1.110	0.656	0.820	−2.614	−0.353	2.124	0.053	0.931	−1.311	−0.120

Innovations in production play a major role in increasing output and driving down costs for agricultural commodities. Wheat farming provides a good illustration. Rostow (1978) details the impact on wheat production of the expansion of areas of cultivation from the mid nineteenth century through the early twentieth century, first with opening of the American Middle West and Great Plains to wheat production following the westward expansion of rail links, then with expansion in Canada, Australia and Russia.[11] More recently, the Green Revolution has substantially lifted yields and allowed extension of production to previously unviable locations.

As shown in Tables 2a and 2b, the real price of wheat dropped by an average of 0.634 % per annum from 1848 to 1902 and by 1.013 % per annum from 1932 to 1993. Interestingly, the first decline was among the largest for any agricultural commodity over the same period, while the second decline was around the median level of agricultural commodities in the same period. The expansion in wheat farming area was clearly specific to wheat, while the Green Revolution affected the agricultural sector as a whole.

There is little doubt that innovation has significantly impacted on the real price of wheat since 1848, given that the massive real price decrease has occurred in spite of any limits imposed by nature on the very large increases in production over the period. How much is specifically attributable to the two major innovations identified above is arguable, for there have been numerous other innovations occurring over the years, including the mechanization of harvesting and the opening of new production areas in South America and Asia. There are also the confounding influences, such as wars (the real price of wheat rose by close to 100 % from 1913 to 1917 and by almost 200 % between 1941 and 1947), the aggregate business cycle on "sensitive" prices in general (the real wheat price rose by almost 100% in the commodity boom from 1972 to 1974 and by about the same percentage in the recent boom of 2006–2008) and of weather or pests affecting crop yields. Nonetheless, the experience of radical real price decrease in the period since the middle of the nineteenth century stands in sharp contrast to the experience of the prior two centuries when the real wheat price fluctuated widely but without a discernible trend.

Technological change has affected prices of agricultural commodities on the demand side as well as the supply side. Particularly notable has been the effect of the development of synthetic substitutes. Synthetic fibers substantially reduced demand for cotton, hides, jute and wool over the course of the twentieth century and this is reflected in Tables 2a and 2b in relatively steep trend declines in prices for these commodities over the trough-to-trough cycle from 1932 to 1993. It is also reflected in the statistically significant negative trend for rubber over 1900–2007 in the study by Sapsford et al. (2010).

Innovations in institutions as well as technology have impacted on real prices of agricultural commodities. In the previous section we note the negative impact on real primary commodity prices of market power in manufacturing, in both product

[11] See especially Rostow (1978) pp. 147–149 and pp. 167–177.

and labor markets, in increasing manufacturing prices (the denominator of the real price of all primary commodities is an index of manufacturing prices). More specific to agricultural commodities have been moves towards agricultural protectionism in the industrialized countries. Particularly damaging have been subsidy programs that have led to the dumping of surplus production on world markets.[12]

The dominance of negative price trends for agricultural commodities in Tables 2a and 2b contrasts with a mixed picture for metals and energy. Harvey et al. (2010) find statistically significant negative price trends for only two of the metal and energy commodities (aluminum and zinc), while Sapsford et al. (2010) find such evidence for only one metal (aluminum). Gold prices in Tables 2a and 2b are shown as rising over all cycles since 1796, while oil prices are shown as rising for both cycles for which data are available.[13]

Some of the technological and institutional innovations affecting agricultural commodities have also influenced real prices of metals and energy commodities. In particular increased market power in manufacturing product and labor markets have had a negative impact by increasing the denominator of the real price measures. However, there have been other influences that help to explain the lesser frequency of negative price trends for metals and energy commodities as compared to agricultural commodities.

One factor pushing up metal and energy prices is depletion. Topp et al. (2008) document the impact of depletion across mining (metals and energy) industries in Australia over the past three decades. They estimate that depletion reduced measured multi-factor productivity growth in Australian mining by about two and a half percent per annum. Declining productivity pushes up costs, which makes mining unprofitable unless prices rise or there are compensating reductions in other costs. Topp et al. estimate that cost decreases associated with improvements in technology and new discoveries amounted to about two and a half percent per annum, almost exactly offsetting the increased costs due to declining resource quality.

Innovations in institutions have also had positive impact on the real prices of some metal and energy commodities. The obvious example is the influence of the Organization of Petroleum Exporting Countries (OPEC) on oil prices since the 1970s. There has also been considerably increased concentration of production on a global scale in many segments of metals mining and processing, particularly aluminum, copper, iron ore and nickel. Of course the process of concentration as an element of creative destruction might have at least a temporary depressing effect on prices rather than the increasing effect associated with monopoly in static equilibrium.[14]

[12] See Nissanke (2010b) for an extensive discussion of the impact of government policies on prices of primary commodities.

[13] For both gold and oil the absence of a statistically significant positive trend in real price can be attributed to falling prices in early years for which data are available. Real gold prices fell in the three cycles from 1669 to 1796, while real oil prices fell in the years from 1859 (the first year in the oil price series) to 1902.

[14] For a discussion of the compression of profit margins in the concentration phase of the dynamic process of competition see Bloch (2000).

5 Conclusion

Innovation has arguably been the dominant force in determining the path of real prices for primary commodities over the past three and a half centuries. The influence of innovation has been sufficient to result in negative trends in real prices for numerous individual commodities and for aggregate indexes of commodities. The negative trends have occurred in spite of massive increases in output with growth in the world economy, defying the predictions of classical and neoclassical economics that scarcity associated with natural limits would lead to rising real prices of primary commodities.

Models of growth that emphasize natural resource scarcity as a constraint on growth divert attention from the key role of innovations in determining the course of prices and quantities of primary commodities. While there is a dominant tendency for real primary commodity prices to decline, the outcomes vary across time and across commodities. We provide examples of the role of innovations in both technology and institutions in driving trends over particular periods for particular commodities. Further, the innovations are not simply the result of historical accident, but reflect concerted entrepreneurial efforts of individuals and organizations to achieve scientific advance, to advance public policy objectives and, especially, to earn profits. Schumpeter correctly identified the need to build such entrepreneurial activity into the analysis of long-run growth. The spirit of his contribution suggests that it is profitability rather than necessity that is the mother of innovation under capitalism.

Properly incorporating entrepreneurial activity and endogenous innovation into the analysis of primary commodities in the process of long-run growth requires a broad perspective. First, the scope of innovations considered needs to extend beyond the technology of producing primary commodities. Innovations in technology of using primary commodities are also important, as has been shown by the impact of the development of synthetic materials and moves to increase energy efficiency. Second, innovations in the distribution and marketing of primary commodities have had a major impact on the real price of individual commodities in the past and are likely to continue to do so in the future. Finally, innovations in the technology and market organization of manufacturing are also important as manufacturing prices constitute the denominator of the real price measures for primary commodities. While increased market power in manufacturing has had a profound negative impact on the real prices of primary commodities in the past, future innovations could reverse this trend.

One clear insight from Schumpeter's (1939) analysis in *Business Cycles* is that innovations impart a cyclical character to long-run growth, particularly in terms of long cycles of the type identified by Kondratieff. We find a pattern of cycles lasting between three and six decades in real primary commodity prices over the past three and a half centuries. We date the last cyclical trough as occurring in 1993 and the peak as occurring in 2008.[15]

If our dating is correct, the world economy has entered into the downswing of a long cycle. Judging from the behavior of real primary commodity prices in past cycles, this should leave the aggregate of real primary commodity prices well below 1993 levels.[16] This prediction provides a sharp contrast to the view prevailing in neoclassical economics that natural resource scarcity leads to increasing real prices for natural resource products over time. Of course, with technological change being exogenous to the process of economic growth in neoclassical models, any observed behavior can be ascribed ex post to the observed course of technological change. The great virtue of Schumpeter's approach is that it brings technological change within the analysis of economic development and growth, albeit without the false precision of neoclassical optimizing models that depend on the assumption that the future is knowable or, at least, that the expected future value of economic variables can be calculated accurately.

Acknowledgments Helpful comments from the discussant, William Kingston, and members of the audience are gratefully appreciated as are comments from Hiroaki Suenaga and two anonymous referees. We also thank Jakob Madsen for providing the data on commodity prices used in the empirical analysis. Any errors and omissions are solely the responsibility of the authors.

References

Bloch H (2000) Schumpeter and Steindl on the dynamics of competition. J Evol Econ 10:343–353
Bloch H, Sapsford D (2000) Whither the terms of trade? An elaboration of the Prebisch-Singer hypothesis. Cambridge J Econ 24:461–481
Freeman C, Louçã F (2001) As time goes by. Oxford University Press, Oxford
Harvey DI, Kellard NM, Madsen JB, Wohar ME (2010) The Prebisch-Singer hypothesis: four centuries of evidence. Rev Econ Stat 92:367–377
Hotelling H (1931) The economics of exhaustible resources. J Polit Econ 39:137–175
Kalecki M (1971) Selected essays on the dynamics of the capitalist economy. Cambridge University Press, Cambridge
Mensch G (1979) Stalemate in technology. Ballinger, Cambridge, MA

[15] In this context, it is important to remember that the downswing in Schumpeter's analysis refers to downward pressure on prices and is consistent with substantial output expansion. Indeed, the last downswing in real commodity prices that began in 1937 included at least three decades of robust output expansion.

[16] As noted by an anonymous referee this prediction is fragile, being dependent on the judgment that 2008 is indeed a cyclical peak as well as on the continuation of a long-run downward trend in primary commodity prices. The dramatic declines of most primary commodity prices in 2009 from their 2008 highs represent a large movement that fits the prediction, but the subsequent rebound suggests the downward path will be far from steady. Clearly, there is still a substantial distance left to cover in terms of both time and the decline in the level of real prices.

Nissanke M (2010a) Issues and challenges for commodities in the global economy: an overview. In: Nissanke M, Mavrotas G (eds) Commodities governance and economic development under globalization. Palgrave, London, pp 39–64

Nissanke M (2010b) Commodity market structures, evolving governance and policy issues. In: Nissanke M, Mavrotas G (eds) Commodities governance and economic development under globalization. Palgrave, London, pp 65–97

Prebisch R (1950) The economic development of Latin America and its principal problems. UN ECLA. Econ Bull Latin Am 7(1962):1–22

Ricardo D (1911) The principles of political economy. J. M. Dent Everyman's Library, London

Rostow WW (1978) The world economy: history and prospect. University of Texas Press, Austin, TX

Rostow WW (1980) Why the poor get richer and the rich slow down. University of Texas Press, Austin, TX

Sapsford D, Pfaffenzeller S, Bloch H (2010) Commodities still in crisis? In: Nissanke M, Mavrotas G (eds) Commodities governance and economic development under globalization. Palgrave, London, pp 99–115

Schumpeter JA (1939) Business cycles, vols 1 and 2. McGraw-Hill, New York

Singer H (1950) The distribution of gains between investing and borrowing countries. Am Econ Rev Paper Proc 40:473–485

Tilton JE, Landsberg HH (1999) Innovation, productivity growth, and the survival of the U.S. copper industry. In: David Simpson R (ed) Productivity in natural resource industries. Resources for the Future, Washington, DC, pp 109–139

Topp V, Soames L, Parham D, Bloch H (2008) Productivity in the mining industry: measurement and interpretation. Productivity commission staff working paper, Canberra, Australian Productivity Commission

Tylecote A (1992) The long wave in the world economy. Routledge, London

Knowledge Flows in High-Tech Industry Clusters: Dissemination Mechanisms and Innovation Regimes

Bo Carlsson

Abstract This paper explores knowledge flows, i.e., creation and dissemination of knowledge, in three types of clusters in order to lay a conceptual foundation for analysis of knowledge-based industry clusters and for technology policy. Distinction is made between two different innovation regimes: discovery-driven innovation, represented by Silicon Valley and Cambridge, UK, in semiconductors, and by Boston/Cambridge, the San Francisco Bay Area and Medicon Valley in biotechnology; and design-driven innovation as represented by Boeing in Seattle, Bombardier in Montreal, Airbus in Toulouse, and Saab in Linköping in the aircraft industry. In each cluster, the role of universities and other creators of knowledge is examined. The nature of knowledge dissemination is also analyzed, distinguishing between market-mediated transfers of knowledge and non-market mediated and undirected transfers ("true" spillovers). The role of new start-ups versus incumbent firms in knowledge dissemination and cluster growth is also examined.

1 Introduction

New knowledge is an important driver of economic growth. Much of the economic growth literature in the last couple of decades has focused on the role of knowledge creation and diffusion. The theory of "endogenous growth" (see for example Romer 1986, 1990; Lucas 1988) is based on the idea of knowledge spillovers emanating from R&D. Although this is a useful contribution to our understanding of economic growth, it has led to an overly simplistic focus of public policy on knowledge creation. The theory specifies neither the nature nor the mechanisms of spillovers,

B. Carlsson (✉)
Department of Economics, Weatherhead School of Management, Case Western Reserve University, 10900 Euclid Avenue, Cleveland, Ohio 44106-7235, USA
e-mail: Bo.Carlsson@case.edu

A. Pyka and E.S. Andersen (eds.), *Long Term Economic Development*, Economic Complexity and Evolution, DOI 10.1007/978-3-642-35125-9_9,

with the unfortunate result that the term "knowledge spillover" has come to be used much too frequently and loosely.[1] The purpose of the present paper is to show that it matters where and by whom new knowledge is created as well as how it is disseminated. Focus needs to be on the process, not only on the outcome (Werker and Athreye 2004). What is needed is an evolutionary approach rather than a traditional (orthodox) one.

A basic idea in traditional theory is that new knowledge is a public good which gives rise to economic growth when it is applied in economic activity and that its benefits increase the more widely it is applied. But in a world of uncertainty, lack of appropriability, indivisibilities, and externalities there are insufficient incentives to engage in R&D. This results in market failure, leading to underinvestment in knowledge creation and weak mechanisms for knowledge transfer (Metcalfe 1994). The implication for public policy in standard theory is that knowledge creation and knowledge diffusion (R&D) should be stimulated and intellectual property rights protected. However, this general policy prescription needs considerable adjustment in a world characterized by large differences among firms, bounded rationality, and various other asymmetries. The claim of this paper is that a more solid basis for technology policy requires a better understanding of the processes of knowledge creation and dissemination as well as how "spillovers" relate to these processes. Evolutionary theory provides an appropriate analytical framework for such a discussion (see e.g. Metcalfe 1994, 1995; Cantner and Pyka 2001; Smits et al. 2010). The main components of the necessary theoretical framework are incorporated in the theory of innovation systems (Carlsson and Stankiewicz 1991).

It is useful for the purposes of this analysis to examine knowledge flows in knowledge-based (high-tech) industry clusters which may also be referred to as technological innovation systems (Carlsson 1995, 1997, 2002).[2] However, while there are many studies of industry clusters or innovation systems, they are often more descriptive than analytical, focusing more on their geographic and institutional dimensions than on the nature of knowledge and knowledge flows that are at their core. In this paper the focus is on knowledge flows in particularly knowledge-intensive industry clusters. Having reviewed the literature, I chose to examine three domains which are represented by several studies covering more than one geographic area, namely biotechnology, semiconductors, and aerospace. I wanted to see whether there are common features of knowledge creation and dissemination in these knowledge-intensive clusters. What emerged from this explorative study were distinct patterns of knowledge flows with respect to the mechanisms for knowledge dissemination and innovation regime. The idea is to generate, not to test, new theory. For considerations of space, the evidence is presented here according to the patterns that emerged.

[1] Acs et al. (2009) and Braunerhjelm et al. (2010) have suggested entrepreneurial activity as one mechanism of converting new economically useful knowledge into economic growth.

[2] For a survey of the literature on innovation systems, see Carlsson (2007).

The central questions in this paper are: Where does the knowledge come from that constitutes the core of knowledge-based industry clusters (innovation systems)? How is the knowledge disseminated—via market mechanisms (such as technology transfer) or non-market mechanisms (spillovers), and what are the implications for the organizational structure of the clusters and for public policy?

It is demonstrated that the sources of knowledge and the vehicles of dissemination of knowledge differ among knowledge-intensive (high-tech) industry clusters depending on whether innovation is design-driven or discovery-driven. In design-driven systems or clusters such as in the aerospace industry, technology sharing and transfer is typically market-mediated; new knowledge tends to be created in large firms, and the role of universities is primarily to supply skilled labor. By contrast, in discovery-driven innovation such as in the biotechnology and semiconductor industries, universities play a much more prominent role as creators of new knowledge, and technology sharing usually involves both market-mediated transfer and true spillovers. As a consequence, the two types of clusters are organized differently, and there are important implications for the role of public policy.

The paper is organized as follows. I begin with a brief review of the knowledge spillover literature and a discussion of dissemination mechanisms. The next section discusses various types of clusters, how and why they have evolved, and the knowledge flows within each. The fourth section reviews the literature on knowledge flows in high-tech industry clusters characterized by different innovation regimes. The fifth section examines the sources of knowledge and mechanisms of knowledge diffusion and how these have evolved over time in two types of discovery-driven clusters: (1) the microelectronics clusters in Silicon Valley and in the Cambridge (UK) area; and the biotechnology clusters in Boston/Cambridge (Massachusetts), the San Francisco Bay Area, and Medicon Valley (spanning the Copenhagen-Malmö region in Denmark and Sweden). Design-driven clusters in the aircraft industry are also examined: Boeing (Seattle), Bombardier (Montreal), Airbus (Toulouse), and Saab (Linköping, Sweden). In each case I am interested primarily in the sources of knowledge, how knowledge flows differ and especially the role of university research versus industrial R&D, how these interrelate, what the mechanisms of interaction are, the character and importance of 'anchor tenants' located within the cluster and their links to outside entities, and how these relationships have evolved over time. Where (inside or outside the cluster) and by whom (academia or business) does knowledge generation take place? To what extent is it appropriate to speak of 'spillovers' (unintended, non-market mediated) in reference to knowledge flows? The final section summarizes the argument, draws conclusions, and states the policy implications.

2 Knowledge Spillovers and Economic Growth

In economics, an externality or spillover of an economic transaction is defined as an impact on a party that is not directly involved in the transaction. It was noted long ago by Abramovitz (1956) and Solow (1956) that only a small fraction of macroeconomic growth in the United States can be attributed to increased inputs of labor and capital, the rest (the "residual") being attributable to other factors, particularly technological change—"a measure of our ignorance" as Abramovitz put it. The contribution of endogenous growth theory is to include technology explicitly in the production function, arguing that the remaining unexplained residual is due to R&D spillovers (and measurement errors). This residual constitutes the benefits reaped elsewhere in the system in addition to those appropriated by those who made the R&D investment. As pointed out by Griliches (1992), this results in problems in measuring spillover effects: it is difficult to distinguish between true externalities in the form of (unappropriable) knowledge spillovers and market-mediated knowledge transmissions that are hard to price accurately and that therefore result in measurement errors.

Griliches reviewed the basic model of R&D spillovers (based on the knowledge production function) and focused on the empirical evidence for their existence and magnitude. He found that "taken individually, many of the studies are flawed and subject to a variety of reservations, but the overall impression remains that R&D spillovers are both prevalent and important" (Griliches 1992, p. S29). He distinguished between two types of R&D 'spillovers': One represents knowledge embodied in capital equipment and involves the problem of measuring capital equipment, materials and their prices correctly. The foremost example here is the computer industry. As computers have improved and their price has come down, different industries have benefited differentially, depending on their rate of computer purchases. But according to Griliches, "these are not real knowledge spillovers. They are just consequences of conventional measurement problems. True spillovers are ideas borrowed by research teams of industry *i* from the research results of industry *j*. It is not clear that this kind of borrowing is particularly related to input purchase flows" (Griliches 1992, p. S36). The second type of spillovers, "true spillovers," involves disembodied knowledge. "The assumption is made that two firms that are active in the same technological areas, as indicated by their taking out patents in the same patent classes, are more likely to benefit from each other's research results." (p. S39)

In an influential paper, Jaffe (1989) brought the analysis of spillovers from the macroeconomic to the regional level. He studied spillovers from university research to commercial innovation using state-level time-series data on corporate patents, corporate R&D, and university research. He found a significant effect of university research on corporate patents at the state level in a few industries, particularly in drugs and medical technology, electronics, optics, and nuclear technology. Subsequently, Jaffe et al. (1993) found that patent citations are geographically concentrated to local metropolitan areas.

Anselin et al. (1997) estimated knowledge production functions at both the state and the metropolitan statistical area (MSA) levels. They found strong evidence of local spillovers at the state level. At the MSA level, they distinguished between industrial research and development activities and university research in the MSA and in the surrounding counties and found evidence of local spatial externalities between university research and high technology innovative activity, both directly and indirectly via private research and development.

Feldman (1999) reviewed four separate strains in the empirical spillover literature: innovation production functions, the linkages between patent citations, the mobility of skilled labor based on the notion that knowledge spillovers are transmitted through people, and knowledge spillovers embodied in traded goods. Feldman then examined the composition of agglomeration economies, the attributes of knowledge, and the characteristics of firms. She found that knowledge spillovers from science-based activities are localized and contribute to higher rates of innovation, increased entrepreneurial activity, and increased productivity within geographically bounded areas. The main mechanisms of knowledge spillover are patent citations and movements of people and traded goods. There is evidence that knowledge spillovers are limited in the spatial dimension in some domains but not necessarily in others (Feldman 1999, pp. 20–21).

Breschi and Lissoni (2001) reviewed the literature of knowledge spillovers in relation to industry clusters. They distinguished between three kinds of externalities: economies of specialization, labor market economies, and knowledge spillovers (Breschi and Lissoni 2001, p. 978). The first two of these are pecuniary externalities (knowledge flows mediated by the market mechanism); the third is a technological externality (pure spillover) to the extent that it involves unintended and non-market mediated transfer of knowledge.

Thus, Breschi and Lissoni take a critical view of the literature:

> The major limitation of the empirical literature we have reviewed... is that virtually no contribution has explored the ways in which knowledge is actually transferred among people located in the same geographic area.... We need to explore the price and non-price mechanisms through which knowledge may be traded between universities and firms (or individuals therein), as well as between firms... First and foremost, we observe that much of knowledge transmitted from universities to firms has nothing to do with the public results of basic science, but consists of consultancy services to firms. Rather than providing *innovation opportunities*, such knowledge transfer may enhance the customer firms' *appropriation capabilities*. (Breschi and Lissoni 2001, p. 994)

Local academic institutions and public research institutes often provide critical inputs for firms' innovative activities, such as *training* and *consultancy*, even if their current research is not *directly* relevant to those activities. By producing graduates and offering services (or tolerating their staff doing so), universities contribute to enhancing absorptive capacity of firms even if their research is not on the frontier. Hiring of skilled personnel increases the absorptive capacity of the firm and thus enables the firm to take advantage of spillovers.

Arikan (2009) studied inter-firm knowledge exchanges and the knowledge creation capability of clusters. He found that these exchanges typically take place through frequent interactions among cluster firms and that they that take various forms, from vertical supplier–buyer relations to horizontal alliances, licensing agreements, and research consortia—all of which are market-mediated. In addition, geographic proximity increases the frequency of interactions among cluster firms as well as the effectiveness of knowledge exchanges through these interactions; face-to-face contact between firm members contributes to the building of inter-firm trust and institutional norms of cooperation." (Arikan 2009, p. 658)

"A cluster that has a high level of knowledge creation capability is one where knowledge held by individual firms is effectively shared among cluster firms through interfirm knowledge exchanges and amplified by individual firms' knowledge spirals, leading to enhanced knowledge creation by individual firms." (Arikan 2009, p. 660) In other words, a high level of absorptive capacity increases the probability of identifying and benefiting from spillovers.

The problem with much of the literature on knowledge spillovers and economic growth is that it fails to distinguish between knowledge transfers (targeted sharing or dissemination of knowledge) and true spillovers (externalities). Only a fraction of new knowledge is economically useful, and only a small fraction of economically useful knowledge is commercialized (via new products in existing firms, licenses, or new start-ups) (Carlsson and Fridh 2002). Some of the new knowledge created in academic institutions is published, but the bulk of it is embodied in the students who carry it into the labor force (Carlsson et al. 2009). Most R&D is targeted; about 60 % of total R&D in the United States involves development, 22 % is applied, and only 18 % is basic R&D, mostly untargeted (source: NSF). Most of the basic R&D is carried out in academic institutions. And while basic R&D has shifted increasingly towards universities (away from business) in recent decades, it is only a few top universities that are capable of producing basic R&D of sufficient quality to give rise to new business opportunities (Mansfield, 1995). Most of the basic R&D carried out by business firms tends to enhance their absorptive capacity rather than pushing out the knowledge frontier; the utilization of new skills acquired through hiring of new PhDs is part of this process. These are certainly important knowledge transfers, but they take place via (admittedly imperfect) market mechanisms. They are not spillovers in a true sense. True spillovers are not market-mediated; they are the result of externalities in the form of knowledge transferred or acquired from outside sources without intent or direction on the part of the inventor and without compensation. Knowledge acquired from publications or patents or via employees or students leaving to start a new firm without payment to the employer represents spillovers. Buying a license or a piece of equipment, hiring of skilled workers, or acquiring knowledge via joint ventures, alliances, or mergers and acquisitions are intentional transfers mediated via markets; they do not involve true knowledge spillovers.[3] As will be shown below, true spillovers are the main raison d'être for some high-tech clusters. In other clusters in which knowledge is disseminated via transfers, the reasons for co-locating may be more conventional.

[3] This is not to suggest that market-mediated knowledge transfers are unimportant—on the contrary. They are the dominant mechanisms of knowledge diffusion. But they are not true spillovers.

3 Types of Industry Clusters

The term "industry cluster" became prevalent in the economic literature around 1990 (see e.g. Krugman 1991; Porter 1990, 1998), but it has been used rather loosely. Porter (1990) defined an industry cluster as a geographically proximate group of firms and associated institutions in related industries, linked by economic and social interdependencies. This is the definition most commonly used in the literature. Gordon and McCann (2000) distinguished between three different interpretations of industry cluster: the classic model of "pure agglomeration" based on the (neo-)classical tradition in economics, the industrial complex model of tight integration and stable relationships among firms, and the social network model built on interpersonal trust and relationships transcending firm boundaries. There are many different types of clusters, depending on the type of economic activity involved as well as stage of development. Much of the literature refers to Alfred Marshall's *Principles of Economics* (1920), the first edition of which was published in 1890.

As Marshall pointed out, many industrial activities tend to cluster in certain geographic regions. Marshall distinguished between regional agglomerations and "industrial districts." He referred to the former as "elementary localization of industry" which "gradually prepared the way for many of the modern developments of division of labor in the mechanical arts and in the task of business management" that characterize industrial districts (Marshall 1920, p. 268). According to Marshall, there are three primary causes of localization of industries: non-tradable inputs (physical conditions such as climate, soil, and access to raw materials), "patronage of a court" (demand for goods of high quality), and "the presence of a town" (urbanization economies, i.e., a sufficient number of customers) (*ibid.*, pp. 268–269). Once an agglomeration has emerged, it may be transformed over time into an industrial district if certain advantages are acquired: a local market for special skills that can be passed on to the next generation (mysteries of the trade are no longer mysteries but are "in the air"); growth of subsidiary trades; and use of highly specialized machinery (Belussi and Caldari 2009, p. 337). The resulting industrial district is the locus of economic activity that makes up a large fraction of an industrial economy; it represents the ordinary growth process—what Schumpeter would refer to as "economic growth" in the stationary state. Universities, government policies, and public laboratories play a modest role in these districts; they are self-organized agglomerations of private firms competing in similar markets, together with specialized suppliers of equipment and services (Niosi and Zhegu 2005, p. 3). There are not many knowledge externalities (true spillovers) associated with these districts, since they are not knowledge-based.

To get to a more dynamic stage ("economic development" in Schumpeter's terminology) two additional factors are needed—emphasized by Marshall in both his *Principles* and *Industry and Trade* (1923), although not specifically in connection with his discussion of industrial districts: what he calls "industrial leadership" (i.e., entrepreneurship), and "introduction of novelties" (i.e., innovation). These additional elements make it possible to break out of mere "organic" growth into a more dynamic phase, transforming an industrial district into what we may call a rapidly growing technology-based industrial cluster. These are the types of clusters with which this paper is concerned.

According to this interpretation of Marshall, there are two key elements to look for in the formation of clusters: a pre-existing local or regional agglomeration ("industrial district") of economic activity and a scaling-up of that activity through entrepreneurship and innovation.

In discussing the organization of industry clusters, Markusen (1996) distinguishes between (1) Marshallian 'industrial districts' consisting mainly of locally owned SMEs; (2) hub-and-spoke districts characterized by a small number of large, vertically integrated firms surrounded by many small suppliers; (3) "state-anchored districts" which are similar to hub-and-spoke districts, but with the "hub" being a public or nonprofit organization, such as a university, government laboratory, or defense plant, rather than a large firm; and (4) satellite industrial platforms consisting of the branch facilities of multi-plant firms that are headquartered outside the cluster.

Maskell (2001) argues that any economic theory of clusters must provide an explanation for the existence and growth of the cluster and identify its boundaries. Once a cluster exists, focusing specifically on knowledge-based clusters, he distinguishes between the horizontal and vertical dimensions of clusters. He finds that "while suppliers and customers simply need to interact with each other in order to do business, competitors don't. Most relationships in the cluster will therefore be along the vertical dimension." (Maskell 2001, p. 930)

Maskell also emphasizes the role of heterogeneity of firms in a cluster. He asks, What are "the advantages of N co-localized firms of size S undertaking related activities that are not transferable to a single firm of size $S \times N$ doing the same? This is arguably the single most important question for understanding the existence of the cluster, yet largely ignored in discussions on the subject." (p. 927) Maskell argues that clustering reduces the costs of co-ordination and helps in overcoming problems of asymmetrical information, leading to further specialization so that a higher level of knowledge creation is obtained. "The main advantages are not the ease of intra-cluster interaction as such..., but the deepening of the knowledge base that it enables... Only by a steady increase in the number of firms in the cluster would it be possible to create knowledge simultaneously by variation and by the division of labor." (p. 932)

This introduces a time dimension to the analysis of clusters. Growth of clusters occurs by relocation of existing firms, by attracting (e.g. via existing dominant firms) entrepreneurs to start new firms, and by spin-offs from existing firms. If and when new entry no longer occurs, the cluster stops growing.

Following up on Maskell's analysis, Bathelt et al. (2004) discuss the idea of different types of knowledge flows, distinguishing between 'local buzz' and 'global pipelines.' Buzz refers to the information and communication flows within the same industry and place or region. It consists of "specific information and continuous updates of this information, intended and unanticipated learning processes in organized and accidental meetings, the application of the same interpretative schemes and mutual understanding of new knowledge and technologies, as well as shared cultural traditions and habits within a particular technology field, which stimulate the establishment of conventions and other institutional arrangements. Actors continuously contribute to and benefit from the diffusion of information, gossip and news by just 'being there'." (p. 38) "Global pipelines," on the other hand, refers to the linkages between anchor tenants within a cluster and similar entities outside the cluster such as the sharing of designs and technical specifications among aircraft manufacturers and their suppliers of major sub-systems. Ernst and Kim's (2002) concept of 'global production networks' is similar.

4 Design Space, Innovation Regimes, and Knowledge Flows

There are several dimensions of knowledge creation and dissemination that we need to understand before proceeding to empirical analysis of clusters. The sources, nature, and diffusion of knowledge differ among industry clusters. Knowledge flows vary dependent on design space and innovation regime.

Design space is defined as a cluster of complementary technical competencies. Its boundaries shift constantly due to scientific discovery (serendipitous or purposive), leading to new combinations. The design space is potentially influenced by academic research (concepts, theories, research methods and tools) as well as by industrial R&D (changes in absorptive capacity). (Stankiewicz 2002)

It is useful to distinguish between two types of innovation regimes: discovery-driven and design-driven.

> Discovery-driven regimes are characteristic of fields with poorly articulated or structured design spaces. The limited extent to which functions are clearly identified and mapped on the known structures and processes means that the solutions to problems have to be discovered rather than designed... Typical for discovery regimes is that innovation is driven by opportunity rather than demand. Technological advances, particularly the radical ones, tend to be triggered by serendipitous discoveries. The search processes that follow these discoveries are usually massively parallel (various forms of screening). Product performance requirements are hard to fully specify and operationalize early in the process. Hence the scope for vicarious testing is limited, and there is often strong dependence on some form of field trials. (Stankiewicz 2002, pp. 40–41)

By contrast, in well-developed engineering fields, technical problems are typically attacked through "analytical design"—presupposing a well-articulated design space.

> The search processes taking place in that space are sequential and iterative rather than parallel... The relatively high efficiency of the development processes reflects the fact that the design space utilized is strongly bounded and the performance requirements well defined and easy to operationalize. Design-oriented innovation processes are demand rather than opportunity driven... Mechanical engineering, electrical engineering, and software are examples of technologies operating predominantly under the design regime. (Stankiewicz 2002, p. 40)

This means that even though knowledge-based clusters are dependent on new knowledge, the organization of knowledge creation and diffusion varies from one cluster to another and may also change over time.

Laursen and Salter (2004) investigate what types of firms use universities as a source of innovation. They find that firms that adopt "open" search strategies (firms that use many external sources of knowledge such as competitors, suppliers and customers, private research institutes, fairs and trade associations) and invest in R&D are more likely than other firms to draw from universities. They also find that only a limited number of firms draw directly from universities as a source of information or knowledge for their innovative activities. The results imply that the direct contribution of universities to industrial practice is likely to be highly concentrated in a small number of industrial sectors (Laursen and Salter 2004, pp. 1211–12).

Studying bioscience-based clusters, Cooke (2004) notes the rise of specialist research firms, dedicated biotechnology firms or DBFs ("discovery companies") in the life sciences, along with university and other research labs, in proximity to which knowledge-intensive firms tend to cluster.

> Hence we see a highly globalized, hierarchical knowledge generation model in which leading-edge research is initiated by multi-disciplinary DBFs in clusters linking with (often many) large pharmaceutical firms, research institutes and other DBFs as developers. It is plain that the clusters are increasingly the locus of knowledge generation… The rise of research over science explains the rise of DBFs over big pharma in new knowledge generation. But DBFs still need large drugs firms to fund their discovery programmes. (Cooke 2004, p. 1115)

Universities and research institutes create basic scientific knowledge that is commercialized in clusters of DBFs, with the support of venture capitalists and other business and legal services. At the same time, multinational pharmaceutical companies fund the research in exchange for future licenses and acquisitions.

Powell et al. (1996) discuss "learning through networks" in biotechnology-based clusters. They argue that when knowledge is broadly distributed, the locus of innovation is found in networks of inter-organizational relationships. To be able to benefit, firms must be directly involved in the research process. "Passive recipients of new knowledge are less likely to appreciate its value or to be able to respond rapidly. In industries in which know-how is critical, companies must be expert at both in-house research and cooperative research with such external partners as university scientists, research hospitals, and skilled competitors." (Powell et al. 1996, p. 119)

Owen-Smith and Powell (2004) distinguish between channels and conduits. They see channels as diffusely and imperfectly directing transfers between nodes, facilitating information spillovers that benefit both loosely connected and centrally positioned organizations. Conduits, on the other hand, are more closed; they are characterized by legal arrangements (e.g., nondisclosure agreements and exclusive licensing contracts that transfer intellectual property rights) designed to ensure that only the specific parties to a given connection benefit from the information that is exchanged. They also find that both the geographic location of organizations connected by formal ties and the institutional characteristics of nodes in a network can alter the character of information flows. New knowledge flows out of universities much more readily than it does from commercial organizations (Owen-Smith and Powell 2004, pp. 5–7).

5 Knowledge Flows in Three Types of Clusters

Having thus laid the foundations—distinction between market-mediated and non-market mediated knowledge dissemination and between design-driven and discovery-driven innovation—we now proceed to an analysis of knowledge flows in three types of knowledge-based industry clusters. We examine the sources of new knowledge and the mechanisms of knowledge transfer in the semiconductor-based clusters in Silicon Valley and Cambridge (UK), the biotechnology clusters in Boston and the San Francisco Bay Area, as well as Medicon Valley, and the aerospace clusters formed around Boeing, Bombardier, Airbus, and Saab. As mentioned earlier, these clusters were chosen because they represent a spectrum of high-tech industrial activity located in different geographic regions with different institutions and because there is a relatively rich literature on each. To my knowledge, this is the first systematic analysis of knowledge flows in a cross-section of clusters. The review of the literature revealed that the knowledge creation processes in semiconductors and bioscience are essentially discovery-driven, whereas that in aerospace is design-driven. This has implications for the role of universities and entrepreneurial activity in cluster formation and growth and also for the structure and organization of the clusters.

5.1 Discovery-Driven Innovation: Semiconductors

5.1.1 Silicon Valley

The evolution of Silicon Valley is discovery-driven. The invention that gave rise to Silicon Valley (and similar clusters elsewhere) was the transistor. The invention was made at Bell Labs in New Jersey around 1950 by a team led by William Shockley. The fact that the new technology was commercialized in what later became known as Silicon Valley can be attributed to both Shockley's (partly incidental) decision to re-locate to the area and start his Shockley Semiconductor Laboratory there (in 1956) and the prior existence of the beginnings of an industrial agglomeration near Stanford University. There were several electronics companies already in place: Litton Engineering Laboratories (founded in 1932), Hewlett-Packard (1937), Varian Associates (1948), Westinghouse, Philco-Ford, and IBM (1950s), and Lockheed Aerospace Co. research lab (1956). There were also important institutions such as Stanford Industrial Park (founded in the late 1940s) and Stanford Research Institute (1950s).

In analyses of the evolution of Silicon Valley, Stanford is typically featured as a paradigm of universities generating innovations that lead to new technology-based firms. See e.g., Saxenian (1994) and Bresnahan et al. (2001). While it is clear that Stanford has indeed played an important role in shaping Silicon Valley, it is also important to note that at the same time there have been many external factors influencing research and other activities at Stanford—such as the federal government (particularly the Department of Defense) and many other actors such as business firms and inventors. It is a matter of co-evolution of institutions, academic and business R&D, and new technology. As Lenoir et al. (2003) point out,

> [t]he key to understanding these dynamic flows between the Valley and Stanford is the role of Federal support of research and development at major universities as well as the stimulus provided by federal R&D... Creating and sustaining an entrepreneurial culture has been crucial to developing this synergistic feedback between federally supported research and research problems of industry, and it has positioned Stanford researchers to make major advances in science and engineering. A further crucial element in this synergism is the presence at Stanford of an engineering school, a medical school, and an environment that encourages interdepartmental and cross-school collaborative work. Such collaborations have been fundamental in producing startup companies focusing on convergent technologies (such as computing and biotechnology, or nanotechnology and communications) that have been crucial to generating new waves of technological innovation. (Lenoir et al. 2003, p. 1)

Many studies of Silicon Valley have emphasized the role of Fred Terman, the Dean of Engineering and subsequently Provost at Stanford, who joined the University in 1946. Part of Terman's vision was to build Stanford's research capabilities through close alliances with industry, similar to what MIT had done before the war. But he was aware of the desire on the part of industrial sponsors of academic research to control the direction of research and to ensure exclusive access to the research results. Therefore, he built his research programs with government grants funding the research of doctoral students who would then become attractive candidates for hiring by industry. Terman was also one of the drivers behind the building of infrastructure. Stanford Industrial Park was a part of Terman's strategy of building a strong university center for research and graduate instruction in electronics (Lenoir et al. 2003, p. 5).

Upon his arrival in California, Shockley hired a set of extraordinarily talented engineers for his Semiconductor Laboratory. Within a year these engineers ("The Traitorous Eight") left the company to form their own firm, Fairchild Semiconductor. A decade later, several of these engineers spawned another set of their own individual companies: Intel, Advanced Micro Devices, Inc. (AMD), Kleiner-Perkins venture capital company, and Fairchild Semiconductor Corp. (Moore and Davis 2001). Stanford did not play a direct role in creating the knowledge that gave rise to the first generations of Silicon Valley firms, but it has certainly done so subsequently, as exemplified by Sun Microsystems (founded 1982), Cisco (1984), Yahoo! (1994), and Google (1998), all founded by Stanford graduate students.

Lécuyer (2005) has argued that while the Department of Defense dictated the intellectual contours of academic science and engineering during the Cold War, American science was also deeply influenced in important ways by industry. He has shown that between 1955 and 1985 Stanford University benefited from industrial innovation in solid state technology (transistors, integrated circuits, and VLSI systems) and that these transfers enabled Stanford engineers to make significant contributions to the expanding fields of microelectronics and computing.

Along similar lines, Kenney and Patton argue that the primary source of entrepreneurs for Silicon Valley start-ups has been other firms, not university institutions. It is an indirect process: it is still true that many of the 'defining firms' (pioneers) in individual sectors originated in universities and corporate laboratories. For example, in addition to the Stanford spin-offs already mentioned, 3Com, Seagate, and Cadence are directly linked to Bay Area corporate research institutes and universities (Kenney and Patton 2006, pp. 39–40). There were (and are) close links between these corporate research institutes and universities in the area. But it is these firms rather than Stanford per se that have spawned most of the new firms. The Silicon Valley pattern seems to have been for a university spin-off to start a new line of business in the semiconductor industry and then in turn spin off new firms, each specialized in a new business. Sometimes the mechanism was the start-up of a firm to design and market new integrated circuits that would then contract for manufacturing from existing producers who happened to have spare capacity. As advances were made in existing design by Stanford or Berkeley faculty, these faculty would form new start-ups. As the software improved, many IC firms abandoned their in-house software and purchased software from design software vendors. The standardization of the design software facilitated the rise of the fabless semiconductor firms as they were able to purchase their design tools, eliminating the need for them to create their own software. The design software became the interface between the designers and the manufacturers (Kenney and Patton 2006, p. 48).

After each new discovery in a university or corporate lab, a new company was spun off and then spawned new spin-offs as new applications of the technology were found. An example is in the magnetic storage industry whose origins can be traced to research conducted in IBM's San Jose Laboratories. As new discoveries were made, people left IBM to establish firms to exploit new market opportunities of supplying storage devices for the new entrants. Similarly, in computer networking the pioneer was Xerox's Palo Alto Research Center (PARC) which created a networked system of small computers, laser printers, and data storage devices. At the end of the 1980s, computers were proliferating and entrepreneurs began forming firms to design and produce networking equipment (Kenney and Patton 2006, pp. 50–52).

> A business model emerged in which venture capitalists funded start-ups that were established with acquisition as an exit strategy. Cisco pioneered a new corporate strategy of using the Silicon Valley start-up ecosystem to identify the new technologies that would affect its business. As firms competed and grew and yet others were formed, Silicon Valley increasingly became the knowledge center for computer networking. This deep knowledge

meant that Silicon Valley firms, entrepreneurs, and venture capitalists would be uniquely positioned to see the next big thing. (Kenney and Patton 2006, p. 53)

Another important part of the Silicon Valley model is the openness and flexibility of the labor market. It was commonplace for people to change jobs between firms in the Valley, so that over time, participating in a start-up has become a career path (Saxenian 1994, pp. 30–37).

5.1.2 Cambridge, UK

The Cambridge area provides an example similar to that of Silicon Valley of endogenous formation of a high-tech cluster through spin-off, agglomeration and institutional adaptation, based on a discovery-driven process of innovation.

> Endogenous developments in Cambridge encompass the founding of companies by current and former members of the university, clustering stimulated by serial spin-outs from originator firms, the rise of local suppliers and, especially significant, the emergence of specialist labour markets. These developments depended on demand for high-tech output and exerted attraction effects through business services drawn to the area, through the implantation of international subsidiaries, inward investment via acquisition and the attraction of venture capital funds. Together these processes, endogenous and exogenous, contributed to the development of local competence and capabilities resulting in the formation and success of many new firms. (Garnsey and Heffernan 2007, p. 44)

Another endogenous determinant of clustering involves local supply chain benefits. Similar to Silicon Valley, high-tech firms in the Cambridge area make use of value chain complements or substitutes for the firms' internal activities by outsourcing to local legal and business services. These, in turn, have been attracted to the area by the presence of high-tech firms. Access to specialized labor is a key factor. It is not only the supply of new university graduates that is an important local asset but also a labor market of experienced specialized professionals that has accumulated over time. Mobility of highly skilled workers, facilitated by social networks, have contributed to technology transfer and fostering of interfirm links (Waters and Lawton Smith 2008). In Cambridge, clustering is closely related to an inter-generational spin-out process. The firms are connected locally by mobile people and knowledge to a greater extent than by supply relations, and they operate in value chains that have global reach. Their production networks are more international than local.

Both in Silicon Valley and in Cambridge the primary mechanism of knowledge transfer in electronics has been inventors leaving a university or corporate laboratory to start a new firm in order to commercialize a new application. Stanford has played an important role primarily as institution-builder but also as a source of knowledge, along with industrial R&D. The openness and high degree of labor mobility in the industry, both in Silicon Valley and in Cambridge, has made it easy for new firms to attract skilled labor from existing companies and thus build their absorptive capacity. This process involves both market-mediated technology transfer and pure spillovers. The main vehicle for continued growth has been proliferation of new products via start-ups and spin-offs.

Garnsey and Heffernan (2007) point out that success in Cambridge has been achieved in spite of significant obstacles. New firms in the area have had to struggle to obtain investment capital, reflecting a short-term focus of UK capital markets and higher rates of return in other, less innovative activity elsewhere in the UK economy. Until the late 1990s, venture capital in the area consisted of only three funds investing in about five ventures each among all Cambridge high-tech companies. Local and central government have also been unsupportive of business expansion in Cambridge. Waters and Lawton Smith (2002) argue that there is a need for more locally tailored policies rather than a local application of top-down central policy. Inadequate public transport and shortages of housing and skilled technical labor are particularly noteworthy constraints on growth.

5.2 *Discovery-Driven Innovation: Biotechnology*

The biotechnology industry is another discovery-driven industry. Its origin is the discovery by James Watson and Francis Crick of the structure and operation of the DNA molecule in Cambridge, UK, in 1953. Over the next couple of decades, basic research was conducted in university and government laboratories, as well as in a few large oil and chemical companies. The first commercial biotechnology firm in the United States was Cetus Corporation, founded in Berkeley, CA, in 1971, by Ron Cape and Peter Farley who brought scientific experience from both academic and business laboratories. Cetus was looking for a wide spectrum of applications, ranging from genetically engineered bacteria for alcohol production and oil-spill cleanups to vaccines and therapeutic proteins for the prevention and treatment of human disease. Genentech, founded in 1976, was the first commercial biotechnology firm to focus specifically on the development of pharmaceutical products using biotechnology techniques. It was founded by Bob Swanson, a venture capitalist with Kleiner and Perkins who had been an early investor in Cetus, and Herbert Boyer, a biochemist at the University of California, San Francisco (Romanelli and Feldman 2006, pp. 88–89).

Thus, the biotech industry originated in academic research. Similarly to the semiconductor industry, the evolutionary process is clearly discovery-driven, only even more so. An important difference between the two sectors is that biotechnology relies more heavily on basic science than does microelectronics, and university research has therefore played a more prominent role. Another important difference is that the process of converting a new scientific discovery into a new product ready for commercialization takes much longer, is riskier, and requires much more investment and scientific expertise than in microelectronics. As a result, intermediaries between scientific research and commercial application have emerged in the form of dedicated biotechnology firms (DBFs). In a few cases (e.g., Genentech and Amgen), the DBFs produce and market the new products themselves, but in most cases the deeper pockets and greater resources and expertise in production, marketing, and distribution of large pharmaceutical firms are needed.

An important feature of discovery-driven processes is that researchers are typically looking for applications of new discoveries in new domains. In the early days, firms experimented in broad categories of human diagnostics and therapeutics, agricultural biotechnology, and industrial and environmental biotechnology. Today firms tend to focus instead on quite specific techniques for the production of bioengineered drugs, plants, and chemicals. (Romanelli and Feldman 2006, p. 90) Because of the costs and risks involved, the experimentation is carried out by numerous small, specialized firms (DBFs) rather than by large, established firms.

> The DBFs represent the "hard core" of commercial agents in biotechnology, exclusively selling science-based knowledge as inputs to other industries, especially pharmaceuticals, but increasingly also to such diverse industries as medical diagnostics, food production and agriculture, bio-environmental remediation and chemical processing. Incumbents in pharmaceuticals have had to acquire and assimilate biotechnology capabilities and to engage in cooperative relations with DBFs, universities and other research institutions in order to survive. (Christensen 2003, p. 224)

As the design space in biotechnology has become both denser and more diverse, involving knowledge from a growing variety of disciplines, inventive and innovative activities have increasingly come to require both specialized knowledge from many different sources and competencies to integrate these diverse knowledge inputs. It is beyond the capacity of even large firms to master all the required competencies. As a result, DBFs have come to play the role of "experimenters" and "explorers" of scientific and technological opportunities for large pharmaceutical companies. Alliances between DBFs and large pharmaceutical corporations have become a prevalent feature of the modern pharmaceutical industry. Over time, pharmaceutical firms have also increasingly acquired small DBFs. While in the past pharmaceutical companies have always relied primarily on in-house R&D, complex innovative networks have emerged involving pharmaceutical companies, DBFs, public research institutions, as well as public authorities. Such networks have become the predominant mode of organizing innovation and may prove to become an enduring alternative to the historically vertically integrated innovation processes (Christensen 2003).

In the early phase of the industry, and especially in biotechnology narrowly defined, i.e., human therapeutics and diagnostics, the transfer of knowledge from universities to new start-ups (DBFs) was tied tightly to "star scientists" and was therefore confined to quite limited geographic areas. See e.g. Zucker and Darby (1996) and Zucker et al. (1998a, b). According to these studies, the positive impact of research universities on nearby firms was related to identifiable market exchange between particular university star scientists and firms, not to generalized knowledge spillovers. There was simply insufficient capacity outside the university laboratories to absorb the new technology. Much of the knowledge development and transfer still takes place via DBFs that commercialize technology.

However, it may be that the findings of Zucker and colleagues about the role of star scientists with impact only locally pertain to the beginning of the industry but not necessarily to later periods. Feldman (2003) points out that at the very beginning of the industry, universities were quite aggressive in intellectual property licensing, and that the importance of university research may decline over time.

> Science, the pursuit of new knowledge, occurs primarily within the domain of the research university and is characterized by a priority-based reward system that emphasizes scientific publication. Technology, on the other hand, develops ideas from science for commercial markets. It is characterized by the pursuit of economic returns and its venue is rent seeking firms. While it is appropriate to consider patents, publication and the location of star scientists in the earliest stages of firm formation – the science stage – we may expect that as an industry develops and science is translated into commercial applications, the locational dynamics may change to emphasize industrial and technological attributes. While science resources may be most important in the earliest stages of the industry development, technology resources may become more important as the industry develops. (Feldman 2003, p. 321)

5.2.1 Boston/Cambridge and the San Francisco Bay Area

Feldman's hypothesis is borne out, at least in part, in studies by Owen-Smith and Powell (2004, 2007). They analyzed strategic alliance networks in human therapeutic and diagnostic biotechnology during the period 1988–1999 in the Boston/Cambridge (Massachusetts) metropolitan area and in the San Francisco Bay Area. They found that

> [d]uring the very early years of the industry, from the early 1970s to the late 1980s, most biotech firms were very small start-ups that relied, of necessity, on external support. Lacking the skills and resources needed to bring new innovations to market, they became involved in elaborate lattices of relationships with universities and large pharmaceutical firms... Lacking a knowledge base in the new scientific field of molecular biology, large companies were drawn to start-ups by the latter's capabilities in basic and translational science. (Owen-Smith and Powell 2007, p. 62)

Studying bilateral links between entities in the Boston area, they found that at the beginning of the period (1988) by far the dominant part of the linkages were between public research organizations (PROs, such as Harvard, MIT, Tufts, and Massachusetts General Hospital) and DBFs. There were only a small number of ties between biotech firms or between biotech firms and local VC firms. These ties grew as the network expanded during the 1990s and dominated the commercial ties at the end of the period. Thus, the Boston network grew from origins in the public sector. Public science formed the foundation for commercial application. Early in its evolution, the Boston biotechnology community was linked together by shared connections to academic research. These connections have remained an important part of the network, but over time the number of DBF to DBF and DBF to VC ties has increased relative to university linkages (Owen-Smith and Powell 2007, p. 67).

The trajectory in the Bay Area is quite different from that in Boston. In 1989–1990,

> the Bay Area community was composed entirely of ties linking DBFs to local VC firms. Where the stability and technical diversity of Boston PROs anchored that network and fostered a more open technological trajectory…, the Bay Area relied heavily on the prospecting and matchmaking efforts of venture investors. Later years witnessed the increasing importance of VCs, a smattering of ties involving PROs, and – most importantly – dramatic growth in DBF-DBF connections… Both Boston and the San Francisco Bay Area evolved from dependence on a non-DBF organizational form to a state where significant portions of the network were made coherent by direct connections among science-based biotechnology firms. In other words, similar endpoints in the evolution of the networks were reached through different routes. While both relied on the inclusion of organizations different from biotechnology firms, Boston was anchored in the public sector, whereas the Bay Area was dominated by venture capitalists. (pp. 67–68)

Boston companies were often started by MIT and Harvard professors, who were typically senior professors with established reputations, who maintained their university affiliations, and who tended to serve the new companies primarily as scientific advisors. In contrast, founders in the Bay Area were much more likely to come from VC or other biotech firms. When Bay Area faculty were involved in founding, they tended to be younger and much more likely to take a leave from their university positions. Whereas almost all founders in Boston came from within the region, founders in the Bay Area came from a variety of locations, including faculty from Yale, Columbia, and Duke who came to California to start companies. (p. 70)

While Boston/Cambridge and the San Francisco Bay Area followed quite different trajectories during the 1990s, they ended up with rather similar structures by the end of the decade. As the density of links between DBFs increased in both clusters, the relative dependence on PROs and VCs, respectively, declined. Owen-Smith and Powell contend that networks dominated by PROs and 'open science' will result in innovations that rely less heavily on internal R&D and that draw more on research conducted in organizations other than DBFs.

There are several implications of these studies. Among these are (1) that the sources of knowledge (especially the role of universities) may vary from one location to another as well as over time, depending on institutional factors (co-evolution); (2) that the geographic boundaries of the cluster may shift over time; (3) that "true" technological spillovers may increase over time as absorptive capacity increases; and (4) that as a result of these complexities, public policy-making in biotechnology is extraordinarily difficult.

5.2.2 Medicon Valley

Medicon Valley refers to the biotechnology cluster located on both sides of the Öresund straight that separates Denmark and Sweden. The region has a long tradition in the agricultural, brewing, and pharmaceutical industries. The Swedish pharmaceutical firm Astra and the Danish firm Lundbeck started their activities in the region around World War I and were joined later by Novo Nordisk, Leo, Ferrosan, and Ferring (Denmark). Together with the universities of Copenhagen (founded 1479) and Lund (founded 1660) and several smaller universities, these companies formed an industrial agglomeration in the region that was already in place when an initiative was taken by Professor Sture Forsén at Lund University and Nils Hörjel, the county governor, in 1983, to start the Ideon Science and Technology Park adjacent to Lund University. Both Bioinvent and Biora, the first Swedish pure biotech firms, originated in different research projects at Lund University in the 1980s.

The initiation of Ideon sparked a wave of research parks in the region, including Symbion Science Park in Copenhagen. In 1995, five universities in the region began discussing cooperation among the universities in the two countries to strengthen the scientific knowledge base. This resulted in a joint effort by nine regional universities to create what is now called Öresund University. The completion of the bridge between Copenhagen and Malmö in 2000 tied the two sides together physically (Braunerhjelm and Helgesson 2006).

Thus, the universities took the lead in creating Medicon Valley. They were soon followed by policymakers and local governmental bodies that started to market the region in order to attract both national and international investment. The number of service providers and VC firms started to increase. There were 9 VC firms in the region in 1995; the number increased to 33 in 2002 (most on the Danish side). By 2002 there were 116 biotech firms in the cluster (82 in Denmark and 34 in Sweden) with a total employment of nearly 3,000. There were also 71 pharmaceutical firms (including large firms such as Astra Zeneca, NovoNordisk, H. Lundbeck, and LEO Pharma) and 129 medical technology firms in the region. The research infrastructure included 26 hospitals (11 of which were university hospitals) and 12 universities. The research output in the region places it among the leading regions in the world: in per capita terms, the number of biotechnology-related articles and citations in scientific journals in the region ranked slightly above other regions in Europe and not far behind Boston and the San Francisco Bay area in the United States (Braunerhjelm and Helgesson 2006; Coenen et al. 2004).

It is clear that universities (especially Lund University) played an important role in forming a biotechnology cluster in the area, drawing on the pre-existing regional agglomeration of pharmaceutical firms and research institutions. But where did the knowledge come from?

Coenen et al. (2004) have studied the knowledge flows in the region. They found that the knowledge dynamics of the cluster exhibit a dual local–global knowledge flow pattern. The sector is characterized by strong spatial concentration around nodes of excellence that are interconnected through a global network. Their study highlights the significance of proximity within epistemic communities (rather than other relational or physical proximities) in shaping innovation processes across multi-spatial scales. The study is based on a database-survey on collaboration in scientific publication by 109 biotechnology firms in Medicon Valley. Examining interpersonal knowledge interaction as reflected in scientific publications by all DBFs located in the region, they find that a large share (58 %) of the firms can be found in the Science Citation Index, with a total of 846 publications. About 40 % of the Danish firms and 50 % of the Swedish firms are involved in international co-publication. A vast majority of the firms' joint publications are with different types of PROs, whereas firm-firm co-publication seems to be quite rare; this applies to firms in both countries. The co-authors in international joint publications are scientists in a variety of countries, dominated by Germany, the UK and the US. About 1/3 of the firms have one or more publications with co-authors from outside Europe while only 1/5 of the firms are involved in cross-border Danish-Swedish co-publications (Coenen et al. 2004, p. 1013).

Thus it seems as though the collaborations that these firms have are more influenced by epistemic community (common scientific background) than by spatial or relational proximity. Many of the biotech firms in the Swedish part of the region are spin-offs from Lund University, but the common educational and professional background seems to play a greater role than the relational proximity between the researchers at the firm and their former colleagues at the university (Coenen et al. 2004, p. 1014).

In a similar study, McKelvey et al. (2003) have studied knowledge collaboration among Swedish entities in the biotechnology-pharmaceutical sector (not just in Medicon Valley but in the country as a whole) and with entities outside Sweden. They identified 215 R&D collaborations by 67 Swedish firms or Swedish research institutes and 137 foreign partners. Among these 215 R&D collaborations there were 52 agreements between two Swedish actors and between Swedish and foreign partners. Similarly to Coenen et al., the authors concluded that the degree of interconnection among Swedish firms is quite low and that no firm or group of firms plays a central role. Instead, alliances and collaborations with entities in the United States are much more important than with entities in Sweden or elsewhere in Europe. They also found that the Swedish parts of the large Swedish pharmaceutical firms Pharmacia, Astra-Zeneca and Amersham Pharmacia Biotech have very different spheres of R&D collaboration, both nationally and internationally. Thus, while the major MNCs have little formal collaboration within the country, they are also interested in different types of partners (McKelvey et al. 2003, p. 495). However, geographic co-location does appear to be important for smaller biotech-pharma firms located in regions of strong medical research.

Thus, it appears that Swedish firms interact more internationally and especially with entities in the U.S. than domestically or in other European countries. While the existing literature suggests that the reason for this is to access American research and American biotechnology firms, this appears to be valid mostly for large European pharmaceutical firms. This Swedish study shows instead that there is also a reciprocal flow, i.e., that international partners do deals to access knowledge at small to medium sized Swedish firms and Swedish research organizations (McKelvey et al. 2003, p. 496).

McKelvey et al. conclude:

> There are two large MNCs in the pharmaceutical sector, which have strong Swedish heritages. These two actors are not engaged in formal knowledge collaboration with the rest of the national firm population, and they are also reducing their involvement with Swedish universities over time... For the rest of the small and medium sized Swedish biotech-pharma firms, the propensity to collaborate with geographically co-located partners differs depending on whether the collaboration is firm to firm, firm to university, or

> university to university. The overall finding is that geographical co-location is less important for firm to firm deals or for university to university co-authored papers than for firm to university deals. In other words, a large number of Swedish firms tend to collaborate with Swedish universities rather than international universities. (McKelvey et al. 2003, p. 499)

It is apparent that the knowledge flows in the three regional biotechnology clusters (Boston/Cambridge, San Francisco Bay Area, and Medicon Valley) have evolved quite differently. In Boston, major research institutions such as Harvard, M.I.T., and Massachusetts General Hospital played a crucial role both as generators of new knowledge and as launching pads for new start-ups. In the Bay Area, venture capitalists served as major sources of linkages between academic research and its commercialization and as sources of funding. In Medicon Valley, the primary sources of knowledge are outside the region; the main conduits are research collaboration with universities, particularly in the United States, and the global pipelines supplied by multinational firms. There does not appear to have been much knowledge spillover in a true sense; the vast majority of knowledge transfers have been intentional and market-mediated. However, in recent years the increasing presence of research activities of major pharmaceutical firms in each of the three regions suggests that absorptive capacity is increasing to the point where true knowledge spillovers may become important.

Similarly to the semiconductor industry, the main vehicle of growth in biotechnology is start-up of new firms, typically based on academic research, applying new knowledge to new products.

5.3 *Design-Driven Innovation: Aircraft Industry*

The aircraft industry has evolved from humble beginnings as erstwhile assemblers of simple mechanical components and parts into perhaps the most knowledge-intensive integrators of complex systems known to mankind. But knowledge creation and dissemination in the aircraft industry clusters follows a different pattern than in other knowledge-based industries. While a significant portion of the knowledge is created and disseminated within local clusters, the main hubs of knowledge creation are the anchor tenants ("global network flagships" in the terminology of Ernst and Kim 2002), not universities. As the terminology implies, these system integrators are connected to global knowledge networks and depend more on such networks than on local suppliers. Consequently, local knowledge spillovers are of a different nature than in other knowledge-based clusters.

Before we discuss knowledge generation and knowledge flows in the industry, a brief history of four aircraft companies is instructive.

5.3.1 Boeing (Seattle)

Boeing was founded in 1917 by William E. Boeing who had studied at Vevey (Switzerland) and Yale University but did not graduate. He worked initially in the timber industry. He became interested in airplanes and decided he could build a better plane than the existing biplanes. In 1927 Boeing created an airline and in 1933 introduced the first modern airliner (a 10-seater). The Air Mail Act of 1934 prohibited airlines and aircraft manufacturers from being under the same corporate umbrella, so the company split into three: Boeing Airplane Company, United Airlines, and United Aircraft Corporation (later United Technologies). Shortly thereafter an agreement was reached with Pan American World Airways to develop and build a commercial airliner able to carry passengers on transoceanic routes. The first flight of the Boeing 314 Clipper took place in 1938. It was the largest civilian aircraft of its day with a capacity of 90 passengers. In the same year Boeing completed work on the Model 307 Stratoliner, the world's first pressurized-cabin transport aircraft. During World War II, Boeing built a large number of bombers. The company designed the B-17 bomber which was also assembled by the Lockheed and Douglas aircraft companies and the B-29 that was assembled also by Bell Aircraft Co. and the Glenn L. Martin Company. After the war Boeing developed military jets such as the B-47 Stratojet and the B-52 Stratofortress as well as the KC-135 tanker aircraft that was adapted as the Boeing 707 civilian jetliner, the first commercial jet airliner in the United States. In the 1960s and 1970s the Boeing 727, 737, and 747 were added to the product line, in the1980s the 757 and 767, and in the 1990s the 777 (Wikipedia).

Boeing dominated the large commercial aircraft industry for over 50 years. It is still the world's largest producer of both military and civilian aircraft and is also the largest aerospace company in the world. Its main assembly plants are located in Seattle, Washington. In 2001 its headquarters moved to Chicago. Boeing is somewhat different from other aircraft manufacturers in that for several decades it manufactured its main structural parts in-house. As a result, it became much more vertically integrated than its competitors. In the last few decades the company has dispersed its manufacturing and supplier system throughout the world in order to increase market penetration and reduce design and production costs. (Niosi and Zhegu 2005)

5.3.2 Bombardier (Montreal)

The production of aircraft in Montreal started in the 1920s, when several American, British, and Canadian producers competed to produce small propeller aircraft. In 1944, a group of employees of the Canadian subsidiary of British Vickers founded Canadair. After World War II and during the cold war, Canadair produced mostly military aircraft. Dozens of companies were spun off from Canadair or were attracted to Montreal to supply parts and components. In 1976, the company moved into civilian aircraft by acquiring the exclusive rights to the blueprint for a business jet (Learjet 600) designed by Learjet Corporation of Wichita, Kansas (USA). In 1986, Bombardier Corporation of Montreal bought Canadair and entered the regional aircraft market. The company developed several new regional jets and also bought de Havilland in Toronto. By the early 2000s Bombardier Aerospace was the world's third largest producer of aircraft, with 15,000 employees in Montreal and 28,000 world-wide. (Niosi and Zhegu 2005, p. 11)

Bombardier Aerospace is the largest but certainly not the only company in the aircraft cluster in Montreal. As early as the 1920s, Pratt & Whitney Canada, a subsidiary of U.S.-based United Technologies, started overhauling and repairing American-designed and built aircraft engines. Its production expanded and new products entirely designed and manufactured in Montreal were added. In the mid-1980s, Bell Helicopter of the U.S. transferred its production (but not design) of its civilian helicopters to Montreal. Several other companies (including subsidiaries of British and French firms) are also located in Montreal. There are now over 250 small and medium-sized manufacturing companies in the Montreal aerospace cluster (Niosi and Zhegu, pp. 12–13).

5.3.3 Airbus (Toulouse)

The aircraft cluster in Toulouse is centered on Airbus Industrie, a European consortium founded on government initiative in 1969 with Aerospatiale of France and Deutsche Airbus of Germany each taking a leadership role and with British (Hawker Siddeley, later acquired by British Aerospace) and Dutch (Fokker-VFW) companies also participating. Each company would deliver its sections as fully equipped, ready-to-fly components. In 1971 the Spanish company CASA also acquired a small share of Airbus Industrie.

Today Airbus is rivaling Boeing as the world's largest producer of commercial aircraft. Airbus assembles six different models of aircraft in Toulouse with parts and components coming from 1,500 contractors in 30 different countries. The United States is the largest provider with over 800 suppliers. Meanwhile, Toulouse has become a major aerospace cluster, with hundreds of firms. These include a French-Italian manufacturer of turboprops, manufacturers of turbines, landing gear, and small aircraft. Toulouse has also attracted producers of other aerospace-related products such as Matra and Alcatel (satellite communications). (Niosi and Zhegu, pp. 17–18)

5.3.4 Saab (Linköping)

Svenska Aeroplan AB (SAAB) was founded in 1937 in Trollhättan in western Sweden but soon moved its headquarters to Linköping near the east coast about 100 miles southwest of Stockholm. With World War II looming, the Swedish Air Force needed aircraft. When the war broke out in 1939, Saab was producing bombers and fighters, mainly copies of German and American designs. The first aircraft designed in-house was a light bomber that rolled off the line in 1941. In 1943 a fighter bomber aircraft was ready. At the end of the war, Saab converted seven U.S. B-17 Flying Fortress bombers into passenger aircraft. It also developed a small passenger plane (Saab 19) of its own, as well as a small plane for private use. As the Cold War intensified, the Swedish government wanted Saab to concentrate on military aircraft. Consequently, the production of the Saab 19 was discontinued in 1954 and transferred to the Dutch company Fokker. The fighter J-29 was introduced in 1948, followed by the J-32 in 1952, the J-35 in 1955, the J-37 in 1967, and the JAS-39, a multi-purpose aircraft which entered service in 1997. Saab has continued to produce all the aircraft needed by the Swedish air force and has also exported these aircraft to other countries (Eliasson 2010; http://www.swedecar.com; http://www.wikipedia.org).

Thus, Saab started out as a producer of military aircraft, diversified into civilian aircraft but was forced to revert to a primary focus on being a system integrator and producer of military aircraft and a supplier of advanced subsystems to Boeing and Airbus.

5.3.5 Organization of the Aircraft Industry

The dominant characteristics of the aircraft industry are helpful in explaining why the industry is organized the way it is and why the knowledge flows differ from those in other knowledge-based clusters.

> Aerospace is a high value-added sector, strongly affected by scale and timing. The industry success depends on rapid technological progress; government support for corporate R&D is essential. Their activity depends on components and parts which can be widely dispersed in terms of both industry and location. Transportation costs of these components are not relevant in overall aircraft costs. Also, demand (market) is not geographically bounded… [T]he primary centripetal force has been the regional pool of skilled and semi-skilled labor. Less important factors have been the location to the original industries of the cluster (often engineering sectors close to aircraft such as railway manufacturing) and the entrepreneurial talent… The persistent increase of R&D costs has been the major centrifugal force for the aircraft global decentralization: in order to reduce R&D costs, the industry has been gradually implementing strategies of international cooperation. (Niosi and Zhegu 2005, p. 6)

The large aerospace clusters typically consist of one or several OEMs (original equipment manufacturers) surrounded by hundreds of small and medium-sized suppliers of components and parts. There are two types of suppliers: higher-tier lead suppliers that deal directly with several OEMs and lower-tier suppliers that usually deal with the higher-tier suppliers, not directly with the OEMs. The higher-tier suppliers are usually located outside the local cluster, often overseas. Aerospace regions tend to specialize in different parts of the value chain. They manufacture high-value products in batches from a few hundred to several thousand. For example, there are civilian aircraft assembly clusters (such as in Seattle, Montreal, and Toulouse) and engines clusters (such as around GE's engine plants in

Cincinnati, Ohio, and Lynn, Massachusetts). With Boeing as a major assembler, Seattle is specialized in engineering and production of large commercial aircraft. Toulouse (France) is the major production site of Airbus and ATR (Niosi and Zhegu 2005).

5.3.6 Knowledge Generation and Knowledge Dissemination in the Aircraft Industry

Airplane manufacturers are essentially system integrators; they provide strategic and organizational leadership in designing complex systems. In the increasingly modularized global production system, the technology of the most advanced engineering firms often involves development of concepts, integration, and systems architecture rather than manufacturing (Eliasson 2010). Manufacturing is instead outsourced to various suppliers in the value chain. The OEMs are powerful carriers of knowledge. They are primarily global pipelines to major sub-system suppliers but they also transfer technical and managerial knowledge to local suppliers so that they can meet the technical specifications. For example, the Boeing 787 Dreamliner is assembled in Seattle using components developed and produced by an international team that includes Rolls-Royce in the UK (engines), General Electric in Ohio (engines), Kawasaki Heavy Industries in Japan (main landing gear), Dassault Systèmes in France (software), and Saab Aerostructures in Sweden (cargo doors) and dozens of other suppliers of components and sub-systems, plus hundreds of local suppliers of parts. In the case of Saab, the core technologies for the JAS-39 Gripen aircraft (other than platform development, systems integration, and aircraft control system which are Saab's own responsibility), the engine is manufactured by VolvoAero based on the General Electric F404 engine and the radar, computer, and electronic systems are developed by Ericsson. Other sub-systems are developed by a variety of major aerospace contractors in the U.S., U.K., France, and Germany. Only one sub-system is contracted to a Swedish company, but there are many Swedish suppliers of components (Eliasson 2010). Clearly, in terms of knowledge flows, the linkages to other advanced firms are much more important than to the local firms in the cluster.

Modern aircraft integrate advanced mechanical technology with electronics, sensor technology, hydraulics, new materials, and communications systems, among others. The system integration involves overall design, safety and reliability, availability and maintainability, monitoring and diagnostics, survivability, and produceability. Military aircraft are designed and developed in collaboration between government (military) agencies and aircraft manufacturers; for civilian aircraft, airlines play the role of competent customers.

The bulk of R&D expenditures in advanced firms is devoted to identifying internationally available complementary technology to integrate with their existing knowledge base, and only a small fraction is allocated on genuinely new technology development. The multinational firms are specialists in this field. It is noteworthy that distributed and integrated production became the mode of operation in engineering industries only after the micro processor resulted in the integration of computing and communications technology in the 1990s (Eliasson 2010).

5.3.7 Knowledge Transfer Mechanisms

Given the tiered structure of the aircraft industry, it is useful to examine knowledge flows at two levels. The knowledge flows between the system integrator and tier 1 (sub-system) contractors are bilateral; there is a great deal of learning, but the system integrators must necessarily take a leadership role. The knowledge flows are based on contracts. Historically, such contracts have typically been of a cost-plus nature.[4] These knowledge flows are large and have great economic impact as the participants apply advanced technology in their own businesses, with ripple effects to their sub-contractors. But it is important to note that they are market-mediated; they are not spillovers.

At tier 2 and lower levels, knowledge flows in the aircraft industry are usually more unilateral in nature and take place through more formal contracts. Flagship companies transfer knowledge in the form of blueprints and technical specifications, mostly free of charge, to ensure that products and services produced by the suppliers meet the necessary specifications. Sometimes these knowledge transfers are bilateral, i.e., systems and sub-systems evolve through collaboration between the integrator and the suppliers. Knowledge may also be transferred informally, without a contract and without any payment involved, particularly through technical assistance to local suppliers. The flagship company may exercise significant control over the way in which knowledge is disseminated and used, or it may play a more passive role with little influence on how local suppliers take advantage of the knowledge. Even though these transfers may not involve direct payment from the supplier to the OEM, the benefits are appropriated primarily by the OEM in the form of purchased products that meet the specification. Only to a limited extent should they be regarded as knowledge spillovers. But to the extent that local suppliers can develop their absorptive capacity, they can effectively absorb knowledge disseminated by global network flagships. This requires both individual and organizational learning. (Ernst and Kim 2002) These knowledge flows are not market-mediated, but they are directed to specific users, not generally to all the firms in the cluster.

> Flagships typically provide the local suppliers with *encoded* knowledge, such as machinery that embodies new knowledge, blueprints, production and quality control manuals, product and service specifications, and training handouts. This is done to assist the suppliers in building capabilities that are necessary to produce products and services with the expected quality and price. (Ernst and Kim 2002, p. 1425)

In contrast to electronics and biotechnology, aerospace clusters, even though they are knowledge-based, are not based on local knowledge spillovers. They rely

[4] The Saab JAS-39 Gripen project is an exception; it is based on fixed-price contracts.

mostly on global pipelines. For example, Saab's technological prowess as a developer and producer of military aircraft has depended in large measure on access to U. S. technology, notably advanced electronics. In return for building a strong air force capable of preventing Soviet anti-submarine aircraft from crossing Swedish airspace, the U.S. made advanced military technology available to Sweden, even though Sweden is not a member of NATO (Eliasson 2010). The clustering of economic activity in this sector is due primarily to agglomeration effects (externalities) in the form of pools of skilled labor and local suppliers of parts, components, and services. Knowledge spillovers from universities do not play a very important role. Niosi and Zhegu argue that local knowledge spillovers are less significant, of a different nature, and make less contribution to explaining the geographical agglomeration of firms in the aircraft industry than in other knowledge-based clusters. On the other hand, international transfers of technology help to explain the dispersion of industry across nations. The fact that the industry is geographically clustered is due to the anchor tenant effects as creators of labor pools and owners of very large manufacturing plants creating regional inertia.

Even though most of the technology transfers in the aircraft industry are market-mediated (i.e., not true spillovers), they still have enormous economic impact. According to calculations made by Eliasson, the economic effects of aerospace R&D anchored by Saab in Sweden are very large, at least 2–4 times the original investment in R&D. This includes not only the core technologies integrated in military aircraft but also related technologies in the engineering industries more generally. For example, Eliasson argues that were it not for its collaboration with Saab on military aircraft, Ericsson—currently the world's largest supplier of telecommunications equipment—would not have survived as an independent company. Other Swedish companies have also been able to develop more advanced products as a result of collaborating with Saab. The diffusion of technology rarely occurs in the form of transfers of well-defined and patentable technology packages; there is much learning on the part of both user and supplier. The main diffusion channel is people with knowledge and experience who move on through internal careers in firms or over the labor market (Eliasson 2010).

6 Conclusions and Policy Implications

In this paper I have tried to draw together several strands of literature, both theoretical and empirical, in order to analyze knowledge flows in various types of knowledge-based industry clusters. Where does the knowledge come from, and what mechanisms are used to disseminate knowledge? In particular, to what extent is it appropriate to use the term 'spillover' to refer to the diffusion of knowledge?

The sources of knowledge and the vehicles of dissemination of knowledge differ among high-tech clusters. In clusters characterized by discovery-driven innovation, such as biotechnology and semiconductors, universities play a much more important role as creators of knowledge than in design-driven clusters. In biotechnology, the new knowledge tends to be basic science that needs to be developed and "translated" before it can be commercialized. This is typically accomplished via dedicated biotechnology firms, the new products being manufactured and marketed via existing firms. The transfer from DBFs to large firms such as pharmaceutical companies is typically market-mediated (via license, acquisition, or joint venture), while the transfer from university to DBF may be either market-mediated (via license or joint ownership) or spillover. Universities are anchors in the early phase of discovery-driven innovation. Their role remains important as the technology matures, but other linkages increase in number and importance as the cluster grows. Large incumbent firms locate subsidiaries (listening posts) in the cluster in order to pick up new ideas.

In electronics there is typically no intermediate stage similar to DBFs; new knowledge results in new start-ups that often spawn new spin-offs. These typically involve spillovers. Firms may eventually grow large, and some become dominant creators and distributors of new technology (usually through market-mediated processes), but the vitality of the cluster depends on new applications of technology typically innovated by new firms spun off from existing firms or from universities.

By contrast, in design-driven processes, large incumbent firms are the main creators of new technology. They do so by combining and integrating components and sub-systems co-designed and co-developed with major suppliers. In addition to co-ordination of research done elsewhere, this requires vast amounts of in-house research. Most of the technology sharing and transfer is market-mediated. By challenging local suppliers to meet high technical standards the system integrators also elevate the absorptive capacity and thus contribute to technology spillovers in the local cluster. Universities have not been important in the early phase of design-driven clusters but have become more important as suppliers of researchers, engineers, and other skilled labor (although not new technology), as technology has become more complex. Design-driven clusters grow primarily by expanding linkages with existing companies both globally and locally rather than through the formation of new entities.

There are several policy implications of this analysis. It is necessary to distinguish between sectors characterized by design-driven innovation and those characterized by discovery-driven innovation. In the former, new knowledge creation tends to take place in large firms rather than universities. These firms tend to be connected to other large firms (suppliers of sub-systems and components), often via international networks through which knowledge is both created and shared via market-mediated processes. The role of universities is to supply skilled labor. Public policy can promote the building of a strong knowledge base by supporting higher education and by instituting policies and mechanisms for public procurement of advanced technology. Successful implementation of public procurement may require prior investment in competence and absorptive capacity. The primary functions of public policy are to identify the domain, thereby providing legitimacy and reduced uncertainty and risk in order to promote resource mobilization and experimentation, helping to establish a market, and creating positive externalities in related industries such as venture capital and services. It can also directly provide funding to promote knowledge creation (Bergek et al. 2008).

In sectors characterized by discovery-driven innovation, universities play a much more important role as creators of new knowledge as well as suppliers of skilled labor. Serendipity is key; pure knowledge spillovers are important. As a result, targeted public procurement is unlikely to be successful. Instead, the role of public policy is to support R&D and to promote entrepreneurship, particularly via spin-offs from universities. Promoting connectivity, both globally and locally, is also important, both for knowledge flows and for capital flows (especially via well-functioning venture capital and exit markets).

References

Abramovitz M (1956) Resource and output trends in the United States since 1870. Am Econ Rev 46(2):5–23

Acs ZJ, Audretsch DB, Braunerhjelm P, Carlsson B (2009) The knowledge spillover theory of entrepreneurship. Small Bus Econ 32(1):15–30

Anselin L, Varga A, Acs Z (1997) Local geographic spillovers between university research and high technology innovations. J Urban Econ 42:422–448

Arikan AT (2009) Interfirm knowledge exchanges and the knowledge creation capability of clusters. Acad Manage Rev 34(4):658–676

Bathelt HA, Malmberg A, Maskell P (2004) Clusters and knowledge: local buzz, global pipelines and the process of knowledge creation. Prog Hum Geogr 28(1):31–56

Belussi F, Caldari K (2009) At the origin of the industrial district: Alfred Marshall and the Cambridge School. Cambridge J Econ 33:335–355

Bergek A, Jacobsson S, Carlsson B, Lindmark S, Rickne A (2008) Analyzing the functional dynamics of technological innovation systems: a scheme of analysis. Res Policy 37 (4):407–429

Braunerhjelm P, Acz Z, Audretsch D, Carlsson B (2010) The missing link: knowledge diffusion and entrepreneurship in endogenous growth. Small Bus Econ 34(2):105–125

Breschi S, Lissoni F (2001) Knowledge spillovers and local innovation systems: a critical survey. Ind Corp Change 10(4):975–1005

Bresnahan T, Gambardella A, Saxenian A (2001) Old economy inputs for new economy outcomes: cluster formation in the new silicon valleys. Ind Corp Change 10(4):835–860

Cantner U, Pyka A (2001) Classifying technology policy from an evolutionary perspective. Res Policy 30(5):759–775

Carlsson B (ed) (1995) Technological systems and economic performance: the case of factory automation. Kluwer Academic, Boston

Carlsson B (ed) (1997) Technological systems and industrial dynamics. Kluwer Academic, Boston

Carlsson B (ed) (2002) Technological systems in the bio industries: an international study. Kluwer Academic, Boston

Carlsson B (2007) Innovation systems: a survey of the literature from a Schumpeterian perspective. In: Hanusch H, Pyka A (eds) Elgar companion to neo-Schumpeterian economics. Elgar, Cheltenham, pp 857–871

Carlsson B, Fridh A-C (2002) Technology transfer in United States universities: a survey and statistical analysis. J Evol Econ 12(1–2):199–232

Carlsson B, Stankiewicz R (1991) On the nature, function, and composition of technological systems. J Evol Econ 1(2):93–118

Carlsson B, Acs Z, Audretsch DB, Braunerhjelm P (2009) Knowledge creation, entrepreneurship, and economic growth: a historical review. Ind Corp Change 18(6):1193–1229, http://icc.oxfordjournals.org/cgi/content/full/dtp043?ijkey=Ayz62ZKvXWykosm&keytype=ref
Christensen JF (2003) Introduction: the industrial dynamics of biotechnology: new insights and new agendas. Ind Innov 10(3):223–230
Coenen L, Moodysson J, Asheim B (2004) Nodes, networks and proximities: on the knowledge dynamics of the Medicon Valley biotech cluster. Eur Plan Stud 12(7):1003–1016
Cooke P (2004) Life sciences clusters and regional science policy. Urban Stud 41(5/6):1113–1131
Dosi G (1988) Sources procedures and microeconomic effects of innovation. J Econ Lit 26 (3):1120–1171
Eliasson G (2010) Advanced public procurement as industrial policy – aircraft industry as a technical university. Springer, New York
Ernst D, Kim L (2002) Global production networks, knowledge diffusion, and local capability formation. Res Policy 31:1417–1429
Feldman MP (1999) The new economics of innovation, spillovers and agglomeration: a review of empirical studies. Econ Innov New Technol 8(1):5–25
Feldman MP (2003) The locational dynamics of the US biotechnology industry: knowledge externalities and the anchor hypothesis. Ind Innov 10(3):311–328
Garnsey E, Heffernan P (2007) The Cambridge high-tech cluster: an evolutionary perspective (Chapter 2). In: Frenken K (ed) Applied evolutionary economics and economic geography. Edward Elgar, Cheltenham, pp 27–47
Gordon IR, McCann P (2000) Industrial clusters: complexes, agglomeration and/or social networks? Urban Stud 37(3):513–532
Griliches Z (1992) The search for R&D spillovers. Scand J Econ 94(Suppl):29–47
Jaffe A (1989) Real effects of academic research. Am Econ Rev 79:957–970
Jaffe AB, Trajtenberg M, Henderson R (1993) Geographic localization of knowledge spillovers as evidenced by patent citations. Quart J Econ 108(3):577–598
Kenney M, Patton D (2006) The coevolution of technologies and institutions: Silicon Valley as the iconic high-technology cluster. In: Braunerhjelm P, Feldman MP (eds) Cluster genesis. Oxford University Press, Oxford, pp 38–60
Krugman P (1991) Increasing returns and economic geography. J Polit Econ 99:483–499
Laursen K, Salter A (2004) Searching high and low: what types of firms use universities as a source of innovation? Res Policy 3:1201–1215
Lécuyer C (2005) What do universities really owe industry? The case of solid state electronics at Stanford. Minerva 43:51–71
Lenoir T, Rosenberg N, Rowen H, Lécuyer C, Colyvas J, Godlfarb G (2003) Inventing the Entrepreneurial University: Stanford and the co-evolution of Silicon Valley. http://www.siepr.stanford.edu/programs/SST_seminars/Lenoir.pdf
Lucas R (1988) On the mechanics of economic development. J Monet Econ 22:3–39
Mansfield, E (1995) Academic research underlying industrial innovations: sources, characteristics, and financing. Rev Econ Stat 77(1):55–65
Markusen A (1996) Sticky places in slippery space: a typology of industrial districts. Econ Geogr 71(3):293–313
Marshall A (1920) Principles of economics, 8th edn, vol 1. Macmillan, London
Marshall A (1923) Industry and trade. Macmillan, London
Maskell P (2001) Towards a knowledge-based theory of the geographical cluster. Ind Corp Change 10(4):921–943
McKelvey M, Alm H, Riccaboni M (2003) Does co-location matter for formal knowledge collaboration in the Swedish biotechnology – pharmaceutical sector? Res Policy 32:483–501
Metcalfe JS (1994) Evolutionary economics and technology policy. Econ J 104(425):931–944
Metcalfe JS (1995) The economic foundations of technology policy: equilibrium and evolutionary perspectives. In: Stoneman P (ed) Handbook of the economics of innovation and technological change. Blackwell, Oxford

Moore G, Davis K (2001) Learning the Silicon Valley way. Stanford Institute for Economic Policy Research discussion paper 00–45

Niosi J, Zhegu M (2005) Aerospace clusters: local or global knowledge spillovers? Ind Innov 12 (1):1–25

Owen-Smith J, Powell WW (2004) Knowledge networks as channels and conduits: the effects of spillovers in the Boston biotechnology community. Organ Sci 15(1):5–21

Owen-Smith J, Powell W (2007) Accounting for emergence and novelty in Boston and Bay Area biotechnology. In: Braunerhjelm P, Feldman MP (eds) Cluster genesis. Oxford University Press, Oxford, pp 61–83

Porter ME (1990) The competitive advantage of nations. Free, New York

Porter ME (1998) Clusters and the new economics of competition. Harv Bus Rev November–December:77–90

Powell WW, Koput KW, Smith-Doerr L (1996) Interorganizational collaboration and the locus of innovation: networks of learning in biotechnology. Adm Sci Q 41(1):116–145

Romanelli E, Feldman M (2006) Anatomy of cluster development: emergence and convergence in the US human biotherapeutics, 1976–2003. In: Braunerhjelm P, Feldman MP (eds) Cluster genesis. Oxford University Press, Oxford, pp 87–110

Romer P (1986) Increasing returns and economic growth. Am Econ Rev 94:1002–1037

Romer P (1990) Endogenous technical change. J Polit Econ 98:71–102

Saxenian A (1994) Regional advantage. Culture and competition in Silicon Valley and Route 128. Harvard University Press, Cambridge, MA

Smits R, Kuhlmann S, Shapira P (2010) The theory and practice of innovation policy. Elgar, Cheltenham

Solow RM (1956) A contribution to the theory of economic growth. Quart J Econ 70(1):65–94

Stankiewicz R (2002) The cognitive dynamics of biotechnology and the evolution of its technological system. In: Carlsson B (ed) Technological systems in the bio industries. Springer, New York, pp 35–52

Waters R, Lawton Smith H (2002) Regional development agencies and local economic development: scale and competitiveness in high-technology Oxfordshire and Cambridgeshire. Eur Plan Stud 10(5):633–649

Waters R, Lawton Smith H (2008) Social networks in high-technology local economies: the cases of Oxfordshire and Cambridgeshire. Eur Urban Reg Stud 15(1):21–37

Werker C, Athreye S (2004) Marshall's disciples: knowledge and innovation driving regional economic development and growth. J Evol Econ 14(5):505–523

Zucker LG, Darby MR (1996) Star scientists and institutional transformation: patterns of invention and innovation in the formation of the U.S. biotechnology industry. Proc Natl Acad Sci USA 93:706–717

Zucker LG, Darby MR, Armstrong J (1998a) Geographically localized knowledge: spillovers or markets? Econ Inq 36(1):65–86

Zucker LG, Darby MR, Brewer M (1998b) Intellectual human capital and the birth of US biotechnology enterprises. Am Econ Rev 88(1):290–306

The International Diffusion of Biotechnology: the Arrival of Developing Countries

Jorge Niosi, Petr Hanel, and Susan Reid

Abstract According to conventional economic theory, countries tend to converge in economic and technological terms towards the leader. More recently, empirical approaches by economic historians (Abramovitz, Landes, Madison, Reinert) have found that while some countries are catching up, others are falling increasingly behind. Several theories compete to explain the precise mechanisms that explain how technological diffusion takes place. The paper reviews them and draws testable hypotheses for the study of international biotechnology diffusion. Biotechnologies are one of the leading sets of technologies developed in the late 20th century. They encompass applications in agriculture, chemicals, environment and pharmaceuticals. The United States has led the way in both scientific and industrial development of biotechnologies and these have quickly spread to Canada, Japan and Western Europe. Are the main developing countries adopting biotechnology? A study of the adoption of human health biotechnology in eight developing countries in Asia (China, India, Korea, and Singapore) and Latin America (Argentina, Brazil, Chile and Mexico) was conducted, based on the analysis of in situ interviews,

---

Reprinted from Journal of Evolutionary Economics 22(4), 767-783 , Springer (2012)

J. Niosi (✉)
Department of Management and Technology, Canada Research Chair on the Management of Technology, Université du Québec à Montréal, 1290 Saint-Denis, Local AB-2300, Montréal, Québec, Canada H2X 3J6
e-mail: niosi.jorge@uqam.ca

P. Hanel
Department of Economics, Université de Sherbrooke, 2500, boulevard de l'Université, Sherbrooke, (Québec), Canada J1K 2R
e-mail: petr.hanel@usherbrooke.ca

S. Reid
Williams School of Business, Bishop's University, 2600 College Street, Sherbrooke, Québec, Canada J1M 1Z7
e-mail: sreid@ubishops.ca

A. Pyka and E.S. Andersen (eds.), *Long Term Economic Development*, Economic Complexity and Evolution, DOI 10.1007/978-3-642-35125-9_10,

patents and scientific publication. The study shows a marked process of adoption and learning in science: each of the above-mentioned developing countries is increasing its share of world publication between 1996 and 2008. However, their share of biotechnology patents for the same period has barely increased. There are also regional differences in terms of sectoral concentration; Latin America, Argentina and Brazil are eager adopters of agricultural biotechnology and are moving up in the pharmaceutical records. Several Argentinean, Chinese, Indian, and South Korean pharmaceutical companies have been particularly active in the development of biogenerics.

1 Introduction

In many different economic literatures, developing countries are seen as predestined to rapidly converge with rich advanced nations. Some authors have even suggested that new technologies are windows of opportunity for emerging countries, not only to catch up but also, to forge ahead of rich nations (Perez and Soete 1988). Others have been more cautious and suggested that catching up most often occur through the backward countries adoption of a similar path compared to industry leaders (Lee and Lim 2001). They found that path-following catching up was more widespread than path-skipping or path-creating catching up. In this respect, science-based industrial activities are particularly interesting because laggard countries need not only to assimilate industrial practices from advanced nations but also, if they intend to forge ahead, the science on which such industrial activities are based.

The case of biopharmaceuticals is particularly relevant because this set of technologies is still rapidly unfolding and producing major novelties in several industries. We have decided to analyse biopharmaceuticals, the major application for modern biotechnology to date, and distinguish between catching up in science and catching up in industrial production. For this purpose we develop indicators of catching up in science and industry, and select eight of the most advanced emerging nations. If catching up in science and industry take place, such countries should be the first to show signs of reducing their gap related to more advanced nations.

2 The Diffusion of Technology

The birth and diffusion of new technologies are the objects of many debates among social scientists. Based on the conventional, theoretical economic approach, countries tend to convergence in productivity levels (Barro 1991) as technology diffuses internationally. Yet, several empirically minded prominent economic historians believe that countries tend to diverge in productivity. Abramovitz (1986) suggested that backwardness only carries a potential for catching up, an opportunity that may or may not materialize. Whether countries take or do not take advantage of such opportunity depends on their "social capabilities": countries that are technologically backward but socially advanced will most probably benefit from the bounty of existing technologies. Landes (1999) argued that the gap between rich and poor countries is growing at the extremes of the wealth distribution, while some countries are catching up.

> "Very roughly and briefly: the difference in income per head between the richest industrial nation, say Switzerland, and the poorest non industrial country, Mozambique, is about 400 to 1. Two hundred and fifty years ago, this gap between richest and poorest was perhaps 5 to 1..." (Landes 1999, p. xx).

For Landes, the main explanations lie in the superior European culture (making easier to produce and assimilate modern science and technology), as well as climate and geography (tropical countries being disadvantaged compared with temperate ones).

Maddison (2007) and Reinert (2007) agree with the non-convergence thesis, but both suggest that falling behind is at least partly linked to policies implemented by the first industrialising nations, including colonisation of the backward countries, combined with protectionism and trade barriers.

Other authors have found that, among OECD countries, convergence has been highly industry specific. Productivity has converged in market services but not in manufacturing (Bernard and Jones 1996; Inklaar and Timmer 2009). Also, convergence depends on the sample of countries, periods, and selected variables, such as labour productivity (LP) using GDP per capita, multifactor or total factor productivity (MFP and TFP respectively).

We have analysed the diffusion and adoption literatures to delineate hypotheses that can help us to explain the specific patterns of technology adoption in biotechnology. The economics and management literatures on the diffusion of technology are abundant and variegated. Based on the diffusion of agricultural and industrial products, models of epidemic diffusion are the most common, where all economic agents have the same chance to acquire the technology. Table 1 summarizes some of the highlights in the literature.

A general consensus is that neighbour imitation and information is key in the adoption of any technology. However, information and proximity are far from exhausting the hypotheses about diffusion. Griliches (1957) has shown that higher returns associated with novelty increase the probability of innovation being adopted.

The product life cycle (PLC) and industry life cycle (ILC) model has made a major impact on the studies about international technology adoption and diffusion. According to this model, Vernon (1966) has argued that new products and processes usually originated in the richest nations (such as the United States), then they

Table 1 Theories about diffusion

Author	Year	Theory/model	Method/data	Field	Parameters	Predictions
B. Ryan and N. Gross	1943	Epidemic model	Survey interviews	Sociology	Innovation, time, social structure, communication channels	Hybrid corn diffused in Iowa through an S-shaped curve. Neighbour imitation is key channel
T. Hagerstrand	1953	Simulation models	Regional data	Geography	Proximity, personal communication, subsidy	Probability of diffusion a negative function of distance
Z. Griliches	1957	Epidemic model, logistic curves	Econometric analysis of time series	Economics	Profitability	Hybrid corn will diffuse if brings higher returns than natural ones. Social returns high on public R&D
R. Vernon	1966	Product life cycle model	Industry studies	Management	Time, standardization, exports, FDI	Innovation diffuses across borders as it standardizes, from rich to poor nations
S. Davies	1979	Epidemic	Cross-section Studies	Economics	Information, adopter's size	Larger firms are first adopters
P. David and W.B. Arthur	1985	Evolution, path dependency	Product and industry cases	Economics	Information lags, sunk costs	Innovation spreads slowly and best technology is not always adopted
W. Cohen and D. Levinthal	1989, 1990	Evolutionary learning model	Case studies	Management	R&D activities, ability to assess technology	R&D executants are early adopters
M. Feldman D. Audretsch	1994	Economic geography	Economic data	Economic geography	Proximity, spillovers, metropolitan size	Spillovers and competition in cities affect probability of innovation
M. Feldman and D. Audretsch	1999	Economic statistics	Economic data	Economic geography	Metropolitan size	Spillovers and competition in cities affect probability of innovation
E. Rogers	1995	Sociological	Case studies	Sociology	Superiority, complexity, observability	Several parameters affect speed of diffusion

B. Mc Williams & D. Zilberman	1996	Probit & logit models	Samples, industry cases	Economics	Size and industry	Large firms adopt early, different patterns according to industry
F. Caselli and W. Coleman II	2001	Linear regression	Computer industry	Economics, management	Human capital	Countries with larger human capital pool adopt earlier
P. Stoneman	2002	Real option	Industry studies	Economics	Learning and expectations	Learning and imitation drive adoption
K. Zhu et al	2006	Economic statistics	Industry studies	Management	Competition, firm size and regulation	Firm size, competitive environment and regulation affect adoption

Representative authors

were exported to countries with similar revenue levels; foreign direct investment was then necessary to protect these novelties from offshore imitators. Diffusion, then, would go along a clear global pattern, from rich to poor countries. Recent research has confirmed this international adoption pattern (Keller 2004). Yet, adoption, as well as innovation, starts in the richest nations and trickles down to less prosperous nations on the basis of their endowment in human capital, type of government, trade policy and previous adoption of advanced technology (Caselli and Coleman 2001; Comin and Hobijn 2004; Meade and Rabello 2004). Critics of the PLC model have argued that, as some kind of convergence occurs among OECD nations (Comin and Hobijn 2004), the model becomes less able to predict the direction of technology diffusion and transfer. Also, several industries do not adjust themselves to the PLC-ILC pattern (Klepper 1997). Yet the model remains a good starting point to understand international technology diffusion. The PLC-ILC model applies to biotechnology in many different dimensions: it was born in the richest nation (the USA) it immediately diffused to Canada, Japan and Western Europe, and it slowly makes its way towards less developed countries such as those of Asia and Latin America. However, biotechnology is not an industry and this makes a difference in the way it is diffused.

Feldman (1994) as well as Feldman and Audretsch (1999) have shown that innovation is most usually born in large cities and is first adopted in large metropolitan areas. The reduced cost and increased speed of information diffusion in major cities is part of the explanation. Similarly, big firms tend to be early adopters of novelty (McWilliams and Zilberman 1996). It may well happen that both learning and imitation are easier in larger metropolitan agglomerations (Stoneman 2002). This is most likely related to the ability for large firms to leverage both R&D and Marketing resources early on in a technology's diffusion. As Cohen and Levinthal (1989, 1990) have argued, the absorptive capacity of firms is enhanced if they conduct R&D.

Innovation systems theory (Lundvall 1992; Nelson 1993; Malerba 2004) moves further in the direction opened up by Abramovitz, and others that have pinpointed the critical role of institutions in development. Emerging countries are those that are building a set of institutions (organizations, policy incentives, regulations) as well as human capital allowing them to absorb existing science and technology and create new ones. These sets of institutions are called national, regional and sectoral systems of innovation. National systems (NSI) are composed of small subsets of regional (RSI) and sectoral innovation systems (SIS). In this approach, countries catch up, fall behind or forge ahead on the basis of the specific sectors that compose their NSI. This approach solves many of the convergence-divergence conundra, and nicely fits with the industry-specific catching up hypotheses of Bernard and Jones (1996), as well as Inklaar and Timmer (2009). In this paper we would like to extend this hypothesis of industry-specific catching-up patterns to biotechnology.

From this literature review, we draw the following hypotheses. (Key authors are in parentheses):

H1: Starting in the most affluent nations, biotechnology will diffuse to the richest and most advanced emerging nations. Thus we expect them in the more affluent and more advanced developing countries in Asia and Latin America, less so in Africa (Vernon).

H2: Biotechnology will be adopted first in larger cities such as Beijing and Shanghai in China, Delhi or Bangalore in India, Rio and Sao Paulo in Brazil and Buenos Aires in Argentina (Feldman, Feldman and Audretsch).

H3: In late industrializing countries, biotechnology will be adopted first by large corporations, then move to smaller firms (Davies).

H4: R&D-active firms will be faster adopters of biotechnology (Cohen and Levinthal).

H5: The nature of the national system of innovation in biotechnology has an impact on the adoption of this set of technologies. The NSI strongest organisations will be first adopters. Countries with strongest NSI will also lead adoption in developing countries (Lundvall, Nelson).

H6: Yet, innovation (and particularly radical one) spreads slowly (David), but will be first adopted in countries with largest human capital pool (Caselli and Coleman).

We add the following hypothesis:

H4: Industrial structure affects the diffusion of biotechnology: countries with a more diversified industrial structure boasting a large number of potential adopters will be faster users of it.

3 Biotechnology, the Science and its Commercial Applications

Biotechnology is a large set of technologies developed after World War II, such as genetic engineering, gene therapy, monoclonal antibodies, stem cell, and tissue engineering. Table 2 presents a summary portrait of the science base and the technologies involved.

These technologies have a myriad of applications including human and animal diagnostics and therapeutics, the development of genetically modified bacteria, plants and animals, the separation of metals in the mining industry, model animals for research and many others. The sciences of biotechnology are usually developed in universities, while public laboratories are most often engaged in developing the infratechnologies. These consist of "a set of technical tools that include measurement and test methods, artefacts such as standard reference materials that allow these methods to be used efficiently, scientific and engineering databases, process models, and the technical basis for both physical and functional interfaces between the components of systems technologies, such as factory automation an

Table 2 Public and private technology assets in biotechnology

Science base	Infratechnologies	Generic technologies: Product	Generic technologies: Process	Commercial products
Cellular biology	Bioinformatics	Antiangiogenesis	Automated cell based assays	Coagulation inhibitors
Genomics	Biomarkers	Antisense	Cell encapsulation	DNA probes
Immunology	Biospectroscopy	Apoptosis	Cell culture	Drug delivery
Microbiology/ virology	Combinatorial chemistry	Bioelectronics	DNA arrays/ chips	Inflammation inhibitors
Molecular biology	DNA sequencing/ profiling	Biomaterials	Fermentation	Hormone restoration
Nanoscience	Electrophoresis	Biosensors	Gene expression profiling	In RNA inhibitors
Neuroscience	Fluorescence	Functional genomics	Gene transfer	Nanodevices
Pharmacology	Gene expression	Gene delivery systems	Immunoassays	Neuro-active steroids
Physiology	Gene typing	Gene testing	Implantable delivery systems	Neuro-transmitter inhibitors
Proteomics	Magnetic resonance spectrometry	Gene therapy	Non invasive imaging	Protease inhibitors
	Mass spectrometry	Gene expression systems	Nucleic acid amplification	Vaccines
	Nucleic acid diagnostics	High-content screening	Recombinant DNA	
	Protein structure modelling/ analysis	Monoclonal antibodies	Separation technologies	
		Pharmacogenomics	Transgenic animals	
		Proteomics		
		Stem cell		
		Structural drug design		
		Tissue engineering		

Source: Tassey (2007) p. 120

communication" (Tassey 1997: 153). Dedicated biotechnology firms and industrial users (most often agricultural, environmental, food, forestry and pharmaceutical companies) are involved in products, process and the commercial technologies. However the lines are not clearly drawn between the science base, the infratechnologies, and the products, the processes and the services applying biotechnologies. One example of this public/private competition for the development of science and technology was the Human Genome project, where a private firm, Celera Genomics, disputed the priority to sequence the human genome to a public contestant, the Human Genome Project.

Since Watson and Crick founded the science of molecular biology with the discovery of the structure of the DNA in 1953, biotechnology has been at the base of a cornucopia of scientific discoveries and the development of entirely new fields including genomics, nanoscience and proteomics. Every year, thousands of articles and patents are produced in these sciences and technologies, providing evidence of the vitality of what has become the most active research and development field in the world.

There is a major distinction between agricultural biotechnology and biopharmaceuticals. Using or copying GM seeds is simpler than producing biopharmaceutical generics. In the first case, the new trait of the seeds can be isolated and reinserted in some other seed. There are few cases of new GMO in agricultural biotechnology invented in emerging countries. Conversely, producing large biological molecules—such as human insulin, human growth hormones or molecular antibodies—requires a far superior knowledge of the underlying science, because the process through which the large recombinant molecules have been produced is kept secret by the original inventors and the catching up bio-pharmaceutical company has to rediscover it. Also, failure in producing high-quality biological drugs may have strong consequences for human life. This is why so few countries have been able to produce biological generic drugs. These countries include Argentina, Brazil, China, India and Korea.

4 Diffusion of Biotechnology

Biotechnology is a science-based set of technologies. Its diffusion involves both elements of science, and technology. Besides, biotechnology has evolved from academic and public sector research towards its commercial applications either in new dedicated biotechnology firms, or in established companies already working in application areas such as those in human health products, veterinary products, grain production and trade, forestry, food and agriculture. We thus suggest considering separately the science, the technology and its commercial application in the study of the diffusion of biotechnology towards the third cohort of countries.

4.1 The International Diffusion of Biotechnology as Science

Let's first analyze the diffusion of science. Developing countries have enormously increased their publication in biotechnology in the last twenty years. Indicators of this type of diffusion are

- Publication
- Citation

- Co-authorship
- International scientific collaboration

Table 3 presents data about the rise in ***scientific publication***[1] in nine of the largest and/or more dynamic developing countries in Asia (China, India, Korea, Singapore and Turkey) and Latin America (Argentina, Brazil, Chile, and Mexico). When tabulated according to the nationality of the authors (and co-authors), these countries represented in 1996 some 8,8 % of world publication in biotechnology; in 2007, they represented 28,4 %. Also, world publication in biotechnology has increased by 64 % in these 11 years. But in all these countries scientific publication has increased much faster than in the world, indicating a rapid catching up in the science dimension of biotechnology.

Also, these publications are cited, and in a large number of cases they are co-authored with overseas partners. The international diffusion of science takes place often through international ***scientific co-authorship***. A large proportion of the articles published by these catching up nations are produced in collaboration with academics of more advanced countries, the United States being first and foremost among them (Table 4). Thus the explosive evolution of publications authored and co-authored by scientists from emerging countries overstates the level of their scientific achievement. It also suggests that the criteria used on nationality are becoming less relevant in the globalized world. The bare number of publications may also overstate scientific catching-up, as we do not know the "quality" of publications in each country.

All these developing countries have the United States companies and institutions as main partners in publication, but there differences based on geography and language. All Asian countries have Japanese institutions among the main collaborators. Singapore and Taiwanese researchers are often co-authors with Australian ones. Three Latin American countries (Argentina, Chile and Mexico) often collaborate with Spanish researchers. Also, Latin American authors most often appear in collaboration with European than with US researchers. None of the Latin American countries have extensive collaborations with Japanese counterparts.

[1] Science-Metrix used the Scopus database; through a computerized search 10,160 journals were analysed, and a list of keywords found in the title, keywords and abstract of articles. Un article co-authored by scientists from different countries counts as many times as there are co-authors. I.e. An article written by an Australian, a Chinese and a Japanese scholar, appears once for Australia, once for China, and once for Japan. Such article will represent one international collaboration for each country. The distribution was highly skewed: some 1207 of these journals had 80 % of the articles.

Table 3 Scientific publication in biotechnology: main developing countries in Asia and Latin America

Country	1996	1997	1998	1999	2000	2001	2002	2003	2004	2005	2006	2007
Argentina	123	128	141	123	171	171	175	198	204	219	289	247
Brazil	235	245	292	349	454	469	540	656	661	755	1077	1164
Chile	50	52	55	78	63	68	77	88	90	112	134	121
Mexico	135	150	135	177	190	197	201	237	260	263	344	312
China	923	938	1212	1411	1580	1922	2161	2823	3424	5035	6564	7650
PRC	548	563	818	1014	1110	1411	1646	2179	2751	4318	5652	6732
Taiwan	296	305	316	285	347	372	371	491	519	573	765	755
Hong Kong	96	85	99	149	152	169	176	202	211	232	266	303
India	495	524	618	668	681	839	995	1162	1161	1597	1871	2065
South Korea	615	664	783	863	950	1011	998	1262	1386	1494	1704	2073
Singapore	73	68	65	87	121	121	137	202	232	288	336	367
[3pt] Turkey	93	97	155	157	178	254	312	387	410	460	527	554
World	31266	31687	32145	32798	34188	35894	36273	38160	40985	44337	48257	51323

Source: Scopus database

Table 4 Scientific collaboration between catching up countries and OECD countries in biotechnology, 1996–2008: absolute figures (and percentages)

	USA	EU (27)	Japan	Australia, Canada and New Zealand	Total
Argentina	311 (30 %)	627 (60 %)	44 (4 %)	64 (6 %)	1046 (100 %)
Brazil	874 (34 %)	1400 (54 %)	97 (4 %)	209 (8 %)	2580 (100 %)
Chile	176 (29 %)	368 (61 %)	15 (2 %)	49 (8 %)	608 (100 %)
Mexico	545 (44 %)	582 (47 %)	29 (2 %)	82 (7 %)	1230 (100 %)
P. R. of China[a]	2618 (38 %)	2360 (34 %)	1120 (16 %)	846 (12 %)	6944 (100 %)
India	863 (39 %)	1009 (45 %)	203 (9 %)	159 (7 %)	2234 (100 %)
Korea	1922 (55 %)	468 (14 %)	807 (23 %)	269 (8 %)	3466 (100 %)
Singapore	377 (47 %)	201 (25 %)	65 (8 %)	159 (20 %)	802 (100 %)
Taiwan[b]	674 (60 %)	238 (21 %)	121 (11 %)	85 (7 %)	1118 (100 %)

[a]Includes Continental China and Hong Kong.
[b]Taiwan is a province of the P. R. of China.
Source: Scopus database

4.2 The Diffusion of Science and Technology from Public Research Organisations (PRO) and Universities; Indicators will be

- Patents including co-invention both international (indicating world-class invention) and national (indicating imitation)
- Venture capital

Emerging countries in biotechnology have received few US patents. Table 5 gives an idea of their contribution to world biotechnology. It is noteworthy that tiny Singapore (4,5 million in population) has been granted more patents than the four Latin American countries together (with a combined population of 356 million).

Both Asia and Latin America are newcomers in the world of venture capital.[2] In the seven years from 2002 to 2008 Latin America has received less than 1 % of world venture capital in biotechnology.

However, they advance much faster in the world of science. The reason is simple: in all emerging nations, most Gross Expenditure on R&D (GERD) is conducted in academic and public research organisations; business R&D (BED) is always lagging because governments can easily stimulate public science, but they

[2] Venture capital in China is still less developed than in industrial countries but it has been growing fast. The VC funds almost doubled from 2006 to 2007, an important share of funding came from abroad. As of 2007, the VC investment in China was US$ 3.25 Billion compared to US$30 billion in the U.S.. About 13 % of VC was invested in bio/health care in China, still less but not by so much than in the U.S. (China Biotech, 2009).

The government of all levels (state, province and cities) are among the principal sources of venture capital. In contrast to the U.S. VC, which brings not only money but also expertise, the lack of business expertise is reducing the effectiveness of government venture capital. In 2007 appeared the first local biotechnology fund (22 local biotech firms) and several multinational VC funds (BioVeda China, 2005).

Table 5 US patents in biotechnology of selected developing countries, 1979–2007

Country	Patents	Patents per million population
Argentina	11	0.3
Brazil	34	0.2
Chile	4	0.2
Mexico	15	0.1
China	97	0.07
India	208	0.2
Korea	444	10
Singapore	71	71

Source: USPTO

find more difficult to break inertia and provide adequate incentives for innovation in private firms (UNESCO 2010). Also, industrial biotechnology is protected both by patents and industrial secrets. The American and European owners jealously protect the processes through which biological drugs are produced. Imitators in backward countries have to discover them again. Yet they are doing it, and here is where the advancement of science is helping them.

4.3 Diffusion of Biotechnology Products to the Marketplace

Indicators of biotechnology production are very different from those used to analyse the adoption of biotechnology in science. They would be

- Products and services, sales, profits, market shares
- Valuable patents
- International alliances among companies for research, production and marketing

The diffusion of biotechnology in developing countries business sector is only partially related to scientific publication and government research. Industry may be interested in adopting biotechnology in the production of human health drugs, veterinary products, new seeds presenting specific characteristics, new fuels, mining or environmental purposes. Private sector developing country firms may adopt biotechnology to produce bio-generics (i.e. biotechnology-based drugs that have lost patent protection), they may "invent around" new seeds or new animal health drugs or new methods for lixiviation in mining developed in more advanced countries. In some cases they may find a world new solution for a human or animal health or a new biotechnology method to produce a known drug. In addition, such companies may link themselves with universities or government research centres based in advanced countries. They may patent in the United States, Europe or at the WIPO office, or request patents only in developing countries. The diffusion of biotechnology in industry depends on several factors:

- Local regulations concerning GMOs in agriculture, health care and environment related activities
- Patent laws covering GMOs, drugs and bio-generics

- Existing industrial structure
- Internal market for products

Local regulations on GMOs are key. A few developing countries, such as Argentina, Brazil, and China have given support to the use of GMOs in agricultural production. Others, such as Chile, India and Mexico, as well as most of Western Europe, have been less supportive. Those countries that favour GMO production increase their probabilities of producing and exporting genetically modified seeds and derivate products.

Patent laws are also highly relevant in the decision to adopt biotechnology. If national patent laws do not protect genetically modified plants, animals or bacteria, or if drugs for human health are not patentable, then few companies, domestic or foreign would be interested in investing in R&D or manufacturing of such products including biotechnology. Since the signature of the TRIPs agreement in 1994 and its enforcement since 2005, most developing countries have progressively increased their protection for drugs, and other biotechnology-related products. In the meantime, the least developed countries obtained under the Doha agreement the postponement of large portions of the agreement up to 2016 (Mercurio 2004). After implementation by China and India of TRIPS accords the numbers of patents for biotechnological inventions granted by the USPTO to Chinese and Indian inventors has increased faster than in Latin America. In the last decade, more than half of these patents were granted to Chinese and Indian institutions, indicating that the research and technological development took place in these countries rather than in the US or other industrialised countries. Similarly as co-authorship of scientific publications, collaborative research is an important source of patented inventions. More than a third of biotech patents awarded by the USPTO to Chinese inventors are assigned to US assignees (universities, research laboratories and companies). This proportion is even larger (more than two thirds) in the case of Indian inventors. While many of Chinese and Indian students and researchers stay abroad for an extended period or permanently and continue to contribute to development of biotechnology in the US and other industrialised countries, others return to their countries of origin bringing with them the knowledge and experience accumulated abroad. These returnees diffuse new scientific, technological and above all business knowledge underlying the development and application of biotechnology in their country of origin.

However, numerous cases of counterfeit have been observed in some large developing countries such as Argentina, Brazil, China and India. As TRIPs mechanism for enforcement of the treaty is lengthy, cumbersome and unpredictable, unilateral actions were taken by several developed countries, most notably the USA, to protect the intellectual property of their firms.

Existing domestic industrial structure is key. Some developing countries including Argentina, China and India, have for many decades protected their pharmaceutical industries through different regulations including the non-patentability of drugs. As a consequence, these countries developed a local pharmaceutical industry producing essentially generics for the local market and exporting to other developing countries. Once the TRIPs agreement signed, these LDCs obtained some deferral of portions of the agreement and started incorporating biotechnology products, particularly those having lost IP protection such as insulin, human growth hormone, animal growth hormone and hepatitis B vaccines.

Several examples suggest that biotechnology development in China is based on a solid domestic research base, well connected with foreign networks and benefiting from the scientific competence and business acumen of returnees.

- Chinese scientists at the National Human Genome Center in Beijing and Shanghai are responsible for 1 % of the Human Genome Project.
- The first commercialized gene therapy product ever approved in the world—an anti-cancer injection—*Gendicide*—was introduced by the Chinese firm Sibiono in 2003.

Similar examples can be found in India. The three innovative Indian domestic firms—Shantha Biotechnics, Bharat Biotech International, and Jupiter Biotechnology—are all located in Hyderabad, the bio-valley of India. Shantha Biotechnics and Bharat Biotech International are acknowledged as dedicated and innovative biopharmaceutical start-up companies that have managed to gain significant success and recognition (Frew et al. 2007). As Table 4 illustrates, innovation capability of the Indian firms is primarily demonstrated by a large number of their own brands of recombinant products. For instance, Shantha was the first in India to develop the r-DNA hepatitis B vaccine, followed by Bharat and others. Both Shantha and Bharat have a range of recombinant products based on their own innovations. Jupiter, on the other hand, is the leading world producer in drug intermediates. Examination of domestic medical biotech companies indicates that India has currently outperformed China in terms of quantity, scale of manufacturing, and globalization.

In Argentina, BioSidus is producing human insulin and growth hormones using genetically-modified cows that give these drugs in their milk. Over a dozen other domestic pharmaceutical companies (including Bago, Cassara, ELEA, Gador, Roemmers and Wiener) are exporting biosimilar drugs, mostly to other developing countries. Korea is also exporting biogenerics and Brazil is moving in the same direction through both private firms and public laboratories. In all these cases, the industrial structure includes a strong generic pharmaceutical industry that has adopted biotechnology.

Some of these countries developed new processes and in a few cases, brand new products such as Cuba's meningitis vaccine, and Argentina's foot-and-mouth recombinant disease vaccine. In Brazil, the government implemented a regulation forcing government hospitals to buy generic products. Also, patent expiration of several blockbuster drugs, and rapid market growth supported the development of a domestic Brazilian pharmaceutical industry in the last two decades. Such an environment does not exist in Chile. Argentina had local producers of seeds and veterinary products some of which incorporated biotechnology processes and animal drugs.

The internal market is also important. All the largest countries mentioned (Argentina, Brazil, Mexico, China and India) have a vast internal market, and access to larger ones (Mercosur in the case of Argentina and Brazil, NAFTA for Mexico). Several of them have grown exporting and multinational pharmaceutical companies. Some Argentinean companies have discovered and exploited specific market needs. One of them, Biogenesis-Bago, has developed the only available biotechnology vaccine against foot-and-mouth disease, a pressing need in a country with a total stock of 55 million bovines and close to an even larger cattle-raising country (Brazil). Another pharmaceutical company in Argentina, Gador, is developing, in collaboration with a British biotechnology firm, a vaccine against Chagas disease, one that affects 18 million people in South America and threatens close to 200 million; the same Argentinean company has already produced a diagnostic test for that South American infective illness. A Cuban firm, in collaboration with a research team from the University of Ottawa, has developed the only vaccine against meningitis available in the world. The vaccine followed a strong upsurge of meningitis in that country. It represents a major export product for that country.

In Korea over 40 pharmaceutical companies are adopting biotechnology. The leading one is LG Pharmaceuticals, a subsidiary of the LG chaebol, which developed a recombinant hepatitis B vaccine being successfully exported (Wong et al. 2004). Also, Korean firms and research universities are patenting in the United States, not simply inventing for foreign assignees as in Latin America or Singapore. Leading among them are Daewoong Pharmaceuticals, Dong Shin Pharmaceuticals, Korean Vaccine, and Lifecord International (all of Seoul).

Among the LDC countries studied in this paper, China is first and foremost. In 2009–10, China exported 8 billion USD of pharmaceutical products. It is followed by Singapore, Korea, Brazil, Mexico and Argentina.

In developing countries the major biotechnology centres are the largest cities. In these metropolitan areas, the largest and most dynamic universities (Sao Paulo, and Rio in Brazil, Buenos Aires in Argentina, Mexico DF in Mexico, Beijing and Shanghai in China, Seoul in Korea) lead biotechnology publication. Also, the vast majority of products in each of these countries are produced in a handful of large cities, by large and medium sized companies.

5 Conclusion

Economic theories of technology adoption get a fairly strong confirmation in the diffusion patterns of human health biotechnology. Biotechnology innovations are born in the richest countries, and are diffusing towards a second or third cohort of medium-income nations. Continental Europe, Canada and Japan are in the second cohort. The countries in our study belong to the third one. Yet, the level of diffusion is very uneven from one country to the other. And all of these nations do not have the same probability of adoption and then going on to diffuse them themselves, either through science/tech innovations, or through products and/or services. Those countries having the largest human capital pools, the strongest institutions in their national innovation systems are more able to adopt/use it and to innovate, whether at the national, regional or global levels. Diffusion has taken between one or two decades to reach the most advanced emerging countries in Asia and Latin America. In all regions biotechnology adoption in human health has been much faster in science than in industry.

Also, within these countries, large established firms active in R&D are more likely adopters of human health biotechnology. We do not observe many new start-up firms among the early adopters of human health biotechnology, especially for first-level innovations. The chances of seeing small start-ups or spin-off firms join the ranks of the large European or US-based biotechnology firms are very slim. Industrial structure counts: those emerging countries with a generic pharmaceutical industry will be the fastest and most probable adopters of biotechnology in human health, both in terms of science and tech diffusion to the companies and in terms of their own ability to diffuse new products and services to the marketplace.

Developing country universities and public laboratories have contributed to the biotechnology literature for at least three decades and the pace of publication is increasing. In scientific terms, some catching up is taking place. Government laboratories are also helping both with the science and with the generation of new products.

Yet emerging country private firms have discovered biotechnology only in the last two decades. Due to the absence of venture capital, only large incumbent companies are adopting it (Table 6). They are generic pharmaceutical firms in Argentina, China, Korea and India, veterinary product firms in Argentina and Brazil. Institutional factors (science, technology and innovation policies or the absence of such policies, organisational designs and routines in universities and PROs, and small venture capital industry) explain the performance of different countries in terms of diffusion and adoption of biotechnology. Market size is also important. Chile or Singapore do not have a domestic market for human or animal health products. The largest Latin American and Asian countries do. In some countries such as Argentina, China and India, and soon may be Brazil, established domestic companies have strong positions in such markets as those for generic human health biologics, animal health products and GMO (seeds). In this sense, these countries may "leapfrog" the science phases, or be medium performers in science but fairly strong performers in generic product markets and GMO.

Also, helping the catching-up process is the steady decline on the cost of genomic research (see *Nature*, Vol. 464, April 2010), and experience accumulated by academic research teams, and government institutes as well as companies in dealing with animal, human and plant DNA. On the commercial scene, LDCs have been able to produce their own versions of several biogenerics, but almost all of the new drugs are originated in the United States and Western Europe.

In some countries such as Argentina, Brazil, China, Korea and India, established domestic generic pharmaceutical companies have already carved for themselves positions in such markets as those for human health biologics, and animal health products. It remains to be seen whether they will be able to compete with Canadian,

Table 6 Venture capital in biotechnology by region

	2002	2003	2004	2005	2006	2007	2008	Total US$M	Total (%)
Americas	2941	3155	3978	3903	4186	5241	4106	27510	76
Europe	992	797	1193	1376	1298	1430	1160	8246	23
Asia	36	40	69	78	58	107	55	443	1

Nature Biotechnology

German or Israeli firms aiming at the same human health biotechnology generic products (Table 6).

References

Abramovitz M (1986) Catching up, forging ahead, and falling behind. J Econ Hist 46(2):385–406

Barro RJ (1991) Economic growth in a cross section of countries. Q J Econ 106(2):407–443

Bernard AB, Jones CI (1996) Comparing apples to oranges: productivity convergence and measurement across industries and countries. Am Econ Rev 86(5):1216–1238

Caselli F, Coleman WJ (2001) Cross-country technology diffusion: the case of computers. Am Econ Rev 91(2):328–335

Cohen W, Levinthal DA (1989) Innovation and Learning: the two faces of R&D. Econ J 99:569–596

Cohen W, Levinthal DA (1990) Absorptive capacity: a new perspective on learning and innovation. Adm Sci Q 35(1):128–152

Comin D, Hobijn B (2004) Cross-country technology adoption: making the theories face the facts. J Monet Econ 51:39–83

David P, Arthur WB (1985) Clio and the economics of QWERTY. Am Econ Rev 75(2):332–337

Davies S (1979) The diffusion of process innovations. Cambridge University Press, Cambridge

Feldman M (1994) The geography of innovation. Kluwer, Boston

Feldman M, Audretsch D (1999) Innovation in cities: science-based diversity, specialisation and localized competition. Eur Econ Rev 43:409–429

Frew S, Rezaie R, Sammut SM, Ray M, Daar AS, Singer P (2007) India's health biotechnology at a crossroads. Nat Biotechnol 25(4):403–418

Griliches Z (1957) Hybrid corn: an exploration on the economic of technological change. Econometrica 25(4):501–522

Hagerstrand T (1953) Innovation diffusion as a spatial process. University of Chicago Press, Chicago (1967 Edition)

Inklaar R, Timmer M (2009) Productivity convergence across industries and countries: the importance of theory-based measurement. Macroecon Dyn 13:218–240

Keller W (2004) International technology diffusion. J Econ Lit 42(3):752–783

Klepper S (1997) Industry life cycles. Ind Corp Change 6(1):145–138

Landes D (1999) The wealth and poverty of nations. Norton, New York

Lee K, Lim C (2001) Technological regimes, catching up and leapfrogging: findings from the Korean industries. Res Policy 30(3):459–483

Lundvall B-A (1992) National systems of innovation. Pinter, London

Maddison A (2007) Contours of the World Economy, 1-2003. Oxford University Press, New York

Malerba F (ed) (2004) Sectoral systems of innovation. Cambridge University Press, Cambridge

McWilliams B, Zilberman D (1996) Time of technology adoption and learning by using. Econ Innov New Technol 4(2):139–154

Meade PT, Rabello L (2004) The technology adoption life cycle attractor: understanding the dynamics of high-technology markets. Technol Forecast Soc Change 71:667–684

Mercurio BC (2004) TRIPs, patents and access to life-saving drugs in the developing world. Marquette Intellect Prop Law Rev 8(2):211–253

Nelson R (ed) (1993) National innovation systems. Oxford University Press, New York and Oxford

Perez C, Soete L (1988) Catching up in technology: entry barriers and windows of opportunity. In: Dosi G, Freeman C, Nelson R, Silverberg G (eds) Technical change and economic theory. Pinter, London, pp 458–480

Reinert E (2007) Why some countries grow rich, and why poor countries stay poor. Perseus, New York

Rogers E (1995) Diffusion of innovations, 4th edn. Free Press, N. York

Ryan B, Gross NC (1943) The diffusion on hybrid seed corn in two Iowa communities. Rural Sociol 8:15–24

Stoneman P (2002) The economics of technological diffusion. Blackwell, Maiden MA

Tassey G (1997) The economics of R&D policy. Quorum Books, Westport, CT

Tassey G (2007) The technology imperative. Elgar, Cheltenham

UNESCOQuach U, Thorsteindottir H, Singer PA, Daar AS (2010) Science Report 2010, Paris

Vernon R (1966) International investment and international trade in the product life cycle. Q J Econ 80:190–207

Wong J, Quach U, Thorsteindottir H, Singer PA, Daar AS (2004) South Korean Biotechnology: a rising industrial and scientific powerhouse. Nat Biotechnol 22:42–44

Zhu K, Kraemer KL, Xu S (2006) The process of innovation assimilation in different countries. Manage Sci 52(10):1557–1576

The Internet as a Global Production Reorganizer: The Old Industry in the New Economy

Gunnar Eliasson

Abstract Globalization of production is breaking up the 200 year industrial knowledge monopoly and backbone of the wealthy Western economies; their engineering industries. Development is moved by a distributed manufacturing technology made possible by the integration of computing and communications (C&C). Previously internal value chains, now distributed over global *markets of specialized subcontractors*, have made smaller scale production relatively more profitable. As engineering firms are embracing the new technologies to take them into the New Economy, they are destroying the business platforms for laggard incumbent firms. As volume based strategies of the old actors clash in markets with new innovative producers, the dynamic and complex decision environment that characterizes an *Experimentally Organized Economy* (EOE) raises the business failure rate. The complexity of the situation makes the capturing of the new opportunities genuinely experimental and dependent on entrepreneurial capacities that are not universally available among the industrial economies. While some developing economies are successfully adopting the new technologies, entering

The *Internet* is the ultimate manifestation of the integration of *Computer and Communications* (*C&C*) technologies, or the *fifth generation of computing*. This essay takes on the broader C&C perspective and addresses the introduction of fifth generation computing at all levels; Microchips integrated with sensors and mechanical devices minimize fuel consumption in car engines; Product life cycle planning (PLM) help visualize and monitor the entire design, manufacturing, use and servicing process of a product up to final scrapping, a C&C based technology that some visionaries say will help high wage Western firms beat low wage competitors.

The empirical background of this paper are the more than 200 interviews with Swedish and European industrial firms that I have conducted for various studies referred to in the text.

This is a significantly revised version of a paper prepared for the: **13th Conference of the International Joseph A. Schumpeter Society 2010** at Aalborg University, Denmark, 21–24 June 2010.

G. Eliasson (✉)
The Royal Institute of Technology (KTH), Stockholm, Sweden
e-mail: gunnar.elias@telia.com

A. Pyka and E.S. Andersen (eds.), *Long Term Economic Development*, Economic Complexity and Evolution, DOI 10.1007/978-3-642-35125-9_11,

onto faster growth paths, mature industrial economies experience difficulties of reorganizing for the same task. Some suffer more from the new competition than they benefit from the new opportunities. For the foreseeable future, however, engineering will continue to serve as the backbone of the rich industrial economies.

1 The Old Industry in the New Economy-Introducing an Opportunity

The principles behind my story of the ongoing industrial development were well understood already by Smith (1776), who was observing the spontaneous decentralization of the organization of production in the British economy. Change today, however, is considerably faster, and dramatically raised its pace around the mid 1990s when C&C technologies were finally integrated to become accessible for broad based commercial use. The outcome has been a considerably more dynamic and complex decision environment for businesses operating in the markets of the old industrial economies.

Computing and communications (C&C) technologies have revolutionized production in three ways; by (1) making the design and manufacturing of radically new, innovative and higher quality products possible, notably within engineering industry, by (2) changing the ways hierarchies are organized and managed, and by (3) creating economic incentives for a global distribution of production. This essay is about all three, and therefore addresses an eminently complex problem, the analytical solution to which will depend on how we cut it down to size by prior assumptions. Combining the three ways in my analysis, however, will allow me to relate both to standard economic theory, and popular business management models that have their origin in the same theories.

The new C&C technologies suddenly established the *Internet*, broadly defined, around the mid 1990s, as the perhaps most disruptive platform for global economic, industrial and social change ever. The Internet is the unexpected evolutionary outcome of the more general integration of computing and communications (C&C) technologies.[1] The stage was set for a future production organization of not only extreme global complexity, but also of constant experimental change. One question is in what shape the currently leading industrial economies will eventually emerge. How will the old engineering industry, for a couple of 100 years the

[1] For decades the large computer and (tele) communications companies had been unsuccessfully attempting to integrate computing and communications without coming up with a universal commercial solution until the mid 1990s, when the Internet became a viable commercial technology, created by outsider new business start ups, notably Mosaic Corporation in 1994 (rechristened Netscape in 1995). Eliasson (1996a) tells the story, and notably in the appended Chronicle (Eliasson and Eliasson 1996). I will use "the Internet" as a model term to represent the more general C&C technologies.

industrial backbone of the industrialized economies, look in the New Economy? A consequent question therefore is if the new C&C technologies are taking the world through an even greater period of economic experimentation, creative destruction and increasing income diversity than was the case during the first industrial revolution, that began in the late eighteenth century.

The ongoing C&C based industrial revolution has meant a renaissance for engineering. The consequences are visible in the form of both great new business opportunities, and new market risks. *First*, the need for large volumes over which to distribute the increasing costs for investments in product platform development has been reduced through more efficient innovation by actors that have been capable of capturing the opportunities. This is a concrete illustration of the increasing returns in "ideas production" theorized about in the "new growth models" (Jones and Williams 1998, 1999).

Second, increasing returns in innovation, combined with new C&C technology allow the distribution of production over *markets for specialist subcontractors*, raising the flexibility of manufacturing and allowing smaller producers to enjoy significant positive networking externalities of the kind suggested already by Marshall (1890, 1919) as a property of his industrial district, in the macro economic model of Romer's (1986) version of new growth theory, and again later as an aspect of the spillover proposition.[2] But this *macro dynamics can only be understood by taking the analysis down to the micro level* (Eliasson 2003). It is nice *to place the increasing importance for macro economic development of broad based markets for specialized subcontractor services in the context of the Marshallian industrial district*, that is further illuminated in a parallel paper on the European automotive industry (Eliasson 2011a).

Third, the consequences for industrial development of these two technology shifts have not all been assimilated by the business community in which the new production organization techniques are yet to be learned, and a remaining volume mentality in strategic business models derived from standard micro production theory, blocks their introduction. *When volume based and small scale flexible manufacturing strategies clash in markets complex, unpredictable and interesting dynamics is generated of the kind typical of an Experimentally Organized Economy*

[2] My Marshall/Schumpeter inspired quantitative analysis of what I call an *experimentally organized economy* (EOE) is therefore principally interesting since it is based on a method of simulating macro outcomes from micro cases over markets with the simultaneous endogenous determination of quantities and prices (see Eliasson 2009). The Appendix brings the principles together, and indicates with references to experiments on the Swedish micro to macro model MOSES, that significant, even revolutionary change may be involved. Both new growth theory and Marshall's theory of an industrial district were attempts to correct for a deficiency of the neoclassical model through endogenizing spillovers into a theory of economic growth. But that same "new" theory is still only a variation of an old theme that rests squarely on a traditional neoclassical static equilibrium footing that has been elaborated for decades by Dale Jorgenson and his research group, beginning with Jorgenson and Griliches (1967).

(EOE, Eliasson 2005b, 2007, 2009). Complexity theory here takes on new intriguing dimensions for business analysts and economic observers alike to consider (Frenken 2006; Hanusch and Pyka 2007. Again see Appendix).

In the 1980s, and before, three different ways of capturing economies of scale practiced frequently were to (1) raise volumes to reduce unit costs, often neglecting product innovation, (2) develop a complete product range for the market and to (3) engage in non core activities to spread risks. Automotive industry was, and still is, the outstanding example. Particularly interesting from an academic point of view, therefore, is that this volume mentality of the past has been coded into "modern" Enterprise Resource Planning (ERP), or company wide business planning systems, practiced top down in today's dynamic global market environments. Some of these planning systems have taken on gigantic proportions. They embody a top down mentality and ambitions to integrate everything through immensely complex accounting systems in ways that remind of old soviet planning. These systems not only involve principally impossible updating of accounting systems in a dynamic business environment that requires constant organizational change, but also, as a consequence, foster a conservative business mentality (Eliasson 1996a: CH5), that prevents large corporations from breaking up and distribute their value chains to capture the benefits of smaller scale and more flexible distributed manufacturing over markets of more innovative and efficient specialist subcontractors. Econometric evidence (e.g. Okamuro et al. 2011) also suggests that an industry structure dominated by large scale manufacturing and big business makes the business climate less entrepreneurial.

Fourth, and finally, the shift in the nature of the increasing returns concept is reflected in new work place competence requirements. Productivity of workers along the manufacturing line is no longer determined by the machines, irrespective of worker quality. Instead the workers, or rather engineers, are increasingly defining their own job specifications and their own productivities. There is a potential to significantly raise business performance and *an increasing demand for entrepreneurial qualities of "workers"*. This development is illustrated by the large and growing part of design and engineering in modern production, and the diminishing cost share of physical manufacturing (Eliasson 2006a, b). (Thus, for instance, ASEA (now ABB) in my hometown Västerås in Sweden has been thoroughly transformed from a blue collar to a white collar work place dominated by specialist workers, engineers and managers and with practically no low skill jobs. Similarly, product development at Ericsson is 95 % software development, the productivity of which is directly dependent on engineer ingenuity (Eliasson 2010).) This outcome is again reflecting back on the idea of so called new growth theory (Jones and Williams 1998). Even more telling is the fact that engineering industry of today is supported by an equally large and rapidly growing consultancy industry, sometimes internalized within the contractor firm, but increasingly composed of external innovative service providers.[3] These subcontractors are extremely important for the development of modern manufacturing firms. Key to understanding the story to be told therefore are the two sides of resource allocation and production; the information processing and the communications side, on the one hand, and the coordination of production activities on the other, knowledge based communication being needed to coordinate physical production.[4] *The globalization of previously internalized value chains over markets for specialized subcontractors therefore has made small scale production based on positive networking externalities not only profitable, but also flexible, and caused an increased interest in the role of small and medium sized firms (SMEs) in local, regional, national and global economic growth.* This is not a new phenomenon, but new C&C technologies dramatically raised the pace of change from the mid 1990s and on, prompting premature visions of an entirely New Economy.

Another consequence, slowly learned among the students of industrial economics, is that information processing and communication use up the bulk of resources in an advanced industrial economy, probably much more than 50 % (Eliasson 1986, 1990a, b; Wallis and North 1986).[5] A large and growing part of industrial output therefore consists of information and communications services embedded in physical products. Productivity change in this service production therefore today dominates productivity change of the entire industry. Mechanical devices, sensors and electronics are integrated in increasingly complex products, often making software services the largest cost component in advanced engineering products. Transactions within hierarchies and over markets, furthermore, not only use up large resources. They also fundamentally influence how resources are allocated, making the standard (static) I/O model a less than useful instrument to understand and influence what is going on (Eliasson 2009).

In the early 1990s economists worried about the absence of visible manifestations of the enormous investments in information technologies in US industry over the previous two decades. Had large investment resources been

---

[3] This is a fact that has made industrial statistics increasingly misleading for years. We observed already in Eliasson (1990b:51ff, 79)that the size statistically occupied by manufacturing in the NA statistics had been on a steady decline since the early 1950s. When corrected for external, outsourced service inputs the revised extended manufacturing industry had, however, remained constant, or even slightly increasing at around 50 % of GNP. The even more interesting observation is that the mistaken idea of "deindustrialization" still keeps coming up in even serious policy debate, with reference to the misleading NA statistics.

[4] In what follows I will use the term *production* to cover all value added creation over the entire value chain, including product design and development, engineering, manufacturing, marketing and distribution to the final user. The term *manufacturing* will be reserved for the physical side of production.

[5] The two volume *Handbook of Industrial Organization* edited by Schmalensee and Willig (1989) refers to the principal existence of transactions costs, notably in Williamsson's chapter, but the consequences of a dominant information and transactions cost element in the total cost structure of the economy for the standard I/O model on which so many policy conclusion have been based, are carefully avoided in the 1555 page discourse. See Eliasson 2009.

wasted? Robert Solow coined the widely used term *the productivity paradox* (Solow 1987; Brynjolfsen 1993; Berndt and Malone 1995). This discussion was however worded in the physical productivity terms of modern neoclassical macro production theory. The dynamics I am referring to, however, took place within the aggregates, and "invisibly" for those studying reality through the wrong theoretical glasses. So when during the second half of the 1990s the US economy suddenly and unexpectedly surged ahead, and the largest economy in the world, believed for many years to suffer from overage and chronic stagnation, was now leading the growth league, the economics profession was again caught off guard and coined the term the *New Economy* to "explain" what was going on, as the economies of previous winners, such as *Japan* (*As Number 1*, Vogel 1979) were stagnating. From 1980 to 2000 practically all industrial economies had lagged behind US GNP per capita growth, excepting *at that time* Ireland, and perhaps Portugal (Hämäläinen and Heiskala 2007:18f).

The New and superior Economy had been ushered into the US on the back of C&C technologies. Röller and Waverman (2001) estimated the diffusion of land-based communications networks in 21 industrial economies had accounted for one-third of output growth between 1970 and 1990. Greenstein and Spiller (1996), Lichtenberg (1993) and Mun and Nadiri (2002) also observed that new technology spillovers were particularly large in industries that were intensive in their use of C&C technologies.[6]

Then came a sudden reversal in the IT industry around the turn of the millennium. Still Chun et al. (2004) observed that "stock returns and fundamental performance measures were significantly higher in industries that had a history of more investment in information technology". Radically new methods of organizing production, made possible by new integrated computing & communications (C&C) technology and the Internet, were said to be the mainstay of the New Economy, and explained the unprecedented growth cycle of the US economy over more than a decade (Jorgenson and Wessner 2006, 2007).

(There is an even longer term policy issue. The 1990s saw a surge in spillover[7] econometrics, and the observation that social rates of return were above, or far above, private rates of return on R&D. Nadiri (1993), Jones and Williams (1998, 1999), and others concluded that the rich industrial economies were *underinvesting in private R&D* and argued that a great policy opportunity to do something about that underinvestment was presenting itself. The numbers were such that the low wage competition from China, and similar industrially developing economies challenging Western engineering industries, should be considered too small to worry about. The real economic problem, however, is different and has to do with (1) the incentives to invest sufficiently in private R&D to generate the spillovers needed to overcome the underinvestment, and (2) the commercializing competences needed to profitably exploit the spillovers. The spillover values seem

[6] See further Eliasson (2010:41).

[7] The term first appears to have been used by Nadiri (1978).

to be largely captured by others than those creating them, notably by consumers in the form of lower prices (Nordhaus 2004), and society at large, while the profitability of the spillover generating firms is too low to make them invest in R&D and grow at a rate sufficient to overcome the underinvestment. Defense products are one case, notably military aircraft. Such products distinguish themselves by carrying with them a large "cloud of technologies", available for free to everyone capable of commercializing them, and sufficient to name Swedish Saab military aircraft a technical university diffusing new technologies and workers with experience from the most advanced manufacturing techniques to engineering industry in particular. I have therefore (Eliasson 2010:239ff) ventured the suggestion that a *new demand based innovation policy* in the form of *public procurement of privately demanded advanced public goods and services* should help overcome the underinvestment, without most of the misallocation and dead weight problems associated with traditional short term Keynesian demand stimulus.)

The integration of mechanical devices and electronics through software in products has created entirely new industrial opportunities for the mature engineering industry, the industrial backbone of Western economies. But this is also the industry that is being subjected to the most dramatic change as concentrated production sites based on volume manufacturing are giving way to *new distributed forms of flexible production*, the complexity of which make them analytically intractable and *available only as the outcome of an experimental process fraught with management mistakes*. Not all local or national industrial economies will therefore make the transition, since not only are the organizational competences to do it right often lacking. *The new organizational practices to cope are also resisted politically since they affect the distribution, composition and compensation of jobs.*

It may be true that the global diffusion of spillovers explains most of economic growth among the rich industrial economies (Klenow and Rodriguez- Clare 2004; Keller 2001),[8] but not all rich industrial economies will therefore make it successfully into the New Economy, because they lack the necessary entrepreneurial *receiver competences* (Eliasson 1986:46f, 57f, 1990a; Cohen and Levinthal 1990). *Failing economies will then suffer more from the increased global competition than they will benefit from the new opportunities*. The roads to successful globalization of production in an experimentally organized economy are therefore lined with business mistakes and occasional successes. As in the first industrial revolution beginning in the late eighteenth century (Pritchnett 1997) diversity will probably increase (Eliasson 2007). Now, as well as then, inabilities to receive, adjust to and commercialize the new technologies will be the reason (Eliasson 2000, 2003; Parente and Prescott 2004).

I therefore go on (in Sect. 2) comparing the engineering industry, as the initiator and mover of the industrial revolution, with what is currently going on with product technology development and the organization of firm hierarchies and the

[8] For a somewhat contrary view, see Branstetter (1996).

globalization of their value chains. My story is about the renaissance of engineering. I continue (Sect. 3) with a stylized presentation of the C&C technologies, notably the Internet, as a global production flow reorganizer, placing special emphasis on the security issue and on what is yet to become established industrial practice; integrated production based on virtual and flexible design. This frames my concluding (in Sect. 4) discussion of *the new balance between volume and smaller scale production*, that will save the capable high wage economies of the Western world from the onslaught of low wage competition from industrializing economies and re-establish engineering as the industrial back bone of the "New Economies".

2 The Renaissance of Engineering

When the machine tools had been developed into reliable machines for routine factory use by the beginning of the nineteenth century, decentralized industrialized structures of specialist producers began to evolve very much as Smith (1776) had described it, while it was happening, and compete the then dominant handicraft industry out of business. The modern engineering industry had been born. But not all economies succeeded in reorganizing themselves for that transition. Massive global diversity was one consequence (Pritchnett 1997).

A similar industrial revolution of the engineering industry, made possible by new Computing and Communications (C&C) technology is currently in progress. Its potential leverage on productivity advance is huge, but the entrepreneurial capacities of the producers of the old industrial nations to reorganize production around the new engineering technology may not be sufficient to carry them further into the New Economy. If the transition of the industrialized world succeeds, it may, however, be possible in principle for the already rich industrial nations to beat imitator economies attempting to catch up, and to keep the distance to the industrially less developed economies. But this will require a new combination of technical and entrepreneurial competences, radical industrial reorganization and a political willingness to cope with the consequent social adjustments. I take note of the Patel and Pavitt (1994) observation of the continued, widespread and neglected importance of mechanical technologies. Are we witnessing the demise, or the renaissance of engineering industry?

2.1 A Brief History of Engineering Technology

The "new" machine tool technology was revolutionary. It represented a generic technology that could be used in practically all metal manufacturing, and it made specialized and decentralized production ("outsourcing") possible. From the beginning such specialization and geographical decentralization offered great advantages over the earlier craft industry where the entire product was manufactured in one workshop. *Organization*, hence, became an integral part of engineering technology, or the fourth production factor recognized by Alfred Marshall. England's growing industrial heartland developed around this technology. To be noted is that the workshops in Lancashire had more machine tools in operation at the beginning of the nineteenth century than all the world taken together (Carlsson 1986; Woodbury 1972, *FT*, May 27–28, 2000).

Sweden, since its period of military imperialism during the seventeenth century had experienced an acute need to develop and manufacture more sophisticated weaponry than its enemies. At the time Sweden therefore developed a tradition to import whatever skills and industrial competencies that were needed to achieve those objectives through active promotion of the immigration and permanent settlement of skilled workers and industrialists. Thus public procurement to satisfy advanced military needs defined a Swedish platform for further indigenous industrial development. What began as an iron based cannon industry gradually evolved into a sophisticated engineering industry (Eliasson 2011b).

The world was eager to learn, and Swedes were outstanding learners. The Swedish economist Westerman (1768) travelled to, and learned from what was going on in England, and observed that the new machines from England of course were good to have, but they did not help much if there were too few people who knew how to operate them, and above all, if an understanding of how to organize manufacturing around them was lacking. The economic importance of the industrial revolution under way in England was soon understood, and industrial espionage became common. Linnaeus' student Daniel Solander, who worked in England most of his life, was instructed by authorities close to the Swedish king to persuade skilled English workers to emigrate to Sweden. He even tried to convince James Watt to move to Sweden with his impressive "fire machine" (*Populär Historia* Nr. 1, 2003, p. 31 ff).

Improved steel quality (not least because of the first industrial implementation of the Bessemer method at the Edskens factory in Gästrikland in Sweden 1853)[9] made the machine tools more precise and more reliable. This technology was further improved in the US during the second industrial revolution (1860–1920)[10] as measurement technology (refined by the gauge blocks from Johansson's factory in Eskilstuna, patented 1901) made it possible to manufacture standardized and exchangeable components very precisely. Swedish industry had already then become a great innovative player in global markets.

2.2 New Digital Technology Revolutionizes Engineering

Among the "old industries", engineering was best suited for exploiting the new digital technology; (1) because the *digital technology* is excellent replacement for many mechanical solutions in engineering products, and (2) because its basic technology potential is decentralized and distributed production. Enormous

[9] By the founder of Sandvik, Göran Fredrik Göransson.

[10] And notably through the development, and effective use of guns with exchangeable components during the US civil war.

systemic productivity gains could be achieved and Swedish manufacturing firms were pioneers in the 1970s in using electronic devices in their products (Eliasson 1980, 1981). The micro-processor—or the fourth generation of computers—took engineering technology one great step forward. Today *the functionalities of advanced mechanical products depend entirely on how mechanical devices and electronics have been integrated through software* (Eliasson 2010).

The decentralized organization of casting, sheet metal forming, machining,[11] welding, heat treatment of components, etc., previously carried out within one factory, defines the next phase in the digital revolution. The geographical distribution of the production of components and subsystems over markets for specialized subcontractors to be brought together (systems integration) for final assembly into a complete product is another equally revolutionary characteristic of engineering production, still being moved at a rapid pace by the continuing integration of computer and communications technologies.

I therefore ask, in this essay, what the fifth generation of computers—the merge of computing and communications (C&C) technology and the Internet, its ultimate manifestation—will mean for traditional manufacturing, and engineering in particular. With specialization and outsourcing increasing, and with product development, manufacturing, distribution and marketing merging on a global scale, industrial actors with the right competence have discovered great business opportunities.

Metal forming machine tools are still the backbone of modern engineering industry. Engineering has been given attributes such as "mature", "old" and "traditional", and automobiles are often quoted as a typical product of such a mature industry. The question, however, is how a production technology founded on "metal forming" could have been maintained for 150 years as, and still to a large extent defines, the industrial backbone, and the competence monopoly of the industrial world.

The question is how western producers will cope, when their engineering knowledge monopoly is being challenged from all ends by an industrially not yet developed world that is rapidly learning this technology, and at least to begin with operates at far lower wage levels. Literature offers a variety of answers. *First*, sufficient numbers of the highly diversified products of engineering industry are very sophisticated and are constantly changing in response to the constantly varying tastes of wealthy customers. They will be demanded "for ever" and it will be a competitive advantage to be close to those customers. So the industrially developing economies will not be capable of competing successfully in the upper end of these markets. *Second*, mechanical engineering in the industrial world uses very complicated technologies. Everything from military jet fighters to computers and simple metal components belong to the product mix. Swedish metal manufacturing was once (Pavitt 1979; Pavitt and Soete 1981) ranked as one of the most varied and technologically advanced industries in the world, just behind the US, Japan and

[11] Using gear-cutting, grinding and milling machines.

Germany, and far ahead of all other economies, including England and France. Since then, however, the Swedish range of technologies has narrowed. The big firms have discontinued their production of peripheral products, shedded high risk experimental development projects and shut down non profitable production to focus on core competences. At the same time (*third*) Swedish engineering companies have developed from being small (by global standards) as financial organizations, but large as manufacturing units in the 1970s (Pratten 1976) to become, through internal growth, acquisitions and expansion abroad, a smaller number of very large firms. It is interesting to compare a list of the largest firms 50 years ago with the same list today (see Eliasson 1996a:49). Most of the firms at the head of the ranking have been replaced. (Today only ASEA (now ABB), Ericsson, Stora (now Stora Enso), SCA, Sandvik, SKF and Volvo remain among the largest 15, but both ABB and Ericsson were recently close to being toppled by internal mismanagement and external events (Eliasson 2005a). Volvo, Electrolux, Saab, Scania, Astra (Zeneca) and (temporarily) Pharmacia have moved up).

2.3 The Spontaneous and Unpredictable Emergence of the Internet Revolution

While economic analysts had been preoccupied with the particular technologies they had been used to be concerned with, an economic tsunami had been secretly gaining momentum during the last couple of decades of the twentieth century.

The transistor was the first step in the digital computing revolution. It was invented in Bell Labs 1947 and the second generation of computing had been initiated.[12] One of the inventors, William Shockley, took the principle with him to Palo Alto in California where he started Shockley Semiconductors. As talented employees jumped ship and started their own companies a close to explosive development was initiated. AMD was one spin off from Shockley's enterprise, and Intel another, within which the micro processor was invented 1971, and with that the PC made possible. The fourth generation of computing was born.

The origin of the Internet is sometimes dated to 1973 when Winston Cerf (at Harvard) and others formulated the so called Internet Transmission Protocol (TCP/IP). But very little occurred outside the university world until 1994 when Mosaic corporation (rechristened Netscape in 1995) introduced an easy to use graphical browser. Most computer companies had been aware of the industrial potential, and had been unsuccessfully attempting for years to integrate computing and communications (Eliasson 1996a), only to see Netscape's bright idea initiate a commercial revolution, and Internet use exploded. Before 1995 the Internet is more or less absent from the business journals, then suddenly to permeate them

[12] After the vacuum tube. The third generation of computing was ushered in 1958, when Texas Instruments first introduced the integrated circuit.

(Eliasson and Eliasson 1996). If we are to discuss the intellectual origin of the Internet, furthermore, we should go back to 1957 when the US Defense Department founded Advanced Research Projects Agency (ARPA) and asked it to develop a method to keep communications open during a nuclear war. A computer network capable of exchanging information between any couple of computers was developed. In this sense the by far most important industrial technology of the twentieth century has a military origin. To capture such spillovers is, however, an entirely different story. Thus, for instance, the document on "Future Critical Technologies," delivered to the White House and the US President in 1995 failed to mention the Internet, and even worse, also the then ongoing rapid integration of Computing and Communications (C&C) technologies was not really part of the presentation. It is not the spectacular emergence of Silicon Valley that constitutes the new industrial revolution. It is the explosive, but unpredicted, commercialization of technologies developed there and diffused through the production system in extremely complex ways. The model capable of representing the dynamics of this process is based on micro economic phenomena, extremely complex and of the nonlinear type with no analytically determinate equilibrium outcome. The story is that of the unpredictability prevailing in what I call an Experimentally Organized Economy (EOE. See Eliasson 1987, and Appendix). A tsunami had been created that surfaced at the industrial level about the mid 1990s. The fifth generation of computing had been born and a new industrial revolution was on the way.

2.4 The Art of Distributed and Integrated Production: A Small Scale Revolution?

Decentralization and distribution of production over markets, was understood already by Smith (1776) to be the source of economic wealth of nations. Advanced engineering products of today are too complex and require too many specialized technologies to be developed and manufactured within one company. Product development and manufacturing, therefore, have to be distributed over *markets of specialist subcontractors*, and increasingly on a global scale. To organize such distributed and integrated production right is a difficult management art in itself. Even though this is where Swedish industry, and its aircraft industry in particular, was a pioneer and has excelled (Eliasson 2010), complexity is such that organizational failure is common. The market for specialist subcontractor services, however, is what makes it possible for the systems integrating firms to operate on a smaller scale than before, drawing on the networking externalities embodied in the system. C&C technologies make it possible to reorganize and *integrate* the different manufacturing methods in innovative new configurations, raising the *flexibility of production*. Individual technologies can also be subjected to both stepwise and radical change, the latter not rarely making the competence endowment of entire firms obsolete. Benkard (1999) emphasizes the need to "forget" in aircraft industry.

Networking externalities arise in different ways. First, one single producer can never be the most cost efficient in all operations. New C&C technologies have made it possible to shift production from concentrated internalized large volume manufacturing towards a more flexible, but also more complex distributed organization. With some production outsourced to more efficient subcontractors they can achieve optimum scale by also serving other customers (Eliasson 1986:82f). The distribution of production over many subcontractors also means increased efficiency since factors of production, notably labor, will be better utilized and compensated closer to their marginal productivities (Eliasson 2006a), and flexibility can be achieved more easily by changing delivery contracts than by laying off own workers. To get the new distributed organization right, however, is not easy. The distributed organization means that new *indirect* transactions costs are incurred through organizational mistakes, and larger *direct* transactions costs because of the increased market transactions. If done right, however, large systems productivity gains, and flexible product designs can be achieved. Second, part of the systems productivity gains originates in the possibilities to charge higher prices for flexibly redesigned products for markets where such products are demanded.[13] This is the normal situation in modern production subject to rapid technological change. A distributed (over markets of subcontractors) production organization is, therefore, also more flexible than a centralized internalized organization. This means that large systemic productivity effects can normally be achieved *in principle* from reorganizing a company towards distributed production.

3 The Internet as a Global Production Reorganizer

The industrial potential of the "Internet", broadly defined, completely unforeseen some 20 years ago, appears to be enormous and originates in the simultaneous reorganization and coordination of information and "production" flows (Item 5 in Table 1). A production organization distributed over markets of specialized subcontractors makes it possible both to capture systemic productivity gains and to raise flexibility in production for those capable and creative enough to manage the complexity involved. The deep information and communications structure superimposed on the distributed physical production structure is reflected in significant transactions costs. That transactions draw large direct and indirect resources (More than 50 %, Eliasson 1986, 1990b; Wallis and North 1986) was long an unknown or ignored fact among economists and still is, in much contemporary economic theorizing. The direct transactions costs are incurred in both internal and external markets. The indirect transactions costs are however much larger and are incurred in the form of business mistakes and lost profits (Eliasson and Eliasson

[13] Cf Nilsson's 1981 study of the diseconomies of the inflexible automated ASEA electrical motor manufacturing line.

Table 1 Systems effect categories at different levels of aggregation in knowledge based information economy

1. Speed up info flows over given structures (rationalization)
2. Speed up physical flows over given structures (rationalization)
3. Reorganize info flows
4. Reorganize physical flows
5. Do all simultaneously (*integrated production*)

Source: Eliasson (1998b). Information efficiency, production organization and systems productivity—quantifying the effects of EDI investments; in Macdonald and Madden (1998)

2005). They constitute a standard cost for economic development and are key characteristics of an experimentally organized economy within which their size is not analytically determinate (see Appendix).

3.1 E-Business and Internet Security

Internet based electronic business is the perhaps most commonly referred to use of C&C technology in the old production organizations. To begin with physical transactions ("paper flows") were supposed to be replaced by digital flows. Attempts to replace the book by a digitally sourced screen have long been discussed, but perhaps Apple's new Ipad will do it. US *Amazon* has come to symbolize this development, but the principles date further back. The paperless office was an early indicator of the idea that did not take hold in the 1970s because the technology was not ready. Electronic Data Interchange (EDI), a precursor of the Internet, was introduced by many large companies in the 1990s to help organize their purchasing, production and distribution flows. Most of these systems were proprietary to the company which limited the possibilities to communicate over external markets and to achieve desired systems externalities (Eliasson 1998). This, however, all changed dramatically with the rapid introduction of the Internet standard in the late 1990s.

Early applications of C&C technology in industry and business, however, simply meant speeding up either information or manufacturing flows without changing the organization of the same flows (Items 1 and 2 in Table 1). Limited organizational competence and innovative capacities held back development. Security is another concern. As long as trade secrets and other sensitive information and large economic values transacted over the Internet can be pirated by skilled hackers the full potential of the new technology will not be realized. On this McKnight and Bailey (1997:19) and McKnight et al. (1997) observed that security is the "enabler for electronic markets".

While most speculation on, and around E-trade has been about its impact on distribution to consumers (B2C), the revolution has taken place in business to business (B2B) trade, a development closely related to the expansion of distributed production and the need to coordinate flexible information and production flows over subcontractors. The initiation of that development does not date back much more than a decade or two.

General Electric (GE) was a pioneer in developing advanced and efficient Internet based purchasing. Already in 1998 GE expected to save almost half a billion dollars by shifting the purchasing of five billion dollars to the Internet (DI April 17. 1998). *Dell* was early in selling its PCs over the Internet. It began its second revolution already in 2000 (*BW*, July 18, 2000) by using the Internet to integrate its assembly and subcontractor system over its entire value chain up to the customer, using enterprise resource planning (ERP) technology. This meant (*BW*, June 18, 2001, FT July 19. 2000) that Dell only had 5 days of inventory, while competitors were carrying 30, 45 and even 90 days of inventory. *IBM* took similar steps early, and announced in 1999 that 25 % of its income had been generated by e-trade (BW May 28. 2001). The theoretical principles behind this capital saving potential had been taught in economics since the 1960s. Only now, however, was the instrumentation there to allow the principles to be realized in practice.

Swedish *Sandvik* introduced IT already in the 1970s in its global customer relations using a proprietary system. Early in the new millennium it shifted its global marketing and distribution system over to the Internet (*Sv.D.*, February 8, 2002).[14] Swedish and Swiss ABB announced in 2000 that it was reorganizing itself away from being a hardware manufacturer to become an information and knowledge ("Brain power" based) business, using the Internet to integrate customers, product development and a distributed (over the market) manufacturing organization (DI February 14. And 21. 2002, Eliasson 2002:101), production automation being one of its strategic growth areas. It did not help, however, at least not in the short run, and ABB was in serious trouble by the turn of the millennium, being forced to shed almost all its non core businesses (DI, February 22. 2005), often at the wrong time and at bargain prices.

Reorganizing itself into something entirely different all the way through Table 1 is not easy. While one of ABBs specialties still is factory automation, ABB limits its ambitions to engage only in certain industry applications where it has learned the process technology, and never reorganizes the information and process flows of an established company completely to take full advantage of the possible systemic potential (Item 5 in Table 1). This is simply too difficult, and the risks of getting the flows organization seriously wrong are too high.

It is generally so that the new high tech electronics devices, sensors etc. may give the early developer and user a temporary advantage in partial applications. Over some "run", however, the new devices have been learned by competitors. They are available in the market, and the longer term industrial success and staying power rest on understanding the business to be automated. WoodEye, a Swedish Saab related company used early sensor and electronic devices, originally developed to represent, and analyze in flight behavior of supersonic missiles in real time, to automate the diagnosis and sorting of timber logs in a sawmill by quality, also in real time (Eliasson 2011b). The economics of this new technology was tremendous since sorting was reliable, rapid and labor saving. The long run business outcome,

[14] Also cf case study of the earlier system in Fries (1984).

however, did not depend on the sensors and electronics equipment, components that soon became standard and generic, but on understanding and reorganizing the saw mill process to make full use of the new information technology.

Within automotive manufacturing *Covisint* (founded by GM, Ford and Daimler Chrysler 2000) has developed into the world's largest Internet market in the industry. One ambition was to cut prices for components through competitive purchasing in more transparent markets, but the official rationale for this trading place was to facilitate the development of new organizational solutions for production over the markets of subcontractors.

The new production organization of the *Boeing* company, however, illustrates the advantage of an Internet based information system. The ambition has been to raise the speed of the moving line of one of the world's most complicated manufacturing processes in its Renton (Washington) factory. The entire assembly line is integrated (over the Internet) with all subcontractors and all modifications of designs and construction blueprints being simultaneously updated at all locations where they are used. When developing, manufacturing and assembling the 250 seat 787 Dreamliner in the world's largest building in Everett, Washington 17 companies from 10 countries have been involved (*BW*, June 11, 2001, *Time* Sept. 17. 2007, DI March 26. 2010). The complexity has reached such proportions that Boeing fell 2 years behind schedule in flying its new Dreamliner. The Dreamliner business plan represented a dramatic paradigm shift compared to the previous 777 model. Still, time to market for the two models has been roughly the same. An additional comfort for Boeing is that its main competitor Airbus, with its giant 380 model for 555 passengers based on a conventional, but scaled up concept,[15] was even more late, because of organizational problems, and the awkward rules imposed on the sharing of management authority and job locations between the nations involved in the project, notably France and Germany.

E-business can also be "internal" within distribution and supplier networks, and few paid attention to the Arkansas supermarket chain *Wal-Mart* which learned long before the New Economy hype how to use IT to distribute everything from clothes

[15] While Airbus is heavily subsidized, Boeing has had to rely on private partners and on some state subsidies to finance, and to cover the technical and commercial risks on the Dreamliner. On this French Prime Minister Lionel Jospin once said that "We will give Airbus the means to win the battle against Boeing" (*Newsweek* Dec. 13. 2004). On this I say (Eliasson 2010) that the positive spillovers to (externalities for) the US economy of the Dreamliner will be much larger than the Airbus benefits to the European economy. It will therefore be interesting to see who wins the commercial battle. Rather than leaning on politicians, Boeing listened to its customers (the Airlines) which managed to steer Boeing away from its original product concept, that to begin with was similar to that of Airbus, towards a smaller aircraft for direct flights between cities, the Dreamliner. To counter Boeing's Dreamliner, Airbus has started development of the 270 seat 350 model, again with public subsidies as the bottomline.

Recently (FT Sept. 10/11. 2011:9), one of the commercial partners of EADS (that own Airbus), German Daimler has been trying to sell its share to a (on insistence of the German Government) German investor. French Government controlled Aerospatiale, and other French owners are not signaling a corresponding divestment.

to medicine. Wall-Mart established an entirely new, highly productive organization of retail trade with direct contact between producers (suppliers) and superstore shelves and practically no inventories beyond what is being on the move between factories and Wal-Mart stores. Wal-Mart tried to enter Europe on the basis of its superior IT-based distribution technology. It shook up the old fashioned low productive European retail industry, but met with unexpected resistance with European customers who did not like to wander around in enormous ware houses. Whatever the long run outcome it will leave unproductive European competitors dead in its wake (*BW*, June 28, 1999, *Newsweek*, May 20, 2002, *Sv.D. Näringsliv* January 24, 2003).

3.2 *Mass Manufacturing vs. Smaller Scale Networking Externalities*

C&C technology enters production through three different information channels where (Eliasson 1996a) (1) *information* systems make hierarchies more transparent, and improves access to information and people with competence, (2) *business systems*[16] monitor and run *operations* and (3) *accounting* systems are designed for economic measurement and *control*. The three different channels overlap, since both information and business systems are based on the accounting systems of the firm. There may, however, be several, each based on different taxonomies to serve different purposes. The information access system has openings for discrete human interfaces and human competence inputs,[17] that business systems attempt to minimize. Manufacturing automation is a special, and "relatively simple" special case of such efforts. Even so, complexity is such that failure is common. One illustration is that companies in the manufacturing automation market, such as ABB, rarely undertake complete reorganizations of the entire business, but rather modify existing processes in a piece meal fashion.[18] In the last couple of decades specialist companies such as German SAP, US Oracle and Lawson have developed extremely complex enterprise wide business or Enterprise Resource Planning (ERP) systems designed to integrate everything top down to make the business more transparent and efficient in reducing slack and cutting costs.

While new information technology may make giant and complex hierarchies more transparent, such systems also reduce organizational flexibility because of the difficulties associated with maintaining and updating the enormous and often fragmented databases with new activities. And worse, such systems influence the thinking of management, foster a preoccupation with costs and encourage

[16] Including electronic trade.

[17] Of the Turing (1936) kind.

[18] Interview with ABB Sweden in 2002. ABB works according to a bottom up approach, while SAP starts from the financial control level and works itself down.

"gigantism". In fact, such systems are principally impossible business planning tools in a dynamic business management context because they make it impossible to add and remove activities without a major overhaul of databases, and hence also make it difficult for large businesses to adopt smaller scale and more flexible manufacturing distributed over markets of specialist subcontractors. To avoid organizational rigidification an extremely high resolution of internal statistical accounts and a preparedness for integrating accounts of comparable resolution and classification of new businesses to come is needed. Such, standardized, expensive to install[19] and inflexible, some would say unwieldy, business systems that attempt to integrate everything therefore not only create impossible data collection and updating problems, but also distorts organizational transparency (Eliasson 1976, 1996a:Ch 5, 2005b). They develop a preoccupation with costs, notably inventory minimization, and should rather be called "partial misinformation system", to quote Ackoff (1967), in markets dominated by innovative product competition and constant organizational change. In fact, the CEO of profitable Swedish truck producer Scania has called the SAP system costly and useless (Interview in separate advertizing section of DI, Sept. 29. 2004). Many companies have tried and failed, including the Swedish defense organization, that has invested 2.4 billion SEK in a SAP system that cannot even, it turned out, handle secret documents, and now, after a series of cost overruns and reduced ambitions is expected to save 270 million SEK per year from integrating its 1,500 different IT systems.[20] This is well within the error margin for such calculations on a 40 billion annual budget (*Computer Sweden* June.5.2009:4f, *Veckans Affärer*, 8 April 2010:20–24). On this I add that the savings calculated overemphasize improvements in cost rationalization, deemphasizing the costs of rigidity, notably losing winners, and takes management attention away from innovative product development. Much larger values are likely to be lost in the long term in the form of missed winners, a typical illness of the very large business organizations (Eliasson 1996a).

ERP systems had been largely developed for stable organizational hierarchies to achieve top down cost control, faster flows, and minimized inventories, thereby being inattentive to the organizational flexibility (Item 5 in Table 1) that the break up and market distribution of previously internal value chains has created. Managing unstable business organizations in the Internet world through rigid accounting systems is certainly not the best way for top management to be well informed (Eliasson 2005b). Static efficiency may have increased, but at the cost of inflexibility and doing the wrong thing. The risk with comprehensive business systems therefore is that their introduction and use breeds a hierarchical volume mentality that both closes management eyes to business opportunities and reduces flexibility

[19] And not only that. The SAP system was designed and on the market "before Internet", and converting SAP software for Internet use has been both difficult and costly, not least for the customers (FT June 12. 2001).

[20] There is no way to calculate savings at that level of precision. And what one has calculated as a gain might very well already have been lost several times over in the form of lost investment opportunities that could not be fitted into the systems standard.

in both product design and manufacturing organization. Such streamlined production control systems may kill innovation, argued already Michael Cappelas, then CEO in (the earlier) Compaq (now within HP. *BW*, September 24, 2001). Econometric evidence (e.g. Okamuro et al. 2011) also suggests that industry structures dominated by large scale manufacturing and big business make the business climate less entrepreneurial. Advocates for Product Life cycle Management (PLM) systems are therefore critical of the preoccupation with cost minimization in ERP systems. Their argument is that ERP systems make managers "neglect" innovation and product development. Product Lifecycle Management (PLM) is a visualization technology that originated in aircraft industry. To begin with PLM methods were developed to compute service charges from rented products such as aircraft engines (Eliasson 1996b, 2010:157ff). The business concept was to remain the owner of the complex product, renting it as a user service to the customer. With time PLM has become a generic term for virtual production systems that make all information on the product available over its entire life cycle. When aircraft engines were rented to airlines and charged for engine services the design, engineering and life management of the engine were changed radically (Eliasson 2010). The same is happening in large and expensive investment equipment with a long life, such as trucks, and also in automotive rental business. The argument is that virtual production systems of the PLM type, contrary to cost focused ERP systems, pay attention to the product and the customer, and make firms, both small and large, more innovative (*Ny Teknik, Special Supplement* Sept. 28. 2005:2).

A conclusion for the following therefore is that the common management preoccupation with volume manufacturing and cost minimization, for instance to counter import competition from low wage economies, now codified in rigid business systems, makes the business less well prepared in markets where product innovation and variation are demanded. With quality variation becoming an increasingly demanded product feature, *flexibility, and the supply of product variety* have to be made part of a relevant definition of productivity. The more distributed over markets of subcontractors production, the more flexibly product customisation can be combined with efficient supply chain management, and the more difficult it becomes to measure and control quality over the entire value chain. As a consequence, the more difficult and competence demanding, the more important it becomes to get the new complex organization of production right, and industrial experience demonstrates that this is not only difficult, but also failure prone.

3.3 The Important Markets for Specialized Subcontractors

Large scale systems integration means concentrating on product development, outsourcing non core physical manufacturing on specialized subcontractors, and then marketing and distributing the product, sometimes even taking over part of the maintenance and servicing of the product from the customer. This technology was developed in aircraft industry and Alan Mulally has made a point of having brought it with him to crisis stricken Ford from Boeing in 2006 (*Time* Sept. 6. 2010:30f).

Visualization is key to effective distribution and integration of production. Visualization in turn depends on standardization, modularization, precise definition, measurement and manufacturing of the modules. Modularization is no simple technique, even though it was first used a century and a half ago[21] with the development of precise measurement and machining techniques. This development was speeded up by the Swedish pioneer "Mått Johansson" in Eskilstuna (in the Lake Mälar region) who invented and patented his set of gauge blocks 1901, a measurement technology that rapidly diffused through the global engineering industry. The new CAD-CAM based visualization technology is of course immensely more demanding on measurement and precision. Crosby's (1997) point about the role of measurement in economic quantification in the early western industrialization, from the thirteenth century and on, apparently still carries a momentum.

(Swedish engineering firms were leaders in integrating microelectronics in their products during the1970s (Eliasson 1980, 1981). *Embedded systems*,or chips (electronic modules) embedded in small mechanical systems that guide the mechanical devices have become an important technology in the last decade. Such devices now appear everywhere in engineering industry and are increasingly developed into standardized functional modules developed by specialized subcontractors.)

The benefits of distributed and integrated production are illustrated in Table 1. To begin with the use of IT in production was limited to doing the same thing, but now with IT support (Items 1 and 2). With degrees the art of raising productivity by reorganizing process flows in ways IT made possible were introduced (Items 3 and 4). The very complex, difficult and potentially rewarding art of doing both simultaneously (Item 5) is what we are discussing. The potentially large economic gains from distributing production come from complete reorganization at both the physical and the information process flow levels, and this is where the markets for specialist subcontractors come into play, in ways that were not feasible before the commercialization of C&C and Internet technologies. Even the fairly well controlled internal environment of a manufacturing plant offers such enormous variety of possible production flow organization that automation, as I have mentioned, is always done through gradual modifications of exiting architectures to avoid costly mistakes. The art of complexity management is however not fully tested until distribution of production stretches over markets, and includes the whole value chain from product design, through manufacturing, distribution and, as well, servicing and use, and involves the constant change of product specifications. We are now talking about much more than outsourcing the low end of manufacturing, but of the fact that it is impossible to develop all specialized competencies of advanced production internally, and that the systems integrating firm can never be the most

[21] During the US Civil War the life and performance of guns were radically extended through the use of interchangeable parts (Carlsson 1994).

efficient developer and manufacturer of all. Here standardized modular systems integrated through C&C based software have worked wonders for engineering product development. But also economic factors are at work. The carriers of specialized knowledge can never capture their full rent by being employed by the systems integrator. By taking on the higher private risks of being outsourced they can also offer their services to other buyers, and raise their returns (Eliasson 1986:82ff). Again, the existence of varied markets for specialized subcontractor services are instrumental for capturing the full benefits of distributed and integrated production. (Outcontracting over specialized and varied subcontractor markets is more flexible than internalized production, and a natural part of the flexible manufacturing systems, originally pioneered by Honda and Toyota in Japan, but later learned, and rapidly introduced, in the US and Europe and now being returned to stagnant Japanese businesses in upgraded form (*Ny Teknik* Nr 49. Dec.3. 2003:14f).) But again, distributing the value chain too widely over markets, notably over global markets, eventually leads to the loss of cost and quality control.[22] To get that compromise right is a difficult industrial art that managers often fail to learn.

4 The New Balance Between Small Scale and Volume Production

C&C technologies have influenced engineering in three ways; by making (1) the design of radically new products possible, (2) complex hierarchies more transparent and (3) incentives for globally distributed production stronger. The outcome has been a shift towards smaller scale.

When looked at from a national or global economic perspective the systemic productivity gains or networking externalities associated with distributed and integrated production have been found to be based not only on the information, communication and coordination potential of C&C technologies (shown in Table 1) but also on the development of broad based markets for specialized subcontractor services and—not least—functioning, high capacity transport networks that allow for stable, high speed, predictable and flexible flows of physical products, notably road transports.

While the benefits of (globally) distributed production, very much as Smith (1776) once described it, are large, many factors hold back the immediate exploitation of the industrial productivity potential of new C&C technology. Factors slowing the transition to a new global production organization in a particular region or economy are (1) lack of local competence on the part of business management,

[22] A common experience from extensive outsourcing that has forced many firms to return outcontracted manufacturing from low wage economies. This is typically the experience from producers that change their product designs frequently and/or customize their products (Eliasson 2005c).

(2) the high risk of management failure in the now much more complex and unfamiliar business opportunities space, (3) an institutional environment in the industrial economies that discourages entrepreneurs to act on the opportunities, and, not least, (4) a general political aversion among the (still) rich industrial economies to absorb the unpredictable reshuffling of monetary wealth, employment, individual welfare and political power that accompanies a successful such transition. There is also the time perspective itself. Learning takes time as does the development of the supporting markets for specialized subcontractor markets. But economic incentives are so large that the experimental transition process will not stop. The total outcome is already statistically visible as production is distributed over markets of specialized subcontractors delivering a larger production value at a significantly smaller input of labour. A number of these production units have once been internal parts of a large firm that have now been separated as small autonomous firms/subcontractors that can access the entire global market, and benefit individually from larger economies of scale. A radically *different balance between small scale and large scale production* is developing. This global development *has exerted* an effective check on inflation, and pushed for a more effective labour market organization that has moved individual wages closer to their marginal productivities. The other side of this coin might have been a widening distribution of incomes. To understand what has happened to the global economy is simply impossible if the analysis is not taken down to the dynamics of micro market behaviour.

The complexity of the situation makes the capturing of the new business opportunities genuinely experimental and dependent on entrepreneurial capacities that are not universally available among the industrial economies. While some developing economies are successfully adopting the new technologies, entering onto rapid growth paths, other mature industrial economies experience great difficulties of reorganizing for the same task, and suffer more from the new competition than they benefit from the new opportunities. For those that succeed, however, engineering will continue to serve over the foreseeable future as the backbone of the rich industrial economies.

Acknowledgment I want to thank an anonymous referee for several very appropriate comments that have made my paper very much more to the point.

Appendix: Some Background on the Complex Dynamics of an Experimentally Organized Economy

This empirical paper has told the story of (1) faster endogenous industrial decentralization ("globalization") facilitated by the *entrepreneurial introduction* (commercialization) of new generic technologies, and the (2) endogenous development of markets for specialized subcontractors that raise flexibility of production through (3) decentralized, individual and often inconsistent ("experimental") decisions in markets. What is going on is not principally new, but faster than before. In this Appendix I therefore discuss the principal relationships between entrepreneurial action at the micro level, and macroeconomic growth in terms of the Swedish micro to macro model, approximating an experimentally organized economy (Eliasson 1991). There is already sufficient evidence from simulation experiments on that model to demonstrate how the three circumstances together can raise long term macro economic growth on an order of magnitude that may warrant the term a new industrial revolution. I have therefore also presented an exercise in quantitative evolutionary economics, or Schumpeterian dynamics governed by the entrepreneurial actions and reactions of large numbers of individuals and businesses with widely different views of what is going on that frequently lead to business failure, but also are needed to capture business opportunities that would otherwise go unexplored. In that sense business mistakes become a necessary standard (transactions) cost for economic development (Eliasson and Eliasson 2005) and policy makers had better learn how to cope with the consequent social change for society to enjoy the benefits of growth. On this I like to talk about a Smith—Schumpeter—Wicksell (SSW) connection (Eliasson 1992, 2009).

The origin of the limits of economic systems understanding and decision failure at all levels, including the policy level, has its roots in complexity, and complexity theory has become a growing field of economic analysis in the Schumpeterian tradition (Frenken 2006; Hanusch and Pyka 2007). Failure, however, at the micro market level in an experimentally organized economy is the mirror image of viable entrepreneurship. An increase in successful entrepreneurial inputs in an economy unavoidably is accompanied by an increase in the business failure rate and should be positively regarded (Eliasson 1992, 2009; Eliasson and Taymaz 2000). So the upshot of my analysis is that understanding and explaining economic growth requires that the analysis be taken down to the micro market level where entrepreneurial dynamics that moves economic growth takes place (Eliasson 2003). The complexity of modelling, however, now escalates out of all bounds.

Beginning from that end it is, however, no longer acceptable to do what is commonly done, namely to reduce theoretical complexity by prior simplifying assumption to come up with models that embody clear single valued conclusions, notably on policy. Such simplification always takes the form of reducing the state space of the mathematical model that controls ones analysis to full transparency. Linearization of the model is one example. The analysis of this paper of an Experimentally Organized Economy (EOE) takes the exact opposite position, namely to *allow a maximum of facts to be brought to bear on a problem by the minimum use of prior assumptions*. This is desired micro to macro complexity theorizing, and I will conclude this brief Appendix by explaining how.

Hume and Locke had loosely discussed the world in terms of *memory*, *logic* and *imagination*. Leibnitz, however, objected. He did not accept any imagination beyond all possible logical combinations of the facts that resided in the memory. Hence, everything according to Leibnitz could be explained through logical manipulation of facts in a defined memory. Kant, however, opened the door again for vision, or "imagination" to enter as a separate dimension of human awareness

(Eliasson 1996a:16f). I have followed Kant and (1) let the unpredictable entrepreneur into exact economic modelling through the imagination slot, and (2) added the possibility that the new technology created by the imagery of entrepreneurs can be learned and thereby expand the opportunities space that corresponds to Leibnitz memory in an economic model, and finally (3) link the entrepreneurial input to economic growth through total factor productivity increase (Eliasson 1992, 1996a:77–87, 114).

On model form an experimentally organized economy is best represented by a class of highly non linear micro (firm) based macro models that feature frequent phases of deterministic chaos, such that the structure of the model cannot be learned from analysing the process outcomes (Eliasson 1991:179; Ballot and Taymaz 1998). For that reason they correspond to the ultimate notion of complexity.

It was long believed that evolutionary processes were deterministic, well understood and predictable, or stochastic and not fully understood, but predictable in expectation (Puu 1989). The discovery of deterministic chaos (Schuster and Just 2005), and that fairly simple non linear deterministic models generated sequences of chaotic and unpredictable events (Day 1982, 1983; Ysander 1981) eliminated the foundation for such beliefs. The problem of determinism is that if we do not know the initial conditions infinitely exactly we cannot determine the orbit. The exactitude by which we can determine (measure) initial conditions therefore determines the nature of predictability, chaos[23] or complexity. A key concept in the analysis of an experimentally organized economy, and of complexity or chaos, therefore is what we assume about the opportunities space, or the space which includes not only all possible logical manipulations of the facts stored in the Leibnitz memory, but also Kant's imagined combinations, or in our terms, the entrepreneurial experimental outcomes.[24] The mathematical term is state space. One side of complexity economics therefore is the limits of measurement, or the exactness with which one can determine the initial conditions of a sequence of events. *Measurement therefore has to be made a key element of theoretical economics.* Limits of economic measurement also prevent us from understanding the dynamics of evolutionary development with sufficient precision to "police" the economy in directions we might want it to take. Seemingly insignificant disturbances today ("the fluttering of the wings of a butterfly in northern Sweden") may with time take the entire European economy in completely unexpected directions.

The increased rate of unpredictable organizational change in the production system of a modern industrial economy invalidates the standard I/O model as a tool of analysis in industrial economics. As the principal theoretical base for my reasoning about the micro foundation of macro economic change I have therefore used my own micro (firm) based macro model which approximates a theory of the EOE (Eliasson 1977, 1991; Eliasson et al. 2004, 2005; Ballot and Taymaz 1998). The endogeneity of growth in that model is defined by the Schumpeterian creative

[23] Note the relationship between deterministic chaos and stochastic events in Carleson (1991).

[24] They have been entered into the model through genetic algorithms (Ballot and Taymaz 1998).

Table 2 The four mechanisms of Schumpeterian creative destruction and economic growth

1. Innovative entry enforces (through competition)
2. Reorganization
3. Rationalization
4. Exit (shut down)

Source: "Företagens, institutionernas och marknadernas roll i Sverige", Appendix 6 in Lindbeck A (ed) Nya villkor för ekonomi och politik (SOU 1993:16) and Eliasson (1996a: 45)

destruction process shown on "stylized form" in Table 2,in turn kept moving by endogenous competitive entry (Item 1), or the entrepreneurial "imagination" of an experimentally organized economy.

Key to understanding how entrepreneurship can be defined as imaginary inputs is the size (or transparency) of the memory, or the opportunities space of the model. Optimization requires that state space to be small and/or transparent, or be strictly convex with continuous derivaties. The intangible entrepreneur, to exist, requires a non linear model with an immense opportunities space. The large opportunities space furthermore has to stay large and largely unexplored for ever. This defines the origin of the complexity of the model of the experimentally organized economy. Such a model allows for business mistakes, that are by definition excluded from all variations of the I/O model, barring stochastic, insurable business mistakes, a reduced form Frank Knight (1921) called ridiculous (Eliasson 1992:256). The capacity of an experimentally organized economy to keep the full information situation for ever unattainable through economic systems learning I have called the *Särimner effect* in honour of the pig of the Viking sagas that was eaten for supper, only to come back alive next evening to be eaten again. The difference is that the state space of the experimentally organized economy (contrary to the pig) grows from being explored and learned, therefore defining a positive sum game (Eliasson 2005a:42). Antonov and Trofimov (1993) demonstrate on the same model that free experimentation with different, often inconsistent decision models, and flexible structural accommodation of business failure outcompete centrally directed policies, because such policies are always restrictive and tend to eliminate some entrepreneurial winners, which may make a large difference in the long run in non linear models. Eliasson and Taymaz (2000) and Eliasson et al. (2004) furthermore demonstrate that the magnitudes involved at the macro level may take on "revolutionary" dimensions.

References

Ackoff RL (1967) Management misinformation systems. Manag Sci 14(4):B14

Antonov M, Trofimov G (1993) Learning through short-run macroeconomic forecasts in a micro-to-macro model. J Econ Behav Organ 21(2):37

Ballot G, Taymaz E (1998) Human capital, technological lock-in and evolutionary dynamics. In: Eliasson G, Green C (eds) The microeconomic foundations of economic growth. The University of Michigan Press, Ann Arbor

Benkard CL (1999) Learning and forgetting: the dynamics of aircraft production. National Bureau of Economic Research, Working Paper No. 7127. NBER, Cambridge, MA

Berndt E, Malone T (1995) Information, technology and the productivity paradox; getting the questions right. Econ Innov New Technol 3:177–182

Branstetter L (1996) Are knowledge spillovers international or intranational in scope? Microeconometric evidence from the USA and Japan. NBER WP 5800 (October). NBER, Cambridge MA

Brynjolfsen E (1993) The productivity paradox of information technology. Commun ACM 36 (12):67–77, BW; Business Week

Carlsson BO (1986) The development and use of machine tools in historical perspective. In: Day RH, Eliasson G (eds) The dynamics of market economies. North Holland, New York, pp 247–270

Carleson L (1991) Stochastic behavior of deterministic systems. J Econ Behav Organ 16 (1–2):85–92

Carlsson B (ed) (1989) Industrial dynamics, technological, organizational, and structural changes in industries and firms. Kluwer, Boston

Carlsson B (1994) Small business, flexible technology, and industrial structure. F. de Vries lecture, Erasmus University, Rotterdam

Chun H, Jung-Wook K, Jason L, Randall M (2004) Patterns of Comovement: the role of information technology in the US economy, NBER Working Paper No. 10937 (Nov). NBER, Cambridge MA

Cohen WM, Levinthal DA (1990) Absorptive capacity: a new perspective on learning and innovation. Adm Sci Q 35:128–152

Crosby AW (1997) The measure of reality—quantification and western society 1250–1600. Cambridge University Press, Cambridge, DN; Dagens Nyheter

Day RH (1982) Irregular growth cycles. Am Econ Rev 72(3):406–414

Day RH (1983) The emergence of chaos from classical economic growth. Q J Econ 98:201–213

Eliasson G (1976) Business economic planning, theory, practice and comparison. Wiley, London

Eliasson G (1977) Competition and market processes in a simulation model of the Swedish economy. Am Econ Rev 67(1):277–281

Eliasson G (1980) Elektronik, teknisk förändring och ekonomisk utveckling (Electronics, technical change and economic development). In: Datateknik, ekonomisk tillväxt och sysselsättning. Rapport från Data- och Elektronikkommitten (DEK). DEK, Stockholm

Eliasson G (1981) Electronics, economic growth and employment - revolution or evolution? In: Giersch H (ed) Emerging technologies: consequences for economic growth, structural change, and employment. Institut für Weltwirtschaft an der Universität Kiel, Kiel

Eliasson G (1986) Kunskap, information och tjänster – en studie av svenska industriföretag (knowledge, information and service production – a study of Swedish manufacturing firms). IUI, Stockholm

Eliasson G (1987) Technological competition and trade in the experimentally organized economy. Research Report No. 32. IUI, Stockholm

Eliasson G (1990a) The firm as a competent team. J Econ Behav Organ 13(3):275–298

Eliasson G (1990b) The knowledge-based information economy. In: Eliasson G, Fölster S et al (eds) The knowledge based information economy. IUI, Stockholm, Chapter I

Eliasson G (1991) Modeling the experimentally organized economy. J Econ Behav Organ 16 (1–2):153–182

Eliasson G (1992) Business competence, organizational learning, and economic growth: establishing the Smith-Schumpeter-Wicksell (SSW) connection. In: Scherer FM, Perlman M (eds) Entrepreneurship, technological innovation, and economic growth. Studies in the Schumpeterian tradition. The University of Michigan Press, Ann Arbor

Eliasson G (1996a) Firm objectives, controls and organization – the use of information and the transfer of knowledge within the firm. Kluwer Academic, Boston

Eliasson G (1996b) Spillovers, integrated production and the theory of the firm. J Evol Econ 6:125–140
Eliasson G (1998) Information efficiency, production organization and systems productivity quantifying the systems effects of EDI investments. In: Macdonald S, Madden G (eds) Telecommunications and social economic development. North Holland, Amsterdam, pp 205–217
Eliasson G (2000) Industrial policy, competence blocs and the role of science in the economic development. J Evol Econ 10:217–241
Eliasson G (2002) Den Nya och Omedelbara Ekonomin – ett Internet perspektiv (The new and immediate economy – an internet perspective). Vinnova & Teldok (Telematic), Stockholm
Eliasson G (2003) Global economic integration and regional attractors of competence. Ind Innov 10:75–102
Eliasson G (2005a) Competence blocs in the experimentally organized economy. In: Eliasson G et al. (eds) The birth, the life and the death of firms-the role of entrepreneurship, creative destruction and conservative institutions in a growing and experimentally organized economy. The Ratio Institute, Stockholm
Eliasson G (2005b) The nature of economic change and management in a new knowledge based information economy. Inform Econ Policy 17:428–456
Eliasson G (2005c) Insourcing of production from foreign subsidiaries or subcontractors- an empirical study of Swedish firms. Paper prepared for Invest in Sweden Agency (ISA) Stockholm. http://www.isa.se/kostnadellerkompetens
Eliasson G (2006a) From employment to entrepreneurship. J Ind Relat 48(5):633–656
Eliasson G (2006b) Policies for a new entrepreneurial economy. Paper presented to the international J.A. Schumpeter Society 11th ISS conference, Nice-Sophia Antipolis, 21–24 June 2006. Later published in Cantner U, and Gaffard JL, Nesta L (eds) (2009) Schumpeterian perspectives on innovation, competition and growth. Springer, Berlin, Heidelberg
Eliasson G (2007) Divergence among mature and rich industrial economies – the case of Sweden entering a new and immediate economy. In: Hämäläinen T, Risto H (eds) Social innovations, institutional change and economic performance. Edward Elgar, Cheletenham, Chapter 8
Eliasson G (2009) Knowledge directed economic selection and growth. Prometheus 27 (4):371–384
Eliasson G (2010) Advanced public procurement as industrial policy – aircraft industry as a technical university. Springer, New York
Eliasson G (2011a) Comparing the industrial dynamics of automotive industries in the stockhlm and Southern German regional economies
Eliasson G (2011b) From gunpowder, Cannons and Missiles to Civilian Industry, Mimeo KTH
Eliasson G, Eliasson C (1996) The computer and communications industry – a chronicle of events that mark the experimental evolution of a new information industry. In: Eliasson G (ed) Supplement appended to Eliasson (1996a) as an electronic Word Perfect 5.1 diskette
Eliasson G, Eliasson Å (2005) The theory of the firm and the markets for strategic acquisitions. In: Cantner U, Dinopoulos E, Lanzilotti RF (eds) Entrepreneurship. The new economy and public policy. Springer, Berlin
Eliasson G, Taymaz E (2000) Institutions, entrepreneurship, economic flexibility and growth – experiments on an evolutionary model. KTH, INDEK, TRITA-IEO-R 1999:13; In: Cantner–Hanush–Klepper, 1999, Economic evolution, learning and complexity – econometric, experimental and simulation approaches
Eliasson G, Johansson D, Taymaz E (2004) Simulating the new economy. Struct Chang Econ Dyn 15(2004):289–314
Eliasson G, Johansson D, Taymaz E (2005) Firm turnover and the rate of growth – simulating the macroeconomic effects of Schumpeterian creative destruction (Chapter VI). In: Eliasson G et al. (ed) The birth, the life and the death of firms-the role of entrepreneurship, creative destruction and conservative institutions in a growing and experimentally organized economy. The Ratio Institute, Stockholm

Frenken K (2006) Technological innovation and complexity theory. Econ Innov New Technol 15 (137):137–155, FT; The Financial Times
Fries H (1984) Datateknik och koncernstyrning. In: Eliasson G et al. (eds) Hur styrs storföretag? - en studie av informationshantering och organisation (how are large business groups managed? - A study of information handling and organization). IUI, Stockholm
Greenstein SM, Pablo TS (1996) Estimating the welfare effects of digital infrastructure, NBER Working Paper No. 5770 (Sep). NBER, Cambridge, MA
Hämäläinen T, Heiskala R (eds) (2007) Social innovations, institutional change and economic performance. Edward Elgar & Sitra, Finland
Hanusch H, Pyka A (2007) Principles of neo-Schumpeterian economics. Camb J Econ 31:275–289
Jones CI, Williams JC (1998) Measuring the social returns to R&D. Q J Econ 113(4):1119–1135
Jones C, Williams JC (1999) Too much of a good thing? The economics of investment in R&D, NBER Working Paper No. 7283. NBER, Cambridge, MA
Jorgenson DW, Griliches Z (1967) The explanation of productivity change. Rev Econ Stud XXXIV(3):249–282
Jorgenson D, Wessner C (eds) (2006) Measuring and sustaining the new economy: software, growth, and the future of the U.S economy. The National Academic Press, Washington, DC
Jorgenson D, Wessner C (2007) Measuring and sustaining the new economy: enhancing productivity growth in the information age. The National Academic Press, Washington, DC
Keller W (2001) International technology diffusion, NBER Working Paper No 8573 (Oct). NBER, Cambridge, MA. Published 2004 in J Econ Liter 42:752–782
Klenow PJ, Rodriguez- Clare A (2004) Externalities and growth, NBER Working Paper No. 11009. NBER, Cambridge, MA
Knight F (1921) Risk, uncertainty and profit. Houghton-Mifflin, Boston
Lichtenberg FR (1993) The output contributions of computer equipment and personnel: a firm level analysis, NBER Working Paper No. 4540 (Nov). NBER, Cambridge, MA
Macdonald S, Madden G (eds) (1998) Telecommunications and social economic development. North Holland, Amsterdam, pp 205–217
Marshall A (1890) Principles of economics. Macmillan & Company, London
Marshall A (1919) Industry and trade. Macmillan& Company, London
McKnight LW, Bailey JP (eds) (1997) Internet economics. The MIT Press, England
McKnight LW, Richard S, Joseph R, David C, Clark J, Branko G, David G (1997) In: McKnight LW, Joseph PB (eds) Internet economics. The MIT Press, Cambridge, MA
Mun SB, Nadiri MI (2002) Information technology externalities: empirical evidence from 42 U.S industries, NBER Working Paper No. 9272 (Oct). NBER, Cambridge, MA
Nadiri I (1978) A dynamic model of research and development expenditure. In: Carlsson B, Eliasson G, Nadiri I (eds) The importance of technology and the permanence of structure in industrial growth, IUI Conference Reports, 1978:2, Stockholm
Nadiri I (1993) Innovations and technological spillovers, Working Paper No. 4423. NBER, Cambridge, MA
Nilsson S (1981) Förändrad tillverkningsorganisation och dess återverkningar på kapitalbindningen – en studie vid ASEA, SOU 1981:10, Stockholm
Nordhaus WO (2004) Schumpeterian profits in the American economy: theory and measurement. NBER Working Paper No. 10433, Cambridge, MA
Okamuro H, van Stel A, Ingrid V (2011) Explaining differences in entrepreneurial activity between a managed and an entrepreneurial economy: political lessons from Japan and the Netherlands, International council for small business 2011 conference in Stockholm. http://icsb2011.org/
Parente SL, Prescott EC (2004) A unified theory of the evolution of income levels. In: Aghion P, Durlauf S (eds) Handbook of economic growth. North Holland, Amsterdam, Chapter 31
Patel P, Pavitt K (1994) The continuing, widespread (and neglected) importance of improvements in mechanical technologies. Res Policy 23:535–545
Pavitt K (1979) Technical innovation and industry development. Futures (Dec)

Pavitt K, Soete L (1981) International differences in economic growth and the international location of innovation. Mimeo, Science Policy Research Unit, University of Sussex, England
Pratten C (1976) A comparison of the performance of Swedish and UK companies. Cambridge University Press, Cambridge
Pritchnett L (1997) Divergence big time. J Econ Perspect 11:3–17
Puu T (1989) Nonlinear economic dynamics. Springer, Berlin
Röller LH, Waverman L (2001) Telecommunications infrastructure and economic development: a simultaneous approach. Am Econ Rev 91(4):909–923
Romer PM (1986) Increasing returns and long-run growth. J Polit Econ 94(5):1002–1037
Schmalensee R, Willig R (eds) (1989) Handbook of industrial organization, vols. I and II. North-Holland, Amsterdam
Schuster HG, Just W (2005) Deterministic chaos – an introduction, 4th edn. Wiley-VCH, Weinham
Smith A (1776) An inquiry into the nature and causes of the wealthy of nations. Modern Library, New York, 1937
Solow RL (1987) We'd better watch out. *New York Times Book Review*:36 *Sv.D. Svenska Dagbladet*
Turing AM (1936) On computable numbers, with an application to the Entscheidungs problem. Proc London Math Soc Ser 2 42(3):230–265
Vogel EF (1979) Japan as No.1- lessons for America. Harvard University Press, Cambridge, MA
Wallis J, North D (1986) Measuring the transactions sector in the American economy. In: Engerman SL, Gallman RE (eds) Long term factors in American economic growth. The Chicago University Press, Chicago
Westerman J (1768) Om Svenska Näringarnes Undervigt emot de Utländske, förmedelst en trögare Arbets-drift (On the inferiority of the Swedish compared to foreign manufacturers because of a slower work organization), Stockholm
Woodbury RS (1972) Studies in the history of machine tools. The MIT Press, Cambridge, MA
Ysander BC (1981) Taxes and market stability. In: Eliasson G, Södersten J (eds) Business taxation, finance and firm behavior, IUI conference reports 1981:1. IUI, Stockholm

Looking Around: The Smart Way of Italian SMEs to Innovate

Piergiuseppe Morone, Carmelo Petraglia, and Giuseppina Testa

Abstract In this paper we assess the relevance of both knowledge creation and diffusion processes in affecting Italian SMEs' propensity to innovate. In doing so a knowledge production function (KPF) is estimated for a representative sample of small and medium manufacturing firms over the period 1998–2003. To account for endogeneity of R&D effort in the KPF, we estimate a Heckman selection model on R&D decisions. The KPF is estimated for three different samples of firms using a standard probit where the probability that SMEs will innovate depends upon intramural R&D effort, regional and industrial spillovers and a vector of interaction and control variables. The main results obtained are the following: first, being located in the South, although does not affect the firm's choice of starting R&D projects, affects negatively the amount of R&D investments. Second, the probability to innovate is positively related to sectoral spillovers and the magnitude of such impact is decreasing in firms' size. Third, knowledge diffusion via geographical proximity enhances the probability of the recipient firm to innovate only if it has an appropriate endowment of human capital.

P. Morone (✉)
Sapienza – University of Rome, DiGEF – Department of Law, Philosophy and Economic Studies, P.le A. Moro 5, 00185 Rome, Italy
e-mail: piergiuseppe.morone@uniroma1.it

C. Petraglia
Facoltà di Economia, Università degli Studi della Basilicata, Viale dell'Ateneo Lucano, 85100 Potenza, Italy
e-mail: carmelo.petraglia@gmail.com

G. Testa
School of Economics, Mathematics and Statistics, Birkbeck, University of London, Malet Street, London WC1E 7HX, UK
e-mail: gtesta@econ.bbk.ac.uk

A. Pyka and E.S. Andersen (eds.), *Long Term Economic Development*, Economic Complexity and Evolution, DOI 10.1007/978-3-642-35125-9_12,

1 Introduction

Most high-income countries across the world have been experiencing a slow growth rate over the last decades and lost ground to cheap-labour economies (see among others: Atkinson and Andes 2009). Indeed, the financial crisis started in the U.S. in 2007 further hampered the already poor performance of the U.S. and most European countries and calls for new efforts to regain competitiveness and boost economic growth.

In this paper we do not aim to provide an exhaustive analysis of the on-going vast debate on high-income countries' competitiveness (or the lack of it). However, bearing in mind that in high-income knowledge-based economies innovation is a crucial asset for long-term competitiveness, we aim at contributing to the debate by providing some new insights into the determinants of firms' innovating behaviour. We shall do so by placing our attention on both internal and external (to the firm) sources of knowledge creation and diffusion as crucial inputs of innovation. Specifically, we shall investigate two external sources that potentially shape innovating patterns: knowledge diffusion across firms operating in the same sector (via industrial proximity) and/or across firms located in the same region (via geographical proximity). When looking at internal sources, we will focus on R&D activities conducted within the firm as well as on the human capital endowment of the firm—which are key factors for absorbing knowledge generated outside of the firm.

Our empirical investigation will focus on Italian small and medium enterprises (SMEs). This is a non-trivial choice since SMEs are those that typically face more difficulties in investing in R&D and hence rely more heavily upon external sources of knowledge. Moreover, Italian SMEs specialisation lays largely in the production of low-capital and low-skill intensive goods (i.e. traditional sectors), a fact which puts the country in direct competition with fast-growing economies (like China and India).

The remainder of the paper is organised as follows: Sect. 2 provides a background to this study presenting key references in the literature and introducing the case study; Sect. 3 sets out the research questions and presents the empirical model; Sect. 4 introduces the dataset and Sect. 5 presents empirical results; finally, Sect. 6 concludes.

2 Background and Literature Review

As mentioned in the introduction, it is becoming increasingly relevant for firms located in wealthier countries to base their competitive advantage on the knowledge contents of their products in order to overcome the competitive pressure of emerging countries which, on the other hand, can rely on much cheaper labour cost (see, for instance, Pinch et al. 2003). Such a *knowledge-based* model of production requires a firm to be highly committed to innovation activities linked to well-behaving processes of both knowledge creation and diffusion. In fact, intramural research activities as well as knowledge spillovers are both important factors that can potentially affect firms' innovative propensity (for seminal contributions, see Griliches 1992, and Jaffe 1986).[1] In particular, in assessing the impact of knowledge spillovers on the firm's likelihood to innovate, we maintain that knowledge accumulated by other firms can be exploited by means of spillovers within two different—and sometimes overlapping—"spaces" bordered by either geographical or industrial proximity. However, we should be very cautious when formulating our expectations on R&D spillovers since many factors might affect firms' capacity to benefit from knowledge created outside of the firm. This problem will be further developed in the following section where we first review the concept of proximity as it emerged in the literature and then address the issue of R&D spillovers absorption.

2.1 *Proximity and R&D Spillovers*

Many studies (e.g. Jaffe 1986; Acs et al. 1994; Levin and Reiss 1988; Bernstein, 1988; Ornaghi 2006) documented the importance of industrial proximity when measuring R&D spillovers. Such studies suggest that as firms become closer in an industrial space—that is their production processes become increasingly similar—then there is a greater potential for interaction, regardless of their geographical localisation. Scholars such as Griliches (1979) have distinguished between two main types of sectoral R&D spillover: horizontal (i.e. learning from product-market rivals) and vertical (i.e. learning from suppliers or retailers). Indeed, firms that produce similar products can often benefit from each other's R&D activities. For example, when a pharmaceutical firm introduces a new drug, in the absence of patent protection, rival companies can easily determine its mark-up and offer close substitutes. At the same time, firms that are related through a vertical chain might experience technological synergies.

However, restricting knowledge externalities to industrial spaces ignores an important source of knowledge diffusion—i.e. inter-industry knowledge spillovers occurring among firms which are geographically proximate (Audretsch and Feldman 2004). Jacobs (1969), for instance, suggests that the exchange of complementary knowledge across a variety of industries within geographical spaces can yield a greater return on a new economic knowledge, promoting knowledge

[1] When talking about knowledge spillovers we refer to disembodied spillovers as defined by Griliches "[...] ideas borrowed by research teams of industry *i* from the research results of industry *j*. It is not clear that this kind of borrowing is particularly related to input purchase flows" (Griliches 1992: S36).

externalities and ultimately innovative activity and economic growth.[2] She argues that the most important source of knowledge spillovers is external to the industry in which the firm operates.

Along this line of reasoning a large body of the literature (Powell et al. 1996; Florida and Cohen 1999; Feldman and Francis 2002) has investigated how R&D spillovers in geographically-concentrated industries stimulate innovative activities. Glaeser et al. (1992) provide a very comprehensive overview of different models of externalities, and suggest that local competition and non-regional specialisation enhance innovative activities. Rather than local concentration, they argue, "local competition accelerates imitation and improvement of the innovator's ideas. Although such competition reduces the returns to the innovator, it also increases pressure to innovate: firms that do not advance technologically are bankrupted by their innovating competitors" (Glaeser et al. 1992: 1131). Similarly, Porter (1990) provides some examples of Italian ceramics and gold jewellery industries, in which hundreds of firms are located in close geographical proximity and fiercely compete to innovate. This view contrasts with that of Marshall (1920), which argues that firms undertake investments in R&D if they have a monopoly power on their ideas—that is they are able to internalise externalities generated by their R&D activity. Thus, a clear area of dispute surrounding geographical R&D spillovers has been the distinction between innovation from 'local competition' and from 'local concentration'. In its simplest form, it implies a distinction between cooperative practices—that is, firms cooperate to get hold of R&D undertaken by other firms—as opposed to confrontation practices—that is, firms confront each other and through this innovate.

In innovation-related research, however, a variety of reasons have been provided to explain why firms gather in close geographical proximity. The most important of these is, arguably, that, within clusters, individuals may move from firm to firm and owners as well as workers may both benefit from the fact that 'the secrets of industry are in the air' (Marshall 1920). Indeed, with clusters, a better match between what an individual seeks and what an employer looks for, is created. Under this view, there are numerous empirical works that discuss the importance of skilled labour force for knowledge transfer in clusters. Studies by Cohen and Levinthal (1989) represent, indeed, an important contribution to the innovation literature. They suggest that the absorptive process of externally-generated knowledge depends upon firm own R&D effort, and on the degree to which the outside knowledge targets its own needs and concerns. This implies that the lack of property rights over ideas does not cause innovators to slow down their investment in R&D—as Marshall argued—since firms can exploit externally-generated R&D only if they invest in R&D. Stretching this argument we shall focus our attention

[2] Within innovation literature, 'innovation' is very much related to 'knowledge'—that is, the cognitive capabilities to elaborate and develop new ideas. Among the different conceptualisations of innovation, Fisher (2006) conceives innovation as "the application of novel pieces of knowledge or a novel combination of existing pieces of knowledge" (1998:1).

also on firms' human capital endowment which, in our view, is a good proxy of firms' knowledge base and, along with intramural R&D investments, provides a valuable measure of their ability to absorb knowledge created outside of the firm.

2.2 *Empirical Studies and the Italian Case*

It can be argued that Italian economic system, largely based on small and medium-sized enterprises (SMEs) might represent an obstacle to innovating activities. Indeed, since the seminal contribution by Schumpeter (1942), the link between firm size and innovation has been at the heart of the economic debate. And a positive correlation between firm size and commitment to formal R&D activities is a common finding in empirical works.

In point of fact, Italian business R&D expenditure is weak compared to other advanced economies, where large companies play a stronger role. However, regardless of the reluctance of Italian firms to commit themselves to R&D, "the country's performance tops the EU average for the sales of new-to-market products and comes close to the average for new-to-firm-products. The satisfactory performance for sales from new-to-market innovation could reflect innovative processes specific to firms, difficult to classify and register in official statistics. This is the case of design innovation, one of the strengths characterising some of the most successful 'made in Italy' products (e.g. high fashion, luxury goods)" (Technopolis Group 2006: 4).

As the empirical literature on the Italian case shows, SMEs can contribute significantly to innovative output (see amongst others Piergiovanni et al. 1997; Morone and Testa 2008). One commonly agreed-on explanation for such evidence is that SMEs can potentially benefit from knowledge spilled-over by other firms or institutions. Medda and Piga (2004), for example, explore whether R&D spillovers contribute to the growth of Italian manufacturing firms' labour productivity. In their study, they consider the extent to which R&D spillovers take place within 'intra-industry', and 'inter-industry' space. Empirically, useing Romer's methodology (1986) to measure intra-industry R&D spillovers, they follow Terleckyj's (1974) methodological approach to measure inter-industry R&D spillovers. Aiello and Cardamone's (2008) study differs from Medda and Piga's study in the way in which R&D spillovers and technological proximity are constructed. Rather than using a symmetric uncentered correlation metric, they suggest an asymmetric uncentered correlation metric to account for the different degree of intensity of the bi-directional knowledge flows. Antonelli's (1994) analysis sheds light on the relationship between internal R&D expenditures and regional R&D spillovers on the productivity growth of each firm. In his study, regional R&D spillovers are measured simply by R&D expenditures incurred by other firms within a region. His investigation reveals the importance of firm own R&D capability to internalise R&D spillovers.

As it emerges, while a vast literature relates R&D spillovers to firm's productivity growth, there is a void in the literature, with regard to the Italian case, on the relationship between R&D spillovers and firm's innovative activities. The present study seeks to fill-in this gap, by studying the relationship between intramural R&D, human capital endowment, R&D spillovers (both sectoral and regional), and innovative activities performed by Italian SMEs.

3 Research Hypothesis and Empirical Approach

As discussed in Sects. 1 and 2 above, our main research interest is to assess the impact of both internal and external knowledge inputs on SMEs' innovation activities, by estimating a KPF augmented with R&D spillovers. When considering external sources of innovation we shall focus our attention both on regional and sectoral spillovers. Specifically, we shall look at regional and sectoral R&D spillovers. This leads to the formulation of our first two research hypotheses.

H1: Knowledge created inside of the firm (through R&D investments) exerts a positive impact on firm's propensity to innovate.

H2: Knowledge created outside of the firm can exert a positive impact on firm's propensity to innovate through spillovers. However, such spillovers occur if firms are proximate either at geographical level or at industrial level. Hence, we can specify our hypothesis as follows:

H2a—Sectoral R&D spillovers (occurring among firms proximate at industrial level) exert a positive impact on a firm' propensity to innovate.

H2b—Regional R&D spillovers (occurring among firms proximate at geographical level) exert a positive impact on a firm' propensity to innovate.

As discussed above, knowledge created outside of the firm can be better absorbed if the firm possess an adequate knowledge endowment. This leads to our third research hypothesis:

H3: Firms possessing an adequate knowledge endowment can best benefit of external knowledge inputs.

As mentioned above, we shall address these three research hypotheses estimating an augmented KPF. In what follows we shall discuss in some details the adopted empirical strategy.

Following Crépon et al. (1998), Griffith et al. (2006) and Morone et al. (2007), we observe that the estimation of any knowledge production function is possibly subject to endogeneity. This occurs for two main reasons: first, intramural R&D expenditure may be correlated with unobservable factors because firms that expect to be able to innovate are those that might be more likely to be engaged in R&D. Second, since firms can in principle undertake some R&D activities without reporting R&D investment, internal R&D effort may be measured with error.

In order to tackle endogeneity, we first run a Heckman selection model on R&D decisions, which allows us to obtain internal R&D investment conditioned on the decision to undertake R&D activities. In doing so, we account for endogeneity and obtain our measure of the internal knowledge input to be included in the KPF.

As for possible external (to the firm) sources of knowledge, we assumed in our second research hypothesis that knowledge diffusion across firms might occur via either geographical or industrial proximity. That is to say, a given firm can in principle exploit innovative inputs used by other firms by means of spillovers occurring within both the 'industrial space' populated by firms operating in its same sector and the 'geographical space' where it is located.[3] Accordingly, we measure R&D spillovers as follows:

$$W_{is} = \sum_{j \neq i} \hat{R}_{js} \tag{1}$$

where Wis is total knowledge available to firm i in space $s = [x, y]$ and is obtained by aggregating R&D predicted values delivered by the Heckman selection model for any other firm j in the same space.[4] Note that, as SMEs are likely to benefit from knowledge created by other firms regardless of their size, our measure of spillovers uses information on the R&D effort of our full sample of Italian manufacturing firms, including large firms. This is because we believe knowledge might spill over from any firm operating in the geographical/industrial space of reference for a given SME.

Once having obtained both internal and external sources of knowledge, we define the following KPF:

$$I_i = \hat{R}_i^{\alpha} W_{ix}^{\beta} W_{iy}^{\eta} C_i^{\gamma} K_i^{\lambda} (H_i W_{ixy})^{\phi} \tag{2}$$

where i indexes firms, x industries and y regions. I_i represents innovative activities (product innovation and/or process innovation) reported by firm i and $\hat{R}_i$ its internal R&D effort. W_{ix} measures aggregate industry-specific knowledge created by firms operating in the same sector x as firm i, while W_{iy} is aggregate geographical-specific knowledge created by other firms located in the same region y. K_i is the physical capital of firm i, C_i a vector of control variables which capture heterogeneity across firms and H_i a measure of the firm's human capital—which in our estimates will proxy the knowledge endowment of the firm. Using lower-case letters to denote natural logarithms, we shall write the KPF to be estimated as follows:

[3] We use the 14 sectors provided in our sample as a framework for calculating the sectoral spillover variable (these are: Food & beverage, Clothing, Footwear & leather, Wood & furniture, Paper, Fuel, Chemical products, Plastic products, Mineral products, Metal products, Mechanical products, Electrical equipment including optical instruments, Motor Vehicle and Other sectors). Regional spillovers are calculated using the 19 Italian Regions (Valle D'Aosta and Piemonte are counted as one).

[4] Equation (1) assumes a unitary absorption capacity across firms. Our results will show that the ability of a firm to capture available external knowledge increases with its internal endowment of human capital.

$$i_i = \hat{r'}_i\alpha + w'_{ix}\beta + w'_{iy}\eta + C'_i\gamma + k'_i\lambda + H_i w_{ixy}'\phi + \varepsilon_i \tag{3}$$

We will estimate Eq. (3) for our sample of small and medium enterprises (SMEs). As we are also interested in singling out the size relevancy for knowledge absorption and innovation, we shall replicate our estimates for a subsample of small firms (those with less than or equal to 100 employees) and a subsample of micro firms (those with less than or equal to 50 employees).

4 Data

The data were retrieved from the last two waves (eighth and ninth) of the Capitalia survey on Italian manufacturing firms with more than ten employees, covering the periods 1998–2000 and 2001–2003 respectively (Capitalia 2002, 2005).

Each wave of the survey covers approximately 5,000 manufacturing firms[5] selected using a sampling method stratified by geographical area, industry and firm size. The Survey collects firm-level information on turnover level, structural characteristics, labour force, inter-firms relationship, attitudes toward foreign markets, financial structure and the input and output measures of innovation. With regard to this latter aspect, the database provides information on the following: firm share of innovative (the share of sales due to new or improved products and new processes), firm R&D expenditure and whether or not the firm has introduced new products, processes and organisational changes and has been engaged in R&D activities.

In order to increase the time span of our analysis, we use a balanced panel of firms obtained by merging the eighth and ninth waves of the survey.[6] Given the large number of observations, and the wide coverage in terms of geographic area, industry and size, we are quite confident that the data employed in this paper are highly representative of the Italian manufacturing sector (Casaburi et al. 2007).

Table 1 reports descriptive statistics on firms' intramural R&D effort and innovative behaviour, grouping firms according to their size (i.e. number of employees). Note that in this table we included also large firms (i.e. those with more than 250 employees) since their investments in R&D are relevant to construct our measures of R&D spillovers. The share of firms reporting R&D activities increases substantially when moving from the smallest size to larger categories. This is in line with our expectations as it shows that small firms (i.e. those with less than 51 employees) are less keen on doing formal R&D. Interestingly, a larger share of firms with 51–100 employees perform R&D when compared with those in the following size category (i.e. 101–250). R&D expenditure increases exponentially

[5] The eighth wave of Capitalia contains information on 4,680 firms; the ninth wave of Capitalia gathered information on 4,289 firms.

[6] The adopted merging procedure and data cleaning is described in detail in the Annex.

Table 1 Intramural R&D and innovative behaviour in the sample

	Firms conducting intramural R&D, 1998–2000		R&D expenditure in 2000, thousand euros[a]		Innovative firms, 2001–2003[b]	
Firm size (employees)	Obs.	%	Mean	s.d.	Obs.	%
Between 10 and 50	241	29.18	73.458	94.001	428	51.38
Between 51 and 100	88	60.69	186.127	286.415	99	67.81
Between 101 and 250	55	57.89	378.137	458.781	69	71.13
More than 250	69	74.19	2,207.288	4,363.157	76	88.37

[a]R&D expenditure is total expenditure on research and development (R&D) activities reported by the firms deflated by the output price
[b]Firms were classified as innovative if answered affirmatively to the following question: "Have new product and/or process innovations been introduced over the period 2001–2003?"

with firms' size: it almost triples in moving from the first to the second category, nearly doubles in moving to the third category and increases nearly sixfold for large firms (i.e. more than 250 employees).

When we look at innovation behaviour we can observe again how it is constantly correlated with firms' size. However, we can note now that there is a smooth transition from the smallest size to larger categories. This finding confirms what was discussed in Sect. 2—i.e. that small firms display innovation behaviours which cannot be explained from looking solely at formal engagement in R&D. This reinforces our hypothesis that spillover effects might actually play a key role in shaping innovation behaviour of small firms.

Before presenting our empirical findings, a few words must be said on the innovation measure used in our investigation. As put by Kuznets (1962), the greatest obstacle to understanding the economic role of technological change is the scholars' inability to adequately measure innovation. Several measures have been proposed so far to overcome this obstacle in the innovation literature.[7] In our study we use a dummy variable based on the answer provided to the following question: "Have new product and/or process innovations been introduced over the period 2001–2003?". Such measure presents both advantages and disadvantages. The main advantage is that, in principle, it should capture any innovation

[7] Traditionally, there are two approaches to measuring innovation outputs: the 'object' approach and the 'subject' approach. Measures of the first approach range from patent counts and patent citations to new product announcements (recently, new data have been proposed; these are the Literature-based Innovation Output (LBIO) data which are compiled by screening specialist trade journals for new-product announcements—see van der Panne 2007). The second approach focuses on the innovating agent and includes small-scale incremental changes. The most important example of the 'object' approach is the SPRU database, developed by the Science Policy Research Unit at the University of Sussex. The CIS (*Community Innovation Survey*), developed by the European Commission together with Eurostat and DG-Enterprise is one of the most comprehensive 'subject' oriented database which attempts to collect internationally comparable direct measures of innovation. For a comprehensive discussion on various measures of innovations see Smith 2006.

introduced by any firm and, hence, should not be affected by differences which exist across sectors as well as across size classes (such as those observed in the propensity to patent). Nonetheless, our measure of innovation suffers from two shortcomings: first, it relies only on the perception of the firms' managers answering the questionnaire and second, it does not discriminate between innovations which are new to the firm or to the market.

Both of these problems refer to what Smith (2006) has labelled the "fundamental definitional issue" of what should be considered 'new': "[D]oes an innovation have to contain a basic new principle that has never been used in the world before, or does it only need to be new to a firm? Does an innovation have to incorporate a radically novel idea, or only an incremental change? In general, what kinds of novelty count as an innovation?" (2006: 149). We are aware that none of these issues are captured by our innovation measure. Bearing these caveats in mind, we shall now move on to present our empirical results.

5 Results

In this section we first describe the results of the Heckman sample selection model, reporting evidence on the factors affecting both the choice of being engaged in and the intensity of the effort devoted to R&D activities (i.e. R&D expenditure). Then, we focus on the estimation of the KPF, analysing the effects of internal and external knowledge sources on SMEs' propensity to innovate. In doing so, we shall attempt to address our three research hypotheses through a robust econometric analysis.

5.1 R&D Choice and Expenditure

Table 2 reports estimation results of the Heckman selection model for the R&D choice and amount equations. In the choice equation we observe whether a firm is engaged in R&D activities. In our specification the decision to engage in R&D activities refers to the period 1998–2000. The dependent variable (which takes a value of 1 if the firm chooses to undertake R&D activity and 0 otherwise) is determined by human capital endowment, size, location, export orientation, age and the technology degree of the firm.[8]

[8] Human capital endowment is measured as the share of employees with a higher education degree. As for the location of firms, we use a geographical dummy taking the value of 1 for firms located in the South of Italy and zero otherwise. The export orientation dummy is equal to 1 if the firm is involved in export activities and 0 otherwise. Age refers to the years of activity of the firm. The technology degree is measured through a dummy which takes the value of 1 if the firms operates in the high-tech sector (which correspond to the science-based sector in the Pavitt's taxonomy) and 0 otherwise.

Table 2 R&D choice and amount equations

	Heckman Selection Model			
	R&D engagement		R&D expenditure	
	Dummy referred to the period 1998–2000		Log of R&D expenditure in the year 2000	
Variables	Marg. Eff.	P > |z|	Coeff.	P > |z|
Human capital	1.017	0.004	3.516	0.085
Log of employment	0.142	0.000	0.541	0.053
South dummy	−0.038	0.462	−0.461	0.038
Export dummy	0.191	0.000		
Age	−0.003	0.018		
High-tech firms	0.292	0.000		
Constant	−1.960	0.000		
Mill's ratio	−0.916	0.000		
Sigma	1.324			
Rho(covariance)	−0.724			
LR test of indepen. equations	14.95	0.000		
Number of obs.	553			
Censored obs.	280			
Uncensored obs.	273			
Wald Chi2(3)	81.63	0.000		

First, we can observe that the higher is the endowment of human capital, the greater is the probability of doing R&D. Specifically, on average, a unitary increase in the share of employees with university degrees, increases the probability of being involved in R&D by the same amount. This result indicates that the differences in human capital endowment among firms do affect the firm's likelihood of undertaking R&D.

The coefficient attached to the log of employees (0.142) is statistically significant, implying that a unitary increase in the number of employees increases the probability of being involved in R&D by 0.14 %. In turn, this suggests that the probability of being engaged in R&D increases as the size of the firm increases. On the other hand, being located in the South of Italy—although the coefficient of the South dummy is negative—does not appear to affect the R&D choice.

In addition, we investigate whether the presence in foreign markets makes firms more likely to perform R&D activities compared to those operating exclusively in domestic markets. It emerges that exports have a strong and positive effect on the probability of being engaged in R&D; specifically, being an exporter increases, *ceteris paribus*, the probability of doing R&D by 19 % points. This result is consistent with the finding that exporting makes firms more easily aware of foreign innovators' activities, whose outcomes can be assimilated in order to improve their position both in domestic and foreign markets (Barrios et al. 2003: 476).[9] We also find that high-tech firms have a higher probability of being engaged in R&D and that the responsiveness of a firm's choice to conduct R&D increases for younger firms.

The amount equation predicts the expenditure of R&D effort (in year 2000) under the assumption that R&D expenditure is influenced by human capital, size and location. R&D expenditure is significantly and positively affected by human capital. The same holds for size: a higher level of R&D investment is associated with a larger firm size. Finally, being located in the South of Italy has a negative effect upon the amount of R&D investments.[10] This latter result seems to show that firms located in South, although not affected by their location in the choice of starting R&D projects, are forced to reduce the scale of such projects. Explanations for this outcome can be found in credit market imperfections affecting investment opportunities of Southern firms in general and, as a consequence, R&D projects. Indeed, financial pressures are higher, *ceteris paribus*, for Southern firms in terms of higher interest rates (ISAE 2003). Also, the consolidation process experienced by the Italian banking system during the 1990s followed a clear territorial pattern: the acquisition of local Southern banks by Northern large credit institutes. This has made credit rationing more binding in the South (Giannola 2002).

Finally, we note that the dependent variable is observed for 273 firms, while the remaining 280 firms in the sample do not report R&D. The p-value attached to the Rho estimate, which captures the correlation between the error terms of the R&D choice and amount equations, suggests the presence of a selection bias, which supports the methodology adopted.[11] This is also confirmed by the LR test of independent equations as reported in Table 2.

[9] As we could have a potential endogeneity of exports, we regressed R&D engagement in 2003 on exports reported in the period 1998–2000 and found that the direction of the link between export and R&D is robust (results available upon request).

[10] The South dummy captures the dualistic structure of the Italian economy—the so-called *Mezzogiorno* and the rest of the country—is probably unique among the countries of the European Union. The structural poverty of the *Mezzogiorno* economy producing a less-favourable environment (e.g. transport and communications, education, and public order) considerably reduces the technological possibilities of local firms. Indeed, given the uncertainty of the economic system, many Southern entrepreneurs may be reluctant to undertake investment programmes aimed at improving technology and at enhancing their operating scale. This applies in particular to R&D projects.

[11] We can notice the negative sign of the estimates of ρ. It indicates that there is a negative correlation between the error term of selection equation and that of the outcome equation. That is, those firms which are more likely to do R&D, invest less in R&D; whereas those firms that are less likely to do R&D, invest more in R&D.

5.2 *The Knowledge Production Function*

Tables 3, 4, and 5 show the estimation results of the augmented KPF for the three samples as discussed above in Sect. 3. Note that the dependent variable (innovative output) is observed in the period 2001–2003, while regressors are observed over the previous three years (1998–2000)—specifically, intramural R&D effort, R&D spillovers and human capital are observed in 2000, whereas physical capital refers to the whole period 1998–2000.

As for the full sample of SMEs (see Table 3), we can first observe that a unitary increase in the log of physical capital generates an increase of more than 3 % points in the probability of innovating (however, this result is only marginally significant at 10 % level), whereas the log of human capital is not significant.[12]

When looking at knowledge sources, we observe that the coefficient of the log of predicted R&D takes the expected sign and is statistically significant at the 1 % level: an increase of one unit in the log of R&D effort exerted in the year 2000 is associated with an increase of 23 % points in the probability of innovating in the period 2001–2003. This finding confirms our first research hypothesis (H1) suggesting that knowledge created inside the firm has a strong and positive impact on firm's propensity to innovate.

As we move to external sources of knowledge we can observe that an increase of one unit in sectoral R&D spillovers is associated with an increase of 14 % points in the probability of innovating. These results suggest that knowledge circulates quite effectively at the sectoral level and—in accordance with what we stated in our research hypothesis H2a—that sectoral R&D spillovers exert a positive effect on a firm' propensity to innovate.

On the other hand, we find evidence of a negative and significant effect of regional R&D spillovers on innovation.[13] Such evidence is at odds with our research hypothesis H2b, indicating that geographical proximity is harmful for effective knowledge transfers to take place across firms. We cautioned our readers about possible odd results when assessing the impact of R&D spillovers, being the literature quite unsettled on this point. Although many studies (see, among many others, Howells, 2002) claim that agents that are spatially concentrated benefit from knowledge externalities (because short distances favour information contact and facilitate the exchange of tacit knowledge), it has also been noted that the exchange of knowledge in the geographical space requires cognitive proximity as well as

[12] The wide innovation-related literature recognizes the importance of investments in machinery and equipment for innovation. Scholars such as Cohen and Klepper (1992, 1996) have argued that large firms rely upon human capital endowments, and physical capital investments to support their innovative activities, whereas innovation among small firms originate from informal learning by doing, by using, and by interacting with suppliers and competitors.

[13] Note that the coefficient of regional R&D spillovers does not change sign if aggregating knowledge at provincial level.

Table 3 Augmented KPF for SMEs (estimation technique: probit)

Variables (dep. var.: whether innovated)	Marg. Eff.	P > lzl
R&D measures		
Predicted Log R&D	0.235	0.015
Log regional R&D spillovers	−0.118	0.023
Log sectoral R&D spillovers	0.140	0.039
Firm specific characteristics		
Log of physical capital	0.031	0.079
Log of human capital	−0.251	0.571
Log regional R&D spillovers × Log human capital	0.082	0.045
Log sectoral R&D spillovers × Log human capital	−0.058	0.346
Pseudo R^2	0.065	
Sample size	482	

Table 4 Augmented KPF for SFs (estimation technique: probit)

Variables (dep. var.: whether innovated)	Marg. Eff.	P > lzl
R&D measures		
LRDI (log of predicted RD)	0.272	0.021
Log regional spillovers	−0.132	0.020
Log sectoral spillovers	0.136	0.066
Firm specific characteristics		
Log of physical capital	0.030	0.110
Log of human capital	−0.434	0.396
Regional RD spillovers × Log human capital	0.092	0.061
Sectoral RD spillovers × Log human capital	−0.040	0.579
Pseudo R^2	0.0628	
Sample size	417	

Table 5 Augmented KPF for MFs (estimation technique: probit)

Variables (dep. var.: whether innovated)	Marg. Eff.	P > lzl
R&D measures		
LRDI (log of predicted RD)	0.332	0.051
Log regional spillovers	−0.142	0.039
Log sectoral spillovers	0.172	0.055
Firm specific characteristics		
Log of physical capital	0.044	0.040
Log of human capital	−0.165	0.819
Regional RD spillovers × Log human capital	0.077	0.258
Sectoral RD spillovers × Log human capital	−0.068	0.487
Pseudo R^2	0.0723	
Sample size	309	

strong social ties[14] (resulting, for example, from past collaborative links between firms). In the absence of such complementary features, geographical proximity does not exert any effect upon knowledge diffusion.

Along this line of reasoning, Boschma (2005) pointed out that geographical proximity is neither a necessary nor a sufficiency condition for the transfer of knowledge to be effective. It is not necessary because other forms of proximity can act as substitutes of geographical proximity[15]—according to our results, industrial proximity seems to play such a role. Furthermore, it is not sufficient because firms located in the same geographical space also need to be close from a cognitive point of view in order to effectively exchange knowledge. That is, they need to share a common knowledge base (see, for instance, Giuliani and Bell 2005). Our results reflect this effect by depicting the positive role played by human capital, as it emerges from the positive and significant coefficient of the interaction term between regional spillovers and human capital endowment. Simply being part of a dynamic (R&D intensive) geographical region has a negative impact on innovation unless the amount of human capital involved in the production process of the individual firm is also high. This is the most interesting finding of our research and confirms our third research hypothesis (H3) suggesting that it is not so much how good are your neighbours in creating knowledge, but how good *you* are in exploiting and absorbing that knowledge.

Table 4 refers to the augmented KPF estimated for the subsample of small firms (SFs), i.e. those with less than 101 employees. The marginal effect for the R&D expenditure measure is higher than that reported in Table 3. At the mean, increasing the R&D effort by one unit increases the probability of innovating by 27 % points. This finding implies that small firms extract higher value (in terms of innovative ability) from R&D investments.

Also in this case we find that innovation is negatively affected by regional R&D spillovers, with a marginal coefficient slightly higher than that reported in Table 3. Again a positive relationship between the probability of innovating and the interaction term between regional spillovers and human capital endowment is observed. In accordance with the argument developed above, this result suggests that in order for regional spillovers to be effective in boosting innovations, small firms are required to be endowed with an adequate level of human capital. Finally, the coefficient on

[14] Recalling the wide literature that studies diffusion of information through social links (Rogers 1995; Valente, 1995; Singh 2003; Morone et al. 2006), in fact, it can be argued that the probability of reporting innovations is highly related to knowledge diffusion only if firms located in the same region are socially well connected. In light of this, we may conclude that firms located in most of the Italian regions, lack sufficiently tight social links. This observation does not hold for all Italian regions, as local contexts differ substantially in terms of social capital endowments (for a survey on the relationship between local endowment and the rising of Italian industrial districts see Becattini 1987).

[15] Boschma (2005) provides a comprehensive taxonomy of five forms of proximity (geographical, institutional, social, cognitive and organizational) studying the channels through which they either enhance or hamper knowledge transfers.

the log of sectoral spillover is statistically significant and comparable in size to that reported in Table 3. This indicates that SFs also benefit from spillovers arising in the industrial space.

Table 5 reports estimates of the KPF for the subsample of micro firms (MFs), i.e. those with less than 51 employees. First and foremost, we can observe that when considering solely micro firms, the coefficient on the log of predicted R&D effort is still statistically significant (at the 5 % level) and its magnitude is higher than the values reported in Tables 3 and 4.

Also this third regression shows that the probability of innovating is positively affected by sectoral R&D spillovers. When restricting the sample to micro firms, the coefficient on the log of sectoral spillovers is statistically significant and displays a higher magnitude (i.e. 0.17 %) than those observed in the other two KPF estimations. This indicates that sectoral spillovers are comparatively more relevant, as a source of innovation, for smaller firms.

As in the case of SMEs and SFs, the log of regional R&D spillovers enters negatively in the KPF. Its effect on the micro firm's probability of innovating is higher than the ones reported in Tables 3 and 4. Moreover, the coefficients on the interaction terms are not statistically significant, suggesting that for micro firms the accumulation of human capital does not help in extracting value from R&D spillovers.

6 Conclusions, Limitations and Future Work

This paper has attempted to provide some new insights into the wide-ranging debate on high-income countries firms' competitiveness and specifically on the relevance of internal and external sources of knowledge creation and diffusion for innovation.

Our study moves from the assumption that "there is no such thing as a low-tech industry. There are only low-tech companies—that is, companies that fail to use world-class technology and practices to enhance productivity and innovation" (Porter, 1998: 86). Following Porter, we can maintain that it is possible to find innovative firms enjoying competitive advantages in global markets in all sectors. This theoretical perspective broadens the scope for a policy of *strong competition* (based on innovation, in contrast to *weak competition* based on price competition) for post-Fordist high-income and knowledge based economies (Asheim 2000: 7).

Consequently, we investigated firms' competitiveness by placing due attention on the determinants of firms' decision to undertake innovative activities. Along with traditional variables that affect the propensity to innovate, we focused our attention on the presence of R&D spillovers arising from firms operating in the same sector (industrial proximity) and the presence of regional R&D spillovers arising from firms located in the same region (geographical proximity).

The empirical investigation looked at Italian small and medium enterprises using data on innovative activities and other characteristics drawn from the Capitalia dataset for the period 1998–2003. To account for the endogeneity of R&D

expenditure in the knowledge production function, we first estimated the R&D expenditure for a firm conditional on being engaged in R&D activity. Subsequently, we used these estimates in a knowledge production function (KPF) estimated (using a standard probit model) for three different samples of firms: small and medium firms (less than or equal to 250 employees); small firms (less than or equal to 100 employees); and micro firms (less than or equal to 50 employees).

Our main results suggest that the probability of being engaged in intramural R&D increases with the size of the firm and with the share of human capital endowment. Moreover, younger firms, exporting firms and high-tech firms are more likely to be engaged in R&D activities. Interestingly, the geographical location of the firm does not affect its probability to conduct R&D. As for the R&D expenditure, it is positively affected by the human capital endowment of the firm and its size but is negatively affected by the location in the South of the country. This latter result is rather interesting as it points out that firms located in the South, although not affected by their location in the choice of starting R&D projects, are forced to reduce the scale of such projects. As we explained in the results section, this finding is probably due to credit market constrains affecting Southern firms which, although keen on initiating R&D activities, are limited in their investments capability and, in turn, in their innovative ability. This result is, according to the authors, quite interesting and calls for extra efforts in investigating the impact of credit market's failure upon innovation activities undertaken by South Italy entrepreneurs.

By estimating the KPFs disaggregated by firm size, we find the probability to innovate to be positively related to sectoral spillovers. More importantly, the magnitude of such impact is at a pick for very small firms (i.e. those with less than 51 employees). That is, knowledge spilling over from other firms operating in the same industrial space is essential for very small firms and compensates for their limited R&D expenditure. As for knowledge diffusion via geographical proximity, we find that the absorption capacity of firms is strictly dependent on their specific endowment of human capital. This latter result confirms that geographical proximity is not a sufficient condition for knowledge transfer between firms to be effective, as it needs to co-exist with cognitive proximity.

Although interesting and robust, these findings are to be considered preliminary as they suffer from some caveats that are mostly related to the nature of the dataset used in the analysis. First, as already mentioned at the end of Sect. 4, the innovation measurement used in the KPF reflects firm's self-perception of innovation. Moreover, it does not allow us to distinguish between product and process innovations. In this regard, a firm that introduced only a process innovation over the period 2001–2003 would appear to be as innovative as a firm that introduced perhaps several new products over the same period. This is highly problematic since the need for R&D and the utilization of external knowledge is highly different for the two innovative forms.[16] A needed extension of this work should look more closely

[16] We wish to thank an anonymous referee for pointing this out.

at the distinction between product and process innovation and better explore the relation between knowledge diffusion and various types of innovative activities.

Finally, some problems might arise from the way in which the R&D spillover measures are constructed in our paper. In fact, our measures best capture the amount of external knowledge *available* to the firm. Yet, we can hardly distinguish between those firms who are able to exploit such external knowledge and those who are unable/unwilling. We tried to capture the ability to *absorb* external knowledge by introducing a set of interaction variables in our regression model; however, a possibly more promising line of research could look at R&D collaborations in order to account for R&D spillovers. This may complement or fine-tune some of the conclusions that have resulted from our analysis. We note that especially with regard to the negative effect observed for regional R&D spillover, it could also strengthen our finding that geographical proximity needs to be coupled with cognitive proximity in order to exert any positive effect upon innovation.

Acknowledgements The authors are grateful to Marco Vivarelli for helpful comments provided on an earlier version of the paper and to Nick von Tunzelmann for precious suggestions and comments. The authors also thank Cesare Imbriani for the helpful discussion provided in different stages of the work. Capitalia data and helpful advice from Attilio Pasetto (Area Studi Capitalia) are gratefully acknowledged. Finally, we wish to thank our two anonymous referees for constructive criticism. The usual disclaimers apply.

Annex: Construction of Panel Data

The eighth and ninth Capitalia surveys cover the periods 1998–2000 and 2001–2003 respectively. The firms included in the surveys were selected by means of a mixed procedure: sample-based for firms with between 11 and 500 employees, and exhaustive for firms with more than 500 employees. The composition of the sample was determined using a random selection procedure stratified by class of employees, location and sectors. Note that the survey design is stratified and rotating, so that about half of the firms in the eighth wave (1998–2000) are dropped in the ninth wave (2001–2003), with other new firms being added. The choice of firms to be dropped from the eighth wave, and of those to be added in the ninth wave was casual, but still aimed at maintaining the stratified nature of the sample. In order to construct our balanced panel data we retrieved information only on those firms present in both waves.

Given this panel data, we proceeded to evaluate the difference in firms' sectors and size between the balanced panel data and the eighth and ninth waves of Capitalia survey, in order to evaluate if the sectoral and dimensional composition of the initial samples has been respected.

From Table 6, we can notice that the share of firms of our panel is, on average, in line with the one observed in the two Capitalia samples. However, we should mention that the share of firms in the balanced panel data appears to be slightly

Table 6 Panel data compared to Capitalia surveys

	Panel data 1998–2003 (%) (N = 1,019)	Capitalia 1998–2000 (%) (N = 4,289)	Capitalia 2001–2003 (%) (N = 4,289)
Size			
11–20 employees	34.00	39.90	22.10
21–50 employees	37.60	37.10	29.60
51–250 employees	21.80	16.20	26.90
251–500 employees	3.30	3.90	5.10
>500 employees	3.20	2.90	6.10
Location			
North West	37.39	37.60	35.90
North East	31.50	27.40	30.10
Center	18.80	20.60	17.70
South	12.27	14.40	16.30
Sectors			
Traditional secter	51.20	52.30	51.90
Scale sector	16.80	18.10	16.80
Specialised sector	27.70	24.30	26.70
High-tech sector	4.00	5.30	4.60

underestimated in some cases and slightly overestimated in other cases. More precisely, we can observe that our panel, when compared to both Capitalia survey waves, slightly overestimates the share of firms with 21–50 employees and underestimates the share of firms with 251–500 employees. Similarly, our sample overestimates the share of firms located in the north-east and underestimates the share of those located in the south. Finally, firms in traditional sectors are slightly underestimated, whereas those in specialised sectors are overestimated.

All in all, we believe the results reported in Table 6 provide a confirmation of the reliability of our sample.

Cleaning Procedure

Our data cleaning procedure consisted of several different stages. First, to refine the firm's constitution year variable, which contains several missing values, we compared the information from the Capitalia questionnaire with information gathered from an independent data source (AIDA database). In doing so, we substituted all missing and erratic observations with AIDA information and, in the case of inconsistency, proceeded to report the oldest year of firm's foundation. The second step was converting into euros the R&D expenditure and the physical capital investment recorded in Italian liras back in 1998.

All mentioned variables were also reported to constant prices by using value added industry output deflators of Southern and Northern areas of Italy (the source of deflator is SVIMEZ). However, the presence of several missing values in most of the relevant variables obliged us to perform our study on a restricted number of observations.

References

Acs ZJ, Audretsch DB, Feldman MP (1994) R&D spillovers and recipient firm size. Rev Econ Stat 76(2):336–340

Aiello F, Cardamone P (2008) R&D spillovers and firms' performance in Italy. Emp Econ 34(1):143–166

Antonelli C (1994) Technological districts localized spillovers and productivity growth. The Italian evidence on technological externalities in the core regions. Int Rev Appl Econ 8:18–30

Asheim BT (2000) The learning firm in the learning region: workers participation as social capital. DRUID summer 2000 conference, Rebild, Denmark, 15–17 June

Atkinson RD, Andes SM (2009) The Atlantic century: benchmarking EU & US innovation and competitiveness. ITIF report (Information Technology and Innovation Foundation). Washington, DC

Audretsch D, Feldman M (2004) Knowledge spillovers and the geography of innovation. In: Thisse JF, Henderson JV (eds) Handbook of urban and regional economics, 4th edn. Elsevier, Amsterdam, pp 2713–2739

Barrios S, Goerg H, Strobl E (2003) Explaining firms' export behaviour: R&D spillovers and the destination market. Oxf Bull Econ Stat 65(4):475–496

Becattini G (1987) Mercato e forze locali: il distretto industriale. Il Mulino, Bologna

Bernstein JI (1988) Costs of production, intra- and interindustry R&D spillovers: Canadian evidence. Can J Econ 21(2):324–347

Boschma RA (2005) Proximity and innovation: a critical assessment. Reg Stud 39(1):61–74

Capitalia (2002) Indagine sulle imprese manifatturiere. Ottavo rapporto sull'industria italiana e sulla politica industriale, Rome

Capitalia (2005) Indagine sulle imprese manifatturiere. Nono rapporto sull'industria italiana e sulla politica industriale, Rome

Casaburi L, Gattai V, Minerva GA (2007) Italian firms' international operations and their performance: some raw evidence from the Capitalia dataset. Mimeo, New York

Cohen WM, Levinthal DA (1989) Innovation and learning: the two faces of R&D. Econ J 99 (397):569–596

Cohen WM, Klepper S (1992) The anatomy of industry R&D intensity distributions. Am Econ Rev 82:773–788

Cohen WM, Klepper S (1996) A reprise of size and R&D. Econ J 106:925–951

Crépon B, Duguet E, Mairesse J (1998) Research, innovation and productivity: an econometric analysis at a firm level. Econ Innov New Technol 7(2):115–158

Feldman MP, Francis JL (2002) The entrepreneurial spark: individual agents and the formation of innovative clusters. In: Quadrio Curzio A, Fortis M (eds) Complexity and Industrial Clusters. Springer Verlag, Heidelberg

Fisher M (2006) Innovation, networks and knowledge spillovers: selected essays. Springer, Berlin

Florida RL, Cohen WM (1999) Engine or infrastructure? The university role in economic development, In: Branscomb LM, Kodama F, Florida R (eds) Industrializing knowledge: university-industry linkages in Japan and the United States. The MIT Press, Cambridge, pp 589–610
Giannola A (2002) Il credito difficile. L'Ancora del Mediterraneo, Napoli
Giuliani E, Bell M (2005) The micro-determinants of meso-level learning and innovation: evidence from a Chilean wine cluster. Res Policy 34(1):47–68
Glaeser EL, Kallal HD, Scheinkman JA, Shleifer A (1992) Growth in cities. J Polit Econ 100 (6):1126–1152
Griffith R, Huergo E, Mairesse J, Peters B (2006) Innovation and productivity across four European countries. NBER Working Paper 12722
Griliches Z (1979) Issues in assessing the contribution of research and development to productivity growth. Bell J Econ 10(1):92–116
Griliches Z (1992) The search for R&D spillovers. Scand J Econ 94(Suppl):29–47
Howells JRL (2002) Tacit knowledge, innovation and economic geography. Urban Stud 39 (5–6):871–884
ISAE (2003) I rapporti banca-impresa e I vincoli finanziari alla crescita delle piccolo e medie imprese. Rapporto 2003, Priorità nazionali: dimensioni aziendali, competitività, regolamentazione, Rome
Jacobs J (1969) The economy of cities. Random House, New York
Jaffe A (1986) Technological opportunity and spillovers of R&D: evidence from firms patents, profits, and market value. Am Econ Rev 76(5):984–1001
Kuznets S (1962) Inventive activity: problems of definition and measurement. In: Nelson RR (ed) The rate and direction of Inventive activity. Princeton University Press, National Bureau of Economic Research Conference Report, pp 19–43
Levin RC, Reiss PC (1988) Cost-reducing and demand-creating R & D with spillovers. Rand J Econ 19:538–556
Marshall A (1920) Principles of economis. Macmillan, London
Medda G, Piga C (2004) R&D e spillover industriali: un'analisi sulle imprese italiane. Working paper CRENoS 2004/06, Centre for North South Economic Research, University of Cagliari and Sassari, Sardinia
Morone P, Testa G (2008) Firm growth, size and innovation. Econ Innov New Technol 17 (4):311–329
Morone P, Sisto R, Taylor R (2006) Knowledge diffusion and networking in the organic production sector: a case study. EuroChoices 5(3):40–46
Morone P, Petraglia C, Testa G (2007) Research, knowledge spillovers and innovation. Birkbeck Working Papers in Economics and Finance, 0713
Ornaghi C (2006) Spillovers in product and process innovation: Evidence from manufacturing firms. Int J Ind Organ 24:349–380
Piergiovanni R, Santarelli E, Vivarelli M (1997) From which source do small firms derive their innovative inputs? Some evidence from Italian industry. Rev Ind Organ 12(2):243–258
Pinch S, Henry N, Jenkins M, Tallman S (2003) From 'industrial districts' to 'knowledge clusters': a model of knowledge dissemination and competitive advantage in industrial agglomeration. J Econ Geogr 3(4):373–388
Porter M (1990) The comparative advantage of nations. Free Press, New York
Porter ME (1998) Clusters and the new economics of competition. Harv Bus Rev 1998:77–90
Powell W, Koput KW, Smith-Doerr L (1996) Interorganizational collaboration and the locus of innovation: networks of learning in biotechnology. Adm Sci Q 42(1):116–145
Rogers EM (1995) Diffusion of innovations. Free Press, New York
Romer PM (1986) Increasing returns and long-run growth. J Polit Econ 94(5):1002–1037
Schumpeter JA (1942) Capitalism, socialism and democracy. Harper, New York
Singh J (2003) Social networks as drivers of knowledge diffusion. Mimeo, Harvard University

Smith K (2006) Measuring innovation. In: Fagerberg J, Mowery DC, Nelson RR (eds) The Oxford handbook of innovation. Oxford University Press, Oxford
Technopolis Group (2006) Strategic evaluation on innovation and the knowledge based economy in relation to the structural and cohesion funds, for the programming period 2007–2013. A report to the European Commission, DG Regional Policy. Country report, Italy
Terleckyj N (1974) Effects of R&D on the productivity growth of industries: an exploratory study. National Planning Association, Washington, DC
Valente TW (1995) Network models of the diffusion of innovations. Hampton, Creskill, NJ
van der Panne G (2007) Issues in measuring innovation. Scientometrics 71(3):495–507

Strategic Fit Between Regional Innovation Policy and Regional Innovation Systems: The Case of Local Public Technology Centers in Japan

Nobuya Fukugawa

Abstract Local public technology centers are publicly-managed technology transfer organizations, and their resource allocation strategies represent policy instruments for the promotion of localized knowledge spillovers. Since substantial regional differences exist with regard to the need for public technological services, policy instruments should consider these differences. This study develops a model and a method to evaluate whether the regional innovation policy matches the characteristics of a regional innovation system. The results indicate that the resource allocation strategies of technology centers have not been developed according to the needs of the regional environment; hence, technology transfer activities may not have been optimally utilized to facilitate regional economic development.

1 Introduction

A regional innovation system is a conceptual framework in which industrial innovations are generated through interactions among the industries, universities, and government of a region (Howells 1999; Cooke et al. 2004; Mowery and Sampat 2005). The regional perspective is important when the geographical range of knowledge diffusion among economic agents is limited because of the tacit nature of the knowledge transferred. Since university knowledge is disseminated through publication, it does not encounter geographical limitations in diffusion. However, a number of empirical studies have indicated that spillovers from university research tend to be localized (Jaffe 1989; Anselin et al. 1997; Autant-Bernard 2001). That is, one economic agent near the university may benefit from university spillover,

N. Fukugawa (✉)
Graduate School of Engineering, Tohoku University, 6-6-11-804 Aramaki, Aoba-ku Sendai 980-8579, Japan
e-mail: fukugawa@m.tohoku.ac.jp

A. Pyka and E.S. Andersen (eds.), *Long Term Economic Development*, Economic Complexity and Evolution, DOI 10.1007/978-3-642-35125-9_13,

whereas another in a geographically isolated area will not benefit from the spillover. Therefore, policy instruments for the promotion of the exchange of knowledge among industries, universities, and public research institutions can improve knowledge productivity in the region (Fritsch 2004; Fritsch and Franke 2004; Ronde and Hussler 2005). In the long run, regional differences in knowledge productivity will lead to regional differences in economic development.

Among the regional innovation policies that have been implemented in developed countries, the establishment and expansion of local public technology centers in Japan constitute one of the most distinguished policy instruments. Local public technology centers, administrated by the prefectural and municipal governments, engage in providing technological support to small local firms. The centers were established before modern economic growth began in the nineteenth century; they increased in number during the twentieth century; and they now cover all prefectures and most technological categories. The technological services the centers offer to small local firms include the inspection of materials and products, technological consultation, diffusion of new technologies, joint research, and funded research. Furthermore, local public technology centers conduct their own research and license out their patented technologies mainly to small local firms. The US government was of the opinion that local public technology centers significantly contributed to economic development in postwar Japan, and this policy instrument was benchmarked in the design of the regional innovation policy implemented in the 1990s in the US (U.S. Congress 1990; Shapira et al. 1995, 1996; Feller et al. 1996).

As noted above, local public technology centers are remarkable in terms of their history, geographical and industrial coverage, variety of services offered, and number of policy recipients. However, local public technology centers currently face two structural changes that could force them to redefine their capabilities and responsibilities in the regional innovation system. First, the prolonged economic stagnation since the 1990s has left the local authorities with serious financial difficulties. Furthermore, as a result of the government's structural reform in the 2000s, the local authorities had their subsidies reduced substantially. Consequently, the local authorities reduced the budgets of the local public technology centers (see Fig. 1) and rigorously evaluated their performance. In order to budget more efficiently, the local authorities required local public technology centers to redefine their strengths and contributions to the regional economy more explicitly. Second, the national system of innovation was fundamentally reformed during and after the 1990s; this was symbolized by the enactment of the Science and Technology Basic Law in 1995, the Technology Licensing Organization Act in 1998, the Law of Special Measures for Industrial Revitalization in 1999, the Law to Strengthen Industrial Technology in 2000, and the incorporation of national universities in 2004. A series of reforms required national universities in each region to share knowledge with small local firms, whereas before the reforms, they had not been motivated to be involved in the regional economy. This change marked the national universities' entry into the local market for public technological services; this

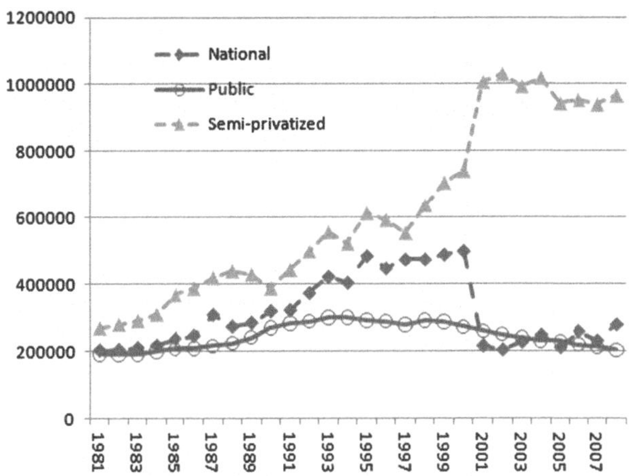

Fig. 1 R&D expenditure in national, public, semi-privatized research institutes in Japan (million JPY). Note: Many national research institutes were incorporated in 2001. "Public" indicates local public technology centers. Information was collected from the Ministry of Internal Affairs and Communications, "Science and Technology Survey"

market was initially dominated by local public technology centers, which were the primary source of knowledge for small local firms.

In these new circumstances, local public technology centers are required to establish their own strategy to function as part of a regional innovation system. This study aims to propose a model describing the characteristics of regional innovation systems, and, using a comprehensive dataset on local public technology centers, the study quantitatively examines whether technology centers' strategies match the characteristics of the regional innovation systems. Although much research has been conducted on university spillovers in Japan (Kneller 1999, 2007; Motohashi 2005), local public technology centers as a source of public knowledge have received little attention from researchers. Therefore, this analysis should intrigue the researchers interested in technology transfer and regional development, as well as policymakers responsible for developing strategies for local public technology centers.

The remainder of the paper is organized as follows. Section 2 describes local public technology centers in Japan and their policy impact. Section 3 identifies key resource allocation strategies of local public technology centers. Section 4 models the characteristics of regional innovation systems. Section 5 predicts the relationships between the resource allocation strategies of technology centers and the characteristics of the regions where technology centers are located. Section 6 tests the predicted relationships by using a comprehensive dataset of local public technology centers and discusses the implications of the empirical analysis. Section 7 summarizes theoretical and methodological contributions of the study, and refers to issues for future research.

2 Local Public Technology Centers in Japan

Local public technology centers, administrated by the prefectural and municipal governments, play three roles in regional innovation systems. First, they provide small local firms with various technological services, such as the inspection of raw materials and final products, consultations to solve problems in production processes, and the organization of workshops to diffuse new technologies. Second, they conduct their own research, patent their inventions, and license their patents to small local firms. Third, they help small local firms collaborate so as to facilitate product development among them. I will discuss the key roles of technology centers in regional innovation systems in greater detail in Sect. 3.

Regional innovation policy as represented by local public technology centers has its roots in the 1880s, before the beginning of modern economic growth in Japan. Figure 2 illustrates the founding of local public technology centers by year and by technological field.[1] In the early days, local public technology centers were primarily established to support agriculture, the most important industry in pre-modern society. The development of the heavy industry after the 1910s was followed by the establishment of an increasing number of local public technology centers to provide technological support to the manufacturing industry. In the 1950s and 1960s, the remarkable economic recovery in postwar Japan led to serious environmental side effects, prompting the creation of local public technology centers for environmental science. Today, most prefectures have at least two types of local public technology centers, providing support in the areas of agriculture and manufacturing. Certain technology centers offer services in specific fields of manufacturing, such as ceramics and textiles. Other centers are engaged in research and technological assistance in the areas of industrial design and civil engineering.

This regional innovation policy, unique to Japan, received attention from the US government in the 1990s, since it was recognized for its significant contributions to the rapid economic growth of postwar Japan. Owing to serious concerns over the decreasing competitive advantage in the manufacturing industry, the US government benchmarked local public technology centers in its manufacturing extension partnership program, the regional innovation policy that was implemented in the 1990s (U.S. Congress 1990). Public technology transfer organizations, such as manufacturing extension centers, were established to improve the technological capabilities of small local firms (Shapira et al. 1995, 1996; Feller et al. 1996; Shapira 2001). Empirical studies on this policy find positive effects on the

[1] Information was collected from "Current Status of Local Public Technology Centers" by the Japan Association for the Promotion of Industrial Technology. The upsurge of manufacturing technology centers in the 1980s and 1990s was affected by frequent administrative reform in local authorities. All the reorganized technology centers are counted as newly established technology centers because of the difficulty in identifying centers during the complicated process of reorganization.

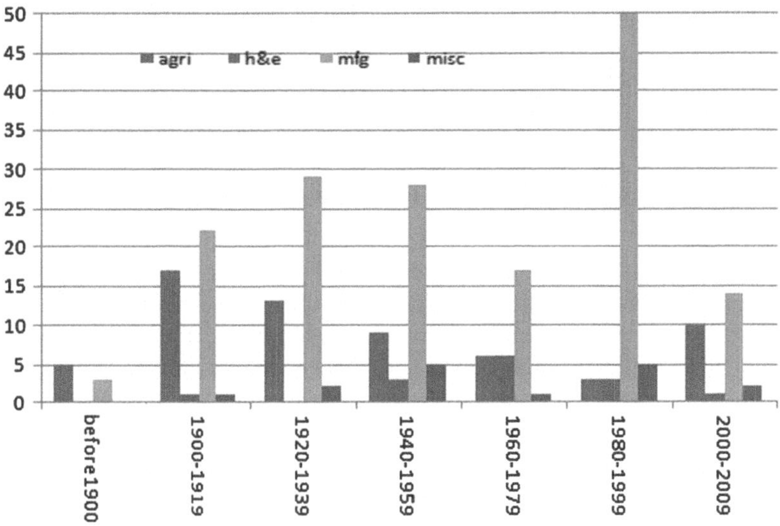

Fig. 2 The number of newly established local public technology centers by period and technology. Note *agri* agriculture, *h&e* public health and environmental science, *mfg* manufacturing, *misc* miscellaneous

productivity growth of program applicants (Luria and Wiarda 1996; Oldsman 1996; Dziczek et al. 1998; Jarmin 1999).

Although no econometric evaluation of the policy effects of local public technology transfer centers has been carried out to date, several studies suggest that local public technology centers contribute to the improvement of the technological capabilities of small local firms. Shapira (1992), based on interviews with center directors, reports that local public technology centers play an important role in improving product quality and in introducing new technology to small local firms. Comparing the manufacturing extension partnerships in the US with the local public technology centers in Japan, Ruth (2006) argues that the latter are superior to the former in terms of helping small local firms form interorganizational networks for innovation. Based on a questionnaire survey on networks among innovative small firms, Fukugawa (2006) finds that local public technology centers significantly contribute to the technological success of joint product development by such interfirm networks.

Others highlight the regional embeddedness of technology center scientists as an advantage of local public technology centers in the regional innovation system. The lifetime employment of technology center scientists encourages them to be involved in the regional economy and to establish stable and long-term relationships with small local firms, which in turn helps local public technology centers build mutual trust with customers. The job security of center scientists tends to result in the obsolescence of their technological knowledge. However, this is not detrimental to the technology transfer productivity of local public technology centers, because most of their customers typically do not engage in the development of state-of-the-art technology, and a small lag in knowledge diffusion does not affect the centers' ability to meet customers' needs for technological know-how (Shapira 1992; Hassink 1997).

3 Strategies of Local Public Technology Centers

As noted in Sect. 2, local public technology centers play three key roles in regional innovation systems: providing solutions to problems that small firms face in production processes; conducting their own research and licensing out the patented technology; and intermediating networks of innovative small firms. Although these roles are complementary to a certain extent, these activities compete for the limited resources of local public technology centers. In this sense, how intensively a technology center is engaged in a specific type of technology transfer represents a resource allocation strategy of the technology center. A comprehensive survey of local public technology centers, "Current Status of Local Public Technology Centers 2000–2009" by the Japan Association for the Promotion of Industrial Technology will be used here to analyze the resource allocation strategies of local public technology centers. Although this dataset provides information on local public technology centers in all technological categories, this study focuses on manufacturing technology centers. The definitions and descriptive statistics of variables are shown in Table 1. All variables are divided by the number of scientists to control for size of the centers.

Figure 3 shows the factor loadings computed by factor analysis. Factor analysis is a statistical method for extracting latent factors behind observable variables that affect several observable variables in the same direction. Given the screen plot, two factors with eigenvalues that are higher than one are extracted as the horizontal axis (Factor 1) and the vertical axis (Factor 2) in Fig. 3. Factor 1 strongly correlates with resource allocation variables that represent the proportion of Ph.D. scientists (*quality*), the number of papers published in academic journals per scientist (*paper*), the number of patents granted per scientist (*patgr*), and the number of patents applied for per scientist (*patap*); however, Factor 1 has no correlation with other variables.[2] The quality of human resources, research activities, and research outcomes are associated with the tendency of local public technology centers to intensify their research capacities. Factor 2 positively correlates with resource allocation variables that represent sharing information on new technologies (*workshop*), an open laboratory for the use of equipment that small firms cannot afford (*openl*), testing and inspection services (*test*), and providing small firms with

[2] Factor 1 also positively correlates with the number of research projects per scientist (*res*), but the correlation is not as strong as with other variables, probably because the variable reflects all types of research projects. Information on each type of research (e.g., funded research) is available for only a few empirical periods; therefore, factor analysis is difficult, since there are few observations to which it can be applied.

Table 1 Definitions and descriptive statistics of variables

Variables	Definition	N	Mean	S.D.	Min	Max
Quality	The proportion of Ph.D. scientists	902	0.20	0.15	0	0.9
Paper	The number of academic articles per scientist	828	0.20	0.32	0	7.6
Patgr	The number of patents granted per scientist	981	0.26	0.28	0	1.7
Patap	The number of patents applied for per scientist	975	0.52	0.59	0	8.3
Res	The number of research projects per scientist	998	0.64	0.29	0	1.7
Consult	The number of technological consulting services per scientist	956	105.50	108.60	0	822.5
Guide	The number of technological guidance services per scientist	879	24.93	40.47	0	289.3
Openl	The number of equipment rental services per scientist	926	75.62	189.15	0	4207.3
Test	The number of inspection and testing services per scientist	962	215.96	419.68	0	4193.5
Workshop	The number of workshops per scientist	973	2.12	5.27	0	117.1

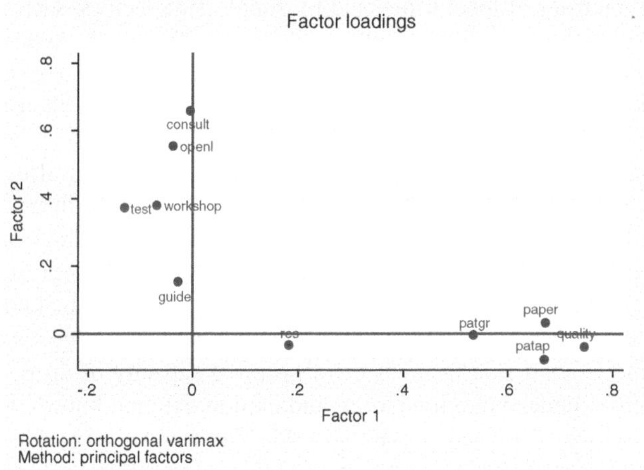

Fig. 3 Factor loadings

immediate solutions for technological problems (*consult* and *guide*); however, Factor 2 has no correlation with other variables. The variables correlated with Factor 2 are associated with the tendency of local public technology centers to disseminate technological knowledge to small firms.

Given these findings, Factors 1 and 2 are presumed to represent technology centers' resource allocation strategies for *knowledge creation* and *knowledge dissemination*, respectively. The correlation coefficient between Factor 1 and Factor 2 is very low (i.e., 0.02), implying that knowledge creation and knowledge dissemination are independent. Thus, it is difficult for local public technology centers to intensively pursue one type of strategy without giving up another type of strategy to some extent. Such a trade-off seems to be getting more serious, because most local authorities have experienced greater budget constraints since the 2000s (see Fig. 1), suggesting that efficient resource allocation to match regional environments is important.

4 Characteristics of Regional Innovation Systems

In order to identify the characteristics of regional innovation systems, this study assumes a local market for public technological services. Previous studies have suggested that demand and supply in a local market for public technological services determine how public knowledge is transferred to the private sector (Charles and Howells 1992; Santoro and Chakrabarti 2002; Schartinger et al. 2002; Carayol 2003). Specifically, the type of knowledge linkage established between industry and universities is determined both by demand-side factors, such as R&D intensity of local firms, and by supply-side factors, such as research quality of local universities. Given their arguments, this study assumes a local market for public technological services in which small firms seek and exploit public knowledge accumulated in the region, either to improve their production processes or to build long-term R&D capabilities.

The demand for public technological services in a region is affected by the attributes of small local firms. Although some regions have large firms, these firms are likely to have sufficient internal resources to solve technological problems independently. Furthermore, even if large firms encounter technological difficulties beyond their capabilities, they are unlikely to rely on regional public knowledge for solutions since they are likely to have developed global knowledge networks. The most important demand-side factor is the absorptive capacity of firms, that is, the ability to identify, understand, transform, and exploit external knowledge for their innovative activities (Cohen and Levinthal 1990; Zahra and George 2002). Absorptive capacity has a cumulative nature and is generated by R&D efforts of a firm, which makes it difficult for competitors to duplicate the resource immediately. Absorptive capacity affects how a firm interacts with a source of knowledge. Small firms relatively rich in absorptive capacity can employ an interactive channel of knowledge transfer, such as joint research, whereas small firms that do not perform R&D are likely to be supported by technology centers by means of a unilateral channel, such as technological consultation.[3]

[3] Absorptive capacity also affects the geographical range of knowledge interactions. Small firms with higher absorptive capacity may not rely on local public technology centers since they are likely to have developed global knowledge networks (Beise and Stahl 1999). Here, it is assumed that small local firms first seek a local market for technological services, and then expand their search for the next best option if the first trial fails.

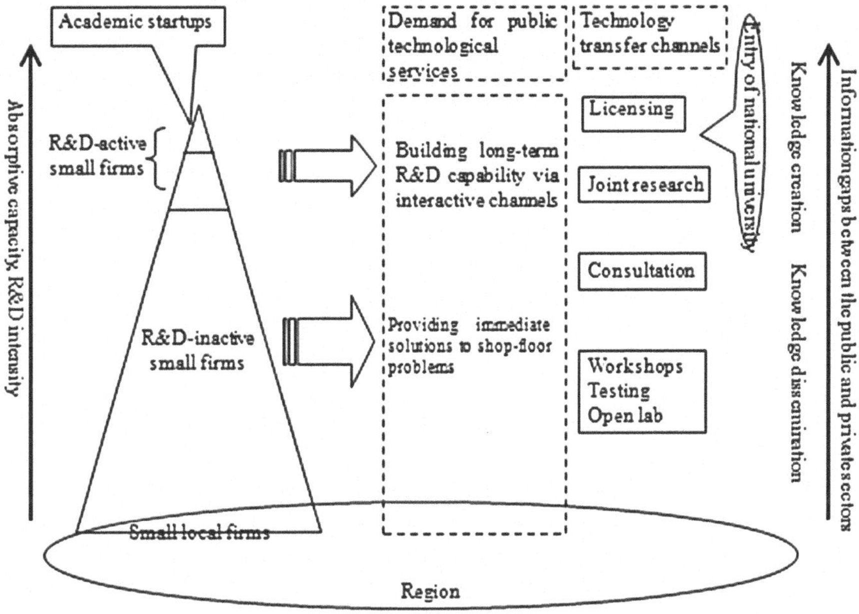

Fig. 4 Type of demand in a local market for public technological services

The supply of public technological services in a region is generated by national universities as well as local public technology centers. National research institutes may also contribute to the supply of public technological services. However, national research institutes in Japan are highly concentrated in Tokyo and Ibaraki prefecture (essentially in the city of Tsukuba), whereas at least one national university with faculties in the natural sciences is located in each prefecture. Furthermore, national research institutes engage in the R&D of state-of-the-art technology, which has little to do with the technological problems that are encountered by small local firms. If a national university in a particular region is relatively active in knowledge interactions with small local firms, it acts as a new entry into the local market for public technological services.

Given these arguments, the conceptual framework of regional innovation systems is illustrated in Fig. 4. The triangle on the left-hand side represents small local firms that demand public technological services. Area refers to the number of firms. The bottom of the triangle denotes small local manufacturers that do not engage in R&D, while the upper side denotes R&D-active small firms. The top of the triangle denotes small firms that devote themselves to research, such as academic startups. Small firms located in the upper portion of the triangle are assumed to have higher absorptive capacity, implying that they are likely to develop interactive and long-term relationships with external sources of knowledge. In contrast, small firms located at the bottom of the triangle demand public knowledge for immediate solutions to problems that occur at the shop-floor level, implying that the firms are likely to employ a unilateral channel of knowledge transfer.

The rectangles on the right-hand side represent the channels of knowledge transfer. Rectangles in the upper (lower) side refer to spillover channels with a relatively large (small) information gap between firms and external sources of knowledge (Izushi 2003, 2005). Information gaps are determined by the importance of communication between local public technology centers and small firms, and by the time required for small firms to evaluate the outcome of technological services. Izushi finds that the relationship between the two evolves over time. Small firms begin by using technological services with a smaller information gap, such as testing. After having developed mutual trust, small firms employ services with a larger information gap, such as joint research. Given these arguments, technology transfer channels are classified according to their information gap or the significance of the interactions.

The rectangles in the upper portion indicate that more interactive communication is needed when a larger information gap exists. In the case of joint research, scientists from both sides share their ideas, with matching research efforts, to create new knowledge. As shown in Fig. 3, the technology center's strategy, represented as Factor 1 (*knowledge creation*), is relevant for this kind of technology transfer. Furthermore, intellectual property licensing entails a larger information gap, which means that the licensing requires efficient communication or an efficient interface between open science and proprietary technology. When university patents are licensed to the private sector, gatekeepers with a deep understanding of science and business play an important role in evaluating the commercial potential of the invention and identifying a relevant industry partner who can commercialize the technology (Thursby and Thursby 2002). In contrast, rectangles in the lower portion indicate that hardly any communication is necessary between small firms and technology centers. In the case of technological consultation, the firm plays only a passive role, and knowledge is transferred unilaterally. The technology center's strategy, represented as Factor 2 (*knowledge dissemination*), is relevant for this kind of technology transfer. Furthermore, little interaction is necessary when local public technology centers either provide firms with testing services or let firms use their equipment.

5 Relationships Between Regional Innovation Policy and Regional Innovation Systems

In Sects. 3 and 4, I have introduced the methods by which regional innovation policy and regional innovation systems are measured. In this section, I will show how the fit between the two can be evaluated. Each prefecture is graphed in Fig. 5 according to the demand- and supply-side factors of a local market for public technological services. The vertical axis shows the proportion of small manufacturing firms in a prefecture that perform R&D. A high ratio implies that an average small manufacturer in the prefecture would have greater absorptive

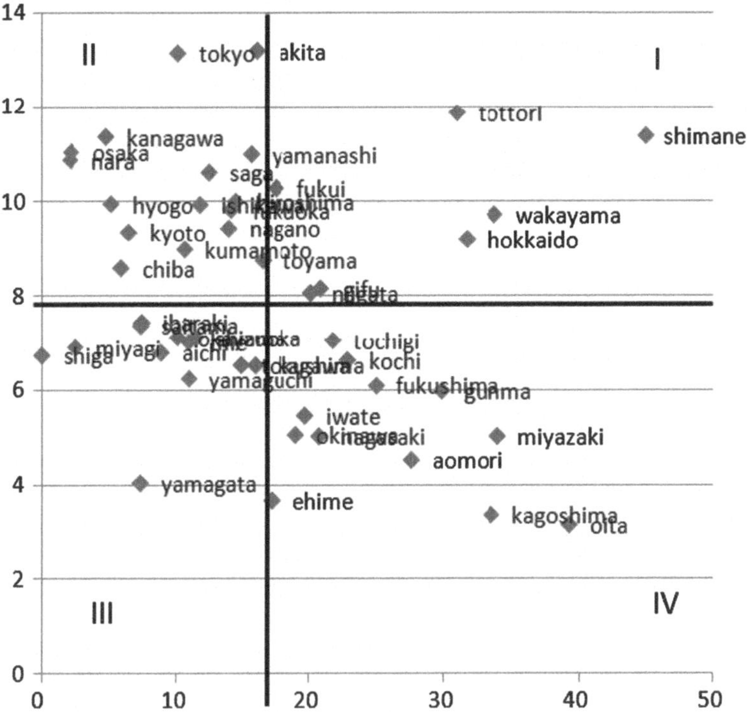

Fig. 5 Characteristics of regional innovation systems. Note (1) The vertical axis = the number of small manufacturers that perform R&D in a prefecture/sum of small manufacturers in a prefecture. See Sect. 4 for detailed definitions. The *horizontal line* denotes the average, approximately 8 %. The horizontal axis = the number of joint research projects between small local firms and national universities in a prefecture/sum of joint research projects conducted by national universities in a prefecture. The *vertical line* denotes the average, approximately 17 %. (2) Prefectures in Quadrant I are Fukui, Gifu, Hokkaido, Niigata, Shimane, Tottori, Wakayama. Prefectures in Quadrant II are Akita, Chiba, Fukuoka, Hiroshima, Hyogo, Ishikawa, Kanagawa, Kumamoto, Kyoto, Nagano, Nara, Osaka, Saga, Tokyo, Toyama, Yamanashi. Prefectures in Quadrant III are Aichi, Ibaraki, Kagawa, Mie, Miyagi, Okayama, Saitama, Shiga, Shizuoka, Tokushima, Yamagata, Yamaguchi. Prefectures in Quadrant IV are Aomori, Ehime, Fukushima, Gunma, Iwate, Kagoshima, Kochi, Miyazaki, Nagasaki, Oita, Okinawa, Tochigi

capacity. Information was collected from the Small- and Medium-sized Enterprise Agency, "SME Basic Survey 2008–2009." Information on R&D prior to 2008 was not available from this survey. The horizontal axis shows the proportion of joint research projects between national universities and small firms in a region. The average of this ratio between 2000 and 2002 is used. Information was collected from the National Institute of Science and Technology Policy, "University-Industry Collaboration Database." Since the incorporation of national universities in 2004, the universities have increasingly engaged in knowledge interactions with small local firms. When national universities in a region will be more eager to engage in joint research with small firms, small local firms will have greater opportunities to exploit university knowledge.

Figure 5 is divided into four parts by lines representing the averages of the horizontal and vertical axes.[4] Assuming that the characteristics of regional innovation systems are exogenous and invariant over time, and that regional innovation policy is dependent on them, the strategies of local public technology centers that match the characteristics of regional innovation systems are predicted as follows.

In Quadrant I, where the levels of both the demand and the supply variables are relatively high, there is a latent demand for high quality knowledge pool and interactive transfer channels in the region because of the presence of R&D-intensive small firms. Furthermore, a relatively high supply-side variable implies that knowledge created in national universities in the region is more accessible via joint research conducted with small local firms. It is reasonable to expect that in prefectures located in Quadrant I, small local firms that want to build long-term R&D capacity will exploit university knowledge in the region to a great extent. Therefore, in prefectures located in Quadrant I, local public technology centers need to distinguish themselves from the national university in the region by offering types of technological services that are different from those provided by the scientists of national universities. Therefore, in these regions, local public technology centers are expected to adopt a resource allocation strategy, represented as *knowledge dissemination.*

In Quadrant II, where the level of the demand variable is relatively high and the level of the supply variable is relatively low, a national university in the region is not willing to interact with small local firms despite their relatively higher R&D intensity. This mismatching between the demand for and supply of technological knowledge implies that in prefectures located in Quadrant II, local public technology centers should fill the gap by maintaining a higher technological capability, such as excellent scientists, and they should assist R&D-intensive small firms to innovate. In this case, knowledge transfer from public institutions to the private sector is expected to be interactive, because the small firms in Quadrant II are likely to have a higher absorptive capacity. Therefore, local public technology centers are expected to adopt a resource allocation strategy, represented as *knowledge creation.*

In Quadrants III and IV, where the level of the demand variable is relatively low, small local firms are likely to engage exclusively in production and distribution. Therefore, it is reasonable for local public technology centers located in a prefecture that is classified as being in Quadrants III or IV to adopt a resource allocation strategy, represented as *knowledge dissemination.* In such environments, local public technology centers are expected to offer technological services with a relatively smaller information gap, such as technological consultation and testing,

[4] The correlation coefficient between the demand- and supply-side variables is statistically insignificant; hence, the two axes can be depicted as orthogonal. Both variables are normally distributed, meaning that the average value can represent each variable.

Table 2 Predicted relationships between regional innovation policy and regional environment

Quadrant	Absorptive capacity of small firms	Accessibility of small firms to university knowledge in the region	Resource allocation strategy
I	High	High	Knowledge dissemination
II	High	Low	Knowledge creation
III	Low	Low	Knowledge dissemination
IV	Low	High	Knowledge dissemination

Note: See Fig. 5 for Quadrants I, II, III, and IV. See Sect. 3 for Factor 1 and Factor 2

since small local firms in the region tend to need local public technology centers for immediate problem solving in the production process rather than for building long-term R&D capability. Table 2 summarizes the theoretically predicted strategies (shown in column 4) of local public technology centers that match the characteristics of regional innovation systems (shown in columns 1, 2, and 3).

6 Results

Have local public technology centers allocated their resources to match the characteristics of regional innovation systems in the period when they were required to allocate resources more efficiently? The purpose of this section is to examine the statistical relationship between the characteristics of regional innovation systems and the theoretically predicted strategies (shown in Table 2) of local public technology centers. Specifically, I conducted an analysis of variance to examine whether the average of year-on-year growth (2000–2009) of each variable that represents a resource allocation strategy varies according to the characteristics of regional innovation systems as of 2000–2002, as represented by four quadrants in Fig. 5. A positive value for the average of year-on-year growth indicates that the local public technology center reinforced the resource, whereas a negative value indicates that the local public technology center relinquished the resource. As suggested by Table 2, Factor 1 (*knowledge creation*) should be reinforced in Quadrant II, whereas Factor 2 (*knowledge dissemination*) should be reinforced in Quadrants I, III, and IV. Therefore, resource allocation variables such as *workshop*, *consult*, *guide*, *openl*, and *testing* are predicted to exhibit significantly higher growth in Quadrants I, III, and IV, whereas resource allocation variables such as *quality*, *paper*, *res*, *patgr*, and *patap* are predicted to exhibit significantly higher growth in Quadrant II.

Table 3 shows the results of the analysis of variance. As summarized by Table 2, it was predicted that variables related to *knowledge creation* would show

Table 3 One-way analysis of variance

Strategy	Knowledge creation					Knowledge dissemination				
Variables	*Quality*	*Patgr*	*Patap*	*Paper*	*Res*	*Consult*	*Test*	*Openl*	*Workshop*	*Guide*
I	0.07	0.03	0.23	0.31	0.01	0.03	0.09	0.41	0.16	0.48
II	0.07	0.07	0.14	0.19	−0.002	0.08	0.20	0.81	0.26	0.92
III	0.13	0.12	0.18	0.24	0.01	0.29	0.20	0.20	0.07	1.48
IV	0.08	0.14	0.21	0.12	0.01	0.10	0.05	0.42	0.07	0.32
F value	1.44	0.93	0.59	0.50	0.17	3.37*	0.90	0.73	0.76	0.76

Note: Values in cells denote the average of year-on-year growth (2000–2009). Knowledge creation variables (*quality*, *patgr*, *patap*, *paper*, *res*) are expected to show higher growth in Quadrant II. Knowledge dissemination variables (*consult*, *test*, *openl*, *workshop*, *guide*) are expected to show higher growth in Quadrants I, III, and IV

*$p < 0.05$

significantly higher growth in Quadrant II, but variables related to *knowledge dissemination* would show significantly higher growth in the other quadrants. The results, however, show no significant difference across quadrants in most variables; that is, local public technology centers allocated their resources regardless of the characteristics of their regional environments. The only exception is technological consultation, which shows higher growth in Quadrants III and IV, as predicted in Table 2. Overall, the results suggest that small local firms lost an opportunity to improve their productivity by leveraging external knowledge, because of the misallocation of resources by the local public technology centers in the region. Specifically, small local firms might not have needed the types of technological services that were being provided by local public technological centers, but they were unable to find the services that they actually needed. Therefore, the resource allocation strategy of local public technology centers must be considered inefficient. In other words, economic welfare in a region would have improved if the local public technology centers had allocated resources according to the characteristics of their regional innovation systems.

The statistical analysis extracts the average look of local public technology centers from observations. However, an outlier sometimes gives important information when it represents a very distinctive example among the observations. Figure 6, which presents the factor scores, illustrates such distinctive strategies, that is, those of the Osaka Municipal Technical Research Institute, which pursues a strategy that intensifies its own research capability. The quality of its human resources is very high, which attracts external research funds via funded research, and these lead to higher research productivity, as represented by the number of papers and patents. Osaka prefecture is located in Quadrant II, where small local firms are relatively rich in absorptive capacity and where a national university in the region is relatively inactive in research collaborations with small local firms. Although Osaka has many R&D-intensive small firms, Osaka University, one of the leading research universities in Japan, develops knowledge networks across prefectures and the nation, and thus, it is less embedded in the regional economy. The model developed in this study suggests that it would be reasonable for the

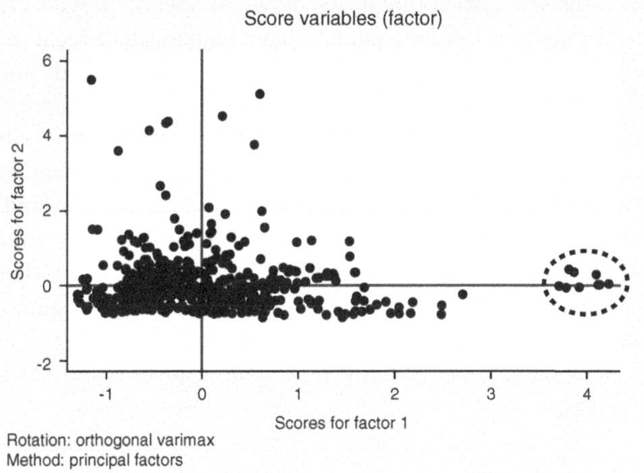

Fig. 6 Factor scores. Note *Dots* within the *circle* denote the Osaka Municipal Technical Research Institute

Osaka Municipal Technical Research Institute to intensify its research capacity, so that small local firms with absorptive capacity can rely on it. It is also rational that the Osaka Municipal Technical Research Institute was incorporated in 2008, which implied less administrative pressure from Osaka city and increased incentives to obtain external funds by exhibiting a high-quality research output by means of publications and patents. Figure 6 also shows that many technology centers are located around the origin. This implies that, since local public technology centers are expected to provide small local firms with a highly standardized list of technological services, it is generally difficult for each technology center to develop its own strategy to match the characteristics of regional environments.

7 Conclusion

This study contributes to the existing literature by introducing a new methodology for the quantitative evaluation of the effectiveness of regional innovation policies. I have developed a model to describe the characteristics of regional innovation systems. Thereafter, the relationships between regional innovation policies represented as resource allocation strategies of local public technology centers and the characteristics of the regions where technology centers were located were tested. There were no significant differences in the strategies adopted by local public technology centers, which corresponded to the characteristics of the regional innovation system. The case of a highly research-intensive technology center described in Sect. 6 (the Osaka Municipal Technical Research Institute) represents the complementary fits between regional policy and regional environment;

however, such cases seem exceptional. As shown in Sect. 2, previous literature has argued that local public technology centers have helped small local firms improve their technological capabilities. However, the results of this study imply that the resources of local public technology centers may not have been optimally utilized to facilitate regional economic development. In other words, local public technology centers might have provided small local firms with irrelevant technological services, and the small local firms might have faced difficulties in finding services that they actually needed. In order to redesign technology center's strategies so that they will match the characteristics of regional environments, the finer and more precise indicator which enables to identify the characteristics of regional innovation systems by technological category should be developed. My future research will incorporate a patent database to describe how small firms invest in R&D in specific technological fields.

References

Anselin L, Varga A, Acs Z (1997) Local geographic spillovers between university research and high technology innovations. J Urban Econ 42:422–448

Autant-Bernard C (2001) Science and knowledge flows: evidence from the French case. Res Pol 30:1069–1078

Beise M, Stahl H (1999) Public research and industrial innovations in Germany. Res Pol 28:397–422

Carayol N (2003) Objectives, agreements and matching in science-industry collaborations: reassembling the pieces of the puzzle. Res Pol 32:887–908

Charles D, Howells J (1992) Technology transfer in Europe: public and private networks. Belhaven Press, London

Cohen W, Levinthal D (1990) Absorptive capacity: a new perspective on learning and innovation. Adm Sci Q 35:128–152

U.S. Congress, Office of Technology Assessment (1990) Making things better: competing in manufacturing, OTA-ITE-443, Washington DC: U.S. Government Printing Office

Cooke P, Heidenreich M, Braczyk H (2004) Regional innovation systems (2nd edition): the role of governance in a globalized world. Rutledge, London

Dziczek K, Luria D, Wiarda E (1998) Assessing the impact of a manufacturing extension center. J Technol Transfer 23:29–35

Feller I, Glasmeier A, Mark M (1996) Issues and perspectives on evaluating manufacturing modernization programs. Res Pol 25:309–319

Fritsch M (2004) Cooperation and the efficiency of regional R&D activities. Cambridge J Econ 28:829–846

Fritsch M, Franke G (2004) Innovation, regional knowledge spillovers and R&D cooperation. Res Pol 33:245–255

Fukugawa N (2006) Determining factors in innovation of small firm networks: a case of cross industry groups in Japan. Small Bus Econ 27:181–193

Hassink R (1997) Technology transfer infrastructures: some lessons from experiences in Europe the US and Japan. Eur Plan Stud 5:351–370

Howells J (1999) Regional systems of innovation? In: Archiburi D, Howells J, Michie J (eds) Innovation policy in a global economy. Cambridge University Press, London, pp 67–93

Izushi H (2003) Impact of the length of relationships upon the use of research institutes by SMEs. Res Pol 32:771–788

Izushi H (2005) Creation of relational assets through the library of equipment model: an industrial modernization approach of Japan's local technology centers. Entrepren Reg Dev 17:183–204
Jaffe A (1989) Real effects of academic research. Am Econ Rev 79:957–970
Jarmin R (1999) Evaluating the impact of manufacturing extension on productivity growth. J Policy Anal Manage 18:99–119
Kneller R (1999) Intellectual property rights and university-industry technology transfer in Japan. Sci Publ Pol 26:113–124
Kneller R (2007) Bridging islands: venture companies and the future of Japanese and American industry. Oxford University Press, New York
Luria D, Wiarda E (1996) Performance benchmarking and measuring program impacts on customers: lessons from the midwest manufacturing technology center. Res Pol 25:233–246
Motohashi K (2005) University-industry collaborations in Japan: the role of new technology-based firms in transforming the national innovation system. Res Pol 34:583–594
Mowery D, Sampat B (2005) Universities in national innovation systems. In: Fagerberg J, Mowery D, Nelson R (eds) Oxford handbook of innovation. Oxford University Press, New York
Oldsman E (1996) Does manufacturing extension matter? An evaluation of the industrial technology extension service in New York. Res Pol 25:215–232
Ronde P, Hussler C (2005) Innovation in regions: what does really matter? Res Pol 34:1150–1172
Ruth K (2006) Innovation policy for SME in Japan: the case of technology transfer centres. In: Storz C (ed) Small firms and innovation policy in Japan. Routledge, London, pp 56–81
Santoro M, Chakrabarti A (2002) Firm size and technology centrality in industry-university interactions. Res Pol 31:1163–1180
Schartinger D, Rammer C, Fischer M, Frohlich J (2002) Knowledge interactions between universities and industry in Austria: sectoral patterns and determinants. Res Pol 31:303–328
Shapira P (1992) Modernizing small manufacturers in Japan: the role of local public technology centers. J Technol Transfer 17:40–57
Shapira P (2001) US manufacturing extension partnerships: technology policy reinvented? Res Pol 30:977–992
Shapira P, Roessner D, Barke R (1995) New public infrastructures for small firm industrial modernization in the USA. Entrepren Reg Dev 7:63–84
Shapira P, Youtie J, Roessner D (1996) Current practices in the evaluation of US industrial modernization programs. Res Pol 25:185–214
Thursby J, Thursby M (2002) Who is selling the Ivory Tower? Sources of growth in university licensing. Manag Sci 48:90–104
Zahra S, George G (2002) Absorptive capacity: a review, reconceptualization, and extension. Acad Manag Rev 27:185–203

Schumpeterian Patterns of Innovation and the Sources of Breakthrough Inventions: Evidence from a Data-set of R&D Awards

Roberto Fontana, Alessandro Nuvolari, Hiroshi Shimizu, and Andrea Vezzulli

Abstract This paper examines the relationship between Schumpeterian patterns of innovation and the generation of breakthrough inventions. Our data source for breakthrough inventions is the "R&D 100 awards" competition organized each year by the magazine *Research & Development*. Since 1963, this magazine has been awarding this prize to 100 most technologically significant new products available for sale or licensing in the year preceding the judgment. We use USPTO patent data to measure the relevant dimensions of the technological regime prevailing in each sector and, on this basis, we provide a characterization of each sector in terms of the Schumpeter Mark I/Schumpeter Mark II archetypes. Our main finding is that breakthrough inventions are more likely to emerge in 'turbulent' Schumpeter Mark I type of contexts.

Reprinted from Evolutionary Economics 22(4), 785-810, Springer (2012)

R. Fontana (✉)
Department of Economics and Management, University of Pavia, Via San Felice 6, 27100, Pavia, Italy

CRIOS – Bocconi University, Via Sarfatti 25, 20139 Milano, Italy
e-mail: roberto.fontana@unibocconi.it

A. Nuvolari
LEM – Sant'Anna School of Advanced Studies, Piazza Martiri della Liberta' 33, 56172 Pisa, Italy
e-mail: alessandro.nuvolari@sssup.it

H. Shimizu
Institute of Innovation Research, Hitotsubashi University, Tokyo, Japan
e-mail: shimizu@iir.hit-u.ac.jp

A. Vezzulli
UECE-ISEG, Universitade Técnica de Lisboa, Rua Miguel Lupi, 20, 1249-078 Lisboa, Portugal
e-mail: andreav@iseg.utl.pt

A. Pyka and E.S. Andersen (eds.), *Long Term Economic Development*, Economic Complexity and Evolution, DOI 10.1007/978-3-642-35125-9_14,

1 Introduction

One of the robust findings emerging from the rich body of empirical research on innovation carried out over the last thirty years is that innovative activities differ across industries along several dimensions, such as the knowledge base underlying innovation processes, the type of actors and institutions involved in innovative activities, the characteristics and the economic effects of innovations (Malerba 2005). These differences have been highlighted both by detailed case studies of individual sectors (see, for example, the essays collected in Mowery and Nelson 1999) and by empirical contributions that have systematically compared quantitative measures of innovation with other economic characteristics of sectors (Cohen 2010).

In the evolutionary economics literature these differences in patterns of innovative activities across sectors have been captured by means of taxonomic exercises. The aim of these exercises was to identify in the welter of the empirical evidence some archetypical configurations capturing the key-dimensions in which the structure of innovative activities differs systematically across sectors. Within this approach, one of the most common distinctions proposed to summarize the inter-sectoral differences in patterns of innovation is the characterization of industries in terms of Schumpeter Mark I and Schumpeter Mark II patterns. Schumpeter Mark I industries are characterized by turbulent environments with relatively low entry barriers, where innovations are (mostly) generated and developed by new 'entrepreneurial' firms. Accordingly, technological competition among firms in Schumpeter Mark I industries assumes the form of "creative destruction", with successful innovating entrants replacing incumbents. In contrast, Schumpeter Mark II industries are characterized by stable environments with relatively high entry barriers in which innovations are generated and developed by large established firms. In Schumpeter Mark II industries, technological competition assumes the form of "creative accumulation", with incumbent firms introducing innovations by mean of a process of consolidation of their technological capabilities along well established technological trajectories (Malerba 2005: 382). The terms Schumpeter Mark I and Mark II refer to the well-known distinction between the early view of innovation that Schumpeter advanced in *The Theory of Economic Development* (1911) ("Schumpeter Mark I") and the later view proposed by Schumpeter in *Capitalism, Socialism and Democracy* ("Schumpeter Mark II").

A substantial empirical literature has shown the existence of these two patterns of innovation as characteristic of many industrial sectors in different countries using data such as patents (Malerba and Orsenigo 1995, 1996) or responses to innovation surveys (Castellacci 2007). One relatively robust empirical finding is that Schumpeterian patterns of innovation are, by and large, technology-specific. More specifically, in different countries, the same industries display similar patterns of innovation (Malerba and Orsenigo 1996). Following this cue, most research efforts have tried to relate the two Schumpeterian patterns to a number of specific technological dimensions summarized by the concept of technological regime.

A technological regime, as defined by Malerba and Orsenigo (1995, 1996, 1997), Breschi et al. (2000) is a synthetic description of the "framework conditions" (Castellacci 2007: 1111) in which innovative activities take place. These conditions shape the processes of variety generation and selection among the firms in the sector and, through this channel, they affect both the organization of innovative activities and the market structure of the industry. (Malerba and Orsenigo 1996, 1997) have proposed that the key dimensions of a technological regime are the level of technological opportunities, the degree of appropriability of innovations, the cumulativeness of technological advances and the characteristics of the knowledge base underlying innovative activities. In general, the evidence suggests that Schumpeter Mark I patterns of innovation emerge in the presence of high technological opportunities, low appropriability, and low cumulativeness. By contrast, high appropriability and high cumulativeness are conducive to the emergence of Schumpeter Mark II patterns.[1]

While most of the contributions in this field have studied the precise relationships between the dimensions of technological regimes and the sectoral patterns of innovative activities, the overall connection between technological regimes and the innovation performance of sectors have received much less attention. A notable exception is the recent contribution of Castellacci (2007) investigating the relationship between technological regimes and productivity growth.

In this paper, we focus on the relation between sectoral patterns of innovation and a more specific dimension of innovative performance, the generation of breakthrough inventions. This approach is somewhat reminiscent of the debate on the 'sources of invention' triggered by the contribution of Jewkes et al. (1958) who, on the basis of 70 case studies of breakthrough inventions, argued that, notwithstanding the emergence of corporate research laboratories, the most important inventions of the first half of the twentieth century had been actually generated by individual inventors and small companies. In other words, the ultimate source of truly significant inventions was outside the walls of the corporate research and development laboratories. For our purposes, we consider as breakthrough inventions the inventions that have won a prestigious competition organized by one of the leading magazines for R&D practitioners. In comparison to other measures of innovative performance such as patents or productivity, this type of indicator seems to represent a more 'direct' measure of innovative performance. Furthermore, since in this paper we shall follow the common practice to use patent data to measure the relevant dimensions of the technological regimes, it seems useful to have a direct indicator of innovative performance at the sectoral level that is not also constructed using patents. The paper is structured as follows. Section 2 reviews the relevant background literature. Section 3 introduces our database. Section 4 presents the empirical results, and Section 5 concludes.

[1] Schumpeter Mark II patterns are, in principle, consistent both with low and high degrees of technological opportunities (Breschi et al. 2000: 395).

2 Background Literature

2.1 *Technological Regimes and Schumpeterian Patterns of Innovation*

In retrospect, some of the modern research on sectoral patterns of innovation emerged out of a feeling of dissatisfaction towards the 'mixed' evidence produced by the testing of the so-called 'Schumpeterian hypothesis' postulating a positive effect of firm size and market concentration on innovation. Following a suggestion of Nelson and Winter (1982), Malerba and Orsenigo (1995, 1996, 1997) argued that the inconclusive results of the literature studying the relationship between market structure and rates of innovation were due to a failure properly to acknowledge the specific conditions of technological opportunities and appropriability prevailing in each sector and, relatedly, to recognize that both innovation and market structure ought to be regarded as endogenous variables jointly determined by the nature of the prevailing technological regimes.

Malerba and Orsenigo's approach to this issue was to examine systematically sectoral patterns of innovation across countries using patent data. In general, they found that it was possible to use the Schumpeter Mark I–Schumpeter Mark II distinction to characterize sectoral patterns of innovative activities in all the major industrialized countries. In particular, Malerba and Orsenigo (1995) examined patterns of innovation in different technology classes using USPTO patents over the period 1969–1986 for four European countries (Germany, France, UK and Italy), while Malerba and Orsenigo (1996) carried out a similar exercise using EPO patents over the period 1978–1991 for six major industrialized countries (USA, Germany, UK, France, Italy and Japan). The dimensions considered in the assessment of the patterns of innovation were: i) concentration and asymmetries among innovating firms in each sector (measured, respectively, by the C4 concentration ratio and the Herfindahl index computed using the shares of patents hold by different firms); ii) size of the innovating firms (measured as the total share of patents in the technology class belonging to firms with more than 500 employees); iii) changes over time in the hierarchy of innovators (measured using the Spearman correlation coefficient of the patents owned between the innovating firms in different periods); iv) relevance of the entry of new innovators (measured as the share of patents of firms applying for the first time in a specific technology class).

Malerba and Orsenigo's findings showed that technology classes with low concentration and reduced asymmetries among innovating firms were characterized by the relatively small size of innovating firms, changes in the hierarchy of innovators and considerable innovators' entry, pointing towards a Schumpeter Mark I pattern. By contrast, technology classes with high concentration and asymmetries among innovating firms were characterized by the large size of innovators, a relative stability in the hierarchy of innovators, and limited entry, pointing towards a Schumpeter Mark II pattern. These results were further corroborated by a principal component analysis on the variables mentioned above. In all countries, the principal component analysis produced one dominant factor (explaining in all cases more than 50 % of the variance) the loadings of which are fully consistent with the Schumpeter Mark I/Schumpeter Mark II distinction. The overall conclusion of these investigations was the recognition of systematic differences across industries in the patterns of innovation (differences that it is possible to characterize in terms of the Schumpeter Mark I and Schumpeter Mark II dichotomy) and of similarities across countries in sectoral patterns of innovation for a specific technology (Malerba and Orsenigo 1997: 94).

Malerba and Orsenigo's interpretive hypothesis of this finding is that the emergence of these two sectoral patterns of innovation is accounted for by different 'technological regimes' that shape and constrain innovative processes in different sectors. In their definition, a technological regime is a synthetic description of the technological environment in which firms act. More specifically, a technological regime is a specific combination of some basic characteristics of technologies: opportunity conditions, appropriability conditions, cumulativeness of technical progress, and the nature of the knowledge base (Malerba and Orsenigo 1997: 94). The hypothesis is that Schumpeter Mark I patterns of innovation emerge in contexts characterized by high technological opportunities, low appropriability and low cumulativeness, whereas Schumpeter Mark II pattern emerge in contexts of high appropriability and cumulativeness (technological opportunities can be both high or low). Breschi et al. (2000) provided a first (successful) test of these hypotheses concerning the relationship between technological regimes and sectoral patterns of innovation using data from the PACE innovation survey to measure the relevant dimensions of the technological regimes and EPO patents to measure the sectoral patterns of innovation.

Further contributions have confirmed the merits of introducing the Schumpeter Mark I/ Schumpeter Mark II distinction.[2] Van Dijk (2000) studied the industrial structure and dynamics in Dutch manufacturing and found consistent differences in the patterns of industrial dynamics between Schumpeter Mark I and Schumpeter Mark II industries. The distinction between Schumpeter Mark I and Schumpeter Mark II seems also useful to study patterns of innovation with broad technological fields. For example, Corrocher et al. (2007) have shown the existence of Schumpeter Mark I and Schumpeter Mark II patterns of innovation examining patents taken in different sub-segments of ICT applications.

More recently, the focus of the empirical investigations has shifted towards the connection between technological regimes and innovation performance. Castellacci (2007) studied the relationship the relationship between differences in sectoral productivity growth and technological regimes in nine European countries

[2] Other contributions have, however, argued that the Schumpeter Mark I–Schumpeter Mark II distinction may be too narrow and does not map adequately the large empirical variety of inter-sectoral patterns of innovative activities. Therefore more articulated taxonomies of innovation patterns have been proposed. The most famous example is the Pavitt's taxonomy (Pavitt 1984). For a comprehensive discussion, see Marsili and Verspagen (2002).

(Germany, France, Italy, Netherlands, Norway, Portugal, Sweden, UK and Austria) in the period 1996–2001. Technological regimes are defined in terms of technological opportunities, appropriability and cumulativeness, and the measurement of the different dimensions of technological regimes is based on responses to the CIS surveys. Castellacci finds that Schumpeter Mark II sectors are characterized by higher rates of productivity growth. Furthermore, the relationship between the different characteristics of the technological regimes and productivity is different in the two Schumpeterian patterns.

2.2 *Schumpeterian Patterns of Innovation and Breakthrough Inventions*

Another critical dimension of technological performance is the emergence of breakthrough inventions. The recent emphasis on the key role of breakthrough inventions is related to the growing appreciation of the highly skewed nature of innovation size distributions (Silverberg and Verspagen 2007). Clearly, if the majority of innovations yield only modest returns and most economic value is actually generated by relatively few breakthrough inventions situated in the tail of the value distribution, the search for the possible determinants of these breakthrough inventions becomes a fundamental research issue (Scherer and Harhoff 2000).

Existing approaches to the study of the role of breakthrough invention can be classified into two camps. On the one hand, there are historians of technology and economic historians who have frequently acknowledged that serendipity plays a large role in the generation of breakthrough inventions. Mokyr (1990: 13) is possibly summarizing what is the conventional wisdom on this issue when he writes: "macro-inventions [. . .] do not seem to obey obvious laws, do not necessarily respond to incentives and defy most attempts to relate them to exogenous economic variables. Many of them resulted from strokes of genius, luck or serendipity. Technological history, therefore, retains an unexplained component that defies explanation in purely economic terms. In other words, luck and inspiration mattered, and thus individuals made a difference". Still, some economic historians have been able to unravel some significant relationship between breakthrough inventions and economic and social variables (Khan and Sokoloff 1993).

On the other hand, there is the recent literature in management. Ahuia and Lampert (2001) assess the relationship between breakthrough inventions and R&D strategies at firm level. Their findings suggest that established firms tapping new technologies are more likely to introduce breakthrough inventions. Chandy and Tellis (2000) look at the role of incumbent firms in the generation of radical innovations. They find that, despite their inertia, established firms can be an important source of radical innovations. Finally, Schoenmakers and Duysters (2010) analyze the connection between breakthrough inventions and different types of knowledge. They find that radical inventions are to a higher degree based on existing knowledge rather than incremental inventions. They also find that inter-firms collaborations play an important role in the development of radical inventions, as highlighted also by Singh and Fleming (2010) at the individual inventor level.

This paper contributes to this emerging literature on the sources of breakthrough inventions by examining this issue from the perspective of the literature on Schumpeterian patterns of innovation. More specifically, we shall not deal directly with the issue of the possible economic and social determinants of major macro-inventions, but we shall limit ourselves to study the possible role played by different Schumpeterian patterns of innovation in the generation of breakthrough inventions. If it turns out that Schumpeterian patterns affect the generation of breakthrough inventions, it is important that future contributions devoted to study of the sources of breakthrough inventions at micro level will try to control explicitly for the dimensions of the technological regime prevailing in the industries under consideration. A similar exercise was carried out by Granstrand and Alange (1995) for the Swedish case using a sample of 100 'significant' inventions that occurred in the period 1945–1980, although their focus was not so much on the impact of the technological regimes but on the relative contribution of different organizational structures (individual inventors, small firms, large firms) to the generation of inventive breakthroughs. Their findings were mixed. They found that large firms were responsible for 80 % of the inventions in their sample, but still a sizable share of breakthrough inventions (i.e. the remaining 20 %) could be ascribed to individual inventors and small firms.

3 The "R&D 100" Awards Database

Our source of data is the 'R&D 100 Awards' competition organized by the magazine *Research and Development* (previously called *Industrial Research*). The magazine, founded in 1959, is one of the most authoritative regular publications for R&D practitioners.[3] The 'R&D 100 Awards' competition has been running continuously since 1963. Each year the magazine awards with a prize the 100 most technologically significant products available for sale or licensing in the year preceding the judgment.

Throughout the years, breakthroughs inventions such as Polacolor film (1963), the flashcube (1965), the automated teller machine (1973), the halogen lamp (1974), the fax machine (1975), the liquid crystal display (1980), the printer (1986), the Kodak Photo CD (1991), the Nicoderm antismoking patch (1992) and Taxol anticancer drug (1993) have received the prize. In order to apply for the prize, the inventors or their companies must fill out an application form providing a

[3] The information reported here on R&D magazine and the R&D competition was retrieved from http://www.rdmag.com, last accessed on 7/7/2011.

detailed description of the invention. The prize consists of a plaque which is presented at a special ceremony. There is no monetary prize. The prize is awarded by a jury composed of university professors, industrial researchers and consultants with a certified level of competence in the areas they are called upon to asses. Jury members are selected by the editor of the magazine and inventions are assessed according to two criteria: i) technological significance (i.e., whether the product can be considered a major breakthrough from a technical point of view) and ii) competitive significance (i.e., how the performance of the product compares to rival solutions available on the market). R&D 100 awards are accolades comparable to the Oscars for the motion picture industry as "they carry considerable prestige within the community of R&D professionals" (Block and Keller 2009: 464).

There are a number of characteristics of the R&D 100 awards competition that, *prima facie*, appear particularly promising for the study of inventive breakthroughs. First, the R&D 100 awards competition represents a good opportunity for companies, and government laboratories to showcase their inventions. Second, R&D 100 awards are granted to inventions that, at least in principle, should embody a clearly documented improvement of the state-of-the-art (i.e. a technological breakthrough). Third, the selection of the awards is made by a competent, authoritative jury of experts. Fourth, R&D awards may be assigned both to patented and not-patented inventions. Finally, there seems to be limited space for strategic behaviors and attempts to conditioning the jury, because the nature of the prize is simply honorific.

Given these properties, it is surprising that economists of innovation have so far paid scant attention to this type of data. To the best of our knowledge, the R&D 100 awards data have been so far only used in three contributions: Carpenter et al. (1981), Scherer (1989) and, more recently, Block and Keller (2009). Carpenter et al. (1981) used these data to study differences in citations received between patents covering awarded inventions and a random sample of patents, providing an important corroboration for the use of forward citations as an indicator of patent quality. Scherer (1989) used information on the mean and maximum R&D costs of the awarded inventions to study the distribution of R&D investments. Finally, Block and Keller (2009) used the R&D 100 awards to gain insights on the growing importance of public institutions in the US innovation system over the period 1971–2006. From our perspective, it is reassuring that three authoritative contributions in the field of innovation studies have employed the data to study the nature of breakthrough inventions.

4 Empirical Analysis

Retrieving the information from different issues the magazine, we have constructed a dataset with all the R&D 100 awards granted from 1963 to 2005. In this section we use the dataset to study the impact of different Schumpeterian regimes on the generation of breakthrough inventions. We proceed in two steps. First, we introduce some preliminary descriptive statistics of the dataset to check the reliability of the source. Second, we carry out an econometric study of the probability of the occurrence of breakthrough invention as a function of the Schumpeterian regime prevailing at the sectoral level.

4.1 Descriptive Statistics

Figure 1 displays the share of awards granted to US applicants for the prize. The nationality of the applicants has been assigned using the organization, rather than by looking at the nationality of the inventors. Over the period 1963–2002, the share of US awards declined indicating that other countries closed the gap with the US in terms of technological performance. Interestingly enough, during the period 2003–2005, the US recovered their edge, but, of course, this is a too short span of time for detecting clear trends.

Figure 2 displays the share of awards received by applicants from different countries by sub-periods excluding the US that, as one would have expected given the nature of the competition and the place of publication of the magazine, dominate the sample. The figures clearly indicate that Japan and Germany are the two most prominent contenders of US technological leadership. Figure 2 shows how this effort of closing the gap evolved over time, with Japan and Germany progressively overtaking two older established players, France, and UK.

Figure 3 shows the shares of awards granted to different type of organizations. The trends here are consistent with the literature that has recently pointed out the increasing involvement in inventive activities of a number of new actors such as government laboratories and universities. Whereas in the early 1960s, corporations were the primary source of inventions, in the most recent years this has clearly not been the case.

Figure 4 displays the number of awards that are the outcome of collaborative activities. The figure shows an increasing trend which is fully consistent with the emphasis that has been put on the growing role of cooperation and networking in the field of innovative activities (Freeman 1991).

To carry out our analysis at the sectoral level, we classified each awarded invention according to a technology-oriented classification of 30 different sectors based on the co-occurrence of the International Patent Classification (IPC) codes proposed by the *Observatoire des Sciences et des Techniques* (OST).[4] We assigned each R&D 100 invention to only one of the 30 OST sectors. These sectors were further aggregated into 5 'macro' technological classes (called 'OST5' henceforth) defined according to the ISI-INIPI-OST patent classification based on the EPO IPC technological classes, as reported in Table 1.[5]

[4] See Hinze et al. (1997).

[5] Technology-oriented classification system jointly elaborated by the German Fraunhofer Institute of Systems and Innovation Research (ISI), the French Patent Office (INIPI) and the Observatoire des Science and des Techniques (OST).

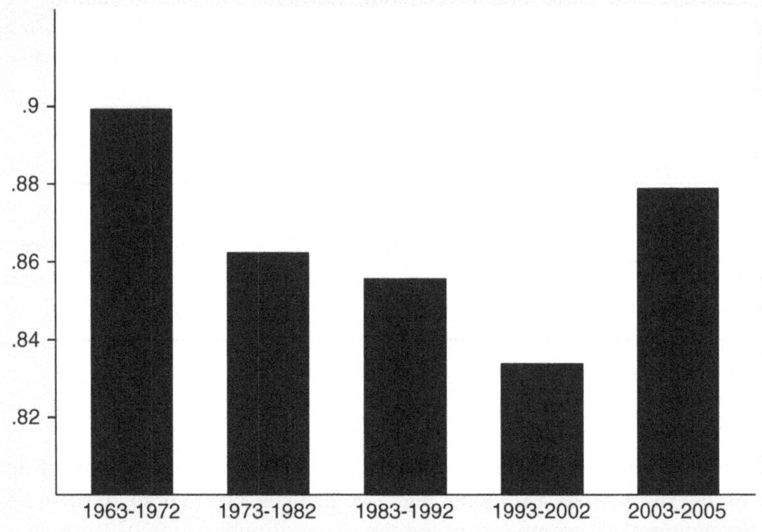

Fig. 1 Share of "R&D 100"awards received by US applicants

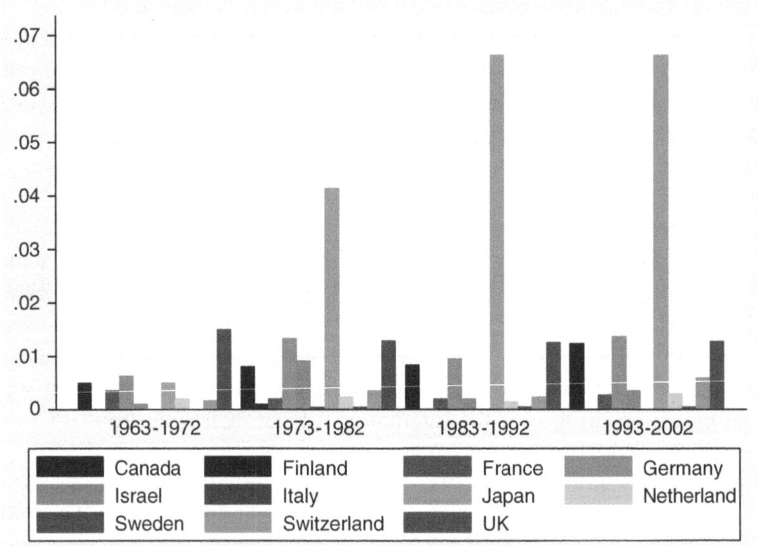

Fig. 2 Share of "R&D 100" awards received by applicants of different countries

Figure 5 contains histograms showing the distribution of the awarded inventions across the 30 OST sectors.

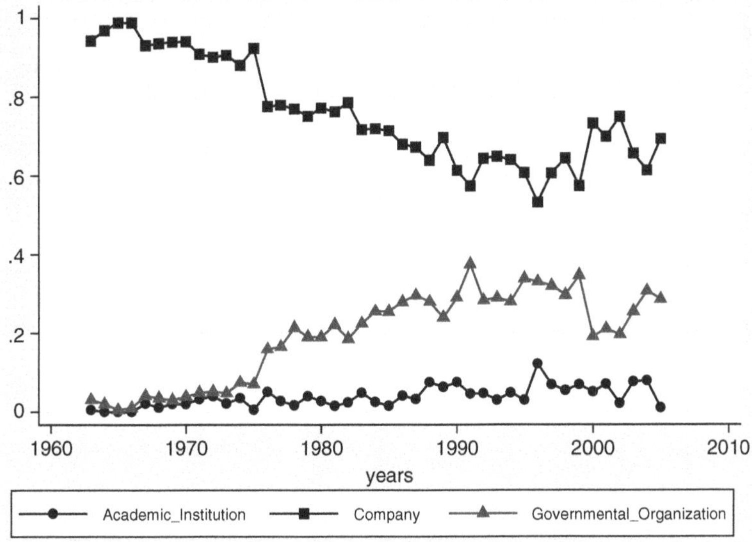

Fig. 3 Shares of "R&D 100" awards granted to different type of organization

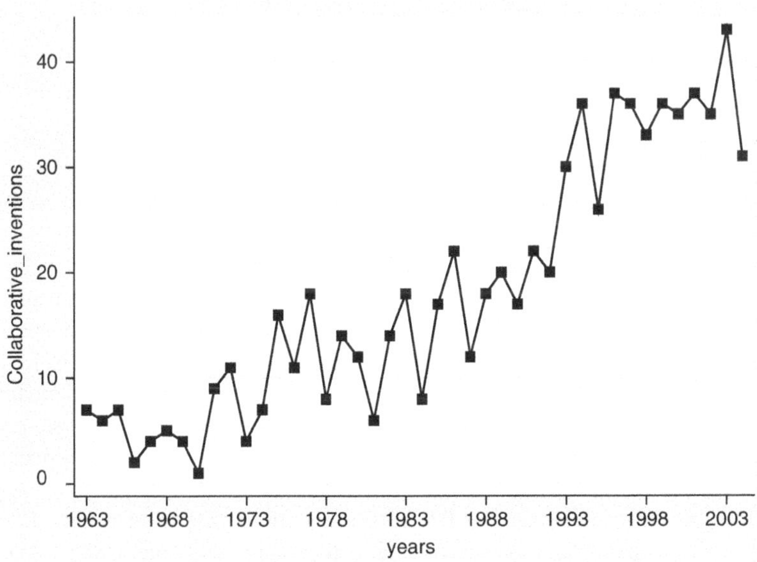

Fig. 4 Number of collaborative inventions receiving an "R&D 100" award

As one would have expected, there is some distortion towards 'high-tech' sectors such as instruments, biotechnology, information and communication technologies, optics (lasers), and semiconductors. The predominant sector is instrumentation

Table 1 Aggregation of the 30 ISI-INPI-OST sectors in 5 macro-classes

MacroISI-INIPI-OST	ISI-INIPI-OST	Technological class
1	1, 2, 3, 4, 5	Electrical engineering
2	6, 7, 8, 27	Instruments
3	9, 10, 11, 12, 14, 15	Chemistry & pharmaceuticals
4	13, 16, 17, 18, 20, 24, 25	Process engineering
5	19, 21, 22, 23, 26, 28, 29, 30	Mechanical engineering

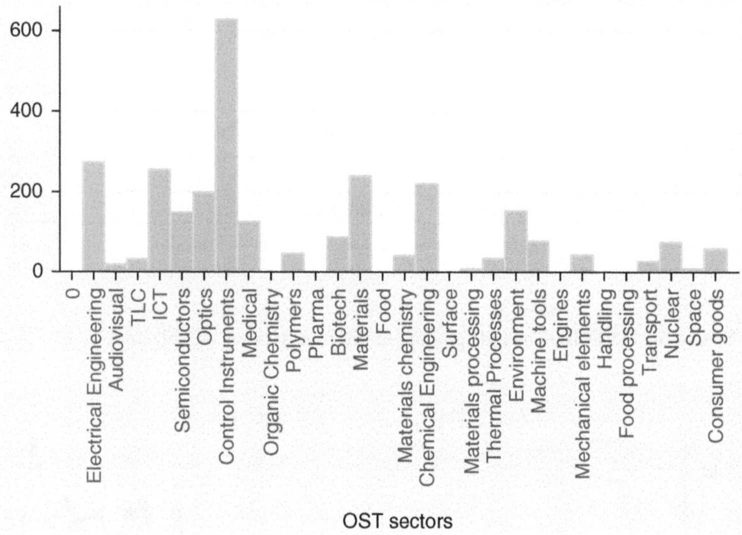

Fig. 5 Distribution of "R&D 100" awards across technology classes, 1963–2005

(control instruments). On the one hand, this may be clearly explained by the interests of the editors and the readership of the magazine, given that instrumentation plays a central role in the majority of modern R&D processes. On the other hand, this may be the consequence of the fact that it is easier for inventions in these categories to prove that they are superior to the state of the art by means of quantitative assessment of technological performance. All in all, these results confirm that the R&D 100 awards tend to cover, as one would have expected, a high-tech R&D intensive segment of the economy.

Finally, we check whether the R&D 100 inventions that were patented (more specifically, those for which we were able to match with one USPTO patent) receive more citations than an analogous random sample of patents. Accordingly, for each R&D invention with a USPTO patent we construct a 'matched random' sample of ten patents from the same grant year and from the same IPC class.

Table 2 Patent citations received by R&D 100 inventions and a random sample of patents (matched by granted year and technology class)

	Number	Mean	Median	Standard deviation	Min	Max
R&D 100 patents	535	12.88037	7	16.17822	0	137
Random Sample	5331	8.483024	4	14.11133	0	329

Mann–Whitney test rejects the null hypothesis of equal populations

The results of this test are reported in Table 2.[6] The non parametric Mann–Whitney test confirms that the median number of citations of patents associated with a R&D 100 invention is significantly higher than the median of the random matched sample. These results confirm the early findings of Carpenter et al. (1981) obtained for the two years 1969–1970 of awards and provides an important corroboration for our use of the R&D 100 data set as an indicator of breakthrough inventions.

4.2 The Econometric Exercise

In this section, we carry out our econometric exercise. Our main explanatory variables are constituted by a set of time-varying indicators constructed using patent based data for each of the five macro-classes mentioned above. These indicators aim at capturing different patterns of innovative activities across classes and over time.[7] Following the contributions of Breschi et al. (2000), Hall et al. (2001) and Corrocher et al. (2007), we computed the indicators as follows (where $j = 1,..,5$ for each OST5 sector and $t = 1976,\ldots, 2006$ is the year of granting of each patent):

1) $PAT_{GROWTH_{jt}} = \frac{pat_{jt} - pat_{jt-1}}{pat_{jt-1}}$ where pat_{jt} is the total number of patents granted in OST5 class j in year t.
2) $Entry_{jt} = \frac{newpat_{jt}}{pat_{jt}}$ where $newpat_{jt}$ is the total number of patents granted in OST5 class j in year t by new innovators (i.e. by firms patenting for the first time in class j).
3) $C4_{jt}$ representing the concentration ratio of the top four patenting firms (in terms of number of patents granted in a given year t and class j).

[6] The random matched sample includes 5331 patents and not 5350 because, for some specific years in some technology classes, it was not possible to collect enough patents to create the match.

[7] Our main source of information is the NBER Patent Data Project which collects a very comprehensive set of information on USPTO patents for the 1976–2006 period (e.g. dates of application and grant, inventors and applicant's name, number of claims, technological classes, forward and backward citations, etc.). The reclassification of all USPTO patents according to the 2008 IPC classification system is available on the NBER Patent Data Project website and it has been performed on the basis of the International Patent Classification Eighth Edition available at: http://www.uspto.gov/go/classification/uspc002/us002toipc8.htm. For a comprehensive description of the database, see Hall et al. (2001).

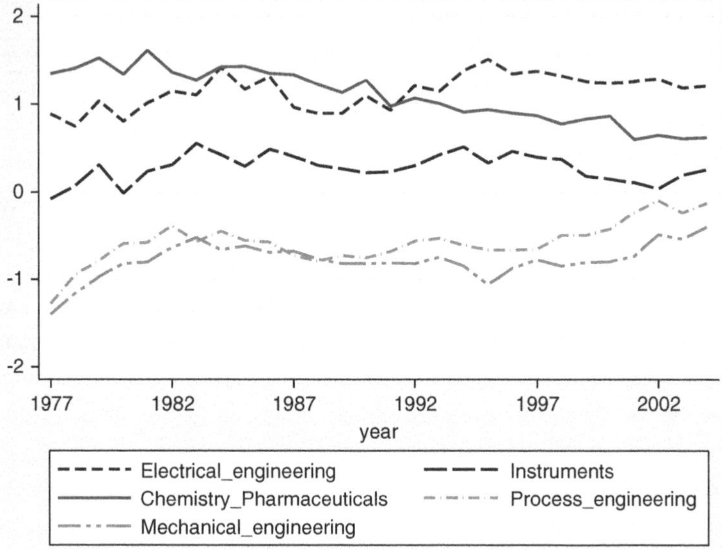

Fig. 6 The dynamics of SCHUMP for each OST5 macro sector (1977–2005)

4) $Stability_{jt}$ is the Spearman rank correlation coefficient between hierarchies (in term of number of patents granted) of firms patenting in year t and firms patenting in year $t-1$ in class j.

Following Breschi et al. (2000), the last three indicators (*Entry*, *C*4 and *Stability*) are consolidated in a unique indicator called $Schump_{jt}$ by means of principal component analysis. $Schump_{jt}$ is our main variable of interest and represents the prediction obtained using the scoring coefficients of the first component and the standardized values of the original variables.[8] It provides an indication of the type of Schumpeterian pattern of innovation prevailing in a given class i in year t. High values of $Schump_{jt}$ indicate a Schumpeter Mark II type regime (i.e., a "deepening" pattern of innovative activities with a concentrated and stable population of innovators). Low values of $Schump_{jt}$ indicate a Schumpeter Mark I type regime (i.e., a "widening" pattern with a large and turbulent population of innovators) (Breschi et al. 2000). Figure 6 depicts the different trend of $Schump_{jt}$ across the OST5 macro sectors within our time window.

Two sectors (Electrical Engineering and Chemistry & Pharmaceuticals) are consistently close to a Schumpeter Mark II type of pattern, while two other sectors (Mechanical and Process Engineering) are close to a Schumpeter Mark I type of pattern and one sector (Instruments) displays an intermediate pattern between these two.

[8] The extracted principal component accounts for about 70 % of the total variance. The correlations between the principal component and our three original indicators *C4, Entry*, and *Stability* are 0.37, −0.67 and 0.64, respectively.

5) $Herfsources_{tech_{jt}}$ is an index of the relative variety of knowledge sources across technological classes and is calculated in a similar way as in Corrocher et al. (2007). Let $a_{jht} = \frac{c_{jht}}{c_{jt}}$ be the share of backward citations from patents granted in year t and belonging to OST5 class j to previous patents in IPC class h (defined at 4 digit level), where c_{jht} is the total number of patents belonging to IPC class h and cited by patents granted in year t and belonging to OST5 class j and $c_{jt} = \sum_h c_{jht}$.
   Let then $v_{jht} = \frac{p_{jht}}{p_{jt}}$ be the share of patents (for each granting year t) in OST5 class j belonging to IPC class h. Let $Herf_{tech_{jt}}$ and $Herfcit_{tech_{jt}}$ be the corrected Herfindahl indexes (Hall et al. 2001) calculated using, respectively, the shares c_{jht} and v_{jht} and indicating how much each OST5 class j and its knowledge sources are concentrated (in term of number of patents granted and number of backward citations made) across different IPC 4 digit sub-classes in a given year t. The resulting relative index of concentration of knowledge sources across IPC technological classes is given by the ratio of the previous two indexes: $Herfsources_{tech_{jt}} = \frac{Herfcit_{tech_{jt}}}{Herf_{tech_{jt}}}$.
6) $Herfsources_{firm_{jt}} = \frac{Herfcit_{firm_{jt}}}{Herffirm_{jt}}$. This is an index of the relative variety of knowledge sources across firms and is calculated (for each granting year t) in a similar way as $Herfsources_{tech_{jt}}$. Here the Herfindahl index at the numerator is calculated using the shares of backward citations from patents in class j to patents applied by firm z: $b_{jzt} = \frac{d_{jzt}}{d_{jt}}$, where d_{jzt} is the total number of cited patents from OST5 class j applied by firm z (excluding self citations) and $d_{jt} = \sum_z d_{jzt}$. The Herfindahl index at the denominator measures the degree of concentration across firms in a given class j calculated with respect to the number of patents granted in a given year t.
7) $Selfsources_{jt} = \frac{sc_{jt}}{c_{jt}}$ is an index of intensity of internal knowledge sources and is defined for each OST5 class j and granting year t as the ratio between the total number of self-citations (i.e. backward citations to patents applied by the same firm z) over the total number of backward citations.

In addition to these indicators we also include 'applicant level' variables and further controls. Our final reference period of analysis ranges from 1977 to 2005 with a total of 2802 inventions awarded.[9] Table 3 gives a comprehensive overview of the variables used in the econometric exercise.

Tables 4 and 5 report the main descriptive statistics of the variables used in the analysis, as well as the distribution of the awarded inventions across sectors and over time.

[9] We dropped the first (1976) and last (2005) year of reference to avoid possible inconsistencies when calculating our time-varying industry indicators based on patent data.

Table 3 Description of the variables

	Description	Type
Dependent variable		
OST5	Invention-type classification according to OST5 (see Table 1)	5 categories: j = 1,2,3,4,5.
Independent variables		
Sector-level characteristics	j = category of the invention (OST5); t = year of award	
PAT_GROWTH_{jt}	Patent growth rate	Continuous
$SCHUMP_{jt}$	Schumpeterian pattern of innovative activities index	Continuous
$HERFSOURCES\_TECH_{jt}$	Variety of knowledge sources across technological classes index	Continuous
$HERFSOURCES\_FIRM_{jt}$	Variety of knowledge sources across firms index	Continuous
$SELFSOURCES_{jt}$	Intensity of internal knowledge sources index	Continuous
Invention-level characteristics		
MAPPL	= 1 for multiple applicant organizations, = 0 otherwise	Dummy
NINV	Number of inventors	Count
USA	= 1 if at least one applicant is a U.S. organization, = 0 otherwise	Dummy
GOV	= 1 if at least one applicant is a governmental organization, = 0 otherwise	Dummy
ACAD	= 1 if at least one applicant is an academic organization, =0 otherwise	Dummy
Other controls		
dum1986_1995	= 1 the invention has been awarded in the 1986–1995 decade, = 0 otherwise	Dummy
dum1996_2005	= 1 the invention has been awarded in the 1996–2005 decade, = 0 otherwise	Dummy

In our first model, we analyze the factors affecting the probability of observing a breakthrough invention in each OST5 sector by considering both industry-level technological regimes and invention specific characteristics. Even though in our setting this probability does not obviously reflect directly the specific choice made by an individual amongst a fixed set of alternatives maximizing a latent utility function, we can assume that the observed distribution of prizes across sectors (as resulting by the yearly decision of the awarding board) would mimic quite closely how 'nature' chooses in which sectors a breakthrough invention is more likely to occur.

We, therefore, rely on the estimation of a Conditional Multinomial Logit (CML) model with both alternative-varying and individual-varying covariates. In this setting, the probability of observing a breakthrough invention i in a given macro-sector j is defined as:

Table 4 Descriptive statistics

Variable	Obs	Mean	Std. dev.	Min	Max
OST5	2802	2.514	1.322	1	5
PAT_GROWTH$_{jt}$	2802	0.049	0.126	−0.290	0.478
SCHUMP$_{jt}$	2802	0.261	0.733	−1.412	1.602
HERFSOURCES_TECH$_{jt}$	2802	0.521	0.103	0.273	0.910
HERFSOURCES_FIRM$_{jt}$	2802	0.841	0.156	0.565	1.382
SELFSOURCES$_{jt}$	2802	0.142	0.048	0.085	0.448
MAPPL	2802	0.256	0.437	0	1
NINV	2802	1.665	0.902	1	5
USA	2802	0.877	0.329	0	1
GOV	2802	0.320	0.467	0	1
ACAD	2802	0.074	0.262	0	1
dum1986_1995	2802	0	0	0	1
dum1996_2005	2802	0.322	0.467	0	1

$$pr_{ij} = \frac{\exp(X_{ij}\beta + Z_i\gamma_i)}{\sum_{i=1}^{m}\exp(X_{ij}\beta + Z_i\gamma_i)} \tag{1}$$

where X_{ij} are a set of alternative-specific and Z_i are a set of case-specific covariates, respectively. Table 6 reports the estimated coefficients for the model.

The marginal effects for individual-specific covariates are computed as follows:

$$\frac{\partial pr_{ij}}{\partial Z_i} = pr_{ij}(\gamma_j - \bar{\gamma}_t) \tag{2}$$

where $\bar{\gamma}_t$ is a probability weighted average of the estimated coefficients. The marginal effect for a given alternative-specific covariate x_{rik} (i.e. the value of the covariate x_r for individual i and alternative k) is computed as:

$$\frac{\partial pr_{ij}}{\partial x_{rik}} = \{@r@ \quad lpr_{ij}(1 - pr_{ij})\beta_r for \quad j = k - pr_{ij}pr_{ik}\beta_r for \quad j \neq k\}. \tag{3}$$

Thus the own-marginal effect (for $j = k$) has the same sign of the estimated coefficient, whereas the cross-marginal effect (for $j \neq k$) has the opposite sign.

In Table 7 below, we report only individual-specific and own alternative-specific marginal effects. For each alternative, they are computed at the average value of each covariate.

Collaboration (i.e. having a multiple applicant) (MAPPL) decreases the probability of observing a breakthrough invention in the sector of Instruments (−0.073), whereas it increases the probability of observing a breakthrough invention in the sector of Mechanical Engineering (+0.087). Breakthrough inventions with at least one U.S applicant organization are more likely to occur in the Chemistry &

Table 5 Distribution of 'R&D 100' awards across sectors

Year	Electrical eng.	Instruments	Chemistry & pharma	Process eng.	Mechanical eng.	All sectors
1977	20 (20.2 %)	38 (38.38 %)	14 (14.14 %)	18 (18.18 %)	9 (9.09 %)	99 (100 %)
1978	24 (24.24 %)	37 (37.37 %)	17 (17.17 %)	14 (14.14 %)	7 (7.07 %)	99 (100 %)
1979	33 (32.35 %)	32 (31.37 %)	18 (17.65 %)	12 (11.76 %)	7 (6.86 %)	102 (100 %)
1980	35 (32.11 %)	32 (29.36 %)	8 (7.34 %)	30 (27.52 %)	4 (3.67 %)	109 (100 %)
1981	24 (24.74 %)	47 (48.45 %)	7 (7.22 %)	13 (13.4 %)	6 (6.19 %)	97 (100 %)
1982	25 (25.25 %)	40 (40.4 %)	7 (7.07 %)	17 (17.17 %)	10 (10.1 %)	99 (100 %)
1983	20 (20.2 %)	38 (38.38 %)	6 (6.06 %)	19 (19.19 %)	16 (16.16 %)	99 (100 %)
1984	24 (24.24 %)	44 (44.44 %)	0 (0 %)	21 (21.21 %)	10 (10.1 %)	99 (100 %)
1985	36 (36.36 %)	39 (39.39 %)	1 (1.01 %)	19 (19.19 %)	4 (4.04 %)	99 (100 %)
1986	34 (34.34 %)	37 (37.37 %)	0 (0 %)	23 (23.23 %)	5 (5.05 %)	99 (100 %)
1987	25 (25 %)	50 (50 %)	0 (0 %)	20 (20 %)	5 (5 %)	100 (100 %)
1988	15 (15 %)	60 (60 %)	0 (0 %)	25 (25 %)	0 (0 %)	100 (100 %)
1989	22 (22.22 %)	49 (49.49 %)	0 (0 %)	21 (21.21 %)	7 (7.07 %)	99 (100 %)
1990	23 (23 %)	46 (46 %)	0 (0 %)	25 (25 %)	6 (6 %)	100 (100 %)
1991	22 (22 %)	35 (35 %)	5 (5 %)	30 (30 %)	8 (8 %)	100 (100 %)
1992	21 (21 %)	32 (32 %)	8 (8 %)	24 (24 %)	15 (15 %)	100 (100 %)
1993	29 (29 %)	29 (29 %)	8 (8 %)	22 (22 %)	12 (12 %)	100 (100 %)
1994	26 (26 %)	35 (35 %)	5 (5 %)	22 (22 %)	12 (12 %)	100 (100 %)
1995	18 (17.82 %)	29 (28.71 %)	6 (5.94 %)	27 (26.73 %)	21 (20.79 %)	101 (100 %)
1996	31 (30.69 %)	29 (28.71 %)	8 (7.92 %)	28 (27.72 %)	5 (4.95 %)	101 (100 %)
1997	27 (27 %)	26 (26 %)	12 (12 %)	23 (23 %)	12 (12 %)	100 (100 %)
1998	26 (26 %)	33 (33 %)	1 (1 %)	30 (30 %)	10 (10 %)	100 (100 %)
1999	28 (28 %)	32 (32 %)	1 (1 %)	26 (26 %)	13 (13 %)	100 (100 %)
2000	26 (26 %)	29 (29 %)	7 (7 %)	33 (33 %)	5 (5 %)	100 (100 %)
2001	26 (26 %)	35 (35 %)	4 (4 %)	24 (24 %)	11 (11 %)	100 (100 %)
2002	32 (32 %)	26 (26 %)	11 (11 %)	23 (23 %)	8 (8 %)	100 (100 %)
2003	31 (31 %)	40 (40 %)	6 (6 %)	12 (12 %)	11 (11 %)	100 (100 %)
2004	25 (25 %)	28 (28 %)	16 (16 %)	21 (21 %)	10 (10 %)	100 (100 %)
Total	728 (25.98 %)	1,027 (36.65 %)	176 (6.28 %)	622 (22.2 %)	249 (8.89 %)	2,802 (100 %)

Table 6 Conditional Multinomial Logit regressions

Variables	(1) All sectors	(2) Instruments	(3) Chemistry pharma	(4) Process eng.	(5) Mechanical eng.
MAPPL		−0.237* (0.130)	−0.349 (0.242)	0.0453 (0.138)	0.605*** (0.174)
NINV		0.0682 (0.0583)	0.185** (0.0910)	0.132** (0.0627)	0.0366 (0.0829)
USA		0.380*** (0.145)	0.918*** (0.294)	0.848*** (0.186)	0.254 (0.215)
GOV		−0.124 (0.113)	−0.567*** (0.212)	−0.0606 (0.124)	−0.388** (0.172)
ACAD		0.486** (0.201)	0.319 (0.333)	−0.455* (0.247)	−0.846** (0.355)
dum1986_1995		−0.0995 (0.152)	−0.595** (0.246)	0.196 (0.164)	−0.114 (0.226)
dum1996_2005		−0.416*** (0.146)	0.340 (0.311)	−0.0359 (0.181)	−0.348 (0.260)
PAT_GROWTH	0.603 (0.509)				
SCHUMP	−0.481*** (0.178)				
HERFSOURCES_TECH	−0.676 (1.084)				
HERFSOURCES_FIRM	−1.106*** (0.325)				
SELFSOURCES	7.326*** (2.311)				
Constant		−0.508** (0.234)	−3.060*** (0.481)	−2.146*** (0.435)	−1.919*** (0.433)
Observations	14010	14010	14010	14010	14010

Robust standard errors in parentheses *** $p < 0.01$, ** $p < 0.05$, * $p < 0.1$

Table 7 Conditional Multinomial Logit regressions—marginal effects

Variables	(1) Electrical eng.	(2) Instruments	(3) Chemistry pharma	(4) Process eng.	(5) Mechanical eng.
Pr(OST5 = j | 1 selected)	0.264	0.372	0.056	0.221	0.087
MAPPL	0.008 (0.021)	−0.073*** (0.023)	−0.017 (0.010)	0.017 (0.020)	0.065*** (0.016)
NINV	−0.018* (0.010)	0.001 (0.011)	0.007 (0.004)	0.014 (0.009)	−0.003 (0.006)
USA	−0.110*** (0.029)	0.006 (0.029)	0.025** (0.010)	0.089*** (0.022)	−0.010 (0.017)
GOV	0.033* (0.020)	−0.001 (0.022)	−0.023** (0.009)	0.014 (0.018)	−0.022* (0.011)
ACAD	−0.026 (0.034)	0.167*** (0.039)	0.013 (0.019)	−0.098*** (0.024)	−0.057*** (0.012)
dum1986_1995	0.009 (0.026)	−0.025 (0.027)	−0.029*** (0.010)	0.052** (0.022)	−0.007 (0.017)
dum1996_2005	0.045 (0.028)	−0.089*** (0.027)	0.031* (0.018)	0.029 (0.026)	−0.015 (0.017)
PAT_GROWTH	0.117 (0.099)	0.141 (0.119)	0.032 (0.027)	0.104 (0.088)	0.048 (0.041)
SCHUMP	−0.093*** (0.035)	−0.112*** (0.042)	−0.025*** (0.010)	−0.083*** (0.031)	−0.038*** (0.014)
HERFSOURCES_TECH	−0.131 (0.210)	−0.158 (0.253)	−0.036 (0.057)	−0.116 (0.533)	−0.054 (0.086)
HERFSOURCES_FIRM	−0.215*** (0.063)	−0.258*** (0.076)	−0.059*** (0.001)	−0.190*** (0.056)	−0.088*** (0.026)
SELFSOURCES	1.423*** (0.449)	1.712*** (0.541)	0.388*** (0.125)	1.261*** (0.399)	0.582*** (0.187)
Observations	14010	14010	14010	14010	14010

Robust standard errors in parentheses *** $p < 0.01$, ** $p < 0.05$, * $p < 0.1$

Pharmaceuticals and Process Engineering sectors, whereas they are less likely to occur in the Electrical Engineering sector. The presence of at least one governmental applicant decreases the probability of observing a breakthrough in the Chemistry & Pharmaceuticals and Mechanical Engineering sectors, whereas it increases the probability of observing an invention in the Electrical Engineering sector. Finally, a breakthrough invention with at least one academic applicant is less likely to occur in the Process Engineering and Mechanical Engineering sectors, whereas it is more likely to occur in the Instruments sector.

Turning our attention to the impact of alternative-specific covariates, *SCHUMP*, which is our main variable of interest, has a negative and significant marginal effect. This result suggests that breakthrough inventions are more likely to occur in sectors characterized by a Schumpeter Mark I type of innovation patterns than in Schumpeter Mark II. This result appears both in Tables 6 and 7. This finding is of particular interest also because it is likely that our measure of breakthrough invention will probably be biased towards inventions emerging from the corporate R&D segment of the economy.

Interestingly enough, concerning the variety of knowledge source across firms indicator (*HERFSOURCES_FIRM*), we find that the more the amount of relevant knowledge in a sector is concentrated across firms, the lower is the probability of observing a breakthrough invention in that sector. At the same time, however, the probability of observing a breakthrough increases with the degree of knowledge 'cumulativeness' in a given sector as captured by the relative degree at which each firm exploits its internal source of knowledge (*SELFSOURCES*).

4.3 Robustness Checks and Sensitivity Analysis

The CML model estimated above relies on the Independence of Irrelevant Alternatives (IIA) assumption which states that the relative odds between two alternatives considered (e.g. the probability of awarding an invention in the Instruments vs. Electrical Engineering macro-sectors) is not affected by adding another alternative (e.g. by adding another macro-sector not considered in our analysis) or by changing the characteristics of a third alternative (e.g. by splitting in two the Chemistry & Pharmaceutical macro-sectors). Although this assumption seems plausible in our setting, since we have classified ex-post the awarded inventions in the OST sectors with respect to the decision of the awarding board,[10] we report in this sub-section (as a robustness check exercise) the estimates of an alternative econometric model which relaxes the IIA assumption. The Alternative-Specific Multinomial Probit (ASMNP) regression model (Drukker and Gates

[10] As we already mentioned, the R&D 100 awarding board was not faced with a real choice amongst macro-sectors alternatives when deciding which invention deserved the prize (i.e. there were no 'pre-determined' shares of awards reserved for each sector).

2006) assumes a multinomial distribution for the error terms ε_{ij} in each j-alternative latent variable equation pr^*_{ij} with a user-specified correlation structure Ω:

$$4pr^*_{ij} = X_{ij}\beta + Z_i\gamma_i + \varepsilon_{ij}\ and$$
$$\underline{\varepsilon}'_j = (\varepsilon_{i1},,\varepsilon_{iJ}) \sim MVN(0,\Omega), for\ j = 1,\ldots,J\ \ and\ \ \mathrm{i} = 1,\ldots,\mathrm{N}.$$

The simulated maximum likelihood estimator for the ASMNP is computed using the command asmprobit on STATA 11—SE version which implements the GHK algorithm (Geweke 1989; Hajivassiliou and McFadden 1998; Keane and Wolpin 1994) to approximate the multivariate distribution function. Tables 8 and 9 report respectively the estimated coefficients and marginal effects of the ASMNP model.[11] In most of the cases, the sign, the statistical significance and the magnitude of the estimates are similar to the CML estimates.

Moreover, for those sectors in which the alternative-specific regressors have the most significant estimated impact (Instruments, Chemistry & Pharmaceuticals, and Mechanical Engineering), Fig. 7 shows the degree of sensitivity of the marginal effects with respect to different levels of the alternative specific regressors considered in different sectors.

Interestingly enough, the estimated impact of the Schumpeterian regime indicator (SCHUMP), although being always negative, shows a different behavior with respect to the sector considered. In the sector Instruments, the estimated negative marginal effect tends to become stronger the more the Schumpeterian regime gets closer to a Mark II type, whereas in Mechanical Engineering, the negative impact tends to become weaker. For Chemistry & Pharmaceuticals, although on average the estimated marginal effect of SCHUMP is negative, we observe a U-shaped pattern with a rate of change in the simulated probability of getting an invention awarded which decreases (i.e. the estimated negative impact becomes stronger) when moving from an highly 'turbulent' Schumpeterian Mark I type to an 'intermediate' type, and then increases when moving from an 'intermediate' type to an highly 'stable' Mark II type regime.

A similar non-monotonic pattern is found when considering the effect of HERFSOURCES_FIRM in the Instruments sector. The rate of change in the simulated probability of observing a breakthrough invention in this sector decreases when moving from a low concentrated (in terms of relevant knowledge owned by firms) to an 'average' concentrated scenario, and then increases when moving to an highly concentrated one. In the other two sectors considered (Chemistry & Pharmaceuticals and Mechanical Engineering), the estimated negative marginal effects monotonically decreases with the degree of concentration. Finally, concerning the estimated positive impact of the relevance of the internal sources of knowledge (SELFSOURCES), we can see that its intensity tends to decrease

[11] The marginal effects are computed considering the mean value for continuous variables and a discrete change 0–1 for binary variables.

Table 8 Alternative Specific Multinomial Probit regression

Variables	(1) All sectors	(2) Instruments	(3) Chemistry pharma	(4) Process eng.	(5) Mechanical eng.
MAPPL		−0.134*** (0.0375)	−0.142*** (0.0368)	0.871 (1.231)	−0.0289 (0.0271)
NINV		0.0820*** (0.0183)	0.0878*** (0.0174)	0.980** (0.406)	0.0590*** (0.0141)
USA		0.431*** (0.0409)	0.468*** (0.0395)	5.941 (3.730)	0.329*** (0.0289)
GOV		−0.148*** (0.0385)	−0.161*** (0.0362)	0.721 (1.004)	−0.131*** (0.0295)
ACAD		0.211 (0.157)	0.206 (0.162)	−6.023** (2.661)	0.0583 (0.127)
dum1986_1995		0.0403 (0.0443)	0.0669 (0.0422)	3.687*** (1.152)	0.0177 (0.0351)
dum1996_2005		−0.133*** (0.0435)	−0.0753* (0.0416)	3.857*** (1.177)	−0.145*** (0.0336)
PAT_GROWTH	0.0905*** (0.0231)				
SCHUMP	−0.0971*** (0.00389)				
HERFSOURCES_TECH	−0.151*** (0.0177)				
HERFSOURCES_FIRM	−0.249*** (0.00691)				
SELFSOURCES	0.712*** (0.0962)				
Constant		0.162*** (0.0612)	0.0459 (0.0656)	−2.03*** (0.1109)	0.171*** (0.0470)
Observations	14010	14010	14010	14010	14010

Robust standard errors in parentheses *** $p < 0.01$, ** $p < 0.05$, * $p < 0.1$

Table 9 Alternative Specific Multinomial Probit regression—marginal effects (alternative specific regressors)

Variables	(1) Electrical eng.	(2) Instruments	(3) Chemistry pharma	(4) Process eng.	(5) Mechanical eng.
Pr(OST5 = j | 1 selected)	0. 258	0. 378	0.055	0.218	0.086
PAT_GROWTH	0.0015 (0.001)	0.192** (0.080)	0.123*** (0.046)	0.0005 (0.001)	0.076* (0.044)
SCHUMP	−0.0014* (0.0008)	−0.190*** (0.041)	−0.121*** (0.027)	−0.0005 (0.001)	−0.075** (0.030)
HERFSOURCES_TECH	−0.003 (0.002)	−0.355* (0.209)	−0.227* (0.091)	−0.001 (0.005)	−0.140 (0.097)
HERFSOURCES_FIRM	−0.004** (0.002)	−0.472*** (0.078)	−0.301*** (0.075)	−0.001 (0.005)	−0.186*** (0.026)
SELFSOURCES	0.011* (0.006)	1.473*** (0.360)	0.939*** (0.215)	0.004 (0.009)	0.581** (0.258)
Observations	14010	14010	14010	14010	14010

Robust standard errors in parentheses *** $p < 0.01$, ** $p < 0.05$, * $p < 0.1$

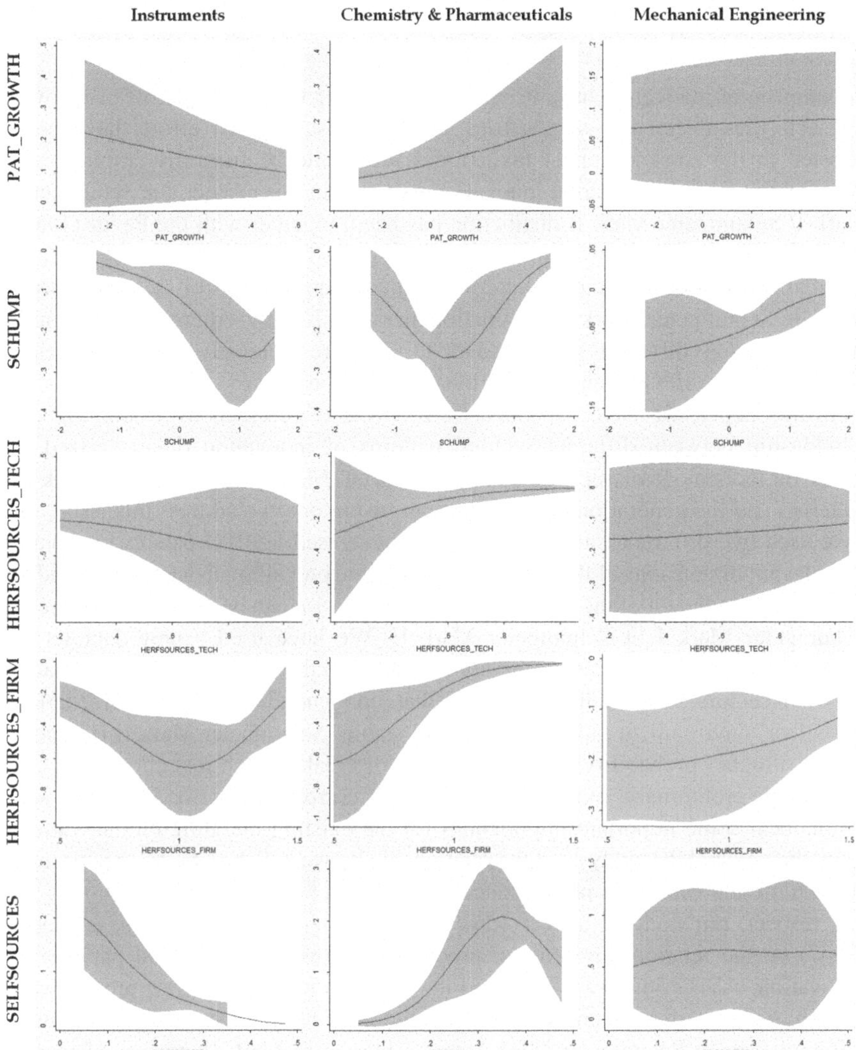

Fig. 7 Estimated marginal effects (*red line*) for different values of the covariates in different sectors (95 % confidence interval is the *grey area*)

with the degree of knowledge 'cumulativeness' in the Instruments sector whereas the pattern is inverted-U-shaped for the Chemistry & Pharmaceuticals sector and constant for the Mechanical Engineering sector.

5 Concluding Remarks

Economists of innovation have been aware for a long time that patterns of innovative activities differ across industries. So far, most research efforts have been devoted to the construction of taxonomies that could be fruitfully employed to interpret the variety of sectoral innovation patterns. In this respect, the Schumpeter Mark I/ Schumpeter Mark II distinction has been, together with the Pavitt (1984) taxonomy, the interpretative approach that has gained the widest currency. In fact, the characterization of sectoral patterns of innovation in terms of the Schumpeter Mark I/ Schumpeter Mark II distinction has consistently emerged in different countries using different type of data to measure innovative activities (e.g., USPTO patents, EPO patents and national Innovation Surveys responses).

In this paper, we have expanded on this line of research by examining the relationship between different sectoral patterns of innovation (characterized in terms of technological regimes and Schumpeter Mark I/ Schumpeter Mark II patterns) and the generation of breakthrough inventions. To address this issue, we have used two different sources of data. We have used USPTO patents to capture the relevant dimensions of the technological regime prevailing in each sector and to construct an indicator of the degree in which each sector can be identified as either a Schumpeter Mark I or Schumpeter Mark II. We have used a new data set of awarded inventions to measure the number of breakthrough inventions generated by each sectors. Our findings indicate that, in general, a Schumpeter Mark I 'turbulent' environment rather than a more 'stable' Schumpeter Mark II is conducive to a higher probability of the occurrence of breakthrough inventions.

Though preliminary and in need of further corroboration, we think that our results bear some important implications for the existing literature on innovation. First, they extend the analysis of the relationship between Schumpeterian pattern of innovation and economic performance to the case of breakthrough inventions. In this respect, our findings appear somewhat consistent with those of Castellacci (2007) on the relationship between productivity growth and sectoral patterns of innovation. Also in that case he found that the relationship between productivity growth and the dimensions of the technological regime was articulated in a different way in Schumpeter Mark I and Schumpeter Mark II patterns. Second, our results complement the evidence provided by recent studies in the management tradition that look at the sources of innovative breakthroughs mainly at the individual level. While the probability of achieving a breakthrough may be related to inventors' past experience and ability (Conti et al. 2010) and/or to the organizational setting in which the research activity takes place (Jeppesen and Lakhani 2010), industry characteristics seem also to play an important role and ought to be considered when carrying out firm level studies. Finally, our results bear also some policy implications. If an entrepreneurial regime is an environment relatively more conducive to breakthrough inventions, then it is clear that intelligent innovation policies would better follow the advice of Jewkes et al. (1958) and pay attention to the role of small firms and/or individual entrepreneurs rather than focusing exclusively inside the walls of the research and development facilities of large corporations.

Acknowledgements We thank the editors of the special issue and an anonymous reviewer for helpful suggestions. We have also benefited from comments of seminar participants at the International Schumpeter Society Conference 2010, Workshop on 'Knowledge Integration and Innovation', EPIP conference 2009, EMAEE Conference 2009. Fontana and Nuvolari acknowledge financial support from European Union, project FP6 – 043345, NEST-2005-Path-CUL: "CID-Cultural Innovation Dynamics. Explaining the uneven evolution of human knowledge".

References

Ahuia G, Lampert C (2001) Entrepreneurship in the large corporation: a longitudinal study of how established firms create breakthrough inventions. Strateg Manag J 22:521–543

Block F, Keller M (2009) Where do innovations come from? Transformations in the US economy. Socio-Econ Rev 7:459–483

Breschi S, Malerba F, Orsenigo L (2000) Technological regimes and schumpeterian patterns of innovation. Econ J 110:388–410

Carpenter MP, Narin F, Woolf P (1981) Citation rates to technologically important patents. World Pat Inf 3:160–163

Castellacci F (2007) Technological regimes and sectoral differences in productivity growth. Ind Corp Change 16:1105–1145

Chandy R, Tellis G (2000) The incumbent's curse? Incumbency, size and radical product innovation. J Market 64:1–17

Cohen WM (2010) Fifty years of empirical studies of innovative activity and performance. In: Hall B, Rosenberg N (eds) The handbook of economics of innovation. Elsevier, Amsterdam, pp 129–213

Conti R, Gambardella A, Mariani M (2010) Learning to be Edison? Individual inventive experience and breakthrough inventions. Paper presented at DRUID Academy conference 2010

Corrocher N, Malerba F, Montobbio F (2007) Schumpeterian patterns of innovation in the ICT field. Res Policy 36:418–432

Drukker DM, Gates R (2006) Generating Halton sequences using Mata. Stata J 6:278–294

Freeman C (1991) Networks of innovators. A synthesis of research issues. Res Policy 20:499–514

Geweke J (1989) Bayesian inference in econometric models using Monte Carlo integration. Econometrica 57:1317–1339

Granstrand O, Alange S (1995) The evolution of corporate entrepreneurship in Swedish industry—was Schumpeter wrong? J Evol Econ 5:133–156

Hajivassiliou VA, McFadden DL (1998) The method of simulated scores for the estimation of LDV models. Econometrica 66:863–896

Hall B, Jaffe A, Trajtenberg M (2001) The NBER patent citations data file: lessons, insights, methodological tools. NBER Working Paper n. 849w8

Hinze S, Reiss T, Schmoch U (1997) Statistical analysis on the distance between fields of technology. Report for the European Commission, TSER project

Jeppesen LB, Lakhani KR (2010) Marginality and problem solving effectiveness in broadcast search. Org Sci 21(5):1016–1033

Jewkes J, Sawers D, Stillerman R (1958) The sources of invention. MacMillan, London (rev. edn. 1969)

Keane MP, Wolpin KI (1994) The solution and estimation of discrete choice dynamic programming models by simulation and intermpolation: Monte Carlo evidence. Rev Econ Stat 76:648–672

Khan Z, Sokoloff K (1993) "Schemes of practical utility": entrepreneurship and innovation among "great inventors" in the United States, 1790–1865. J Econ Hist 53:289–307

Malerba F (2005) Sectoral systems: how and why innovation differs across sectors. In: Fagerberg J, Mowery DC, Nelson RR (eds) The Oxford handbook of innovation. Oxford University Press, Oxford, pp 380–406
Malerba F, Orsenigo L (1995) Schumpeterian patterns of innovation. Camb J Econ 19:47–65
Malerba F, Orsenigo L (1996) Schumpeterian patterns of innovation are technology-specific. Res Policy 25:451–478
Malerba F, Orsenigo L (1997) Technological regimes and sectoral patterns of innovative activities. Ind Corp Change 6:83–117
Marsili O, Verspagen B (2002) Technology and the dynamics of industrial structures: an empirical mapping of Dutch manufacturing. Ind Corp Change 11:791–815
Mokyr J (1990) The lever of riches. Oxford University Press, Oxford
Mowery DC, Nelson RR (eds) (1999) Sources of industrial leadership. Cambridge University Press, Cambridge
Nelson RR, Winter S (1982) An evolutionary theory of economic change. Harvard University Press, Cambridge
Pavitt K (1984) Patterns of technical change: towards a taxonomy and a theory. Res Policy 13:343–373
Scherer FM (1989) "Comments" on Z. Griliches, "Patents: recent trends and puzzles". Brook Pap Econ Act 9:291–330
Scherer FM, Harhoff D (2000) Technology policy for a world of skewed distributed outcomes. Res Policy 29:559–566
Schoenmakers W, Duysters G (2010) The technological origins of radical inventions. Res Policy 39:1051–1059
Silverberg G, Verspagen B (2007) The size distribution of innovations revisited: an application of extreme value statistics to citation and value measure of patent significance. J Econ 139:318–319
Singh J, Fleming L (2010) Lone inventors as sources of breakthroughs: myth or reality? Manag Sci 56:41–56
Van Dijk M (2000) Technological regimes and industrial dynamics: the evidence from Dutch manufacturing. Ind Corp Change 9:173–194

R&D, Patents and Stock Return Volatility

Mariana Mazzucato and Massimiliano Tancioni

Abstract Recent finance literature highlights the role of technological change in increasing firm specific (idiosyncratic) and aggregate stock return volatility, yet innovation data is not used in these analyses, leaving the direct relationship between innovation and stock return volatility untested. The paper investigates the relationship between volatility and innovation using firm level patent data. The analysis builds on the empirical work by Mazzucato (Rev Econ Dyn 5:318–345, 2002; J Evol Econ 13(5):491–512, 2003) where it is found that stock return volatility is highest during periods in the industry life-cycle when innovation is the most 'radical'. In this paper we ask whether firms which invest more in innovation (more R&D and more patents) and/or which have more important innovations (patents with more citations) experience more volatility in their returns. Given that returns should in theory be higher, on average, for higher risk stocks, we also look at the effect of innovation on the level of returns. To take into account the competition between firms within industries, firm returns and volatility are

The research leading to these results has received funding from the European Community's Seventh Framework Programme (FP7/2007–2013) under Socio-economic Sciences and Humanities, grant agreement n° 217466 (www.finnov-fp7.eu). The authors are also grateful to the ESRC Innogen centre for support.
Comments from participants at the 2010 International Schumpeter Conference and at seminars (Kites-Bocconi), and workshops (CERF Cambridge workshop on 'Technology and Bubbles') were very useful. All errors remain our own.
Reprinted from Evolutionary Economics 22(4), 811-832 , Springer (2012)

M. Mazzucato (✉)
Science and Technology Policy Research Unit, University of Sussex, Brighton BN1 9QE, United Kingdom
e-mail: M.Mazzucato@sussex.ac.uk

M. Tancioni
Department of Economics and Law, University of Rome La Sapienza, Piazzale Aldo Moro 5, 00185 Rome, Italy
e-mail: massimilano.tancioni@uniroma1.it

A. Pyka and E.S. Andersen (eds.), *Long Term Economic Development*, Economic Complexity and Evolution, DOI 10.1007/978-3-642-35125-9_15,

measured relative to the industry average. We focus the analysis on firms in the pharmaceutical industry between 1974 and 1999. Results suggest that there is a positive and significant relationship between volatility, R&D intensity and the various patent related measures—especially when the innovation measures are filtered to distinguish the very innovative firms from the less innovate ones.

1 Introduction

In recent years there has been increased attention, by both the economics profession and the popular press on the topic of stock return volatility. While recent attention has been affected by the bursting of the most recent financial bubble, the attention dates back to different works which have assumed that the New Economy, or the 'information age', has affected the stability of the market valuation process, and in so doing increased volatility (Campbell et al. 2001). Shiller's work (2000) has shown that 'excess volatility', i.e. the degree to which stock returns are more volatile than underlying fundamentals, is highest in periods of technological revolutions when uncertainty is greatest. Campbell et al. (2001) find that firm level idiosyncratic risk, i.e. the degree to which firm specific returns are more volatile than average market returns, has risen since the 1960's and claim that this might be due to the effect of new technologies, especially those related to the 'IT' revolution, as well as the fact that small firms tend now to go public earlier in their life-cycle when their future prospects are more uncertain. Mazzucato (2002) and Mazzucato and Semmler (1999) show that, at the sectoral level, the early stage of automobiles was just as volatile as the early stage of the internet and personal computers (underpinning the dot.com era), suggesting that it is not the New Economy but the turbulence that characterizes the early life-cycle of key new industries that causes the volatility to emerge.

The basic idea behind all these works is that innovation, especially when 'radical', leads to high uncertainty hence more volatility. This idea provides interesting insights into the debate about whether markets are 'efficient'. Behavioral economists have recently highlighted the role of animal spirits and herd effects in investment behavior, quite different from the assumptions of perfect foresight and rationality that has been assumed for years in finance theory. What these studies contribute to this debate is that during periods of instability caused by technological change, these behavioral aspects are even stronger causing the departure of stock returns from underlying fundamentals to be greater. Pastor and Veronesi (2004) claim that the reason that high tech firms have returns that appear unjustifiably high (at the beginning of a 'bubble') is not due to *irrationality*, but due to the effect that new technology has on the uncertainty about a firm's average future profits. Yet while hypothesizing a link between return volatility and innovation, none of these studies actually use firm specific innovation data to directly test the relationship. Innovation is alluded to (e.g. the 'IT revolution', the New Economy, radical change) but not measured at the firm level.

The aim of our paper is to explore, econometrically, the relationship between innovation and stock return volatility. Our expectation is that volatility should be affected by such uncertain investments since volatility is commonly perceived as a proxy for uncertainty (Pastor and Veronesi 2004). And as innovation is a perfect example of true Knightian uncertainty (Knight 1921), then we expect there to be a relationship between innovation and volatility. Thus the key hypothesis we test is whether those firms that invest in technological change experience more stock return volatility. Innovation is proxied through R&D spending and patents (weighted by citations in order to distinguish radical innovations from more incremental ones).

Our study focuses on the pharmaceutical industry due to the fact that it has one of the highest sectoral rates of R&D spending and patenting. Focussing on one sector allows us to look at the evolution of the relationship between stock returns and innovation over time, both over the industry's life-cycle (Mazzucato 2002) and over the course of time as the intensity of patenting and R&D investments change—as occurred after the 1980 Bayh–Dole act which allowed publicly funding research in the US to be patented. This would not be possible to do in a study which aggregates different industries, disregarding dynamics which may affect the relationship between innovation and stock returns.

Since we focus on one sector, we focus on how innovation spending by a firm affects the degree to which its stock return is more volatile than the industry average. Comparing the firm to the industry average rather than to the market average (as is more common in studies of idiosyncratic risk) captures the competitive dynamics of the industry since pharma firms are not competing with computer firms but with other pharma firms. We also look at the effect of innovation on the *level* of firm returns (relative to industry returns). In both cases we test the relationship before and after the mid 1980s.

Our results provide evidence that there is indeed a positive and significant relationship between stock return volatility and innovation. We find that volatility is positively and significantly related to R&D intensity, and to the patent related measures of innovation used in the analysis. We also find that the level of firm returns (compared to the industry average) are positively related with volatility, as is predicted by the 'rational bubble' hypothesis (Pastor and Veronesi 2005)—though we provide a very different explanation. We pay particular attention to the lag structure of the independent variables as this provides information on the speed with which the market reacts to news regarding innovation.

The rest of the paper is organized as follows. Section 2 reviews the literature on innovation and stock returns, focusing on those contributions which have provided insights on the relationship over an industry's 'life-cycle'; Section 3 discusses the data used and the variables constructed; Section 4 provides descriptive statistics and a discussion of the model selection criteria; Section 5 presents the results and Section 6 concludes.

2 Risk and Stock Returns Over the Industry Life-Cycle

Technological innovation is a very risky process: it is extremely expensive ($403 million per drug in pharma), takes a very long time (up to 17 years from the beginning of the research to the commercialization phase), and has a very high failure rate (in pharma only 1 in 10,000 compounds reach market approval phase, i.e. .01 % succeed). For these reasons, innovation is often given as an example of true Knightian uncertainty, which unlike 'risk' cannot be easily calculated via probability distributions.[1] Figure 1 exemplifies the dangerous consequences of this uncertainty: an exponential rise in the rate of R&D spending has not been accompanied by an increase in new molecular entities.

How are stock returns affected by this uncertainty? As stock prices are driven by future growth expectations, and since innovation is a key driver of firm growth, it can be expected that stock returns and innovation are related. The expectations about a firm's growth will be positive when the firm in question is a very innovative one, but due to the high uncertainty and failure rate, the expectations will often prove wrong. The correcting behavior will result in volatility. Hence the way that creative destruction affects expectation formation about firm growth will result in volatility. This provides an explanation for Shiller's (1981) finding that the difference between the volatility of shares and the volatility of the underlying fundamentals is highest during each of the major technological revolutions of the last two centuries. A similar point is made in Perez (2002) where bubble dynamics are related to major technological revolutions.

However, not all innovations are radical. Some are incremental and more process oriented. Hence in thinking about the relationship between stock return volatility and innovation, Mazzucato (2002, 2003) studies whether excess volatility of stock returns and idiosyncratic risk are highest in periods of the industry life-cycle in which innovation is the most 'radical' (for a review of the life-cycle perspective see Klepper (1996). Using *industry level* innovation data (a quality change index that compares Bureau of Economic Prices to hedonic quality adjusted prices), these studies find that in fact it is precisely in the periods of the industry life-cycle which are characterized by the most quality change, that the stock returns are the most volatile. In some industries like autos, this has occurred in the 'early' phase of the industry life-cycle when innovation was more radical and market shares more unstable. In others, like the personal computer industry, it occurred later on in the industry life-cycle when the departure from a leading incumbent (IBM) allowed both innovation and competition to open up (Bresnahan and Greenstein 1997). In each case, it appears that it is the phase in the industry life-cycle when innovation is

[1] *"The practical difference between the two categories, risk and uncertainty, is that in the former the distribution of the outcome in a group of instances is known (either from calculation a priori or from statistics of past experience). While in the case of uncertainty that is not true, the reason being in general that it is impossible to form a group of instances, because the situation dealt with is in a high degree unique…"* (Knight 1921, pp. 232–233).

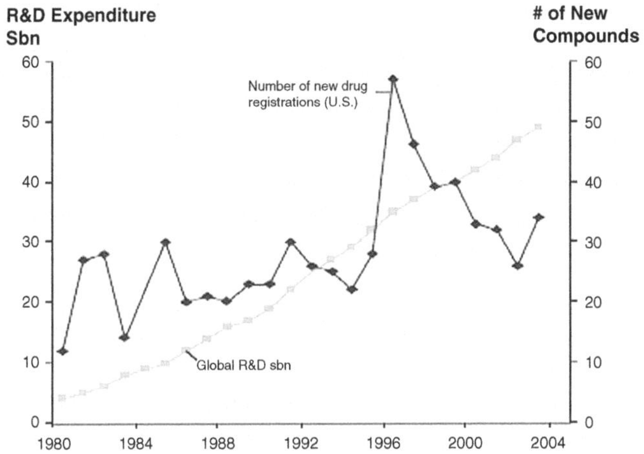

Fig. 1 The productivity dilemma: R&D vs. discovery of New Molecular Entities

the most radical and competition the most intense that stock returns are the most volatile (Mazzucato 2002). Mazzucato and Tancioni (2008) find that in a comparison of 5 different sectors (computers, pharma, biotech, autos and textiles), it is the firms spending the most on R&D that experience the most volatility in their shares. This is especially important in an industry like pharma where there is very high R&D spending but not so many concrete rewards from it as suggested in Fig. 1, hence financial markets need to find a way to distinguish the potentially high performers from the low performers.

In this study we introduce firm level patent data and ask whether the firms that spend the most on R&D, have the most patents, and the patents with the most citations, experience the most volatility. The productivity literature on market value and innovation has established a positive relationship between a firm's market value, its R&D intensity and its citation weighted patents (Griliches et al. 1991; Pakes 1985; Hall et al. 2001, 2005). So here we see whether this type of data can also help us better understand volatility dynamics which, as argued above, have not been studied in light of firm specific innovation dynamics. We also look at the effect on the *level* of returns since in theory if returns are on average higher for higher risk shares, then we should see a relationship between returns and innovation as well, since the latter is a good proxy for risk (uncertainty).

As in our previous work, we analyze a single sector so to better take into account the possible effect of qualitative and quantitative changes in innovation over the industry life-cycle (not possible in more static cross-section industry studies). We focus on the pharma sector due to the fact that the high R&D and patenting intensity of this industry provides us with ample innovation data, and also because much has been written about changes in innovation dynamics in this sector, allowing us to test whether the relationships we study have evolved alongside such transformations. For example, Henderson et al. (1999) describe the changes that have taken place since the mid 1980's in the innovative division of labor between large pharma firms and small (dedicated) biotech firms. Similarly, Gambardella (1995) describes how advances in science (enzymology, genetics and computational ability) since the 1980's caused a change in the way that firms search for new innovations: a pre 1980 period of "random screening", and a post-1980 period of "guided search" characterized by more scale economies and path-dependency.[2] An important institutional event which affected patenting behavior in this period was the 1980 Bayh–Dole act, which allowed universities and small businesses to patent discoveries emanating from publicly sponsored research (e.g. by the NIH), prompting many biotech spin-offs from academia. However, Mowery and Ziedonis (2002) show that the overall effect on patenting activity was small.

Our analysis is carried out in three stages. We first test for a statistical relationship between the volatility of returns and innovation in order to explore the hypothesis that the high uncertainty that underlies innovation is a key source of firm specific volatility (as suggested but not tested in Campbell et al. (2001), and Shiller (2000)). We then test the relationship between innovation and the *level* of returns. Finally we test directly for the relationship between relative returns and volatility.

3 Data

3.1 Patent Data

We study the pharma industry from 1974 to 1999. Our sample of firms is constructed by merging financial data from Compustat with USPTO patent data (extracted from the NBER patent citation database included in the book/CD by Jaffe and Trajtenberg 2002). From now on we will refer to these databases as Compustat and NBER respectively.

The NBER patent citations database provides detailed patent related information on 3 million US patents granted between January 1963 and December 1999, and all citations made to these patents between 1975 and 1999 (over 16 million). For each patent, information on the citations it *received* (a forward looking measure, which captures the relationship between a patent and subsequent technological developments that build up on it, i.e. its descendants), and the citations *made* (a backward looking measure which captures the relationship between a patent and the body of knowledge that preceded it, i.e. its antecedents) is available. Weighting patents by citations is important since studies have found that the distribution of the value of patents is highly skewed, with few patents of very high value, and many of low value (a large fraction of the value of the stream of innovations is associated with a small number of very important innovations, Scherer and Ross 1990).

[2] Gambardella (1995) documents that although the guided regime did not increase the number of new molecules discovered, it did decrease the failure rate of those tested (hence making the process more efficient).

We start from the assumption that patents that are 'more important' are those that are the most uncertain due to the way they challenge the status quo, more so at least than incremental innovations (Tushman and Anderson 1986). We use citation weighted patents as a proxy for the 'importance' of an innovation and see whether firms with more 'important' innovations experience more volatility. Specifically, we test for the relationship between firm level volatility of returns (relative volatility) and the following innovation variables: R&D intensity (R&D divided by sales), patent counts, and patents weighted by their citations. We also look at the impact of these variables on the level of returns and earnings. The relationship between the level of returns and their volatility is at the basis of financial economics (Campbell et al. 2001). By looking at this relationship at the sectoral level, and relating it to innovation, we are in essence providing an industrial dynamics explanation of this famous relationship.

As many patents in the pharma industry do not result in new drugs (Harris 2002; Pisano 2006),[3] we do not assume that patents represent actual innovations (e.g. a new drug), but rather *signals* that the market receives regarding the potential 'innovativeness' of a firm. The more patents a firm has the stronger the signal regarding its potential innovativeness, and the more citations per patent, the more important (trustworthy) the signal. This lies in contrast with the usual interpretation of R&D as an *input* and patents as an *output* of the innovation process. In fact, it might be that because there are so many patents in this industry (inflated especially after the 1980 Bayh–Dole act), the market treats them as more noisy signals than in other industries, and hence citations take on an even more important role as a filtering device.

To understand the uncertainty around patents as signals of innovativeness it is important to remember that we merged the databases using the patent *application date* (rather than the patent granted date) when there is the highest uncertainty: uncertainty whether the patent will be granted, uncertainty whether, even if granted, the patent will lead to a commercialized product etc. And as the approximate lag between the application date and the granted date is 3 years, when considering the lag structure of the models below, a lag of $t - 1$ on patent applications is like a forward lag of $t + 2$ for patents granted.

3.2 Financial Data

We use the firm CUSIP code[4] to match firms in the two data bases (Compustat and NBER patent data). Only firms pertaining to the GIC code (which in 2000 replaced

[3] Pisano (2006) reports that it takes an average of 10–12 years for a company to get a drug out on the market. Only 10 %–20 % of drug candidates beginning clinical trials have been approved by the FDA.

[4] CUSIP, operated by Standard and Poor's, refers to the *Committee on Uniform Security Identification Procedures*, which identifies any North American security for the purposes of facilitating clearing and settlement of trades. It serves as the National Securities Identification Number for products issued from both the United States and Canada.

the SIC codes) 352020 for pharma are included in the analysis. The merging of the two databases results in a restricted sample: out of a total of 323 pharmaceutical firms, the merged sample contains 126 pharma firms.[5] In order to avoid dealing with highly volatile stock return data, we have omitted firms present in the sample for less than seven years. Since we consider a two-year maximum lag in our estimates, this guarantees that data is available for at least five years. We thus end up studying the dynamics of 63 firms in the pharma industry from 1974–1999.[6] We have verified robustness of results with respect to changes in the selection criterion.

Following Schwert (1989), *monthly* data is used to calculate the volatility of annual returns: the standard deviation is calculated over 12 month observations on returns. We use monthly rather than daily data, since it would be exaggerated to expect that quarterly R&D figures and annual patent data have an impact on daily stock returns. Furthermore, Campbell et al. (2001) analyze volatility using both daily and monthly data and do not find qualitative differences (in trends).

To measure relative volatility we do not use the variance decomposition method used in Campbell et al. (2001) which isolates firm, industry and market level volatility through a variance decomposition analysis. Rather, we use a proxy for idiosyncratic risk which captures the degree to which firm specific returns are more volatile than the average industry returns: the log ratio between the standard deviation of a firm's return[7] and the standard deviation of the average industry return. We think this is the relevant measure of volatility to look at since firms compete with other firms in their own industry, and hence their growth potential is valued in comparison with their immediate competitors. In fact, in our previous study (Mazzucato and Tancioni 2008) we found that the reaction of returns to R&D is very high for innovative firms in non innovative industries precisely because they 'stand out' compared to their competitors. Furthermore, since the pharma industry is a very innovative industry in which R&D spending is very high, financial markets must find a way to distinguish the potential high flyers from the potential losers, even though they are both spending a lot on R&D. For this reason, the relevant measure of volatility is that which compares the firm to its competitors, not to the general market.

To summarize, the financial variables are monthly; R&D is quarterly; and patents are annual.[8] And the volatility of returns and their levels are measured relative to the industry average, as log deviations from industry level volatility and returns.

[5] On average, nearly 95 % and 97 % of the merged sample is available when financial variables are matched with, respectively, R&D intensity and patents weighted by citations received.

[6] Other sample selection criteria have been used in the literature. For example, in a related study on spill-overs and market value, Deng (2005) omits firms with less than 3 years in the Compustat database.

[7] The return of a firm's stock is defined as: $\frac{(P_t - P_{t-1}) + D_t}{P_{t-1}}$.

[8] The patent application date is listed by year, while patent grant date is listed by month.

3.3 Stocks vs. Flows

The R&D and patent variables are entered in terms of flows rather than stocks. This lies in contrast to the market value and innovation literature (Hall et al. 2005), which uses stocks (applying a Permanent Inventory approach with a 15 % depreciation assumption). We use flow variables because while it makes sense to think that it is the stock of intangible assets that affects the level of market value, changes in stock returns (hence their volatility) are affected mainly by recent 'news' that the market did not previously take into account (flows not stocks). Since we are mainly concerned with the determinants of volatility (which is stationary in mean over time), the use of cumulated and thus trended explanatory variables such as stocks would lead to potentially biased estimates, because of the unbalanced statistical properties of the data. Furthermore, in a study by Hall et al. (2001), where R&D is entered both as a stock and as a flow in the market value equation, it is found that the flow variable has more explanatory power than the stock "*...which implies a higher valuation on recent R&D than on the history of R&D spending.*" (Hall et al. 2001, p. 261).[9]

Nevertheless to make sure the results are robust we also check them using an R&D stock measure, obtained by applying a permanent inventory scheme with a conventional 15 % annual depreciation assumption.

3.4 Truncation and Other Data Issues

Patent citation data are naturally susceptible to two types of truncation problems. One has to do with the patent counts and the other one with the citation counts.[10] The former arises from the fact that as the end date is approached, only a percentage of the patents that have been applied for (and are later granted) are available in the data. The second truncation problem regards citation counts. As the NBER data ends in 1999, we have no information on the citations *received* by patents in the database beyond this period. Although this affects all the patents in the database (patents keep receiving citations over long periods, even beyond 50 years), it is

[9] Hall et al. (2001) notes that the significance of the R&D flow is reduced when cash flow is included as a regressor suggesting that at least part of the R&D flow effect arises from its correlation with cash flow. In contrast, the R&D stock variable is not sensitive to the inclusion of the cash flow variable. We test for this below and find that the cash flow variable is less significant than it is in Hall et al. (2001).

[10] Another problem regarding citations is that since the propensity to cite is not constant, it is important to distinguish when an increase in the number of citations (e.g. technological impact of the patent) is "real" as opposed to "artefactual". The latter includes the possibility that in some periods there was "citation inflation", e.g. due to institutional factors (e.g. USPTO practices) and/or differences across fields.

especially serious for patents close to the end date. Since every year suffers a different degree of this problem (with the later years suffering more), it makes comparison between years difficult.

There are two main ways to deal with both these truncation problems. The first is the *fixed effects* approach, the second is the *structural* approach (both reviewed in detail in Jaffe and Trajtenberg 2002). The fixed effects approach involves *scaling* citation counts by dividing them by the total citation count for a group of patents to which the patent of interest belongs (e.g. by period, or by field). In essence, this means calculating the firm's *share* of total industry patents.[11] The quasi structural approach is a more involved approach based on estimating the shape of the citation lag distribution, i.e. the fraction of lifetime citations (defined as 30 years after the grant date) that are received in each year after the patent is granted (Hall et al. 2005).[12] Unlike the fixed effects approach it allows one to distinguish real from artefactual differences between years and fields. For example, one can see whether the patents issued in the late 1990's made fewer citations, after controlling for the size and fertility of the stock of patents to be cited, than those before. By doing this, one can get the "real" 1975 patents, just as with price index adjustments.

We follow a slightly modified version of the fixed effects approach. We divide the firm-level patent citations received by the *average* industry citations not the *total*, since the latter varies with the changing number of firms in our unbalanced sample. Since the number of firms that are present in the sample increases over time,[13] while the innovative activity at the firm-level remains relatively stable, the standard fixed effects correction would bias downward the measure of innovation at the firm-level.[14] Dividing by the yearly *average* (as opposed to the yearly total), means that the correction is not affected by the changing number of firms in the sample.

[11] To remove year and/or field effects, the number of citations received by a given patent are divided by the corresponding year-field mean, or only by yearly means to remove only year effects. The justification for the correction is to remove factors of time variability that are not related to substantial innovation, as in the case of legislative interventions which affect number of patents and citations (e.g. the Bayh–Dole act), or by the truncation issue. The problem with this method is that it does not distinguish between differences that are real and those that are artefactual (e.g. if patents in the 1990's really did have more technological impact, removing the year effects ignores this real factor).

[12] Given the distribution, which is assumed stationary and independent of the overall citation intensity, the authors estimate the total citations of any patent for which a portion of its citation life is observed. This is done by dividing the observed citations by the fraction of the population that lies in the time interval for which citations are observed (Hall et al. 2005, p. 13).

[13] The number of firms that are contemporaneously present in the whole sample goes from 31 in 1980 to 187 in 2003, while the average number of patent applications per firm is (only) doubled in the same period.

[14] Furthermore, the FE approach suggested in Jaffe and Trajtenberg (2002) removes the time series variability, since the evolution of innovative intensity over time is substantially extracted by the correction.

Table 1 Descriptive statistics

	VOL	RET	RD/REV	PATW
a) Summary				
Mean	0.116	0.020	0.119	0.648
Std. dev.	0.079	0.055	0.366	1.957
CV	0.678	2.806	3.083	3.020
b) Correlations				
VOL	1.000			
RET	0.011	1.000		
RD/REV	0.238	−0.169	1.000	
PATW	−0.185	0.161	−0.033	1.000

4 Descriptive Statistics and Econometric Results

4.1 Descriptive Statistics

Table 1 contains descriptive statistics on the different variables used in the analyses. The table contains first the information for the two financial variables, relative volatility (VOL), relative returns (RET) and then for the two innovation variables, R&D intensity (RD/REV) and weighted patents (PATW). Considering a standardized measure of variability (CV), relative returns exhibit a large amount of variation, while relative volatility of returns (VOL) appears less variable. Large sample variability is also found for the two measures of innovation (RD/REV and PATW).

Contemporaneous correlations among variables do not show much significance. This evidence is supported by the regression results (below) which show that the relationships hold mostly dynamically (over time). However, by considering the scatter-plots between variable means, evaluated over section and over time, we obtain a first appreciation of the temporal and sectional correlation among variables. From Fig. 2, which refers to the average values evaluated over the section (i.e. firm averages in each year), VOL appears positively correlated with both RD/REV and PATW, while RET shows a negative and moderate correlation with these innovation measures. Considering the average values evaluated over time (i.e. period averages for each firm), Fig. 2 shows that VOL is positively correlated with RD/REV only, and a weak negative correlation with PATW is found. Considering RET, the correlation pattern is positive with PATW, and remains negative with RD/REV. These figures provide a first, albeit simplistic, indication of the co-evolution of volatility and innovation—investigated more rigorously below.

It is interesting to see that in Fig. 3 the rise in citation weighted patents is accompanied by a rise in market share instability.[15] This is precisely what would be expected by the literature on 'competence-destroying' innovations (Tushman and Anderson 1986): the period in which innovation is the most radical is the period in

[15] The market share instability index is defined in Hymer and Pashigian (1962): $I = \sum_{i=1}^{n} \left[\left| s_{it} - s_{i,t-1} \right| \right]$, where s = market share of firm i, and n = number of firms.

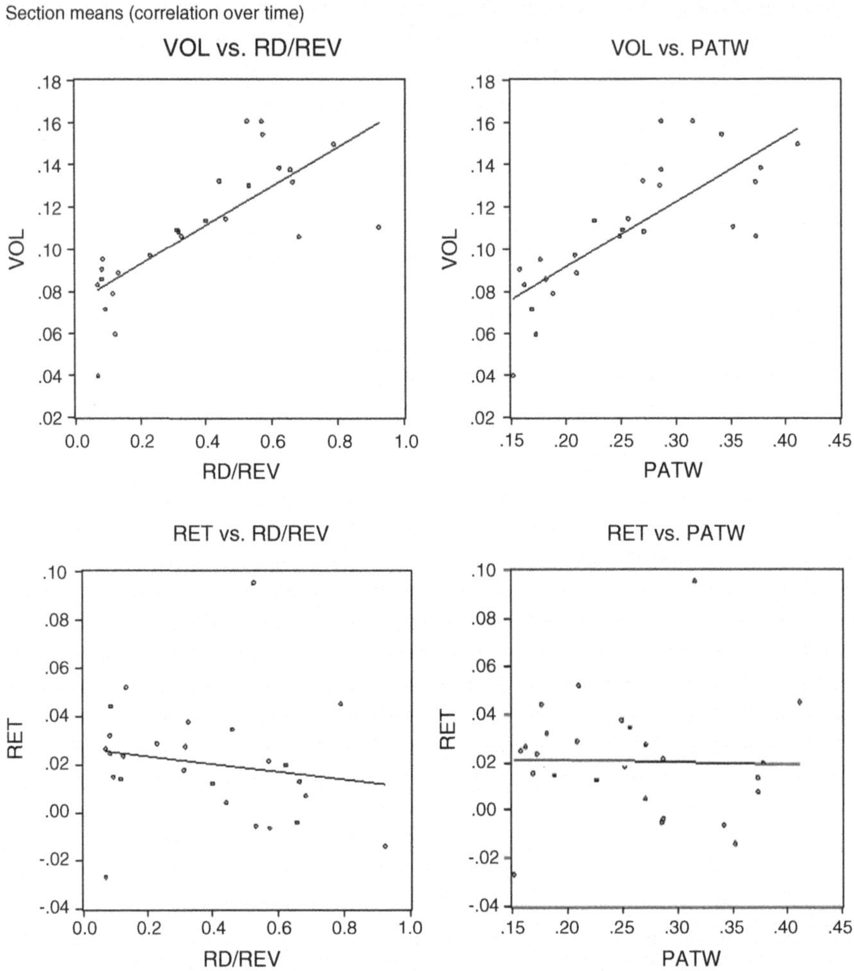

Fig. 2 (continued)

which there is most competition between firms causing a change in their ranking (with more stable periods in market shares being related instead to periods of less technological change). It gives us a preliminary reason to expect that citation weighted patents also affects the volatility of stock returns as these are being driven by the expected growth of firms which in such a period undergo much change for the reasons discussed above.

4.2 Econometric Implementation

We first regress relative volatility VOL on the innovation variables R&D/REV and PATW to test whether the volatility of firm returns is affected by investments in innovation (Model 1). Second, we test the impact of innovation on the level of

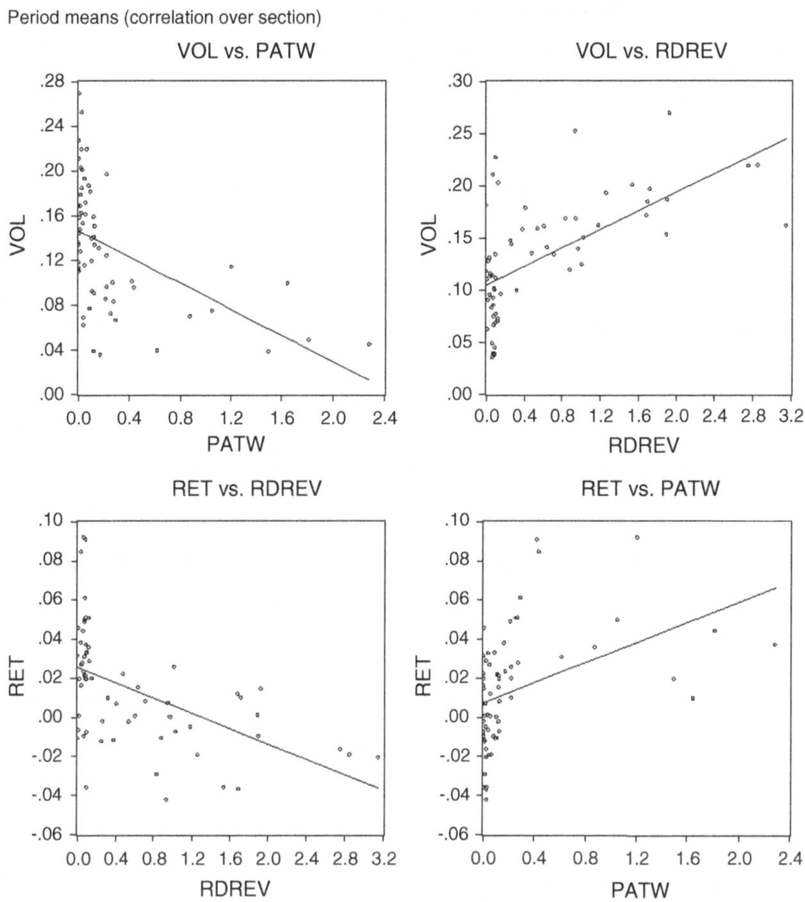

Fig. 2 Scatter-plot between average financial and innovation data—Section means and period means

returns (Model 2). Lastly we look at the direct relationship between volatility and returns (Model 3). In all cases we control for the size of the firm as proxied by relative capitalization (SIZEC). Specifically, the relationships we estimate are:

Model 1: Relative volatility and innovation

$$vol_{i,t} = \alpha + \sum\nolimits_{h=0}^{p} \beta_{1,h} rdrev_{i,t-h} + \sum\nolimits_{k=0}^{q} \beta_{2,k} patw_{i,t-k} + \beta_3 sizec_{i,t} + u_i + \varepsilon_{i,t}$$

Model 2: Returns and innovation

$$ret_{i,t} = \alpha + \sum\nolimits_{h=0}^{p} \beta_{1,h} rdrev_{i,t-h} + \sum\nolimits_{k=0}^{q} \beta_{2,k} patw_{i,t-k} + \beta_3 sizec_{i,t} + u_i + \varepsilon_{i,t}$$

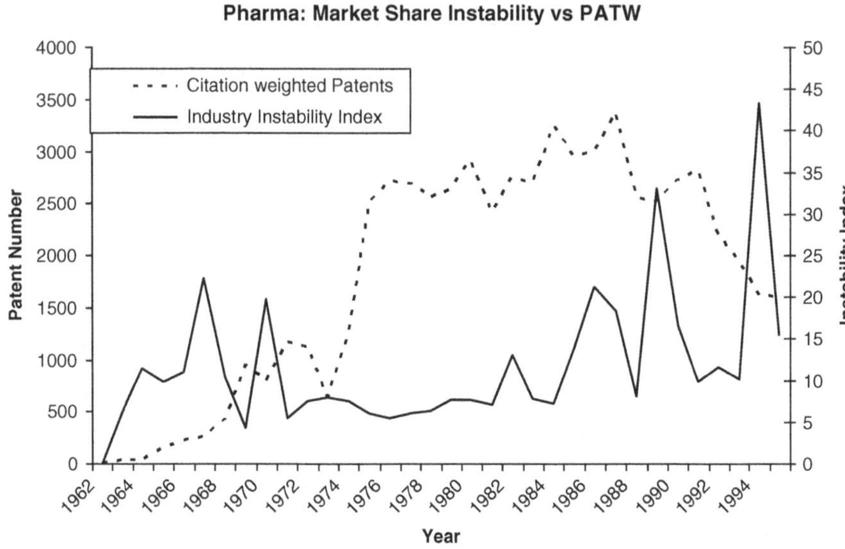

Fig. 3 Market share instability and citation weighted patents in pharma

Model 3: Returns and volatility

$$ret_{i,t} = \alpha + \sum\nolimits_{j=0}^{s} \beta_{1,s} vol_{i,t-s} + \beta_2 sizec_{i,t} + u_i + \varepsilon_{i,t}$$

where lower case letters denote logs.

The panel structure of the data-set suggests to employ as natural model alternatives the pooled, the Fixed Effects (FE) and the Random Effects (RE) specifications. With the FE model, firm level factors systematically enter the relationships, while in the RE model these factors are distributed randomly, i.e. they are an error component which is constant over time.

Individual effects models all presume that there are omitted variables that have section-specific effects such as tacit knowledge and related managerial capabilities. Hall et al. (2005) adopt a pooled model with period and industry dummies. Aside from the fact that their results (on the relation between market value and innovation) become insignificant when individual effects are considered (as also in the related literature), they do not include section-specific controls for two reasons. First, since R&D *stocks* change slowly over time (by construction), the inclusion of sectional controls would capture those systematic components that are deemed related to firm specific R&D strategies, i.e. to the independent variable. Second, since firms change their strategies over time in response to market signals, an individual effects model in the form of FE is inappropriate as it presumes permanent firm specific effects. In our case, the first point is irrelevant since we are dealing with volatile flow data and not with slowly-changing stocks, hence individual effects are not likely to be correlated with the independent variable and thus to capture the sample correlation between the dependent and independent variables. Concerning the second point, we believe that even if firm strategies vary in response to time-varying market signals, the presence of publicly available information on fundamentals (that are likely to be relatively firm-specific) may result in systematic cross-sectional factors, reflecting relatively permanent aspects of the firm's fundamentals that are not explicitly taken into account in the model specification.

For these reasons, unlike Hall et al. (2005), we consider section-specific effects in the form of random effects (RE). Even if there is no objective reason to believe that the section specific effects and the explanatory variables are uncorrelated, this choice should reduce the bias implied by the presence of latent variables, as long as they are uncorrelated with the observed regressors.[16]

A further question is endogeneity. We recognize that a firm's innovative effort is an endogenous strategy that is implemented on the basis of actual and expected outcomes of innovation activity, potentially captured by the financial variables employed in the analysis. Since there are no valid instruments in our sample data to accommodate the potential endogenous nature of R&D investments and patenting activity, we instrument the innovation variables using their lagged values. This basically implies that we are using pre-determined values not only when considering dynamic relations (i.e. lagged regressors), but also when estimating contemporaneous relations.

The preferred lag structure is chosen adopting a 'general to specific' procedure in which statistically insignificant lags are removed on the basis of likelihood ratio tests. The errors u_i are the random effects, and the variable $sizec_{i,t}$ is a control for firm size, calculated as the log ratio between a firm's capitalization and total industry capitalization. Controlling for firm size is important due to the fact that small firms tend to be more volatile than large firms (in both growth rates and stock returns), a result commonly found in the literature.

We run the regressions of Models 1 and 2 for the entire period, and then for the two sub-periods, before and after the Bayh–Dole act (before and after 1982, allowing for the act to have an effect in its first two years). As a further robustness check, we re-estimate models 1 and 2 over a sample in which only above-average innovators are considered, i.e. the firms for which the R&D/REV ratio is above the unrestricted sample mean of 0.12. Finally we look at the role that different levels of R&D spending play, i.e. whether the relationships differ for above and below average R&D spenders.

---

[16] This assumption is questionable, since it is likely that the omitted factors that are relevant for the dependent variable are also relevant in determining the explanatory variable (Mundlack 1978). As regards our specific analysis, the omitted factors no doubt include tacit knowledge and managerial capabilities, factors that have relevant effects on both innovative activity and the market performance of a given firm.

5 Results

5.1 Dynamic Specification and Size Controls

Before discussing the results for each model, it is worth mentioning that best estimates are obtained with lagged regressors in Models 1 and 2. Only in Model 3 does VOL enter contemporaneously with no lag. Best estimates are obtained when selecting a second order lag for RD/REV and a first order lag for PATW, irrespective of the equation being estimated. This is evidence that RET and VOL are contemporaneously correlated and both depend on lagged measures of innovation, with R&D intensity preceding the patenting activity. Firm size is negatively correlated with relative volatility and positively correlated with relative performances.

The results of the preferred models are summarized in Table 3, and discussed below.

5.2 The Effect of Innovation on Volatility (Model 1)

When relative volatility VOL is regressed on the innovation variables (Eq. 1), it is found that R&D and citation weighted patents have positive and significant effects on relative volatility (5 % significance). Unweighted patent numbers are instead not significant. This suggests that investors in financial markets, when building their expectations about future growth performances, have likely learned that unweighted patents are very noisy signals about growth in this industry. This is because patents have been increasingly used for strategic reasons (carving out a technological area), and due to the fact that many areas that could not be patented before are being patented now (e.g. public research through the Bayh–Dole act, as well as upstream areas of research)—both leading to patents being a weaker signal of real changes in innovative activity. In this context there is an increased need for patents to be weighted if they are going to really signal potential growth. In fact, when we split the sample into the two periods, before and after the 1982 (to account for the effect of the 1980 Bayh–Dole act), it is indeed found that citation weighted patents are not significant in the first period, but are so in the second. This confirms that this weighting measure becomes relevant in the second period due to the noise that is introduced by the exponential increase in the number of patents.

The coefficient for lagged R&D effort for above average R&D spenders is larger in size and strongly significant. Lagged patents are instead not significant for these firms. Perceived risk is thus not affected by the patenting activity.

5.3 The Effect of Innovation on returns (Model 2)

When relative returns are regressed on R&D intensity and weighted patents (Eq. 2), only citation weighted patents have positive and significant effect on the dependent variable RET. While R&D has a positive effect on VOL it has a negative effect on RET. One explanation for this negative effect is the fact that R&D costs very much

Table 2 Estimation results (whole sample)

	Coeff.	Std. err.	t-stat.	Prob.
Equation 1				
Dependent variable: VOL				
IV Random Effects Panel ML regression				
Obs: 751				
Cross-section dimension (firms): 63				
CONST	0.125	0.007	17.9	0.000
SIZE_C	−0.510	0.143	−3.57	0.003
RD/REV(-2)	0.015	0.005	2.82	0.005
PATW(-1)	0.016	0.007	2.18	0.029
Sigma_u	0.041	0.005	7.38	0.000
Sigma_e	0.056	0.001	36.19	0.000
Log likelihood = 1032.306				
LR test of Sigma_u = 0: Chi_sq = 103.60, Prob. = 0.000				
Equation 2				
Dependent variable: RET				
IV Random Effects Panel ML regression				
Obs: 891				
Cross-section dimension (firms): 63				
CONST	0.012	0.004	2.67	0.008
SIZE_C	0.157	0.090	1.76	0.079
RD/REV(-2)	−0.011	0.004	−2.75	0.006
PATW(-1)	0.023	0.005	4.39	0.000
Sigma_u	0.023	0.003	7.89	0.000
Sigma_e	0.045	0.001	37.08	0.000
Log likelihood = 1222.253				
LR test of Sigma_u = 0: Chi_sq = 82.90, Prob. = 0.000				

in this industry (approx $403 million per drug) so it is seen as having a negative effect on short run profits driving shares. The positive effect of citation weighted patents on returns is possibly because patents are seen as being closer to the final innovative output (a potential new drug) making the financial markets less impatient with results. Firms with higher innovation activity are thus not expected to display higher returns, unless they are also characterized by higher patenting activity.

Unlike in Model 1, firm size has a positive (significant) sign, suggesting that larger firms have higher returns, as would be predicted.[17]

Considering the pre-post Bayh–Dole act sub-periods, we obtain that neither citation weighted patents nor R&D effort are significant in the first period, but are in the second. In the latter the R&D effort coefficient is again negative. Consistent with the results from Model 1, this result signals that the relationship between innovation activity and firm performance takes place as the exponential increase in the number of patents makes the information on firm specific innovation more

[17] However, out of interest we ran the same equation with Return-Earnings as the dependent variable, the sign is again negative as would be expected. Small innovative firms tend to have higher P/E both because their earnings are lower but also because the growth expectations driving returns is higher.

Table 3 Estimation results (pre Bayh–Dole)

	Coeff.	Std. err.	t-stat.	Prob.
Equation 1				
Dependent variable: VOL				
IV Random Effects Panel ML regression				
Obs: 184				
Cross-section dimension (firms): 25				
CONST	0.079	0.010	7.90	0.000
SIZE_C	−0.338	0.113	−2.98	0.003
RD/REV(-1)	0.087	0.037	2.35	0.019
PATW(-1)	−0.011	0.009	−1.25	0.211
Sigma_u	0.022	0.004	4.87	0.000
Sigma_e	0.029	0.002	17.4	0.000
Log likelihood = 368.577				
LR test of Sigma_u = 0: Chi_sq = 34.80, Prob. = 0.000				
Equation 2				
Dependent variable: RET				
IV Random Effects Panel ML regression				
Obs: 162				
Cross-section dimension (firms): 25				
CONST	0.045	0.009	4.87	0.000
SIZE_C	−0.160	0.101	−1.58	0.113
RD/REV(-2)	−0.051	0.034	−1.50	0.134
PATW(-1)	0.009	0.008	1.11	0.266
Sigma_u	0.017	0.004	4.77	0.000
Sigma_e	0.029	0.002	16.51	0.000

relevant to predict performances. Interestingly, the control for firm size has a negative sign in the first period and a positive sign in the second.

Considering the sample restricted to the highly innovative firms, the coefficients for both lagged R&D effort and lagged patents are not significant according to standard levels. In this case, lagged R&D effort and patenting are not valid predictors for returns.

5.4 The relationship between returns and volatility (Model 3)

Given the positive effect of innovation on both returns and volatility, it is not surprising that there is a positive relationship between these two financial measures. The relationship is found to be contemporaneous.

Results are summarized in Tables 2, 3, 4 and 5.

6 Conclusion

Our study finds evidence that the *degree* of volatility (idiosyncratic) for stock returns in the US pharmaceutical industry is related to underlying innovation dynamics. This finding provides empirical support to untested assumptions made

Table 4 Estimation results (post Bayh–Dole)

	Coeff.	Std. err.	t-stat.	Prob.
Equation 1				
Dependent variable: VOL				
IV Random Effects Panel ML regression				
Obs: 589				
Cross-section dimension (firms): 63				
CONST	0.135	0.007	18.10	0.000
SIZE_C	−0.795	0.164	−4.83	0.000
RD/REV(-1)	0.013	0.006	2.33	0.020
PATW(-1)	0.016	0.009	1.93	0.054
Sigma_u	0.040	0.005	7.76	0.000
Sigma_e	0.061	0.002	32.04	0.000
Log likelihood = 767.39				
LR test of Sigma_u = 0: Chi_sq = 83.57, Prob. = 0.000				
Equation 2				
Dependent variable: RET				
IV Random Effects Panel ML regression				
Obs: 590				
Cross-section dimension (firms): 63				
CONST	0.010	0.005	2.05	0.040
SIZE_C	0.294	0.112	2.61	0.009
RD/REV(-2)	−0.010	0.004	−2.43	0.015
PATW(-1)	0.020	0.006	3.18	0.001
Sigma_u	0.025	0.003	7.30	0.000
Sigma_e	0.047	0.001	32.34	0.000
Log likelihood = 895.340				
LR test of Sigma_u = 0: Chi_sq = 60.53, Prob. = 0.000				

in recent finance models on the relationship between technological change and stock price volatility (Shiller 2000; Campbell et al. 2001).

We use firm level R&D and patent data (citation weighted) to test whether firms that are ‘more innovative’ are characterized by higher (than average) volatility of stock returns and higher levels of market value and price-earnings ratios. We find that both the level and volatility of stock returns is in fact related to innovation. This of course does not mean that valuation is ‘rational’ or correct in any sense. It simply means that financial markets seem indeed to react to the ‘signals’ that firms provide, via their R&D spending and patenting behaviour, about their future growth prospects. But while the *degree* of volatility appears to be affected by such signals (raising investors’ sometimes exaggerated growth expectations), the *existence* of the volatility itself is of course related to other factors highlighted by behavioral finance theorists, such as loss aversion, bandwagon effects, herding, etc. (Kahneman and Tversky 1979). The presence of those ‘behavioral’ factors means that the insistence by some theorists, such as Pastor and Veronesi (2005), that the relationship between innovation and volatility provides evidence of ‘rational bubbles’ is not warranted. Our findings, in sum, provide a sort of ‘middle ground’ which connects the *irrational exuberance* of investors (Keynesian ‘animal spirits’)

Table 5 Estimation results (highly innovative firms)

	Coeff.	Std. err.	t-stat.	Prob.
Equation 1				
Dependent variable: VOL				
IV Random Effects Panel ML regression				
Obs: 158				
Cross-section dimension (firms): 28				
CONST	0.144	0.013	11.13	0.000
SIZE_C	−23.670	10.603	−2.23	0.026
RD/REV(-1)	0.028	0.007	3.85	0.000
PATW(-1)	0.008	0.017	0.45	0.651
Sigma_u	0.000	0.026	0.00	1.000
Sigma_e	0.078	0.004	17.78	0.000
Log likelihood = 298.421				
LR test of Sigma_u = 0: Chi_sq = 28.32, Prob. = 0.000				
Equation 2				
Dependent variable: RET				
IV Random Effects Panel ML regression				
Obs: 158				
Cross-section dimension (firms): 28				
CONST	0.014	0.005	2.05	0.040
SIZE_C	0.236	0.121	1.94	0.051
RD/REV(-2)	0.005	0.003	1.35	0.168
PATW(-1)	0.014	0.011	1.27	0.209
Sigma_u	0.029	0.004	7.66	0.000
Sigma_e	0.049	0.002	31.6	0.000
Log likelihood = 317.453				
LR test of Sigma_u = 0: Chi_sq = 18.74, Prob. = 0.000				

to the *structural* dimensions of the real economy (spending on innovation)—but as changes in that structure are affected by Knightian uncertainty, this connection is not about a perfect or 'rational' valuation procedure but rather a force that connects, in a messy but tractable way, investors' expectations about future growth rates and firms' spending on innovation.

The lag structure of the innovation variables provides insights into the speed at which the market reacts to innovation 'signals'. Lags are higher for R&D than for patents (citation weighted), suggesting that the market reacts more quickly to signals regarding innovation outputs than inputs. In fact, it is sensible to think that uncertainty is highest at the time a patent is applied for, since this includes the uncertainty regarding whether the patent will be granted, as well as uncertainty regarding the effect of the patent (if granted) on firm growth. This is especially true in the pharma industry where there is a high patenting rate but a very low rate of new drug discovery (Orsenigo et al. 2001). Pisano (2006), in fact, claims that one way that the pharma industry differs from other high tech industries, such as computers and software, is the profound and persistent uncertainty of the R&D process due to the limited knowledge of human biological systems (as opposed to chemical or electronic).[18]

We find that volatility is higher in the case of small firms (proxied by market share) and in the post 1985 period which is characterized by a more *guided search* regime (due to scientific and organizational changes discussed in Gambardella 1995). The higher volatility in the latter period is most likely related to the fact that this period is characterized by an 'inflation' of patents (due to the effect of the 1980 Bayh–Dole act on patenting behavior), which reduces their reliability as a 'signal' of real innovation (hence more mistakes made by investors). The fact that citation weighted patents have a stronger effect on volatility than simple patent counts, suggests that the market is able to, at least partially, filter through this noise.

More broadly, our results confirm that innovation variables are important in capturing the levels of 'risk' embodied in firm performance and as such have an impact on both returns (risk-return) and volatility (risk-volatility)—as would be expected in the finance literature. However, the fact that innovation is not just risk but real Knightian uncertainty means that these results should not be used to justify those finance models that might predict this relationship based on the assumption of underlying normal distributions of returns. Rather, we have shown that innovation, with all the uncertainty that it embodies, should be taken more seriously in finance models and in doing so help to provide a Schumpetarian foundation to the analysis of bubble dynamics.

References

Bresnahan TF, Greenstein S (1997) Technological Competition and the structure of the computer industry. J Ind Econ 47(1):1–40

Campbell JY, Lettau M, Malkiel BG, Yexiao X (2001) Have individual stocks become more volatile? An empirical exploration of idiosyncratic risk. J Finance 56:1–43

Deng Y (2005) The value of knowledge spillovers. Paper presented at the CEF annual conference, Washington DC, 24 June 2005

Gambardella A (1995) Science and innovation in the US Pharmaceutical Industry. Cambridge University Press, Cambridge

Griliches Z, Hall B, Pakes A (1991) R&D, patents and market value revisited: is there ad second (technological opportunity) factor? Econ Innov New Technol 1:1983–1201

Hall B, Jaffe A, Trajtenberg M (2001) The NBER patent citations data file. In: Jaffe AB, Trajtenberg M (eds) Patents, citations and innovations: a window on the knowledge economy. MIT Press, Boston

Hall BH, Jaffe A, Trajtenberg M (2005) Market value and patent citations. Rand J Econ 36(1):16–38

Harris G (2002) Why drug makers are failing in quest for new blockbusters. Wall Street Journal. 18 March 2002

[18] This is one of the reasons for its low R&D productivity, a delusion for those that hoped that biotech's more nimble structure would save pharma's low turnout of new drugs.

Henderson R, Orsenigo L, Pisano G (1999) The pharmaceutical industry and the revolution in molecular biology: interactions among scientific, institutional and organizational change. In: Mowery D, Nelson R (eds) Sources of industrial leadership. Cambridge
Hymer S, Pashigian P (1962). Firm size and rate of growth. J Polit Econ 70(6):556–569
Jaffe AB, Trajtenberg M (2002) Patents, citations and innovations: a window on the knowledge economy. MIT Press, Boston
Kahneman D, Tversky A (1979) Prospect theory: an analysis of decisions under risk. Econometrica 47(2):263–291
Klepper S (1996) Exit, entry, growth, and innovation over the product life-cycle. Am Econ Rev 86(3):562–583
Knight FH (1921) Risk, uncertainty and profit. Houghton Mifflin, Boston
Mazzucato M (2002) The PC industry: new economy or early life-cycle. Rev Econ Dyn 5:318–345
Mazzucato M (2003) Risk, variety and volatility: innovation, growth and stock returns in old and new industries. J Evol Econ 13(5):491–512
Mazzucato M, Semmler W (1999) Stock market volatility and market share instability during the US auto industry life-cycle. J Evol Econ 9(1):67–96
Mazzucato M, Tancioni M (2008) Idiosyncratic risk and innovation: a firm and industry level analysis. Ind Corp Change 17(4):779–811
Mowery DC, Ziedonis AA (2002). Academic patent quality and quantity before and after the Bayh–Dole act in the United States. Res Policy 31(3):399–418
Mundlack Y (1978) On the pooling of time series and cross section data. Econometrica 46:69–85
Orsenigo L, Pammolli F, Riccaboni M (2001) Technological change and network dynamics. Lessons from the pharmaceutical industry. Res Policy 30:485–509
Pakes A (1985) On patents, R&D, and the stock market rate of return. J Polit Econ 93(2):390–409
Pastor L, Veronesi P (2004) Was there a Nasdaq Bubble in the Late 1990's. J Financ Econ 81(1):61–100
Pastor L, Veronesi P (2005) Technological revolutions and stock returns. National Bureau of Economic Research w11876
Perez C (2002) Technological revolutions and financial capital: the dynamics of bubbles and golden ages. Edward Elgar, Cheltenham
Pisano GP (2006) Can science be a business? Lessons from Biotech. Harvard Business Review, October, 114–125
Scherer FM, Ross D (1990). Industrial market structure and economic performance. Houghton Mifflin Company, Boston
Schwert GW (1989) Why does stock market volatility change over time? J Finance 54:1115–1153
Shiller RJ (1981) Do stock returns move too much to be justified by subsequent changes in dividends. Am Econ Rev 71:421–435
Shiller RJ (2000) Irrational exuberance. Princeton University Press, Princeton
Tushman M, Anderson P (1986) Technological discontinuities and organizational environments. Adm Sci Q 31:439–465

On Profit Differentials Between Persistent and Occasional Innovators: New Evidences from a Random-Coefficient Treatment Model

Giovanni Cerulli and Bianca Potì

Abstract The paper studies the medium-term effect of being a persistent (occasional) innovator on firm economic return within a "counterfactual" setting using a random-coefficient model. This approach allows us to assess not only the point effect of a persistent/occasional innovation strategy on profitability, as in standard regression settings, but the "entire distribution" of it. We exploit a 9 years (1998–2006) longitudinal dataset of Italian manufacturing firms obtained by a merging of the last three waves of the Capitalia/Unicredit survey (eighth, ninth and tenth survey).

Results show a strong better economic performance of the group of firms that continuously implement their innovating capacity and output. Also occasional innovation produces good operating profit margin (OPM) differentials, although we estimate a difference with the persistent behavior of about *three* (percentage) points lower. Differences between occasional and persistent innovators are also enlightened at a dynamic level: we found that persistent innovation allows for a dynamic advantage against occasional "first-time-only" innovative strategy. Moreover, the analysis of the idiosyncratic distribution of the effect, based on the random-coefficient model, allows us to inspect what factors lead to be persistent innovators and we identify the "best performers" among them. These champions are characterized by a large stock of accumulated knowledge, a large size and operate in more concentrated markets. This result confirms what we have found in the literature on innovation persistence: dynamic capability building can be found mainly when a mechanism of increasing returns to scale is operating and this is mainly present in few leading companies.

G. Cerulli (✉) • B. Potì
Ceris-CNR, Institute for Economic Research on Firms and Growth, National Research Council, Unit of Rome, Italy
e-mail: g.cerulli@ceris.cnr.it; b.poti@ceris.cnr.it

A. Pyka and E.S. Andersen (eds.), *Long Term Economic Development*, Economic Complexity and Evolution, DOI 10.1007/978-3-642-35125-9_16,

1 Introduction

This paper develops within the Schumpeterian/evolutionary analysis of the relation between firm innovative performance and profitability, exploiting a new methodological perspective, with a focus on firms' heterogeneous responses within "persistent" and "occasional" innovation strategies. We look at a causal relation between innovation and profitability, at factors explaining this and at the heterogeneity within innovation strategies. In a previous work (Potì and Cerulli 2009) the authors of this paper, by using the third Italian Community Innovation Survey, identified differences in firm economic returns (operating profit margins, OPM) for various subgroups of innovation strategies, putting into evidence factors explaining the probability of being within the best performers in each group of innovation strategy. The main results of that study were: first, when studying the economic impact of innovation activity it is worth to distinguish among different kinds of innovation strategies rather than limiting the analysis to an aggregated level, as firm heterogeneity does matter especially in an evolutionary market environment; second, competition awards more complex innovation strategies, characterized by a persistent innovation behavior, generally accompanied by articulated R&D and patenting activities: being a persistent innovator should represent a sort of protection or a basis for firm self-selection among the best performers. The limit of that paper was to be based on a cross-section analysis, focused on a short period of just 3 years (1998–2000), given data availability constraints.

The idea of the present paper is to verify the presence of a causal relation between the permanence of the profit differential and the persistence of an innovation behaviour on a medium term (a period of 9 years) within a "counterfactual" comparison with a non-innovating strategy. At our knowledge there is only another paper using a counterfactual approach in this context, but it focuses only on innovation persistence and not on the relation between this strategy and firm profitability differentials (Duguet and Monjon 2004).

More specifically, our paper aims at answering the following questions: (i) Are persistent innovation strategies actually rewarding more firms adopting them when compared with the pivotal case of non-innovating strategies? (ii) Is occasional innovation sufficient to guarantee higher returns compared to returns from non-innovative strategies? And which is the differential effect of occasional and persistent innovation? (iii) What kind of "dynamic effect" does persistent innovation generate when compared to a "one-time-only" innovation strategy? (iv) What observable characteristics differentiate, among the group of persistent innovators, the best performers?

We exploit a sample of Italian manufacturing firms and define as persistent innovators those firms that innovate in all the three periods considered (the three most recent waves of the Capitalia/Unicredit surveys on Italian manufacturing covering the period 1998–2006), and as occasional those firms innovating at least in one of the three waves. We measure innovation in a large and qualitative meaning and study the effect on a quantitative variable (the operating profit margin).

In the Schumpeterian world today's profits are related to yesterday's, but are expected to be converging to the competitive norm in a regime of "creative destruction", while they can have increasing cumulative characters in a Mark II regime, where innovation is cumulative or also routine-based and large firms operate in a more stable technical environment. The presence of "persistence in innovation" is explored by a growing body of empirical literature, showing that there is a small core group of persistent innovators, a large group of occasional innovators and a persistent group of non innovators (Geroski et al. 1997; Cefis and Orsenigo 2001; Malerba and Orsenigo 1996; Cefis 2003; Peters 2009; Raymond et al. 2006). The first objective of our work is to investigate if there is a permanent profit differential among these groups.

A measure of profit persistence used in the literature is a measure of permanent rents, which are not eroded by competitive forces (the long-run profit rate), and several empirical studies showed that firms display persistent differences in profitability (Mueller 1986, 1990; Cefis 2003; Dosi 2007; Goddard and Wilson 1999; Odagiri and Maruyama 2002); Geroski et al. 2003; Gschwandtner 2004; (Crespo-Cuaresma and Gschwandtner 2008).

The literature on profit persistence shows that even if it is difficult for a firm to repeat a very good or very bad performance over time, there is a core group that persists in outperforming and "this result confirms that very dynamic firms are usually very different from other firms in that they can show strong [profit] autocorrelation patterns" (Capasso et al. 2009, p. 21). Our work develops upon three lines:

Firstly, using a counterfactual approach we try to answer to the question: "which is the difference between the economic performance of a firm having innovated along a period of 9 years and the economic performance the same firm would have realized if it had not innovated in the same period?". In this way we identify a non-spurious causal relation (the bias of the self-selection among the persistent innovators due to specific firm characters being avoid), and we measure the "effect" of being a persistent innovator in terms of a different rate of profit. Furthermore, we use a *random coefficient treatment model*, that allows to estimate the entire distribution of the effect of innovating on profits, an aspect that shed more light on firm heterogeneous response, thus overcoming the limits posed by standard regression analysis where only a single average effect is recovered. Then, by replicating the same estimation procedure, we compare the economic effect of being a persistence innovator with that of being an occasional innovator (a firm which has innovated at least once in a period of 9 years).

Secondly, thanks to the use of a random coefficient estimation, we can look at the distribution of the profit differential across companies by identifying the group of them getting a positive differential (i.e. a positive "treatment" effect), that is a core set of persistently innovating firms laying on the right tail of the distribution: these firms can be identified as (commercially and technologically) successful. Then, we analyse what explains the profit persistence by testing some theoretical explanations we found in the literature, where various factors, driving "innovation persistence" on the one hand and "profit persistence" on the other, are put forward. Indeed, according to the literature, being a "persistent innovator" can be explained by: (1) The persistence of the "state" of innovator, mainly due to: (i) the presence of *sunk cost* related to R&D efforts; (ii) the *cumulativeness* of knowledge, mainly linked to learning effects as "cumulativeness captures the incremental nature of technological search" (Dosi and Nelson 2009, p. 20); (iii) the resources or profits gained in the past, which reduce innovator *liquidity constraints*; (2) The competence basis of the firm and its "dynamic capabilities". Differently from the previous cumulative mechanism, dynamic capabilities refer to "deliberate efforts of managers", accompanied by costly investment (i.e. long-term commitments to specialized resources) to adapt or change firm internal routines (Winter 2003), conferring some competitive advantage over competitors (Teece et al. 1997); finally, (3) The "context conditions", including market structural factors. As for the "persistence of profit", the literature looks mainly at competition conditions, market structure and technological opportunities, but also at the strategies followed, by studying the long-run profit differential among firms with different market power, different market structure and strategies. With regard to our results on this part, we find out that *two* main factors explain the positive profit differential within the group of persistent innovators: building market barriers (a classical statement of industrial organization theory) and knowledge accumulation (a fundamental aspect of the evolutionary theory). Size matters too, but it is less relevant and eventually linked to: (i) market barriers, being a barrier in itself (lower costs, portfolios of multiple innovations) and (ii) the process of learning (through scale and scope economies).

Thirdly, we look at the dynamics of the profit margin differences (identified always through a treatment effect approach) by comparing two groups of firms with different innovating behaviour: firms which innovated only in the first period and the whole group of firms which innovated each of the three periods considered. We find out that in our sample the group of persistent innovators starts with a lower level of differential profit (i.e. the difference with the case in which the same firms would have not innovated at all) and progressively improve their relative position, showing the possibility of a catching-up based on the process of persistently innovating.

As far as our results are concerned, very concisely we find out:

- a steady *causal* profit-differential among the *occasional* and the *persistent* innovating strategy over 9 years, with a decisive higher performance in the group of persistent innovators;
- a large-tailed distribution of profit differentials across persistent innovators, assuming also negative values: not all the firms with this strategy would gain compared with the situation in which the same unit had not been innovating.
- some main characters identifying the best performers among the group of persistent innovators: the explanation is found both in industrial organization

theory (market barriers) and in evolutionary theory (accumulated stock of knowledge).

- a catching-up process of persistence innovation over a "first-time-only" innovation strategy: even if in the first period of observation we observe that the profit differential (still measured using non-innovators as comparison group) of persistent innovators is lower than that of occasional innovators, subsequently the group of persistent innovators is found to gain momentum until to outperform occasional performance.

In a nutshell, our conclusion is that the process of being a persistent innovator matters, but it is not sufficient to guarantee a medium-term return higher than non innovator's one, since to face imitation needs building market barriers and accumulating a relevant stock of knowledge.

The paper is organized as follows: Sect. 2 presents a review of two streams of literature on innovation and profit differential persistency; Sect. 3 shows the econometric model employed. In Sect. 4 we present the dataset used and the variables used for the empirical analysis. We then go on by setting out, in Sect. 5 and subsections, the main results along with their relative comments. Section 6 concludes the paper.

2 Literature Background

Two main streams of literature dealing with the relation between innovation persistence and firm profitability can be identified: (1) the literature studying the innovation persistence, mainly focusing on identifying its presence, spell length and determinants as well as, mainly through case studies, the dynamic path of the phenomenon; (2) the literature on the "effects" of the innovation persistence, primarily focusing on profit persistence and on the "characters" of differential economic returns between innovators and non innovators. The second stream of studies benefits of some arguments of the first one (innovation persistence), that's why, even if our analysis is better placed within the second stream, we start making reference to the recently growing literature on innovation persistence.

The literature on innovation persistence offers relevant theoretical and empirical perspectives on the subject of profit differentials. Basically, it refers to three main theoretical bodies: (i) the Schumpeterian/evolutionary theory (dealing with how firms accumulate technological capabilities over time for sustaining lifelong competitiveness), (ii) endogenous growth theory (based on a macroeconomic perspective of technical change); (iii) industrial organization theory and models of technological competitiveness (in particular, *patent race* models).

The Schumpeterian literature includes two hypotheses/regimes: that of "creative accumulation" shaped by cumulative forces, irreversibility and positive feedbacks and that of "creative destruction", where the profit gained through innovation has a short term duration. The "accumulation regime" is characterized by the persistence of a stable group of firms. In the "creative destruction" case innovation process has a stochastic nature and innovation is a random event, which "incessantly revolutionizes the economic structure from within, incessantly destroying the old one, incessantly creating a new one" (Schumpeter 1942, p. 83). Progress creates losses as well as gains.

Within the endogenous growth theory two main models confront each other: (i) Romer's model (1990), where innovation-based growth is referred to horizontal product innovations (product variety) not involving obsolescence (new products are not better than existing ones) and the production of goods exhibits increasing return. (ii) Aghion and Howitt model (1992), in which growth is based on vertical innovation (change in quality, as new products render previous ones obsolete) and the inter-temporal relation between two amounts of research is modelled as deterministic: the amount of research in any period depends negatively upon the expected amount of next period (due to the "current rent" destruction).

Within the Industrial Organization theory, the innovation process can be modelled as done in the *patent race* literature and two main models confront each other: Gilbert and Newbery (1982) consider innovation that is non drastic in nature, i.e. incumbent and challenger compete and the incumbent commits to an R&D strategy and to patent innovations, assuming that it will gain greater profit by monopolizing the innovation. Within the alternative model, Reinganum (1983) introduces uncertainty on when the research effort will succeed; the incumbent, who has a greater amount to lose, in case of drastic or quasi-drastic innovation spend less than the challenger and, since greater spending speed the time of a successful innovation, it is likely not to innovate first.

The empirical literature about the dynamics of firms' innovation behaviour can help in assessing previous different theories and in understanding how and under which conditions "innovation implies systematic heterogeneity across firms" (Cefis and Orsenigo 2001, p. 1156). Moreover the results of these studies on persistence in innovation at micro level shed light on industrial dynamics and evolution, by looking at whether "some forms of dynamic increasing returns play a major role in degree of concentration and its stability over time" (Cefis 2003, p. 491). This empirical literature on innovation persistence is now highly diversified in terms of innovation measurements, methodologies and data, but some common body of aims and results can be recognised.

Innovation persistence can be defined as a continuous state of realizing innovation and innovation can be measured in various ways: (i) as applying for/granting patents (Geroski et al. 1997; Cefis and Orsenigo 2001; Malerba and Orsenigo 1997) or successfully introducing new products on the market (Geroski et al. 1997, for instance, use major innovations). These empirical studies are more linked to firm strategic behavior, patent race and market competition; (ii) as introducing innovation in a large meaning: new product, new process and organizational innovations (Peters 2004; Roper and Hewitt-Dundas 2008); (iii) as measuring internal firm capacity and competence transformation in terms of productivity (Antonelli and Scellato 2009), since "evolutionary economists emphasize that differences in firm productivity should be expected given the idiosyncratic routines, capabilities and competencies of firms and their different learning processes" (Capasso et al. 2009, p. 2).

The models are sensitive to the type of measurement used (Duguet and Monjon 2004) and can be differently designed in terms of innovation persistence's characters and drivers, but they arrive at similar conclusions, since—also when innovation is not identified with "leadership" position (i.e. when innovation data are used instead of patents or major product innovation)—persistence in innovation meets some limits, as a non linear relation between technological performance and level (or duration) of innovation can be identified (Roper and Hewitt-Dundas 2008).

Furthermore, empirical studies have looked at the phenomenon of innovation persistence through different methodologies, and two have been particularly applied: "hazard models" to study the innovation spell length and the cumulative time effects, and "random effect discrete choice models" to study the effect that a previous innovation has on the probability of further innovation at a point in time. Both these types of models include at least two kinds of components: the initial innovation status and the (observed or unobserved) firm heterogeneity. The absence or not satisfying treatment of firm heterogeneity in early studies have brought to use the critical term of "spurious state dependence" (Peters 2004), since companies can possess specific characteristics making their innovation particularly persistent.

Three main drivers or sources of innovation persistence have been stressed in empirical studies: (1) "state-dependence", i.e. the probability of being an innovator at time t is higher if a firm was an innovator at time $t-1$. In this case the innovating behavior reproduces almost automatically itself in the subsequent step. An explanation for state-dependence is found in: (i) *increasing returns* generated by self-reinforcing feedbacks and spillovers (new growth literature) and *dynamic economies* of scale based on learning by doing (evolutionary literature), according to which current knowledge (and innovation) builds on past knowledge within an adaptive process (Dosi and Nelson 2009); (ii) *accumulation of knowledge* over time (Nelson and Winter 1982a) and firm internal capacity transformed by the event of innovating; (iii) reduction of *liquidity constraints*, allowed by the competitive advantages of a firm experimenting successful innovation and thereby higher profits (Nelson and Winter 1982b); (iv) *sunk costs* associated to R&D investment (Sutton 1991), which represent a barrier to exit the market, as they cannot be fully recovered; (2) firm heterogeneity, i.e. idiosyncratic characters of firms. In this regard, the resource/competence-based theory explains firms' heterogeneity (in innovating and in performance) on the basis of endowment and organizational aspects, including firm dynamic capabilities, i.e. the ability of a firm of adapting to changes, by modifying its internal routines. Firm heterogeneity reduces the role of "state" dependence, in favor of a "path" dependence; (3) the "context conditions": Antonelli and Scellato (2009) develop this argument in terms of accessibility to the pool of knowledge in the system, while Geroski et al. (2007) introduce the question of context in terms of the role of demand and market competition, as factors constraining the "state" dependence. Hence, the evolutionary idea of the innovation experience as a radical transformation process on the part of innovating firms can be sustained/constrained also by other conditions. One crucial question in empirical models is how much the persistence of innovation may be explained by the "state" dependence or by the observed/unobserved heterogeneity of firms.

As for results, within the empirical literature on innovation persistence, some are now largely shared and in particular: (i) the polarization of the persistent state: (high percentages of) non innovators and large innovators tend to remain in their position over time (Cefis and Orsenigo 2001); (ii) the presence of a large body of occasional innovators, whose profit are temporary (Malerba and Orsenigo 1995).

Beyond the diffusion of the innovation persistence (percentage of firms which are persistent innovators), which is different if major innovations or minor (routine) innovations are considered, there can be differences in terms of the spell length, that is, for how many successive years the firm continues to innovate. Geroski et al. (1997, p. 38) find out that only a low percentage (30 %) of all patenting spell are ongoing after 1 year; only a small number of spells (around 4 %) last for more than 5 years, and a high percentage of spells (70 %) starting with only one product innovation ended after two periods. A key aspect is related to the presence of dynamic economies of scale in "state" dependence, in this case innovation spell length is endogenously determined and "success breeds success". The presence of dynamic economies of scale is assessed in the literature under two specification: in terms of initial level of innovations (the threshold level of pre-spell innovation activity necessary to generate a certain spell length) and in terms of duration dependence, that is "the more innovation a firm produces, the more likely it is to continue to innovate" due to a sort of innovation learning curve (Geroski et al. 1997, p. 33). The threshold level of patents inducing a patenting spell of 3 or more years is around five patents. An initial degree of relative disadvantage declines smoothly as the initial level of innovation rises. But other scholars (Jang and Chen 2011) using patent data for the IT sector in Taiwan, survival regression and a Weibull specification, find out that the initial patent count exhibits a non linear positive effect on the tenacity of patenting. The authors found no enhancing effect in their sample after the threshold of four patents, once accounting for firm specific control variables. So, the initial increase of persistent patenting behaviour can dissipate when the patent stock reaches a certain threshold. Roper and Hewitt-Dundas (2008, p. 360), by combining a quantitative analysis of innovation persistence based on an innovation panel data with a series of case-studies, also find out that the persistence of "high levels" of sales of innovative products declines monotonically from the initial level: plants with high levels of sales of innovative products in a 3-year period find it hard to sustain this position through the next period. Indeed, even if a relatively high level of innovation persistence is present, thus suggesting a Schumpeterian Mark II innovation regime, some factors can interrupt this process.

The main message from the literature based on patents or major innovations is that the process of knowledge generation can yield sharp diminishing return "when referred to knowledge embodied in new goods or in patents" (Geroski et al. 1997, p. 45); in fact, "it is very hard to find any evidence at all that innovative activity can be self sustaining over anything other than very short period of time" (p. 46). This literature is biased toward "leadership through innovation", but a non linear character of the dynamic economies of scale in innovation is found also by the literature using innovation data.

The literature on profit persistence pays attention to the long-run persistent profitability differences across firms and to the presence of persistently long-run (above/below) average returns due to firm or industry characteristics and to business strategies: "The extent to which profits persist above the norm depends on how successful firms overcome the challenge posed by the need to adapt and to pre-empt imitators" (Geroski and Jacquemin 1988, p. 376). Geroski and Jacquemin (1988) examine the persistence of profit amongst large firms and compare how differences in the competitive process affect firms' profits. To enjoy a persistent profit (a rate of return in excess from the average) a firm must adapt to exogenous changes in its environment and to the endogenous change produced by its previous success (i.e. attracting imitators).

This literature uses as main theoretical reference the structure-conduct-performance approach (Mueller 1990; Geroski et al. 1993; Cefis and Ciccarelli 2005): "profits are assumed to depend on the threat of entry in the market and the threat is itself assumed to depend on the profits observed in the last period" (Gschwandtner 2005, p. 209). The presence of profit persistence is interpreted as an indicator of imperfection in the fulfilment of the competitive environment hypothesis. This literature finds out that industry and firm characteristics contribute in explaining profit persistence, even if with mixed evidence. As for the relation between concentration and profit persistence Scherer and Ross (1990) claim that it is not clear if the relationship between profitability and concentration is a positive one, since companies in the industry keep prices high in order to increase profits or a negative one because they keep prices low in order to deter entry. Mueller (1990) find a negative relationship between profitability and concentration for US data and claims that non price competition increases with concentration and lowers profits. In principle, a negative relationship between the profit persistence measures and the size of the industry is expected; however, Gschwandtner (2005) does not find a significant relationship between size of the industry and profit persistence. The effect of firm size on profit persistence might be positive or negative too. Geroski and Jacquemin (1988, p. 338) claim that there are systematic associations between various structural traits of firms, industry characteristics and the persistence of success: the role of openness to international trade and of concentration is particularly important (a less concentrated industry could bring a slower adjustment to long-run profit level), however "it remains difficult to find factors that are systematically associated with the persistence of profits". According to the same scholars, country factors may result more discriminating than industry or firm specific ones.

The literature on profit persistence takes also explicitly into consideration the impact of firm's strategy (innovation as well as advertising, research and development, merging, etc.) (Geroski et al. 2003). Geroski et al. (1997) found a positive direct effect of innovations on profitability at short run and large indirect effects due to the insensitivity of firms "to adverse macroeconomic shocks". Cefis and Ciccarelli (2005) investigate if differences in profit between innovators and non innovators are caused by the innovation activity. They compare three different groups of firms—innovators, non-innovators and persistent innovators—and test (by a Kolmogorov-Smirnov statistic) whether the deviation of firm OPM from the OPM mean of the industry to which the firm belongs is equal or not. These scholars find that the persistent innovators have a mean, median and maximum value of profit higher than non innovator group and conclude that innovation seems to be the (or one of the main) source of profit differentials. Cefis and Ciccarelli (2005, p. 53) claim that the method for taking into account firm heterogeneity is crucial and that adopting a Bayesian specification allows to "reveal a reasonable pattern of the impact of innovations on profits as well as a greater cumulative and long run impact". The cumulated impact of innovation on profitability increases up to the second/third lag and then decreases smoothly. The effect of dynamic economies of scale (persistence of innovation state) seems more relevant than the "level" of innovation: in fact, for a persistent innovator, the initial number of patents (innovations) counts less than being an innovator, differently for an occasional innovator where the initial number of innovations has a positive effect on profitability.

Geroski et al. (1993) too claim that innovating firms' profitability is less linked to the output of an innovation process, than to the process of innovation itself, transforming the internal firm capabilities. The production of innovation outputs receives the impact of market dynamic forces, systematic (such as threat of entry, actual entry, intra-industrial mobility and investment competition among leaders), and unsystematic/unpredictable forces (such as "good luck" and stochastic firms' entry, non induced by previous profits), bringing profit near the industrial average in a relatively short time. But permanent differences in the profitability between innovating and non-innovating firms endure (Geroski et al. 1993).

Another way to study the effect of firm persistent strategy of research (and innovation) on its profit is developed using the firm's profit decomposition suggested by Mueller (1986, 1990). The firm's profit at time *t* is split into three components: the normal competitive return, a firm permanent rent (a premium for risk) and a transitory rent. This kind of studies looks at the presence of "asymmetry in the convergence" process among firms, "where less successful firms (below an industry-average profitability) did converge to the competitive return" while more profitable firms show more persistent returns (Eklund and Wiberg 2007, p. 4). The microeconomic theory states that the competition process will bring profits to a normal return, through entry and exit dynamics. This hypothesis can be tested comparing the long run profits of different firms, for instance more and less persistent R&D performers. Eklund and Wiberg (2007, p. 9) find out that firms' profit do converge, but "the process is partial" and the estimated equilibrium profit rates for each different group of firms deviates from the average returns. The best performing firms in the long-run are still presenting profits above the average. There are asymmetries in the profit convergence as well as in the profit persistence: by studying the profit dynamics there is evidence of time varying profit persistence.

According to this theoretical background, in this paper we make the hypothesis that a persistence in profit differentials can be at work among the three groups of non-innovators, persistent and occasional innovators on medium-term (9 years), and we look for a "causal" relation. Then we study the distribution of the "profitability difference" at firm level, in order to get a clearer understanding of what are the sources of the "positive" profit differential. In fact, being a persistent innovator doesn't avoid that the market selection forces operate, producing winners as well as losers.

We also check the dynamic pattern of the profit differential between persistent innovators and occasional innovating firms (innovating only in the first period) during the considered period of time. The increasing differential shows the possibility of catching-up based on a (continuous on three periods) process of innovating. Finally, we look at the dynamics of the level of the operating profit margin (OPM) for the three groups of firms (persistent, occasional and simple innovators), i.e. if there is a trend towards convergence and if it doesn't counter totally the profit level difference among the three groups.

Compared to the current literature the novelty of our paper is in the use of a random coefficient model within a treatment evaluation setting which, compared to standard regression analysis, allows us to estimate not only the point effect of a persistent/occasional innovation strategy on the OPM—the so-called "average treatment effect", ATE, and "average treatment effect on treated", ATET—but the "entire distribution" of this effect over companies as a function of their observable characteristics. Relying on a "distribution" rather than only on one single statistical moment (usually, the "mean") brings with it a great amount of further information about the heterogeneous response of firms to the innovative event. As it is unquestionable that heterogeneity is essential both to be studied *per se* and, even more, to inspect more in-depth the actual meaning of aggregated results, we believe our model to help in the direction of a major understanding of the relation between innovative efforts and market success.

3 Methodology

We study the persistency of innovators' profit differentials by applying a "treatment model" estimated by a "random coefficient regression" (instead of a standard regression approach), with a specific attention thus paid to the estimation of the entire "distribution" of profit differentials over the three periods (consisting of 3 years each). In a treatment context the differential "operating profit margin" between innovators (i.e., treated firms) and non-innovating firms (i.e., untreated units) becomes the "treatment effect", whose cumulative distribution function (c.d. f.) estimated over time carries a lot information and evidence on the way innovative strategies award treated compared to non-treated companies. This approach overcomes the standard practice of relying merely on the significance of a single coefficient, as usually occurs in regression models, in so approaching more a non-parametric analysis of the innovation-performance relationship.

Furthermore, this methodology is especially suitable in a context of Schumpeterian competition, where the relation between innovation and market success is crucially thought to be firm specific and highly idiosyncratic. Thus, our approach seems appropriate to verify what has changed in profit differential distribution during the three periods considered and which factors impacted more substantially on this change.

The starting point is that of modelling three behavioural equations: one for the self-selection decision of firms "to become innovating" according to a specific objective function (unknown to the researcher), one for explaining the OPM behaviour of innovating (treated) firms and one for the operating profit margin behaviour of non-innovating (untreated) firms. The firm self-selection equation takes on the following form:

$$w^* = \eta + \mathbf{x}_1\boldsymbol{\theta} + a$$
$$w = \begin{cases} 1 & if \ \ w^* \geq 0 \\ 0 & if \ \ w^* < 0 \end{cases} \tag{1}$$

In Eq. (1) w^* is the optimal level of innovation chosen by the firm with characteristics given by the vector of covariates $\mathbf{x}_1$, $\boldsymbol{\theta}$ is a vector of parameters, while w is the index function (taking zero/one values) denoting the rule according to which the firm decides to innovate or not, given certain $\mathbf{x}_1$. The scalar a, finally, identifies all the firm features that the analyst is unable to observe. From this equation, at the first step, we get the propensity scores (the idiosyncratic single-firm probability of innovating), p($\mathbf{x}_1$).

As for the OPM behavioural equation, we have an equation for treated (denoted by the suffix "1") and one for untreated units (denoted by the suffix "0"):

$$\begin{aligned} y_0 &= \mu_0 + g_0(\mathbf{x}) + e_0 \\ y_1 &= \mu_1 + g_1(\mathbf{x}) + e_1 \end{aligned} \tag{2}$$

where y is the OPM, μ is a constant term, $g(.)$ a function (that is assumed to be different in the two groups, what generates a random coefficient model) of the covariates $\mathbf{x} = [\text{p}(\mathbf{x}_1); \mathbf{x}_2]$, with $\mathbf{x}_2$ denoting firm characteristics affecting the OPM behaviour, other than those affecting the innovative self-selection behaviour of the firm (collapsed in p($\mathbf{x}_1$)), and where e_0 and e_1 are unobservable (to analyst) components impacting on OPM and having unconditional zero mean. According to these equations we can get the so-called "benefit from treatment", $(y_1 - y_0)$, i.e. of being innovators, as:

$$y_1 - y_0 \quad = \quad (\mu_1 - \mu_0) \ + \ [g_1(\mathbf{x}) - g_0(\mathbf{x})] \ + \ (e_1 - e_0)$$

which is a function of three differential terms as it easy to see. In our estimation procedure we are interested in two types of parameters: the so-called "average treatment effect" (ATE) and the "average treatment effect on treated" (ATET) defined, as function of $\mathbf{x}$, as:

$$\text{ATE}(\mathbf{x}) = E(y_1 - y_0|\mathbf{x})$$

$$\text{ATET}(\mathbf{x}) = E(y_1 - y_0|\mathbf{x}, w = 1).$$

The problem in estimating these parameters is that, at the same time, each firm can be observed only in one of the two conditions (if treated or if non-treated) so that, on the side of firm behaviour, a "missing observation" problem arises. To overcome this problem, we need additional hypotheses; we introduce the hypothesis of "conditional mean independence" (CMI) that allows to estimate the parameters of interest through standard OLS (see Wooldridge 2002, pp. 608–614). According to the CMI hypothesis we assume that "the unobservable variables affecting the firm innovative self-selection equation are uncorrelated to the unobservable variables affecting the firm OPM behaviour, once we have conditioned on the observable variables **x**"; technically it means that:

$$a \perp (e_0, e_1)|\mathbf{x}.$$

In terms of conditional mean, it becomes:

$$E(e_0|\mathbf{x}, w) = E(e_0|\mathbf{x}) = 0 \quad \text{and} \quad E(e_1|\mathbf{x}, w) = E(e_1|\mathbf{x}) = 0$$

It can be shown that, after this hypothesis, the previous parameters become:

$$\text{ATE}(\mathbf{x}) = (\mu_1 - \mu_0) + [g_1(\mathbf{x}) - g_0(\mathbf{x})]$$

$$\text{ATET}(\mathbf{x}) = E(y_1 - y_0|\text{w} = 1) = \text{ATE}_{(w=1)}(\mathbf{x}).$$

To get the ATE and ATET (unconditional on **x**) we only have to average over the support of **x**, obtaining:

$$\text{ATE} = (\mu_1 - \mu_0) + E_{\mathbf{x}}[g_1(\mathbf{x}) - g_0(\mathbf{x})]$$

$$\text{ATET} = E_{\mathbf{x}}[\text{ATE}_{(w=1)}(\mathbf{x})].$$

The final step is that of arriving at a sample estimate of those parameters, that, of course, has to be done in terms of observable variables. To achieve this task we introduce the so-called "switching regression" defined as:

$$y = wy_1 + (1 - w)y_0$$

where y is observable. By replacing y_1 and y_0 with their expression from (1) and (2), we get the following relation:

$$y = \mu_0 + g_0(\mathbf{x}) + w(\mu_1 - \mu_0) + w[g_1(\mathbf{x}) - g_0(\mathbf{x})] + u \tag{3}$$

where $u = e_0 + w(e_1 - e_0)$. Moving toward a parametric form of $g(\cdot)$ by putting: $g_1(\mathbf{x}) = \eta_1 + \mathbf{x}\boldsymbol{\beta}_1$ and $g_0(\mathbf{x}) = \eta_0 + \mathbf{x}\boldsymbol{\beta}_0$ we can rearrange the previous equation getting, after simple manipulations, the following "reduced form" regression equation:

$$E(y|\mathbf{x}, w) = \gamma + \mathbf{x}\boldsymbol{\beta}_0 + w \cdot \alpha + w \cdot [\mathbf{x} - \boldsymbol{\mu}_\mathbf{x}]\boldsymbol{\delta}. \tag{4}$$

where it can be proved that $\gamma = \mu_0 + \eta_0$, $\alpha = ATE$, $\boldsymbol{\delta} = (\boldsymbol{\beta}_1 - \boldsymbol{\beta}_0)$ and $\boldsymbol{\mu}_\mathbf{x} = E(\mathbf{x})$. Equation (4) can be estimated consistently by OLS, and once obtained the OLS parameters we can get the various treatment effects by simple transformations of the type:

$$\begin{aligned}
\hat{\text{ATE}} &= \hat{\alpha} \\
\hat{\text{ATE}}(\mathbf{x}) &= \hat{\alpha} + (\mathbf{x} - \bar{\mathbf{x}})\hat{\boldsymbol{\delta}} \\
\hat{\text{ATET}} &= \hat{\alpha} + (1/N^T)\sum_{i=1}^{N} w(\mathbf{x} - \bar{\mathbf{x}})\hat{\boldsymbol{\delta}} \\
\hat{\text{ATET}}(\mathbf{x}) &= \left[\hat{\alpha} + (\mathbf{x} - \bar{\mathbf{x}})\hat{\boldsymbol{\delta}}\right]_{(w=1)}.
\end{aligned} \tag{5}$$

Relations (5) are all estimable since they are function of observable (to analyst) components. The only difficulty is that of obtaining standard errors for the *ATET*, a problem that can be overcome by bootstrapping.[1]

4 Dataset and Covariates

Our dataset employs the last three waves of the Capitalia/Unicredit survey on a sample of Italian manufacturing firms. The dataset is representative of the population of Italian manufacturing firms with more than ten employees and sampling weight as well as stratification variables are available. This dataset contains information on many aspects of firm characteristics and strategies (fixed investment decisions, internationalization patterns, financing tools, etc.), and thus also on firm R&D expenditure, financing and innovation behaviors in the following periods: 1998–2000 (eighth survey), 2001–2003 (ninth survey) and 2004–2006 (tenth survey). These surveys provide also balance sheet data. We use innovation data and a large definition of innovation, including product, process and organizational innovations.We work on (three) periods of 3 years and this can bring to an over-evaluation of innovation persistence, even if problems of under-evaluation of

[1] As no in-built commands for random coefficient models are available in standard statistical packages yet, the authors have programmed their own STATA 11 program for this purpose. They have planned to provide this program publicly in next future.

Table 1 Sample number of firms by innovative strategy

	Number of firms	Number of observations (9 years: 1998–2006)	Percentage (%)
Innovators	423	3,807	93.79
Occasional	254	2,286	60.05
Persistent	169	1,521	39.95
Non-innovators	25	225	5.54
Missing	3	27	0.67
Total	451	4,059	

Note: In the questionnaires a firm innovate when at least one of the following types of innovations occurred in at least one of the three Capitali/Unicredit surveys: (i) product innovation, (ii) process innovation, (iii) organizational innovation for product, (iv) organizational innovation for process

persistence can be present when using yearly observations and patent or product innovation data, since firms can develop innovation projects but may obtain new product or patentable outputs only after more than 1 year (Geroski et al. 2007). Each survey contains about 5,000 firms but, being it a rotated panel, only a smaller number of firms are present in all the three surveys. Indeed, once the three waves are merged we get a longitudinal dataset where 451 companies (this is the number of firms that are present in all the three waves) are observed from 1998 to 2006 for a total of 9 years. It means that we rely on 4,059 observations (firm per year), although the merging with accounting data reduces this number in the regression analysis as a consequence of the presence of numerous missing values. But the sample size for regressions remains anyways substantial.

Table 1 shows the composition of our sample by innovating strategy. Given the wide definition of innovative activity assumed in this work (product, process and organizational) the number of innovators is fairly high (about 94 % against 6 % of non-innovators). Among the innovators, the persistent innovators are about 40 % while the occasional ones are 60 %. The distribution between persistent and occasional innovators is fairly in line with previous studies.

Table 2 shows the variables employed in our analysis. The first group are those explaining the probability to innovate (persistently, occasionally, etc.): it is the first step probit regression providing the propensity scores to be included in the second step. The second group (including also the propensity score from the first step) are those explaining firm OPM (operating profit margin before taxation) behavior: it is the second step of our treatment model, where a *random causal effect coefficient* of the innovation dummy on the OPM is estimated. The choice of covariates reflects the huge theoretical and empirical literature reviewed above on the determinants of firm R&D, innovation and profitability behavior.

Measure and economic meaning of the variables included in the model is presented below, firstly with regard to the first-step and secondly to the second-step equation.

Table 2 Variables employed in the first and second step regressions of the random coefficient regression analysis

Step I: variable explaining the probability to innovate (propensity score)	
R&D intensity	Total R&D expenditure to turnover
R&D sectoral	Total sectoral R&D expenditure
Size	Number of employees
Age	Age of the firm since birth
Knowledge	Cumulated R&D expenditures calculated by permanent inventory
Region	Regional dummies (20 modalities)
Sector	Sectoral dummies (2-digit, 21 modalities)
Step II: variable explaining the Operating Profit margin (OPM)	
Turnover	Firm turnover
Investment	Fixed capital investment to turnover
Concentration	4-firms concentration ratio
Labour-costs	Labor costs to turnover
Capital-intensity	Stock of material assets to turnover
Equity	Stock of equity to total assets
Debt	Stock of debt to total assets
Capital	Stock of fixed capital from accounting
Export	Dummy: 1 = firm exports; 0 = firm does not export
Group	Dummy: 1 = firm belongs to a group; 0 = firm does not belong to a group
Geo	Macro-region dummies (four modalities)
Pavitt	Pavitt classification (four modalities)
Propensity score	Probability of innovating coming from the first step

4.1 First-Step: Variable Explaining the Probability to Innovate (Propensity Score)

R&D intensity: firm R&D expenditure per employee. The intra and extra-muros R&D intensity at firm level is a key variable indicating, given the amount of resources, firm relative effort in realizing, committing and acquiring research activity. It is a flow indicator representing the main input variable in the innovation process and, more generally, a measure of firm capability to innovate.

R&D sectoral: total sectoral R&D expenditure. It is the intra-muros R&D expenditure by sector and indicates the degree of externalities in the industry where the firm operates. There is a vast body of literature proving how firm R&D environment may be influential in affecting idiosyncratic innovation effort.

Size: number of employees. The size is an indicator of firm market strength and of its capacity of sustaining a more expensive and large portfolio of innovation projects. The size of resources available to a firm helps in diversifying risks and in getting a relatively better performance. Moreover, company size can account for the presence of innovation scale-economies, as suggested by the Schumpeter Mark II regime of innovation.

Age: number of years since foundation. Company age might be important in explaining its propensity to innovate. Younger firms are sometimes assumed to be more prone to innovate, as they—in order to get higher market shares—have to compete with more established players; nevertheless, older firms can rely on a higher experience and cumulativeness in doing innovation, an aspect that can give them a relative advantage over younger competitors.

Knowledge: cumulated R&D expenditures calculated by permanent inventory. The actual stock of knowledge available to a firm in each specific year (calculated by taking into account knowledge obsolescence through the method of permanent inventory), represents the cumulated past efforts in doing R&D activity. Neo-Schumpeterian literature has strongly emphasized the role of cumulativeness in knowledge production, absorption and exploitation, as well as its complementary role in the co-evolution of other company functions. It is no doubt a relevant predictor of firm choice and capacity to successfully innovate.

Region, *Sector*: regional dummies (20 modalities), Sectoral dummies (2-digit, 21 modalities). Introducing a dummy for the region and for the sector to which the firm belongs is needed from a statistical point of view, as the Capitalia/Unicredit dataset is built according to a stratified sampling, where strata were identified according to firm size, sector and location. Since the probability of inclusion in the sample is not constant over companies under stratified sampling, conditioning on these variables may be seen as a strategy to attenuate the selection bias, when—as in our case—sampling weights are not available.

4.2 Second-Step: Variable Explaining the Operating Profit Margin

OPM: gross profits before taxation on turnover. Measuring profitability is a critical aspect. Following recent applications, we use the ratio of accounting profits to total sales that indicates the ability of firms to hold price above the average (or marginal) cost to total sales.[2] This proxy is an inter-firms comparable measure and reflects the (exceeding) return once all intermediary goods, labour, organizational and managerial work and risk financial capital have been remunerated.

Turnover: firm total sales. Apart from accounting for company size, firm turnover is usually meant as a proxy of firm market demand. The extent of demand is in turn key for explaining profit performance via higher revenues, although costs considerations are similarly relevant.

Investment: fixed capital investment to turnover. The fixed investment intensity represents the short-term company effort to expand its productive capacity.

[2] As it is known accounting data can represent noisy measures of economic variables. At the same time accounting data are used by firms in decision making and are taken into account by the stock markets. The real problem is "the extent to which errors in accounting data are correlated with independent variables used in the regression analysis" (Schmalensee, 2005, p 962). If such correlation is not important, the statistic analysis doesn't miss the real relations involving economic profitability.

Traditional industrial organization studies have steadily showed as capital-deepening strategies—by augmenting labour productivity—may have beneficial effects on profit margins.

Concentration: 4-firms concentration ratio. To measure industry concentration we use the ratio of aggregated sales of the four largest sellers to the industry total sales. In the typical structure-conduct-performance approach, high concentration implies the possibility for a company to keep extra-profits in the long-run, especially in low competitive markets. The justification is to be found in the association of concentration with high barriers to new entry.

Labour-costs: labour costs to turnover. Labour intensity depends on the sector, but its rate and quality can influence substantially the difference between revenues and costs. Indeed, although higher labour quality might increase costs, the associated savings coming from a higher productivity of labour might increase revenues. Thus, the relation between higher labour cost and profit might be controversial.

Capital-intensity: stock of material assets to turnover. As in the case of labour intensity, capital intensity is another key element that can be thought as driving operating profits. This link passes, again, through increases in employees' productivity and through a more efficient organization of the productive process.

Equity: stock of equity to total assets. The financial structure of the firm is relevant to be introduced, also in a operating profit function. In particular, the stock of equity, by cumulating both the self and private financing, conveys information on how firm is able to attract external sources of financing for expanding its business, without incurring higher indebtedness.

Debt: stock of debt to total assets. The meaning of the stock of cumulated (short and long-term) borrowing is complementary to equity: it regards the ability of firm to attract resources from the bank system. The level of debt on total assets, thus, may have a double meaning: on the one hand, it may signal the financial quality of the firm, as banks generally provide funds only after a severe analysis of firm financial soundness; on the other hand, it might show that the firm has a great financial burden that might hamper its capacity to be profitable in the near future.

Capital: stock of fixed capital from accounting. The stock of fixed capital is a measure of capital accumulation; this measure accounts for past purchases of machineries and tools and, as such, it should grasp the past (experienced) productive capacity of the company. It should have some considerable effect of profits.

Export: dummy variable equal to 1 if the firm exports some part of production, and 0 if the firm does not export at all. Companies exposed to foreign competition are generally more prone to be efficient, thereby able to cut costs and increase revenues, more than non exporting ones. Moreover, exporting firms have to compete not only on prices, but also on the quality of goods and services: it leads to operate in more innovative but also profitable markets.

Group: dummy variable equal to 1 if the firm belongs to a group of companies, and 0 if the firm does not belong to any group. Belonging to a group, as for instance a multinational company, may have some role in explaining firm performance.

Companies operating in a group can have access to a richer pool of resources as well as to a higher set of market opportunities.

Geo, Pavitt: macro-region dummies (four modalities), Pavitt sectoral classification (four modalities). These variables are essential *ceteris paribus conditions* and are important for the same reasons given in the first step equation.

Propensity score: Probability of innovating coming from the first step. This variable completes the system of the two equations (first and second step).

5 Results

In our analysis we consider three treatment variables we have called: *innpers*, *innocc* and *innoccfrt*. The definition of these variables are reported in the note of Table 8. The complete analysis is provided only for *innpers* while for *innocc* and *innoccfrt* we set out the main results on ATE and ATET.

5.1 *Results by* innpers

The variable *innpers* is a demarking one for it elucidates the differences between firms that persistently innovate and firms that do not innovate at all during the three waves (that is, during the 9 years considered). Such a variable, in fact, should quite clearly emphasize the "net" causal effect of innovation on profits.

For this treatment variable we estimate and report all the results: (i) propensity score analysis, (ii) OPM behavioral equation estimation, (iii) identification of demarcation factors characterizing the best (innovating) performers.

5.1.1 Propensity Score Analysis

Table 3 sets out what factors explain more the probability to innovate persistently (compared to non-innovating at all). This probability defines for each firm its propensity score. Results are in line with expectations: the R&D intensity, the size of the firm and its knowledge stock (calculated by permanent inventory) are all positive and significant factors in explaining the probability of being a persistently innovative firm. No effect, at this stage, appears from sectoral R&D, in so showing a small effect (non-significant but positive in sign) of potential R&D spillovers.

Table 4 shows the distribution characteristics of the propensity scores calculated by the previous estimation. Observe the high level of the mean (0.75) and median (0.71): it means that the previous model, although parsimonious, predicts quite well the probability of being a firm persistently innovating.

Table 3 Probit regression for calculating the *propensity scores*

Target: OPM Treatment: innpers	Level	Elasticity × 1Million
R&D intensity	65.4987*** (16.2147)	558.3***
R&D sectoral	0.0000 (0.0000)	0.000003
Size	0.0071*** (0.0015)	0.0607***
Age	0.0018 (0.0030)	0.0156
Knowledge	0.0012*** (0.0003)	0.0104***
N	1,155	
Log likelihood	−400.21	
Pseudo r^2	0.275	
Chi^2	303.8***	

Note: Coefficients in level and in elasticity. Standard errors in parentheses; $*p < 0.1$, $**p < 0.05$, $***p < 0.01$. Sector and geographic dummies included but not reported

Table 4 Estimated propensity score distribution features

N	Mean	Median	5-Percentile	95-Percentile	Variance	Skewness	Kurtosis
2,834	0.75	0.72	0.51	1	0.034	0.11	1.46

5.1.2 Operating Profit Margin Behavioral Equation Estimation

Table 5 shows the results of the operating profit margin behavioral equation, estimated with a random coefficient model where the coefficient of the treatment variable (*innpers*) is exactly the average treatment effect (ATE). This is the second step of our estimation procedure including among the covariates also the propensity score variable of the first step. We are estimating, in other words, the random coefficient model of equation (4). As for the results, the ATE is highly significant and positive with a value of 4.97: it means that, on average, the effect of being a persistent innovator generates about a 5 % higher level of the OPM compared to being non-innovating, a striking high value. Also an higher fixed investment propensity, export orientation and equity financing bring to an higher OPM. Nonetheless a high stock of fixed capital has a negative effect on the level of OPM, and this can be explained by the fact that it represents a cost item and can negatively impact on firm productivity. The fact of belonging to a group generates a negative significant effect too: in the literature this result is explained in the following way: "independent innovating units (marginally) outperform subsidiaries as persistent innovations, presumably because stronger investment incentives outweigh any failure to exploit economies of scope" (Geroski et al. 2007, p. 44). Anyway it is important to remember that these results explain the profit mean value and that we could find differences (different effects) looking at different parts of firm profit distribution (Reichstein et al. 2010).

Table 5 Random coefficient regression analysis for OPM

Target: OPM Treatment: innpers	Level	Beta
ATE	4.9746***	0.367***
	(1.3003)	(1.3003)
Turnover	−0.0000	−0.775
	(0.0001)	(0.0001)
Investment	9.3128**	0.277**
	(4.0120)	(4.0120)
Concentration	0.0265	0.041
	(0.0711)	(0.0711)
Labour-costs	−0.0590	−0.099
	(0.0610)	(0.0610)
Capital-intensity	−0.0019	−0.016
	(0.0080)	(0.0080)
Equity	0.1331**	0.452**
	(0.0641)	(0.0641)
Debt	0.0311	0.112
	(0.0640)	(0.0640)
Age	0.0579*	0.225*
	(0.0329)	(0.0329)
Capital	−0.0006***	−3.232***
	(0.0002)	(0.0002)
Propensity-score	4.1618	0.142
	(3.4644)	(3.4644)
Export	1.0047*	0.077*
	(0.5514)	(0.5514)
Group	−1.1264***	−0.102***
	(0.3931)	(0.3931)
ATET	5.605***	0.406***
	(1.669)	(1.669)
N	934	934
Adj. R^2	0.378	0.378
r^2	0.4189	0.4189
F	11.59***	11.59***

Note: ATE = coefficient of *innpers*. Level and beta coefficients reported. Standard errors in parentheses; $^*p < 0.1$, $^{**}p < 0.05$, $^{***}p < 0.01$

Table 5 sets out also the bootstrap estimation of the ATET, the average treatment effect on treated. As expected also the ATET is positive and highly significant with a value of 5.6, that is about 0.7 point higher than the ATE: it means that the specific gain of the treated firms (those innovating persistently) is positive and adds to the average level (i.e., the ATE).

Besides these results, the proper value added of employing a random coefficient setting, is that of having the possibility of estimating the entire distribution of the causal effects, ATE and ATET, of the treatment variable (innovation strategy) on the target one (OPM). This is extremely useful when we suspect that heterogeneity

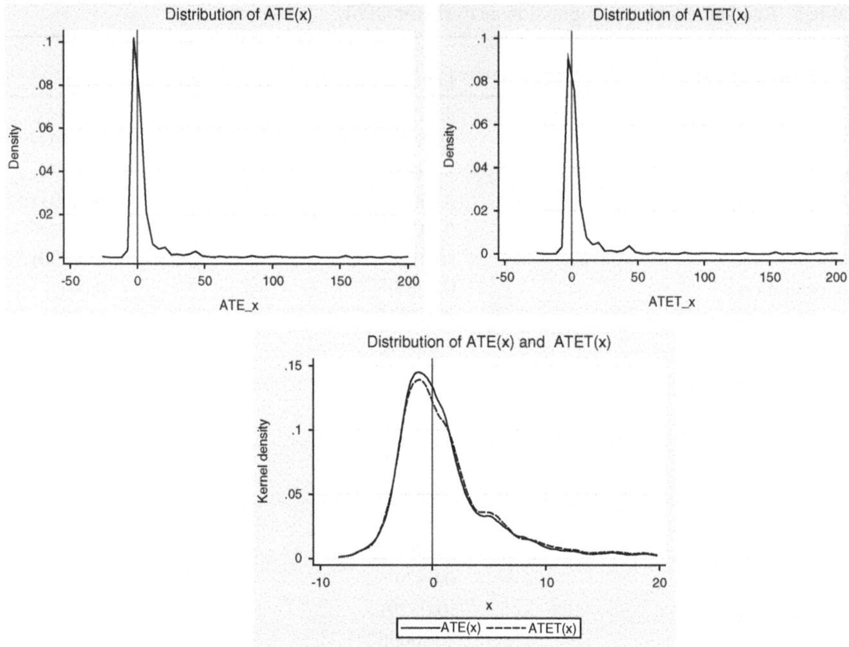

Fig. 1 Distribution of ATE(**x**) and ATET(**x**). Target variable: OPM; treatment variable: innpers

matters in the context in question and when we want to go far beyond a single point estimation of causality.

According to this premise, Fig. 1 shows the estimation of the ATE(**x**) and ATET(**x**) distribution. What immediately emerges is the importance of the right tail of both distributions. In other words, the mean (ATE and ATET respectively) is positive basically thanks to a good amount of firms that perform extremely well (and that we can call the best performers), placed exactly on the right tail. It means that both these distributions are asymmetric to the right and it is confirmed by the fact that the median of ATE(**x**) and ATET(**x**) is still positive but about 0.5, that is a value clearly close to zero. Of course, the area below the right tail of the ATET(**x**) is larger than that of the ATE(**x**), thus explaining why ATET is greater than ATE. The profit differential distribution being asymmetric to the right means that a relevant relation between persistence in innovation and in profit is found, even if in a group of persistent innovators this relation cannot be hold.

5.1.3 Demarcation Factors Characterizing The Best (Innovating) Performers

The capacity of our model to estimate the distribution of the causal effect of being a persistent innovator (compared to a non-innovating behavior) allows us to inspect what factors characterize the event of *"being, among the innovators, the best*

Table 6 T-test for the "difference-in-mean" between the group of innovative firms getting an ATET greater than the distribution median (group 1), and that having a lower value (group 0). Target variable: OPM; Treatment variable: innpers

	Mean (1), (N = 388)	Mean (0), (N = 388)	Difference	p-Value	Relative difference
ATET	13.75	−1.77	15.52***	0.000	2.00
Stock of fixed capital	19,082	1,486	17,596***	0.000	1.71
Sock of knowledge	3,967	433	3,534***	0.000	1.61
Turnover	73,647	8,437	65,209***	0.000	1.59
No. of employees	290	50	240***	0.000	1.41
R&D intensity	0.01	0.03	−0.02	0.261	1.00
Capital-intensity	56.59	30.32	26.27***	0.000	0.60
Equity	36.51	21	15.51***	0.000	0.54
Operating profit Margin	5.58	3.24	2.34***	0.000	0.53
Debt	52.66	70.64	−17.98***	0.000	0.29
Knowledge intensity	12.11	9.44	2.67	0.107	0.25
Investment intensity	0.05	0.06	−0.01	0.298	0.18
Sectoral R&D	269,122	320,667	−51,545**	0.028	0.17
Propensity-score	0.92	0.81	0.11***	0.000	0.13
Concentration	10.12	9.09	1.03*	0.078	0.11
Labor-intensity	18.54	20.59	−2.04***	0.000	0.10
Age	30.39	30.54	−0.15	0.916	0.00

Note: For the generic variable x the relative difference index is equal to: $|x_1 - x_0|/(|x_1| - |x_0|)/2$

performers". In a traditional regression setting, where heterogeneity is absent or at least takes the form of a fixed intercept effect, this analysis is precluded. In our case, on the contrary, we can exploit the knowledge of ATET(**x**) that idiosyncratically maps the relation between firm characteristics (the vector **x**) and causal effect on OPM (it means that each firm i owns its estimated ATE_i and $ATET_i$) . By calculating the median of ATET(**x**), that is about 0.47, we can define two groups of companies: those with an $ATET_i$ lower than the median (that we can call the "weak performers") and those with an $ATET_i$ higher than the median (the "best performers"). Once the two groups are formed, we can check via a mean-comparison test what are the characteristics that are more correlated with being among the best performers.

Tables 6 and 7 report the results: Table 6 for continuous variables and Table 7 for discrete variables (in the first case we have a simple mean-difference t-test, and in the second case a frequency-difference one). From Table 6 it appears, as expected, that the ATET difference between the two groups is remarkable: positive and high for the best performers (about 14 %), low and negative for the weaker performers (about −2 %). This means that being a persistent innovation performer does not bring automatically to get a profit higher than in the case the same firm had not innovated, since firm and industry factors matter when market forces operate through selection. In the last column of Tables 6 and 7, an index of relative difference has been calculated to compare which are the factors that, in relative terms, provide the greatest difference between the two groups of persistent

Table 7 P-test for the "difference-in-frequency" between the group of innovative firms getting an ATET greater than the distribution median (group 1), and that having a lower value (group 0). Target variable: OPM; Treatment variable: innpers

	Frequency (1)	Frequency (0)	Difference	p-Value	Relative difference index
Group	0.51	0.15	0.36***	0.000	1.09
South & Islands	0.1	0.13	−0.02	0.311	0.26
Pavitt—traditional	0.36	0.28	0.07**	0.026	0.25
North-east	0.33	0.26	0.07**	0.028	0.24
Center	0.09	0.11	−0.02	0.406	0.20
Pavitt—specialized	0.42	0.48	−0.07*	0.061	0.13
North-west	0.47	0.5	−0.03	0.389	0.06
Pavitt—scale	0.22	0.23	−0.01	0.797	0.04
Export	0.88	0.86	0.02	0.391	0.02

Note: for the generic variable x the relative difference index is equal to: $|x_1 - x_0|/(|x_1| - |x_0|)/2$

innovating companies. For the generic variable x the formula of this normalized index is:

$$\frac{|x_{best} - x_{worst}|}{(|x_{best}| + |x_{worst}|)/2}$$

where *best* and *worst* (performers) refer to the two groups. This formula allows for getting a ranking of the demarcating factors.

The two "main" factors sustaining the best performers are the stock of fixed capital and the knowledge stock, that we mean as firm capacity of building barriers (through higher capital intensity) and of accumulating persistently knowledge (through R&D and patents). The stock of fixed capital, which had a negative effect on the OPM level in the Table 5, represents the main demarcating factor for persistent innovating firms with positive profit differential. R&D experience, captured by the stock of knowledge, is the second factor marking a great and significant difference between the two groups (with best performers having about a ten times higher level of cumulated R&D experience). Other factors explain the good results of the persistent innovators. The size is remarkably higher in the best performers (290 against 50 employees), in so highlighting the essential role played by "scale economies" in producing higher profits. R&D and fixed investment intensity are not demarcation factors (they can characterize also new entrants—R&D intensity—or less productive firms—fixed investment intensity). Industry concentration is relatively less important (see also Mueller 1990). Best performers are also more capital intensive than weak performers and rely more on equity than on debt to finance their business activities/innovation.

As for the discrete variables, Table 7 shows that best performers belong more to a group, which helps in accumulating more easily know-how and getting a large range of technological possibilities, together with offering a protection from business down-turns.

As for the sector, no sharp differences emerge between the two groups although the best performers are a little more present in the traditional (supplier-dominated) sectors; this can be explained by country characters/specialization (see Geroski and Jacquemin 1988 for the relevance of country variable).

5.2 *Results by* innocc *and* innoccfrt

Table 8 sets out a summary of the previous results and moreover presents the results when we use *innocc* instead of *innpers* as treatment variable. In this latter case we compare firm that have innovated at least in one of the three surveys with, again, non-innovating companies. We can read this as a way of gauging the net effect of "occasional innovation" on the profit margin. From Table 8 we observe a positive and significant effect of occasional innovation compared to a non-innovating strategy: the ATE is 2.39 % and ATET is 2.51 %. These levels of treatment effects are in this case about *3 points lower* than in the case of persistent innovators: it means that, over the 9 years considered, being persistent rather than occasional innovators brings about an advantage of about *three* percentage points of higher OPM (a result similar to what found in the literature). What does it mean from a behavioral point of view? As suggested by neo-Schumpeterian literature, innovation, based on a selective advantage, can generate scale advantages when reproduced through time and a change within firm capabilities that allows to better exploit market opportunities. However, as this analysis has been so far performed in a "pooled sample setting", conclusions on behavioral dynamic have to be taken with substantial care.

Indeed, in order to shed more light on this specific aspect, we performed a temporal analysis of the causal relation between innovation and profit performance, by exploiting *innoccfrt* as treatment variable. This dummy-variable compares persistently innovating firms with companies that have innovated only "in the first wave" (the eighth one). We analyze the pattern of the ATE and ATET over the three waves to see whether a continuing innovation activity generates additional gains (in terms of OPM) compared to an innovation activity stopped at the first period (the first wave). Results for this exercise is reported in Table 9. Looking at both the estimated ATE and ATET of Table 9, we can notice that they are always non statistically significant. Nevertheless, the sign and size of these coefficients along the three waves bring with them some useful descriptive information. The ATE and ATET coefficients, in fact, start with negative signs in the first wave (ATE = −2.68, ATET = −3.00), to then grow up to nearly zero values in the second wave (ATE = 0.13, ATET = −0.01), to finally take positive and high values in the third wave (ATE = 4.11, ATET = 4.48). Therefore, although with some dispersion over the mean, this result seems to show that innovating with persistency can produce a sort of *catching-up effect* in terms of OPM, as the ATE and ATET increase monotonically from a negative to a positive value. This can be the dynamics through which firms, with an initial lower market share, by persistent

Table 8 Summary of regression results for the pooled model where the treatment variables are: "innpers", "innocc" and "innoccfrt"

	Coefficient	Robust Std. Err.	t-Test	Number of observations
Innovating occasionally (*innocc*)				
ATE	2.39*	0.63	3.80	1,358
ATET	2.51*	0.73	3.42	
Innovating persistently (*innpers*)				
ATE	4.97*	1.65	3.01	934
ATET	5.61*	1.67	3.36	
Innovating only in the first survey (*innoccfrt*)				
ATE	0.78	2.54	0.31	1,174
ATET	0.82	1.65	0.49	

Note: For ATET standard errors are obtained via 200 bootstrapping replications
*$p < 0.01$
innpers
1 = INNOVATING PERSISTENTLY
0 = NON-INNOVATING
innocc
1 = INNOVATING AT LEAST IN ONE OF THE THREE SURVEYS (but never in all the three)
0 = NON-INNOVATING
innoccfrt
1 = INNOVATING PERSISTENTLY
0 = INNOVATING ONLY IN THE FIRST SURVEY (SURVEY 8)

Table 9 Results on regression dynamic analysis where the treatment variable is "innoccfrt"

	Coefficients	Robust Std. Err.	t-Test	Number of observations
First survey				
ATE	−2.69	4.72	−0.57	439
ATET	−3.01	6.45	−0.47	439
Second survey				
ATE	0.13	5.24	0.03	278
ATET	−0.01	4.86	0.00	278
Third survey				
ATE	4.12	9.51	0.43	306
ATET	4.48	14.22	0.32	306

Note: For ATET standard errors are obtained via 200 bootstrapping replications

competition in innovation can overcome their competitors. Moreover, although occasional innovation provides a significant higher OPM compared to the total absence of innovation, we cannot conclude that this innovation strategy is sufficient to guarantee a dynamic advantage over non-innovating firms, as this is possible only by perpetuating over time the decision to innovate.

Figure 2 shows the temporal pattern of the median level of OPM in the period considered in our study (1998–2006) for simple innovators, occasional innovators and persistent innovators. The choice of plotting median rather than mean values relies on the need to reduce as much as possible the effect of influential

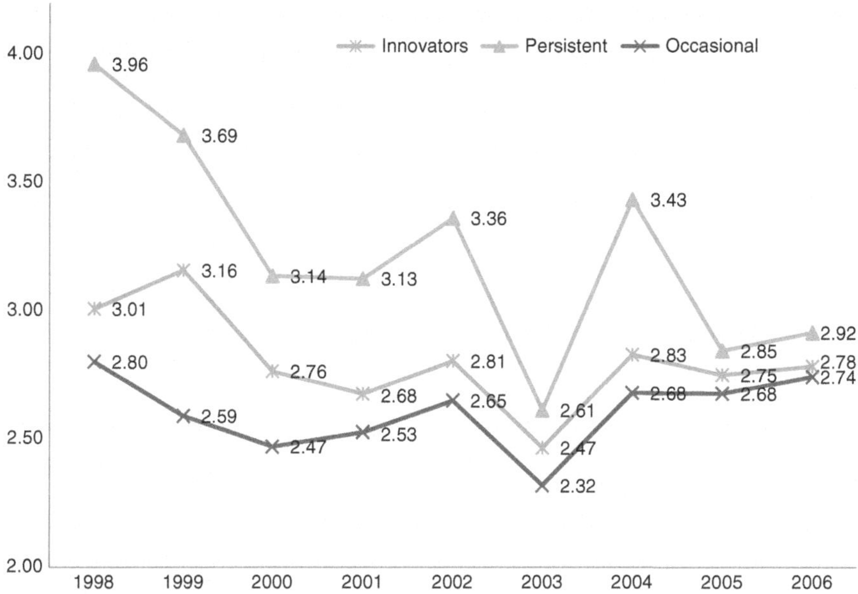

Fig. 2 Pattern over time of the operating profit margin (OPM). Median values

observations, since profits are subject to very high variance. These plots clearly show the presence of a hierarchy among the three groups, steadily kept over time: persistent innovators dominate both simple innovators and occasional innovators, whereas simple innovators dominate occasional innovators. What is striking to notice is that this difference is maintained also under business cycle, although the sensitivity of persistent innovators to business downturns and recoveries is sensibly higher: in fact, their OPM reduces more during adverse business cycles, while it increases significantly more during economic upturns. This may be explained by the fact that maintaining over time a persistent innovating strategy normally presents a double-face character: on the one hand it is a costly decision, on the other hand it is the basis for improving products/processes quality, thereby gaining new market opportunities. This double nature induces harsher profit reductions when market demand is weaker, but higher market opportunities in the boom phase.

6 Conclusions

In this paper, we find a causal relation between innovation strategy (persistent or occasional) and firms' profit margin compared with non-innovating firms through a counterfactual approach. By taking heterogeneity into serious account, our model explores the relation between firm innovation and profitability in the medium-term, by distinguishing between persistent and non-persistent (occasional) innovation strategies. Our results show a decisive better economic performance in the group of firms that continuously implement their innovating capacity and output. Also occasional innovation produces good outcomes in terms of OPM differentials (when compared with a non-innovative strategy), but the difference with the persistent behavior is strong and about three (percentage) points lower. This result, together with the comparison of the dynamic trend of the profit differential (from the non-innovator) between innovating firms who stop after a period and firms which go on innovating, shows and confirms the presence of an effect of "capacity building" from continuously participating to the innovation activities. When looking at a temporal analysis of the difference in profit performance between persistent and occasional firms that innovate only once at the beginning of the period considered, we find that this differential increases through time.

Even if we cannot distinguish between the two sources of innovation persistence, the observed catching-up of persistent innovators show that there is a positive return to scale in innovative activities ("state dependence") and a premium for the ability to build on "dynamic capabilities". The ability to compete and gain is not reached once-for-all, but needs the process of learning to be maintained over time by complex and persistent innovative strategies. Persistent innovation allows for a dynamic advantage compared to occasional "first-time-only" behaviors, an aspect that deserves further evidence and attention especially when looked through the evolutionary-Schumpeterian analytical lens.

The analysis of the idiosyncratic distribution of the causal effect of being a persistent innovator (compared to be a non-innovator) on profitability, allows us to inspect what factors lead to get a positive profit differential. Indeed, among persistent innovators we identify the "positive performers", i.e. the group of firms whose ATET is above the median. These champions are characterized by two main factors, respectively the capacity of building barriers through the stock of fixed capital and the dynamic economies of scale linked to the stock of accumulated knowledge. Other factors follow: the size of the market and the size of the firm.

Our answer to the question: "can a firm's long-run economic performance be predicted by a simple discrete strategy variable?", should be mixed. Adopting an approach which takes into account firm heterogeneity and differences among innovation strategies shows a systematic relation among firm profit persistence and its innovation strategy on a medium-long term, but, going behind the average result, it appears that the distribution of the profit differential (from non innovators) on medium term is highly skewed and sometime negative, even if there is a right tail of firms with a high profit differential. The firms with a persistent strategy of innovation do better on a medium term if they are able of building market barriers (supporting the cost of this strategy, for instance the cost of high fixed capital investments), while persistently building their stock of knowledge (benefitting of positive dynamic scale effect and of a large sized market). Other factors are less relevant: the R&D intensity, which could be high also in small (potential) new entrants, and market concentration, positive but low significant (see Mueller 1990 on the relation between concentration and profitability). Nonetheless, there is a part of persistent innovators who face negative dynamic scale effects: in our analysis they have a negative differential with non innovators on medium term. These firms are not able of translating their differential abilities and innovation performance in differential market success. It is possible to assume that in these cases the scale advantage doesn't work because radical innovations are introduced by competitors or because the innovation dynamics of firms with small shares of market is quite intensive (Cantner 2007). Interestingly, profit differentials of persistent innovators in our analysis remain positive in a medium term mostly in traditional sectors (supply dependent), where technological opportunities are largely exploited and markets are less open to technological turbulence.

With respect to the results of patent and innovation based literature on innovation persistence, which find out a non linear relation between technological or economic performance and level or duration of innovation, our result adds that, by looking at the shape of the profit differential distribution, it is possible to distinguish two groups of firms, with positive and negative dynamic return to innovation scale and to identify some discriminating factors, pertaining to the firm ability of profit appropriability (barriers building).

What about the profit trend towards convergence in the long-term? We don't develop any specific analysis of this aspect but, given our result of persistent differential at medium term (sustained by a group of persistent innovators), we descriptively looked at the (year by year) trend of OPM median level of the three groups of firms considered from 1998 to 2006 and found out a strong sensitivity of the persistent innovators group (on the whole) to the economic cycle and a trend to convergence with decreasing but maintained differences across the groups. The non-full convergence of persistent innovators is probably sustained by the companies which were capable of "defending" their advantage, due to firm and industry characteristics. Our large definition of innovation brings on the one hand a more diffused presence of persistent innovators, but on the other hand a less persistent capacity of keeping a profit differential. A large part of firms (occasional but also persistent innovators) are involved in the process of creative destruction, following to the introduction of new combinations in the economic system. It does mean also that only a few firms had "advantageous" dynamic capabilities (Winter 2003).

A more "dynamics-based" study of the profit differential paths, for different parts of the profit differential distribution, could provide a better understanding of how profit persistence due to innovation changes through time, and which firm/ industry characters may help the trend towards convergence to benefit from "state" and "path" dependency.

References

Aghion P, Howitt P (1992) A model of growth through creative destruction. Econometrica 60 (2):323–351

Antonelli C, Scellato G (2009) The persistence of innovation: the Italian evidence. Università di Torino, Department of Economics "S. Cognetti de Martiis", Working paper series, 03/2009

Cantner U (2007) Firm's differential innovative success and market dynamics. Jena Economic Research Paper, 078

Capasso M, Cefis E, Frenken K (2009) Do some firms persistently outperform? Utrecht School of Economics, Tjalling C. Koopmans Research Institute. Discussion Paper Series: 09–28

Cefis E (2003) Is there persistence in innovative activities? Int J Ind Organ 21:489–515

Cefis E, Ciccarelli M (2005) Profit differentials and innovation. Econ Innov New Technol 14 (1–2):43–61

Cefis E, Orsenigo L (2001) The persistence of innovative activities; a cross country and cross-sectors comparative analysis. Res Policy 30:1139–1158

Crespo-Cuaresma J, Gschwandtner A (2008) Tracing the dynamics of competition: evidence from company profits. Econ Inq 46(2):208–213

Dosi G (2007) Statistical regularities in the evolution of industries. A guide through some evidence and challenges for the theory. In: Malerba F, Brusoni S (eds) Perspective in innovation. Cambridge University Press, Cambridge

Dosi G, Nelson RR (2009) Technical change and industrial dynamics as evolutionary processes. LEM Working Paper, N. 07, August

Duguet E, Monjon S (2004) Is innovation persistent at firm level? An econometric examination comparing the propensity score and regression methods. Cahiers de la Maison des Sciences Economiques v04075, Université Panthéon-Sorbonne

Eklund JE, Wiberg D (2007) Persistence of profit and the systematic search for knowledge. CESIS Electronic Working Paper Series, Paper N. 85, March

Geroski PA, Jacquemin A (1988) The persistence of profits: a European comparison. Econ J 98:375–389

Geroski P, Machin S, Van Reenen J (1993) The profitability of innovating firms. Rand J Econ 24 (2):198–211

Geroski PA, Van Reenen J, Walters CF (1997) How persistently do firms innovate? Res Policy 26 (1):33–48

Geroski P, Lazarova S, Urga G, Walters CF (2003) Are differences in firm size transitory or permanent? J Appl Econ 18:47–59

Geroski P, Mata J, Portugal P (2007) Founding conditions and the survival of new firms. Druid Working Paper No. 07-11. http://www.druid.dk/wp/pdf_files/07-11.pdf

Gilbert RJ, Newbery DM (1982) Pre-emptive patenting and the persistence of monopoly. Am Econ Rev 72(3):514–526

Goddard JA, Wilson JOS (1999) The persistence of profit: a new empirical interpretation. Int J Ind Organ 17:663–687

Gschwandtner A (2005) Profit persistence in the "very" long run: evidence from survivors and exiters. Appl Econ 37:793–806

Gschwandtner A (2004) Profit persistence in the "very" long run: evidence from survivors and exiters. Vienna Economics Papers 0401, Department of Economics, University of Vienna

Jang SL, Chen JH (2011) What determines how long an innovative spell will last? Scientometrics 86:65–76

Malerba F, Orsenigo L (1996) Schumpeterian patterns of innovation are technology specific. Res Policy 25(3):451–478

Malerba F, Orsenigo L (1997) Technological regimes and sectoral patterns of innovative activities. Ind Corp Change 6:83–117

Mueller DC (1986) Profits in the long run. Cambridge University Press, Cambridge

Mueller DC (1990) Dynamics of company profits: an international comparison. Cambridge University Press, Cambridge

Nelson RR, Winter SG (1982a) An evolutionary theory of economic change. Harvard University Press, Cambridge, MA

Nelson RR, Winter SG (1982b) The Schumpeterian trade-off revisited. Am Econ Rev 72:114–132

Odagiri H, Maruyama N (2002) Does the 'Persistence of Profits' Persist? A study of company profits in Japan, 1964–97. Int J Ind Organ 20:1513–1533

Peters B (2004) Employment effects of different innovation activities: microeconometric evidence. ZEW Discussion Paper 04-73, ZEW

Peters B (2009) Persistence of innovation: stylised facts and panel data evidence. J Technol Transfer 34:226–243

Potì B, Cerulli G (2009) Heterogeneity of innovation strategies and firm performance. In: Cantner U, Gaffard JL, Nesta L (eds) Schumpeterian perspectives on innovation. Competition and growth. Springer, Berlin

Raymond W, Mohnen P, Palm F, Schim Van Der Loeff S (2006) Persistence of innovation in Dutch manufacturing: is it spurious? CESIFO Working Paper N 1681, March

Reichstein T, Dahl MS, Ebersberger B, Jensen MB (2010) The devil dwells in the tails, a quantile regression approach to firm growth. J Evol Econ 20:219–231

Reinganum JF (1983) Uncertain innovation and the persistence of monopoly. Am Econ Rev 73:741–748

Romer P (1990) Endogenous technological change. J Polit Econ 98(5):71–102

Roper S, Hewitt-Dundas N (2008) Innovation persistence: survey and case-study evidence. Res Policy 37:149–162

Scherer FM, Ross D (1990) Industrial market structure and economic performance. Houghton Mifflin, Boston

Schumpeter JA (1942) Capitalism, socialism and democracy. Harper and Row, New York

Sutton I (1991) Sunk cost and market structure. MIT Press, Cambridge, MA

Teece D, Pisano G, Shuen A (1997) Dynamic capabilities and strategic management. Strat Manage J 18(7):509–533

Winter SG (2003) Understanding dynamic capabilities. Strat Manage J 24:991–995

Wooldridge JM (2002) Econometric analysis of cross section and panel data. MIT Press, Cambridge

Financial Factors and Patents

Gustav Martinsson and Hans Lööf

Abstract This paper conjectures that equity supply is crucial for firms in order to maintain a smooth patenting profile through time. This hypothesis is tested on Swedish firm-level observations from 1997 to 2005. Patent applications growth in Sweden has been highly volatile in recent years. During the economic downturn, following the burst of the IT-bubble, applications dropped substantially, but results here show that the downturn had little effect on the patenting of high-equity firms. Instead, the entire decline in patent applications is confined to firms with lower levels of equity. This effect is consistent across sectors, firm-size, corporate-affiliation, and human-capital intensity.

This paper explores the relationship between finance and innovation. There are a number of studies which have explored the link between finance and R&D investment (see Hall and Lerner 2010 for a review), but we instead consider how finance affects firm-level patenting.[1] Studying patents in this framework is of interest for a

[1] Klette and Kortum (2004) maintain that patents and R&D are related across firms. However, this relationship is the strongest for large firms. Smaller firms exhibit relatively many patents per dollar of formal R&D which Griliches (1990, p. 1676) interprets as "*. . .small firms are likely to be doing relatively more informal R&D while reporting less of it and hence providing the appearance of more patents per R&D dollar*". There is a discrepancy between what constitutes innovation and what constitutes patents. Not all inventions are patentable and the inventions that actually are patented differ tremendously in quality. An economist wishes to isolate the patents that actually are economically significant. Patents have been found to be a good proxy for innovative output or indexes of inventive activity in the literature (see e.g. Griliches 1990; Lerner et al. 2008).

G. Martinsson (✉)
The Institute for Financial Research, SIFR, Drottninggatan 89, 113 60 Stockholm, Sweden
e-mail: gustav.martinsson@abe.kth.se

H. Lööf
Centre of Excellence for Science and Innovation Studies, Royal Institute of technology, 100 44 Stockholm, Sweden
e-mail: hans.loof@abe.kth.se

A. Pyka and E.S. Andersen (eds.), *Long Term Economic Development*, Economic Complexity and Evolution, DOI 10.1007/978-3-642-35125-9_17,

number of reasons. For instance, a considerable share of firms' inventions stem from activities which fall outside formal R&D. Many firms do not even have an R&D department, while some firms use incentive structures to encourage non-R&D employees to be inventive, and so aim at stimulating patenting. Thus, exploring patents instead of R&D enables us to capture an important aspect of financing firm-level innovation, which is mostly overlooked in the literature.

Since innovation activity is equity dependent (see e.g. Hall 2002), we conjecture that it is crucial for firms to have a consistent supply of equity in order to maintain their patenting strategy over time. Our analysis tests how firm-level equity supply affects the number of patent applications. We show that firms with the best supply of equity, other things equal, can maintain their patenting strategy over time, whereas firms with less equity experience drops in the number of patent applications when internal equity wanes.

Firms' access to finance is volatile and highly affected by both supply and demand of capital. Literature on innovative activity emphasizes firm-level innovation as preferably a stable activity, which may become problematic if firms need to cut research or other innovation-related activities due to shortages of funds caused by short-term drops of capital supply (see Aghion et al. 2005, 2008).[2] Schumpeter (1942) referred to recessions as temporary drops of overall demand and an opportunity for firms to regroup and innovate.[3] Business cycle effects matter in the context of access to finance because, during booms when overall demand is high, firms that otherwise are constrained financially can fund their operations and innovate due to the cash-flow generation caused by the high demand. Firms that are capable of being persistent innovators develop internal capabilities, which enable them to benefit from knowledge spillovers; they also tend to be less sensitive to adverse macroeconomic shocks (Geroski et al. 1997; Cohen and Levinthal 1990).

There are empirical studies suggesting financial effects on R&D investment, albeit supplying a mixed picture. Evidence of financing constraints for U.S. firms investing in R&D has been shown (Hall 1992; Himmelberg and Petersen 1994; Mulkaly et al. 2001), while studies for Europe typically find weak evidence (Bond et al. 2003b; Harhoff 1998). However, more recent studies for the U.S. and Europe, employing more recent and detailed data, indicate that equity supply (both internal and external) plays an important role for the financing of R&D of high-tech firms (see Brown et al. 2009; Martinsson 2010 for U.S. and European evidence, respectively). Brown et al. (2009) find significant effects of cash flows and external equity for young but not for mature firms.

Both patenting activity and R&D are difficult to finance with debt due to the high idiosyncratic risk of firm-level innovation, which forces firms to pledge collateral in order to obtain debt (see Berger and Udell 1990). Further, moral hazard problems

[2] Aghion et al. (2008) show that firms classified as credit constrained have a pro-cyclical R&D share out of total investment, whereas non-constrained firms have a counter-cyclical share. Thus, the non-constrained firms can innovate in recessions and increase their competitiveness.

[3] Geroski and Walters (1995, p. 918) make a similar point.

and adverse selection are severe in terms of firm-specific innovation projects as well (e.g. Stiglitz 1985). Therefore, equity is preferably used to finance innovation.

There is a small but growing body of literature on finance and patents. Similar to our approach, Schroth and Szalay (2009) hypothesize that financing constraints affect firm-level patenting. Using a sample of publicly traded pharmaceutical firms, they show that access to finance greatly affects the probability of winning a patent race. Kortum and Lerner (2000) confirm the importance of venture capital (VC) funding for patenting rates in the U.S., and that increases in VC activity in an industry are associated with significantly higher patenting rates.[4] Geroski et al. (1995) document a positive relationship between cash-flow and patenting.

In this paper, we hypothesize that patenting is equity-dependent, similarly to R&D investment, and therefore it is important for innovative firms to have access to equity in order to maintain a smooth patenting strategy over time. This way, equity supply is crucial if firms are to innovate when overall demand is low as proposed by Schumpeter (1942).

The Swedish economy, in combination with very detailed firm-level data, provides a setting that enables us to empirically explore the hypothesis that equity supply is important for firm-level patenting. First of all, Statistics Sweden has audited register data of all firms in Sweden, thus enabling us to analyze not just publicly traded firms.[5] Using the EPO Worldwide Statistical Database (PATSTAT), we have matched the firm-level data with all patent applications filed by enterprises based in Sweden. Second, Sweden is a patent-intensive country, with 1,770 patent applications per million of population compared to the U.S. with 1,360.[6] Also, Sweden has had a rather volatile development of total patent applications in recent years, which provides time series variation in the data. Patent applications filed by Swedish firms experienced high growth during the mid and late 1990s, before contracting, following the IT-boom, and returning to high growth again in 2006.

We separate our sample into quartiles based on firms' average equity-ratio over the time period. Firms in the bottom quartile are referred to as low-equity firms, the second and third quartiles are middle-equity firms and the top quartile is denoted

[4] Using a different perspective to Kortum and Lerner (2000), Haeussler et al. (2009) focus on firms seeking VC. They document the economic importance of patents as signaling instruments attracting VC financing for younger firms. However, some works find that firms with higher R&D intensity, more patents and lower share of tangible assets report more problems in accessing external finance. See for instance Westhead and Storey (1997), Freel (1997) for UK, Giudici and Paleari for Italy (2000).

[5] The nature of our data enables us to draw inference from a more representative sample of firms. Griliches (1990) shows that U.S. studies on patents analyze publicly traded corporations, which is a highly disproportionate sample of firms. The firms in Bound et al.'s (1982) empirical study on R&D and patents have more than 1,000 employees. Compared to census data of all U.S. firms, only 4.6 % of the firms in the U.S. during the same time period had more than 1,000 employees.

[6] The patent application number is the 2007 number from WIPO divided by the most recent population figure for each country, which is approximately 301 million for the U.S. and 9 million for Sweden.

high-equity firms. The aggregate number of patent applications declined during our sample period. We show that the entire drop of patent applications took place in the middle equity group. Conversely, the top-equity firms exhibited a stable development. The remainder of the paper tries to understand this development. The fact that the low-equity firms account for a very small share of the patent applications corroborates our hypothesis that equity supply plays an important role for the number of patent applications.

We find that the most significant difference between these groups of firms is their equity supply. The equity groups are remarkably similar in terms of other firm characteristics such as size, human-capital intensity, and corporate affiliation.

We test the importance of equity-financing formally by adopting the pecking order approach behind investment-cash flow sensitivity analyses first introduced by Fazzari et al. (1988). The rationale is basically that a firm displaying sensitivity of investment to cash-flow over a period of time likely has worse access to external finance than a firm not displaying such sensitivity. The econometric analysis shows the following: firms in the low and middle equity group display large economically, as well as statistically, significant sensitivities of patent applications to cash-flow. The top equity firms display no such sensitivity, suggesting that the firms in the bottom three quartiles have relatively less access to external finance than firms in the top equity group.

The intuition behind our finding is that when firms face difficulties obtaining external finance, they become dependent on retaining earnings to fund operations. As cash-flow wanes, firms focus on tangible assets which generate cash-flow (Anderson and Prezas 1999). Thus, they are more likely to refrain from filing a patent application if finances are low since patenting inventions, which, by some stochastic probability, only stands to generate cash-flow sometime in the future. Enabling firms to stay innovative, and ultimately protecting their innovative efforts with patents, is important in order for firms to stay competitive in the future.[7]

However, one might argue that recessions shake out the less viable inventions, leading to fewer patent applications by forcing firms to focus on their core operations in the spirit of Schumpeter's (1942) notion of recessions as cleansing mechanisms. We find such an explanation implausible since it is highly unlikely that firms with lower equity-ratio (these firms are far from insolvent) have disproportionately many less patentable inventions.

This paper proceeds as follows. Section 1 presents the data. Section 2 highlights the Swedish case and discusses how equity supply affects patenting activity. Section 3 provides econometric evidence of how equity supply affects patent applications. Section 4 performs some robustness tests. Section 5 concludes and discusses some of the implications of the paper.

---

[7] Http://www.CNNMoney.com (December 11, 2009: 6:08 AM ET) cites an executive of a major software company: "*The overall company reduced spending, and patent filings are a very controllable expense. We might have filed four patents, but we filed three and made sure they were strategically significant*".

1 Data Description

The firm-level data used in this study was originally constructed from audited register information on firm characteristics based on annual reports on surviving and non-surviving firms in Sweden during 1997–2005. Using the EPO Worldwide Statistical Database (PATSTAT), we have merged this data with additional data on the educational level of each firm and national and international patent applications filed by enterprises in Sweden. In the merging process we have managed to match 76 % of the patent applications in PATSTAT with unique firms in Sweden. Analyzing the remaining 24 % of the patent applications shows that they mostly consist of micro firms with few or no employees.

The sample for this paper is focused on manufacturing firms exclusively. We do this for two particular reasons. Most of the patent applications in our sample are filed by manufacturing firms. Moreover, a majority of studies on finance and innovation involve manufacturing firms exclusively and we make extensive use of these previous studies in variable selection, for instance (e.g. Bond et al. 2003b; Brown et al. 2009; Mulkaly et al. 2001).

Since the data includes the entire population of Swedish firms, as defined above, we are confronted with some particular data management issues. First, we must exclude firms with obvious erroneous observations. In line with Brown et al. (2009), Fazzari et al. (1988) and Scellato (2007), all firms with negative sums of cash-flow-to-assets during the sample period are dropped. Since the original sample consists of all firms in Sweden there are some issues regarding the quality of the data for the smaller firms in particular. We therefore exclude firms with average number of workers below ten during the sample period, and we also eliminate implausible values such as negative debt and equity figures, etc.[8] Following the sample construction we end up with an unbalanced panel of about 3,400 firms for the period 1997–2005. About 15 % of the firms applied at least once for a patent during the sample period.

2 Patent Applications and Financial Factors: The Swedish Case

2.1 *Background*

The period after the burst of the IT-bubble in the beginning of 2000 is characterized by a dramatic decline in patent applications filed by Swedish manufacturing firms. The decrease in our sample is substantial, with a drop from about 5,000 filed patent applications in the late 1990s to about 3,000 in the early 2000s. This drop in patent applications was not driven by ICT and/or biotech firms alone; these sectors

[8] The results are robust to considering alternative cut-offs around ten employees.

experienced similar drops to the overall sample. Instead we hypothesize that firms' access to finance played a large part. Innovation is largely financed with equity (see Hall 2002; Hall and Lerner 2010 for surveys). Debt contracts are ill-suited for innovation activity. For instance, the uncertain and volatile returns of research and patent intensive firms (Carpenter and Petersen 2002; Stiglitz 1985), as well as adverse selection problems associated with R&D investment and patent-related activities, disqualify debt as a financial instrument (Jensen and Meckling 1976; Stiglitz and Weiss 1981). Creditors do not share the upside potential of innovation investments, but stand to lose, since they only receive a fixed income stream from interest payments while carrying too much of a down-side risk due to the highly stochastic nature of the return to innovation investments. Further, there is poor collateral quality in innovation-related investment, which disqualifies debt as a financial instrument (Berger and Udell 1990; Titman and Wessels 1988).

2.2 Equity Financing and Patent Applications: Pooled Evidence

We hypothesize that equity supply is important for firms in order to maintain a consistent patenting activity over time. We divide our sample into quartiles based on their average equity-ratio over the time period. Firms in the bottom quartile are referred to as low-equity firms, the second and third quartiles are middle-equity firms and the top quartile is denoted high-equity firms. In Fig. 1 we display the development of *the number of patent applications* for these three groups of firms.

The low equity group comprises very few patent applications. In Fig. 1 it is clear that firms in the middle-equity group constitute the entire fall in the number of patent applications. The high-equity firms display some annual variation, but do not share the development of the middle-equity firms. Given the clear picture presented in Fig. 1 we carry this sample split of three groups based on equity-ratio throughout the paper. First, we need to examine whether we are capturing something other than access to equity.

Table 1 presents descriptive statistics for all firms divided into the three groups in the first three columns to the left, and only for the patenting firms in the three columns to the right. The choice of variables displayed in Table 1 follows the more developed finance and R&D investment literature (see Brown et al. 2009; Hall 1992; Himmelberg and Petersen 1994). The choice of variables is, of course, also restricted by data availability.

We start by scrutinizing the equity-ratio division based on the overall sample. The average number of patent applications per firm increases with the size of the equity-ratio. Not very surprisingly, the high equity-group comprises, on average, more profitable firms (we address this more in Sect. 2.3). We measure profitability by *cash-flow* (after-tax income plus depreciation and amortization). The long-term debt stocks mirror the equity stocks. The low-equity group uses lots of *long-term debt* and the high-equity group much less. We find interestingly that the average and

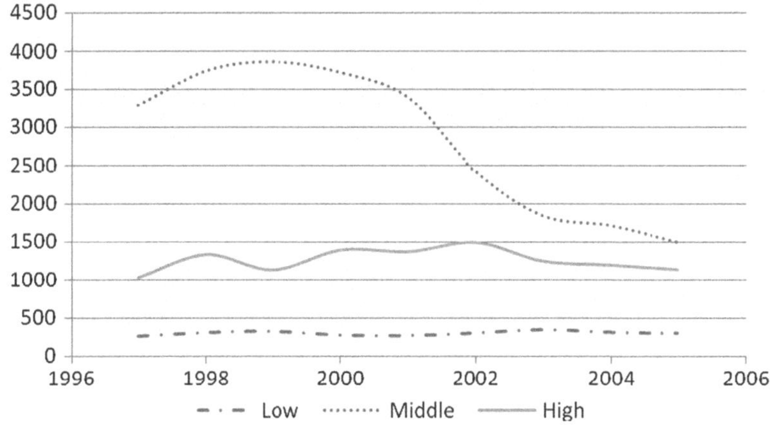

Fig. 1 Number of patent applications across equity-ratio groups 1997–2005. *Notes*: Equity groups are based on the average equity to total assets ratio across the sample period. 'Low' comprises the bottom quartile of firms in terms of average equity ratio, 'Middle' the second and third quartiles and 'High' the top quartile

median firm-size (measured as the log of employment) of the equity groups is more or less identical, so we are not capturing a size effect in Fig. 1.

Klette and Kortum (2004) argue that a firm's innovation rate depends on its knowledge capital, which stands for all the skills and know-how that it possesses when it attempts to innovate. A large part of this knowledge capital is embodied in the workers in the firm. We try to capture this by how well-educated the firm's workers are. We define the variable *Human capital* as number of workers with a university education longer than 3 years normalized by the total number of workers. We argue that this reflects a firm's capacity to absorb, assimilate and develop new knowledge and technology (Bartel and Lichtenberg 1987; Cohen and Levinthal 1990).[9] We do not address the issue of persistent innovators, causing a potential omitted variable bias in our econometric approach (Blundell et al. 1995).[10] We argue that the inclusion of the *Human capital* variable, along with the control of firm fixed effects, in the econometric analysis reduces this problem. It is noteworthy that the three equity-groups display the same share of skilled employees, about 16 %.

The paper also includes a dummy variable, *high-tech sector*, enabling us to control for the degree of high-technology of each sector. This measure is based on the OECD classification of sector R&D-intensity. Since the decline in patent applications coincided with the burst of the IT-bubble, we want to make sure that

[9] Technological change tends to be skill-biased and changes the relative labor demand in favor of highly skilled and educated workers (e.g. Berman et al. 1998; Machin and Van Reenen 1998).

[10] We are unable to control for the effect of persistence in innovation as suggested in Blundell et al. (1995) since we do not have reliable measures of R&D or pre-sample history of the patent variable. Human capital is further useful since many small firms do not report official R&D expenditure.

Table 1 Summary statistics for manufacturing firms during the period 1997–2005

	All firms: 3,397			Patenting firms: 498		
Equity-ratio groups	Low	Middle	High	Low	Middle	High
Nr of firms	850	1,699	849	92 (11 %)	264 (16 %)	142 (17 %)
Patent appl./firm	0.578	1.840	3.645	4.024	9.354	15.500
Cash-flow						
Mean	0.040	0.054	0.073	0.036	0.065	0.088
Median	0.016	0.033	0.048	0.016	0.039	0.053
Sales						
Mean	2.566	2.391	1.702	2.322	2.009	1.462
Median	2.434	2.260	1.603	2.223	1.968	1.433
Long-term debt						
Mean	0.361	0.253	0.119	0.354	0.271	0.128
Median	0.332	0.213	0.071	0.343	0.230	0.079
Equity						
Mean	0.191	0.418	0.729	0.194	0.425	0.708
Median	0.178	0.397	0.705	0.182	0.404	0.701
Employment						
Mean	129	134	130	562	489	404
Median	23	26	21	56	79	60
Human capital						
Mean	0.159	0.161	0.154	0.224	0.239	0.243
Median	0.125	0.122	0.110	0.168	0.189	0.184
High-tech sector	0.064	0.072	0.065	0.075	0.144	0.099
MNE	0.351	0.375	0.333	0.637	0.688	0.711

Notes: Low, middle and high are divisions based on equity-ratio. We calculate average equity-ratio over the sample period and the bottom 25 % are in the low equity-group, the middle 50 % (second and third quartiles) are in the middle-equity group and the top 25 % are in the high-equity group. Cash flow, sales, long-term debt and equity are normalized by beginning of the period total assets. High-tech sector is a dummy indicating 1 if the firm operates in a high-tech sector based on OECDs classification. Human capital is number of employees with at least 3 years of education as a fraction of total employment. MNE is a dummy variable indicating if it is a multinational enterprise

the development in Fig. 1 is not driven by sector composition within each group. The middle equity-group has a slightly higher share of high-tech firms, albeit not large enough to be driving the results. Of the firms in the middle group, 7.2 % operate in high-tech industries, compared to 6.5 % and 6.4 % in the top and bottom groups, respectively (we examine patent applications in high-tech sectors versus non-high tech sectors in depth in Sect. 4).

As a final control variable we have access to information on corporate-affiliation, in Table 1 represented by a dummy indicating if the firm is a part of a multinational enterprise (MNE). Corporate-affiliation might very well be driving the results here. A firm affiliated to an MNE could either receive equity-injections directly from other parts of the MNE or enjoy lower costs of external finance because of its affiliation. In terms of corporate-affiliation of the three equity-groups we find no significant difference; about 35 % of the sample-firms are affiliated to an MNE.

The differences between patenting firms and the overall sample are consistent across the equity groups. Table 1 provides evidence of differences in terms of the average number of patent applications per firm, cash-flow and equity to total assets across the equity-groups. There is also a clear difference between all firms and the patenting firms across all three groups. Patenting firms are more profitable in terms of average cash-flow. Further, they are substantially larger, have relatively more skilled workers and, to a far larger extent, are a part of an MNE. One noteworthy aspect: the number of patent applications per firm is higher for the high-equity group but the share of patenting firms in the middle and high-equity groups is very similar.

Based on our control variables in Table 1 we conclude that we have variation among equity groups in terms of cash-flow and number of patent applications. Is it simply so that more profitable firms file for more and better patents?

2.3 Profitability, Equity Financing and Patent Applications: Time Series Evidence

All three equity groups have stable equity ratios over the studied time period. Based on the descriptive analysis this far it appears as though we lack some information on firm-level access to equity. Given the high and stable level of equity of firms in the high-equity group, they should have high and stable cash-flows unless they can access equity finance elsewhere.

Pooling all firm-year observations, Table 1 reveals that the high-equity firms have on average higher cash-flows. However, breaking down the observations to annual averages Fig. 2 shows that the high-equity group also has the most volatile cash-flows. This suggests that we lack information on, for instance, external equity sources. Are the firms in the high-equity group publicly traded to a larger extent, are they backed up by VC or private equity investors, or any other external equity source? This is beyond what we see in our data. We address this in the econometric analysis in Sect. 3.

One potential driver of the results is that the equity-ratio sample division simply captures growth and non-growth firms (see Fig. 3). However, the groups follow the same pattern with growth (in terms of total assets) in excess of 10 % per annum in the late 1990s, around 2 % growth rates during the weak economic period following the burst of the IT-bubble, and then we see a return to high growth in the latter part of the sample period.

Based on the descriptive statistics it appears as if access to equity is a key factor, explaining the decline of patent applications over the observed time period. Intuitively, this makes sense. When overall demand (measured as GDP) wanes, as it did following the burst of the IT-bubble, it is likely that the supply of cash-flow

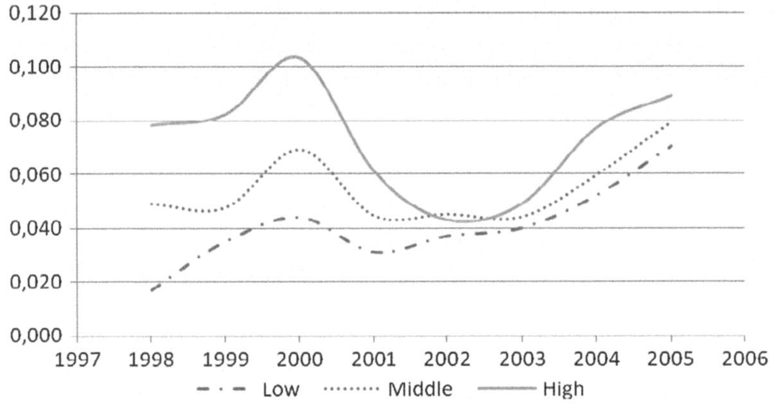

Fig. 2 Average annual cash flow to total assets across equity-ratio groups 1997–2005. *Notes*: Equity groups are based on the average equity to total assets ratio across the sample period. 'Low' comprises the bottom quartile of firms in terms of average equity ratio, 'Middle' the second and third quartile and 'High' the top quartile. Cash flow is defined as after-tax income plus depreciation and amortization divided by the beginning of the period total assets

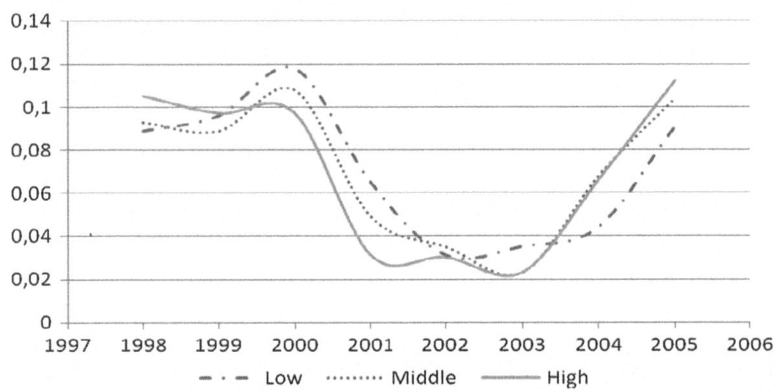

Fig. 3 Average annual total assets growth across equity-ratio groups 1997–2005. *Notes*: Equity groups are based on the average equity to total assets ratio across the sample period. 'Low' comprises the bottom quartile of firms in terms of average equity ratio, 'Middle' the second and third quartiles and 'High' the top quartile. Total assets growth is defined as the year on year percentage change of the natural log of total assets

declines. Investments in intangibles, which patent applications represent, do not generate any cash-flow in the near future (see Anderson and Prezas 1999). If the firm is unable to access external finance, it might be forced to reduce intangible investment in favor of tangible assets that do generate cash-flow streams today. In the descriptive analysis we show that the entire drop in patent applications is concentrated to the middle-equity group. The low-equity group constitutes a very small fraction of overall patent applications and the high-equity group displays a stable development of patent applications. We now proceed with econometric analysis. This enables us to explore how financial factors affect patent applications, while simultaneously controlling for the non-financial determinants of firm-level patenting.

3 Econometric Analysis

3.1 Theory and Empirical Predictions

In order to investigate the importance of equity-financing for persistent patent activity, we adopt a pecking-order approach (Myers and Majluf 1984; Stiglitz and Weiss 1981) inspired by Fazzari et al. (1988), who explore the sensitivity of fixed investment to cash-flow and conjecture that if a firm's investments are associated with cash-flow over time, it can be interpreted as a sign of financing constraints.[11] There are plenty of examples of studies applying the Fazzari et al. (1988) approach to R&D investment (see e.g. Brown et al. 2009; Himmelberg and Petersen 1994; Mulkaly et al. 2001). Our approach is to test the sensitivity of the number of patent applications to cash-flow.

Sensitivity of investment to cash-flow is an indication that the firm lacks access to external finance and thus is likely to be financially constrained. With this methodology we can analyze the relationship between patent applications and cash-flow across the three equity-groups while simultaneously controlling for the key determinants of patenting presented in Table 1. This way we can also gain some information on the external finance access of the high-equity group, which we suspect is better than for the other groups.

The high and stable level of equity across the different phases of the business cycle, in combination with the highly volatile cash-flow development, suggests that the high-equity firms might have better access to external sources of equity than firms in the middle- and low-equity groups.

We hypothesize that firms in the high-equity group do not display sensitivity of patent applications to cash-flow, while the other two groups do. This way we might implicitly observe the external finance access of the three sub-groups. The degree to which the low and middle groups differ is difficult to foresee given the few patent applications made by low-equity firms.

[11] There are, however, caveats with the cash-flow sensitivity approach The approach of dividing a sample into sub-groups on the basis of different access to finance, and then testing the sensitivity of investment to cash-flow, has encountered criticism, most notably in Kaplan and Zingales (1997). However, Bond et al. (2003a, p. 154) argue that it "remains the case in the (Kaplan and Zingales) model that a firm facing no financial constraint... would display no excess sensitivity to cash-flow", and in this case the Kaplan and Zingales critique does not apply.

3.2 Estimation Method

Only about 15 % of the firms in our sample are patenting firms, implying that the patent filings variable has an excess of zero observations and is also over-dispersed. We apply the negative binomial model, since it is robust to excess numbers of zero observations and to over-dispersion while also controlling for unobserved firm-specific effects (Cameron and Trivedi 2008; Lerner et al. 2008).

In our model specification *number of patent applications* is the dependent variable and *cash-flow* is the key explanatory variable of each of the three sub-groups based on equity-ratio. Further, we also include sales and long-term debt as "financial" control variables. Omitting sales may lead to an upward bias of the cash-flow estimate due to the high correlation of sales and cash-flow. Sales constitute a control for firm demand which enables us to view the cash-flow estimate more as a sign of internal finance access rather than a sign of high firm demand (Brown et al. 2009, p. 163). As discussed in Sect. 2, we include the log of employment as a control for firm-size, human-capital intensity as a control for the knowledge base within the firm, sector dummies to control for the high-tech intensity of the industry, and also corporate-affiliation indicating if the firm is a part of a domestic or foreign-owned multinational enterprise (MNE).

3.3 Results

Table 2 shows the relationship of patent applications with respect to its determinants. The first column comprises the coefficient estimates for the whole sample. All variables enter significantly and with the expected signs. However, cash-flow provides the weakest estimate, significant only at about 5 %. As expected, the size estimate indicates that, other things equal, larger firms file for more patents. Human-capital intensity is quantitatively large and highly important to the number of patent applications, in line with the descriptive statistics and existing literature. Also, both foreign as well as domestic MNE-affiliated firms are associated with higher levels of patent applications, corroborating Table 1.

In columns 2–4 we examine the sensitivity of patent applications to cash-flow for the three different subgroups classified by their equity-ratio; Low, Middle and High. Columns 2 and 3 show positive, significant and quite sizeable coefficients associated with changes in cash-flow for firms with a low- or middle-equity ratio. In contrast, the cash-flow coefficient is very small and nonsignificant for high-equity firms. This result confirms the predictions of Sect. 3.1. Following the rationale of cash-flow sensitivity, we argue that this is a sign that low-equity firms have less external finance access than firms with a higher equity-ratio. The cash-flow estimates suggest that the high-equity firms might have better access to outside financing compared to the middle- and low-equity firms. This could be an

Table 2 Negative binomial regressions across equity-ratio groups

	All firms	Low	Middle	High
Cash-flow	0.316	2.375	0.738	0.094
	(0.057)*	(0.005)***	(0.050)**	(0.507)
Sales	−0.229	−0.254	−0.271	−0.212
	(0.000)***	(0.009)***	(0.000)***	(0.028)**
Long-term debt	0.317	0.602	0.279	0.166
	(0.001)***	(0.005)***	(0.083)*	(0.612)
Log size	0.317	0.603	0.334	0.827
	(0.000)***	(0.000)***	(0.000)***	(0.000)***
HT[a]	0.954	1.528	1.400	0.907
	(0.000)***	(0.000)***	(0.000)***	(0.004)***
HMT[a]	0.840	1.686	1.002	1.322
	(0.000)***	(0.007)***	(0.000)***	(0.000)***
LMT[a]	0.912	1.750	1.035	0.879
	(0.000)***	(0.000)***	(0.000)***	(0.001)***
Human cap	2.599	4.087	3.574	1.874
	(0.000)***	(0.000)***	(0.000)***	(0.000)***
FMNE[b]	0.507	0.242	0.522	0.367
	(0.001)***	(0.399)	(0.001)***	(0.187)
DMNE[b]	0.719	0.347	0.854	1.013
	(0.000)***	(0.197)	(0.000)***	(0.000)***
Observations	12,768	3,200	6,384	3,184
Firms	2,672	1,147	1,980	1,074

Notes: Low, middle and high are divisions based on equity-ratio. We calculate average equity-ratio over the sample period and the bottom 25 % are in the low equity-group, the middle 50 % (second and third quartiles) are in the middle-equity group and the top 25 % are in the high-equity group. Dependent variable is number of patent applications. P-values are in parentheses. All results include time-dummies. Cash flow, sales and long-term debt are normalized by beginning of the period total assets. Size is log employees. Hum cap is number of employees with at least 3 years of education as a fraction of total employment. FMNE and DMNE are foreign and domestic multinational enterprises, respectively. The intercept represents firms only operating domestically. *HT* high technological firms, *HMT* high-medium technology firms, *LMT* low-medium technology firms

*significant at 10 %; **significant at 5 %; ***significant at 1 %

[a]Reference is low technology firms

[b]Reference is domestic non-affiliated firms

explanation of why low and especially middle-equity firms reduce their patent applications as a consequence of falling internal equity supply following lower overall demand.

We also estimate the sample of all firms on a sub-sample of years with high economic activity (1997–2000) and lower economic activity (2001–2005).[12] This way we can gain additional understanding of how reliable the cash-flow sensitivity approach is in our context. In times of high economic activity the premium on

[12] These estimation results are not presented due to space constraints, but they are available upon request.

external finance goes down following more risk appetite from investors, higher expected rates of return to investment etc. Cash-flow is also higher when demand is high, all else equal. Thus, we predict that there should be no or lower sensitivity of patent applications to cash-flow in the 1997–2000 sample and higher sensitivity in the 2001–2005 sample. In line with our predictions, the cash-flow is non-significant during the high economic activity period. Conversely, there is a large and highly statistically significant cash-flow estimate in the 2001–2005 sub-sample. The findings for the sample split on macroeconomic activity strengthen our belief in the usefulness of the cash-flow sensitivity approach here.

We thus argue that equity financing matters for a firm in order to maintain its patenting strategy over the course of the business cycle. And, as suggested by the econometric analysis, it is important to be able to access equity externally in order to maintain a consistently high equity-ratio. We draw this conclusion from implicitly observing access to outside finance via estimating the sensitivity of patent applications to cash-flow for the three equity groups.

4 Robustness Checks

4.1 High-Tech Patent Applications vs. Non-high Tech Patent Applications

Since the decline in patent applications coincided with the burst of the IT-bubble, we want to make sure that our results are not driven by the high-tech sectors.[13]

In Fig. 4 we calculate the growth rate of patent applications and convert them into an index with 1997 set as reference year, across high-tech and non-high tech firms as well as high-equity and middle-equity firms. The high-equity group finishes above 100, at 110 to be specific. The middle-equity group index-value in 2005 is 46, implying that the number of patent applications of the middle group declined by 54 % from 1997 to 2005. Both high-tech and non-high tech firms experienced declines of about 40 % in the number of their patent applications during the sample period. This piece of evidence convinces us that we are not simply capturing a downturn in high-tech patent applications.

[13] The following sectors are considered high technology: Manufacture of basic pharmaceutical (SIC 24410), pharmaceutical preparations (24420), office machinery (30010), computers and other information processing equipment (30020), insulated wire and cable (31300), electronic valves and tubes and other electronic components (32100), television and radio transmitters and apparatus for line telephony and line telegraphy (32200), television and radio receivers, sound or video recording or reproducing apparatus and associated goods (32300), medical and surgical equipment and orthopedic appliances except artificial teeth, dentures etc., (33101), instruments and appliances for measuring, checking, testing, navigating and other purposes, except industrial process control equipment (33200) and industrial process control equipment (33300) (source: Statistics Sweden).

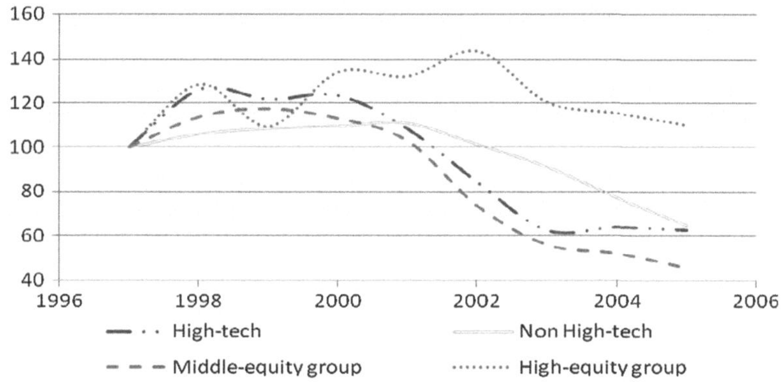

Fig. 4 Development of the number of patent applications (1997–2005): High-tech sector division vs. equity split. Index with 1997 set as 100. *Notes*: The high-tech sectors are: Manufacture of basic pharmaceutical (SIC 24410), pharmaceutical preparations (24420), office machinery (30010), computers and other information processing equipment (30020), insulated wire and cable (31300), electronic valves and tubes and other electronic components (32100), television and radio transmitters and apparatus for line telephony and line telegraphy (32200), television and radio receivers, sound or video recording or reproducing apparatus and associated goods (32300), medical and surgical equipment and orthopedic appliances except artificial teeth, dentures, etc. (33101), instruments and appliances for measuring, checking, testing, navigating and other purposes, except industrial process control equipment (33200) and industrial process control equipment (33300) (source: Statistics Sweden). Equity groups are based on the average equity to total assets ratio across the sample period. 'Low' comprises the bottom quartile of firms in terms of average equity ratio, 'Middle' the second and third quartiles and 'High' the top quartile. Cash-flow is defined as after-tax income plus depreciation and amortization divided by the beginning of the period total assets

4.2 *Are the Middle- and Low-Equity Firms Financially Constrained?*

In Sect. 3 we tried to gain information on the external finance access of the different equity groups. Based on the investment-cash flow sensitivity approach, we argue that the low and middle equity-groups have poorer access to equity than firms in the high-equity group. In this section we address the potential problems of the investment-cash flow approach (the Kaplan and Zingales critique) by applying another test of firms' financing constraint status. Almeida et al. (2004) develop a model for testing whether groups of firms are financially constrained. They test the cash-flow sensitivity of cash. Firms that experience problems obtaining funds in the external capital market buffer cash from their own cash-flow in order to smooth operations when cash-flow wanes. Almeida et al. (2004) find that financially constrained firms display such sensitivity whereas unconstrained firms do not.[14]

[14] Examples of papers adapting this methodology are Bates et al. (2009) and Baum et al. (2009).

We estimate a specification with changes in cash holdings (cash and equivalents) divided by beginning of the period total assets as the dependent variable and cash-flow as the main explanatory variable along with the same control variables as in Table 2 to evaluate the cash-flow sensitivity of cash for the high-equity group vs. the rest of the sample.[15] In line with the results in Sect. 3, the high-equity group displays no cash-flow sensitivity of changes in cash holdings, whereas the middle and low-equity groups do. These findings further strengthen our results that there are firm-level financial effects behind the fall in patent applications in Sweden from 1997 to 2005.

4.3 Change in Definition and Model Specification

In our final robustness check we make a substantial change of the observed data and the methodological framework in order to test the sensitivity of the result presented in Table 2. The alternative dataset is also based on PATSTAT, but we expend the period with three additional years. Moreover, our second data set has a higher match-rate between the firm-level data and the patent applications filed by enterprises based in Sweden. The second dataset also includes more outliers that were eliminated in Table 3. Thus, Tables 3 and 4 report results with the following changes. First, the time-span is 1997–2008. Second, we include sales growth in the model and drop the ownership variables. Third, we modify the cash-flow variable, which now is defined as after-tax income adjusted for depreciation and amortization, wage costs, a cost for intermediate products and costs for raw materials. Fourth, the firms are separated into only two equity groups. The first is *low-medium* consisting of firms within the bottom 2/3 of the average equity distribution over the period 1997–2008, and the second contains firms in the top 33 % of the distribution. Fifth, we include a lagged cash-flow variable, in Table 4. Sixth, finally, we compare different count-data models for panels, the Poisson model and the Negative binomial estimator.

The conclusion from Table 3 is that results confirm the main finding from Table 2 showing that the link between innovation (patenting) and economic fluctuations differ across groups of firms with different access to equity. In Table 3, both the Possison and Negative binomial estimates for cash flow are positive and highly significant. Presumably due to the different definition of the cash-flow variable, the order of magnitude of the coefficient estimates is lower than in Table 2. It can also be noted that the Poisson point estimate for cash-flow is *negative* and significant in Table 3, in accordance with the Schumpeterian hypothesis that R&D and patent

[15] We estimate this specification with within estimation firm-specific effects. Since we are only interested in comparing the two groups, we argue that potential endogeneity and simultaneity biases affect both groups of firms similarly.

Table 3 Poisson and negative binomial panel data regressions across equity-ratio groups

	Poisson		NBREG	
	Low–middle	High	Low–middle	High
Cash-flow	0.143	−0.204	0.284	0.074
	(6.68)***	(4.19)***	(4.48)***	(0.81)
Sales	−0.123	0.151	−0.416	−0.193
	(4.25)***	(2.98)***	(6.08)***	(1.97)**
Sales growth	0.000	−0.000	0.000	−0.000
	(0.04)	(4.29)***	(0.36)	(2.89)***
Long-term debt	0.005	0.010	0.001	0.008
	(3.35)***	(3.89)***	(0.20)	(1.72)
Log size	0.732	0.754	0.475	0.550
	(43.15)***	(14.74)***	(17.34)***	(11.84)***
HT[a]	2.680	1.196	0.728	2.224
	(19.08)***	(4.35)***	(2.60)***	(6.67)***
HMT[a]	2.124	1.927	1.745	2.006
	(9.16)***	(9.31)***	(9.34)***	(9.85)***
LMT[a]	1.631	1.844	1.262	1.717
	(12.39)***	(9.26)***	(10.42)***	(9.18)***
Human cap	0.804	1.865	0.912	1.258
	(8.61)***	(8.74)***	(7.64)***	(6.11)***
Observations	35,593	17,637	35,593	17,637
Firms	5,762	2,777	5,762	2,777

Notes: Low–middle and high are divisions based on equity-ratio. We calculate average equity-ratio over the sample period and the bottom 67 % are in the low–middle equity-group, and the top 33 % are in the high-equity group. Dependent variable is number of patent applications. z-statistics in parentheses. Cash flow, sales and long-term debt are normalized by beginning of the period total assets. Size is log employees. Hum cap is number of employees with at least 3 years of education as a fraction of total employment.

HT high technological firms, *HMT* high-medium technology firms, *LMT* low-medium technology firms

**significant at 5 %; ***significant at 1 %

[a]Reference is low technology firms

filings are pro-cyclical. The corresponding Negative binomial estimate is non-significant.

Table 4 applies the same model as Table 3, but includes a lagged cash-flow variable. The results are almost identical to Table 3. The only exception is that the instantaneous effect if the cash-flow in the negative binomial regression only is significant at the 10 % level, while the lagged cash-flow coefficient is highly significant.

Table 4 Poisson and negative binomial panel data regressions across equity-ratio groups

	Poisson		NBREG	
	Low–middle	High	Low–middle	High
Cash-flow	0.095	−0.253	0.131*	0.037
	(3.51)***	(4.75)***	(1.90)	(0.37)
Cash-flow, t − 1	0.245	0.004	0.148	0.035
	(11.01)***	(0.15)	(2.93)***	(0.77)
Sales	−0.202	0.100	−0.304	−0.220
	(6.31)***	(1.65)	(4.11)***	(2.01)**
Sales growth	0.000	−0.000	0.000	−0.000
	(6.68)***	(4.17)***	(0.12)	(2.79)***
Long-term debt	0.006	0.010	0.000	0.006
	(3.44)***	(3.60)***	(0.05)	(1.27)
Log size	0.932	0.964	0.565	0.613
	(28.82)***	(15.49)***	(18.41)***	(11.73) ***
HT[a]	3.442	0.212	0.961	2.179
	(18.69)***	(0.64)	(2.89)***	(5.81)***
HMT[a]	2.043	2.261	1.759	2.090
	(7.88)***	(9.50)***	(8.41)***	(9.44)***
LMT[a]	1.551	1.942	1.353	1.707
	(10.47)***	(8.90)***	(10.13)***	(8.51)***
Human cap	0.839	1.879	0.842	1.122
	(7.95)***	(7.74)***	(6.52)***	(5.06)***
Observations	29,438	14,681	29,438	14,681
Firms	5,226	2,526	5,226	2,526

Notes: Low–middle and high are divisions based on equity-ratio. We calculate average equity-ratio over the sample period and the bottom 67 % are in the low-middle equity-group, and the top 33 % are in the high-equity group. Dependent variable is number of patent applications. z-statistics in parentheses. Cash flow, sales and long-term debt are normalized by beginning of the period total assets. Size is log employees. Hum cap is number of employees with at least 3 years of education as a fraction of total employment.

HT high technological firms, *HMT* high-medium technology firms, *LMT* low-medium technology firms

*significant at 10 %; **significant at 5 %; ***significant at 1 %

[a]Reference is low technology firms

5 Conclusion and Implications

We argue that firm-level equity supply plays an important role for firms in maintaining their patenting strategy over the business cycle. We use a panel of 3,400 manufacturing firms in Sweden and find that their aggregate number of patent applications dropped by more than 40 % from the peak year in 2000.

We show that the entire drop of patent applications was concentrated among firms with moderate amounts of equity in relation to total assets, whereas patent applications of firms with high levels of equity were little affected. Firms with low levels of equity constitute a very small fraction of aggregate patent applications.

This finding is not driven by firm-size, human-capital intensity, firm-affiliation, sector composition or asset-growth intensity.

Our results indicate that capital-market imperfections may have adverse impacts on firm-level patenting. Since we think it is highly unlikely for firms with moderate equity supply to have disproportionately many low-quality patent applications (even though we wish to incorporate the quality of the patents in future studies), we argue that improving equity supply could be a useful means to facilitate firm-level innovation.

Schumpeter (1942) argues that recessions are cleansing mechanisms that eliminate firms which are unable to re-organize and innovate. This notion about recessions assumes that firms can always obtain finance externally (see also Aghion et al. 2008). The Schumpeterian view on business cycles makes perfect sense in a world without capital-market imperfections; in a recession when demand is low, the opportunity cost to innovate for future growth is also low. Our results indicate that there are capital-market imperfections present that disturb this Schumpeterian view of business cycles. We think it is unlikely for high-equity firms to have such a disproportionately higher number of quality patent applications compared to middle-equity firms. Therefore, it is likely that firms in the middle-equity group actually dropped economically viable patent applications due to a lack of funds.

From a policy perspective it is possible to identify these firms, but is it desirable to intervene? Such policies are plagued with moral hazard and adverse selection issues.[16] And, as Heller and Eisenberg (1998) highlight, there is a downside to patents in that they potentially block technological development through enhancing incumbent market power.[17] However, there are fields where policy makers can intervene. Policies attempting to broadly improve both internal and external equity supply are favorable. Through the corporate tax rate it is possible to affect the supply of internal equity. External equity supply can be improved through efforts to improve accounting standards, removing obstacles in the financial market, creating stock exchanges for firms that wish to go public but during present conditions are unable to (which might also increase venture capital access from enhanced "exit possibilities"), etc.[18]

Lev (2004, pp. 111–112) argues that due to disclosure problems, associated with intangible assets such as patents and R&D, intangibles-intensive public firms face

---

[16] Svensson (2007) analyzes small firms and individuals and their access to external finance and the commercialization of their patents. He shows that the larger share of external funding from governmental programs the lower the probability of patents being commercialized, indicating the agency problems associated with non-private financial support.

[17] Hall and Ziedonis (2001) and Hall (2005) document the explosion of patents since the beginning of the 1980s. U.S. sources also document how the vast number of patent applications has become a serious public policy problem because patent offices are capacity constrained (see for instance National Research Council 2004).

[18] Both Black and Gilson (1998) and Groh et al. (2010) point to a deep equity market being instrumental in achieving a vibrant venture capital market.

an undervaluation problem which leads to higher costs of capital.[19] The patent-intensity of Sweden might partly be a result of the relatively transparent accounting standards reducing asymmetric information, which would otherwise deter investors. Sweden is classified as a country with high accounting standards (Levine 1999).[20] Therefore, it is not only firms with "deep pockets" that are able to be innovators. Ironically, this could be one of the reasons why Sweden's patent-application growth is comparatively volatile. When external finance is plentiful, relatively many firms in Sweden can obtain adequate funds to be innovative, but when the external equity market dries up, these funds are no longer available.

References

Aghion P, Angeletos G-M, Banerjee A, Manova K (2005) Volatility and growth: financial development and the cyclical composition of investment. Working Paper

Aghion P, Askenazy P, Berman N, Cette G, Eymard L (2008) Credit constraints and the cyclicality of R&D investment: evidence from France. Banque de France Working Paper 198

Almeida H, Campello M, Weisbach MS (2004) The cash-flow sensitivity of cash. J Finan 59:1777–1804

Anderson MH, Prezas AP (1999) Intangible investment debt financing and managerial incentives. J Econ Bus 51:3–19

Bartel AP, Lichtenberg FR (1987) The comparative advantage of educated workers in implementing new technology. Rev Econ Stat 69:1–11

Bates TW, Kahle KM, Stulz RM (2009) Why do U.S. firms hold so much more cash than they used to? J Finan 64:1985–2021

Baum CF, Schäfer D, Talavera O (2009) The impact of financial structure on firms' financial constraints: a cross-country analysis. Working Paper

Berger AN, Udell GF (1990) Collateral, loan quality, and bank risk. J Monet Econ 25:21–42

Berman E, Bound J, Machin S (1998) Implications of skill biased technical change: international evidence. Quart J Econ 113:1245–1279

Black BS, Gilson RJ (1998) Venture capital and the structure of capital markets: bank versus stock markets. J Finan Econ 47:243–277

Blundell R, Griffith R, Van Reenen J (1995) Dynamic count data models of technological innovation. Econ J 105:333–344

Bond S, Elston J-A, Mairesse J, Mulkaly B (2003a) Financial factors and investment in Belgium, France, Germany, and the United Kingdom: a comparison using company panel data. Rev Econ Statis 85:153–165

Bond S, Harhoff D, Van Reenen J (2003b) Investment, R&D and financial constraints in Britain and Germany. LSE Research online http://eprints.lse.ac.uk/771/

Bound J, Cummins C, Griliches Z, Hall BH, Jaffe AB (1982) Who does R&D and who patents? NBER Working Paper 908

[19] See Hall et al. (2007) for recent evidence of the market valuation of patents.

[20] Based on an index (scale 0–90) of the comprehensiveness of corporate annual reports, referred to as accounting standards on scale, Sweden scores the highest of 83. For instance the U.S. has an index value of 71 and the second highest accounting standards are found in the UK with 78 (Levine 1999, pp. 14–15).

Brown JR, Fazzari SM, Petersen BC (2009) Financing innovation and growth: cash-flow, external equity, and the 1990s R&D boom. J Finan 64:151–185

Cameron AC, Trivedi PK (2008) Applied microeconometrics using STATA. STATA, New York

Carpenter RE, Petersen BC (2002) Capital market imperfections, high-tech investment, and new equity financing. Econ J 112:54–72

Cohen W, Levinthal DA (1990) Absorptive capacity – a new perspective on learning and innovation. Adm Sci Q 35:128–152

Fazzari SM, Hubbard RG, Petersen BC (1988) Financing constraints and corporate investment. Brookings Pap Econ Act 1:141–195

Francois P, Lloyd-Ellis H (2009) Schumpeterian cycles with pro-cyclical R&D. Rev Econ Dyn 12:567–591

Freel M (1997) Towards an evolutionary theory of small firm growth. Unpublished working paper, Paisley Enterprise Research Centre, Paisley

Geroski PA, Walters CF (1995) Innovative activity over the business cycle. Econ J 105:916–928

Geroski PA, Van Reenen J, Walters CF (1995) Innovations, patents and cash flow. Mimeo (London Business School), New York

Geroski PA, Van Reenen J, Walters CF (1997) How persistently do firms innovate? Res Policy 26:33–48

Giudic G, Paleri S (2000) The provision of finance to innovation: a survey conducted among Italian technology-based small firms. Small Bus Econ 14:37–53

Griliches Z (1990) Patent statistics as economic indicators: a survey. J Econ Lit 28:1661–1707

Groh AP, von Liechtenstein H, Lieser K (2010) The European venture capital and private equity country attractiveness indices. J Corp Finan 16(2). http://ssrn.com/abstract=1747662

Haeussler C, Harhoff D, Mueller E (2009) To be financed or not... – The role of patents for venture capital financing. Centre for European Economic Research Discussion Paper, No. 09–003

Hall BH (1992) Investment and research and development at the firm level: does the source of financing matter? NBER Working Paper 4096

Hall BH (2002) The financing of research and development. Oxf Rev Econ Policy 18:35–51

Hall BH (2005) Exploring the patent explosion. J Technol Transf 30:35–48

Hall BH, Lerner J (2010) The financing of R&D and innovation. In: Hall BH, Rosenberg N (eds) Handbook of the economics of innovation. Elsevier-North Holland, New York

Hall BH, Ziedonis RH (2001) The patent paradox revisited: and empirical study of patenting in the U.S. semiconductor industry, 1979–1995. RAND J Econ 32:101–128

Hall BH, Thoma G, Torrisi S (2007) The market valuation of patents and R&D: evidence from European firms. NBER Working Paper 13426

Harhoff D (1998) Are there financing constraints for innovation and investment in German manufacturing firms? Ann Econ Stat 49/50:421–456

Heller MA, Eisenberg RS (1998) Can patents deter innovation? The anticommons in biomedical research. Science 280:698–701

Himmelberg CP, Petersen BC (1994) R&D and internal finance: a panel study of small firms in high-tech industries. Rev Econ Stat 76:38–51

Jensen MC, Meckling W (1976) Theory of the firm managerial behavior, agency costs and ownership structure. J Finan Econ 4:305–360

Kaplan SN, Zingales L (1997) Do investment-cash flow sensitivities provide useful measures of financing constraints? Quart J Econ 112:169–215

Klette T, Kortum S (2004) Innovating firms and aggregate innovation. J Polit Econ 112:986–1018

Kortum S, Lerner J (2000) Assessing the contribution of venture capital to innovation. Rand J Econ 31:674–692

Lerner J, Sörensen M, Strömberg P (2008) Private equity and long-run investment: the case of innovation. NBER Working Paper 14623

Lev B (2004) Sharpening the intangibles edge. Harv Bus Rev 82:109–116

Levine R (1999) Law, finance and economic growth. J Finan Intermed 8:8–35

Machin S, Van Reenen J (1998) Technology and changes in skill structure: evidence from seven OECD countries. Quart J Econ 113:1215–1244

Martinsson G (2010) Equity financing and innovation: is Europe different from the United States? J Bank Finan 34(6):1215–1224

Mulkaly B, Hall BH, Mairesse J (2001) Firm level investment and R&D in France and the United States: a comparison. NBER Working Paper 8048

Myers SC, Majluf NS (1984) Corporate financing and investment decisions when firms have information that investors do not have. J Finan Econ 13:187–221

National Research Council (2004) Patent system for the 21st century, report of the board on science, technology, and economic policy. National Academic, Washington, DC

Scellato G (2007) Patents firm size and financial constraints: an empirical analysis for a panel of Italian manufacturing firms. Camb J Econ 31:55–76

Schroth E, Szalay D (2009) Cash breeds success: the role of financing constraints in patents races. Rev Finan 14:73–118

Schumpeter JA (1942) Capitalism, socialism and democracy. Harper and Brothers, New York (Harper Colophon edition, 1976)

Stiglitz JE (1985) Credit markets and the control of capital. J Mon Cred Bank 17:133–152

Stiglitz JE, Weiss A (1981) Credit rationing in markets with imperfect information. Am Econ Rev 71:393–410

Svensson R (2007) Commercialization of patents and external financing during the R&D phase. Res Policy 36:1052–1069

Titman S, Wessels R (1988) The determinants of capital structure choice. J Finan 43:1–19

Westhead P, Storey D (1997) Training provision and development of small and medium–sized enterprises, Research Report No. 26, London: DfEE

Building Systems

Brian J. Loasby

Abstract A system is a set of elements which are connected in particular ways. The formal general equilibrium model is an extreme case in which every element is directly connected to every other and in which all potential external connections, including connections from the future, are incorporated in the data. The foundational assumption of this paper is that viable systems must be selectively connected, and that viable large systems are highly-decomposable assemblies of smaller systems. As Simon argued, quasi-decomposability has made evolution possible from the beginning of the universe. Economies are evolutionary systems, in which human intentionality is a novel feature which modifies but does not supersede the processes of novelty generation, selection and diffusion. The micro-foundations for this study are found in the characteristics of the human brain as a system of selective connections. Human knowledge consists of domain-limited patterns imposed on events. Organization—selective connections—is thus basic; but the potential for human knowledge is greatly enhanced by specialisation between domains, combined with variation within each. Co-ordination and development, so often separated in economic theory, are interconnected; they are both ordered processes—not states, in which markets (alongside many other institutions) are prime sources of order.

1 Equilibrium and Evolution

A system is a set of elements which are connected in particular ways. The behaviour of a system therefore depends both on the particular elements of which it is composed and also on the particular pattern of connections between them; indeed

Reprinted from Evolutionary Economics 22(4), 833–846, Springer (2012)

B.J. Loasby (✉)
Division of Economics, University of Stirling, Stirling FK9 4LA, UK
e-mail: b.j.loasby@stir.ac.uk

A. Pyka and E.S. Andersen (eds.), *Long Term Economic Development*, Economic Complexity and Evolution, DOI 10.1007/978-3-642-35125-9_18,

the relationship between structure and performance is a major topic in many fields of study.

A familiar example in economics is the perfectly competitive economy, for which an existence proof of equilibrium was provided by Gerard Debreu. This has two distinctive characteristics. First, the system is completely isolated from any external influences. Second, every element is directly connected to every other: each agent makes a single comprehensive set of choices, formalised in a complete set of contracts to purchase and supply goods and services in specific circumstances and at particular prices. This combination of external isolation and internally complete connections is sufficient to support a proof of equilibrium. Everyone is optimising, subject to the constraints inherent in the data, which are known to be complete and correct, and those imposed by the optimal choices of everyone else. Thus there can be no reason for anyone to depart from the equilibrium once it has been established. What is notable, and essential to the analysis, is the extreme simplicity of its structure: indeed in terms of the opening sentence it has no structure.

There are certain problems with this model system. First, these results rely on the assumption that every agent's actions are insignificant in relation to the supply or demand for any good or service, and no agents act in concert. Next all goods must be defined, not only by their inherent characteristics, but also by their location, date, and the state of the world at each date, where it is necessary to specify all possible states. Providing such definitions may seem straightforward (though time-consuming), but it is not. How much differentiation may be allowed before we must allocate goods to distinct categories? Since all agents are interested in the distance from their own particular locations, how can we draw boundaries which are equally appropriate to all? Since some goods are likely to be used at particular times of day, how finely should we define time? What constitutes a relevantly distinctive state of the world at each date, and may we not also need to specify each anticipated history of the world to this date, which may influence agents' responses? Moreover, there is no obvious time horizon, and should we not be including within our closed system people who are not yet born? They too must have perfect information.

We next encounter a fundamental logical impasse. Although the model does not require us to know what will happen, it does require us to list all possibilities, and therefore to be quite certain what will not happen. There can be no surprises and no discoveries; either would demonstrate that the apparent general equilibrium was false. However if we have a correct description of our situation and of all possible futures, the equilibrium will last for all time and everyone will fulfil all relevant contracts. What is more, that equilibrium should have been achieved long ago; the time for choosing is already past, and our role in each contingency is already prescribed. As Frank Knight (1921) observed 90 years ago, a world without uncertainty requires only automata. It certainly does not require economists—and, since it is efficient, it will not tolerate them.

Finally, no-one has explained how equilibrium can be achieved in a way which is consistent with the model (Richardson 1960). The process of equilibration must require no resources, which are all allocated to their equilibrium uses; no agent is allowed to set any price; and because false trading may frustrate the attainment of the equilibrium inherent in the data, a complete set of contracts must be established in markets which close—forever—before the economy begins to function. How they are to be established is not considered; and the fundamental reason for that I believe is crucial. Markets are superfluous in a full general equilibrium; their role is to order processes which can lead to situations which may be described as equilibria in the sense of rest points—or more precisely as stable processes, and the ways of ordering each market may have significant effects. The key questions in economics are about processes—as is increasingly true in other sciences, notably in physics, and processes are conditioned by structure, which is precisely what is lacking in perfect competition and, on the grand scale, in general equilibrium. Systems that work must be selectively, not universally, connected, and large systems must be complex assemblies of smaller systems. The classic general equilibrium model is not appropriate.

The essential argument was made by Herbert Simon in 1962 in his parable of the watchmakers Tempus and Hora. Both made excellent watches, composed of 1,000 parts each; but whereas Tempus used general equilibrium principles, in which only a complete set of relationships was stable, Hora decomposed his design into ten major assemblies, each of ten subassemblies of ten elements, thus providing independent stability at each level. Both watchmakers attracted many customers, and had to put down their work in order to deal with them; but whereas Tempus then had to restart from the basic elements, Hora lost only the connections within the particular unit on which he was working (Simon [1962] 1969).

Simon's first crucial proposition is that building a system in an environment which is subject to disturbance is likely to be almost impossible without stable intermediate forms—which are necessarily excluded from general equilibrium systems. In Hora's design the connections between levels are independent of the internal arrangements at each level; however near decomposability (very few interactions of elements across boundaries) is often sufficient to ensure a high degree of stability, with the significant qualification of exposure to surprise through the activation of a latent connection. This is a common feature of failures in economic systems (as in other areas of human experience) and deserves more attention from economists—not least when giving advice. Simon argues that the survivors of evolutionary processes which rely on environmental selection may be expected to be predominantly of this kind, and he explicitly—and significantly—includes the evolution of physical as well as biological structures. He then proposes the natural corollary that social and economic systems which function well in a turbulent environment exhibit such properties. Richardson (who has had little connection with Simon's work) reaches the same conclusion, differently expressed, about economic systems. As we shall see, both have illustrious predecessors in economics.

Simon's reasoning invites comparison with the theories developed by Georges Cuvier (1769–1832), a major French contributor to zoology and paleontology. Cuvier believed that every organism was a single fully-integrated system (a foundational principle of general equilibrium) and that the evolution of species was therefore impossible. Consequently no species could respond to shocks, as he claimed was demonstrated by the fossil evidence of extinction. (The exclusion of turbulence is, of course, a condition of general equilibrium.) Thus he could have agreed with Simon's explanation of the fate of Tempus's watchmaking business, but he would have rejected the viability of Hora's alternative design. Raffaelli (2008) uses Cuvier's theory to argue that evolutionary theories necessarily require partial, not general equilibrium.

Discussions and debates about evolution, within economics as well as biology, predominantly focus on variation, selection and retention, at the expense of the fundamental principle of the self-organization of complex systems by selective connections within each level and a high degree of decomposability between levels. (These debates lie outside the focus of this paper.) As Cuvier's argument shows by counterpoint, these features greatly facilitate variation through minor adjustments to the set of elements or the connections between them; and although most modifications are likely to be rejected, decomposability is even more likely to be a feature of those which survive. As Simon argues, it also facilitates retention and reproduction of these survivors.

Present ideas strongly suggest that the history of the universe may be summarised as the building of successive quasi-decomposable systems: first the coalescence of elementary particles into chemical elements, then the emergence of particular combinations of these elements as chemical compounds, next the beginnings of life as some compounds combined to form cells, and then the development of progressively more elaborate life forms, in which direct genetic instructions have become increasingly modified—and sometimes superseded—by interactions between genes which are not deducible simply from a knowledge of the genes themselves.

That is not the end of the sequence, but it will suffice. This is clearly an evolutionary story, in which each stage provides the building blocks for the next and so is a necessary precursor for it. Selecting different collections of elements from a rather small set, and linking the members of each collection in different ways is a far more effective means of generating variety, and thus facilitating evolution, at each level than the independent construction of each system. (The relationship between the number of elements and the number of chemical compounds is a striking illustration.) Moreover this method of building complex systems is particularly appropriate to a process which must proceed by trial and error, and which cannot go into reverse (Prigogine 2005), but which may follow alternative paths to very similar outcomes. Evolution proceeds by self-organization and results in spontaneous order, though with a good deal of disorder from failed innovations along the way.

We may therefore feel justified in treating economic systems as a relatively new class of manifestations of a general evolutionary principle of building systems by making selective connections between elements of existing systems. We may also feel justified in seeking to analyse the structure of each system without investigating its elements in detail. However, when we encounter human-based systems an important modification of the neoDarwinian version of this principle is required: neither random genetic mutation nor selection by differential genetic inheritance is appropriate. We must introduce intentionality. In economic evolution (as in science) trial and error is typically guided by conjectures which are intended to produce particular results, although (like genetic mutations) most conjectures are refuted and unintended consequences are rather common. In addition, the diffusion of ideas and practices in economic systems, which are also social systems, is much more complex than a precisely-defined process of replication. As many studies of innovation have shown, adoption is typically accompanied by adaptation.

2 Microfoundations

To understand how economic systems emerge, we must first have an adequate understanding of human potential, and in particular of the human mind. (The design of watches is the outcome of mental processes, and depends on mental capabilities.) In Raffaelli's (2003, p. 50) phrase, we must consider 'human beings as evolving, organized systems whose behaviour depends on previous clusters of nervous connections which change over time ... [because of] the relationships between their internal structure and the external world'. This is a perspective that in a substantial degree is shared by three great economists, Smith, Marshall, and Hayek.

Let us begin with Hayek.

> Any apparatus of classification must possess a structure of a higher degree of complexity than is possessed by the objects that it classifies; ... therefore, the capacity of any explaining agents must be limited to objects with a structure possessing a degree of complexity lower than its own. (Hayek 1952, p. 185)

The human brain cannot fully understand its own operations, let alone its extraordinarily complex environment. It must make do with representations, each of which is likely to have substantial deficiencies. Sight provides a powerful example, developed by the mathematician Michael Atiyah in a Presidential Lecture to the Royal Society of Edinburgh (Atiyah 2008). Although a substantial part of the brain is allotted to the sense of sight, what we 'see' is not a record of the light falling on the eyes but a neural construction. Hence the phenomenon of illusions, some of which persist even when we know that they are illusions: indeed the acceptance of illusions is essential to classical painting and photography, which require configurations of paint or pixels to be interpreted as places and people. Other kinds of representations are allotted much smaller shares of the brain's resources. That many of them work well within limits may be attributed to the prevalence of decomposability in our universe. Simon clearly recognised the disparity between the capacity of the human brain and the complexity of the environment in which it had to operate, and argued that it was the high degree of decomposability in that environment which enables scientists to produce valuable results by focussing on particular systems while making rather simple assumptions about both the higher and lower systems with which they are connected, though with a high proportion of failures along the way. (The significance of decomposability for the development of scientific knowledge was recognised by Lord Rees, President of the Royal Society, in the BBC Reith Lectures of 2010.) But since decomposability is incomplete the patterns created within the brain will not be reproductions of the phenomena being investigated, and so there will always be limits to the applicability of our representations; these limits may not be easy to recognise. Uncertainty is inherent in our representations.

However, uncertainty is a precondition of intelligence. '[T]o live intelligently in our world ... we must use the principle that things similar in some respects will behave similarly in certain other respects even when they are very different in still other respects' (Knight 1921, p. 206); and what similarities matter, and what differences do not, depends on 'the purpose or problem in view'. Thus we may choose incompatible models for different purposes. Popper (1972, pp. 420–421) also observes that the criteria for similarity are always the product of a point of view. This conception of intelligence as domain-limited order is strikingly similar to Kelly's (1963) proposition that we cope with complexity by constructing patterns that we try to impose on particular events, and that alternative constructions are, in principle, possible.

In what may now be regarded as a pioneering contribution to neuroscience, Hayek (who had dissected brains during his early studies in psychology) identified 'the transmission of impulses from neuron to neuron within the central nervous system ... as the apparatus of classification'; thus 'the qualities which we attribute to experienced objects are strictly speaking not properties of that object at all, but a set of relations by which our brain classifies them' (Hayek 1952, pp. 53, 143). These attributed qualities may therefore incorporate distortions which can lead to error (Hayek 1952, pp. 145–146).

The human brain has an extraordinarily wide potential for organizing new systems in many different fields and consolidating them into automatic procedures; this consolidation economises the scarce resource of cognition, allowing it to be allocated to new problems. However each brain can effectively exploit only a small proportion of this potential. This fundamental economic problem, and its solution, is ignored in most economic analysis but was central to Simon's thinking. As Raffaelli above all has insisted, it was also central to Marshall's thinking. It is the basis of his explanation of the progressive construction, retention and application of knowledge in his early mechanical model of a 'brain' which built up connections by trial and error and embedded those which seemed to work in routines, thus creating the scope and some of the material for the creation and trial of new possibilities. Raffaelli (2003) shows how Marshall later applied this dialectical relationship between innovation and automaticity to economic development as a never-ending process of experimentation and consolidation.

Like Hayek and Marshall, Adam Smith took an early interest in the process of knowledge creation and also produced a theory in which knowledge consists of schemes of order which are created within the brain and prove serviceable as means of guiding understanding and action while economising on cognition. Smith ([1795] 1980), however, began by identifying the motives which 'lead and direct' this process. These are the discomfort, or worse, experienced when confronted with phenomena which do not fit within any established pattern, and delight in the realisation that some novel pattern encompasses them. The growth of knowledge is directed towards particular problems, and therefore shaped by the context within which the individual is operating.

Smith's recognition that success in creating and applying patterns is necessarily provisional is exemplified by his account of the development of astronomy, especially in his comments on the status of Newton's theory. New knowledge is produced by an imaginative conjecture which replaces some troubling appearance of disorder by a new pattern of 'harmony and proportion' (to use Copernicus's account of his own motivation). Ziman (2000, p. 120) implicitly endorses Smith's analysis by insisting that 'the human capability for pattern recognition is deeply embedded in scientific practice' (see also Ziman 1978); and the mathematician Atiyah (2008) insists that pattern-making, not logic, is the mathematician's supreme delight. For Smith, Ziman and Atiyah, imagination is the key to knowledge. Imagination builds systems.

This powerful incentive to imagine new schemes of order within particular contexts could hardly be effective if the universe were not a highly decomposable system, as Simon noted. There is an implicit warning here of the desirability of maintaining decomposability in the systems that we create, currently illustrated by our financial systems. All our knowledge consists of conjectured representations; many conjectures may not work at all, and those that do have a limited range of application and may fail unexpectedly in conditions not previously experienced. The rational choice mindset encourages the belief that the fallibility of our models is a technical problem—and even an opportunity to gain a Nobel Prize.

Because we rely on our representations, there is a natural pathology here, which was explored by the clinical psychologist George Kelly (1963). If a particular structure of knowledge has become firmly established as a basis of understanding and behaviour, then it may be extremely difficult to accept an alternative structure, and even more difficult to invent one. This was Kelly's theory of personal breakdown. His own belief, which is consistent with the view of knowledge in this paper, is that there are always alternatives which might be imagined, and that the clinical psychologist's role is to supply an alternative which the patient can accept. Because failure is a normal element in progress, this pathology should not be neglected in our analysis. It is not confined to individuals; indeed it is a familiar problem in formal organizations, because of the requirement for internal coherence. Here too the financial sector provides current examples.

If the principles of similarity on which categories may be most effectively based, or interpretative systems constructed, differ between domains, then (as Smith noted) we should expect people in different circumstances to develop different categories and so to think and act differently. Path-dependence will be common, but is very unlikely to extend to path-determination because the boundaries of interpretative systems are typically not well defined and categories may be modified in various ways. Orderly specialisation within a quasi-decomposable economic system is therefore a very effective way of accelerating the growth of knowledge. It has allowed humans to create new ways of exploiting their environment, which emerge and diffuse far more rapidly than the slow products of random genetic mutation followed by differential inheritance.

3 Organization

Specialisation between domains as the principal means of enlarging the knowledge and capabilities of a society is Adam Smith's fundamental principle of economic development (Smith [1776] 1976b, pp. 13–24). That there may be alternative bases of specialisation, with different effects, is indicated by his observation that ideas for improved machinery may be prompted by experience of particular operations, by the search for applications of particular machine-building skills, or by the application of expertise in making novel connections between apparently 'distant and dissimilar objects'. Marshall's theory of development rested on a combination of specialisation between fields and variation within each (which is implicit in Smith's exposition): thus both monopoly and perfect competition are defective because they restrict the sources of imagination of novel possibilities.

Specialisation necessarily replaces self-sufficiency with interdependence, and therefore presents two organizational problems: the arrangement of contexts within which knowledge will be developed, which as we have noted will affect (though not always in predictable ways) what kinds of knowledge will emerge, and the arrangement of ways in which the products of knowledge will be distributed. Since this is a system which generates change, not just in quantity but in the form and content of goods, technology, production methods, skills and understanding, neither organizational problem can be adequately represented in terms of an overall equilibrium; both require continual adjustment, and perhaps intermittent radical change. From this perspective we may observe that the problems of co-ordination and growth, which have traditionally been separated in much economic reasoning—but not by Smith or Marshall—are remarkably similar; they each have to be approached, both in economic theory and in particular situations, in terms of partial rather than general equilibrium—where 'equilibrium' is to be interpreted as stable locally-appropriate processes.

Smith envisaged a cumulative progression: the division of labour is limited by the extent of the market, but its effects on productivity lead to an expansion of the market, and so to further division of labour. Marshall developed this theme, in ways that can be summarised in two passages. 'Knowledge is our most powerful engine of production... Organization aids knowledge; it has many forms' (Marshall 1920, pp. 138–139). 'The law of increasing return may be worded thus: an increase of labour and capital leads generally to improved organization, which increases the efficiency of the work of labour and capital' (Marshall 1920, p. 318). Organization and knowledge are both endogenous in the economic system—as they are in the individual. The power of the constant interaction between them was emphasised by

Allyn Young (1928): increasing return is a property, not of a single production function, but of a sequence of productive arrangements.

Different forms of organization promote economic development by providing varied contexts in each of which particular people may build and apply their own particular internal systems of knowledge. In surveying some of these systems it will be appropriate to follow Marshall's distinction between internal and external organization, which is a distinction between dense and sparse networks, corresponding to the architecture of complexity. We begin by recognising that the internal organization of the human brain into categories and connections is powerfully supplemented by access to external knowledge. An essential element in Adam Smith's overall system of thought is the human capacity and willingness to adopt principles and practices which have been developed by others; this promotes the diffusion of knowledge and cohesion within groups—although as Smith recognised, it has its own pathology, because what is adopted may not be appropriate in the new context (Smith [1759] 1976a). We could not talk to the butcher, brewer and baker of 'their advantages' without this interest in the activities and perceptions of other people.

The outstanding example of this reliance on external organizations is the multiplicity of what are normally called 'institutions', each of which orders a repeatable process with its particular, though often ill-defined, range of application. This external support enables us to acquire many routines ready-made—a notable cognitive economy, though we do need the appropriate absorptive capacity to incorporate them into our existing structures of knowledge. Though of established interest as an aid to interpersonal co-ordination, their role in private cognition seems under-appreciated.

The first form of organization noted by Marshall as an aid to knowledge is the firm, and the outstanding analysis of the firm as a context for the generation and application of knowledge was produced by Edith Penrose (1959) as a response to the discovery that the standard 'theory of the firm' was irrelevant to the study of the growth of firms in which she was participating. Coase (1937, p. 393) had defined the firm as 'a system of relationships which comes into being when the direction of resources is dependent on an entrepreneur', but had not sought to examine how the entrepreneur would use his power of direction. Penrose (1959, p. 2) argued that '[a] ll the evidence we have indicates that the growth of the firm is connected with attempts of particular groups of people to do something', and what they are trying to do is not to maximise their profits within a well-defined system but to discover and exploit opportunities. The imagination of new combinations is central.

A Penrosian firm is 'a pool of resources the utilisation of which is organized within an administrative framework' (Penrose 1959, p. 142). That sounds very Marshallian (and seems to anticipate Simon), as does the implication that differences in administrative frameworks are likely to lead to differences in outcome, because they provide different contexts for the development and application of knowledge. (Penrose later recognised the 'Marshallian' character of her analysis.) Because 'the very processes of operation and expansion are intimately associated with a process by which knowledge is increased, ... the productive opportunity of a firm will change even in the absence of any change in external circumstances or in fundamental technical knowledge' (Penrose 1959, p. 56). In Penrose's analytical system, resources are not defined by a complete and closed list of their potential uses, not least because resources—what Richardson (1972) later decided to call 'capabilities'—are modified by use. 'It is of the essence of intelligent practices that one performance is modified by its predecessors. The agent is still learning' (Ryle 1949, p. 42). As Heraclitus observed long ago, we cannot step into the same river twice, moreover the river is continually changed by our own actions. An open economy, like open science, generates knowledge which undermines some established knowledge, but which also supplies the elements for further innovation: creative destruction makes possible new creations.

Organization frames the growth of knowledge. It also frames the imagination of connections between enhanced capabilities and the services which they might provide, and of connections between new services and productive opportunities, which, as Richardson (1960) argued, do not reveal themselves. (The effects of the structure of product divisions in the chemical industry provide many examples.) Turning a perceived opportunity into a successful line of business typically requires the acquisition of additional skills and the building of new relationships, both inside and outside the firm; but if this is successfully achieved, then the firm will find itself not only with additional productive resources, but also with managerial capacity which is progressively released (normally with enhanced capabilities) as new tasks become settled routines. Then the sequence can begin again.

Thus each firm's range is always limited, but these limits may recede as a direct consequence of its own activities (Penrose 1959, pp. 60–63). (That people are changed by what they do was the basis of Marshall's hopes for progress.) Moreover entrepreneurs believe that they can act in ways which will change their environment (Penrose 1959, p. 42): 'it is reasonable to suppose that consumers' tastes are formed by the range of commodities which are available to them or, at least, about which they know' and therefore that an entrepreneur may consider demand 'as something he ought to be able to do something about' (Penrose 1959, p. 80). Marshall (1920, p. 280) includes among the standard tasks of businessmen 'showing people things which they had never thought of having before; but which they want to have as soon as the notion is suggested to them'. Preferences are not 'natural givens', but constructed within contexts which are externally influenced, and subsequently order decision processes.

Opportunity sets within an economy change as a result of the activities, capabilities and ideas of the individuals within that economy, and these capabilities and ideas depend not only on each person's ability to construct and modify systems of knowledge but on the context of their activities and the interactions with other people which are shaped by that context. That is why firms are so important—and why the differences between firms are so important. The consequences of differences between fields are generally recognised, though the dynamics are neglected in much of economics, but the crucial role of heterogeneity within each specialism, to which Marshall attached so much importance, was rejected by his successors as a major threat to economic efficiency. This rejection was carried over into policy in the notion of 'the one best way' and the fashion for a 'national champion' in each industry which would simply deploy the correct knowledge. Fortunately, evolutionary ideas include the importance of variety-preserving systems in developing knowledge.

The effect of the internal structure of a firm on its performance, including its creation and application of knowledge, and the process and effects of its internal institutions, deserves a substantive examination which cannot be attempted here: analyses of enduring quality were produced by Barnard (1938), Chandler (1960) and Burns and Stalker (1961), and an exemplary study of Du Pont provides detailed evidence of both success and failure from a company whose directors thought about such issues and recorded their reasoning (Hounshell and Smith 1988). However something must be said about the firm's external organization, which is inadequately represented by the notion of 'market'.

Coase (1937) famously explained the firm as a means of organizing a particular set of activities more cheaply than by creating a network of market contracts. That creating a system uses resources (not least the scarce resource of cognition) is an important truth; but for his particular purpose Coase did not need to consider who bears the costs of market transactions. In particular, who makes markets, and why? Kirzner (1973) offered an answer: when people do not know what options are available, someone who perceives a particular opportunity can gain by taking it, and in the process provides valuable knowledge to others, prompting further transactions. Kirzner's basic case is a price disparity between locations, not hitherto noticed because no-one has travelled between them: the opportunity already exists, and requires nothing but alertness, which for Kirzner is a natural characteristic, though unevenly distributed and always associated with a particular context. It is this differentiation which provides the Kirznerian entrepreneur with a profit opportunity which others do not perceive.

The Penrosian firm, however, does not simply recognise what already exists; it is a creator of opportunities in product space by imagining new applications for evolving knowledge and capabilities; therefore it has an incentive to incur some costs in order to attract custom. If there are any fixed costs in making a market (as there usually are), then it is the party who expects to engage in most transactions who has the strongest incentive to bear them. Casson (1982) exploited this principle to produce the first substantial analysis of the entrepreneur as market-maker, though Marshall (1919) had already used it to observe that product markets were organized by suppliers and labour markets by customers.

Though these are not the 'perfect markets' of economic theory, they are much closer to them than many of the relationships between firms which depend on goods or services which must match particular requirements. Such production systems are less decomposable. Because transaction costs in such cases tend to be high, one might expect the relationship to be internalised, and indeed this often happens; but when the activities involved are strikingly different, relying on different skills and different ways of thinking that are best managed in different organizational contexts, there is a strong case for maintaining organizational distance to preserve the advantages of specialisation. Consequently we find a remarkable array of firm-specific arrangements, as Richardson (1972) exemplified and explained. Bart Nooteboom has made particularly valuable contributions in this field.

4 Conclusion

The growth of knowledge is an evolutionary process. Knowledge is a structure of classifications and connections: it is the product of imaginative conjectures created by the human mind in response to particular problem situations, each installed in a particular neural network. Such conjectures are often falsified; and there may be deliberate attempts to falsify them in order to avoid the consequences of actions based on error. (This is a major element in both scientific research and the commercial development of new products, which often focusses on exploring the limits of decomposability in order to identify, and if possible remove, obstacles to a particular innovation.) They may also be qualified, extended or amended. All these procedures are influenced by context, and the context is often provided by some form of formal or informal organization. All knowledge is limited in scope; but the limits can never be known for certain. If knowledge and its application are always context-limited, then the creation, modification, and connection of contexts are major determinants of the rate at which knowledge is generated and of the kinds of knowledge which are produced. Marshall indicates the importance of different forms of organization, each with their internal variations, in providing distinctive and complementary kinds of environment for knowledge creation. Of particular current interest is the widespread use of modularisation within ICT, by which interface rules give firms freedom to innovate within their own modules; this reduces their knowledge requirements, but reduces the prospects of new combinations across modules.

For Marshall, and for evolutionary economists, co-ordination and development are necessarily interlinked; and it is decomposability which makes this possible. Schumpeter, by contrast, wished to avoid any direct challenge to Walrasian theory. His prime emphasis was not on entrepreneurial imagination; indeed he may be thought to have underrated the imagination needed to envisage new combinations even of elements already well developed. His distinctive focus was the great effort of will necessary to challenge established patterns, and the corresponding need for a powerful motive, which he identified as personal ambition. He also argued that the prevalence of these patterns, which he noted gave an illusion of rational choice (Schumpeter 1934, p. 80), provided a secure basis for entrepreneurial calculation and planning, and that the entrepreneur's success in disrupting them undermined the basis for subsequent entrepreneurship. Thus Schumpeterian innovation implied a business cycle, for which Keynesian remedies were inappropriate. We may note that Marshall (1920, p. 711) also attributed depression to 'commercial disorganization' resulting from the failure of familiar practices, and more subtly, that both identified routine as a precondition of innovation. However, for Marshall this was implicit in the characteristics of the human mind; and in this respect Simon was a Marshallian.

Human knowledge relies on decomposability; but how well the decomposition of any knowledge structure matches the decomposition of the phenomena to which it is applied is always open to question at many levels, including the boundaries between disciplines and the scope of particular theoretical formulations within each discipline as well as within each of the many kinds of organization that compose an economic system. We should be especially sensitive to the opportunities and dangers of incomplete decomposability in an environment where evolutionary processes are often driven by deliberate attempts not only to introduce novelty but to modify the processes of selection and retention, and where these attempts are often being conducted within administrative systems (whether public or private) that rely on the compatability of knowledge structures which may be undermined by the outcomes of their own policies. We may recall Kelly's warning of the possibility of breakdown, even of structures which have proved serviceable over a long period, and of the potential difficulties of devising and accepting novel systems. If such a change also requires a new foundation for interpersonal and interdepartmental compatabilities, the difficulties may prove insurmountable. Chester Barnard (1938, p. 5) observed that most organizations disappear; and the problems of replacing knowledge and skills in response to unimagined challenges are often the trigger—even for Barnard's own extraordinarily successful business. Evolution is intrinsically about failure; and policy-makers should be reminded that '(w)e want privately owned businesses precisely because we want institutions that... can disappear' (Drucker 1969, p. 293). In building systems we might give more attention to building systems that are less likely to fail, and that can better accommodate failure in the systems which provide the elements in their own structure.

References

Atiyah M (2008) Mind, matter and mathematics. Presidential Address to the Royal Society of Edinburgh. (Recording available at royalsoced.org.uk/events)

Barnard CI (1938) The functions of the executive. Harvard University Press, Cambridge

Burns T, Stalker GM (1961) The management of innovation. Tavistock, London

Casson M (1982) The entrepreneur: an economic theory. Edward Elgar, Cheltenham

Chandler AD (1960) Strategy and structure. MIT Press, Cambridge

Coase RH (1937) The nature of the firm. Economica NS 4:386–405. Reprinted in Coase, RH (1988) The firm, the market, and the law. University of Chicago Press, Chicago

Drucker PF (1969) The age of discontinuity. Heinemann, London

Hayek FA (1952) The sensory order. University of Chicago Press, Chicago

Hounshell DA, Smith JK Jr (1988) Science and corporate strategy: Du Pont R & D 1902–1980. Cambridge University Press, Cambridge

Kelly GA (1963) A theory of personality. W. W. Norton, New York

Kirzner IM (1973) Competition and entrepreneurship. University of Chicago Press, Chicago

Knight FH (1921) Risk, uncertainty and profit. Houghton Mifflin, Boston

Marshall A (1919) Industry and trade. Macmillan, London

Marshall A (1920) Principles of economics, 8th edn. Macmillan, London

Penrose ET (1959) The theory of the growth of the firm. Basil Blackwell, Oxford

Popper KR (1972) The logic of scientific discovery, 6th impression. Hutchinson, London

Prigogine I (2005) The rediscovery of value and the opening of economics. In: Dopfer K (ed) The evolutionary foundations of economics. Cambridge University Press, Cambridge, pp 61–69

Raffaelli T (2003) Marshall's evolutionary economics. Routledge, London
Raffaelli T (2008) The general pattern of Marshallian evolution. In: Shionoya Y, Nishizawa T (eds) Marshall and Schumpeter on evolution: economic sociology of capitalist development. Cheltenham, UK and Northampton, MA, USA, pp 36–47
Richardson GB (1960) Information and investment. Oxford University Press, Oxford
Richardson GB (1972) The organisation of industry. Econ J 82:883–896
Ryle G (1949) The concept of mind. Hutchinson, London
Schumpeter JA (1934) The theory of economic development. Harvard University Press, Cambridge
Simon HA ([1962] 1969) The sciences of the artificial. MIT Press, Cambridge
Smith A ([1759] 1976a) The theory of moral sentiments. In: Raphael DD, Macfie AL (eds) Oxford University Press, Oxford
Smith A ([1776] 1976b) An inquiry into the nature and causes of the wealth of nations. In: Campbell RH, Skinner AS, Todd WB (eds) 2 volumes. Oxford University Press, Oxford
Smith A ([1795] 1980) The principles which lead and direct philosophical enquiries: illustrated by the history of astronomy. In: Wightman WPD (ed) Essays on philosophical subjects. Oxford University Press, Oxford
Young A (1928) Increasing returns and economic progress. Econ J 38:527–542
Ziman JM (1978) Reliable knowledge. Cambridge University Press, Cambridge
Ziman JM (2000) Real science: what it is and what it means. Cambridge University Press, Cambridge

What Causes Creative Destruction?

Michael Joffe

Abstract Schumpeter's descriptive metaphor "creative destruction" has inspired a great deal of important research. He was clear that the continual transformation underlying economic growth is an intrinsic feature of the system, but left no clear causal account of the underlying process. His principal narrative concerned the entrepreneur, an "agency" explanation rather than a causal one in the usual sense. However, closer examination reveals that this does not fit with the observed historical pattern of continuing *per capita* growth, which is specific to the type of capitalist economy that has only existed in the past two centuries. He also introduced a more systemic view, but this is not very well developed in his writings and the causal mechanism is unclear. Connected with the ambiguity in respect of causation, Schumpeter was also unclear about the relative roles of large and small firms in innovation, at times seeing large corporations as the engine of growth, but at other times seeing them as a threat to the dynamism of the entrepreneur. Comparison with the historical record shows that neither view well represents the general process of capitalist transformation.

1 Schumpeter's Dynamic Description of Capitalist Growth

By the early twentieth century, capitalist growth had conquered much of Western Europe and North America, and was rapidly spreading to other parts of the world as manifested by large-scale investment in railways and industry. During the same period economic theory was dominated by the neoclassical model, which predicted orderly convergence towards a static equilibrium. Joseph Schumpeter accepted much orthodox economic theory, referring to non-dynamic sectors as being subject to ultra-static "circular flow", but in his descriptive writings he provided a vivid

M. Joffe (✉)
Imperial College London, London, UK
e-mail: m.joffe@imperial.ac.uk

A. Pyka and E.S. Andersen (eds.), *Long Term Economic Development*, Economic Complexity and Evolution, DOI 10.1007/978-3-642-35125-9_19,

description of the historical changes that he saw around him, coining the brilliant metaphor "creative destruction".

This has been highly influential, especially in recent decades, and has generated a great deal of valuable "post-Schumpeterian" research. One tradition has been endogenous growth theory, extending standard orthodox macro-economic growth models while retaining their view of causation, which is widely regarded as requiring micro-foundations to provide its dynamic impetus. Another has been evolutionary economics, which conceives of causation quite differently, e.g. using concepts borrowed from biological evolution. The purpose of this paper is to explore the causal views in Schumpeter's own writings. The question is, what causes underlying creative destruction? How does it work?

Schumpeter's concept of growth was one of continual transformation. He made it clear that this originated inside the system itself, not exogenously:

> the . . . process of industrial mutation—if I may use that biological term—that incessantly revolutionizes the economic structure *from within*, incessantly destroying the old one, incessantly creating a new one. This process of Creative Destruction is the essential fact about capitalism. [emphasis in the original](Schumpeter 1992a)

His insistence that this turbulence is a *continuing* feature was an important contribution, as in the early and even the mid-twentieth century it was widely believed that industrialisation and modernisation were processes that occurred once, thereby propelling a previously-backward economy into the modern era. However, beyond this he was not systematic about the actual causal processes involved. Two particular tendencies can be discerned in his descriptive writing: what we may term the agency and the systemic views.

2 Schumpeter's Two Accounts

In the agency view, the dynamism of industrial capitalism is provided by entrepreneurs who produce new combinations that lead to new products, new production methods, etc.[1] This role is explicitly different from routine management, from the provision of capital for investment and bearing of risk, and from invention and the development of new technology (Schumpeter 1983a). One interpretation is that the entrepreneur is here introduced almost as a form of disembodied agency, a *deus ex machina*, that removes the need for a causal theory. By indicating the class or personality type that takes these initiatives, identification of causal processes is no longer required. But this would not address the specificity of capitalist dynamism. As the prominent post-Schumpeterian William Baumol observed: "capitalism is unique in the extraordinary growth record it has been able to achieve" (Baumol 2002), citing historical evidence on the scale of growth under

[1] For a thorough analysis of the "conduct model of the dynamic entrepreneur", see Endres and Woods (Endres & Woods 2010).

capitalist in contrast with non-capitalist systems. Entrepreneurs may well be very important, but if their existence is to be an explanation for *capitalist* dynamism, this raises important questions: why does this particular type of economic system generate entrepreneurs? And secondly, why should they innovate in such a way that one result is growth? Or alternatively, did they occur equally frequently in, for example, Imperial China? And if so, why was that civilisation characterised by technical inventiveness but patchy *per capita* growth? Again, in the developing world, many researchers have observed that entrepreneurs are plentiful, yet neither technological inventiveness nor *per capita* growth necessarily occur.

The systemic view, on the other hand, stresses how capitalism creates the tendency to think in certain ways, e.g. to generate innovations. Schumpeter appears to have held this view, but it is not very well developed in his writings, and no mechanism is suggested:

> "The carrying into effect of . . . technological novelties was of the essence of that hunt [for profits]. And even the inventing itself . . . was a function of the capitalist process which is responsible for the mental habits that will produce invention. It is therefore quite wrong . . . to say . . . that capitalist enterprise was one, and technological progress a second, distinct factor in the observed development of output; they were essentially one and the same thing or . . . the former was the propelling force of the latter." (Schumpeter 1992b)

More recently, a number of authorities—many of whom would count themselves as post-Schumpeterians—have provided accounts of scientific and technological invention, e.g. as manifest in R&D expenditure, to which they attribute capitalist growth. Schumpeter would have regarded this process as quite distinct from his description of the role of entrepreneurs, but the case can be made that they are complementary, as in the above quotation: that the capitalist incentive structure stimulates technical invention; and also that science and technology provide opportunities for entrepreneurs to make new combinations. If so, however, the causation is in the capitalist institutions and in the scientific and technological progress, and it is unclear whether the concept of entrepreneur adds anything significant.

Schumpeter thus tended to slip between an unstructured individual-innovator account and a system-based account, making it difficult to grasp exactly where he located the source of creative destruction. And neither viewpoint provides a satisfactory causal account of capitalist dynamism. Does this matter?

3 The Specificity of Capitalism

One consequence of Schumpeter's apparent vagueness in this regard is that he rejected the idea that sustained *per capita* growth is specific to capitalism, providing a 14-page account of equivalent processes occurring under a simple exchange economy, an isolated manorial estate, and an isolated communist society:

"... the question of what corresponds to this phenomenon in other than the capitalist form of society." (Schumpeter 1983b)

The overwhelming evidence nowadays, with the benefit of hindsight, is that this was an error, and that Baumol is correct in his belief in the uniqueness of capitalism's growth record. McCloskey amplifies this picture with her own metaphor of a "hockey stick": the horizontal handle represents centuries of stagnation and/or fluctuation, while the upward-sloping blade denotes (typically near-exponential) growth after the establishment of capitalism (McCloskey 2010).

It is, however, necessary to be careful here about the definition of capitalism: first, the historical record shows that it is a capitalist *real economy* that is associated with sustained *per capita* growth. The alternative use of the term "capitalism" to denote financial activities confuses the issue, because even though the financial sector has historically played a large role in most capitalist economies, this is neither sufficient nor necessary. Banking systems were developed in northern Italy and Flanders in the middle ages, and the first stock exchange was established in Amsterdam in the early seventeenth century, and yet the first example of specifically capitalist growth in Baumol's sense did not emerge until the beginning of the nineteenth century, some distance away in Britain. Financial institutions were *not sufficient* to trigger it in earlier continental Europe. Much more recently, the dissemination of capitalism has often been achieved using foreign direct investment, brought about by expanding real-economy firms. The example of China in particular shows how successful a capitalist real economy can be despite relatively little input from the financial sector in the early decades. Even in America, investment in industry during the nineteenth century was not primarily funded by financial institutions (Lamoreaux 1985). They are *not* a *necessary* condition.

The minimal definition of capitalism that is relevant here is a system in which the real economy is dominated by production that employs wage labour, and the means of production (equipment and materials) belong to the employer. In this system, production is predominantly organised within capitalist firms (Hodgson 1999), and these compete in the market; a necessary condition is the security of property, and in particular the stability of such firms, which has been called "entity protection" (Blair 2003; Hansmann et al. 2006). This encompasses all the major examples of sustained *per capita* growth. Other elements that are traditionally added, such as free-market economic policies, or private ownership of the means of production, have proved not to be universally necessary. This is clear from the dramatic East Asian experience of growth in the past half century, including Taiwan and South Korea, where openness to world markets played a crucial role but free-market policies were not prominent. China and Vietnam have subsequently proved highly dynamic, even with much of their productive economies in public ownership.

The deeper issue is that a causal understanding is necessary in order to explain why capitalist-style sustained *per capita* growth has occurred in many different types of capitalist system, but not in non-capitalist systems; and also why it has failed to occur, or done so only sporadically, in other capitalist societies. The highly successful, and quite diverse, economic policies in e.g. Taiwan, South Korea, China and Vietnam were not based on "textbook economics", and even now few textbooks mention East Asian catch-up growth, or present theory that can explain it. There is a large empirical literature on the factors associated with growth, as well as several models (including Baumol's) that are excellent in their way but which do not encompass the variety of economic structures and policies in the dynamic economies, including catch-up growth. The current situation is that neither the statistical nor the *a priori* models provide a clear causal account that corresponds to the historical evidence, explaining the degrees of success, failure and all points in between attaching to the different experiences of the various countries of e.g. East Asia and Latin America.

4 How Capitalist Growth Works

A focus on Schumpeter's writings can be instructive here. He emphasised the importance of competition on the basis of costs, as opposed to prices, as well as of quality[2]:

> "Economists are at long last emerging from the stage in which price competition was all they saw . . . competition which commands a decisive cost or quality advantage and which strikes not at the margins of the profits and the outputs of existing firms but at their very foundations and their very lives. This kind of competition is as much more effective than the other as a bombardment is in comparison with forcing a door, and so much more important that it becomes a matter of comparative indifference whether competition in the ordinary sense functions more or less promptly; the powerful lever that in the long run expands output and brings down prices is in any case made of other stuff." (Schumpeter 1992c)

The only caveat one would like to make in relation to this quotation is that the phrase "of existing firms" suggests a contrast, not necessarily true in general, that such decisive action is necessarily initiated by a new entrant. This same implication occurs elsewhere, for example:

> "The introduction [of new production methods] is achieved by founding new businesses. . . ." (Schumpeter 1983d)
> ". . . The same is true if a new enterprise is started by a producer in the same industry and is connected with his previous production. This is by no means the rule; new enterprises are mostly founded by new men and the old businesses sink into insignificance." (Schumpeter 1983e)

In practice, competition on the basis of costs of or novelty/quality can just as well be between existing incumbents as between a newly entering entrepreneur and pre-existing firms. It is not central to Schumpeter's argument, but it does suggest

[2] It should be noted that some of his analyses include not only competition on the basis of cost or of new or higher quality products, but also the discovery of new sources of supply, of new markets, or of new methods of organisation (Schumpeter 1983c); however, these would only be effective in so far as they acted through one of the two basic forms of competition.

that his mental image of the entrepreneur as implicitly a new and dynamic arrival on the scene may have distorted his analysis of how these processes actually operate in practice. By underestimating the extent to which incumbent firms need constantly to seek a competitive edge, he may have attached too much importance to agency relative to his systemic view. This could also have been the source of his problem with market structure which is dealt with in the next section.

But as Schumpeter says, in the last phrase of the first quotation in this section, the type of competition that underlies creative destruction is "made of other stuff". The question remains, what this stuff might be. One approach is to analyse the capitalist real economy in terms of the institutional properties of the firm, specifically of the capitalist firm. Ownership/control of the means of production together with the ability to hire and fire labour provide flexibility in the inputs that firms can call upon and thus also in the size of the market that they can supply. Capitalism is therefore a hybrid of market and non-market organization: exchange between firms takes place in a market, but within each firm the market is replaced by an authority structure. It is this combination, market relations *between firms*, that is the root cause of specifically capitalist growth (Joffe 2011). This view is consistent with the empirical evidence that growth is not specific to particular historical stages or market structures (as represented by the standard ideal types of e.g. perfect and monopolistic competition). On the contrary, the growth records of the major economies display a degree of repeatability and consistency that strongly suggest deep regularities that persist, despite profound changes in firm size, market structure, and many other characteristics including the legal framework (e.g. limited liability) as well as the role of science and technology. In place of sectors subject to "circular flow" plus dynamic sectors with their source of dynamism left inadequately explained, what is needed is a causal understanding of the whole system, which could be called "spiral flow".

Such an analysis characterises the institutional structure of capitalism that gives rise to its endogenous causal processes, including sustained *per capita* growth; like the classic analysis of the price mechanism, it represents a system that is not formally organised. The core concept is that when capitalist competition is based on cost, the long-term result is continuing growth, with a secondary source of growth being the introduction of new products (Joffe 2011).

5 Schumpeter's Problem with Market Structure

A further difficulty in Schumpeter's analysis of creative destruction is the issue of the market structure and the size of firms involved. On the one hand, he saw large firms as being the engine of growth, using this observation to criticise the orthodox view that the optimal situation is a market with many small firms that cannot influence prices. The reasoning was that supra-normal profits are necessary to provide the incentive for entrepreneurial innovation, and that restriction of profit opportunities (e.g. by anti-trust measures) would run the risk of choking this off:

> "The introduction of new methods of production and new commodities is hardly conceivable with perfect—and perfectly prompt—competition from the start. And this means that the bulk of what we call economic progress is incompatible with it. As a matter of fact, perfect competition is and always has been temporarily suspended whenever anything new is being introduced. . . . The firm of the type that is compatible with perfect competition is in many cases inferior in internal, especially technological, efficiency. If it is, then it wastes opportunities. . . . the large-scale establishment or unit of control . . . has come to be the most powerful engine of that progress and in particular of the long-run expansion of total output not only in spite of, but to a considerable extent through, this [monopolistic] strategy which looks so restrictive when viewed in the individual case and from the individual point of time." (Schumpeter 1992d)

On the other hand, Schumpeter saw routinisation as a threat to his conception of the entrepreneur's role:

> The more life becomes rationalised, levelled, democratised . . . the more the entrepreneur's grip on profit loses its power. (Schumpeter 1983f)
> Since capitalist enterprise, by its very achievements, tends to automatize progress . . . it tends to make itself superfluous . . . The perfectly bureaucratized giant industrial unit not only ousts the small or medium-sized firm and "expropriates" its owners, but in the end it also ousts the entrepreneur and expropriates the bourgeoisie as a class . . . . (Schumpeter 1992e)

These two viewpoints are not strictly contradictory, and it is possible to find ways of reconciling them. However, a comparison with the empirical record shows that neither of them represents the general process of capitalist transformation, each being a generalisation that applies in some times and places, and in some industries, but not in others.

6 Conclusion

Schumpeter's metaphor of creative destruction has been extremely powerful in generating fruitful research of many different kinds. At the same time, his descriptions lack coherence in relation to the causal processes involved. Any theory aiming to explain the processes underlying creative destruction needs to be compatible with the observed uniqueness of capitalism's extraordinary growth record, that has been achieved across a wide variety of types of capitalism, and also that not all capitalist economies have shown dynamism in this sense. To introduce causal clarity into the concept of creative destruction would further enhance the value of Schumpeter's work.

References

Baumol WJ (2002) The free-market innovation machine: analyzing the growth miracle of capitalism. Princeton University Press, Princeton

Blair MM (2003) Locking in capital: what corporate law achieved for business organizers in the nineteenth century. UCLA Law Rev 51:387–455

Endres AM, Woods CR (2010) Schumpeter's 'conduct model of the dynamic entrepreneur': scope and distinctiveness. J Evol Econ 20(4):583–607

Hansmann H, Kraakman R, Squire R (2006) Law and the rise of the firm. Harv Law Rev 119:1335–1403

Hodgson GM (1999) Evolution and Institutions: on Evolutionary Economics and the Evolution of Economics. UK, Edward Elgar, Cheltenham, pp 220–246, 'The Coasean tangle: the nature of the firm and the problem of historical specificity'

Joffe M (2011) The root cause of economic growth under capitalism. Camb J Econ 35:873–896

Lamoreaux N (1985) The great merger movement in American business, 1895–1904. Cambridge University Press, Cambridge

McCloskey DN (2010) Bourgeois dignity. University of Chicago Press, Chicago

Schumpeter JA (1983a) The theory of economic development. Transaction, New Brunswick, [originally published in 1911 in German and in 1934 in English], pp 74–94, chapter II section III

Schumpeter JA (1983b) The theory of economic development. Transaction, New Brunswick, pp 138–152, chapter IV

Schumpeter JA (1983c) The theory of economic development. Transaction, New Brunswick, pp 133–136, chapter IV

Schumpeter JA (1983d) The theory of economic development. Transaction, New Brunswick, p 132, chapter IV

Schumpeter JA (1983e) The theory of economic development. Transaction, New Brunswick, p 136, chapter IV

Schumpeter JA (1983f) The theory of economic development. Transaction, New Brunswick, p 155, chapter IV

Schumpeter JA (1992a) Capitalism, socialism and democracy. Routledge, London, [originally published 1943], p 83, chapter VII

Schumpeter JA (1992b) Capitalism, socialism and democracy. Routledge, London, p 110, chapter IX

Schumpeter JA (1992c) Capitalism, socialism and democracy. Routledge, London, pp 84–85, chapter VII

Schumpeter JA (1992d) Capitalism, socialism and democracy. Routledge, London, pp 105–106, chapter VIII

Schumpeter JA (1992e) Capitalism, socialism and democracy. Routledge, London, p 134, chapter XII

Markets and Organizations Individualism and Economic Theory

Maria Brouwer

Abstract Economic theory depicts markets and organizations as opposite allocation mechanisms. Market allocation is based on mobility and organization on instruction. The paper argues that markets and organizations are complements in dynamic economies. A diversity of organizations gives meaning to mobility of capital and labor as it allows individual valuations of people and projects. This differs from both perfect competition and principal agent theory that do not allow for diversity among firms. Individualism spurs innovation, because it allows different views on future values. Investment outcomes will differ from expectation, but will strike stable expectation equilibrium, if diversity of opinion prevails. Collective opinion, by contrast, arrests productivity growth and causes booms and busts. The rise of individualism in late medieval England and the concept of the individualized corporation in our days are discussed. The effects of collective opinion on financial markets are sketched.

1 Introduction

Economic theory treats markets and organizations as two different ways to allocate production factors (Coase 1937). Markets are depicted as allocators of capital and labor that lack foresight, but act on the spur of the moment. Organizations, by contrast, direct employee behavior according to plan. Markets require spot contracts for each transaction, whereas organizations employ persons on long term contracts. The differences between market and organization stand out in economic organization

Published in Brouwer M (2012) Markets and organizations. In: Organizations, individualism and economic theory. Routledge Frontiers of political Economy. Routledge, London, pp 13–33

M. Brouwer (✉)
Department of Economics and Business, University of Amsterdam, Zeeburgerstraat 72, 1018 AG Amsterdam, Netherlands
e-mail: mariabrouwer251@msn.com

A. Pyka and E.S. Andersen (eds.), *Long Term Economic Development*, Economic Complexity and Evolution, DOI 10.1007/978-3-642-35125-9_20,

literature. Markets are assumed to support individualism, if everybody can start his own company. Organization, by contrast, prompts collective behavior prescribed by authority. But, we can also argue that myopic markets are driven by collective opinion, if all firms respond identically to changes in their environment. Moreover, markets group individuals together in aggregates like workers and capital owners, who receive identical prices for their services. The question, therefore, arises whether markets allow people to stand out as individuals or let them disappear in groups?

Market wages are based on the idea that people will move to another employer, if they are paid below market wages. But, people will not move, if all organizations value people identically. Markets are based on mobility, but mobility only becomes effective, when organizations value people differently. Such individualization occurs, when a person's worth is no longer determined by group membership but by individual characteristics. Individuals are largely invisible in neoclassical economic theory, wherein firms of equal size respond identically to exogenous shocks. Schumpeter, however, put individuals central in his innovation theory, wherein entrepreneurs move the economy out of equilibrium and towards a new one at higher levels of productivity. Stagnation, however, has been more characteristic of human history than progress. Schumpeter explained progress by the innate desire of people to improve their social position. However, these desires were frustrated in most epochs or wrought havoc, when people took to war to achieve their goals.

Historians have clarified the relationship between contract and mobility in market economies. Contracts allow people to engage in relationships that differ from tradition. Contract law that allowed people to bequeath possessions to non family members in medieval England freed people from traditional group ties and allowed them to make choices of their own (Macfarlane 1978). Mobility, therefore, requires both institutions like contract law and laws of incorporation and diversity to spur innovation. Modern management theory has emphasized individualization as a tenet of corporations in dynamic economies (Ghoshal and Bartlett 1997).

The paper describes how equilibrium is reached in markets featuring perfect competition and continues by sketching how Schumpeterian innovation affects market competition. Innovation creates profits for successful innovators, which differs from excess profits based on scarcity rents assumed in perfect competition models. Individual valuations came to the fore in medieval England, when contract law allowed decisions that departed from tradition. However, economic models have not proceeded on the institutional approach to economic development. They assume the existence of a superior plan that obeys rationality and ignores uncertainty.

2 Market Competition as an Exogenous Force

Market prices indicate the value of a product, employee or capital good. Market valuation is anonymous, since it arises through valuations made by numerous suppliers and buyers. Nobody in particular can be held accountable for the depreciation of asset values or sinking real wages caused by changes of supply and demand. Markets seem to operate like forces of nature; out of individual control.

Perfect competition theory depicts how equilibrium is attained on spot markets by the interplay of multitudes of suppliers and buyers. Global markets for commodities like wheat fit this picture. The world wheat market brings wheat from various sources together to meet manifold demand. The fate of suppliers is interdependent. Expanding demand increases price for all suppliers and vice versa.

People are also grouped together to obtain market prices for their labor. We can think of markets of skilled and unskilled labor. A person's value is not determined by individual characteristics, but by what it has in common with other people that belong to the same group. Spot market prices for commodities and labor are based on assumed homogeneity of products and people. Spot markets assume the absence of long term contracts. People can be hired and fired by the day. We can think of markets for day labor during the harvest season to fit this picture. Supply comes from non skilled labor; demand from farmers. Equilibrium is struck, when demand equals supply. Each worker receives the same wage. It is not guaranteed that the wage is sufficient for a family to live on. However, the employer is not responsible for the fate of his workers.

Group membership is essential to a person's valuation, which raises the question how group formation occurs? Does supply only encompass unskilled labor in a certain village; a country; the whole world? What is the demand for labor composed of? Are these the farmers in a certain region; the whole country? The size of the market determines to what extent people's fates become identical.

People can improve themselves, if they can leave their initial group and move to another; from unskilled to skilled workers; from landless to landholding people. Individual ascent is related to occupational and geographical mobility. It assumes that individuals can make decisions that diverge from tradition and that are also not imposed on them by the state. The concept of individualism refers to *the rights and privileges of the individual as against the wider group or the state* (Macfarlane 1978, 5). Macfarlane uses the concept to characterize medieval English inheritance laws, wherein male primogeniture and other family obligations could be discarded. Women had equal rights to inherit as men. Individualism thus refers to contractual instead of traditional property rights. People could bequeath their possessions to persons they thought deserved it most. Leaving tradition behind prompted people to make individual assessments of people and assets. The concept of individualism in economics has caused some confusion. Some interpret individualism as referring to isolated and self-contained individuals. However, individualism as purported by Adam Smith points at individual actions directed towards other people and guided by their expected behavior. This concept of individualism differs from the 'rational' concept of individualism that assumes that society is organized according to a superior design made by omniscient wise men (Hayek 1980). The 'rational' approach to individualism must lead to collectivism' in Hayek's view. It assumes the existence of a knowledge source that is revealed by some masters of the universe. Both perfect competition and principal agent theory regard technological progress an exogenous force. Perfect competition theory assumes technology an environmental force to which firms have to adapt. Principal agent theory depicts technological progress as emanating from a master plan. The role of individuals in decision making raises questions, when organizations give more persons a voice.

The role of discussion and decision-making in councils is not studied by economic theory. Perfect competition theory assumes that people only respond to environmental changes in predictable ways, while principal agent theory assumes that a perfect plan is available and only needs to be executed. Decision making, however, is essential to firms that decide to invest in innovation.

Inserting innovation in economic theory changes the way market equilibrium should be understood. Does equilibrium emerge out of the blind actions of myopic firms as assumed in perfect competition theory? Or does equilibrium emanate from the execution of a superior plan as assumed in principal agent theory? Or does equilibrium develop from a trial and error process by a multitude of firms that are in dynamic competition with one another? We will discuss the three models of perfect competition, principal-agent theory and dynamic competition in the next sections.

3 Firms and Markets in Perfect Competition

The perfect competition model draws a picture of people and organizations that are directed by anonymous market forces. Firms in the pc model are assumed to be numerous and of small size. Small size emanates from small fixed costs and declining marginal productivity of labor. Firms do exist in perfect competition theory, but long term labor contracts are absent. Workers are completely interchangeable in this model. Firms hire workers, who are put to work with equipment of a fixed size in the short run. Each consecutive worker is assumed to become less productive, since equipment is used more intensively, when the number of workers increases. The firm stops hiring, when the value of the produce of the last hired worker has equaled wages. Each worker is paid the same wage, which is determined by supply and demand. Wages are low, if labor is in ample supply and increase, if labor is relatively scarce. Producer surplus consists of the value created by non marginal workers. Producer surplus is higher, if wages are lower and more workers are hired.

Assume that the first worker produces 10 units, the second 9 units per day and so on. Each unit of output sells for a price of 10, while the wage rate is 50 per day. The firm will hire six workers, since the value of the produce of the sixth worker is 50, which equals his wage. Producer surplus is 50 + 40 + 30 + 20 + 10 = 150 at this wage and product price (see Table 1). The producer surplus would shrink to 100 if wage was 60 and 5 workers were employed. It would increase till 210 if wages decreased till 40 and 7 workers were employed.

The labor share of valued added would drop from 75 %, when 5 workers were employed at wage 60; till 66.67 %, if 6 workers were employed at wage 50 and to 57 %, if 7 workers were employed at wage 40. A large number of workers thus lowers wage rates and increases producer surplus both absolutely and as a share of value added.

Long term differs from short term equilibrium, because no excess profits are incurred in long term equilibrium. Long term equilibrium is reached when average total costs of the efficient firm are equal to price. Long term is identical to short term equilibrium at a wage of 50, if fixed costs are 150. The efficient firm would employ

Table 1 Total value added, wage costs and producer surplus (PS) in the short run

Workers	Value added	Wage costs	PS
1	100	50	50
2	190	100	90
3	270	150	120
4	340	200	140
5	400	250	150
6	450	300	150
7	490	350	140

$P = 10, w = 50$

6 employees and incurs producer surplus of 150, which equals its fixed costs (see Table 2). Average costs are at a minimum of 10 at this point.

Firms do not make profits in long run equilibrium. A wage decrease would entail short run profits, but these would disappear in long run equilibrium. Producer surplus increases from 150 to 210, if wages decline from 50 till 40. But, new entry would increase output and reduces price. Price would be reduced to average costs of 8.67 in long run equilibrium for a firm employing six employees and fixed costs of 150. Entry would thus eat away producer surplus of 210 and reduce it to 150. But, if entry is barred, producer surplus will stay at 210, if wages drop and product price remains unchanged. The firm would now reap excess profits of $210 - 150 = 60$. However, under perfect competition, excess profits do not exist. Fixed costs will, therefore, increase till 210 as a consequence of an appreciation of assets. Total costs and total revenues balance again and average total costs stay at 10. The value of a limited production factor rises, because it incurs a scarcity rent. We can think of arable land, whose supply is fixed. Landowners can incur a scarcity rent, if wages drop while the amount of land remains unaltered.

Wages could drop below subsistence levels, if labor supply increased, while land is fixed. Markets thus do not guarantee survival of people. However, nobody is to blame, because nobody took decisions that led to this dismal state of affairs. No investment decisions need to be made, if one production factor is fixed, since the number and size of firms then remains unaltered. Firms in perfect competition theory lack leadership and do not look forward. The firm in the pc model does not operate according to plan. Investment decisions are dictated by changing market circumstances to which firms adapt. Labor is hired on spot markets and easily shed. Wages constitute variable costs. Employers do not feel responsible for workers' fates. Organization is limited to hiring and firing by the day and selling the produce on spot markets. There is no room for strategy in the pc model, which, therefore, seems to fit an economy that is directed by tradition as described in Schumpeter's circular flow.

4 The Principal Agent Model

The principal agent model differs from the pc model, because the p-a model features leadership and decision making. The principal is the decision maker, who can only achieve his goals through efforts exerted by agents. The business

Table 2 Total value added; wage cost, total costs and average total costs (atc)

Employees	Value added	Wage costs	Total costs	atc
1	100	50	200	20
2	190	100	250	13.2
3	270	150	300	11.1
4	340	200	350	10.3
5	400	250	400	10
6	450	300	450	10
7	490	350	500	10.2

$P = 10, w = 50, F = 150$

owner is the principal and the employee the agent in this model. Employers pay market wages. Principal agent theory assumes that the efforts of agents vary according to intent. Effort means a disutility to employees, who prefer leisure to work. Labor productivity is thus not determined by a fixed amount of equipment serving a variable number of workers, but by workers' attitudes. Such attitudes do not play a role in the pc model where labor productivity was determined by the rank order by which a worker appeared on the farm. Motivation is, therefore, not an issue in the perfect competition model, but is central to the principal agent model. Workers can either put forth or withhold effort in p-a models. Firms are assumed to operate according to plan. However, the superiority of the plan is not questioned. Company success does not depend on strategy but on control. P-a theory depicts firms that follow identical investment policies, but whose success depends on the effectiveness of control. Principals (owners) can earn excess profits, if workers put forth more effort than expected, but run into losses, if workers perform below expectations. But, firms that perform below average will fail. Principals are held responsible for preventable failure due to weak control. Bankruptcy can be prevented, if principals fire agents that do not meet expectations and keep those that did. Dismissal would be considered proof of lacking motivation, which would kill job prospects of people that are dismissed. Workers would, therefore, put forth sufficient effort, which would solve the principal agent problem. The p-a problem would, therefore, be short-lived in market economies with labor mobility. However, no firm could make excess profits, if all firms pursue identical strategies.

Principal agent theory distinguishes itself from market allocation. People are organized into firms based on plans made by superiors and not hired on the whim of the moment like day laborers. Organization replaces markets as allocation mechanism in principal agent theory.

Principal agent theory is based on distrust between employers and employees. Employers expect workers to shirk, but employers want to pay employees less than their worth. People acquire firm specific skills in tenured labor relationships. However, these skills are not tradable on labor markets. As a consequence, firms can pay workers less than their worth due to the lack of market prices for firm specific skills. This phenomenon is called the '*hold up*' problem. Firms could thus appropriate more producer surplus by not paying employees their full value. However, this would keep employees from acquiring firm specific skills, which would stop such exploitation. The principal agent model would thus dissolve, if agents were forward looking. Agents would neither shirk, because this would cost them future income nor invest in firm specific human capital that is not rewarded. The p-a model thus only makes sense, if agents are myopic and do not learn from past experience. It seems, therefore, unlikely that p-a theory can describe equilibrium that allows investment in human capital.

Markets are assumed to destroy community, because traditional relations are replaced by contracts between buyers and sellers of goods and services. The extreme market model developed by Coase assumes that each person has his own firm. No employment contracts would exist in a world of one person firms. All human relations are directed by anonymous market forces. This model completely lacks community. It assumes that people are all residual claimants who derive their income from producer surplus. Incomes are completely dependent on market conditions akin to perfect competition theory. The self employed do not make plans, but move on economic waves they do not control.

5 Innovation and Competition

5.1 Schumpeterian Innovation and Competition

Schumpeter contrasted the dynamic economy with the stagnant economy of the circular flow. Market economies spur innovation, because they allow the establishment of new firms that are superior to old ones. This is the essence of Schumpeter's theory of economic development (Schumpeter 1934). Without innovation, a market economy is caught in a circular flow, where identical processes are repeated from one period to the next. Schumpeter envisioned the circular flow as a perpetum mobile, wherein perfect competition prevailed. Population and capital stock are assumed to be constant. Capital and labor markets are largely superfluous in the circular flow, since everybody stayed with the same organization and firms ploughed back their cash flows by buying identical capital goods to replace old ones. There is no need for factor mobility in a stagnant economy. Leadership is also superfluous in the circular flow, because no decisions need to be taken; everything being directed by tradition.

Schumpeter distinguishes between exogenous and endogenous events that impinge on a circular flow economy and break up equilibrium. Exogenous events are strikes of nature that produce good or bad harvests; epidemics that reduce the population; earthquakes that destroy people and assets. Endogenous changes, by contrast, stem from human decision making. These could be decisions made by entrepreneurs to found a firm. New organizations require investment. These investments create net value in the Schumpeterian scheme, because new organizations are superior to old ones. Entrepreneurship causes diversity and labor and capital are re-allocated from old to new firms. People move to new firms where they are more productive and better rewarded. The same applies to capital. Schumpeter depicts innovation as funded by banks that grant loans to selected entrepreneurs every so many years, fuelling an investment wave. Market rivalry causes *creative destruction.* Asset values of incumbent firms decline, when new, innovative firms arrive on the scene. However, losses of asset value cannot be limited to incumbent firms. Uncertainty would be eliminated, if old firms are destined to die. New firms can also fail at innovation and lose their value. Investment success must be uncertain. This rules out that one category of firms wins, while another category is sure to lose value (Brouwer 2002).

Schumpeter's endogenous theory of economic development differs from neoclassical theory that describes how the economy reacts to exogenous shocks. Neoclassical theory explains how the distribution of value added among production factors is driven by relative scarcities. Net investment occurs through entry and disinvestment through exit of firms. However, entrant firms are not assumed to be superior to incumbents. Both old and new firms embody state of the art technology. Births and deaths of firms are shaped by present market conditions in the pc model. Firms jump blindly onto each market opportunity that presents itself instead of looking forward and developing a plan of their own. Profits and losses emerge as a consequence of anonymous forces and nobody can be held accountable for failure. Risk is absent, if assets can always be resold at purchase price. But, assets are sunk, if their purchase price cannot be recaptured on second hand markets. Sunk costs constitute barriers to exit and keep firms in the industry as long as some part of fixed costs can still be recovered. Sunk costs incur depreciation losses. However, sunk costs are not deemed to deter entry in the competitive model. We can explain this by arguing that investments in assets become unexpectedly sunk, since people are assumed to be myopic. Losses due to sunk costs constitute the mirror image of scarcity rents in the neo-classical model. Market equilibrium thus features neither profits nor losses, but involves appreciations and depreciations of asset values caused by scarcity or obsolescence.

Scarcity of entrepreneurship cannot explain innovation profits, since supply of entrepreneurship is abundant. Many people want to start their own firm with external finance. Investors, therefore, need to select among the many proposals they receive. Schumpeter assumed that banks were endowed with perfect foresight and would only provide credits to 'good' entrepreneurs. However, uncertainty makes outcomes unpredictable; some investors in new firms suffer losses, while others incur high gains. Some entrepreneurs possess talent that is scarce, but such scarcity only appears after the act of investment. Profits would dissipate, if it had been clear from the outset which entrepreneurs would succeed and which not. Scarcity rents would then be paid to entrepreneurs up front. As a consequence, no investor could make a profit and innovative investment would come to a standstill. Scarcity is the opposite of innovation and economic growth. Net investment only appears, if investors expect long term growth. Demand expansion caused by transitory factors would not prompt net investment, if investors are forward looking. Our description of the pc model indicated how new firm entry occurred in response to increased demand in the absence of scarce production factors. However, investors that are forward looking would refrain from investing, if they regard these changes as transitory. Investors would lose their money, if demand declines or wages rise. Investors that are forward looking would demand a risk premium that increases for sunk assets. However, risk premiums rise to levels that would prohibit investment in new firms in response to exogenous events that are considered transitory. Exogenous changes would then be completely translated into quasi rents (and losses) incurred by incumbent firms. The economy would be completely static.

Net investment requires expectations of long term growth and is not stirred by windfall profits caused by transitory shocks. Growth expectations need to precede actual growth to trigger net investment. The economy is in *steady state* growth, when size and productivity of labor and capital increase at equal rates. The shares of labor and capital in total valued added can remain unchanged in growing economies as has been the case in twentieth century developed economies like the US (Mankiw 2007). However, this state of affairs is based on technological progress that overcomes scarcity. This picture befits developed market economies. However, steadily increasing factor productivity is abnormal, if judged by historical standards. It does not apply to traditional economies that were stagnant. Moreover, modern economies do not grow according to a linear path but through cycles of boom and bust. Dynamic equilibrium is thus a rare phenomenon in both former and present times.

5.2 Entrepreneurship, Productive and Destructive

Innovation causes change, because firms take decisions based on individual plans instead of responding to exogenous forces. Escape from the circular flow requires the execution of plans by organizations that are forward looking. But, purposeful behavior is not restricted to the economic realm. Groups of people can attempt to grasp political power to improve the position of their members at the expense of others. Land owners can be ousted and the land redistributed among landless people. Forward looking decision making also underlies organizations that decide to wage war. A tribal or feudal leader can decide to invade and occupy neighboring territory to appropriate land and other assets. If successful; his organization will thrive, whereas the defeated party is either eliminated or subjected. All types of competition; market, politics and war involve decision making under conditions of uncertain outcomes. War is waged, if the outcome is uncertain. Otherwise, weak states would voluntarily subject to stronger states. Revolutions only occur, if wealthy elites do not render their assets voluntarily. Innovation would also halt, if successful innovations were known beforehand.

Market competition is the only form of rivalry that constitutes a positive sum game, wherein gains exceed losses. War is a negative sum game, whereas political rivalry for surplus appropriation also causes bloodshed and destruction of human and physical capital. Only innovation creates more than it destroys. Investors and workers can lose their opportunity costs, if innovation fails. However, such losses are restricted to the amount invested or wages foregone. Investors are not personally liable for losses and workers remain hirable on labor markets. Limited liability limits losses in market economies. This contrasts with the consequence of failure in war and revolution, where losers often lose their lives and possessions.

The development of limited liability is concomitant to economic growth. Limited liability laws assume that losses were not predetermined, but occur by chance. Bankruptcy law has become separated from criminal law in developed economies. Bankruptcy proceedings allocate losses to those parties that willingly took risks. These are primarily creditors and shareholders in modern corporations. Management is responsible for drafting strategy and, therefore, also for losses. However, management is not liable for losses that were not caused by a felony and has limited liability, if they acted in good faith.

Economic growth is based on the premise that people act in good faith and, therefore, relies on trust. The origins of limited liability can be found in medieval contract law that was developed in Italian city-states like Venice and Genoa, where the commenda organization emerged in the eleventh century to facilitate sea trade. This company form was adopted by Dutch and English traders in the late Middle Ages (Brouwer 2005). Weber described the commenda organization as a principal agent relationship between the investor who funded a voyage and the captain who led the venture, while the investor remained ashore. However, this relationship was based on trust in contrast to modern principal agent theory (Weber 2003).

6 Innovation and Organizations

6.1 Introduction

Perfect competition theory lacks organizations with long term commitments to employees. But, most actual organizations in both past and present feature some kind of commitment. This applies to traditional organizations. Lord and peasant were related by long term bonds in feudalism. The same applies to tribal societies, where people belong to a certain tribe by birth. Tribal and feudal leaders were held responsible for the welfare of the members of their organization. They constituted communities and not markets. These organizations were usually not monetized and were hardly involved in trade as they strove for self sufficiency. Equilibrium of food supply and demand was struck by infanticide or geronticide, if the population became too numerous.

Traditional leaders are not liable for failure as long as they stick to the script written by tradition. They could also attempt to improve the situation of their clan. Tribal leaders could lead their people in war to seize land of other tribes. Victorious tribes usually had no use for conquered people, especially the male, because they wanted to guarantee the survival of their tribe at the expense of others by expanding their territory. Hence, primitive war involved total war; meaning that there was no room for subjugation of conquered people and paying of tribute. *Tribal societies, by their nature, cannot fight for subjugation and all that it implies* (Keeley 1996, 116). Warfare was frequent in primitive societies and was usually fought for economic reasons. No prisoners were taken in these fights. The number of war deaths in non civilized communities was large and amounted from 7 to 40 % of all deaths, far exceeding war casualties of civilized states (Keeley 1996, 90).

Market economies that are caught in a circular flow have nothing to offer above traditional organizations. People would even be better off in traditional than market organizations, if traditional organizations distributed income more equally among members than markets.

Civilization is built on the appropriation of surplus by elites and assumes productivity that exceeds subsistence levels. Land holding elites in traditional societies incur land rents, which they can spend on artifacts of civilization like palaces and works of art. Political elites can appropriate all value added above subsistence levels in autocracies. They would be interested in innovation, if they can appropriate innovation rents. However, innovation often requires new organizations and therewith a reallocation of people over firms and industries. But, labor mobility would erode time honored social structures. Agricultural elites, therefore, were not drawn towards innovation. If innovative; they preferred innovation that allowed them to feed a growing population and increase surplus without endangering traditional relationships between ruling and subjected classes.

The population of a certain territory can only increase, if agricultural productivity increases. Land productivity can be increased by adopting more labor intensive techniques like irrigation and terrace-building. We assume, extending our above numerical example, that 12 workers instead of 6 can be put to work on a plot of land, while wages stay at 50. The farmer will now pay 600 in wages instead of 300. His share of total revenues will only remain constant at one third of value added, if total revenues also double from 450 till 900. Hence, labor productivity should remain constant and land productivity should double to achieve this result. The value of a piece of land would then also double.

Labor absorbing agricultural innovation was practiced in riverbed civilizations in ancient Egypt; imperial China and Indonesian Java. Population increased in imperial China, while per capita income remained constant (Maddison 2007a, b). Controlled flooding also lied at the heart of ancient Egyptian and Mesopotamian civilization. These areas could carry larger populations than less productive lands and also incurred larger producer surpluses.

A different situation emerges, if labor productivity increases. If three instead of six workers can generate revenues of 450 and the third worker produces 10 units at a value of 100; the wage rate would rise till 100. Total wages would stay at 300 and producer surplus at 150. The share of producer surplus in total value added is constant at one third. However, an increase of labor productivity is only translated in increasing wage rates, if labor supply shrank. Three out of six people should leave the land and find alternative employment to make this happen. Otherwise, wages would remain constant at 50 and landowners would absorb a producer surplus of 300 instead of 150, if they employed 3 workers. However, redundant labor that is not re-employed could shatter established social relations and stir social unrest. Labor saving innovation thus requires markets and mobility of production factors to benefit labor. Moreover, new activities need to be developed to attract redundant agricultural labor. An increase of agricultural labor productivity requires the foundation of new organizations that absorb surplus labor at productivity levels that (preferably) exceed that of agricultural labor.

6.2 Innovation in Medieval England

Agricultural productivity in Western Europe of both land and labor was raised in the late Middle Ages by *a new integration of agriculture and herding; three field rotation; modern horse harness and nailed horse shoes.* Regional specialization that came with increased trade also spurred productivity in the late Middle Ages (Maddison 2007a, b, 77). Increased productivity of land and labor implied that populations could grow and the people could leave the land and find employment elsewhere. Medieval people went to towns, where they became engaged in trade and commerce. Both population growth and labor mobility characterized late medieval England, where population increased from 2.5 million in 1100 till 5 a 6 million in 1300 (Dyer 2005, 3). The doubling of population in this period was accompanied by the foundation of many towns. The rise of towns spurred a division of labor between town and country-side that promoted trade. Both domestic and international trade with commercial centers in Flanders, France and Italy bloomed in this period of English history.

Departure from the countryside assumes that people are not tied to the land by unbreakable traditional bonds. Tradition thus needs to be discarded to generate productivity growth. The towns constituted the new organizations of medieval Europe. Many English towns were founded by local lords, which saw an opportunity to make money through taxing trade. However, competition among towns reduced the tax burden, which was modest by modern standards. Lords also invested in infra-structures like roads and bridges to facilitate trade and in water and wind mills. Trade brought monetization and put a monetary value on people and assets. Land values increased, when population rose from 1100 till 1300 (Dyer 2005, 8). Contractual relations between lord and tenant were hardly disturbed by increasing land rents. But, lords incurred a scarcity premium by imposing an entry fee, when tenants had to renew land leases (Dyer 2005, 88). The labor share of income decreased somewhat from 1100 till 1300, but this decrease was impeded by the clearance of more land and the establishment of new towns. Consequently, population could grow without bumping into limits to growth imposed by insufficient food supply and decreasing real wages. The period from 1100 till 1300 was, therefore, characterized as a period of opportunity (Dyer 2005, 31).

The picture of medieval England drawn by Dyer only partly supports perfect competition theory. The theory would have predicted increasing poverty of tenants and growing producer surpluses to be used for conspicuous consumption by land holding elites as a consequence of population growth. But, the downward pressure on real wages was mitigated by innovation and the rise of towns. Traditional relationships were increasingly replaced by market relationships. Many peasants leased lands and serfdom was relatively rare in thirteenth century England. Moreover, *even tenants in villeinage were able to accumulate land and profit from the sale of produce* (Dyer 2005, 90).

Market relations prevailed in these times in England, but the dire effects of scarcity were mitigated by expansionary investment in land through clearings and in towns, infra-structures and equipment. Such investment seems to undermine the lords' power to extract an increasing surplus from a growing population that is combined to a fixed production factor. Agricultural societies provide few incentives to labor saving innovation, if new organizations are absent. But, investment in towns and other structures was triggered by competition among local lords and labor mobility was spurred by individualized contractual relations.

Some towns failed to attract sufficient numbers of inhabitants as happened to the newly founded town of Newborough that was established by the Earl of Derby in 1263. As a consequence, his investment did not pay off, but caused losses. Lords also invested in water mills that were used for sawing and milling of grain. Competition among lords depressed prices for milling services (Dyer 2005, 91–93).

The situation sharply changed in the fourteenth century, when epidemics diminished the population and the 100 years war with France broke the peace. The English population was more than halved in the fourteenth century by the black death, famine and war from 5 a 6 million in 1300 till 2.5 million in the 1360s and stayed at 2.5 million until 1540 (Dyer 2005, 3). Land revenues decreased after 1300, which fits pc theory. Land devalued in real terms due to increasing manufactured goods prices (Dyer 2005, 95). Real wages rose due to increased craftsman's wages and declining grain prices (Dyer 2005, 128). The labor share of value added increased as a consequence of these opposite price movements. Some people returned from the towns to the countryside, where land was cheaply available. Asset deflation hampered investment in land clearings. Investment in infra-structures also halted after 1300 and trade diminished. Land values only started to increase again in the first half of the sixteenth century (Dyer 2005, 131). A shrinking population destroyed asset values and constituted a disincentive to investment. Consumption expenditures, however, increased after 1300 indicating a new equilibrium between consumption and investment (Dyer 2005, 128).

The fourteenth century fits pc theory better than the dynamic period that preceded it. The theory predicts that the production factor that is in limited supply can increase its share of the pie. The diminution of population in fourteenth century Europe shifted the power balance between land owners and workers in the latter's favor. The value of land dropped, when there were fewer hands to toil them and wages increased. A diminishing population would not have benefitted labor, if the supply of land had decreased in proportion with reduced labor. The old equilibrium between land and labor would have been re-established, if half of land was laid to waste. However, such expropriation cannot be easily achieved in a private property setting. What happened in fourteenth century England was that less labor intensive production methods were employed as fields were turned into pastures.

Summing up; late medieval England up to 1300 constituted a mix of market and organization that was conducive to growth. The circular flow was broken due to net investments in infra structures and equipment. Net investment continued until asset values deflated in the fourteenth century due to a shrinking population. Exogenous shocks can benefit one group or another, but cannot create sustained growth.

Perfect competition theory argues that a person's fate is determined by group membership. Labor or landowners suffer or thrive as a class. However, this does not apply to economies that grow through innovation. Some investors thrive while others suffer losses. It was mentioned above that some towns bloomed in thirteenth century England, while others ran into losses. This resembles modern economies, where some firms grow rapidly, while others decline as a consequence of innovation.

6.3 Occidental Feudalism

It was pointed out above how individualism came to characterize English medieval relations. Weber argued that occidental feudalism differed from oriental feudalism by its contractual nature. He described how contracts emerged in occidental feudalism due to the special relationship between king and vassals. Vassalage could be terminated by the vassal at any time upon yielding the fief (Weber 1978, 1075). Moreover, the fief obtained a monetary value and could be sold and bought. Contractual feudalism involved the establishment of alienable property rights and created a market for land. Land became the property of the vassal instead of a privilege that could be withdrawn. The vassal possessed property rights and the king could not impose arbitrarily imposed obligations on the vassal. The contractual relationship between king and vassal transcended to the relationship between lord and tenant, which was also contractual. Contractual relationships in thirteenth century England had developed to a stage where contracts were legally enforceable and upheld by courts.

The spread of contracts implied that persons were no longer liable for debts with their lives; liability was limited to an amount of money to be paid off (Weber 1978, 679–81). Freedom to make wills that disinherited family members emerged in medieval England as a consequence of the freedom of contract (Weber 1978, 692). There were no inalienable birth rights either of the eldest child or any other in thirteenth century England (Macfarlane 1978, 103). Individualism thus implied the freedom to enter contractual relationships based on individual opinions irrespective of tradition. Individual assessments of people's worth spurs labor mobility, if one organization values a person more than others. Medieval people could join a town guild and earn more than a peasant income by learning a trade. Investment in human and physical capital involves expenditures based on the calculation of expected future values of people and assets. Expected value needs to exceed actual value to make the investment worthwhile. Investment in dynamic economies requires an evaluation of investment plans. A growing economy is characterized by discourse between employers and employees, entrepreneurs and financiers. Economic growth is spurred in systems that allow discussion and a plurality of opinion. Occidental feudalism in its later days featured councils and parliaments, wherein vassals could speak their mind and had some decision power. This also applied to court systems, wherein defense and prosecution exchanged arguments.

6.4 Individual and Collective Opinion

Investment under conditions of uncertainty benefits some and hurts others. Some medieval English towns prospered, while others declined. Successful lords could appropriate tax revenues from prosperous towns, whereas those that had invested in towns that failed to attract inhabitants lost their money. Success and failure were unpredictable, but in contrast to the effects from exogenous shocks emanated from human decision making. Exogenous shocks caused by nature would affect all land owners or workers in a region, whereas the effects of human decision making can differ from one organization to another. The fates of firms investing in innovation will differ, if they do not share a common view, but carry out different plans. Diversity is triggered by individual evaluations of people and plans. A person's fate is no longer determined by group, but by individual characteristics. Markets in dynamic economies are no longer driven by anonymous forces, but by individual opinions.

Financial markets that are driven by collective sentiment cannot spread risk. Investment occurs in waves, if collective opinion prevails and periods of unwarranted optimism alternate with pessimism. Asset values move up and down with market moods. Cyclical swings of asset values are unpredictable; or their occurrence would be prevented. If people knew when the peak of stock prices would occur, such a peak would be eradicated, because people would start selling their shares before it had reached that point. Investment based on collective opinion hurts long term growth, since collective opinion is less equipped to select innovation than individualized decision making. Cycles could be dampened, if individualized investor opinions prevailed. Failure and success would occur simultaneously and not in a wave-like fashion. Failure of individual firms cannot be prevented in economies that grow through innovation. Diversification of investment can spread risk. But, diversification of novelty differs from diversification among a fixed set of activities. That is because the number and size of innovation bets is unclear. Diversification cannot save firms from failure in dynamic economies, if portfolios only encompass incumbent firms.

7 Economic Theory and Real World Organizations

7.1 *Traditional Society and Autocracies*

Perfect competition theory depicts organizations that do not take responsibility for the well-being of their members. Wages drop below subsistence levels, if labor supply increases. Perfect competition models best describe static economies that respond to exogenously caused changes. Population growth is halted and the majority of the population is bound to live at subsistence levels. India under Mogul rule fits this picture. Population and per capita income remained stagnant for about thousand years. Occupations were determined by birth and property rights were absent. Small elites could appropriate surpluses that were used for conspicuous consumption (Maddison 1971).

Both the perfect competition and the principal agent model apply to societies where people cannot improve their life by moving to another organization. Perfect competition does not allow differentiation among workers. The principal agent problem also makes mobility futile. Labor mobility would allow employers to dismiss less productive workers and productive workers to move to better paid employment; solving the principal agent problem in both cases.

Control of employee behavior is the main source of success in the p-a model. Principals give instructions that are carried out by agents. P-a theory could explain the feudal relationship between lord and serf, or the relationship between master and slave. Bonded labor is not remunerated by wages, but lives on what it receives in kind. Workers cannot appropriate the revenues from their labor and, therefore, have no incentive to put forth effort. Employees do not need to come up with ideas, but can limit themselves to executing plans thought up by a central authority. Firms that implement innovations springing from a common knowledge base fit this picture. P-a theory cannot easily deal with uncertainty that lets organizations fail irrespective of agents' effort levels. The p-a model seems better suited to describe autocratic political organizations that lack free labor mobility. Failure is attributed to faulty execution of plans made by infallible authorities in autocracies. Shirking becomes a crime under such conditions. Hence, the principal agent model can easily be transformed into a model of a totalitarian state. Several twentieth century experiences of totalitarian political leadership and command economies fit this picture. People were moved at the will of a central authority. Central (re)allocation of labor and capital distinguishes modern totalitarianism from traditional societies where people were tied to the soil. People who do not share the organization's goals are considered criminals and political enemies. Totalitarian states in twentieth century Germany and the Soviet Union attributed failure to sabotage. People, who are accused of undermining the collective effort, are eliminated in such organizations and/or subjected to harsh conditions in (labor) camps. Individuals were held personally liable for the failure of the organization. Such unlimited personal liability and criminalization constitutes the mirror image of incentive systems in dynamic market economies that pay bonuses for good individual performance.

Dynamic economies require a combination of market and organization that spurs innovation. Property rights and other 'good' institutions that allow individual valuations promote innovation. Mobility of labor and capital and freedom of organization are also prerequisites for innovation. Innovation is the opposite of tradition and totalitarian control. Some historical periods were more conducive to innovation than others. The late medieval period is a case in point. Occidental feudal kings did not have absolute power, but had to share it with vassals. Decisions could be revoked and authority was considered neither absolute nor infallible. New organizations emerged, such as cities and monasteries that offered people a life that differed from their parents. Innovation was hampered when authority was absolute and freedom of organization was absent as in imperial China. Land productivity increased due to irrigation and fed an increasing number of people, but per capita income did not grow in China between 1100 and 1800 AD (Maddison 2007a, b, 382).

In the end, productivity growth depends on the capacity of societies to generate and execute good ideas. Multiple decision makers and uncertainty are essential to this process. If the quality of ideas was known beforehand; people possessing such ideas could incur a scarcity premium equal to the value created by the idea. This would annihilate the incentive to invest and entail stagnation. Large firms can hedge their innovation bets by pursuing several attempts at innovation; a possibility small firms lack. Large firms can, therefore, offer more job security than small firms, but cannot diversify by mimicking the economy at large. Such diversification could not take all nascent innovation into account and is, therefore, bound to fail.

Late medieval England was a growing economy. We characterized the process as one of individualization. The nineteenth century also constituted a period of rapid economic growth and the rise of new organization. *Self employment and self finance were replaced by business freedoms and enabling institutions in those days. A modern economy is driven by endogenous change instead of by exogenous circumstances* (Phelps 2006).

8 The Innovative Firm

Towns were centers of progress in the Middle Ages. Modern economies rely on business firms. A picture of innovative business organizations was drawn by Ghoshal & Bartlett in their book '*The Individualized Corporation*' (1997). They describe how firms like 3M, ABB, IKEA and others have organized their companies in ways that foster innovation. Ghoshal & Bartlett discard the idea that markets are good, while organizations are bad. The modern economy is foremost an organizational economy, in their view; markets taking second place. Economists in the era of trust busting fought firms that made (excess) profits. However, profits in dynamic economies come from investment and not from the control of markets and people. Economic policy in those days was based on the premise that corporations wanted to create and abuse market power at the detriment of consumers and society. Received economic and management theory had difficulties to address the needs of innovative firms as it was based on false premises of distrust of corporate motivations and actions (Ghoshal and Bartlett 1997, 274). However, firms need to compete for innovation profits and their market power is, therefore, transitory. Uncertainty that is inherent to innovation involves that firms cannot follow recipes from the (strategy) book, but need to make their own plans. They create value by investing in people and planning their own future. Individualized corporations *shape behaviors of each employee, so that they will take initiative, collaborate and develop the confidence and commitment to continually renew themselves and the organization* (Ghoshal and Bartlett 1997, 178). Innovation requires investment in human capital, which can take the form of giving employees time to think up innovative ideas. Hence, the company must allow a level of slack to be innovative (Ghoshal and Bartlett 1997, 278).

Individualized corporations set their own course. Their behavior is not prescribed by markets. Ghoshall & Bartlett emphasize collaboration as the distinctive feature of the individualized corporation, which distinguishes it from market driven behavior that only pursues self interest (Ghoshal and Bartlett 1997, 279). They assume that markets induce aggressive behavior, where one person's gain is the other person's loss. Individualized corporations, by contrast, are sharing organizations.

I can agree with them on the point that innovative firms need to transcend markets. However, markets are essential to dynamic economies, since they spur labor mobility driven by individual valuations. The concept of the individualized corporation indicates that firms need to differ from one another, offering people a choice. Employees can choose organizations whose views and purposes they share. Employers hire people that fit their purposes and culture. Hence, individualized corporations make individual assessments of people. Markets, however, decide about success and failure of individualized corporations. Investments in physical and human capital are based on expectations that are not always realized. This interpretation of the concept of individualized corporation brings it in line with the definition of individualism used in this paper. Markets allow individualism by breaking up tradition and furthering mobility. Human capital is more optimally utilized, if it contributes to innovation instead of performing routine jobs. But, employees only want to participate in innovation, if expressing ideas does not harm their career. They must thus be spared the negative effects of failure. This can be realized, if innovation profits and losses are shared by all employees of a firm (Brouwer 2005). However, firms cannot guarantee job security in an innovative economy with its chances of failure. Job security is, therefore, replaced by a new moral contract that guarantees workers interesting jobs (Ghoshal and Bartlett 1997, 286).

The modern corporation strikes a balance between individual and organization that is based on trust instead of control. Corporations need to replace rivalry among co-workers by transcending individual success into group success. The emphasis on cooperation raises some intricate questions with regard to promotion and hierarchical relationships in individualized corporations that usually count several layers.

But, competition for promotion should not be based on individual performance, but on team success. People that are capable of generating profits by making individual assessments of people and plans that lead to success should be in charge. We can imagine that employees want to cooperate, if corporate success benefits them all. Modern corporations resemble communities in this respect. However, modern employees, in contrast to members of primitive tribes, are mobile and can enter and exit organizations. The modern corporation thus combines community and market; individualism and collectivism.

9 Expectation Equilibrium and Innovation

An innovative economy features net investments that are fuelled by expectations of growth and profits. Economies can grow at a constant rate in steady state growth. However, steady economic growth requires *expectation equilibrium,* which is achieved, if investor expectations turn out to have been right on average. Some outcomes will exceed expectations, while others will fall short of expectations. Uncertainty about the right path to success is essential to achieve expectation equilibrium as it breeds diversity of corporate strategies. Outcomes of individual firms differ from average performance in this scenario. However, aggregate profits must more than compensate losses to achieve a positive rate of return on aggregate investment. Stable equilibrium depends on diversity of opinion and, therefore, on the absence of ex ante agreement among investors. Success does not depend on having the right information, but on superior perceptive abilities (Brouwer 2002).

Innovation can only be sustained, if aggregate innovation investment improves productivity. The way strategic decisions are made within firms is, therefore, of pivotal importance. The same applies to financing decisions taken by financial institutions.

Lending in late medieval England occurred mainly between individuals (Dyer 2005, 175). We could translate that to modern finance by saying that loans were granted based on individual valuations of people and projects. This differs from decision-making that is based on opinions that are shared by all investors and/or prescribed by rating agencies or mathematical models. Collective opinion can easily err and too much or too little is invested, if collective opinion prevails. Models that estimate risk based on historical data of a short duration will err, if financial products absorbing this risk give raise to (false) feelings of certainty, which induces ever greater risk taking. Governments that guarantee deposits and bail out banks also enhance risk taking based on collective opinion. Financial institutions can gain from following collective opinion, but cannot lose. Collective opinion causes correlated up and downswings of asset values. All mortgage granting institutions gain if real estate prices rise, but they will also all suffer, if too much money was lent to home owners and a housing bubble bursts and home prices decreased. Collective losses could have been prevented, if some firms had been cautious in granting loans. However, all mortgage institutions will suffer, if home prices fall together. So, there is little advantage in being cautious under these circumstances.

Investments in homes are backed by collateral, but collateral value changes are highly correlated. Risk on these investments was severely underestimated by the mass of investors in the 2008–2009 sub prime credit crisis. Insurance of such correlated risks falters, if risk is severely underestimated. Financial innovations like credit default swaps, therefore, turned into weapons of financial mass destruction, when home prices fell.

Investment is less risky, if changes of asset values are uncorrelated. We can think of investments in 'high tech' firms. R&D investments are considered sunk and can hardly act as collateral. But, they can be considered less risky than investments in real estate, if investors have different opinions and profits and losses appear simultaneously. Some firms will win while others lose; some stocks rise, while others decline. Diversity facilitates attaining expectation equilibrium. But, stock markets are also subject to sentiment. Stock busts and booms are caused by collective opinion that deviates positively or negatively from long run average returns. However, stock market bubbles are more easily redressed than real estate bubbles, since they are equity and not debt financed. US and Japanese economies suffered more from the burst of the bubble of home and land values in the 1980s and 1990s than from the internet bubble of 2000. The same applies with even greater force to the mortgage and credit crisis of 2007/2008. Deflation of real estate values was ubiquitous and depreciation losses had to be taken by either creditor banks or home owners. Insurance against losses was futile and could not be paid out of premiums paid for deposit insurance and credit default swaps. Asset depreciations that cannot be recovered by banks or home owners need to be covered by government, that either remits insured deposits of failed banks or bails out banks to cover asset write-offs. US government bailed out banks and also paid out insurance on credit default swaps. Government pay-outs saved the system from collapse, but create moral hazard problems that aggravate cycles of under and over investment. Moreover, bad loans that remain on the balance sheets of financial institutions hamper recovery. Depreciation losses that are taken can re-establish expectational equilibrium swiftly and induce a new upturn. The burst of the internet bubble in 2000 led to a massive devaluation of stocks, but stock markets regained momentum soon after the dive. Government money was not involved to cover losses caused by asset depreciation. Investors in stocks thus erred collectively, but the burden was not shifted to the public at large, but was borne by the people who made the decision to buy stocks at elevated prices.

Collective opinion wreaks the greatest havoc, if it involves state supported investment decisions. Conformism seems a safe choice. However, investment that is supported by government desiccates capital markets and paralyzes economic revival. This happened after the burst of the South Sea Bubble in eighteenth century England. Stock markets stopped functioning for more than a century after the burst of the bubble in 1720. The same occurred in France after the burst of the Mississippi bubble in 1719. The Mississippi Company was supported by the French state and even obtained the right to issue paper money. Inflation soared as a consequence of these policies (Ferguson 2001, 315). These state backed ventures seemed to be sure bets. However, their collective nature made them in fact very risky.

Collective opinion creates booms and busts and arrests productivity growth by limiting the number of alternatives that is pursued. Economists estimate real productivity growth to proceed at annual levels of 2–3 % in modern economies. However collective decision making can support faulty investment projects that do not enhance productivity. The ill fated colonial ventures of the eighteenth century are cases in point. The same seems to apply to financial innovations that triggered the debt crisis of 2008. Expectations are diminished, if investment does not generate profits, which drags down future investment.

10 Conclusions

Most economic models of markets and organizations cannot explain growth caused by innovation. Perfect competition theory assumes perfect knowledge that is accessible to all. Principal agent theory assumes knowledge residing in a central authority that is considered to be infallible. The competitive model of neo-classical theory assumes a monetized economy, where people are paid money wages. Markets are assumed to differ from systems where people are tied to the land and cannot move to other places. However, a search for improvement is futile, if a person's worth is determined by group membership. The most obvious example is that of labor that is tied to a fixed amount of land. This Malthusian version of neo-classical theory depicts societies, wherein populations cannot grow and wages hover along subsistence levels due to the limits imposed by scarce resources. Labor could only gain temporarily high wages, when population was diminished due to epidemics or other disasters.

Technological progress is assumed to spring from science in neo-classical growth theory. However, many scientific inventions were never adopted for commercial purposes. There is no market for ideas in societies that are ruled by tradition or a central authority. Modern societies plan for progress, but are subject to impediments to growth that emanate from collectivism and totalitarianism. Political power that rests on totalitarian ideology wants to destroy political enemies and their artifacts. Twentieth century revolutions based on secular ideology destroyed assets and people on a massive scale. A battle of ideas entails total war, if new ideas cannot coexist with old ones.

Progress was furthered at times when individualization and markets took root. This applies to medieval England, where property rights were defined at an individual level. It also applies to modern economies, wherein organizations are driven by individualized instead of collective opinion. Collective opinion in market economies causes business cycles. Schumpeter attributed recessions to creative destruction, but growth can be steady, if average investor expectations are fulfilled.

Collective opinion, however, causes cycles of under and overinvestment. Collectivism is not imposed on people in market economies, but chosen voluntarily. Progressive economies need to find ways to further diversity and individualized decision making. Progress in market economies is, therefore, not self evidentiary, but relies on the organization of creativity.

References

Brouwer M (2002) Weber, Schumpeter and Knight on entrepreneurship and economic development. J Evol Econ 12:83–105

Brouwer M (2005) The robustness of managing uncertainty through risk-sharing contract; from medieval Italy to Silicon Valley. J Manag Govern 9(3):237–255

Coase R (1937) The nature of the firm. Economica 4:386–405

Dyer C (2005) Àn age of transition? Economy and society in England in the later middle ages. Clarendon, Oxford

Ferguson N (2001) The cash nexus; money and power in the modern world 1700-2000. Basic Books, New York

Ghoshal S, Bartlett CA (1997) The individualized corporation; a fundamentally new approach to Management'. Random House Business Books, New York

Hayek FA (1980) 'Individualism, true and false' in individualism and economic order. University of Chicago Press, Chicago, IL

Keeley LH (1996) War before civilization; the myth of the peaceful Savage. Oxford University Press, New York

Macfarlane A (1978) The origins of English individualism. Basil Blackwell, Oxford

Maddison A (1971) Class structure and economic growth: India and Pakistan since the Moghuls. Amazon, UK

Maddison A (2007a) Chinese economic performance in the long run 960-2030. OECD, Paris

Maddison A (2007b) Contours of the world economy 1–2030 AD; essays in macro economic history. Oxford University Press, Oxford

Mankiw G (2007) Macroeconomics, 6th edn. Worth Publishers, New York

Phelps E (2006) Macro economics for a modern economy. Noble Prize Lecture

Schumpeter JA (1934) The theory of economic development; an inquiry into profits, capital, credit, interest and the business Cycle. Oxford University Press, New York

Weber M (1978) Economy and society; an outline of interpretive sociology. University of California Press, Berkeley

Weber M (2003) The history of commercial partnerships in the middle ages. Rowman and Littlefield Publishers Inc., Lanham, MD

Financial System and Technological Catching-up: an Empirical Analysis

Is there a Recipe for Increasing the Export Variety of Nations?

Muhammad Nadeem Javaid and Pier-Paolo Saviotti

Abstract This paper explores the role of the financial system in technological catching-up in the expectation that financing mechanisms affect the production and the exports of new or "new to the market" commodities. We have developed indices of related export variety (REV) and of unrelated export variety (UEV) by using the informational entropy function for a sample of 97 countries using NBER & UN trade data for the period 1992–2005. We used these indices sequentially as dependent variables with the bank credit ratio and stock market capitalization ratio as independent variables. In addition, we include the education system, natural resources and four principal component factors characterizing the cost of doing business, political system, quality of governance and the degree of openness of the countries as control variables in our regressions. Our pooled regression models show that the financial system is an important determinant of both types of export variety for all countries but that, for the most successful developers, the banking system and the stock market play different roles, with the former being relatively more appropriate for REV and the latter for UEV. Such specialization of different forms of the financial system seems to confirm that stock markets are likely to be relatively more appropriate to fund the exploratory type of innovations which are required to increase UEV.

Reprinted from Evolutionary Economics 22(4), 847-870 , Springer (2012)

M.N. Javaid (✉)
Karachi School for Business & Leadership, ST-03, Dawood Co-operative Housing Society, Bahadurabad, National Stadium Road, Karachi, Pakistan
e-mail: nadeem.javaid@ksbl.org

P.-P. Saviotti
INRA-GAEL, Université Pierre Mendès-France, BP 47, 38040 Grenoble, France & GREDEG-CNRS, 250 rue Albert Einstein, 06560 Valbonne, France
e-mail: pier-paolo.saviotti@wanadoo.fr

A. Pyka and E.S. Andersen (eds.), *Long Term Economic Development*, Economic Complexity and Evolution, DOI 10.1007/978-3-642-35125-9_21,

1 Introduction

We are still lacking sufficient understanding about ever increasing gaps in productivity and income per capita across the globe. During the last few decades, some initially backward countries have managed to narrow these gaps between themselves and the frontier countries by means of technological catching up. The literature on long-run growth points out that technological catching-up is not a question of replacing an outdated technological set up with a more modern one, but in fact it is continually to transform technological, economic and institutional structures (Svennilson 1954; Cornwall 1976; Fagerberg and Verspagen 2001) by developing certain competences such as "social capability" (Ohkawa and Rosovsky 1974; Abramovitz 1986), "technological capability" (Kim 1980), "absorptive capacity" (Cohen and Levinthal 1990) and "innovation system" (Lundvall 1992; Nelson 1993; Edquist 1997). There is a big overlap between several of these concepts, and the relationship between conceptual and empirical work in this area is often weak (Fagerberg and Srholec 2008). Most of this empirical work has used the conventional indicators, namely GDP per capita growth rate, total factor productivity and labor productivity, as measures of economic growth and technological development. Of course, these indicators offer significant insight but do not truly reflect the technological change encompassing all above mentioned competences in the different countries.

In order to integrate technological change into the models of economic growth, we need an indicator which allows us to measure the degree of change in the different economies from one time period to another. In the recent past, product/export variety has gained considerable profession's attention. Variety of any system represents the qualitative changes in its composition (Saviotti 2001). Variety is the outcome of innovation and search activities that in turn crucially depends on knowledge and R&D; each calls for long-term commitment and constant creation of Schumpeterian rents, since the process of assimilating existing technologies in the less developed countries is not very much different from the creation of entirely new technologies in the developed world. In each case, learning requires an allocation of resources (Grossman and Helpman 1991) and risk sharing. As a consequence, the financial system becomes vital to an expansion of the product variety of any economic system. Recently, several empirical studies have shown that the growth of output variety (Frenken et al. 2007) or of export variety (Funke and Ruhwedel 2001a, b; Saviotti and Frenken 2008) is a significant and stable determinant of the growth of GDP, labor productivity and total factor productivity. These empirical studies provide clear evidence for an important regularity in economic development. However, these results do not explain why some countries are more capable than others in promoting the growth of output/export variety and using it as an engine of economic growth. Thus, the objective of this study is to investigate those arrangements particularly financial ones, which are most appropriate for promoting the variety driven catching-up in an economic system. For the purpose of this study, technological catching-up is defined as the production of variety of goods and services through the adoption and adaptation of new or new-to-the-market technologies, which are the outcome of material, process and/or organizational innovations. The financial system is defined here as the complex web of markets, intermediaries and institutions along with legal & regulatory framework for setting up the financial decisions made by households, corporations and government by bridging the gap between fund surplus and fund deficit units.

The rest of the paper is structured as follows. In the second section, we establish the link between export variety and technological catching-up. The third section explains different types of financial systems and their links to technological catching-up. The fourth section deals with methodology to facilitate the construction of indices of related export variety (REV), of unrelated export variety (UEV) and of overall export variety (OEV), data description, econometric models, results and discussion. The last section concludes and presents some policy insights.

2 Export Variety as a Measure of Technological Catching-up

The variety of any system represents the qualitative changes in its composition (Saviotti 1996). A few empirical studies (Funke and Ruhwedel 2001a, b, 2005; Frenken et al. 2007; Hidalgo et al. 2007; Saviotti and Frenken 2008) confirm that producing highly differentiated export goods gives a competitive advantage which allows selling more products in international markets because "the marginal utility of adding a new good to the pre-existing pattern of consumption is greater than that of adding an extra unit of a pre-existing good" (Saviotti 2001: 121–124). There are two types of variety pertaining to the emergence of new commodities (Frenken et al. 2007), (i) related variety, similar to that already present in the economic system and, (ii) unrelated variety, completely different from that already present in the economic system. It is also possible to interpret related variety as mainly due to exploitation activities, while unrelated variety would require a greater content of exploration activities (March 1991). We have used international trade data, which are available with the required characteristics, to calculate REV and UEV by entropy function. Export data describe actual sales and also represent products with different degrees of maturity and creativity. As a matter of fact, only those products cross domestic boundaries which have enough sophistication to compete in the international market. At the same time, entropy statistics allows us to separate one country from another for a given product at a given year. All products have different degrees of variety for a given system at different levels of aggregation. We can distinguish REV (at lower levels of aggregation) from UEV (at higher levels of aggregation). An increase in REV and UEV of a country means that its economic agents are striving to further exploit and explore its available endowments by developing certain capabilities or institutions. If today a country is exporting something new, intuitively this reflects the fact that the country has developed certain technological capabilities to do so. Hence, we believe that export variety is a good proxy for technological catching-up.

3 Financial System and Technological Catching-up

Functional separation of financial & production capital, each pursuing profits by different means (Perez 2002), is an appropriate approach for understanding the intricate link between the financial system and catching-up. The degree of project uncertainty (Huang and Xu 1999) and the share of investments in intangible assets (Myers and Majluf 1984) are the two decisive factors that make the financial system critical for the production sector. According to Keynes liquidity preference theory (1936), investors prefer the greater certainty of returns on liquid assets to the uncertainties of returns on productive capital assets or titles of those assets. So, high demand for liquidity retards growth possibilities. Now, financial systems differ to the extent to which they facilitate the flow of funds by reducing the risks for financiers and by providing sufficient degree of autonomy to entrepreneurs in the use of those funds for the production of a variety of commodities.

A strand of literature on the finance-growth nexus concludes that financial development induces faster long run growth (e.g. Levine 1997; Rajan and Zingales 1998; Levine et al. 2000). According to Levine (1997), the financial system plays an important role by mobilizing savings, allocating credit and facilitating the hedging, pooling and pricing of risks in a modern economy. On the other hand, entrepreneurs and firms try to generate or to recreate knowledge through the processes of searching and learning in vague environments. But this learning and search is not totally random, as one of the selection mechanisms of technologies is the financial system (Christensen 1992). A few studies (Rajan and Zingales 1998; Demirguc-Kunt and Maksimovic 1998) have shown that, to grow faster, industries and firms need to be heavily dependent on external financing in countries with well-developed financial systems. Kletzer and Bardhan (1987) consider a case where differences between countries in their domestic institutions of credit contract enforcement give rise to a comparative advantage. Baldwin (1989) also uncovers the fact that financial development may affect the output decision of firms and thus trade patterns. According to Svaleryd and Vlachos (2005), the financial sector is a source of comparative advantage in a way consistent with the Heckscher–Ohlin–Vanek model. Their main finding is that countries with well-functioning financial systems tend to specialize in industries[1] highly dependent on external financing. They bring empirical evidence showing that differences in financial systems are more important determinants of the pattern of specialization between OECD countries than differences in human capital. These studies give us enough reasons to believe that production and trading patterns are dependent on the financial system. For that reason, its structure and organization matter for catching up.

[1] Rajan and Zingales (1998) while studying financing pattern of US firms declare that drugs and medicines (ISIC 3522) industries are the most dependent, while the tobacco industry (ISIC 314) is least dependent on external finance.

3.1 *Financial System Design; Does Institutional Structure Matter?*

The process of technological catching up cannot be fully understood without establishing its relationship with the organizational design of the financial system. Theoretically, a financial system is either bank based (Continental model) or market based (Anglo-American model); there is an issue of longstanding debate on the relative importance of the two approaches. As in the corporate finance literature, the distinction is based upon their involvement with investment projects. Banks are more engaged in project selection, monitoring firms and identifying promising entrepreneurs. Market-finance (equities and bonds) are an arm's length transactions, with little involvement in a firm's investment decisions. In recent years, policymakers have been advocating a shift toward financial markets, especially in Latin America, Central Asia and Western Europe where financial systems similar to those in US have been proposed (Allen and Gale 2000). Furthermore, discussions about financial reforms have also projected the creation of financial markets (Mendelson and Peake 1993). In contrast, others have advocated bank based system due to their vital role in German and Japanese industrialization (Allen and Gale 2000; Levine 2002). This enduring debate over the relative importance of bank vs. market based systems may be summarized as shown in Table 1.

This debate has two implications concerning our question of interest. First, most of the characteristics which make any system configure toward bank based system are quite prevalent in technologically backward nations, characterized by, e.g. borrowers' poor credit reputations, investment projects necessitate significant monitoring, weak legal/contract enforcement mechanisms and strong national culture respecting uncertainty avoidance. On the other hand, most of the characteristics which make any system configure towards market based system often prevail in technologically advanced nations, characterized by, e.g. borrowers' good credit reputations, high value of information conveyed through market prices, firms under extensive state verification, strong legal/contract enforcement mechanisms, transparent accounting systems and weak national culture respecting uncertainty avoidance. Second, banks are seen to be more appropriate for financing the less risky or routine business and most often incumbent firms, while markets, which better provide cross sectional risk sharing, are more appropriate for innovative business and most often new/young firms. But generally, new/young technology based firms, which are central in the national endeavor for catching-up, feel reflectance to borrow from markets due to "privacy preservation[2]" These firms may not want to reveal their business plans to convince various lenders because this information could be available to their product competitor and may cause harm to their profitability (Yosha 1995; Campbell 1997). On one side, stock markets can be

[2] A firm, interested in issuing a security on the stock exchange, is required to submit a registration statement to the Securities and Exchange Commission, which includes information about the proposed financing, the firm's history, existing business and future plans.

Table 1 Financial system design

Bank-based (continental models)	Market-based (Anglo-American models)
Reduce agency problem, as they are better equipped to assess the quality of borrowers (Ramarkrishnan and Thokor 1984). Firm-bank relationship mitigates adverse selection and moral hazard problems (Boot 2000)	
An economy of scale in the monitoring of borrowers as the acquisition of information is easily made possible and only the manager needs to become informed. But biased against high-risk projects (Diamond 1984).	High risk projects could find finance by the individual investors due to the possibilities for risk diversification and diversity of opinion i.e. agree to disagree. (Allen and Gale 1999).
Better at providing intertemporal risk sharing (Allen and Gale 1995; Bhattacharya and Chiesa 1995; Dewatripont and Maskin 1995; Von Thadden 1995; Yosha 1995).	Better at providing cross-sectional risk sharing (Allen and Gale 1995)
Better at restructuring the financially distressed borrowers (Berlin and Mester 1992)	
Here, agents who are known to each other can cooperate and coordinate their actions (Berlin and Mester 1992; Besanko and Kanatas 1993; Diamond 1991; Chemmanur and Fulghieri 1994)	Here, agents are anonymous and compete with one another.
	Markets have valuable information feedback from the equilibrium market prices of securities to the real decisions of firms that impact those market prices. So, the stock market is a better monitor of managerial performance (Holmstrom and Tirole 1993); Transparent accounting systems are an important prerequisite (Levine 1997; Rajan and Zingales 1998)
Better if the laws are weak and contract enforcement mechanisms are lacking (Rajan and Zingales 1998); most often civil law countries (La Porta et al. 2000)	Better if the laws provide more legal protection to minority shareholders; most often common law countries (La Porta et al. 1998; Demirguc-Kunt and Levine 1999)
Suited if national cultures are strong on uncertainty avoidance (Chuck and Solomon 2006)	Suited if national cultures are weak on uncertainty avoidance (Chuck and Solomon 2006)

useful at early stages of technological development because they are better in sharing the risks emanating from unrelated product diversification, but they also obstruct the flow of funds toward privacy preserving new technology based firms.

On the other side, banks do not lend to such new firms because they severely lack the observable features (i.e. past reputation, collateral and definite cash flows etc). Thus, in this dilemma, such firms may prefer to borrow from single lenders (such as venture capitalists, business angels, incubators) or secure access to banks via Corporate Financial Guarantee Schemes (for details see Benjamin 1978; Boot et al. 1991; Rajan and Winton 1995).

3.2 Preconditions for Technological Catching-up

A country's endowments of physical and human capital, labor, natural resources and the overall quality of its institutions are the main determinants of relative costs and the patterns of production (Rodrik et al. 2005). Sound macroeconomic policies besides openness to trade are the core policy recommendations of the multilateral institutions (Levine 1997). High inflation fosters financial underdevelopment (Boyd et al. 2001), besides increasing the cost of doing business. The openness of a country to external trade and finance has the potential to erode the resistance of the local political elite to modernization (Rajan and Zingales 2003). Political instability and corruption affect the level of development (La Porta et al. 1998). An unstable political climate cannot foster and sustain a business. The form in which investor protection is provided affects the degree of risk taking by financial institutions and the type of financing they offer. Regulations have a significant influence on the ability of financial institutions to be able to respond to the changing needs of corporate borrowers. As new technology spreads in the economy and induces change in the techno-economic subsystem, the old inertia ridden financial institutions and instruments, as part of the overall socio-economic framework, call for comprehensive reforms and new regulatory procedures, which, of course, fall in the ambit of governments. According to Sachs and Warner (1995), economies abundant in natural resources have tended to grow more slowly than economies without substantial natural resources. These findings provide us strong reasons to believe that macro policies, human capital, level of openness, character of the political system, governance mechanism and the presence of natural resources might have considerable connotations for technological catching-up.

In this section, we have highlighted the conceptual and theoretical links between the financial system and variety-driven technological catching-up. Countries differ in the configuration of their financial systems and it is not easy to determine *a priori* which type of financial system is more appropriate to promote technological catching-up. According to a review of the literature, a basic claim is that bank-based systems should be more appropriate than market-based systems for technological catching-up. This basic claim relies on the argument that banks are more appropriate for REV in general and have better potential to help in catching-up efforts of technologically backward nations, while markets are more appropriate for UEV in general and have better potential to help in catching-up efforts of technologically advanced nations. However, markets being better in risk diversification could also complement the product diversification efforts in technologically backward nations. In the next section, we make an attempt to examine empirically this basic claim and nuance the relative performance of the two financial systems in the process of variety driven technological catching-up.

4 Methodology

Following Frenken et al. (2007), we measure export variety using the entropy measure applied to the distribution of sectors in a country's export portfolio, where p_i stands for the share of sector i in total exports of a country. The entropy measure increases with an increase in the number of sectors n and with the evenness of the distribution of shares. Entropy H is computed by:

$$H = \sum_{i=1}^{n} p_i \log_2 \left(\frac{1}{p_i}\right) \tag{1}$$

Entropy can be decomposed at each sectoral digit level. Formally, this decomposition procedure follows from the entropy formula. Let all sectors i at some level of aggregation fall exclusively under a sector S_g at some higher level of aggregation, where $g = 1,\ldots,G$. One can derive the shares P_g at the higher level of aggregation by summing the shares p_i at the lower level of aggregation:

$$P_g = \sum_{i=s_g}^{n} p_i \tag{2}$$

The entropy H_0 at the higher level', also called between-group entropy, is given by the entropy formula:

$$H_0 = \sum_{g=1}^{G} p_g \log_2 \left(\frac{1}{p_g}\right) \tag{3}$$

The entropy H' at the lower level is given by the weighted average of the within-group entropy values, and is given by:

$$H' = \sum_{g=1}^{G} p_g H_g \tag{4}$$

Within group entropy:

$$H_g = \sum_{i \in S_g}^{n} \frac{p_i}{p_g} \log_2 \left(\frac{1}{p_i/p_g} \right) \tag{5}$$

This procedure can be replicated at any level of aggregation. Following previous work on related and unrelated diversification at the country level (Attaran 1986; Frenken et al. 2007), we apply the entropy measure at different levels of sectoral aggregation. Our four-digit export data allow for decomposition at three digit levels. We calculated UEV for each country as the entropy of the one-digit distribution of export shares (i standing for one-digit classes); and we calculated REV as the weighted sum of the entropy at the four-digit level within each three-digit class (i standing for four -digit classes and g standing for three-digit classes). It can further be shown that entropy at the four-digit level equals the sum of unrelated and of related variety (Theil 1972; Frenken et al. 2007), i.e.:

$$H = H_0 + H' \tag{6}$$

4.1 Data

We used bilateral trade data set by commodity for the period 1992–2005. This data set is based on UN world trade data modified by Feenstra et al. (2002) and UN-Comtrade data. The data are organized by the 4-digit Standard according to the International Trade Classification, revision 2, with country codes similar to the United Nations. We have developed indices of, REV, UEV and OEV for 97 countries. Graphical representation of the dynamics of the export variety of a few countries is given in the Appendix. These graphs show the evolution of REV, UEV and OEV during the period studied. On the vertical axis, we measure export variety, which is between 0–1. The vertical scale is not fixed, so that even small changes in export variety could be observed vividly. Scale of variety is therefore different for each country depending upon the initial level of variety produced. The most spectacular performance is displayed by Asian countries e.g. South-Korea, China, Singapore, Malaysia, besides some European countries such as Spain, Ireland and The Netherlands.

We used bank credit to the private sector as a percent of GDP (*Bk-credit*), and stock market capitalization as a percent of GDP (*St.mk-fund*) from World Development Indicators (WDI) as proxies for the bank based and for the market based systems, respectively. Then we created a dummy for stock market (*St-mk*). Concerning the stock market, we can divide our sample of countries into three categories: first, those which have a stock market in all the time periods; second, those which do not have a stock market in the initial time period but established it in the subsequent period; and third, those which do not have a stock market in all the time periods. Therefore, the stock market dummy could give a better picture about the implications of its presence or absence in the economies. Countries without a stock market in a given period were given a value of zero (a total of 57 observations). We used the square root transformation of *St.mk-fund* to fulfill the linearity assumption. Then we introduced the six control variables, i.e. the Cost of Doing Business (*Cost-business*); this is a principal component factor[3] constructed through Whole Sale Price Index (data from WDI) and the Discount Rate (data from International Financial Statistics). The Discount rate, an indicator of a country's monetary policy, gives an insight about the cost of credit; the wholesale price index indicates changes in the prices of raw materials. So, together, these two variables better characterize the macroeconomic policies and the cost of doing business for the different economies. We were able to retain one principal factor with eigenvalue 1.45 explaining 75 % of total variance. We used the method of principal component factors and the oblique "oblimin" rotation procedure to arrive at the solution.

The variables *Governance* (a principal component constructed through data about impartial courts, law &order, property rights, Informal market/corruption and regulations), *Political System* (a principal component constructed through index of democracy & autocracy, political constraint, legislative and executive indexes of political competitiveness, political rights and civil liberties) and *Openness* (a principal component consisting of merchandise imports as % of GDP and FDI inward stock as % of GDP)[4] are borrowed from Fagerberg and Srholec (2008). They have reported the factor scores and factor loadings in their paper for each country considered in the present study for similar periods as those being investigated in our research. Education Index[5] (*Edu-index*) derives from the Human Development Index of the United Nations for the years 1990 and 2000. This index reflects the wellbeing and the quality of the human capital in the respective countries. Finally, we add IMF's dummy for natural resources[6] (N-*resource*). The idea here is that the income generated from natural resources such as oil may create less pressure on economic agents for technological catching-up.

[3] We used the mean and standard deviation of the pooled data for the standardization, which implies that the change of a composite variable over time will reflect both changes in each country's position (relative to other countries) and changes in the importance of the underlying indicators over time. (See Adelman and Morris 1965, 1967)

[4] To avoid bias against large economies, both variables were regressed against (the log of) land area and the residuals from these regressions were then used in factor analysis. (See Fagerberg and Srholec 2008)

[5] The Education Index is measured by the adult literacy rate (with two-thirds weighting) and the combined primary, secondary, and tertiary gross enrolment ratio (with one-third weighting).

[6] The oil dummy equals one for countries designated as oil-exporting by the IMF and zero otherwise.

4.2 The Econometric Model

We studied the impact of financial system of the 97 countries (list is given in Appendix in Table 6) on the export variety employing the pooled data econometric techniques on the lagged levels and on the changes in the dependent variables. We used the REV and UEV sequentially as the dependent variable, while using the log of *Bk-credit* and square root of *St.mk-funding* as independent variables, besides using the *Cost_business, Governance, Political System, Openness, Edu-index*, the dummies for *St-mk* , *N-resource* and *Time* as control variables. We estimated the following two Eqs. 7 and 8. In the lagged regression models, variety indices for 1995 and 2005 were used against the mean values for initial period (1992–1994) and final period (2000–2004) of independent and control variables, respectively. Mean values of the explanatory variables were used to avoid the simultaneity bias in the estimates.

$$\begin{aligned} REV_{i,t} = &\ \beta_1 lnBk \sim credit_{i,t-1} + \beta_2 \sqrt{St.mk \sim fund}_{i,t-1} \\ &+ \beta_3 Cost \sim business_{i,t-1} + \beta_4 Governance_{i,t-1} \\ &+ \beta_5 Political\,System_{i,t-1} + \beta_6 Openness_{i,t-1} \\ &+ \beta_7 Edu \sim Index_{i,t-1} + D + \in_{it} \end{aligned}$$

$$\begin{aligned} UEV_{i,t} = &\ \gamma_1 lnBk \sim credit_{i,t-1} + \gamma_2 \sqrt{St.mk \sim fund}_{i,t-1} \\ &+ \gamma_3 Cost \sim business_{i,t-1} + \gamma_4 Governance_{i,t-1} \\ &+ \gamma_5 Political\,System_{i,t-1} + \gamma_6 Openness_{i,t-1} \\ &+ \gamma_7 Edu \sim Index_{i,t-1} + D + \in_{i,t} \end{aligned}$$

$$D = \{St \sim mk; N \sim resource; t\}$$

For each dependent variable, we ran eight regressions, Basic Pooled Model with only two variables; Pooled Ordinary Least Squares; Iteratively Re-weighted Least Squares; Stepwise Regression (probability of removal at 10 % and reintroduction of a variable at 5 % level); Ordinary Least Squares over the changes of dependent variables between 1994–1995 and 2004–2005 were regressed with the initial levels of independent variables; and Quantile Regressions[7] focusing at Q.25, Q.50 and Q.75. The objective of last three models is to see how dependence of export variety over independent variables varies when we move from the lower quartile towards the upper quartile. The possibility of a endogeneity bias in the estimates, due to possible feedback from variety growth on financial development and other

[7] Quantile Regressions are used when the effects of the independent variables vary across the level of dependent variable. As in our case, export verities have very dissimilar pattern across the different nations.

institutional dimensions of the nations, was investigated by the Hausman (Durbin-Wu-Hausman augmented regression test) procedure. (For details, see Davidson and MacKinnon 1993 and Wooldridge 2002:118–122.) The test failed to detect the evidence of endogeneity bias.

4.3 Results and Discussion

Descriptive statistics for all the variables and the Pearson correlation matrix are shown in Tables 4 and 5 in the Appendix. Statistics shows that the export portfolios of the countries are dominated by UEV as compared to REV, while both of these varieties have 37 percent positive correlation. Bank credit and stock market financing have 39.5 % positive correlation. Cost of doing business and natural resources are negatively correlated with most of the other variables.

Table 2 displays the results using the REV as the dependent variable. Here, the pooled OLS model reflects that *Bk-credit, Edu-index, St-mk* and *N-resources* are significant at the 1 % level, while *St.mk-funding* and *Governance* are significant at 5 % level. The robust regression model shows that *St.mk-funding* and *Governance* were also significant at the 1 % level, though *Openness* negatively impacts the REV at the 5 % level of significance. In the stepwise regression model, *Cost_business, Political System* and *Openness* were removed and the significance level for *St.mk-funding* again decreased to 5 % level with a decrease in its coefficient as well as adjusted R^2 (now 0.69). The adjusted R^2 again rises to 0.96 in pooled OLS over the changes, where *Bk-credit* and *St.mk-funding* are significant at the 1 % and 5 % levels, respectively, but with a considerable increase in the value of coefficient for *Bk-credit* and a negligible fall in the value of coefficient for *St.mk-funding*. Quantile regression models show that the significance level for *Bk-credit* remains at the 1 % level with a sharp increase in its coefficient as we move from Q.25 to Q.75, *St.mk-funding* first becomes insignificant then gains significance at the 1 % level and again loses significance at the 5 % level, all along similar variation in the value of its coefficient as we move from the Q.25 to Q.50 and then Q.75, respectively. However, *Governance* loses significance from 1 % to 5 %, while moving from Q.25 to Q.50, but later it becomes insignificant with a fall in its coefficient value in Q.75. Openness, which negatively affected the REV, is significant at the 1 % and 5 % levels in Q.50 and Q.75, respectively. *Edu-index* and *N-resources,* which are significant at the 1 % level in Q.25, lose significance to the 5 % level in Q.75, while the presence of *st_mk* is significant at the 1 % level for all the quantiles.

Table 3 displays the results using the UEV as the dependent variable. The pooled OLS model shows that *Bk-credit, Edu-index, St-mk* and *N-resources* are significant at the 1 % level, while *St.mk-funding* and *Governance* are significant at the 5 % level to determine the UEV. *Cost_business, Political System* and *Openness* have no impact on UEV. According to the robust regression model, *Bk-credit, St.mk-funding, Edu-index, St-mk* and *N-resources* all are significant at the 1 % level in determining UEV, while *Governance* is significant at the 10 % level. In stepwise

Table 2 Regression results using related export variety as dependent variable

Model	(1)	(2)	(3)	(4)	(5)	(6)	(7)	(8)
REV(log)	Basic	OLS	IRWLS	SW pr (.10)	OLS-Δ	Q.25	Q.50	Q.75
Bk-credit (log)	0.971***	0.586***	0.719***	0.658***	0.630***	0.684***	0.651***	0.860***
	[0.191]	[0.192]	[0.175]	[0.182]	[0.190]	[0.255]	[0.148]	[0.249]
St.mk-fund (sqrt)	0.310***	0.135**	0.140***	0.105**	0.134**	0.0899	0.190***	0.152**
	[0.0482]	[0.0566]	[0.0499]	[0.0494]	[0.0559]	[0.0774]	[0.0431]	[0.0719]
Cost-business		−0.139	−0.0911		−0.128	−0.0360	−0.0196	−0.136
		[0.142]	[0.119]		[0.140]	[0.147]	[0.101]	[0.175]
Political system		0.0229	−0.0915		0.0281	0.0664	−0.0354	−0.133
		[0.118]	[0.110]		[0.116]	[0.153]	[0.0947]	[0.181]
Governance		0.383**	0.384***	0.517***	0.372**	0.535***	0.301**	0.252
		[0.172]	[0.137]	[0.141]	[0.170]	[0.196]	[0.117]	[0.209]
Openness		−0.137	−0.261 * *		−0.128	−0.135	−0.265 * * *	−0.368 * *
		[0.135]	[0.116]		[0.133]	[0.159]	[0.0965]	[0.176]
Edu-index(cubic)		0.303***	0.345***	0.261***	0.317***	0.218*	0.246***	0.401**
		[0.106]	[0.0955]	[0.0956]	[0.105]	[0.129]	[0.0819]	[0.170]
St_mk		1.623***	1.427***	1.612***	1.581***	1.502***	1.733***	1.474***
		[0.334]	[0.312]	[0.330]	[0.330]	[0.452]	[0.261]	[0.473]
N-resources		1.428***	1.292***	1.464***	1.272***	0.921	1.441***	1.354**
		[0.385]	[0.360]	[0.379]	[0.380]	[0.557]	[0.307]	[0.590]
Observations	194	181	181	181	181	181	181	181
R-squared	0.55	0.96	0.73	0.69	0.96	–	–	–

Table 3 Regression results using unrelated export variety as dependent variable

Model	(1)	(2)	(3)	(4)	(5)	(6)	(7)	(8)
OEV(log)	Basic	OLS	IRWLS	SW pr(.10)	OLS-Δ	Q.25	Q.50	Q.75
Bk-credit (log)	0.808***	0.497***	0.560***	0.561***	0.529***	0.528***	0.507**	0.299
	[0.155]	[0.157]	[0.149]	[0.149]	[0.155]	[0.182]	[0.222]	[0.214]
St.mk-fund (sqrt)	0.251***	0.118**	0.133***	0.0913**	0.117**	0.109*	0.154**	0.198***
	[0.0391]	[0.0463]	[0.0440]	[0.0404]	[0.0457]	[0.0558]	[0.0665]	[0.0630]
Cost-business		−0.121	−0.131		−0.109	−0.117	−0.113	−0.183
		[0.116]	[0.110]		[0.114]	[0.0965]	[0.166]	[0.179]
Political system		0.0519	−0.0116		0.0549	0.0836	0.110	0.0150
		[0.0963]	[0.0915]		[0.0952]	[0.104]	[0.139]	[0.168]
Governance		0.280**	0.225*	0.410***	0.278**	0.311**	0.191	0.205
		[0.140]	[0.133]	[0.115]	[0.139]	[0.153]	[0.200]	[0.174]
Openness		−0.0556	−0.0998		−0.0530	0.0246	−0.0605	−0.189
		[0.110]	[0.105]		[0.109]	[0.105]	[0.158]	[0.165]
Edu-index(cubic)		0.256***	0.311***	0.220***	0.267***	0.182**	0.239*	0.399**
		[0.0867]	[0.0824]	[0.0782]	[0.0857]	[0.0862]	[0.125]	[0.168]
St_mk		1.216***	1.037***	1.224***	1.189***	1.006***	1.281***	0.924**
		[0.273]	[0.260]	[0.270]	[0.270]	0.305]	[0.388]	[0.412]
N-resources		1.208***	1.106***	1.214***	1.101***	0.996***	1.297***	1.274***
		[0.315]	[0.299]	[0.310]	[0.311]	[0.374]	[0.434]	[0.448]
Observations	194	181	181	181	181	181	181	181
R-squared	0.55	0.94	0.72	0.69	0.96	–	–	–

Absolute value of t statistics in parentheses, * significant at 10 %; ** significant at 5 %; *** significant at 1 %
Standardized variables used in the estimates (beta coefficients reported)
All regressions include a full vector of year dummies
(1) Basic model (2) Pooled OLS (3) Iteratively re-weighted least squares (4) Stepwise regression probability of removal at 10 % and entry at 5 % level (5) Pooled OLS over the changes of dependent variables (6) Regression focusing on 1st quartile (7) Regression focusing on 2nd quartile (8) Regression focusing on 3rd quartile

Table 4 Summary statistics

Variable	Mean	Std. dev.	Min	Max	Obs
Dependent variables					
REV	0.0160139	0.0382651	1.06e-06	0.2780037	194
UEV	0.0316092	0.0607489	0.0000201	0.4050809	194
Independent variables					
Bk-credit (log)	3.465809	0.9033699	1.314781	5.41913	194
St.mk-fund (sqrt)	3.711031	3.579846	0.00	15.58492	194
Control variables					
Cost-business	0.0072822	0.995614	−1.373083	6.301844	188
Political system	0.0211856	0.9835619	−3.75	0.88	194
Governance	0.0358031	0.9977811	−2.52	1.83	193
Openness	−0.0135233	0.9507607	−3.23	2.14	193
Edu-index	0.7332267	0.2242007	0.101231	0.9933333	187
St-mk	0.7061856	0.4566865	0.00	1	194
N-resources	0.0927835	0.2908795	0.00	1	194

regression *Cost_business*, *Political System* and *Openness* were removed from the model, while all others are significant in determining the UEV, and the adjusted R^2 decreased from 0.72 to 0.69. The adjusted R^2 again rises to 0.96 in OLS over the changes, where *Bk-credit* and *St.mk-funding* are significant at the 1 % and 5 % levels, respectively. Quantile regression models for UEV show that *Bk-credit* loses significance from the 1 % level to the 5 % level along with considerable variations in its coefficient value and becomes insignificant, while *St.mk-funding* gains significance from the 10 % level to the 1 % level along with an increase in its coefficient value as we move from Q.25 to Q.75. *Governance,* which is significant at the 5 % level in Q.25, becomes insignificant in Q.50 and Q.75. However *Cost-business, Political system,* and *Openness* are not significant in determining the UEV in any quantile, whereas most of the control variables are highly significant.

Our results show that bank credit is significant in determining the REV and UEV in all the countries as compared to stock market funding, which is also significant but with lower coefficients. Second, quantile regression models reveal that stock market funding is more systematically significant and with a higher coefficient for UEV as compared to REV in Q.75. Conversely, bank credit is highly significant and has a higher coefficient for REV as compared to UEV in the same quantile. However, the presence of a stock market equally matters for all the quantiles. Firms with sensitive information prefer to borrow from a single lender, usually a bank. But if firms lack collateral and observable features, then corporate financial guarantee schemes provided by the government or venture capital arrangements may help them to get their projects funded. We are constrained in our ability to verify empirically this dimension due to the limited availability of uniform data for the whole set of countries. But this could also be a potential explanation of why bank funding significantly impacts the production of UEV in the lower quantiles as compared to market financing. Our findings also suggest that *Governance* significantly impacts

Table 5 Correlation matrix (figures in parenthesis are p values)

Variables	REV	UEV	Bk-credit	mk-fund	C-business	P.system	Gov.	Open	E-index	St-mk	N-res
REV	1.00										
UEV	0.61	1.00									
	(0.00)										
Bk-credit *(log)*	0.49	0.67	1.00								
	(0.00)	(0.00)									
St.mk-fund *(sqrt)*	0.45	0.56	0.63	1.00							
	(0.00)	(0.00)	(0.00)								
Cost-business	−0.28	−0.24	−0.41	−0.38	1.00						
	(0.00)	(0.00)	(0.00)	(0.00)							
Political system	0.17	0.22	0.18	0.21	−0.01	1.00					
	(0.02)	(0.00)	(0.01)	(0.00)	(0.94)						
Governance	0.40	0.54	0.62	0.51	−0.32	0.14	1.00				
	(0.00)	(0.00)	(0.00)	(0.00)	(0.00)	(0.05)					
Openness	−0.09	0.08	0.13	0.28	−0.25	0.05	−0.02	1.00			
	(0.20)	(0.26)	(0.08)	(0.00)	(0.00)	(0.52)	(0.83)				
E-index	0.32	0.59	0.49	0.41	−0.02	0.40	0.44	0.09	1.00		
	(0.00)	(0.00)	(0.00)	(0.00)	(0.80)	(0.00)	(0.00)	(0.21)			
St-mk	0.26	0.66	0.52	0.43	−0.14	0.22	0.32	0.20	0.49	1.00	
	(0.00)	(0.00)	(0.00)	(0.00)	(0.06)	(0.00)	(0.00)	(0.01)	(0.00)		
N-resources	−0.07	0.15	−0.12	−0.09	0.15	−0.10	−0.15	−0.11	0.06	0.05	1.00
	(0.36)	(0.03)	(0.10)	(0.22)	(0.04)	(0.15)	(0.03)	(0.11)	(0.42)	(0.49)	

Table 6 List of the countries

Sr.N	Country	Sr.N	Country	Sr.N	Country	Sr.N	Country
1	Albania	26	Ecuador	51	Korea Rep.	76	Paraguay
2	Argentina	27	Egypt	52	Kuwait	77	Russian Fed
3	Armenia	28	Spain	53	Sri Lanka	78	Saudi Arabia
4	Australia	29	Estonia	54	Morocco	79	Senegal
5	Austria	30	Ethiopia	55	Madagascar	80	Singapore
6	Belgium-LUX	31	Finland	56	Mexico	81	El Salvador
7	Benin	32	Fiji	57	Mali	82	Slovakia
8	Burkina Faso	33	France, Monac	58	Mozambique	83	Slovenia
9	Bangladesh	34	UK	59	Malawi	84	South Africa
10	Bulgaria	35	Ghana	60	Malaysia	85	Sweden
11	Bahrain	36	Eq.Guinea	61	Niger	86	Togo
12	Belarus	37	Greece	62	Nigeria	87	Thailand
13	Bolivia	38	Guatemala	63	Nicaragua	88	Trinidad Tbg
14	Brazil	39	Honduras	64	Netherlands	89	Tunisia
15	Canada	40	Hungary	65	Norway	90	Turkey
16	Switz.Liecht	41	Indonesia	66	Nepal	91	Tanzania
17	Chile	42	India	67	New Zealand	92	Uganda
18	China	43	Ireland	68	Oman	93	Uruguay
19	Cote Divoire	44	Iran	69	Pakistan	94	USA
20	Cameroon	45	Israel	70	Panama	95	Venezuela
21	Congo	46	Italy	71	Peru	96	Zambia
22	Colombia	47	Jamaica	72	Philippines	97	Zimbabwe
23	Costa Rica	48	Jordan	73	Papua N.Guin		
24	Denmark	49	Japan	74	Poland		
25	Algeria	50	Kenya	75	Portugal		

the production of REV in lower quantiles, but that it has no impact on UEV and Q.75, although Openness significantly and negatively impacts the REV and has no implications for the UEV. Costs of doing business and political system statistically do not have any implication for any kind of variety in the whole sample, while other control variables i.e. education and natural resources, significantly determine the export verities, particularly in the lower quantiles.

5 Conclusion

The main objective of this paper was to appraise the role of the financial system in export variety driven technological catching-up. The organizational structure of the financial system can be expected to matter considerably because it could be a source of comparative advantage and determine the diversification and specialization patterns of production and export of an economy. Countries differ in the configuration of their financial systems and it is not easy to determine *a priori* which type of financial system, bank based or market based, is more appropriate to promote technological catching-up. According to the review of the literature, a basic claim is that bank-based systems should be more appropriate than market-based systems for technological catching-up. This basic claim relies on the argument that bank based systems are more appropriate for REV in general and have better potential to help in catching-up efforts of technologically backward nations, while market based systems are more appropriate for UEV in general and have better potential to help in catching-up efforts of technologically advanced nations. However, markets being better in risk diversification could also complement the product diversification efforts in technologically backward nations. From our empirical analysis, it is obvious that bank funding significantly determines related and unrelated variety in lower quantile. On the other hand, for the upper quantile, bank funding is relatively more appropriate for REV while stock market funding is comparatively more appropriate for UEV. However, the presence of a stock market matters equally for all the quantiles.

Further, our empirical findings support this argument, that financing for the UEV, which is most often produced by new high-tech firms, is reliant on stock market financing as compared to bank credit in the Q.75. In spite of this, financial markets are subject to certain limitations i.e. in markets, the borrowing firm is required to provide detailed documentation in order to convince the various lenders that it is credit worthy. Therefore, young/innovative firms may be reluctant to go public, fearing the reaction of established competitors to the disclosed information. So, external equity, which initially comes from private investors (friends, family, venture capitalists or business angels), could be the source of financing, but unfortunately we are constrained to verify empirically this dimension due to the unavailability of uniform data for all the countries. However, the literature suggests that firms with sensitive information prefer to borrow from a single lender, usually a bank, through corporate financial guarantee schemes provided by the government. So this could also be a potential explanation as to why bank funding significantly impacts the production of UEV in the lower quantile as compared to market financing.

As for the policy implications of our analysis, considerable care needs to be taken in designing the financial institutions and financial sector policies to promote technological catching up. Our analysis suggests that both banks and markets are statistically effective for the production of REV and UEV and seem to complement each other. The presence of a stock market is a statistically highly significant determinant of variety growth for all the quantiles. However, while in the lower quintile the presence of a stock market improves the performance of the economic system with respect to one which is only bank based, in the upper quantile, the stock market is better than a bank based system in supporting the development of UEV. Thus, while banks and stock markets are generally complementary, their pattern of specialization becomes more specific for high levels of development of the countries concerned. As a consequence, our findings do not imply that countries should altogether shift their financial systems towards market based ones, as has been suggested in the reform literature about Latin America, Western Europe and

Central Asia. (See Mendelson and Peake 1993) A judicious strategy would consist of instilling mechanisms such as corporate financial guarantees, incubators and venture capital arrangements to further strengthen and enhance the risk appetite of the already existing financial system. Of course, this last claim calls for empirical verification as we are constrained due to unavailability of uniform data on this dimension for all the countries in our sample.

Overall, our results can be interpreted by saying that countries need to differentiate their exports for catching-up. In the course of this technological change, the financial system has to be flexible enough to cater the differentiated needs of less risky related variety business and the more risky unrelated variety business through internalizing the other institutional weaknesses of the economy. This trajectory applies to the world economic system, but exceptions can exist at the individual country level. However, individual countries will have the possibility to interpret this common constraint based on their endowments, productive structures and institutional configurations.

Acknowledgements Earlier versions of this paper were presented at Thematic Meeting of the French Economic Association "Firms, Markets and Innovation" Sophia Antipolis, France, June 25–26, 2009 and 13th Conference of the International Joseph A. Schumpeter Society, Aalborg University, Denmark, 21–24 June 2010. We wish to thank the participants and discussants at these events. Authors also owe gratitude to Flora Bellone, Lionel Nesta and the editors and referees of this journal for their useful comments on the earlier versions of this paper. All usual caveats apply.

References

Abramovitz M (1986) Catching up, forging ahead, and falling behind. J Econ Hist 46(386):406

Adelman I, Morris CT (1965) A factor analysis of the interrelationship between social and political variables and per capita gross national product. Q J Econ 79:555–578

Adelman I, Morris CT (1967) Society, politics and economic development. The Johns Hopkins Press, Baltimore

Allen F, Gale D (1995) A welfare comparison of the German and U.S. financial systems. Eur Econ Rev 39:179–209

Allen F, Gale D (1997) Financial markets, intermediaries, and intertemporal smoothing. J Polit Econ 105(3):523–546

Allen F, Gale D (1999) Diversity of opinion and financing of new technologies. J Financ Intermed 8:68–89

Allen F, Gale D (2000) Comparing financial systems. MIT Press, Cambridge

Anderson J, Marcouiller D (2002) Trade, insecurity, and home bias: an empirical investigation. Rev Econ Stat 84:342–352

Attaran M (1986) Industrial diversity and economic performance in U.S. areas. Ann Reg Sci 20:44–54

Baldwin R (1989) Exporting the capital markets: comparative advantage and capital market imperfections. In: Audretsch D, Sleuwaegen L, Yamawaki H (eds) The convergence of international and domestic markets. North-Holland, Amsterdam

Benjamin DK (1978) The use of collateral to enforce debt contracts. Econ Inq 16:333–359

Berlin M, Mester L (1992) Debt covenants and renegotiation. J Financ Intermed 2:95–133

Besanko D, Kanatas G (1993) Credit market equilibrium with bank monitoring and moral hazard. Rev Financ Stud 6:213–232

Bhattacharya S, Chiesa G (1995) Financial intermediation with proprietary information. J Financ Intermed 4:328–357
Boot AW (2000) Relationship banking: what do we know? J Financ Intermed 9:7–25
Boot AW, Thakor AV, Udell GF (1991) Secured lending and default risk: equilibrium analysis and monetary policy implication. Econ J 101:458–472
Boyd J, Levine R, Smith B (2001) The impact of inflation on financial sector performance. J Monet Econ 47(2):221–248
Campbell T (1997) Optimal investment financing decisions and the value of confidentiality. J of Finan & Quant Anal 14:913–924
Chemmanur TJ, Fulghieri P (1994) Reputation, renegotiation, and the choice between bank loans and publicly traded debt. Rev Financ Stud 7:475–506
Christensen JL (1992) The role of finance in industrial innovation. Aalborg University Press
Chuck CY, Solomon KT (2006) National culture and financial systems. J Int Bus Stud 37:227–247
Cohen WM, Levinthal DA (1990) Absorptive capacity: a new perspective on learning and innovation. Adm Sci Q 35:128–152
Cornwall J (1976) Diffusion, convergence and Kaldor's law. Econ J 85:307–314
Davidson R, MacKinnon JG (1993) Estimation and inference in econometrics. Oxford University Press, New York
Demirguc-Kunt A, Levine R (1996) Stock market development and financial intermediaries: stylized facts. World Bank Econ Rev 10:291–321
Demirguc-Kunt A, Levine R (1999) Bank-based and market-based financial systems: cross country comparisons. World Bank Work Pap 2143
Demirguc-Kunt A, Maksimovic V (1998) Law, finance, and firm growth. J Finance 53:2107–2137
Dewatripont M, Maskin E (1995) Credit and efficiency in centralized versus decentralized markets. Rev Econ Stud 62:541–555
Diamond D (1984) Financial intermediation and delegated monitoring. Rev Econ Stud 51:393–414
Diamond D (1991) Monitoring and reputation: the choice between bank loans and privately placed debt. J Polit Econ 99:688–721
Edquist C (1997) Systems of innovation: technologies, institutions and organizations. Pinter, London
Fagerberg J, Srholec M (2008) National innovation systems, capabilities and economic development. Res Policy 37:1417–1435
Fagerberg J, Verspagen B (2001) Technology-gaps, innovation-diffusion and transformation: an evolutionary interpretation. Working Papers 11, TIK, University of Oslo
Feenstra RC, Lipsey RE, Deng H, Ma AC, Mo H (2002) World trade flows: 1962–2000, NBER Working Paper 11040
Frenken K, van Oort FG, Verburg T (2007) Related variety, unrelated variety and regional economic growth. Reg Stud 41(5):685–697
Funke M, Ruhwedel R (2001a) Product variety and economic growth: empirical evidence for the OECD countries, IMF papers, Staff 48, No. 2
Funke M, Ruhwedel R (2001b) Export variety and export performance: empirical evidence from East Asia. J Asian Econ 12:493–505
Funke M, Ruhwedel R (2005) Export variety and economic growth in East European transition economies. Econ Transit 13(1):25–50
Grossman GM, Helpman E (1991) Innovation and growth in the global economy. MIT press
Hidalgo CA, Klinger B, Barabasi AL, Hausmann R (2007) The product space conditions and the development of nations. Sci J 317(5837):482–487
Holmstrom B, Tirole J (1993) Market liquidity and performance monitoring. J Polit Econ 101:678–709
Huang H, Xu C (1999) Institutions, innovations, and growth. Am Econ Rev Papers Proceedings 89:438–443
Kim L (1980) Stages of development of industrial technology in a developing country: a model. Res Policy 9:254–277

Kletzer K, Bardhan P (1987) Credit markets and patterns of international trade. J Dev Econ 27:57–70
La Porta R, Lopez-de-Silanes F, Schleifer A, Vishny RW (1998) Law and finance. J Polit Econ 106(6):1113–1155
La Porta R, Lopez-de-Silanes F, Schleifer A, Vishny RW (2000) Investor protection and corporate governance. J Fin Econ 58:3–27
Levine R (1997) Financial development and economic growth: Views and agenda. J Econ Lit 35(2):688–726
Levine R (2002) Bank-based or market-based financial systems: Which is better? J Financ Intermed 11:398–428
Levine R, Loayza N, Beck T (2000) Financial intermediation and growth: Causality and causes. J Monet Econ 46:31–77
Lundvall BA (1992) National systems of innovation: Towards a theory of innovation and interactive learning. Pinter Publishers, London
March JG (1991) Exploration and exploitation in organizational learning. Organ Sci 2(1):71–87
Mendelson M, Peake JW (1993) Equity markets in economies in transition. J Bank Financ 17:913–929
Myers S, Majluf S (1984) Corporate financing and investment decisions when firms have information investors do not have. J Financ Econ 13:187–221
Nelson R (1993) National innovation systems: a comparative analysis. Oxford University Press, New York
Ohkawa K, Rosovsky H (1974) Japanese economic growth. Stanford University Press
Perez C (2002) Technological revolution and financial capital; the dynamics of bubbles and golden ages. Edward Elgar, Cheltenham
Rajan R, Winton A (1995) Covenants and collateral as incentives to Monitor. J Financ 50:1113–1146
Rajan R, Zingales L (1998) Financial dependence and growth. Am Econ Rev 88:559–586
Rajan R, Zingales L (2003) The great reversals: the politics of financial development in the 20th century. J Financ Econ 69(1):5–50
Ramarkrishnan R, Thakor A (1984) Information reliability and a theory of financial intermediation. Rev Econ Stud 51:415–432
Rodrik D, Hausmann R, Hwang J (2005) What you export matters, RWP05-063, faculty research working papers series. Harvard University
Sachs J, Warner A (1995) Natural resource abundance and economic growth, NBER working paper series 5398, Dec. 1–47
Saviotti PP (1996) Technological evolution, variety and the economy. Edward Elgar, Aldershot
Saviotti PP (2001) Variety, growth and demand. J Evol Econ 11:119–142
Saviotti PP, Frenken K (2008) Export variety and the economic performance of countries. J Evol Econ 18:20–218
Svaleryd H, Vlachos J (2005) Financial markets, the pattern of industrial specialization and comparative advantage: evidence from OECD countries. Eur Econ Rev 49:113–144
Svennilson I (1954) Growth and stagnation in the European economy. United Nations Economic Commission for Europe, Geneva
Theil H (1972) Statistical decomposition analysis. North Holland, Amsterdam
Von Thadden EL (1995) Long term contracts, short term investment and monitoring. Rev Econ Stud 62:557–575
Wooldridge JM (2002) Econometric analysis of cross section and panel data. MIT Press, Cambridge
Yosha O (1995) Information disclosure costs and the choice of financing source. J Financ Intermed 4:3–20

Appendix

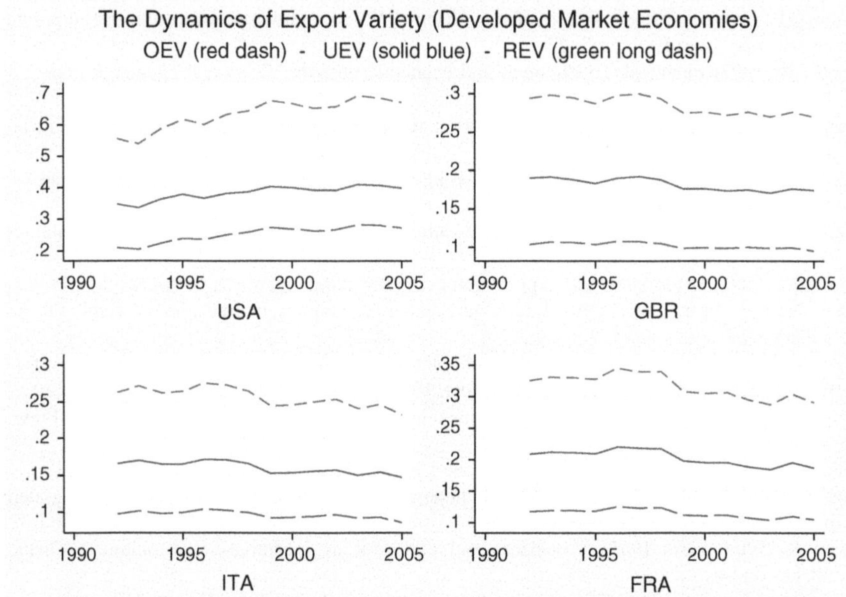
The Dynamics of Export Variety (Developed Market Economies)
OEV (red dash) - UEV (solid blue) - REV (green long dash)
.7
.6
.5
.4
.3
.2
1990
1995
2000
2005
USA
.3
.25
.2
.15
.1
1990
1995
2000
2005
GBR
.3
.25
.2
.15
.1
1990
1995
2000
2005
ITA
.35
.3
.25
.2
.15
.1
1990
1995
2000
2005
FRA

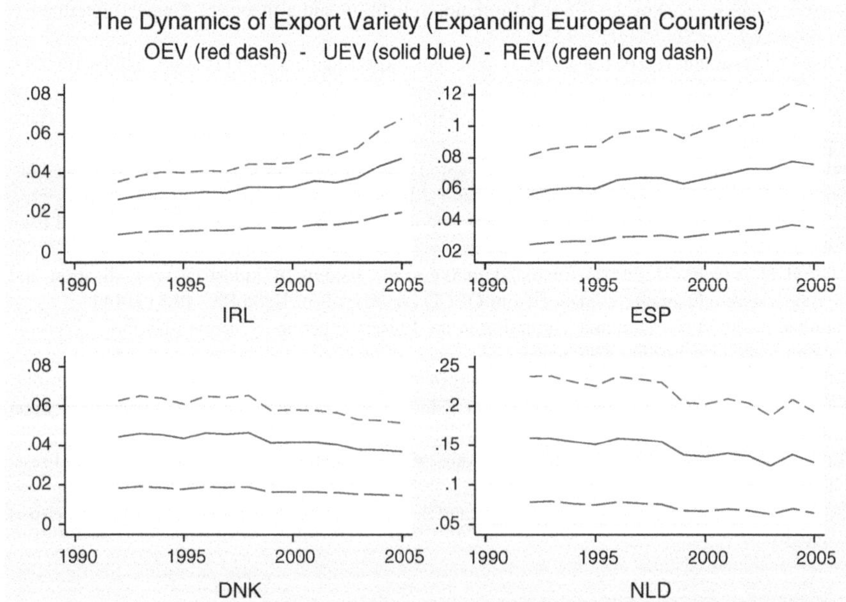
The Dynamics of Export Variety (Expanding European Countries)
OEV (red dash) - UEV (solid blue) - REV (green long dash)
.08
.06
.04
.02
0
1990
1995
2000
2005
IRL
.12
.1
.08
.06
.04
.02
1990
1995
2000
2005
ESP
.08
.06
.04
.02
0
1990
1995
2000
2005
DNK
.25
.2
.15
.1
.05
1990
1995
2000
2005
NLD

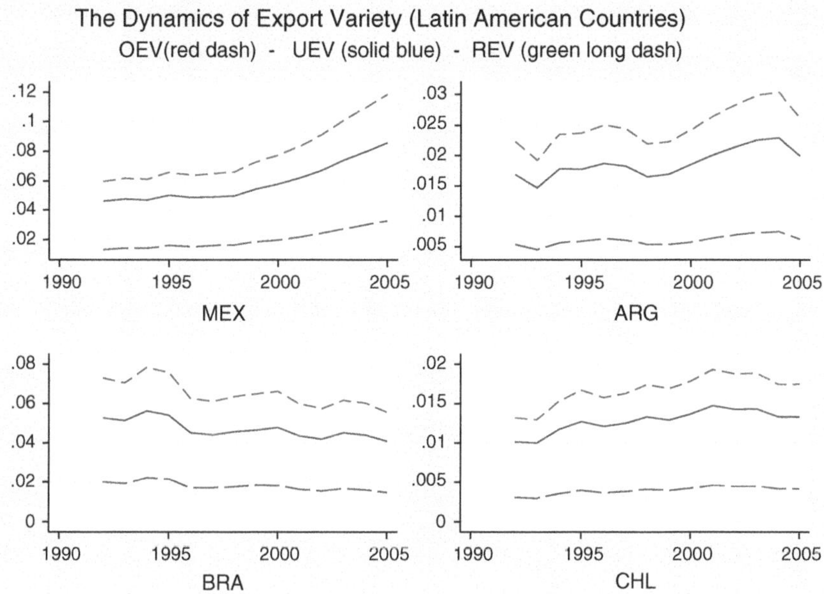
The Dynamics of Export Variety (Latin American Countries)
OEV(red dash) - UEV (solid blue) - REV (green long dash)
MEX
ARG
BRA
CHL
1990
1995
2000
2005

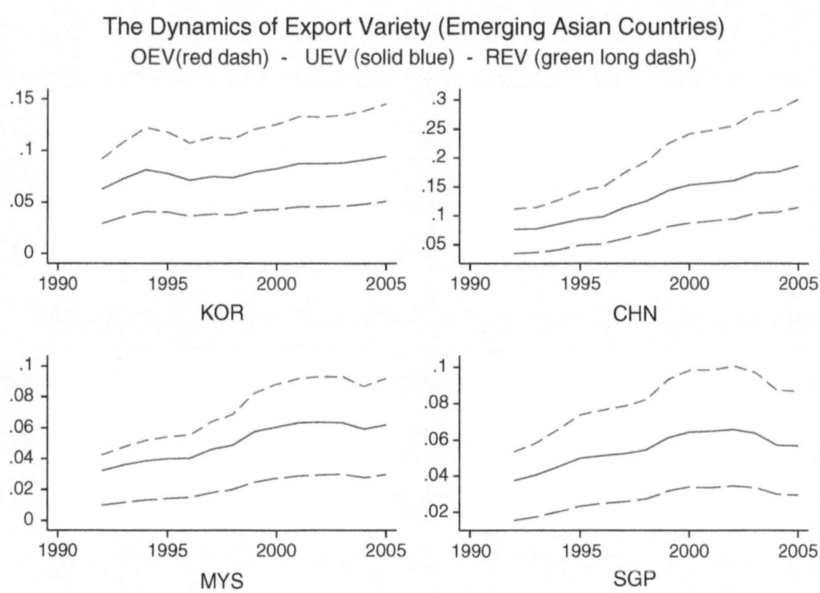
The Dynamics of Export Variety (Emerging Asian Countries)
OEV(red dash) - UEV (solid blue) - REV (green long dash)
KOR
CHN
MYS
SGP
1990
1995
2000
2005

The manufacturer's authorised representative in the EU is Springer Nature Customer Service Centre GmbH, Europaplatz 3, 69115 Heidelberg, Germany. If you have any concerns regarding our products, please contact ProductSafety@springernature.com

Printed and bound by CPI Group (UK) Ltd, Croydon, CR0 4YY
01/10/2026
02225865-0017